Why Do You Need This New Edition?

If you are wondering why you should buy this new edition of *Pathways: Scenarios for Sentence and Paragraph Writing*, here are eight good reasons!

1. **Emphasis on Visual Literacy.** To be a successful student today, you need to be able to read and evaluate the ever growing number of visuals that now accompany articles in newspapers, instruction in textbooks, and information on Web sites, as well as appear in connection with television and online news reports. In response to this change, Pathways helps you explore the multiple connections between reading, writing, and visuals and develop your ability to read, think, and write about the role and meaning of visuals.

2. **New "Writing in a Visual Age" Feature.** This exciting new feature is designed to strengthen your critical reading, thinking, and writing skills while introducing and explaining visual literacy skills. Each "Writing in a Visual Age" section contains a textbook passage followed by questions that encourage you to connect with the material, expand your comprehension, develop your vocabulary, think and respond critically, and analyze the content and significance of a range of graphic aids.

3. **Expanded Coverage of Critical Thinking.** Critical thinking is vital to understanding and analyzing what you read and responding to it clearly and effectively in writing. *Pathways* teaches you specific critical thinking skills that will aid you in evaluating arguments, including how to assess an author's word choice, distinguish fact from opinion, evaluate generalizations, examine bias, evaluate differing viewpoints, and understand the power of images.

4. **New Writers' Workshops.** Two sets of writers' workshops offer easy-to-apply strategies that will allow you to make immediate improvements in your writing skills while you work to develop other skills that take more time and practice. "Using Words Effectively" focuses on how to avoid overused expressions, eliminate weak words and phrases, and use formal English;

"Using Language Effectively" teaches you how to express emotion in writing, avoid slang and trite expressions, eliminate redundancy, and avoid sexist language.

5. **Expanded Coverage on Responding to Readings.** A new section in Chapter 2 explains how you can record your thinking as you read using highlighting and marginal annotations. This kind of active reading improves your comprehension, helps you remember information longer, and allows you to study more effectively for exams.

6. **New Success Workshops.** Two new success workshops have been added: "Use Electronic Resources" tells you about the diverse online resources available to help you improve your writing skills and "Collaborate for Success" di_____ peer review process.

7. **New** _____ Six new student ess_____ hapters and will eng_____ rent topics such as orga_____ ultural exchange prog_____ y of land, and the transition _____ _____ican and Chinese culture. Fifteen new professional readings cover current, high-interest topics including body image and the media, cyberbullying, genetic testing, choosing a major, corporate responsibility, surveillance monitoring, divorce, Shaquille O'Neal, using cell phones for educational purposes, sweatshops at sea, prison dog training programs, attitudes of and toward immigrants, electronic waste, music and exercise, and China's one-child policy.

8. **New "Working Together" Exercises.** Throughout the text, these collaborative exercises provide opportunities for you to learn and practice skills with your peers, an experience that will help you build confidence, build a support network, and learn from others.

PEARSON

PATHWAYS

SCENARIOS FOR SENTENCE
AND PARAGRAPH WRITING

Third Edition

KATHLEEN T. McWHORTER

Niagara County Community College

PEARSON

Boston   Columbus   Indianapolis   New York   San Francisco   Upper Saddle River
Amsterdam   Cape Town   Dubai   London   Madrid   Milan   Munich   Paris   Montreal   Toronto
Delhi   Mexico City   São Paulo   Sydney   Hong Kong   Seoul   Singapore   Taipei   Tokyo

Senior Acquisitions Editor: Matthew Wright

Senior Development Editor: Gill Cook

Senior Supplements Editor: Donna Campion

Senior Media Producer: Stefanie Liebman

Senior Marketing Manager: Thomas DeMarco

Production Manager: Bob Ginsberg

Project Coordination, Text Design, and Electronic Page Makeup: PreMediaGlobal

Senior Cover Design Manager/Cover Designer: Nancy Danahy

Cover Photo: Japanese Garden © Abe Lerner/iStockphoto

Photo Researcher: Jody Potter

Senior Manufacturing Buyer: Dennis J. Para

Printer and Binder: Courier Corporation/Kendallville

Cover Printer: Lehigh Phoenix

Credits and acknowledgments borrowed from other sources and reproduced, with permission, in this textbook appear on pages 617–620.

Library of Congress Cataloging-in-Publication Data

McWhorter, Kathleen T.
  [Pathways for writing scenarios]
  Pathways : scenarios for sentence and paragraph writing / Kathleen
T. McWhorter. —3rd ed.
     p. cm.
  Includes bibliographical references and index.
  ISBN-13: 978-0-205-05807-5
  ISBN-10: 0-205-05807-8
  ISBN-13: 978-0-205-05841-9
  ISBN-10: 0-205-05841-8
 1. English language—Rhetoric—Problems, exercises, etc. 2. English language—
Sentences—Problems, exercises, etc. 3. English language—Paragraphs—Problems,
exercises, etc. 4. Report writing—Problems, exercises, etc. 5. Critical thinking.
6. College readers. I. Title.
  PE1417.M4565 2011
  808'.0427—dc23

                                                              2011020405

1 2 3 4 5 6 7 8 9 10—CRK—14 13 12 11

ISBN-13: 978-0-205-05807-5 (Student Edition)
ISBN-10: 0-205-05807-8 (Student Edition)
ISBN-13: 978-0-205-05841-9 (Annotated Instructor's Edition)
ISBN-10: 0-205-05841-8 (Annotated Instructor's Edition)

Brief Contents

v

Detailed Contents

PART III COMMON SENTENCE PROBLEMS AND HOW TO AVOID THEM 235

PART IV PARAGRAPH BASICS AND DEVELOPMENT   293

PART V COMMON PARAGRAPH PROBLEMS AND HOW TO AVOID THEM 423

PART VI ESSAY BASICS, DEVELOPMENT, AND COMMON PROBLEMS   475

Preface

Pathways: Scenarios for Sentence and Paragraph Writing teaches fundamental sentence and paragraph writing skills by engaging student interest, keeping the focus on ideas rather than on rules, and stressing the interconnection of grammar and the writing process.

OVERVIEW OF THE TEXT

This book presents the study of grammar and the study of the "whole paper" as inseparable. Seven of *Pathways'* 18 chapters deal with grammar topics; in these chapters, students examine student essays, read and respond to ideas, and write and revise paragraphs. In Parts II through IV, students are encouraged to apply what they have learned about sentence-level correctness to their own writing as they explore the logical paragraph development and organization of ideas. The last two chapters of the book provide an introduction to essay writing, enabling students to make the transition from paragraphs to essays. This lively, integrated approach leads to greater student interest and better, more fully assimilated writing skills.

Chapters 2–18 of *Pathways* all contain a brief, high-interest professional reading that sets up opportunities for writing and relates the chapter's lesson to the student's own work. These readings encourage students to think about, discuss, and consider their own experiences, and to respond to what they read by writing, strengthening their confidence in the value and worth of their ideas. Most chapters also include sample student essays that serve as realistic models of student writing. "Read and Respond," Part VII, provides extra opportunities to explore the reading-writing connection. Through the readings and the accompanying apparatus, the text stresses that effective writing must evolve from student interest and experience.

CHANGES TO THE NEW EDITION

The goals of this revision were to strengthen the reading-writing connection through increased emphasis on active, critical reading and writing and to incorporate visual literacy as a theme in the text. The third edition features

■ *NEW Emphasis on Visual Literacy.* Print and electronic sources including textbooks are becoming increasingly visual. In response to this change, *Pathways* emphasizes and explores the multiple connections between reading, writing, and visuals in the new "Writing in a Visual Age" feature, additional graphics to illustrate the professional reading selections, and questions that ask students to read, think, and write about the role and meaning of visuals.

■ *NEW "Writing in a Visual Age" Feature.* This exciting new feature has been added to Chapters 1–3 and 11–16 and is designed to strengthen critical reading, thinking, and writing skills while introducing and developing visual literacy skills. It opens with a textbook passage, which is followed by questions that encourage students to connect with the material, expand their comprehension, develop their vocabulary, think and respond critically, and actively consider the significance and utility of a range of graphic aids.

■ *NEW Expanded Coverage of Critical Thinking.* A new section in Chapter 2 strengthens the reading-writing connection already emphasized in the text by discussing the role and benefits of critical thinking in the writing process. Specific skills addressed include evaluating an author's word choice, distinguishing fact from opinion, evaluating generalizations, examining bias, evaluating differing viewpoints, and understanding the power of images. In addition, each professional reading is now accompanied by critical thinking questions.

■ *NEW Writers' Workshops.* Two sets of writers' workshops offer students easy-to-apply strategies that allow them to see immediate improvement in their writing skills while they work to develop other skills that are more gradually acquired. The first set, "Using Words Effectively," focuses on how to avoid overused expressions, eliminate empty or weak words and phrases, and use formal English rather than text-messaging conventions in academic writing. The second set, "Using Language Effectively," addresses how to use words rather than emoticons to express tone, avoid slang and trite expressions, eliminate redundancy, and avoid sexist language.

■ *NEW Expanded Coverage on Responding to Readings.* The book's reading-writing connection is further strengthened by a new section in Chapter 2 that encourages students to record their thinking as they read using highlighting, marginal annotations, marginal notes, and questions.

■ *NEW Success Workshops.* "Use Electronic Sources" explores the varied and diverse resources available to writers online and "Collaborate for Success" emphasizes the peer review process.

■ *NEW Student Essays.* Five new student essays demonstrate the skills taught in the relevant chapters and engage students with current issues such as organ donation, workplace experiences, and participating in cultural exchange programs.

■ *NEW Part VII: Read and Respond.* The previous multicultural reader has been replaced with a collection of readings—four new—that offer students interesting topics to write about and provide instructors with alternative reading assignments. New topics include cancer charities and advertising, the increasing use of surveillance cameras in public places, and cyberbullying.

■ *NEW Professional Readings.* Fourteen new professional readings have been added. Topics include cyberbullying, genetic testing, divorce, Shaquille O'Neal, biomechanics, prison dog training programs, electronic waste, music and exercise, and credit card usage.

FEATURES

The following features further distinguish *Pathways* from other developmental writing texts and make its approach unique:

■ *Emphasis on Reading Skills.* Chapter 2 presents strategies for active reading that include previewing, connecting to prior knowledge, reading to learn, using idea maps to understand a reading, understanding difficult readings, and responding to readings using highlighting and annotating. Chapter 3 focuses on vocabulary development including using a dictionary, using context and word parts to figure out unfamiliar words, and developing a system for learning new words. Reading skills are emphasized throughout the text using professional readings in every chapter.

■ *Visual Approach to Writing.* Many students are visual learners and respond well to diagrams, charts, and maps. In *Pathways,* students learn to draw idea maps—visual representations of the content and organization of a paragraph or essay—in order to examine ideas as well as revision maps of their own writing as a way to evaluate the effectiveness of the content and organization and to help them make any necessary changes. Sections that feature idea or revision maps are labeled "Visualize It!"

■ *Focus on Critical Thinking.* The text emphasizes the role and benefits of critical thinking in the writing process. Chapter 2 addresses specific skills. Then each full-length reading and each "Writing in a Visual Age" offers opportunities for application and practice.

■ *Emphasis on Visual Literacy.* A new feature, "Writing in a Visual Age," explores and strengthens the connections between reading, writing, and visuals. Full-length readings now include at least one visual, and students are encouraged to analyze and write about them.

■ *Paragraph Writing Scenarios.* Each of Chapters 4–18 contains a set of writing assignments grouped into four categories—friends and family, classes and campus life, working students, and communities and cultures—that give students the opportunity to apply chapter content while exploring a relevant theme.

■ *Emphasis on Grammar and Correctness.* Seven chapters are devoted to grammar topics. Part VIII, "Reviewing the Basics," is a handbook that provides a simple, clear presentation of the forms and rules of grammar, plentifully illustrated with examples, and includes ample exercises for review of skills.

■ *Writers' Workshops.* Two sets of workshops, "Using Words Effectively" and "Using Language Effectively," offer opportunities for immediate skill improvement.

■ *Interconnected Writing in Progress Exercises.* These exercises build on each other throughout the course of each chapter, walking students through the different steps of the writing process from prewriting through drafting, writing using different modes, and revision.

■ *"Working Together" Exercises.* Throughout the text, these collaborative exercises provide opportunities for students to learn and practice skills together.

■ *Emphasis on Student Success.* The introduction, "Writing Success Starts Here!" focuses on the skills students need to be successful in their writing class and in college. The first section, "Take Charge of Your Learning," identifies five behaviors that lead to success and offers concrete strategies for implementing them using sticky tabs (see p. 1). In the second section, "Use the Help Features in This Book," students are shown how they can benefit from various features throughout the book, and in the third section, "Success Workshops," they receive practical suggestions on using electronic sources, time management, organizing a place to read and write, improving concentration, and collaborating with peers.

■ *Reusable Sticky Tabs.* These five tabs (described in the Introduction) are linked to key success strategies and designed to help students implement each strategy and take responsibility for their learning. They include "Important: Review This," "Follow Up With," "Useful For," "Assignment Due," and "Vocabulary."

■ *Student Essays.* Chapters 1, 7, and 8 and all the chapters in Parts III through VI each contain a sample student essay that provides a model of the writing process and sets realistic, attainable expectations for students. Each essay is annotated and is followed by questions that guide students in evaluating the essay.

■ *High-Interest, Engaging Readings.* Beginning with Chapter 2, each chapter includes a professional reading around which prewriting, critical thinking, and writing assignments are structured. Readings are on topics such as image and the media, genetic testing, biomechanics, sweatshops at sea, and electronic waste. Each reading offers students a model for the writing skills taught in the particular chapter, as well as a source of ideas and a base for discussion and collaborative learning activities.

BOOK-SPECIFIC ANCILLARY MATERIALS

Annotated Instructor's Edition for *Pathways: Scenarios for Sentence and Paragraph Writing*, 3/e (ISBN 0205058418)

The Annotated Instructor's Edition for *Pathways* includes the answers to all the exercises.

Instructor's Manual/Test Bank for *Pathways: Scenarios for Sentence and Paragraph Writing*, 3/e (ISBN 0-205-64663-8)

This supplement is full of useful teaching suggestions and includes an introduction to the textbook, activities to engage students' interest, advice to new instructors, and additional writing assignments. The manual also offers suggestions for handling the professional readings, sample syllabi, overhead transparencies, and a full bank of test questions.

The Pearson Writing Package

Pearson is pleased to offer a variety of support materials to help make teaching writing easier for teachers and to help students excel in their coursework. Many of our student supplements are available free or at a greatly reduced price when packaged with *Pathways: Scenarios for Sentence and Paragraph Writing.* Visit www.pearsonhighereducation.com, contact your local Pearson sales representative, or review a detailed listing of the full supplements package in the *Instructor's Manual* for more information.

MyWritingLab

www.mywritinglab.com   Where better practice makes better writers!

MyWritingLab, a complete online learning program, provides additional resources and better practice exercises for developing writers.

What makes the practice in MyWritingLab better?

■ **Diagnostic Testing:** MyWritingLab's diagnostic test comprehensively assesses students' skills in grammar. Students are given an individualized learning path based on the diagnostic's results, identifying the areas where they most need help.

■ **Progressive Learning:** The heart of MyWritingLab is the progressive learning that takes place as students complete the Recall, Apply, and Write exercises within each writing / grammar topic.

■ **Online Gradebook:** Student work in MyWritingLab is captured in the Online Gradebook.

■ **eText:** *The Pathways: Scenarios for Sentence and Paragraph Writing* e-text is accessed through MyWritingLab.

ACKNOWLEDGMENTS

I appreciate the excellent ideas, suggestions, and advice of my colleagues who served as reviewers:

Craig Barthalomaus, Metropolitan Community College–Penn Valley; Sharon Bone, Ivy Tech Community College–Central Indiana; Cheyenne Bonnell, Copper Mountain College; Frieda Campbell-Peltier, Portland Community College; Elissa Caruth, Oxnard College; Irene Caswell, Lander University; Kristyn Clark, Ridgewater College; Laura Foster-Eason, Collin County Community College; Jean Garrett, Mt. San Antonio College; Joanne Giordano, University of Wisconsin; Joan Grimes, East Central Community College; John Grosskopf, North Florida Community College; Janet Harclerode, Santa Monica College; Eric Hibbison, J. Sargeant Reynolds Community College; Cheryta Jones, Southwest Tennessee Community College; Anne Mattrella, Naugatuck Valley Community College; Melissa Michelson, Santa Monica College; Elizabeth Mills, Central Piedmont Community College; Lisa Moreno, LA Trade Technical College; Mary Nielsen, Dalton State College; Carmen Parks, Chesapeake College; Tim Reding, Morehead State University; Karin Russell, Keiser University; Jim Schwartz, Wright State University; Marcea K. Seible, Hawkeye Community College; Shari Waldrop, Navarro College; Eleanor Welsh, Chesapeake College; and Audrey Wick, Blinn College.

The entire editorial staff with whom I have worked deserves praise and credit for its assistance throughout the writing and revision of this text. In particular, I wish to thank Matthew Wright, acquisitions editor, for his enthusiastic support throughout the project and Gillian Cook, development editor, whose knowledge of the field, creative energy, and organizational abilities kept me on target throughout the revision. I also appreciate the willingness of the following students to donate samples of their writing for the paragraph samples and student essays:

Michael Archer, Kally Bajier, Gentry Carlson, Aurora Gilbert, Kim Hyo-Joo, Jessica Nantka, Jesse Napier, Nina Paus-Weiler, Maya Prestwich, Fidel Sanchez, Ted Sawchuck, Quinne Sember, James Lawrence Sturm III, and Markella Tsoukalas.

I also value the professional and creative efforts of Melissa Sacco and her team at PreMediaGlobal. Finally, I thank my students, who continue to make teaching a challenging and rewarding profession.

KATHLEEN T. MCWHORTER

Introduction

Writing Success Starts Here!

Writing is an important part of your everyday life, your college career, and the workplace. In your everyday life, for example, you find yourself writing e-mail and filling out forms. In the classroom, you write exams and papers. On the job, you write e-mail, letters, and reports. It is important to be able to write clearly and correctly in each of these situations. Being able to write well is a valuable asset that greatly increases your potential for success.

In this introduction you will learn numerous strategies for becoming a better writer and a more successful student. You will learn how to use the sticky tabs described below to take charge of your learning. You will also learn about other features in this book that will make improving your writing easier. Finally, you will complete several success workshops that will help you get off to the right start in college. Along the way, you will hear from real students. They will share practical advice that has helped them become successful students.

TABS: TAKE CHARGE OF YOUR LEARNING

Success in a writing course or in any college course, for that matter, involves taking responsibility for your own learning. Your writing instructor is your guide, but you are in charge. It is not enough to attend class and do your assignments. You have to decide what to learn and how to learn it. This section offers five methods for taking charge of your own learning. For each method, sticky tabs are provided to help you become an active learner.

Decide What Is Important to Learn

Important: Review This

TAB: *Important: Review This*

As you work through this book, you will find a wide range of strategies, rules, samples, examples, steps, tables, checklists, and idea maps. Not everyone learns in the same way. For some students examples may be very useful, while for others a list of steps to follow may be more helpful. You should identify the most important and useful materials for you in each chapter and refer to them often throughout the course. Use the "Important: Review This" sticky tabs to mark these sections. For example, one student realized that knowing how to correct a sentence fragment would help her, so she marked the "Need to Know" box, "How to Spot Fragments," on p. 120, with a tab. Then, every time she found a fragment in her writing, she used the tab to locate these revision suggestions.

Here is a partial list of items that students have found useful to tab:

- Idea maps—diagrams of how an essay is organized
- Revision checklists
- Annotated student essays
- Ideas for topics to write about
- Need to Know boxes
- Writing Success Tips
- Using Language Workshops

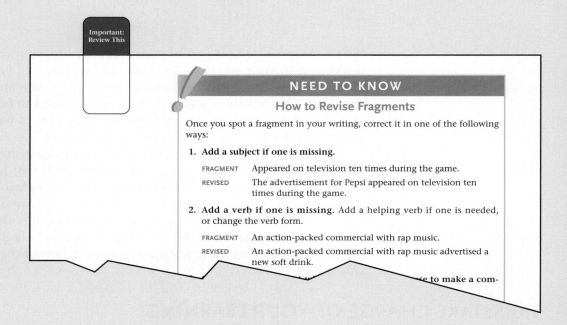

Learn from Classmates and Instructors

TAB: Follow Up With

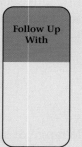

You are never alone in a writing class. Your instructor is your most valuable resource. Work closely with your instructor by discussing topics, talking about writing problems, and seeking help with assignments. Do not be afraid to ask questions. When you find things you want to discuss with your instructor, use the "Follow Up With" tab. Write your instructor's name in the blank space, and use this tab to mark material you have a question about, so you can locate it easily and will remember to speak with your instructor about it. Tabs can be placed on print copies of your essays, class notes, or instructor handouts, as well as on textbook pages.

Your classmates are also valuable resources. They can offer support and friendly feedback. Get together with them informally to discuss assignments, compare notes, and react to one another's papers. Mark material you want to discuss with other students using the "Follow Up With" tab.

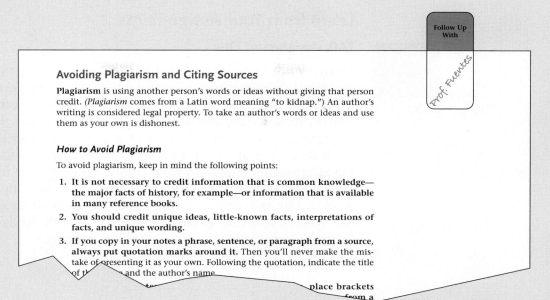

Avoiding Plagiarism and Citing Sources

Plagiarism is using another person's words or ideas without giving that person credit. *(Plagiarism* comes from a Latin word meaning "to kidnap.") An author's writing is considered legal property. To take an author's words or ideas and use them as your own is dishonest.

How to Avoid Plagiarism

To avoid plagiarism, keep in mind the following points:

1. **It is not necessary to credit information that is common knowledge—the major facts of history, for example—or information that is available in many reference books.**
2. **You should credit unique ideas, little-known facts, interpretations of facts, and unique wording.**
3. **If you copy in your notes a phrase, sentence, or paragraph from a source, always put quotation marks around it.** Then you'll never make the mistake of presenting it as your own. Following the quotation, indicate the title of the _____ and the author's name.

_____ place brackets _____ from a

Connect and Apply Your Skills

TAB: Useful For

Your writing will improve when you consciously and deliberately connect skills to one another. This means that you have to use skills learned in one chapter as you complete assignments for a subsequent chapter. For example, you will need to use the vocabulary skills you learn in Chapter 3 when you read and write paragraphs or essays for the subsequent chapters in the book. Your writing will improve more quickly if you use the skills you learn regularly and frequently. Try to apply what you learned last week to what you are writing in your other classes, in your everyday writing, and in any writing you do at work. When you find something useful that applies to writing in other chapters or in other courses or situations, use the "Useful For" tab to mark it for future reference. For example, a history student was asked to write a paper about her recent family history and how it was impacted by larger historical events. She found the suggestions for ways to include evidence in Chapter 17, p. 486, useful, so she tabbed it.

TABLE 17-1 WAYS TO ADD EVIDENCE	
Topic: The Internet's Impact	
Support Your Thesis by	**Example**
Telling a story (narration)	Relate a story about a couple who met using an online dating service.
Adding descriptive detail (description)	Give details about one person's Facebook profile.
Giving an example	Give an example of types of personal likes and dislikes that are included in one person's online profile.
Giving a definition	Explain the meaning of the term "friendship status."
Making comparisons	Compare two online dating sites.
Making distinctions (contrast)	Compare instant messaging with face-to-face conversations.
Discussing types or kinds (classification)	Discuss the types of inf_____

Learn from Your Assignments

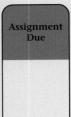

Assignment
Due

TAB: Assignment Due

Assignments, including reading assignments, writing exercises, and paragraph and essay assignments, are learning tools. Every assignment that your instructor gives is intended to teach you something. Make sure you complete all assignments carefully and completely. Mark each assignment given with the "Assignment Due" tab and fill in the date. Don't do any assignment just to get it done. Pay attention to what you are supposed to be learning. For reading assignments, highlight what is important and use the other tabs described above. For written assignments, be sure to submit neat, easy-to-read, well-labeled, and well-organized work. Keep copies of all the essays you write and be sure to keep returned, graded assignments as well. Study your instructor's comments to identify areas in which you can improve.

Assignment
Due

Paragraph Writing Scenarios

9/11/11

Friends and Family

1. Write a paragraph describing an ancestor or relative you've never met, but about whom you've heard a lot. Include things others have said about this person that make him or her sound interesting.

2. Every family has its own idea of success. Write a paragraph about something you've done or could do to make your family proud of you.

Classes and Campus Life

1. You have an important assignment due tomorrow, but classes may be canceled because of the weather. Write a paragraph about how you will spend the evening, preparing for classes or hoping for a storm.

2. A book you need from the library has been out for weeks. Write a paragraph explaining how you will solve the problem.

Working Students

1. Imagine you are going to a job interview. Write a paragraph describing specific strengths you have that will enable you to handle both school and work.

2. Describe in a paragraph something you do to pass the time when work is slow.

Communities and Cultures

1. Some people do best as part of a team, and others prefer to do things alone. Write a paragraph describing one thing you'd rather do on your own and another in which you'd rather be part of a group or team.

2. Society has become very casual, with people wearing jeans in most places. Write a paragraph describing one place where you think jeans or other casual clothes are inappropriate.

Strengthen Your Vocabulary

TAB: *Vocabulary*

Words are the building blocks of language. To write clear sentences and effective paragraphs, you need to have a solid vocabulary with which to start. Everyone can improve his or her vocabulary, and one of the easiest ways to do so is by reading. Throughout the book you will be reading numerous student and professional essays. When you encounter a word you do not know, or one that you know but do not use in your own writing, tab it using the "Vocabulary" tab. If you can get a hint about the word's meaning from the context of the words around it, keep reading and check its meaning later. If you need the word's meaning in order to understand the sentence in which it appears, stop reading and look it up in a dictionary right away. When you find the word's meaning, record it in the margin of the page the word appears on, and later transfer the definition to a vocabulary log.

Vocabulary

READING

THE PLAYLIST'S THE THING

Choosing the right music can help you crank up the workout

By Carolyn Butler

1   Full disclosure is important; there's quite a lot of Britney Spears on my iPod. Yes, my musical tastes typically run to classic rock and country, but when I head for the gym, suddenly I can't get enough of '80s hits like Wham's "Wake Me Up Before You Go-Go," hip-hop tunes like Kanye West's "Gold Digger," or just about anything by the aforementioned Miss Spears. For some reason, these songs just seem to help me stay on the elliptical machine a little longer, make the time pass faster, and leave me smiling—no matter how tired or achy—post-workout.

2   It turns out that there's some science behind this; new research from the ~~al~~ University School of Sport and Education in England shows that rockin~~g~~ ~~cardiovascular exercise ca~~~~~ ~~results~~

A Note About the Tabs You may run out of tabs before you finish the course. However, by then you will have built the habit of using them and can switch over to using sticky notes for the same purpose.

Your digital textbook (e-text) also contains bookmark tabs. At the top, you'll see a toolbar of icons. The third icon from the right is the bookmark icon. It looks like a book page with a ribbon and tabbed corner. Use this icon to bookmark pages that you want to review, follow up on, find useful, have an assignment due on, or want to check vocabulary for. It is a great way to digitally use the sticky-tabs that come with the printed book!

When you are on a page you want to bookmark just click the icon and the top right corner of your page will turn down in a tab. Later, to find the pages you bookmarked, go to the bottom of the left navigation window and select the "Bookmarks" tab.

USE THE HELP FEATURES IN THIS BOOK

Although your instructor and your classmates are your most important sources for learning how to write well, this book also contains numerous features to help you become a successful writer.

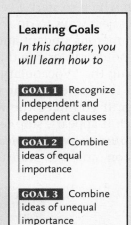

Learning Goals

In this chapter, you will learn how to

GOAL 1 Recognize independent and dependent clauses

GOAL 2 Combine ideas of equal importance

GOAL 3 Combine ideas of unequal importance

Learning Goals

These lists of topics tell you what you should expect to learn in each chapter and correspond to the major headings in each chapter.

Idea Maps

Idea maps, labeled "Visualize It!" are diagrams that show the content and organization of a piece of writing. You can use these maps in several ways:

■ **To organize and guide your own writing.** Think of them as models you can follow.

■ **To help you analyze a paragraph or essay you have written.** Drawing a map of your writing will help you identify problems in organization or spot ideas that do not belong in a paragraph or essay.

■ **As an aid to understanding a professional reading that you have been assigned.** By filling in an idea map, you can assure yourself that you have under- stood the reading, and the process of drawing the map will help you to remember what you read.

WRITE ABOUT IT!

Study the six photographs shown above one at a time (cover the others with your hand as you look at them). What is happening in each one? It is probably difficult to tell because there is so little information in each one. Then, look at the six photographs all together. Now it is clear what is happening. Write a sentence that states the main point of the combined photograph.

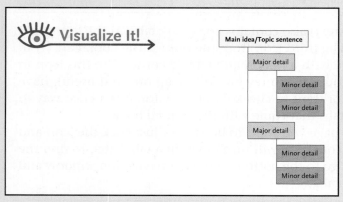

Visualize It! →

Main idea/Topic sentence

Major detail

Minor detail

Minor detail

Major detail

Minor detail

Minor detail

Write About It!

Each chapter opens with a photograph or other visual image that is intended to capture your attention, generate interest, and connect the topic of the chapter to your own experience. This "Write About It!" feature also encourages you to start writing immediately about chapter-related content using a relevant topic.

Student Writing Samples

Paragraphs and essays written by students appear throughout this book. They are realistic models of good writing, but they are not perfect. These pieces of student writing are included to illustrate particular writing techniques. Chapter 10, which discusses how to use verbs, for example, includes a student paragraph that demonstrates how to use verbs to ensure clear, logical writing. Here are some suggestions for reading and writing from student writers:

■ **Read the piece of writing more than once.** Read it once to understand the writer's message. Read it again to examine the writing technique it illustrates.

■ **Read the piece to answer this question: What does this writer do that I can use in my own writing?**

■ **Highlight as you read.** Use an "Important: Review This" tab to mark words, sentences, or paragraphs that you want to study further or that you feel work particularly well.

A STUDENT ESSAY

The Writer
Jessica Nantka earned an associate's degree from Erie Community College in Williamsville, New York. She now attends the State University College at Buffalo where she is majoring in elementary education. Her career goal is to become a teacher.

The Writing Task
For her writing class, Nantka was asked to write an essay explaining what she learned from a work experience. As you read, notice that she uses correct and consistent verbs throughout.

Tittle: Identifies the subject of the essay

I Don't Want a Promotion

Jessica Nantka

Background information about her job

Thesis statement
Topic sentence

At every job, there are different levels of seniority. You might think that getting promoted to the highest position is always better. I work at Picasso's Pizzeria and I've been there for almost two years now. I believe a promotion is not always better, and after experiencing and observing different positions at the pizza shop, a promotion doesn't sound good to me.

When I first started, I was promoted quickly. I worked making wings. Within a month I moved up to making subs, and then to being the weekend sub and wing opener. Three months after I started, I became a sub and wing closer and fourteen months into my job, I became a store opener. Now there is talk that I might become the next manager. I have moved from the bottom of the roster to almost the top in a matter of fifteen months. Although it's flattering to be considered for a manager position, I don't t[...]

NEED TO KNOW

How to Revise Fragments

Once you spot a fragment in your writing, correct it in one of the following ways:

1. **Add a subject if one is missing.**

   FRAGMENT   Appeared on television ten times during the game.

   REVISED   The advertisement for Pepsi appeared on television ten times during the game.

2. **Add a verb if one is missing.** Add a helping verb if one is needed, or change the verb form.

   FRAGMENT   An action-packed commercial with rap music.

   REVISED   An action-packed commercial with rap music advertised a new soft drink.

3. **Combine the fragment with an independent clause to make a complete sentence.**

"Need to Know" Boxes

In many chapters you will find boxes titled "Need to Know." Pay particular attention to these boxes because they present or summarize important information. They are a quick, speedy way to review information, so refer to them often. You may want to use your "Important: Review This" tabs to mark boxes that you find particularly valuable.

Tip for Writers

Tip for Writers boxes appear throughout the book. They are intended to help you learn and apply chapter content by pointing out special concerns, typical grammatical errors, and explaining the meaning of specific words and terms.

Tip for Writers

Then cannot be used to connect two independent clauses even if it is preceded by a comma. When using *then* as a connector, write the sentence one of these ways:

- We adopted a dog, **and then** we adopted four cats.
- We adopted a dog; **then** we adopted four cats.
- We adopted a dog **and then** four cats.

2. **Look for sentences that contain two complete thoughts (independent clauses) without punctuation to separate them.**

complete thought (independent clause)

RUN-ON   Houseplants are pleasant additions to a home or office they add color and variety.

complete thought (independent clause)

complete thought (independent clause)   complete thought (independent clause)

RUN-ON   My sister decided to wear black   I chose red.

complete thought (independent clause)

RUN-ON   Having a garage sale is a good way to make money it unclutters the house, too.

complete thought (independent clause)

complete thought [...]   complete thought [...]

Paragraph Writing Scenarios

This section offers four groups of writing assignments, categorized "Friends and Family," "Classes and Campus Life," "Working Students," and "Communities and Cultures." The writing assignments under each heading offer a wide range of interesting topics and provide an opportunity for you to apply what you have learned in the chapter by writing paragraphs on interesting and relevant topics.

Paragraph Writing Scenarios

Friends and Family

1. Think of a good friend with whom you once had a major argument. Write a paragraph explaining what that argument was about and how you got over it.

2. Write a paragraph describing a relative other than your parents who you were close to as a child.

Classes and Campus Life

1. Think about the teachers you have this year. Write a paragraph comparing two of them. What are the main differences in their styles of teaching?

2. If there is a campus store, write a paragraph about the things you regularly would buy there or would not buy there. If there is not a store on your campus, write a paragraph explaining why you think your school should add one.

Working Students

1. Write an imaginary letter to your boss explaining what you would do to improve your workplace.

2. Write a paragraph explaining why you deserve a raise.

Communities and Cultures

1. People often form ideas about a culture without knowing anyone from that culture. Describe one incorrect idea, misconception, or stereotype that people have about a culture.

2. People live in a variety of communities. Choosing from urban, suburban, rural, or small-town neighborhoods, write a paragraph describing the one you'd most like to live in and why.

Professional Essays

The professional essays in this book were written by expert writers and have been published in books, news magazines, and journals. A professional essay appears at the end of most chapters. By studying the work of professional writers, you can improve your own writing. As with the student writing samples, plan on reading each essay several times. Be sure to look for techniques the writer uses that you can use in your own writing. Both before and after each reading, you will find questions and activities intended to guide you in reading, examining, and writing about the reading.

READING

YOU CAN'T BE THIN ENOUGH: BODY IMAGES AND THE MASS MEDIA

James M. Henslin

1   When you stand before a mirror, do you like what you see? To make your body more attractive, do you watch your weight or work out? You have ideas about what you should look like. Where did you get them?

2   TV and magazine ads keep pounding home the message that our bodies aren't good enough, that we've got to improve them. The way to improve them, of course, is to buy the advertised products: hair extensions for women, hairpieces for men, hair transplants, padded bras, diet programs, anti-aging products, and exercise equipment. Muscular hulks show off machines that magically produce "six-pack abs" and incredible biceps—in just a few minutes a day. Female movie stars effortlessly go through their own tough workouts without even breaking into a sweat. Women and men get the feeling that attractive members of the opposite sex will flock to them if they purchase that wonder-working workout machine.

3   Although we try to shrug off such messages, knowing that they are designed to sell products, the messages still get our attention. They penetrate our thinking and feelings, helping to shape ideal images of how we "ought" to look. Those models so attractively clothed and coiffed as they walk down the runway, could they be any thinner? For women, the message is clear: You can't be thin enough. The men's message is also clear: You can't be muscular enough.

Writers' Workshops

Ten Writers' Workshops are included to help you make an immediate improvement in your writing skills by applying easy-to-follow guidelines. The first set, "Using Words Effectively," provides information on commonly confused words and phrases and how to avoid overused words and phrases, "empty" verbs, and informal language. The second set, "Using Language Effectively," includes tips on how to appropriately convey emotion (no emoticons!); avoid slang, trite expressions and cliches; eliminate redundancy (saying the same thing twice); and avoid using sexist language.

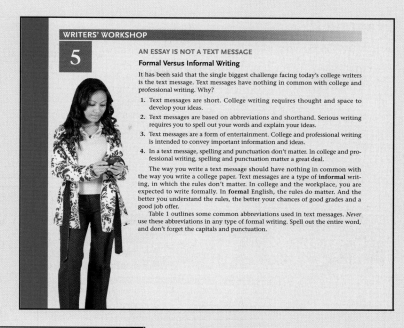

Visualize It!

Many people are visual learners; they process information more effectively when they see it presented in a map, diagram, photograph, or chart format. Throughout the text, idea maps are used to show the structure of paragraphs and the different ways ideas can be organized within them. Idea maps are also used to analyze ideas in paragraphs and to show how first drafts can be revised and improved. Look for the "Visualize It!" arrow.

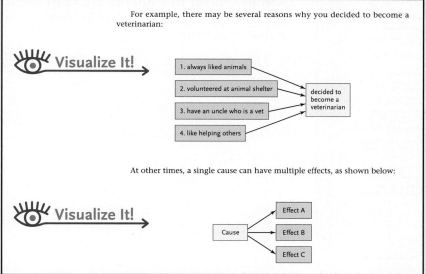

Analyze It!

Practicing the skills you are learning is important, as this is the way you make them part of your own writing process. Starting in Chapter 2, you are asked to analyze a paragraph and apply the skills you have been learning by completing an outline or idea map, figuring out the meaning of vocabulary, or correcting sentence and grammar errors.

Analyze It!

Directions: The following paragraph is correct except that it contains sentence fragments. Underline each fragment. Then revise the paragraph in the space provided by rewriting or combining sentences to eliminate fragments.

Social networks such as Facebook and MySpace appeal to college students for a variety of reasons. Social networks are a way of having conversations. Staying in touch with friends without the inconvenience of getting dressed and meeting them somewhere. Friends can join or drop out of a conversation whenever they want. Social networks also allow college students to meet new people and make new friends. Members can track who is friends with whom. Students may choose to share only portions of their profiles. To protect their privacy. Some students use social networks to form groups. Such as clubs, study groups, or special interest groups. Other students use networks to screen dates. And discover who is interested in dating or who is already taken.

Examine It!

In Chapter 14, "Using Methods of Organization," annotated paragraphs by professional writers and textbook authors are used to illustrate the different methods of organization. These paragraphs provide a quick snapshot of the major elements you need to include when you write a paragraph using a specific pattern of organization.

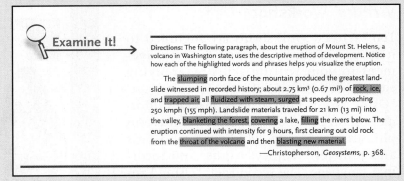

Examine It!

Directions: The following paragraph, about the eruption of Mount St. Helens, a volcano in Washington state, uses the descriptive method of development. Notice how each of the highlighted words and phrases helps you visualize the eruption.

The slumping north face of the mountain produced the greatest landslide witnessed in recorded history; about 2.75 km³ (0.67 mi³) of rock, ice, and trapped air, all fluidized with steam, surged at speeds approaching 250 kmph (155 mph). Landslide materials traveled for 21 km (13 mi) into the valley, blanketing the forest, covering a lake, filling the rivers below. The eruption continued with intensity for 9 hours, first clearing out old rock from the throat of the volcano and then blasting new material.

—Christopherson, *Geosystems*, p. 368.

Writing in a Visual Age

To equip you with the skills to handle the increasingly visual nature of textbooks, Chapters 1–3 and 11–18 include a section titled "Writing in a Visual Age." Each contains a passage that is accompanied by a visual. You will be guided in thinking critically about the passage and the visual and in writing in response to them.

Chapter Review and Practice

Appearing at the end of every chapter, this section offers you some, or all, of the following ways to review what you learned in a particular chapter:

- **The "Chapter Review" section provides a review of the skills taught in the chapter.** Use this to help you remember skills you want to apply in your own writing.

- **The "Editing Practice" gives you an opportunity to identify and correct errors in the writing of others so that you learn to edit your own writing.** Pay particular attention to the types of errors you see and correct in these exercises. The errors shown are common ones, and you may find them in your own writing as well.

- **The "Internet Activities" section directs you to Web sites, including the Web site for MyWritingLab, for additional instruction and/or practice of the skills taught in the chapter.** Use this section to extend and vary your use of the skills you learn in a chapter.

Tab Your Way to Success

Use these tabs to mark important sections and pages of the book that you need to pay special attention to.

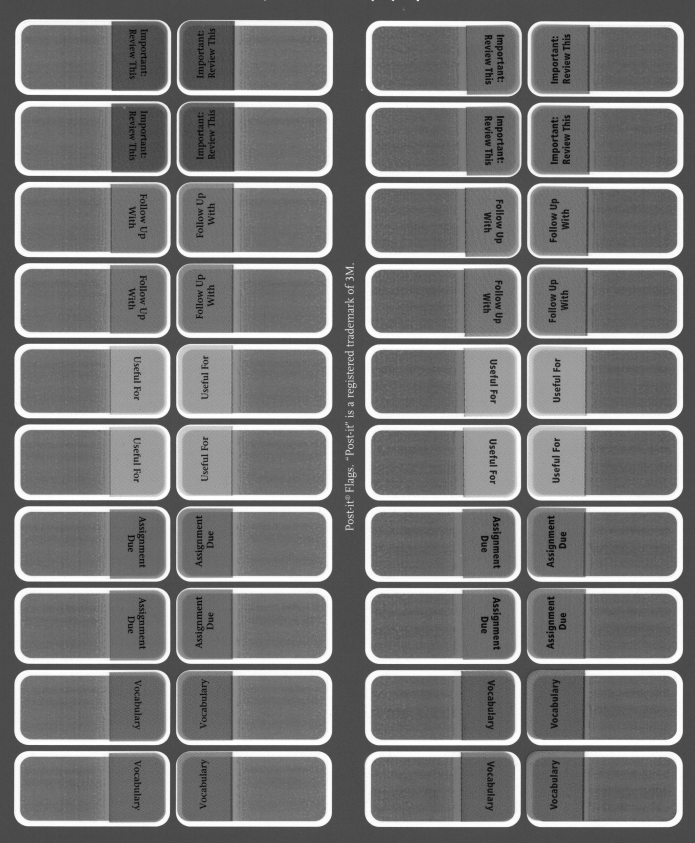

Important: Review This

Important: Review This

Important: Review This

Important: Review This

Important: Review This

Important: Review This

Important: Review This

Important: Review This

Follow Up With

Follow Up With

Follow Up With

Follow Up With

Follow Up With

Follow Up With

Follow Up With

Follow Up With

Useful For

Useful For

Useful For

Useful For

Useful For

Useful For

Useful For

Useful For

Assignment Due

Assignment Due

Assignment Due

Assignment Due

Assignment Due

Assignment Due

Assignment Due

Assignment Due

Vocabulary

Vocabulary

Vocabulary

Vocabulary

Vocabulary

Vocabulary

Vocabulary

Vocabulary

TAKE CHARGE OF YOUR LEARNING

These tabs offer you five ways to be successful in your writing course by taking charge of your own learning. Be sure to read Writing Success Starts Here! for additional information.

Important: Review This

Use this tab to identify the most important and useful materials for you in each chapter and refer to them often throughout the course. These may include strategies, rules, samples, examples, steps, tables, checklists, and idea maps.

Follow Up With

Your instructor is here to help you. When you find things you want to talk about with your instructor, use this tab. Write your instructor's name in the blank, and mark material you have questions about. Tabs can be placed on print copies of your essays, class notes, or instructor handouts, as well as on textbook pages. Your classmates are also valuable resources and you can use this tab to mark material you want to check with one of them.

Useful For

Use this tab when you find something useful that will apply to topics or assignments in other chapters. Also use it to mark sections that will help you in your other college courses.

Assignment Due

Assignments, including reading assignments, writing exercises, and paragraph and essay assignments, are learning tools. Mark each assignment given with the "Assignment Due" tab and fill in the date.

Vocabulary

When you meet a word you do not know, or one that you know but do not use in your own writing, tab it using this "Vocabulary" tab. If you can get a hint about the word's meaning from the words around it, keep reading and check its meaning later. If you need the word's meaning in order to understand the sentence in which it appears, stop reading, and look it up in a dictionary right away. When you find the word's meaning, record it in the margin of the page the word appears in, and later transfer the definition to a vocabulary log.

A Note about the Tabs: **You may run out of tabs before you finish the course. However, by then you will have built the habit of using them and can switch over to using Post-it notes for the same purpose.**

CHAPTER REVIEW AND PRACTICE

CHAPTER REVIEW

To review and check your recall of the chapter, match each term in Column A with its meaning in Column B.

COLUMN A	COLUMN B
_____ 1. classification	a. focuses on similarities and differences
_____ 2. definition	b. describes the order in which things are done or how they work
_____ 3. process	c. takes a position on an issue
_____ 4. narration	d. presents, supports an impression with sensory details
_____ 5. description	e. makes a point by telling a story
_____ 6. example	f. explains by giving situations that illustrate the topic sentence
_____ 7. cause and effect	g. explains why things happen or explains what happens as a result of an action
_____ 8. argument	h. explains a term by giving its class and distinguishing characteristics
_____ 9. comparison and contrast	i. explains by dividing something into groups or categories

EDITING PRACTICE

The following informative paragraph comparing two types of skis is not organized logically. Revise this paragraph so that its main idea is developed logically.

Cross-country skis and downhill skis are different in many aspects. Cross-country skis are intended for gliding over fairly level terrain. Unlike cross-country skis, downhill skis have steel edges and their bindings keep the entire boot clamped

(continued)

WRITING SUCCESS TIPS

The following tips will help you become a more successful student. As you work each section, tab any information you want to refer to again.

TIP #1: Use Electronic Resources

Computers and the Internet are valuable tools for writers. Word processing programs have built-in features to help you polish your writing, and many reference works are available free online.

Jesse Napier
Wesleyan University
Middletown, CT
Jesse is a sophomore at Wesleyan University, where she is pursuing a bachelor's degree in film studies.

　　Advice on using online resources: What I usually do when I have to write a paper is go to a wiki page first. I go to the bottom of the page and look at the sources cited there in the References, Further Reading, and External Links sections, which are good jumping off points because they are more reliable sources. I also use easybib.com for citing sources. I go to the Web site, type in the source information for a Website, book, journal or whatever and it automatically formats in MLA style—or APA or other styles.

Working with Electronic Resources

A computer cannot do the writing for you, but it *can* help you at many stages of the writing process.

If you need help with...	Use this resource	Other suggestions
Spelling	Your word processing program's **spell-check** feature.	• Never turn in an assignment without spell-checking it first. • Be careful! Spell-checkers often do not recognize the names of people and places. Evaluate each suggested change before making it. • Spell-checkers don't catch everything, so you still need to proofread your work.
Vocabulary, word definitions, and proper usage	An **online dictionary**. Two excellent, free online dictionaries are: • Merriam-Webster's dictionary at http://www.m-w.com • http://www.dictionary.com Both sites allow you to hear word pronunciations.	• Many word processing programs also come with built-in dictionaries. Look for them in the "Tools" menu.
Word variety	An **online thesaurus**. You can find a free thesaurus online at: • http://www.thesaurus.com	• A thesaurus lists synonyms, words that mean the same as another word. For example, thesaurus.com lists 80 synonyms for *happy*. Using a thesaurus not only brings variety to your writing, it also helps you develop your vocabulary.
Accuracy of your material	A **fact-checking Web site**. Make sure you have your facts correct. http://www.refdesk.com provides a large number of free resources, including online encyclopedias, maps, and headline news.	• The most popular online encyclopedia is Wikipedia (http://www.wikipedia.org). Most college instructors do not consider Wikipedia a fully reliable source of information, so anything you find there should be double-checked with at least one other source.
Foreign words or expressions	An **online translator**. Two good translation tools are: • http://www.itools.com/lang • http://babelfish.yahoo.com	• Online tools allow you to translate not only individual words and expressions, but also entire Web pages.
Any aspect of the writing process	An **online writing center**. One of the most popular is Purdue University's Online Writing Lab (OWL), which can be found at http://owl.english.purdue.edu. OWL offers help with writing, grammar, and research.	• Your campus may also have a writing center with tutors who are available to help you. Make an appointment if you need help with any part of the writing process.

Try It Out!

"Some say I am sanguine; others say I am bilious. I believe I am pragmatic." Rewrite these two sentences with different words, using dictionary.com and thesaurus.com as resources.

TIP #2: Manage Your Valuable Time

Many students say they do not have enough time to pay adequate attention to classes, studying, jobs, family, and friends. You can avoid or overcome this problem by managing your time effectively.

Veronica Evans-Johnson
Durham Technical College
Durham, NC
Veronica has been attending Durham Tech, first as a part-time student and recently as a full-time student. She is successfully working toward an associate's degree in business administration. She plans to transfer to Central University and prepare for a career in business administration.

Advice on time management: Dreams do come true. Always follow your heart. Never feel you're a failure. No matter what age you are, you can always go back to school. Once you've got an education, no one can steal it away from you. Set your goals high, write them down, and check them off as you go.

I take care of my family first in the evenings. Then I go to my room, close the door, and don't take calls. My family knows not to bother me. I have a laptop and I take it everywhere with me so if I have some free time I can get some [school] work done.

How to Manage Your Time

- **Develop a weekly study plan.** Set aside time for reading assignments, writing and revising papers, reviewing what you have learned, and studying for exams. Identify specific times each week for working on each of your courses.

- **As a rule of thumb, reserve two study hours for each hour you spend in class.**

- **Work on difficult assignments first.** It is tempting to get the easy tasks out of the way first, but then you are left with the more challenging ones when you are tired. Work on difficult tasks, like brainstorming ideas for an essay, when your mind is fresh. When you are tired, do more routine tasks such as organizing lecture notes.

- **Schedule study for a particular course close to class time.** By studying close to class time, you will find it easier to relate what goes on in class to what you have been reading and writing about.

- **Include short breaks in your study time.** Studying for long, uninterrupted periods of time leads to fatigue. Taking periodic, short breaks refreshes you and helps you to focus when you resume working.

Try It Out!

Plan a weekly schedule using the tips provided. Try it for one week, evaluate what worked and what did not, and then revise it.

TIP #3: Organize a Place to Read and Write

You will find that it is easier to read and write if you do so in the same place, as well as at the same time, each day.

Nina Paus-Weiler
Occidental College
Eagle Rock, CA
Nina is a sophomore at Occidental College, where she is working towards a bachelor's degree in urban and environmental policy.
   Advice on organizing a place to study: I go to the library because it makes me work, no distractions. I find a spot that's secluded, usually near a window so I don't feel trapped. My dorm is far away from the library, so I bring everything I need to work, including drinks and snacks. I also write in my room a lot at my desk. If my roommate and I are both working, we'll be quiet, use headphones.

Organizing a Place to Read and Write

- **Try to find a quiet area that you can reserve for reading and writing.** If possible, avoid areas used for other purposes, such as the dining room or kitchen table, because you'll have to move or clean up your materials frequently. If you live in a dorm, your desk is an ideal place to write, unless the dorm is too noisy. If it is, find a quiet place elsewhere on campus.

- **Use a table or desk.** Do not try to write on the arm of a comfortable chair. Choose a space where you can spread out your papers.

- **Eliminate distractions from your writing area.** Get rid of photos or stacks of bills to pay that may take your mind off your writing.

- **Be sure that the lighting is adequate and your chair is straight and not too comfortable.**

- **Collect and organize supplies.** You will need plenty of paper, pens, pencils, erasers, a ruler, a stapler, and so forth. If you write on a computer, keep spare CDs on hand.

- **Organize completed and returned papers, quizzes, class handouts, and other course materials in separate folders.**

Try It Out!

Choose one place at home (or in your dorm) and organize it. Write a list of supplies you need. Try using this location for one week. Do you notice a difference in your ability to get down to work and get things done?

TIP #4: Build Your Concentration

No matter how intelligent you are, how serious you are, or what skills and talents you possess, reading and writing will be difficult and frustrating if you cannot keep your mind on the task at hand. Improving your concentration involves two tasks: eliminating distractions and building your attention span.

Dimitrus Loza
Portland Community College
Portland, OR
Dimitrus is a freshman at Portland Community College where she is studying for her bachelor's degree in law. When she graduates she plans to attend Texas Technical University and pursue a master's degree in law.

Advice on concentration and memorizing information: I have three puppies and I take them to the park and study while they play. It's very relaxing and I get fresh air, and I don't get overwhelmed the way I do inside. I take my books and a notepad, read through a chapter, and write down what's important. When it rains I visit a friend who has a gazebo. In the house it can feel chaotic and cooped up.

One thing I learned was to read right before I go to sleep. I spend about 30–40 minutes going through my notes and everything I wrote down when I was studying, and in the morning I know it. That's how I study for tests.

Eliminating Distractions

- **Choose a place to study with minimal distractions.** Try it out and identify any distractions that occur. If you cannot eliminate them, find a different place to work.

- **Control noise levels.** Determine how much background noise you need or can tolerate, and choose a place best suited to those requirements.

- **Write down bothersome details.** When you think of an errand you need to do or a call you need to make, write it down on a separate notepad to follow up on later. Once you have written it down, you will be able to stop thinking about it.

- **Ask for cooperation.** Your family, friends, and roommates need to understand that you need to be by yourself in order to get your work done.

- **Shut off your cell phone.**

Focusing Your Attention

- **Establish goals and time limits for each assignment.** Deadlines will keep you motivated, and you will be less likely to daydream.

- **Use writing to keep mentally and physically active.** Highlighting, outlining, and note-taking will force you to keep your mind on what you are doing.

- **Reward yourself.** Use rewards such as texting with a friend or ordering a pizza when you complete an evening of study or a particularly challenging assignment.

Try It Out!

Place a check mark in front of three suggestions in the two preceding lists that may work for you. Choose three days this week and try to build one of these suggestions into your routine each day.

TIP #5: Collaborate for Success

While *you* are responsible for your college success, you'll need the help of others along the way. Instructors will offer feedback on your work, and you'll sometimes need to work closely with classmates as well.

Jonathan Fischer
New Jersey Institute of Technology
Newark, NJ
Jonathan successfully completed an associate's degree in civil engineering at Middlesex County College. He transferred to the New Jersey Institute of Technology to earn a bachelor's degree in construction management.
   Advice on getting feedback: When I did badly on a test, I approached my teacher a week or two later. We were already doing new material. We met and made a plan. We started with the material on the test and went over it all and then caught up with the new material. He went step by step through everything, saying "this is good, you went wrong here," and then we went back over what I did to make sure I really understood. The only dummy is the one who doesn't go for help.

Learning from Peer Review

In writing classes, you'll often participate in **peer review**, in which you comment on your classmates' writing and they comment on yours. How can you make peer reviewing as valuable as possible?

When You Are the Writer

1. Prepare your draft in readable form. Double-space your work and print it on standard 8.5″ × 11″ paper. Use only one side of the paper.

2. When you receive your peers' comments, weigh them carefully. Keep an open mind, but do not feel that you must accept every suggestion that is made.

3. If you have questions or are uncertain about your peers' advice, talk with your instructor.

When You Are the Reviewer

1. Read the draft through at least once before making any suggestions.

2. As you read, keep the writer's intended audience in mind (see Chapter 11). The draft should be appropriate for that audience.

3. Offer positive comments first. Say what the writer did well.

4. Use the Revision Checklists in Chapters 12–18 to guide your reading and comments. Be specific in your review and offer suggestions for improvement.

Try It Out!

Exchange writing samples with a classmate.

1. List two things the writer did well.
   a. _____

   b. _____

2. List two areas for improvement.
   a. _____

   b. _____

1

An Introduction to Writing

Learning Goals

In this chapter, you will learn how to

GOAL 1 Use the writing process

GOAL 2 Generate ideas

GOAL 3 Organize ideas

GOAL 4 Write a paragraph

GOAL 5 Write an essay

GOAL 6 Prepare to write

WRITE ABOUT IT!

In the photo above, the student at the computer is writing an assigned essay. Write a few sentences describing what that student might be feeling, using your own experiences with writing as a guide. What problems might she be facing? What things can she do well? What are her trouble spots?

For problems and trouble spots, did you identify problems such as not knowing what to write about, not knowing what to say, or problems catching and correcting spelling and grammar errors?

This book will address common writing problems and help you improve your writing. It will concentrate on writing as a means of expressing ideas. You will learn to plan, organize, and develop your ideas. You will learn to write sentences and paragraphs that express your ideas clearly and effectively. You will also learn how to avoid common problems writing paragraphs and sentences. Finally, after you have expressed your ideas, you will discover that grammar, punctuation, and spelling do have an important function in writing.

WRITING

UNDERSTANDING WHAT WRITING IS AND IS NOT

GOAL 1 Use the writing process

The following list explains some correct and incorrect notions about writing:

Writing is . . .

- following a step-by-step process of planning, drafting, and revising.
- thinking through and organizing ideas.
- explaining *your* ideas or experiences clearly and correctly.
- using precise, descriptive, and accurate vocabulary.
- constructing clear, understandable sentences.
- a skill that can be learned.

Writing is not . . .

- being able to pick up a pen (or sit at a computer) and write something wonderful on your first try.
- developing new, earthshaking ideas no one has ever thought of before.
- being primarily concerned with grammatical correctness.
- showing off a large vocabulary.
- constructing long, complicated sentences.

EXERCISE 1-1   Describing the Writing Process

Directions: Suppose you are writing a letter to a toy manufacturer about a defective toy you purchased for your niece or nephew. You feel the toy is unsafe for toddlers. Describe, step by step, how you would go about writing this letter. (What is the first thing you would do? What would you do after that? And so forth.) You are not actually writing the letter in this exercise or listing what you would say. You are describing your writing *process*. ■

mywriting**lab**

To practice with the writing process, go to
■ Study Plan
■ Writing Process

The Writing Process: An Overview

Writing, like many other skills, is not a single-step process. Think of the game of football, for instance. Football players spend a great deal of time planning and developing offensive and defensive strategies, trying out new plays, improving existing plays, and practicing. Writing involves similar planning and preparation. It also involves testing ideas and working out the best way to express them. Writers often explore how their ideas might "play out" in several ways before settling upon one plan of action.

People have many individual techniques for writing, but all writing involves five basic steps, as shown in Table 1-1.

TABLE 1-1

Steps in the Writing Process	Description of Steps
1. Generating ideas	Finding ideas to write about.
2. Organizing your ideas	Discovering ways to arrange your ideas logically.
3. Writing a first draft	Expressing your ideas in sentence and paragraph form without worrying about spelling, punctuation, capitalization, and grammar.
4. Revising	Rethinking your ideas and finding ways to make your writing clearer, more complete, and more interesting. Revising involves changing, adding, deleting, and rearranging your ideas and words to make your writing better.
5. Proofreading	Checking for errors in grammar, spelling, punctuation, and capitalization.

Tip for Writers

A *draft* is a piece of writing that is not finished.

Revising is the process of rethinking your ideas. It involves adding ideas, deleting ideas, rearranging ideas, and changing the way you have expressed your thoughts.

NEED TO KNOW
The Writing Process

- Writing is a step-by-step process of explaining your ideas and experiences.

- Writing involves five basic steps: generating ideas, organizing your ideas, writing a first draft, revising, and proofreading.

BEGINNING TIPS FOR GENERATING IDEAS

GOAL 2
Generate ideas

Before you can write about a topic, you have to collect ideas to write about. Because many students need help with this right away, three helpful techniques are described here: (1) freewriting, (2) brainstorming, and (3) branching. These techniques are discussed in detail in Chapter 11. Here is a brief introduction to each.

To practice prewriting, go to
- Study Plan
- Writing Process
- Prewriting

Freewriting

What is freewriting? Freewriting is writing nonstop about a topic for a specified period of time.

How does freewriting work? You write whatever comes into your mind, and you do not stop to be concerned about correctness. After you have finished, you go back through your writing and pick out ideas that you might be able to use.

What does it look like? Here is a sample of freewriting done on the topic of owning a dog.

Sample Freewriting

I really wish I had a dog. I need some what's it called . . . oh, yeah, unconditional love. Something that never gets mad at me, no matter what I do. Jumping up and happy whenever it sees me. Definitely loves me best. I could teach it tricks, like roll over and speak or dance with me. Maybe I could get on TV, like Letterman's Stupid Pet Tricks or Those Amazing Animals. What breeds are the smartest? I don't want one that's so big I can't lift it by myself. But I hate those yappy little ones that shiver all the time. I saw a woman walking one once in the winter. It had a little coat on that matched the woman's coat. I wouldn't do something that lame. How do you get them to be good guard dogs? Guess I'd have to pay for training. Ow. What else would I have to pay for; shots, neutering, bed, collar, vet bills? I can't afford that stuff, even if I get a mutt from the shelter. Can I take it to work? Ha! I can just see my boss's face when I walk in with a giant, slobbering Newfoundland! There goes that job. And how could I get home to walk it in between work and class? I only have half an hour. Guess I'd better wait.

Brainstorming

What is brainstorming? Brainstorming is making a list of everything you can think of that has to do with your topic.

How does brainstorming work? Try to stretch your imagination and think of everything related to your topic. Include facts, ideas, examples, questions, and feelings. When you have finished, read through what you have written and highlight usable ideas.

What does brainstorming look like? Here is a sample of brainstorming on the topic of fast food:

Sample Brainstorming on Fast Food

Brands: Burger King, KFC, McDonald's, Wendy's, Pizza Hut, Taco Bell	Comfort food
Advertised on TV; famous	Delicious but high in fat and calories
Lots of them across the country, in every city and town	Hard to order only healthy food
Small menu, limited choices	Burgers, fries, pizza, chicken
Familiar; food is the same everywhere	Soft drinks
Young or inexperienced workers	Sometimes lines are long
Boring to work there	Cheap compared to restaurants
	Can eat in car, on the run

Branching

What is branching? Branching is a way of using diagrams or drawings to generate ideas.

How does branching work? Begin by drawing a 2-inch oval in the middle of a page. Write your topic in that oval. Think of the oval as a tree trunk. Next, draw lines radiating out from the trunk, as branches would. Write an idea related to your topic at the end of each branch. When you have finished, highlight the ideas you find most useful.

What does branching look like? Here is a sample of branching done on the topic of religious holidays:

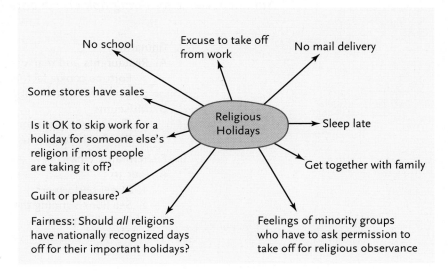

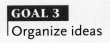

EXERCISE 1-2
Writing in Progress

Practicing Generating Ideas

Directions: Choose one of the following topics. Then try out two of the techniques described for generating ideas.

1. Identity theft
2. Internet communication
3. Telemarketing
4. Advertising ploys and gimmicks
5. Airport security ■

BEGINNING TIPS FOR ORGANIZING YOUR IDEAS

GOAL 3
Organize ideas

Two common methods of organizing ideas are outlining and idea mapping. Understanding each of them will help you decide how to arrange the ideas that you have identified as useful.

Outlining

What is outlining? Outlining is a method of listing the main points you will cover and their subpoints (details) in the order in which you will present them.

How does outlining work? To make an outline, you list the most important ideas on separate lines at the left margin of a sheet of paper, leaving space underneath each idea. In the space under each main idea, list the details that you will include to explain that main idea. Indent the list of details that fits under each of your most important ideas.

What does outlining look like? Here is a sample outline for a brief essay on the topic of a vacation in San Francisco:

Sample Outline for Paragraph on Favorite Places

I. Chinatown
   A. Restaurants and markets
      1. Fortune cookie factory
      2. Dim sum restaurants
   B. Museums
      1. Chinese Culture Center
      2. Pacific Heritage Museum
II. Fisherman's Wharf
   A. Pier 39
      1. Street performers
      2. Sea lions sunning themselves on the docks
   B. Ghirardelli Square

Idea Mapping

What is idea mapping? An idea map is a drawing that shows the content and organization of a piece of writing.

How does idea mapping work? An idea map shows you how ideas are connected and can help you see which ideas are not relevant to the topic of your essay.

What does an idea map look like? Here is a sample idea map drawn for a paragraph on the topic of choosing an Internet password:

 **Visualize It!**

Idea Map

It is important to choose Internet passwords carefully, using the following suggestions.

Do not use common words or names.

Do not use the same password in many places.

Use both numbers and letters.

Change your password frequently.

Tell no one your password.

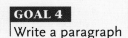

EXERCISE 1-3
Writing in Progress

Using Outlining or Mapping

Directions: For the topic you chose in Exercise 1-2, use outlining or idea mapping to organize your ideas. ■

WRITING PARAGRAPHS

GOAL 4
Write a paragraph

A **paragraph** is a group of sentences, usually at least three or four, that expresses one main idea. Paragraphs may stand alone to express one thought, or they may be combined into essays. Paragraphs are one of the basic building blocks of writing, so it is important to learn to write them effectively.

A paragraph's one main idea is expressed in a single sentence called the **topic sentence**. The other sentences in the paragraph, called **supporting details**, explain or support the main idea. You can visualize a paragraph as follows:

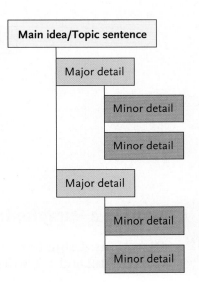

Here is a sample paragraph; its idea map appears on the following page.

> The Abkhasians (an agricultural people who live in a mountainous region of Georgia, a republic of the former Soviet Union) may be the longest-lived people on earth. Many claim to live past 100—some beyond 120 and even 130. Although it is difficult to document the accuracy of these claims, government records indicate that an extraordinary number of Abkhasians do live to a very old age. Three main factors appear to account for their long lives. The first is their diet, which consists of little meat, much fresh fruit, vegetables, garlic, goat cheese, cornmeal, buttermilk and wine. The second is their lifelong physical activity. They do slow down after age 80, but even after the age of 100 they still work about four hours a day. The third factor—a highly developed sense of community—goes to the very heart of the Abkhasian culture. From childhood, each individual is integrated into a primary group, and remains so throughout life. There is no such thing as a nursing home, nor do the elderly live alone.
>
> —adapted from Henslin, *Sociology*, pp. 380–381.

 **Visualize It!** →

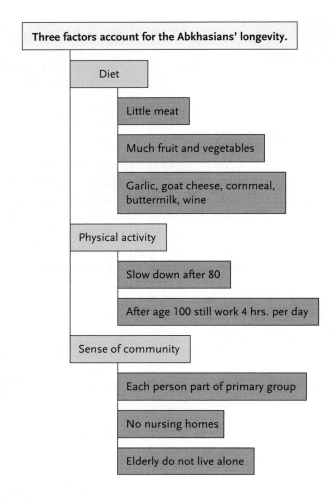

Three factors account for the Abkhasians' longevity.

- Diet
  - Little meat
  - Much fruit and vegetables
  - Garlic, goat cheese, cornmeal, buttermilk, wine
- Physical activity
  - Slow down after 80
  - After age 100 still work 4 hrs. per day
- Sense of community
  - Each person part of primary group
  - No nursing homes
  - Elderly do not live alone

EXERCISE 1-4

Writing in Progress

Writing a Paragraph

Directions: Using one or more of the ideas you generated and organized in Exercises 1-2 and 1-3, write a paragraph about the topic you chose. ■

EXERCISE 1-5

Working Together

Writing a Paragraph

Directions: Write a paragraph on one of the following topics. Be sure to begin with a sentence that states the one idea your paragraph is about.

TOPIC 1. Describe a space alien's fear or surprise when stepping out of a spaceship onto Earth. Explain what the alien sees or hears and how it reacts to what it sees.

TOPIC 2. Describe your reaction to your first day of college classes. Include specific examples to support your description.

Working with a classmate, compare and evaluate each other's paragraphs. Is the opening sentence clear? Is that idea explained in the remainder of the paragraph? ■

WRITING ESSAYS

Write an essay

An essay, which consists of three or more paragraphs, expresses and explains a series of related ideas, all of which support a larger, broader idea.

The emphasis of this text is on writing effective sentences and paragraphs. However, in some of your courses your instructors may ask you to write essays or take essay exams. Some writing instructors prefer that their students write essays right away. Other instructors prefer that their students begin by writing single paragraphs and then progress to essay writing. Regardless of when you begin writing essays, the following introduction to essay techniques will be useful to you. It will show you why good paragraph-writing skills are absolutely necessary for writing good essays.

What Is an Essay?

An **essay** is a group of paragraphs about one subject. It contains one key idea about the subject that is called the **thesis statement**. Each paragraph in the essay supports or explains some aspect of the thesis statement.

How Is an Essay Organized?

An essay follows a logical and direct plan: it introduces an idea (the thesis statement), explains it, and draws a conclusion. Therefore, an essay usually has at least three paragraphs:

1. Introductory paragraph
2. Body (one or more paragraphs)
3. Concluding paragraph

The Introductory Paragraph

Your **introductory paragraph** should accomplish three things:

1. It should establish the topic of the essay.
2. It should present the thesis statement of your essay in an appropriate way for your intended audience.
3. It should interest your audience in your essay.

The Body

The **body** of your essay should accomplish three things:

1. It should provide information that supports and explains your thesis statement.
2. It should present each main supporting point in a separate paragraph.
3. It should contain enough detailed information to make the main point of each paragraph understandable and believable.

The Concluding Paragraph

Your **concluding paragraph** should accomplish two things:

1. It should reemphasize but not restate your thesis statement.
2. It should draw your essay to a close.

You can visualize the organization of an essay using the following idea map:

 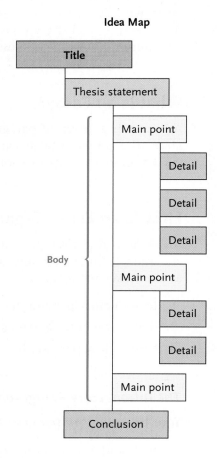

In the following sample essay, the marginal notes indicate the function of each paragraph. Read the essay and study the idea map that follows it.

A Sample Student Essay

Title: identifies the two topics

College and the Marine Corps

Introduction: topic is introduced

I have made two important decisions in my lifetime. They were to join the Marine Corps and to attend college. Each decision turned out to be the right one for me. Although the Marines and college are very different, each has had a similar effect on me.

Thesis statement
Description of Marine Corps

There was only one reason for joining the Marine Corps. I had to make money to go to college. I needed it, and they offered it. The Marine Corps was more difficult and challenging than I had thought it would be. Boot camp was horrible. Being deployed to Iraq was worse. Each day was filled with obstacles, physical as well as mental. Each day, however, I felt a strong sense of accomplishment in making it through the day. At the end of my tour of duty I was proud to call myself a Marine.

Description of college

College has turned out to be the same as the Marine Corps in many ways. I chose to attend college for one reason: to have a career. I am enrolled in the Operating Room Assistant program, and it is much more difficult than I imagined it to be. Biology and Medical Terminology are hard courses. There are many obstacles, such as unannounced quizzes, labs, and exams. However, each time I earn a passing grade, I feel the same sense of accomplishment that I felt in the Marines. I know that when I graduate and walk into an operating room, I will be proud to be part of the medical team.

Conclusion: draws essay to a close; looks ahead to the future

Soon I plan to make a decision just as important as joining the Marine Corps or attending college. Next spring, I am planning to get married to a person I met in the Marines. I hope it, too, will work out.

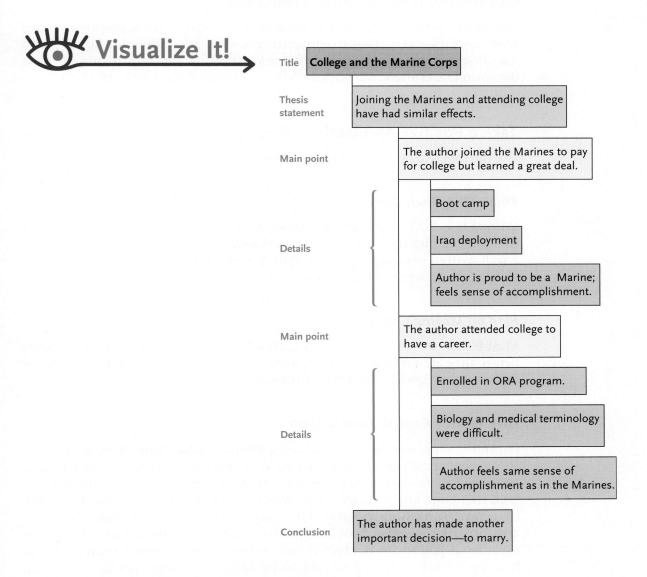

Visualize It!

Title — **College and the Marine Corps**

Thesis statement — Joining the Marines and attending college have had similar effects.

Main point — The author joined the Marines to pay for college but learned a great deal.

Details —
- Boot camp
- Iraq deployment
- Author is proud to be a Marine; feels sense of accomplishment.

Main point — The author attended college to have a career.

Details —
- Enrolled in ORA program.
- Biology and medical terminology were difficult.
- Author feels same sense of accomplishment as in the Marines.

Conclusion — The author has made another important decision—to marry.

EXERCISE 1-6   Writing an Essay
Writing in Progress

Directions: Using the ideas you generated in Exercise 1-2 but did not use to write a paragraph in Exercise 1-4, write a short essay. You may need to do additional brainstorming, freewriting, or branching to come up with enough ideas to write about. ■

PRACTICAL ADVICE FOR GETTING STARTED

GOAL 6
Prepare to write

Writing is a skill that you can learn with the help of this book, your instructor, and your classmates. Like any other skill, such as basketball, accounting, or cooking, writing takes practice. Be sure to focus your attention on new techniques suggested by your instructor as well as the ones given in each chapter of this book. To improve, you often need to be open to doing things differently. Expect success; don't hesitate to experiment.

Get the Most out of Your Writing Class

Attend all classes. Do not miss any classes and be sure to come prepared to class with readings and writing assignments complete. Take notes during class, and ask questions about things you do not understand. Be sure to participate in class discussions and attend all writing conferences offered by your instructor.

Take a Positive Approach to Writing

Use the following tips to achieve success:

Think First, Then Write

Writing is a thinking process: it is an expression of your thoughts. Don't expect to be able to pick up a pen or sit down at a computer and immediately produce a well-written paragraph or essay. Plan to spend time generating ideas and deciding how to organize them before you write your first draft.

Plan on Making Changes

Most writers revise (rethink, rewrite, change, add, and delete) numerous times before they are pleased with their work. For example, I revised this chapter of *Pathways* five times before I was satisfied with it.

Give Yourself Enough Time to Write

For most of us, writing does not come easily. It takes time to think, select a topic, generate ideas, organize them, draft a piece of writing, revise it, and proofread it. Reserve a block of time each day for writing. Use the time to read this book and to work on its writing exercises and assignments. Begin by reserving an hour per day. This may seem like a lot of time. However, most instructors expect you to spend at least two hours outside of class for every hour you spend in class. If your writing class meets for a total of three hours per week, then you should spend at least six hours per week working on writing.

Develop a Routine

Try to work at the same time each day. You will develop a routine that will be easy to follow. Be sure to work at peak periods of concentration. Don't write when you are tired, hungry, or likely to be interrupted.

Take Breaks

If you get stuck and cannot think or write, take a break. Clear your mind by going for a walk, talking to a friend, or having a snack. Set a time limit for your break, though, so you return to work in a reasonable time. When you begin again, start by rereading what you have already written. If you still cannot make progress, use freewriting, brainstorming, and branching techniques (see pp. 19–21) to generate more ideas about your topic.

Keep a Journal

A writing journal is an excellent way to improve your writing and keep track of your thoughts and ideas. A **writing journal** is a collection of your writing and reflections.

How to Keep a Writing Journal

1. Buy an 8.5-by-11-inch spiral-bound notebook. Use it exclusively for journal writing. Alternatively, you can use a computer file.

2. Reserve ten to fifteen minutes a day to write in your journal. Write every day, not just on days when a good idea strikes.

3. Write about whatever comes to mind. You might write about events that happened and your reactions to them, or describe feelings, impressions, or worries.

   If you have trouble getting started, ask yourself some questions:

   - What happened at school, work, or home?
   - What world, national, or local events occurred?
   - What am I worried about?
   - What positive experience have I had lately? Maybe it was eating a good meal, making a new friend, or finding time to wash your car.
   - What did I see today? Practice writing descriptions of beautiful, funny, interesting, or disturbing things you've noticed.
   - What is the best or worst thing that happened today?
   - Who did I talk to? What did I talk about? Record conversations as fully as you can.

Sample Journal Entries

The following student journal entries will give you a better picture of journal writing. They have been edited for easy reading. However, as you write, do not be concerned with neatness or correctness.

> *Jeffrey* The best thing that happened today happened as soon as I got home from work. My cell phone rang. At first, I wasn't going to answer it because I was tired and in one of those moods when I wanted to be by myself. It rang so many times I decided to answer it. Am I glad I did! It was MaryAnn, a long-lost girlfriend whom I'd always regretted losing touch with. She said she had just moved back into the neighborhood, and . . . I took it from there.

Malcolm This morning while walking across campus to my math class, I stopped for a few minutes under a chestnut tree. Perfect timing! I've always loved collecting chestnuts, and they were just beginning to fall. When I was a kid, I used to pick up lunch bags full of them. I never knew what to do with them once I had them. I just liked picking them up, I guess. I remember liking their cold, sleek, shiny smoothness and how good they felt in my hand. So I picked up a few, rubbed them together in my hand, and went off to class, happy that some things never change.

Benefits of Journal Writing

When you write in your journal, you are practicing writing and becoming better at expressing your thoughts in writing. You can practice without pressure or fear of criticism. Besides practice, journal writing has other benefits:

1. Your journals will become a good source of ideas. When you have a paper assigned and must select your own topic, review your journal for ideas.

2. You may find that journal writing becomes a way to think through problems, release pent-up feelings, or keep an enjoyable record of life experiences. Journal writing is writing *for yourself.*

Use Peer Review

Not everything you write in a college writing class needs to be graded by your instructor. Instead, you can get valuable "peer review," or feedback, from other members of your class. Peers (classmates) can tell you what they like and what they think you need to do to improve your writing. You can also learn a lot from reading and commenting on the work of other students. To learn more about peer review, see Writing Success Tip #5: Collaborate for Success.

Writing in a Visual Age

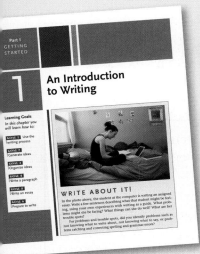

Part I
GETTING STARTED

1   An Introduction to Writing

Learning Goals
In this chapter you will learn how to:

GOAL 1 Use the writing process

GOAL 2 Generate ideas

GOAL 3 Organize ideas

GOAL 4 Write a paragraph

GOAL 5 Write an essay

GOAL 6 Prepare to write

WRITE ABOUT IT!

In the photo above, the student at the computer is writing an assigned essay. Write a few sentences describing what that student might be feeling, using your own experiences with writing as a guide. What problems might she be facing? What things can she do well? What are her trouble spots?

For problems and trouble spots, did you identify problems such as not knowing what to write about, not knowing what to say, or problems catching and correcting spelling and grammar errors?

Think about the written materials you see each day—textbooks, magazines, newspapers, Web sites. Which are you more likely to read: a magazine that contains text along with photos and other graphics, or a newspaper article that contains words only?

In our visual age, most people like to see illustrations with their reading materials. Because well-chosen photos can make good writing even more effective, many writers now include visual aids along with their words. (You may have noticed, for example, that each chapter in this book begins with a photo.)

One goal of *Pathways* is to emphasize the many connections among reading, writing, and visuals. To strengthen your ability to understand and use visuals in your writing, each chapter ends with a "Writing in a Visual Age" exercise that will help you develop your reading, writing, critical thinking, and visual skills together.

READING

1. Read the following paragraphs. Then underline the topic sentences and key supporting details.

   Fashion does not reflect solely the designer's tastes and interests. Rather, fashion is a reflection of the social, political, economic, and artistic forces of any given time. Changing styles throughout the ages tell the story of societal changes and attitudes just as effectively as textbooks and scholarly journals. Throughout history, clothing and fashion have reflected the way people think, live, and love.

   Fashion, as we know it, is relatively new. In ancient and medieval times, clothing styles remained practically unchanged for a hundred years at a time. Fashions began to change more rapidly in the 1500s, as European explorers discovered different cultures, customs, and costumes. They brought these ideas home from their travels, and as new fabrics and ideas became available, people began to develop a fashion sense. The demand grew for new styles, and being "fashionable" became a goal of the upper classes. Today, in the twenty-first century, fashion is everywhere. Magazines, television shows, and Web sites all help to spread new fashion trends to young and old, rich and poor alike.

   —adapted from Frings, *Fashion, p.* 6.

CRITICAL THINKING AND RESPONSE

2. Write a paragraph answering the following questions: What is the author's purpose for writing? Do you think she accomplished her goal? Does this reading make you want to learn more about fashion?

WRITING

3. Summarize the reading in one or two sentences.

4. Think of a celebrity (actor, model, sports figure) with a fashion sense that you admire. Write a paragraph explaining why that person's style appeals to you.

5. Suppose you would like to find a photo to illustrate this reading. What type of photo would you use and why?

6. A **caption** is a brief description of a photo that connects it to the reading. Write a caption to accompany the photo. (A caption should always be a complete sentence.)

Caption: _____

CHAPTER REVIEW AND PRACTICE

CHAPTER REVIEW

To review and check your recall of the chapter, match each term in Column A with its meaning in Column B and write the correct letter in the space provided in Column A.

COLUMN A

_____ 1. peer review

_____ 2. writing journal

_____ 3. writing

_____ 4. freewriting

_____ 5. brainstorming

_____ 6. branching

_____ 7. outlining

_____ 8. idea map

_____ 9. paragraph

_____ 10. essay

COLUMN B

a. writing nonstop about a topic for a specified period of time

b. listing points and subpoints you will cover in the order in which you will cover them

c. a group of paragraphs about one subject

d. a collection of your writing and reflections

e. a process of planning, drafting, and revising ideas

f. a group of sentences that express one main idea

g. using drawings and diagrams to generate ideas

h. generating ideas by making a list of everything that comes to mind on a topic

i. a process in which a classmate reads and comments on a student's writing

j. a diagram that shows both the content and organization of a planned piece of writing

 For support in meeting this chapter's objectives, log in to www.mywritinglab.com, go to the Study Plan tab, click on An Introduction to Writing and choose The Writing Process from the list of subtopics. Read and view the videos and resources in the Review Materials section, and then complete the Recall, Apply, and Write exercises in the Activities section. You can check your scores and overall progress by using the Gradebook.

2

The Reading-Writing Connection

Learning Goals

In this chapter, you will learn how to

GOAL 1 Preview before reading

GOAL 2 Read for meaning

GOAL 3 Read more effectively

GOAL 4 Mark and annotate text

GOAL 5 Create idea maps

GOAL 6 Think critically

GOAL 7 Write about a reading

WRITE ABOUT IT!

Although the people in the two photos seemingly have nothing to do with one another, they are connected. Write a sentence stating how are they connected.

The journalist in the first photo is writing a news article; the person in the second photo is reading the article he wrote. Readers and writers are always connected in this way. In this chapter you will learn about the reading-writing connection. You will learn reading and critical-thinking skills that will make an immediate, noticeable change in how well you understand and remember what you read. As you work through this chapter, you will see that there is a strong connection between reading and writing. Improving one skill often improves the other.

EXPLORING THE READING-WRITING-CRITICAL THINKING CONNECTION

At first, reading and writing may seem like very different, even opposite, processes. A writer starts with a blank page or computer screen and creates and develops ideas, while a reader starts with a full page and reads someone else's ideas. Although reading and writing may seem very different, they are actually parts of the same communication process.

Writers begin with a message they want to communicate; readers attempt to understand that message through their own experiences. Because reading and writing work together, improving one often improves the other. By learning to read more effectively, you'll become a better writer as well as a better reader. For example, as you learn more about writing paragraphs, you will be able to read them more easily. Similarly, as you learn more about how an essay is organized, you will find it easier to read essays and to organize your own ideas into essay form. Finally, by becoming a more critical thinker and reader, you improve your ability to communicate and persuade when you write.

NEED TO KNOW

The Relationship Between Reading, Writing, and Critical Thinking

- Reading and writing are parts of the same communication process.

- Writers begin with a message they want to communicate.

- Reader try to understand the message by connecting it to their own experiences.

- Critical thinking makes you a better reader and a more persuasive writer.

PREVIEWING BEFORE READING

GOAL 1 Preview before reading

Do you wish you could remember more of what you read? **Previewing** is a way of becoming familiar with what a reading is about and how it is organized *before* you read it. Previewing will make an assignment easier to read and remember, as well as make it more interesting. It will also help you discover what you already know about the topic before you begin reading.

Previewing is like looking at a map before you begin to drive in an unfamiliar city. It familiarizes you with the organization and content of a reading. Then, when you read the selection, you are able to understand it more easily. Previewing is not time-consuming. You can preview a brief selection in several minutes by following these basic steps:

1. **Read and think about the title of the selection.** What does it tell you about the subject? Does it offer any clues as to how the author feels about the subject or how the author will approach it? What do you already know about the subject?

2. **Check the author's name.** If it is familiar, what do you know about the author?

3. **Read the first paragraph.** Here the author often introduces the subject. Look for a statement of the main point of the entire reading. If the first paragraph is lengthy, read only the first few sentences.

4. **Read all boldfaced headings.** Headings divide the reading into sections and announce the topic of each section.

5. **Read the first sentence under each heading.** This sentence often states the main point of the section.

6. **If the reading lacks headings, read the first sentence of each of a few paragraphs on each page.** You will discover many of the main ideas of the article.

7. **Read the last paragraph.** Often this paragraph summarizes or concludes the reading. If the last paragraph is lengthy, read only the last few sentences.

The more you practice previewing and get in the habit of previewing, the more effectively it will work. Use the preview strategy for all your college textbooks, as well as for assigned chapters and readings in this book. You will notice in this book a section titled "Thinking Before Reading," which comes before each reading and reminds you to preview it.

Demonstration of Previewing

Now, preview the following reading, "Ways to Improve Your Memory." The portions you should preview have been highlighted. Preview this reading now, reading only the shaded portions.

READING

WAYS TO IMPROVE YOUR MEMORY

Saul M. Kassin

1   Before taking office, President Clinton invited five hundred business leaders to an economic summit in Little Rock. When it was over, many of the guests marveled at Clinton's ability to address them all by name. I have always been impressed by stories like this one—by stories of stage actors who memorize hundreds of lines in only one week of rehearsal, of people who fluently speak five languages, and of waiters who take dinner orders without a note pad. How can these accomplishments be explained?

2   Over the years, psychologists have stumbled upon a few rare individuals who seemed equipped with extraordinary "hardware" for memory. But often the actors, waiters, multilinguists, and others we encounter use memory tricks called mnemonics—in other words, they vary their memory's "software." Can you boost your recall capacity through the use of mnemonics? Can you improve your study skills as a result? At this point, let's step back and consider several ways you can improve your memory.

3   *Practice time:* To learn names, dates, vocabulary words, formulas, or the concepts in a textbook, you'll find that practice makes perfect. In general, the

more time spent studying, the better. In fact, it pays to overlearn—that is, to review the material even after you think you have it mastered. It's also better to spread out your studying over time than to cram all at once. You will retain more information from four two-hour sessions than from one eight-hour marathon.

4   *Active thinking:* The sheer amount of practice time is important, but only if it's "quality time." Mindless drills may be helpful in the short run, but long-term retention requires that you think actively and deeply about material—about what it means and how it is linked to what you already know. Ask yourself critical questions about the material. Think about it in ways that relate to your own experiences. Talk about the material to a friend, thus forcing yourself to organize it in terms that can be understood.

5   *Organization of information:* Once you have information to be learned, organize it as in an outline. Start with a few broad categories, then divide these into more specific subcategories and sub-subcategories. This is how many experts chunk new information, and it works. Thus, when Andrea Halpern presented subjects with 54 popular song titles, she found that recall was greater when the titles were organized hierarchically than when they were scrambled. The implication for studying is clear: organize the material in your notes, preferably in the form of an outline—and make sure to review these notes later.

6   *Verbal mnemonics:* Sometimes the easiest way to remember a list of items is to use verbal mnemonics, or "memory tricks." Chances are, you have already used popular methods such as *rhymes* ("*i* before *e*, except after *c*" is my favorite; "thirty days hath September, April, June, and November" is another) and *acronyms* that reduce the amount of information to be stored (for example, *ROY G BIV* can be used to recall the colors of the light spectrum: *r*ed, *o*range, *y*ellow, *g*reen, *b*lue, *i*ndigo, and *v*iolet). Relying on verbal mnemonics, advertisers create slogans to make their products memorable.

7   *Interference:* Because one learning experience can disrupt memory for another, it is wise to guard against the effects of interference. This problem is particularly common among college students, as material learned in one course can make it harder to retain that learned in another. To minimize the problem, follow two simple suggestions. First, study right before sleeping and review all the material right before the exam. Second, allocate an uninterrupted chunk of time to one course, and then do the same for your others as well. If you study psychology for a while, then move to biology, and then on to math and back to psychology, each course will disrupt your memory of the others—especially if the material is similar.

8   *Study environment:* Information is easier to recall when people are in the setting in which it was learned. That's why actors like to rehearse on the stage where they will later perform. So the next time you have an important exam to take, it may help to study in the room where the test will be administered.

9   These are just a few ways to improve your memory. Experiment with each to discover those that work for you.

—Kassin, *Psychology*, pp. 244–245.

Although you may not realize it, you learned a great deal about improving your memory in the minute or two you spent previewing.

EXERCISE 2-1   Testing Your Recall

Directions: Without referring to the above reading, "Ways to Improve Your Memory," make a list of ideas or suggestions you recall. ■

Connecting the Reading to Your Own Experience

Once you have previewed a reading, try to connect the topic to your own experience. Take a moment to recall what you already know or have read about the topic. This activity will make the reading more interesting and easier to write about. Here are a few suggestions to help you make connections:

1. **Ask questions and answer them.** Suppose you have just previewed a reading titled "Advertising: Institutionalized Lying." Ask questions such as: Do ads always lie? If not, why not? What do I already know about deceptive advertising?

2. **Brainstorm.** Jot down everything that comes to mind about the topic on a sheet of paper or a computer file. For example, if the topic of a reading is "The Generation Gap," write down ideas as they occur to you. You might list reasons for such a gap, try to define it, or mention names of families in which you have observed it. For more about brainstorming, see Chapter 11, p. 300.

3. **Think of examples.** Try to think of situations, people, or events that relate to the topic. For instance, suppose you have previewed a reading titled "Fashions, Fads, and Crazes." You might think of recent examples of each: pajamas as casual attire, iPods, or tattoos.

Each of these techniques will help you identify ideas or experiences that you may share with the writer and that will help you focus your attention on the reading. In this book, the section titled "Thinking Before Reading," which comes before each reading, lists several questions that will help you make connections to your own experiences.

EXERCISE 2-2   Connecting the Reading to Your Own Experience
Writing in Progress

Directions: Based on your preview of "Ways to Improve Your Memory," use one or more of the above techniques to connect the reading to your own experience. You might think of memory tricks you already use or things you find difficult (or easy) to remember. ■

READING FOR MEANING

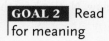
GOAL 2 Read for meaning

Reading is much more than moving your eyes across a line of print. To get the most out of a reading, you should search for, grasp, and react to the author's ideas. To do so, you'll need to know how essays and paragraphs are organized, how to develop strategies for dealing with difficult or confusing sentences or passages, and how to handle unfamiliar vocabulary.

What to Look for in Paragraphs

Paragraphs will be easier to understand and remember if you look for their three essential parts:

- **The topic** A paragraph is about one topic. This topic is discussed throughout the paragraph.
- **The main idea** A paragraph expresses one idea about its topic. Often this idea is expressed in a sentence called the **topic sentence.**
- **The supporting details** All the other sentences in the paragraph explain its main idea. Supporting details are facts that explain more about the main idea.

You can visualize a paragraph as follows:

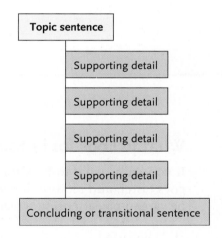

In the diagram above, the topic sentence appears first. The topic sentence is usually placed first in a paragraph, but it can appear anywhere in the paragraph. (You will learn much more about topic sentences and supporting details in Chapters 12 and 13.)

As you read, search for the topic sentence of each paragraph and notice how the other sentences in the paragraph explain it. This process will help you keep your mind on the reading and will direct your attention to the reading's key points. Try underlining or highlighting each topic sentence as you find it.

In this book you will find an exercise titled "Reviewing the Reading" following each reading. It is designed to help you check your understanding of the reading—both main ideas and details.

Analyze It!

Directions: Complete the idea map for the paragraph below. Notice how the writer states and then explains ideas.

Verbal Mnemonics

Sometimes the easiest way to remember a list of items is to use verbal mnemonics, or "memory tricks." Chances are, you have already used popular methods such as *rhymes* ("*i* before *e*, except after *c*" is my favorite; "thirty days hath September, April, June, and November" is another) and *acronyms* that reduce the amount of information to be stored (for example, *ROY G BIV* can be used to recall the colors of the light spectrum: *r*ed, *o*range, *y*ellow, *g*reen, *b*lue, *i*ndigo, and *v*iolet). Relying on verbal mnemonics, advertisers create slogans to make their products memorable.

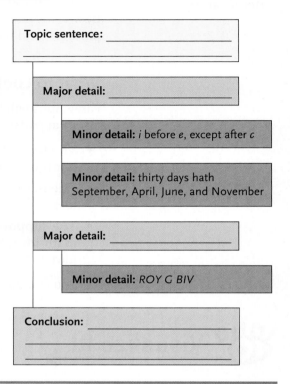

Topic sentence: _____

Major detail: _____

Minor detail: *i* before *e*, except after *c*

Minor detail: thirty days hath September, April, June, and November

Major detail: _____

Minor detail: *ROY G BIV*

Conclusion: _____

What to Look for in Essays

If you know what to look for as you read, you'll find reading an essay is easier, goes faster, and requires less rereading. When you read the essays in this book, be sure to pay attention to each of the following parts:

1. **The title** In some essays, the title announces the topic of the essay and may reveal the author's viewpoint. In others, the meaning of the title becomes clear only after you have read the essay.

2. **The introduction** The opening paragraph of an essay should interest you, announce the subject of the essay, and provide necessary background information on the subject.

3. **The author's main point** The main point is often called the *thesis statement*. It is the one big idea that the entire essay explains. Often it appears in the first paragraph, but it can be placed anywhere in the essay. Don't confuse the phrase *thesis statement* with *topic sentence*. The sentence that states the main idea of a paragraph is a topic sentence. (For more on thesis statements, see pages 478–483.)

4. **Support and explanation** The body of the essay should explain, give reasons for, or offer support for the author's thesis. Each supporting

paragraph should have a topic sentence that identifies the paragraph's main idea.

5. **The conclusion** The last paragraph brings the essay to a close. Often, it will restate the author's main point. It may also suggest directions for further thought.

Now, reread "Ways to Improve Your Memory," which has been marked here to identify each of the parts described above.

READING

WAYS TO IMPROVE YOUR MEMORY

Saul M. Kassin

Introduction

1   Before taking office, President Clinton invited five hundred business leaders to an economic summit in Little Rock. When it was over, many of the guests marveled at Clinton's ability to address them all by name. I have always been impressed by stories like this one—by stories of stage actors who memorize hundreds of lines in only one week of rehearsal, of people who fluently speak five languages, and of waiters who take dinner orders without a note pad. How can these accomplishments be explained?

Introduction continues

2   Over the years, psychologists have stumbled upon a few rare individuals who seemed equipped with extraordinary "hardware" for memory. But often the actors, waiters, multilinguists, and others we encounter use memory tricks called mnemonics—in other words, they vary their memory's "software." Can you boost your recall capacity through the use of mnemonics? Can you improve

Thesis statement

your study skills as a result? At this point, let's step back and consider several ways you can improve your memory.

Topic sentence: first way to improve memory

3   *Practice time:* To learn names, dates, vocabulary words, formulas, or the concepts in a textbook, you'll find that practice makes perfect. In general, the more time spent studying, the better. In fact, it pays to overlearn—that is, to review the material even after you think you have it mastered. It's also better to spread out your studying over time than to cram all at once. You will retain more information from four two-hour sessions than from one eight-hour marathon.

4   *Active thinking:* The sheer amount of practice time is important, but only if it's "quality time." Mindless drills may be helpful in the short run, but long-

Topic sentence: second way

term retention requires that you think actively and deeply about material—about what it means and how it is linked to what you already know. Ask yourself critical questions about the material. Think about it in ways that relate to your own experiences. Talk about the material to a friend, thus forcing yourself to organize it in terms that can be understood.

Topic sentence: third way

5   *Organization of information:* Once you have information to be learned, organize it as in an outline. Start with a few broad categories, then divide these

into more specific subcategories and sub-subcategories. This is how many experts chunk new information, and it works. Thus, when Andrea Halpern presented subjects with 54 popular song titles, she found that recall was greater when the titles were organized hierarchically than when they were scrambled. The implication for studying is clear: organize the material in your notes, preferably in the form of an outline—and make sure to review these notes later.

Topic sentence: fourth way

6   *Verbal mnemonics:* Sometimes the easiest way to remember a list of items is to use verbal mnemonics, or "memory tricks." Chances are, you have already used popular methods such as *rhymes* ("*i* before *e*, except after *c*" is my favorite; "thirty days hath September, April, June, and November" is another) and *acronyms* that reduce the amount of information to be stored (for example, *ROY G BIV* can be used to recall the colors of the light spectrum: *red, orange, yellow, green, blue, indigo,* and *violet*). Relying on verbal mnemonics, advertisers create slogans to make their products memorable.

Topic sentence: fifth way

7   *Interference:* Because one learning experience can disrupt memory for another, it is wise to guard against the effects of interference. This problem is particularly common among college students, as material learned in one course can make it harder to retain that learned in another. To minimize the problem, follow two simple suggestions. First, study right before sleeping and review all the material right before the exam. Second, allocate an uninterrupted chunk of time to one course, and then do the same for your others as well. If you study psychology for a while, then move to biology, and then on to math and back to psychology, each course will disrupt your memory of the others—especially if the material is similar.

Topic sentence: sixth way

8   *Study environment:* Information is easier to recall when people are in the setting in which it was learned. That's why actors like to rehearse on the stage where they will later perform. So the next time you have an important exam to take, it may help to study in the room where the test will be administered.

Conclusion

9   These are just a few ways to improve your memory. Experiment with each to discover those that work for you.

HOW TO HANDLE DIFFICULT READINGS

GOAL 3 Read more effectively

All of us, at one time or another, come across a piece of material that is difficult or confusing. An entire reading may be difficult, or just a paragraph or two within an otherwise comfortable reading may be troublesome. Don't give in to the temptation to skip over difficult parts or just give up. Instead, try to approach challenging readings using the methods in the box on page 43.

> ## Tips for Reading Difficult Material
>
> 1. **Analyze the time and place in which you are reading.** If you have been reading or studying for several hours, mental fatigue may be the source of the problem. If you are reading in a place with numerous distractions, lack of concentration may contribute to poor comprehension.
>
> 2. **Look up unfamiliar words.** Often, a few unfamiliar words can block understanding. Keep a dictionary handy and refer to it as needed.
>
> 3. **Do not hesitate to reread difficult or complicated sections.** In fact, sometimes several rereadings are appropriate and necessary.
>
> 4. **Rephrase each paragraph in your own words.** You might approach extremely complicated material sentence by sentence, expressing each idea in your own words.
>
> 5. **Read aloud sentences or sections that are particularly difficult.** Hearing ideas aloud often aids comprehension.
>
> 6. **Make a brief outline of the major points of the reading.** An outline will help you see the overall organization and progression of ideas.
>
> 7. **Slow down your reading rate if you feel you are beginning to lose comprehension.** On occasion, simply reading more slowly will boost your comprehension.
>
> 8. **Summarize.** Test your recall by summarizing each section after you read it.
>
> 9. **Work with a classmate.** Working through and discussing a reading with a classmate often will increase your understanding of it.

HOW TO RECORD YOUR THINKING: MARKING AND ANNOTATION

 Mark and annotate text

Annotation is a way of jotting down your ideas, reactions, and opinions as you read. Think of annotation as recording your ideas while you read. It is a way to "talk back" to the author—to question, agree, disagree, or comment. Annotations are particularly useful when you will be writing about what you have read.

Three different types of annotations are useful: *symbols and abbreviations, highlights,* and *statements and questions.* Depending on your preferences, you may choose to use one, two, or all three of these methods.

Symbols and Abbreviations

Marking key parts of an essay with symbols or abbreviations can help you clarify meaning and remember key information. Table 2-1 on page 44 provides a list of useful symbols and abbreviations. You should feel free to add to this list in any way that suits your reading and learning styles.

TABLE 2-1   ANNOTATION SYMBOLS AND ABBREVIATIONS

Type of Annotation	Symbol and Example
Underlining key ideas	The <u>most prominent unions in the United States are among public-sector employees</u> such as teachers and police.
Circling unknown words	One goal of labor unions is to address the apparent ⟨asymmetry⟩ of power in the employer-worker relationship.
Marking definitions *def.*	To say that the balance of power favors one party over another is to introduce a disequilibrium.
Marking examples *ex.*	Concessions may include additional benefits, increased vacation time, or higher wages.
Numbering lists of ideas, causes, reasons, or events	The components of power include self-range①, population②, natural resources③, and ④geography.
Placing asterisks (stars) next to important passages	* Once a dominant force in the United States economy, labor unions have been shrinking over the last few decades.
Putting question marks next to confusing passages ?	Strikes can be averted through the institutionalization of mediated bargaining.
Marking possible test items ⊤	A *closed shop* is a form of union agreement in which the employer agrees to hire only union workers.
Drawing arrows to show relationships	Standing between managers and employees is the ⟨shop steward⟩, who is both a union employee and a rank-and-file worker within the company that employs union members.
Marking summary statements *sum.*	The greater the degree of conflict between labor and management, the more sensitive the negotiations need to be.
Marking essential information that you must remember	The largest and most important trade union in the United States, and the one that has had the most influence on labor-union relations, is the AFL-CIO. !
Noting author's opinion of or attitude toward the topic *opinion*	In a world where the gap between rich and poor is increasing, labor unions are essential to ensuring that workers are paid and treated fairly.
Indicating material to reread later *RR*	At the apex of union density in the 1940s, only about 9.8 percent of public employees were represented by unions, while 33.9 percent of private, nonagricultural workers had such representation. In this decade, those proportions have essentially reversed, with 36 percent of public workers being represented by unions while private sector union density had plummeted to around 7 percent.

Here is an example of an annotated reading:

Sitting on the top rung of the class ladder is a powerful elite that consists of just 1 percent of the U.S. population. This ⟨capitalist⟩ class is so wealthy that it owns one-third of all the nation's assets. This tiny 1 percent is worth more than the entire bottom 90 percent of the country. <u>Power and influence</u> cling to this small elite. They have direct access① to politicians, own major media and entertainment② outlets (newspapers, magazines, TV stations, sports franchises), and control the③ boards of directors of our most influential colleges and universities.

The capitalist class can be divided into "old money" and "new money." <u>The longer that wealth has been in a family, the more it adds to the family's prestige.</u> The

def.

children of old money (sometimes called blue-bloods) seldom mingle with "common" folk. Instead, they attend exclusive private schools where they learn ways of life that support their privileged positions. They don't work for wages; instead, many study business or become lawyers so that they can manage the family fortune. The people

def.

with "new money" are also known as the nouveau riche. Although they have made fortunes in business, entertainment, or sports, they are outsiders to the upper class. They have not attended the "right" schools, and they don't share the social networks that come with old money. Children of the new-moneyed can ascend into the top part of the capitalist class—if they go to the right schools *and* marry old money.

—Henslin, *Sociology*, p. 272.

Highlights

In some cases, the easiest and fastest way to mark important facts and ideas is to highlight them with a pen or highlighter. (Many students prefer highlighters because they come in different colors, such as bright yellow or pink, which draw the eye to important material.) When highlighting, you mark the portions of a reading that you need to study, remember, or locate quickly.

Here are a few suggestions for highlighting effectively.

1. **Read a paragraph or section first**, then go back and highlight what is important.
2. **Highlight the topic sentence and any important details you want to remember.**
3. **Be accurate.** Make sure your highlighting reflects the content of the reading. Incomplete highlighting may cause you to miss the main point.
4. **Use a system for highlighting.** For instance, use two different highlighter colors to distinguish between topic sentences and supporting details.
5. **Highlight the right amount.** By highlighting too little, you miss valuable information. By highlighting too much, you are not identifying the most important ideas. As a general rule, the only complete sentences that should be highlighted are topic sentences. In all other sentences, highlight only key phrases or words.

Here is an example of effective highlighting:

Money (or actually the lack of it) is a major source of stress for many people. In a sense, this is one of the most "valid" stressors because so many of our basic survival needs require money. Anyone struggling to survive on a small income is likely to feel plenty of stress. But money has significance beyond its obvious value as a medium of exchange. Even some of the wealthiest people become stressed over money-related issues. To some people, wealth is a measurement of human value, and their self-esteem is based on their material assets. Stress management for such people requires taking an objective look at the role money plays for them.

—Byer and Shainberg, *Living Well*, pp. 78–79.

Statements and Questions

In many of your writing assignments, you'll be asked to respond to an author's presentation, opinion, or suggestions. By recording your responses in the margin as you read, you take the first step toward writing about your own ideas.

Table 2-2 (p. 46) lists some types of statements and questions you might write in the margins of a reading. Note that it is perfectly acceptable to use abbreviations in your statements and questions! You should feel free to expand this list in any way that helps you "talk" with the reading.

TABLE 2-2 RESPONDING TO A READING IN THE MARGIN	
Based on "Ways to Improve Your Memory," pages 36–37	
Ways of Responding	**Example of Marginal Annotation**
1. **Ask questions.**	What does *mnemonics* mean?
2. **Challenge the author's ideas.**	"Mindless drills" actually work well for me—I learn a lot of vocabulary using flashcards!
3. **Look for inconsistencies.**	Reading starts with the story of B. Clinton, but there are no examples of the techniques he used to remember all those names!
4. **Add examples.**	Good mnemonic I use: HOMES for the names of the great lakes (Huron, Ontario, Michigan, Erie, Superior)
5. **Note exceptions.**	The problem is, *i* before *e* except after *c* doesn't always work. Ex: weird, science
6. **Disagree with the author.**	Study right before sleeping? I'm tired before I go to bed—that's not a good time for me to study!
7. **Make associations with other sources.**	Why is it so easy to remember the lyrics to songs? Could singing the words actually make them easier to remember?
8. **Make judgments.**	This reading has some good ideas, but not all of them will work for my life and schedule.
9. **Make notes to yourself.**	Talk to Jenna, who takes acting classes. What techniques does she use for remembering her lines?
10. **Ask instructor to clarify.**	Ask Prof: How do I break info down into categories and subcategories?

EXERCISE 2-3 Using Marking and Annotating

Directions: Annotate or mark the following readings using any of the techniques described above. Use whichever techniques work best for you.

1. Amusement Parks

The first amusement parks, which were called pleasure gardens, were built in England and France. Some of the largest and most popular amusement parks such as Gardaland on Italy's Lake Garda and Tivoli in Denmark attract millions of visitors each year. As the name *pleasure garden* implies, these attractions began as manicured gardens designed to provide a temporary escape for city dwellers from the everyday drudgeries of life. Rides such as carousels, games, and food and drink stands were added to these pleasure gardens to meet visitors' needs.

The idea of parks with rides and other entertainment activities soon found its way to the United States. Interest in amusements in the United States heightened when the Ferris wheel was introduced at the 1893 Chicago World's Fair. The name for this new amusement, which became the centerpiece of most modern amusement parks, was taken from its inventor, George Washington Gales Ferris.

—adapted from Cook, Yale, and Marqua, *Tourism*, p. 214.

2. Dieting

Millions of people in the United States want to lose weight without sacrificing their favorite foods, without pain, and without great effort. If only we could be thin and firm by waving a magic wand! It is very popular to resort to well-publicized weight-loss programs that involve special food requirements such as high-fat, low-protein, low-carbohydrate, or liquid protein. There are hundreds of such programs that continue to come and go. Many of them are reported as "breakthroughs," but if this were the case, even newer breakthroughs would not be needed.

There is usually at least one fad diet book on the best-seller list in any given week. Some fad diets are simple variations of a basic 1000–1100-calorie balanced diet. Others may be dangerous because they emphasize one food or food group and the elimination of others, and advise people to follow diets low in energy and nutrients. Some fad diets are more hazardous to a person's health than the obesity they propose to cure, creating adverse reactions ranging from headaches to death. Of 29,000 claims, treatments, and therapies for losing weight, fewer than 6 percent are effective, and 13 percent are downright dangerous. Ultimately, the problem is that most diet plans focus on short-term (and often futile) weight loss, which results in weight cycling, or "yo-yo" dieting, and psychological problems that result from repeated failures to keep weight off. Only 5 percent of people who try are able to maintain their weight losses. Much better is a program of lifetime weight management, which involves learning new eating and exercise habits.

—adapted from Byer and Shainberg, *Living Well*, p. 311.

■

USING IDEA MAPS

GOAL 5 Create idea maps

Many students have difficulty remembering what they have read and find they have to reread frequently in order to write about a reading. One solution to this problem is to draw an idea map: a diagram that helps you both understand and remember how the writer's ideas relate to one another and how the essay is organized. Idea maps work because they force you to think about and analyze the relationships between ideas. They also are effective because they require you to express ideas from the reading in your own words; this activity increases your recall of those ideas.

Here is a sample idea map for the reading "Ways to Improve Your Memory." Notice that it includes all of the key ideas.

 Visualize It!

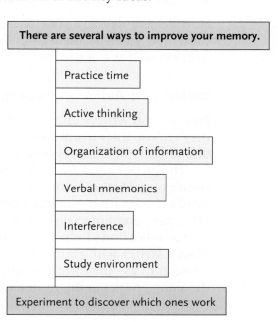

There are several ways to improve your memory.

Practice time

Active thinking

Organization of information

Verbal mnemonics

Interference

Study environment

Experiment to discover which ones work

PREPARING TO WRITE: THINKING CRITICALLY

GOAL 6
Think critically

College writing assignments are not just about reading and memorization. They are also about *thinking*. You may have noticed that annotation skills require you not only to identify key material, but also to *analyze* what you are reading. **Critical thinking** is another term for analytical thinking.

In this context, *critical* does not mean "negative." Critical thinking requires you to evaluate what you read, rather than to accept everything as the truth. Thinking critically sometimes requires you to disagree with the author or express a different opinion.

The Benefits of Critical Thinking

The ability to think and read critically offers many benefits to writers. Specifically, critical thinking allows you to:

- Distinguish good information from incomplete, inaccurate, or misleading information.
- Write paragraphs, essays, term papers, and essay exams that exhibit a strong understanding of what you've read.

Critical reading should take place at all times, no matter what you read. For example:

- When reading a college textbook, you might ask yourself if the author is trying to influence your opinions.
- When reading a newspaper, you might ask yourself if the journalist is telling the full story or if she is leaving something out.
- When reading an advertisement, you might ask yourself what techniques the ad is using to get you to buy the product.

Many of the writing assignments in this book ask you to think critically about a reading before you begin writing.

Critical Thinking: The Basics

How do you develop your critical thinking abilities? Here are six tips to get started. As you read these tips, remember that they will help make you a better writer as well as a better reader.

Evaluate the Author's Choice of Words

Professional writers understand that words influence the reader greatly, and they choose their words carefully. For this reason, reading critically means understanding the nuances of words and how they affect the reader.

The dictionary definition of a word, its literal meaning, is its **denotation**. A word's **connotation** is the set of additional associations that it takes on. Often, a word's connotation is much stronger than its denotation because connotations often have emotions connected to them.

Connotations help writers influence the reader's opinion on the topic. Thus a writer who wants to be kind to an overweight politician might describe him as "pleasingly plump." A writer who wants to be negative about the same politician might describe him as "morbidly obese" or "grossly fat."

As you evaluate the writer's choice of words, ask yourself:

- What adjectives (descriptive words) does the writer use, and how do they affect me?
- Do any of the words have a strong emotional component to them? What is the writer's purpose in using these words?

For more on choosing the best words in your own writing, see Writers' Workshops: Using Words Effectively, pp. 96–101.

Distinguish between Facts and Opinions

Facts are statements that can be verified—that is, proven to be true. Opinions are statements that express feelings, attitudes, or beliefs and are neither true nor false.

Facts
Martin Luther King, Jr., was assassinated in 1968.
The main source of food for Native Americans was the buffalo.

Opinions
Americans should give up their cars and take public transportation instead.
By the year 2025, food shortages will be a major problem in most Asian countries.

Opinions are sometimes signaled by the use of such key words or phrases as *apparently, this suggests, some believe, it is likely that, seemingly, in my view,* and *one explanation is.*

Opinions can be divided into two categories. **Informed opinions** are made by people whose learning and experience qualify them to offer expert opinions. **Uninformed opinions** are made by those who have few qualifications. To determine whether an opinion is informed or not, ask these questions:

- What experience does this person have regarding the subject matter?
- What do other respected authorities think of this person?
- Is the opinion expressed in a respectful way? Or is it expressed in a manner that is disrespectful or intolerant?
- Does the opinion appear in a respected publication, or is it found on a Web site where people can say whatever they want?

Be sure to read the directions to your writing assignments carefully. If the assignment calls for strictly factual reporting, do not offer your opinion.

Recognize and Evaluate Generalizations

A **generalization** is a statement made about a large group based on observation or experience with a portion of that group. For example, "College freshmen are disoriented during their first week on campus" is a generalization. By visiting colleges and observing freshman, you could make the generalization that freshmen are disoriented. However, unless you observe every student on every campus in the world, you could not be certain your generalization applies to all students.

Much of what you read will contain generalizations, and you will sometimes be asked to write generalizations yourself. Because writers usually do not have the space to describe all available evidence, they often make a general statement of what the evidence shows. To evaluate a generalization, ask yourself:

- Does the author provide evidence to support the generalization? Generalizations without any supporting evidence are often untrustworthy.

- What is the basis of the author's generalization? Is it based on many years of observation or reading (reliable) or on just one observation or source (unreliable)?

Your own writing will be the most persuasive when you give evidence to support any generalizations you make.

Look for Bias

Read the following statements and determine what they have in common:

- Laboratory experiments using live animals are forms of mutilation and torture.
- The current vitamin fad is a distortion of sound medical advice.

Each statement reflects a **bias**—a preference for or prejudice against a person, object, or idea. Biased material is one-sided. Other facts, such as the advantages of using animals for laboratory research, or research that has confirmed the value of taking vitamins, are not mentioned. (Notice, too, the use of emotional words such as *mutilation, torture,* and *distortion.*)

Much of what you read and hear expresses a bias. In many newspapers and magazine articles, nonfiction books, and essays you will find the opinions and beliefs of the author revealed. Some writers reveal their attitudes directly by stating how they feel. Others do so less directly, expressing their attitudes through the manner in which they write. As you read, ask yourself the following questions:

- What facts were omitted? What additional facts are needed?
- What impression would I have if different words had been used?

Evaluate different viewpoints and develop your own opinion

College reading and writing assignments provide you with opportunities to encounter new ideas and viewpoints. Some of these ideas may force you to reexamine how you think about a particular issue. An instructor may raise a controversial or current topic or issue by asking you to read different articles with different viewpoints, and then ask you to write about them.

When reading materials that challenge your beliefs:

- Put aside or suspend temporarily what you already think about the issue.
- Look for and evaluate evidence that suggests the viewpoint is well thought out.
- To overcome the natural tendency to pay more attention to points of view you agree with, deliberately spend more time reading, thinking about, and examining ideas that differ from your own.

To fully grasp varying viewpoints, try writing a summary of each in your own words.

Understand the Power of Images

A writer can choose visual aids that reflect his or her opinions. Consider the following excerpt and the photo that accompanies it.

Is alcohol bad for health? This beverage cuts both ways. One to two drinks a day for men and one drink for women reduces the risk of heart attacks, strokes, gallstones, and diabetes. Beyond these amounts, however, alcohol scars the liver, damages the heart, and increases the risk of breast cancer. It also increases the likelihood of birth defects. One-third of the 43,000 Americans who die each year in vehicle accidents are drunk. Each year, 700,000 Americans seek treatment for alcohol problems.

—Adapted from Henslin, *Sociology*, pp. 580–581.

A Vermont state trooper in Newport, VT, checks the wrecked car that four teens died in while returning from a night drinking in Quebec.

The passage is very matter-of-fact. It summarizes the benefits and drawbacks of drinking alcohol. But also note how intense the photo is. Just looking it at, you know that a horrible accident has occurred and someone has probably died. Thus the photo makes the author's message about the drawbacks of alcohol much stronger than his message about its benefits.

When viewing a photo or other visual aid, ask yourself:

- What is the author's reason for including this photo? Is it meant to appeal to my emotions?
- Does the photo reinforce the author's opinions or biases?

EXERCISE 2-4   Reading Critically

Directions: Read the following paragraph, and think analytically and critically when you answer the questions that follow.

> In survey after survey, 60 to 80 percent of food shoppers say they read food labels before selecting products; they consume more vegetables, fruits, and lower-fat foods; and they are cutting down on portion sizes and total calories. Diet-book sales are at an all-time high as millions of people make the leap toward what they think is healthy eating. But we still have a long way to go. In fact, although reports indicate that increasing numbers of us read labels and are trying to eat more healthfully, nearly 78% of all adults indicate that they are not eating the recommended servings of fruits and vegetables and that they are still eating too many refined carbohydrates and high-fat foods.
>
> —Donatelle, *Health*, p. 255.

1. The passage talks about "surveys," which is another word for "questionnaires." Why might the survey results not truly reflect reality?

   _____

   _____

2. Does the fact that diet-book sales are at an all-time high mean that more people are going on diets and/or eating more healthfully? In a sentence or two, explain why or why not.

   _____

   _____

3. Write a sentence or two summarizing the author's opinion regarding a good way to eat more healthfully. Do you agree or disagree with this opinion?

   _____

   _____

4. Have you ever watched a friend, co-worker, or family member start a diet? On a separate sheet of paper, write a paragraph describing that person's approach to dieting. For example, did he or she decide to start exercising every morning? Did his or her approach work? ■

EXERCISE 2-5   Taking Notes

Directions: If your instructor conducts a class discussion of the reading "Ways to Improve Your Memory," take brief notes during the discussion and fill them in when the class is over. Possible discussion questions are:

1. Are some types of material more difficult to memorize than others? Give some examples.

2. What positive (or negative) experiences have you had with memorizing information? When has your memory failed you or served you well?

3. Do you know anyone with extraordinary memory skills? Describe his or her skills. ■

EXERCISE 2-6   Applying Your Skills
Working Together

Directions: Select two or more techniques suggested in "Ways to Improve Your Memory." Write a journal entry in response to the following question: How can you apply these techniques to your studies? Compare your entry with that of a classmate, and create a Tip Sheet that would be useful to other students not in your writing class. ■

HOW TO WRITE ABOUT A READING

GOAL 7 Write about a reading

Once you've read, annotated, and thought critically about a reading, you are ready to write. Each reading in this book is followed by a series of exercises to help you develop your skills.

1. **"Reviewing the Reading"** asks you to think closely about the author's audience, purpose, and writing techniques.

2. **"Examining the Reading Using an Idea Map"** asks you to map the reading visually.

3. **"Strengthening Your Vocabulary"** helps you expand your vocabulary.

4. **"Reacting to Ideas: Discussion and Journal Writing"** offers questions that can stimulate discussion with your peers, as well as ideas for writing in your journal. As you prepare to discuss or write, ask yourself the following questions to direct your thinking:

   • Why did the author write this? What was his or her purpose?

   • For what audience was the essay written?

   • What issue, problem, concern, or question does the essay address?

   • What is the author's main point or position on the issue?

   • What types of words and visuals did the author use? Why?

5. **"Writing About the Reading"** offers both paragraph and essay assignments on topics related to the reading. When your instructor gives you an assignment, use the following suggestions to help you produce a solid, well-written paper:

- **Read the assignment several times before you begin.** Express in your own words what the assignment requires. If you have a choice of assignments, take a fair amount of time to choose. It is worthwhile to spend a few minutes thinking about and weighing possible topics. You don't want to work your way through a first draft and then realize that you don't have enough to say or you cannot work well with the topic.

- **Try discussing the assignment with a classmate.** By talking about it, you can make sure you are on the right track, and you may discover new or additional ideas to write about. Also consider asking the classmate to react to your paper once you have a draft.

- **Review your journal entries and notes of class discussions for possible topics or approaches to the assignment.** (Chapter 11, "Planning and Organizing," offers several strategies for discovering and selecting ideas to write about.)

- **Don't be satisfied with the first draft that you write.** As you will discover in Chapter 12, "Drafting and Revising," you need to rethink and revise both what you have said and how you have said it.

Writing in a Visual Age

READING

The world's most livable cities are not those with "perfect" auto access between all points. Instead, they are cities that have taken measures to reduce outward sprawl, diminish automobile traffic, and improve access by foot and bicycle in conjunction with mass transit. For example, Geneva, Switzerland, prohibits automobile parking at workplaces in the city's center, forcing commuters to use the excellent public transportation system. Copenhagen, Denmark, bans all on-street parking in the downtown core. Paris, France, has removed 200,000 parking places in the downtown area.

Curitiba, Brazil, is cited as the most livable city in all of Latin America. The achievement of Curitiba is due almost entirely to the efforts of Jaime Lerner, who, serving as mayor for many decades, guided development with an emphasis on mass transit rather than cars. The space saved by not building highways and parking lots has been put into parks and shady walkways, causing the amount of green area per inhabitant to increase from 4.5 square feet in 1970 to 450 square feet today.

—Wright and Boorse, *Environmental Science*, p. 604.

Caption: _____

1. The reading summarizes several ways to make cities more "livable." Write a sentence or two offering the mayor of your town one or two suggestions for improving the quality of life for the citizens.

2. What is the denotation of the word *sprawl*, used in the second sentence? What is the word's *connotation*?

CRITICAL THINKING AND RESPONSE

3. Of the cities mentioned in the reading, how many are located in the United States? What does this tell you about the author's bias?

WRITING

4. In a sentence or two, summarize the author's opinion regarding the best ways to improve the quality of life in a city.

5. The reading implies that cars and automobiles reduce the quality of life in a city. Write a paragraph in which you summarize what you think would happen if cars were banned in your city. What would be the benefits? What problems might arise?

USING VISUALS

6. Like words, photos have both denotations (their obvious content) and connotations (the feelings the images evoke). Suppose the authors wanted to include a photo with a negative connotation. What type of photo might they choose? What kind of photo might they choose if they wanted to convey a positive connotation?

7. The photo above shows a city park in Curitiba, Brazil. Write a caption to accompany the photo, using the information you learned in the reading.

WRITING ABOUT A READING

THINKING BEFORE READING

The following reading first appeared in *Parade* magazine. In "What Really Scares Us?" author David Ropeik explains some of the emotional factors behind our fears. Notice while you read how the essay is organized with main points and supporting details. Before you read:

1. Preview the reading, using the steps discussed on page 35.

2. Connect the reading to your own experience by answering the following questions:

    a. What fears do you have? Why do you think these things frighten you?

    b. Are your fears mostly logical or emotional?

3. Mark and annotate as you read.

READING
WHAT REALLY SCARES US?

David Ropeik

1   The list of things to be afraid of seems to grow daily: terrorism, snipers, and child abductions. According to a number of public-opinion surveys, many people think it's more dangerous to be living now than it ever has been.

fly in the face of challenge, defy

2   But those fears **fly in the face of** evidence that, in many ways, things are better than they've ever been. The average American life expectancy in 1900 was about 47 years. Now it's nearing 80. Diseases that plagued us—polio, smallpox, tuberculosis—have been all but eradicated in the U.S. In 1960, out of every 1000 babies born, 26 did not survive their first year. That number is now down to seven.

3   So why this disconnect between the facts and our fears? Well, it turns out that when it comes to the perception of risks, facts are only part of how we decide what to be afraid of and how afraid to be. Another huge factor—sometimes the most important factor—is our emotions.

4   Why do humans perceive risks this way if our highly advanced brain gives us the power to reason? It's because our brains are biologically built to fear first and think second. Which, in the end, is a pretty good strategy for survival.

5   Say you're walking through the woods and see a line on the ground, and you're not sure if it's a snake or a stick. The visual information goes to two parts of the brain. One is called the prefrontal cortex, behind your forehead. That's the area where we do a lot of our reasoning and thinking. The other area is called the amygdala, which is the brain's key emotion center.

6   Because of the way the brain is constructed, the information gets to the amygdala before it gets to the prefrontal cortex. So, before the reasoning part of the brain has had a chance to consider the facts, the fear center is saying, "Jump back, you dummy! It *could* be a snake!"

7   But how does the brain turn raw sensory information into fear? Apparently our brains have built-in patterns for interpreting sensory information that help us subconsciously filter incoming messages, making us more afraid of some things than others. Psychologists have identified many of the specific emotional characteristics of risks that are likely to make us more, or less, afraid.

Emotional Factors That Determine Our Fears

full-fledged
complete, total

8   **Control.** Imagine that you're driving down the highway, feeling pretty safe because you're behind the wheel. Now switch seats with your passenger. You're probably a little more nervous, maybe even turning into a **full-fledged** backseat driver. Not because the risk has gone up—the annual odds of being killed in a motor vehicle crash are 1 in 6700—but because you no longer are in control.

anthrax
a serious infectious disease

9   **Trust.** We trust certain sources more than others. We're less afraid when a trusted doctor or scientist, such as the head of the Centers for Disease Control and Prevention, explains **anthrax** than when a politician explains it.

10   **Newness.** When a risk first shows up, we treat it more like a snake until we've lived with it for a while and our experience lets us put the risk in perspective. We are more afraid of West Nile virus when it first shows up in our area than after it has been around for a few years. (Odds of dying from West Nile virus: 1 in 1,000,000.)

11   **Choice.** We're more afraid of risks that are imposed on us than risks we take by choice. Imagine that you're driving along, talking on your cell phone. In the next lane, some other guy is driving and using *his* cell phone. Though both of you are in danger, the risk from the motorist next to you feels greater, because it's being imposed on you.

12   **Dread.** Things that can kill us in really awful ways seem riskier. We're more afraid of being eaten alive by a shark (odds, 1 in 281,000,000) or dying in a plane crash (1 in 9,000,000) than of dying from heart disease (1 in 300).

13   **Me or them.** If the risk is to you, it's worse than if that same risk only threatens somebody else. We're *all* worried about terrorism, now that we know it can happen here too, to us. A one in a million risk is too high if we think *we* could be that "one."

14   **Is it hard to understand?** The more complicated a risk is, the less we can understand it—and the more we treat it like a snake, just to be safe. For example, we're concerned about ionizing (nuclear) radiation, but we're not worried about infrared radiation, which we know simply as heat.

Facts Can Help You Feel Safer

Here are your chances of dying in a given year due to . . .

Child Kidnapping
1 in 1,300,000

Dog Bite
1 in 19,000,000

Cell Phone Radiation
0

Flood
1 in 6,900,000

Flu
1 in 130,000

Lightning
1 in 3,000,000

Guns
1 in 28,000

Snake/Lizard/Spider
1 in 56,000,000

(Figures provided by David Ropeik based on data from private and U.S. government agencies. Odds are for the average American. Individual risk may vary.)

15   **Natural or manmade?** If it's natural, we're less afraid than if it's manmade. We're more frightened of nuclear power accidents (odds, 1 in 200,000) than of solar radiation. Yet sun exposure causes an estimated 1.3 million new cases of skin cancer in America per year, 7800 of which are fatal.

16   Several of these factors are often at work on the same risk at the same time, some making us more afraid and some less. The effect of these factors changes over time. Also, individual fears vary based on individual circumstances. For instance, women fear breast cancer more than men, while men fear prostate cancer more than women.

17   While it's understandable that we perceive risks this way, it also can be dangerous. Some people, afraid to fly because they lack control or because the risk or terrorism is new and feels high, choose instead to drive—a much bigger risk. It may make them *feel* safer, but overreacting this way raises their risks.

18   Underreacting can be dangerous too. People who aren't concerned about the risk of the sun—because it's natural and because of that nice glowing tan—raise their cancer risk by not taking the danger of sun exposure seriously enough to slap on sunscreen or wear a hat.

19   In the end, the best way to reduce the danger of any given risk is to arm yourself with some basic facts from a reliable, neutral source, so the rational side of your perceptions can hold its own in the contest against your natural emotions. The better you can do at keeping your perception of risks closer in line with what the risks actually are, the happier *and safer* you'll be.

GETTING READY TO WRITE

Reviewing the Reading

Answer each of the following questions using a complete sentence.

1. Name some of the things we fear these days. What sorts of things were concerns for us in the past?

2. Explain how the brain deals with a potential threat.

3. Identify the eight emotional factors that determine how fearful we are of something.

 **Thinking Visually**   4. Why is the chart included in the reading? How does it enhance or strengthen the author's main point?

5. Why is it dangerous to overreact and misperceive the level of risk in a particular situation?

6. What advice does the author have for us for dealing with our fears?

Examining the Reading Using an Idea Map

Review the reading by completing the missing parts of the idea map below.

Visualize It!

Title — **What Really Scares Us?**

Thesis — There is a discrepancy between our perception of risk and the actual risk involved; emotions are involved.

Humans have many fears.

> Present fears: terrorism, snipers, child kidnappings

> _____

Our brains deal with fear in a certain way.

> Visual information goes to the prefrontal cortex.

> _____

> The emotional center reacts first before the information is processed.

There are eight emotional factors that determine our fears.

> Control
> Trust
> Newness
> Choice
> _____
> _____
> _____
> _____

People tend to under- or overreact to risk; both are dangerous.

Conclusion — We can deal with fear by getting educated about the actual risks.

Strengthening Your Vocabulary

Using the word's context, word parts, or a dictionary, write a brief definition of each of the following words or phrases as it is used in the reading.

1. eradicated (paragraph 2) _____
2. disconnect (paragraph 3) _____
3. subconsciously (paragraph 7) _____
4. imposed (paragraph 11) _____
5. arm (paragraph 19) _____
6. rational (paragraph 19) _____

Reacting to Ideas: Discussion and Journal Writing

Get ready to write about the reading by discussing the following:

1. Discuss a current public fear. How justified is the public in being frightened?
2. Discuss whether television and newspaper reporters encourage fear in their audiences.
3. Write a journal entry about a time when you felt scared. Which of the eight factors were involved?
4. Discuss whether knowing the statistics behind risky situations is helpful.

WRITING ABOUT THE READING

Paragraph Options

1. Ropeik points out that what we fear now is different from what we feared in the past. Write a paragraph about something in the very recent past that was a big concern that we do not worry so much about today.
2. Some fears are timeless. Write a paragraph about something that many humans have always feared.
3. One of the emotional factors is control. Write a paragraph that describes a time when you felt frightened because you were not in control.

Essay Options

4. Survey some friends and family members about their greatest fears. Organize them into categories. Use the information to write an essay about some of the specific fears people have today.
5. Think about your daily routine. Write an essay describing some of the dangers you face every day. Explain how you assess the risk in your life.
6. Choose a scary situation and write an essay that gives advice and information to help lessen someone's fear of this situation.

CHAPTER REVIEW AND PRACTICE

CHAPTER REVIEW

To review and check your recall of the chapter, match each term in Column A with its meaning in Column B.

COLUMN A	COLUMN B
_____ 1. topic	**a.** a way of recording your reactions to a reading in its margins
_____ 2. previewing	**b.** a diagram that shows the content and organization of an essay or reading
_____ 3. thesis statement	**c.** a method of becoming familiar with a reading before you actually begin reading
_____ 4. main idea	**d.** a way of exploring your own ideas and experimenting with them before you begin to write an essay
_____ 5. annotating	**e.** the facts that explain the main idea of a paragraph
_____ 6. idea map	**f.** the one thing a paragraph or essay is about
_____ 7. supporting details	**g.** the main point of an essay
_____ 8. journal writing	**h.** the one point a paragraph makes about its topic

3

Expanding Your Vocabulary

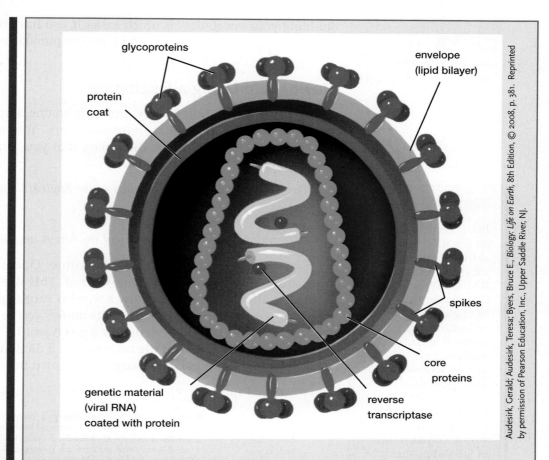

glycoproteins

envelope (lipid bilayer)

protein coat

spikes

core proteins

genetic material (viral RNA) coated with protein

reverse transcriptase

Audesirk, Gerald; Audesirk, Teresa; Byers, Bruce E., *Biology: Life on Earth*, 8th Edition, © 2008, p. 381. Reprinted by permission of Pearson Education, Inc., Upper Saddle River, NJ.

WRITE ABOUT IT!

The labels that accompany the photograph above contain several unfamiliar words. Write a list of ways you can figure out their meanings. In this chapter you will learn numerous strategies for figuring out and learning unfamiliar words.

VOCABULARY

Your vocabulary is one of your most valuable assets. Because words are the basic building blocks of language, you need a strong vocabulary to express yourself clearly in both speech and writing. A strong vocabulary identifies you as an effective communicator—an important skill both in college and in the workplace. Further, a solid vocabulary is the mark of an educated person—someone who is able to think, write, read critically, and speak effectively. Vocabulary building is well worth your while, and will pay off hundreds of times both in college and on the job. Let's get started!

GET THE RIGHT TOOLS

GOAL 1 Use dictionaries and thesauruses effectively

Building your vocabulary is much easier if you have the right tools to help you. Be sure you have a dictionary, and consider purchasing a thesaurus.

Buying and Using a Dictionary

Every writer needs a dictionary, not only to check spellings, but also to check meanings and the appropriate usages of words. You should have a desk or collegiate dictionary plus a pocket dictionary that you can carry with you to classes. Widely used dictionaries include:

> *The American Heritage Dictionary of the English Language*
>
> *Webster's New Collegiate Dictionary*
>
> *Webster's New World Dictionary of the American Language*

Several dictionaries are available online. One of the most widely used is Merriam-Webster's (http://www.m-w.com). This site features an audio component that allows you to hear how a word is pronounced. You might also refer to http://www.dictonary.com. This site allows you to view and compare entries from several different dictionaries for a given word.

Here is a brief review of the information a dictionary entry contains. As you read, refer to the sample dictionary entry shown below.

Tip for Writers

ESL students will find an ESL dictionary extremely helpful for speaking and writing. Written for the nonnative speaker of English, it gives definitions in the simplest language possible, contains sample sentences to show how words are used, explains the differences between easily confused words, contains lots of labeled pictures, and offers many additional features. For students ready to write paragraphs and essays, the *Longman Advanced American Dictionary* is a good choice. (There are also ESL dictionaries for British English and for both American and British English.)

Pronunciation

Parts of speech
Verb forms

Restrictive meanings

Word history

◆ **drink** (drĭngk) *v.* **drank** (drăngk), **drunk** (drŭngk), **drink•ing, drinks** —*tr.* **1.** To take into the mouth and swallow (a liquid). **2.** To swallow the liquid contents of (a vessel): *drank a cup of tea.* **3.** To take in or soak up; absorb: *drank the fresh air; spongy earth that drank up the rain.* **4.** To take in eagerly through the senses or intellect: *drank in the beauty of the day.* **5a.** To give or make (a toast). **b.** To toast (a person or an occasion, for example): *We'll drink to your health.* **6.** To bring to a specific state by drinking alcoholic liquors: *drank our sorrows away.* —*intr.* **1.** To swallow liquid: *drank noisily; drink from a goblet.* **2.** To imbibe alcoholic liquors: *They only drink socially.* **3.** To salute a person or an occasion with a toast: *We will drink to your continued success.* ◆*n.* **1.** A liquid that is fit for drinking; a beverage. **2.** An amount of liquid swallowed: *took a long drink from the fountain.* **3.** An alcoholic beverage, such as a cocktail or highball. **4.** Excessive or habitual indulgence in alcoholic liquor. **5.** *Chiefly Southern U.S.* See **soft drink.** See Regional Note at **tonic.** **6.** *Slang* A body of water; the sea: *The hatch cover slid off the boat and into the drink.* [Middle English *drinken*, from Old English *drincan.* See **dhreg-** in Appendix I.]

American Heritage Dictionary of the English Language

1. **Pronunciation** The pronunciation of the word is given in parentheses. Symbols are used to indicate the sounds letters make within specific words. Refer to the pronunciation key printed on each page or on alternate pages of your dictionary.

2. **Grammatical information** The part of speech is indicated, as well as information about different forms the word may take. Most dictionaries include

   - principal forms of verbs (both regular and irregular).
   - plural forms of irregular nouns.
   - comparative and superlative forms of adjectives and adverbs.

3. **Meanings** Meanings are numbered and are usually grouped by the part of speech they represent.

4. **Restrictive meanings** Meanings that are limited to special situations are labeled. Some examples are:

   - *Slang*—casual language used only in conversation.
   - *Biol.*—words used in specialized fields, in this case biology.
   - *Regional*—words used only in certain parts of the United States.

5. **Synonyms** Words with similar meanings may be listed.

6. **Word history** The origin of the word (its etymology) is described. (Not all dictionaries include this feature.)

EXERCISE 3-1   Using a Dictionary 1

Directions: Use a dictionary to complete each of the following items.

   Word: *reconstitute*

   1. Write one definition of this word and identify its part of speech.

   _____

   2. Write your own sentence using this word.

   _____

   word: *launch*

   1. Write one definition of this word and identify its part of speech.

   _____

   2. Write your own sentence using this word.

   _____

   word: *console*

   1. Write one definition of this word and identify its part of speech.

   _____

   2. Write your own sentence using this word.

   _____

EXERCISE 3-2   Using a Dictionary 2

Directions: Use a dictionary to answer the following questions.

1. What does the abbreviation *obs.* mean?

2. What does the symbol *c.* stand for?

3. How many meanings are listed for the word *fall*?

4. How is the word *phylloxera* pronounced? (Record its phonetic spelling.)

5. What is the plural spelling of *addendum*?

6. Can the word *protest* be used other than as a verb? If so, how?

7. The word *prime* can mean first or original. List some of its other meanings.

8. What does the French expression *savoir faire* mean?

9. List three synonyms for the word *fault*.

10. List several words that are formed using the word *dream*.

■

Finding the Right Meaning in a Dictionary Entry

Most words have more than one meaning. When you look up the meaning of a new word, you must choose the meaning that best fits the way the word is used in the context of the sentence. The following sample entry for the word *green* contains many meanings for the word.

Meanings grouped by parts of speech

7 Nouns

green (grēn) *n.* **1.** The hue of that portion of the visible spectrum lying between yellow and blue, evoked in the human observer by radiant energy with wavelengths of approximately 490 to 570 nanometers; any of a group of colors that may vary in lightness and saturation and whose hue is that of the emerald or somewhat less yellow that that of growing grass; one of the additive or light primaries; one of the psychological primary hues. **2.** Something green in color. **3. greens** Green growth or foliage, especially: **a.** The branches and leaves of plants used for decoration. **b.** Leafy plants or plant parts eaten as vegetables. **4.** A grassy lawn or plot, especially: **a.** A grassy area located usually at the

Many different meanings

Type of vegetable

center of a city or town and set aside for common use; a common. **b.** *Sports* A putting green. **5. greens** A green uniform: "A young...sergeant in dress greens" (Nelson DeMille). **6.** *Slang* Money. **7. Green** A supporter of a social and political movement that espouses global environmental protection, bioregionalism, social responsibility, and nonviolence. ❖*adj.* **green•er, green•est 1.** Of the color green. **2.** Abounding in or covered with green growth or foliage: *the green woods.* **3.** Made with green or leafy vegetables: *a green salad.* **4.** Characterized by mild or temperate weather: *a green climate.* **5.** Youthful; vigorous: *at the green age of 18.* **6.** Not mature or ripe; young: *green tomatoes.* **7.** Brand-new; fresh. **8.** Not yet fully processed, especially: **a.** Not aged: *green wood.* **b.** Not cured or tanned: *green pelts.* **9.** Lacking training or experience. See synonyms at **young. 10a.** Lacking sophistication or worldly experience; naive. **b.** Easily duped or deceived; gullible. **11.** Having a sickly or unhealthy pallor indicative of nausea or jealousy, for example. **12a.** Beneficial to the environment: *green recycling policies.* **b.** Favoring or supporting environmentalism: *green legislators who strengthened pollution controls.* ❖*tr. & intr. v.* **greened, green•ing, greens** To make or become green.

—*idiom:* **green around** (or **about**) **the gills** Pale or sickly in appearance. [Middle English *grene*, from Old English *grēne*, see **ghrē-** in Appendix I. N., sense 7, translation of German *(die) Grünen*, (the) Greens, from *grün*, green.] —**green'ly** *adv.* —**green'ness** *n.*

12 Adjectives

1 Verb

Part of golf course

Unripe fruit

Inexperienced person

American Heritage Dictionary of the English Language

The meanings are grouped by part of speech and are numbered consecutively in each group. Generally, the most common meanings of the word are listed first, with more specialized, less common meanings appearing toward the end of the entry. Now find the meaning that fits the use of the word *green* in the following sentence:

> The local veterans' organization held its annual fund-raising picnic on the village **green**.

In this sentence, *green* refers to "a common or park in the center of a town or village." Since this is a specialized meaning of the word, it appears toward the end of the entry.

Here are a few suggestions for choosing the correct meaning from among those listed in an entry:

1. **If you are familiar with the parts of speech, try to use these to locate the correct meaning.** For instance, if you are looking up the meaning of a word that names a person, place, or thing, you can save time by reading only those entries given after *n.* (noun).

2. **For most types of college reading, you can skip definitions that give slang and colloquial (abbreviated as *colloq.*) meanings.** Colloquial meanings refer to informal or conversational language.

3. **If you are not sure of the part of speech, read each meaning until you find a definition that seems correct.** Skip over restrictive meanings that are inappropriate.

4. **Test your choice by substituting the meaning in the sentence with which you are working.** Substitute the definition for the word and see whether it makes sense in the context of the sentence.

Tip for Writers

A bilingual dictionary translates from your native language to English and vice versa. However, these dictionaries may not give all the different meanings that a word has in English. This type of dictionary is useful but not sufficient for academic writing. ESL students should have an ESL dictionary with a vocabulary of at least 80,000 words and also use a standard desk-size college dictionary.

EXERCISE 3-3   Writing Different Meanings

Directions: The following words have two or more meanings. Look them up in your dictionary and write two sentences with different meanings for each word.

1. culture

_____

_____

2. perch

_____

_____

3. surge

_____

_____

4. extend

_____

_____

5. irregular

_____

_____

EXERCISE 3-4   Finding Appropriate Meanings

Directions: Use the dictionary to help you find an appropriate meaning for the boldfaced word in each of the following sentences.

1. The last contestant did not have a **ghost** of a chance.

_____

2. The race-car driver won the first **heat**.

_____

3. The police took all possible **measures** to protect the witness.

_____

4. The orchestra played the first **movement** of the symphony.

_____

5. The plane stalled on the **apron**.

_____

Using a Thesaurus

A thesaurus is a dictionary of synonyms. It groups together words with similar meanings. A thesaurus is particularly useful when you want to do the following:

- Locate the precise or exact word to fit a particular situation. (Example: Replace "a *boring* movie" with "an *uneventful* movie.")

- Find an appropriate descriptive word. (Example: Choose from among the following words to describe *happiness*: *delight, pleasure, joy, glee.*)

- Replace an overused or unclear word. (Example: Replace "a *good* television program" with "a *thrilling* or *refreshing* television program.")

- Convey a more specific shade of meaning. (Example: Use one of the following words to describe *walking*: *swagger, strut, stroll.*)

Suppose you are looking for a more precise word for the phrase *will tell us about* in the following sentence:

In class today, our chemistry instructor **will tell us about** our next assignment.

The thesaurus lists the following synonyms for "tell" or "explain":

> 10 **explain, explicate, expound,** exposit; **give the meaning,** tell the meaning of; **spell out,** unfold; **account for,** give reason for; **clarify, elucidate,** clear up; **make clear,** make plain; **simplify,** popularize; **illuminate,** enlighten, **shed** *or* **throw light upon;** rationalize, euhemerize, demythologize, allegorize; tell *or* show how, show the way; **demonstrate, show, illustrate,** exemplify; decipher, crack, unlock, find the key to, unravel, **solve;** explain oneself; explain away.
> 11 **comment upon,** commentate, remark upon; **annotate,** gloss; **edit,** make an edition.
> 12 **translate, render,** transcribe, transliterate, put *or* turn into, transfuse the sense of; construe; English.
> 13 **paraphrase, rephrase, reword, restate,** rehash; give a free *or* loose translation.

The American Heritage College Thesaurus

Read the previous entry and underline words or phrases that you think would be more descriptive than *tell about*. You might underline words and phrases such as *comment upon, illustrate, demonstrate,* and *spell out*.

The most widely used thesaurus is *Roget's Thesaurus*. Inexpensive paperback editions are available in most bookstores.

When you first consult a thesaurus, you will need to familiarize yourself with its format and learn how to use it. The following is a step-by-step approach:

1. **Locate the word you are trying to replace in the index.** Following the word, you will find the number(s) of the section(s) in the main part of the thesaurus that list(s) the synonyms of that word.

2. **Turn to those sections, scanning each list and jotting down all the words you think might work as synonyms.**

3. **Test each of the words you selected in the sentence in which you will use it.** The word should fit the context of the sentence.

4. **Select the word that best expresses what you are trying to say.**

5. **Choose only words whose shades of meaning you know.** Check unfamiliar words in a dictionary before using them. Remember, misusing a word is often a more serious error than choosing an overused or general word.

 **Analyze It!**

Directions: Read the paragraph on the left, taken from a college textbook. Use context, word parts, and a dictionary, if necessary, to figure out the meanings of the words listed on the right. Write the meanings in the space provided.

Human communication, in one way or another, inevitably involves the body in sending and receiving messages. Beyond the mechanics of speaking, hearing, gesturing, and seeing, the body itself can function as a "text" that conveys messages. The full range of body language includes eye movements, posture, walking style, the way of standing and sitting, cultural inscriptions on the body such as tattoos and hairstyles, and accessories such as dress, shoes, and jewelry. Body language follows patterns and rules just as verbal language does. Like verbal language, the rules and meanings are learned, often unconsciously. Without learning the rules and meanings, one will commit communication errors, which are sometimes funny and sometimes serious.

—Miller, *Anthropology*, p. 68.

inevitably _____

_____

mechanics _____

_____

body language _____

_____

_____

accessories _____

_____

unconsciously _____

_____

EXERCISE 3-5   Using a Thesaurus

Directions: Using a thesaurus, replace the boldfaced word or phrase in each of the following sentences with a more precise or descriptive word. Write the word in the space provided. Rephrase the sentence, if necessary.

1. Although the movie was **good**, it lasted only an hour and 20 minutes.

   _____

2. The judge **looked at** the criminal as she pronounced the sentence.

   _____

3. The accident victim was awarded a **big** cash settlement.

   _____

4. The lottery winner was **happy** to win the $100,000 prize, but he was surprised to learn that a sizable portion had already been deducted for taxes.

   _____

5. On the first day of class, the instructor **talked to** the class about course requirements.

   _____

USE CONTEXT CLUES TO FIGURE OUT UNFAMILIAR WORDS

GOAL 2 Use context clues to figure out unfamiliar words

Context refers to the words around a given word. Often you can use context to figure out a word you do not know. Try it in the following sentence:

> **Phobias,** such as a fear of heights, water, or confined spaces, are difficult to overcome.

From the clues in the rest of the sentence, you can figure out that *phobias* are fears of specific objects or situations. Such clues are called **context clues.** There are five types of context clues that can help you figure out a word you do not know: *definition, synonym, example, contrast,* and *inference.* These are summarized in the "Need to Know" box shown on the following page.

Context clues do not always appear in the same sentence as the unknown word. They may appear anywhere in the passage, or in an earlier or later sentence. So if you cannot find a clue immediately, look before and after the word. Here is an example:

> Betsy took a *break* from teaching in order to serve in the Peace Corps. Despite the **hiatus**, Betsy's school was delighted to rehire her when she returned.

Notice that the clue for the word *hiatus, break,* appears in the sentence before the one containing the word you want to define.

EXERCISE 3-6   Using Context Clues 1

Directions: Using the definition or synonym clues in each sentence, write a brief definition of each boldfaced word in the following sentences.

1. After taking a course in **genealogy**, Diego was able to create a record of his family's history dating back to the eighteenth century.

   _____

2. Louie's **dossier** is a record of his credentials, including college transcripts and letters of recommendation.

   _____

3. There was a **consensus**—or unified opinion—among the students that the exam was difficult.

   _____

4. After each course heading there was a **synopsis**, or summary, of the content and requirements for the course.

   _____

5. When preparing job application letters, Serena develops one standard letter or **prototype.** Then she changes that letter to fit the specific jobs for which she is applying.

   _____

NEED TO KNOW

Five Useful Types of Context Clues

Type of Context Clue	How It Works	Examples
Definition	Writers often define a word after using it. Words such as *means, refers to,* and *can be defined as* provide an obvious clue that the word's meaning is to follow. Sometimes writers use dashes, parentheses, or commas to separate a definition from the rest of the sentence.	**Corona** refers to <u>the outermost part of the sun's atmosphere</u>. <u>Broad flat noodles</u> that are served covered with sauce or butter are called **fettuccine.** The judge's **candor**—<u>his sharp, open frankness</u>—shocked the jury. **Audition**, <u>the process of hearing</u>, begins when a sound wave reaches the outer ear.
Synonym	Rather than formally define a word, some writers include a word or brief phrase that is close in meaning to a word you may not know.	The main character in the movie was an **amalgam**, or <u>combination</u>, of several real people the author met during the war.
Example	Writers often include examples to help explain a word. From the examples, you can often figure out what the unknown word means.	**Toxic** materials, such as <u>arsenic, asbestos, pesticides, and lead</u>, can cause bodily damage. (You can figure out that *toxic* means "poisonous.") Many **pharmaceuticals**, including <u>morphine and penicillin</u>, are not readily available in some countries. (You can figure out that *pharmaceuticals* are drugs.)
Contrast	Sometimes a writer gives a word that is opposite in meaning to a word you don't know. From the opposite meaning, you can figure out the unknown word's meaning. (Hint: watch for words such as *but, however, though, whereas.*)	Uncle Sal was quite **portly**, <u>but his wife was very thin</u>. (The opposite of *thin* is *fat,* so you know that *portly* means "fat.") The professor **advocates** the testing of cosmetics on animals, <u>but many of her students oppose it</u>. (The opposite of *oppose* is *favor,* so you know that *advocates* means "favors.")
Inference	Often your own logic or reasoning skills can lead you to the meaning of an unknown word.	Bob is quite **versatile**: <u>he is a good student, a top athlete, an excellent auto mechanic, and a gourmet cook.</u> (Because Bob excels at many activities, you can reason that *versatile* means "capable of doing many things.") <u>On hot, humid afternoons, I often feel</u> **languid.** (From your experience you may know that you feel drowsy or sluggish on hot afternoons, so you can figure out that *languid* means "lacking energy.")

EXERCISE 3-7   Using Context Clues 2

Directions: Using the example clues in each sentence, write a brief definition of each boldfaced word in the following sentences.

1. **Histrionics**, such as wild laughter or excessive body movements, are usually inappropriate in business settings.

_____

2. Jerry's child was **reticent** in every respect; she would not speak, refused to answer questions, and avoided looking at anyone.

_____

3. Most **condiments**, such as pepper, mustard, and catsup, are used to improve the flavor of foods.

_____

4. Dogs, cats, parakeets, and other **sociable** pets can provide senior citizens with companionship.

_____

5. Paul's grandmother is a **sagacious** businesswoman; once she turned a small ice cream shop into a popular restaurant and sold it for a huge profit.

_____

EXERCISE 3-8   Using Context Clues 3

Directions: Using the contrast clues in each sentence, write a brief definition of each boldfaced word in the following sentences.

1. Freshmen are often **naive** about college at first, but by their second semester they are usually quite sophisticated in the ways of their new school.

_____

2. Although most members of the class agreed with the instructor's evaluation of the film, several strongly **objected.**

_____

3. Little Jill hid shyly behind her mother when she met new people, yet her brother Matthew was very **gregarious.**

_____

4. The child remained **demure** while the teacher scolded, but became violently angry afterward.

_____

5. Some city dwellers are **affluent**; others live in or near poverty.

_____

EXERCISE 3-9   Using Context Clues 4

Directions: Using logic and your own reasoning skills, choose the correct definition of each boldfaced word in the following sentences.

_____ 1. To **compel** Clare to hand over her wallet, the mugger said he had a gun.

    a. discourage   **c.** force

    b. entice   **d.** imagine

_____ 2. Student journalists are taught how to be **concise** when writing in a limited space.

    a. peaceful   **c.** proper

    b. clear and brief   **d.** wordy

_____ 3. There should be more **drastic** penalties to stop people from littering.

    a. dirty   **c.** extreme

    b. suitable   **d.** dangerous

_____ 4. To **fortify** his diet while weightlifting, Monty took 12 vitamins a day.

    a. suggest   **c.** avoid

    b. strengthen   **d.** approve of

_____ 5. On our wedding anniversary, my husband and I **reminisced** about how we first met.

    a. sang   **c.** argued

    b. remembered   **d.** forgot ■

EXERCISE 3-10   Using Context Clues in a Passage

Directions: Read the following passage and then circle the answer that best defines each boldfaced word appearing in the text.

Worms and *viruses* are rather unpleasant terms that have entered the **jargon** of the computer industry to describe some of the ways that computer systems can be invaded.

A worm can be defined as a program that transfers itself from computer to computer over a network and plants itself as a separate file on the target computer's disks. One worm was **injected** into an electronic mail network where it multiplied uncontrollably and clogged the memories of thousands of computers until they could no longer function.

A virus is a set of illicit instructions that passes itself on to other programs or documents with which it comes in contact. It can change or delete files, display words or obscene messages, or produce bizarre screen effects. In its most **vindictive** form, a virus can slowly **sabotage** a computer system and remain undetected for months, contaminating data or wiping out an entire hard drive. A virus can be dealt with using a vaccine, or antivirus, which is a computer program that stops the virus from spreading and often **eradicates** it.

—adapted from Capron, *Computers.*

_____ **1.** jargon

      a. language   **c.** confusion

      b. system   **d.** security

_____ **2.** injected

      a. avoided   **c.** removed

      b. introduced   **d.** discussed

_____ **3.** vindictive

      a. creative   **c.** spiteful

      b. simple   **d.** typical

_____ **4.** sabotage

      a. prevent   **c.** transfer

      b. disable   **d.** produce

_____ **5.** eradicates

      a. eliminates   **c.** repeats

      b. allows   **d.** produces ■

PAY ATTENTION TO WORD PARTS

GOAL 3 Use word parts to figure out the meanings of words

Suppose that you came across the following sentence in a human anatomy textbook:

Trichromatic plates are used frequently in the text to illustrate the position of body organs.

If you did not know the meaning of *trichromatic*, how could you determine it? There are no clues in the sentence context. One solution is to look up the word in a dictionary. An easier and faster way is to break the word into parts and analyze the meaning of each part. Many words in the English language are made up of word parts called **prefixes**, **roots**, and **suffixes**. These word parts have specific meanings that, when added together, can help you determine the meaning of the word as a whole.

The word *trichromatic* can be divided into three parts: its prefix, root, and suffix.

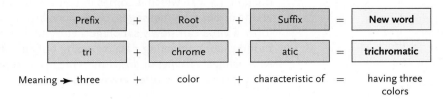

You can see from this analysis that *trichromatic* means "having three colors." Here are a few other examples of words that you can figure out by using prefixes, roots, and suffixes:

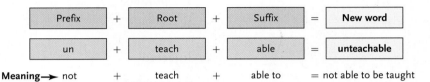

*The parents thought their child was **unteachable**.*

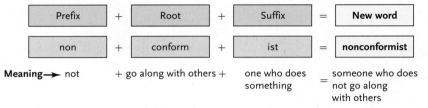

*The student was a **nonconformist**.*

The first step in using the prefix-root-suffix method is to become familiar with the most commonly used word parts. The prefixes and roots listed in Table 3-1 and Table 3-2 (see p. 75 and p. 76) will give you a good start in determining the meanings of thousands of words without looking them up in the dictionary. For instance, more than 10,000 words can begin with the prefix *non-*. Not all these words are listed in a collegiate dictionary, but they would appear in an unabridged dictionary. Another common prefix, *pseudo-*, is used in more than 400 words. A small amount of time spent learning word parts can yield a large payoff in new words learned.

Before you begin to use word parts to figure out new words, here are a few things you need to know:

1. **In most cases, a word is built upon at least one root.**
2. **Words can have more than one prefix, root, or suffix.**
   a. Words can be made up of two or more roots (geo/logy).
   b. Some words have two prefixes (in/sub/ordination).
   c. Some words have two suffixes (beauti/ful/ly).
3. **Words do not always have a prefix and a suffix.**
   a. Some words have neither a prefix nor a suffix (read).
   b. Others have a suffix but no prefix (read/ing).
   c. Others have a prefix but no suffix (pre/read).

TABLE 3-1 COMMON PREFIXES

Prefix	Meaning	Sample Word
Prefixes referring to amount or number		
mono/uni	one	monocle/unicycle
bi/di/du	two	bimonthly/divorce/duet
tri	three	triangle
quad	four	quadrant
quint/pent	five	quintet/pentagon
deci	ten	decimal
centi	hundred	centigrade
milli	thousand	milligram
micro	small	microscope
multi/poly	many	multipurpose/polygon
semi	half	semicircle
equi	equal	equidistant
Prefixes meaning "not" (negative)		
a	not	asymmetrical
anti	against	antiwar
contra	against, opposite	contradict
dis	apart, away, not	disagree
in/il/ir/im	not	incorrect/illogical/irreversible/impossible
mis	wrongly	misunderstand
non	not	nonfiction
pseudo	false	pseudoscientific
un	not	unpopular
Prefixes giving direction, location, or placement		
ab	away	absent
ad	toward	adhesive
ante/pre	before	antecedent/premarital
circum/peri	around	circumference/perimeter
com/col/con	with, together	compile/collide/convene
de	away, from	depart
dia	through	diameter
ex/extra	from, out of, former	ex-wife/extramarital
hyper	over, excessive	hyperactive
inter	between	interpersonal
intro/intra	within, into, in	introduction
post	after	posttest
re	back, again	review
retro	backward	retrospect
sub	under, below	submarine
super	above, extra	supercharge
tele	far	telescope
trans	across, over	transcontinental

4. **The spelling of roots may change as they are combined with suffixes.** Some common variations are included in Table 3-2.

5. **Different prefixes, roots, or suffixes may have the same meaning.** For example, the prefixes *bi-, di-,* and *duo-* all mean "two."

6. **Word parts may have more than one meaning.** A dictionary listing that begins or ends with a hyphen is a word part, not a complete word. The hyphen is usually not used in the spelling of the word. Be careful when interpreting the meaning of these word parts. Many have more than one meaning. For example, *ex-* means "former" (as in *ex-president*), but it can also mean "out" or "outside" (as in *exit* or *exterior*).

7. **Use a dictionary to find out which prefix to use.** Several word parts mean "not" and make the word they precede mean the opposite of its original meaning. For example, the following are some common negative prefixes: *in-* (*incomplete*), *im-* (*impossible*), *un-* (*unbearable*), *non-* (*nonsense*), *il-* (*illegal*), *ir-* (*irregular*), and *dis-* (*disobey*). Which one should you use? In many cases, the correct prefix is determined by the word's part of speech (such as

TABLE 3-2   TWENTY COMMON ROOTS

Common Root	Meaning	Sample Word
aud/audit	hear	audible
bio	life	biology
cap	take, seize	captive
cede	go	precede
chron(o)	time	chronology
cred	believe	incredible
dict/dic	tell, say	predict
duc/duct	lead	introduce
graph	write	autograph
mit/mis(s)	send	permit/dismiss
path	feeling	sympathy
photo	light	photosensitive
port	carry	transport
scrib/script	write	inscription
sen/sent	feel	insensitive
spec/spic/spect	look, see	retrospect
sym/syn	same, together	synonym
ven/vent	come	convention
vert/vers	turn	invert
voc	call	vocation

dis- before a verb) and the first letter of the base word. Base words beginning with *m* or *p* usually use *im-*, words beginning with *l* usually use *il-*, and most words beginning with *r-* use *ir-* as their negative prefixes. If you're not sure which prefix to use, consult a dictionary.

8. **Sometimes you may identify a group of letters as a prefix or root but find that it does not carry the meaning of that prefix or root.** For example, the letters *mis* in the word *missile* are part of the root and are not the prefix *mis-*, which means "wrong or bad."

Prefixes

Prefixes appear at the beginnings of many English words. They alter the meaning of the root to which they are connected. For example, if you add the prefix *re-* to the word *test*, the word *retest* is formed, meaning to test again. If *pre-* is added to the word *test*, the word *pretest* is formed, meaning a test given before something else. If the prefix *post-* is added, the word *posttest* is formed, meaning a test given after something else. Table 3-1 groups common prefixes according to meaning.

EXERCISE 3-11   Using Prefixes 1

Directions: Use the list of common prefixes in Table 3-1 (p. 75) to determine the meaning of each of the following words. Write a brief definition or synonym for each. If you are unfamiliar with the root, you may need to check a dictionary.

1. interoffice _____

2. supernatural _____

3. nonsense _____

4. introspection _____

5. prearrange _____

6. reset _____

7. subtopic _____

8. transmit _____

9. multidimensional _____

10. imperfect _____

EXERCISE 3-12   Using Prefixes 2

Directions: Read each of the following sentences. Use your knowledge of prefixes to fill in the blanks and complete the words.

1. A person who speaks two languages is _____**lingual.**

2. A letter or number written beneath a line of print is called a _____**script.**

3. The new sweater had a snag, and I returned it to the store because it was _____**perfect.**

4. The flood damage was permanent and _____**reversible.**

5. People who speak several different languages are _____**lingual.**

6. A musical _____**lude** was played between the events in the ceremony.

7. I decided the magazine was uninteresting, so I _____**continued** my subscription.

8. Merchandise that does not pass factory inspection is considered _____**standard** and is sold at a discount.

9. The tuition refund policy approved this week will apply to last year's tuition as well; the policy will be _____**active** to January 1 of last year.

10. The elements were_____**acting** with each other when they began to bubble and their temperature rose. ■

EXERCISE 3-13   Using Prefixes 3
Working Together

Directions: Working with a classmate, list as many words as you can think of for two of the following prefixes: *multi-, mis-, trans-, com-, inter-.* Then share your lists with the class. ■

Roots

Roots carry the basic or core meaning of a word. Hundreds of root words are used to build other words in the English language. Twenty of the most common and most useful are listed in Table 3-2 on p. 76. Knowledge of the meanings of these roots will enable you to unlock the meanings of many words. For example, if you knew that the root *dic/dict* means "tell or say," then you would have a clue to the meanings of such words as *dictate* (to speak while someone writes down your words), *diction* (wording or manner of speaking), or *dictionary* (a book that "tells" what words mean).

EXERCISE 3-14   Using Roots 1

Directions: Complete each of the following sentences using one of the words listed below. Not all of the words will be used.

apathetic	dictated	graphic	scriptures	tendon
captivated	extensive	phonics	spectators	verdict
deduce	extraterrestrial	prescribed	synchronized	visualize

1. The jury brought in its _____ after one hour of deliberation.

2. Religious or holy writings are called _____.

3. The _____ watching the football game were tense.

4. The doctor _____ two types of medication.

5. The criminal appeared _____ when the judge pronounced his sentence.

6. The runners _____ their watches before beginning the race.

7. The textbook contained numerous _____ aids, including maps, charts, and diagrams.

8. The district manager _____ a new policy on business expenses.

9. Through his attention-grabbing performance, he _____ the audience.

10. By putting together the clues, the detective was finally able to _____ who committed the crime. ■

EXERCISE 3-15   Using Roots 2

Directions: List two words for each of the following roots: *dict/dic; spec/spic/ spect; cred; photo; scrib/script.*

_____

_____

_____

■

Suffixes

Suffixes are word endings that often change the part of speech of a word. For example, adding the suffix *y* to the noun *cloud* forms the adjective *cloudy*. Accompanying the change in part of speech is a shift in meaning (*cloudy* means "resembling clouds; overcast with clouds; dimmed or dulled as if by clouds").

Often, several different words can be formed from a single root word by adding different suffixes.

EXAMPLES

Root: class
root + suffix = class/ify, class/ification, class/ic

Root: right
root + suffix = right/ly, right/ful, right/ist, right/eous

If you know the meaning of the root word and the ways in which different suffixes affect the meaning of the root word, you will be able to figure out a word's meaning when a suffix is added. A list of common suffixes and their meanings appears in Table 3-3 on p. 80.

You can expand your vocabulary by learning the variations in meaning that occur when suffixes are added to words you already know. When you find a word that you do not know, look for the root. Then, using the sentence in which the word appears, figure out what the word means with the suffix added. Occasionally you may find that the spelling of the root word has been changed. For instance, a final *e* may be dropped, a final consonant may be doubled, or a final *y* may be changed to *i*. Consider the possibility of such changes when trying to identify the root word.

TABLE 3-3 COMMON SUFFIXES	
Suffix	**Sample Word**
Suffixes that refer to a state, condition, or quality	
able	touchable
ance	assistance
ation	confrontation
ence	reference
ible	tangible
ion	discussion
ity	superiority
ive	permissive
ment	amazement
ness	kindness
ous	jealous
ty	loyalty
y	creamy
Suffixes that mean "one who"	
an	Italian
ant	participant
ee	referee
eer	engineer
ent	resident
er	teacher
ist	activist
or	advisor
Suffixes that mean "pertaining to or referring to"	
al	autumnal
hood	brotherhood
ship	friendship
ward	homeward

EXAMPLES

The article was a **compilation** of facts.
root + suffix

compil(e) + -ation = compilation (something that has been compiled, or put together into an orderly form)

We were concerned with the **legality** of our decision to change addresses.
root + suffix

legal + -ity = legality (pertaining to legal matters)

The couple **happily** announced their engagement.
root + suffix

happ(y) + -(i)ly = happily (in a pleased or contented way)
Note: The letter *y* is changed to *i* when suffix is added.

▮ EXERCISE 3-16   **Using Suffixes 1**

Directions: On a sheet of paper, for each suffix shown in Table 3-3, write another example of a word you know that contains that suffix. ▮

▮ EXERCISE 3-17   **Using Suffixes 2**

Directions: For each of the words listed below, add a suffix so that the word will complete the sentence. Write the new word in the space provided. Check a dictionary if you are unsure of the spelling.

1. **converse**

   Our phone _____ lasted ten minutes.

2. **assist**

   The medical _____ labeled the patient's blood samples.

3. **qualify**

   The job applicant outlined his _____ to the interviewer.

4. **intern**

   The doctor completed her _____ at Memorial Medical Center.

5. **audio**

   She spoke so softly that her voice was not _____.

6. **permit**

   The professor granted her _____ to miss class.

7. **instruct**

   The lecture on Freud was very _____.

8. **mortal**

   The _____ rate in Ethiopia is very high.

9. **feminine**

   She called herself a _____, although she never actively supported the movement for equal rights for women.

10. **hazard**

    The presence of toxic waste in the lake is _____ to health. ▮

▮ EXERCISE 3-18   **Using Suffixes 3**

Directions: For each word listed below, write as many new words as you can create by adding suffixes.

1. compare _____

2. adapt _____

3. right _____

4. identify _____

5. will _____

6. prefer _____

7. notice _____

8. like _____

9. pay _____

10. promote _____

■

How to Use Word Parts

Think of roots as being at the root or core of a word's meaning. There are many more roots than are listed in Table 3-2. You already know many of these, because they are used in everyday speech. Think of prefixes as word parts that are added before the root to qualify or change its meaning. Think of suffixes as add-ons that make the word fit grammatically into the sentence in which it is used.

When you come upon a word you do not know, keep the following pointers in mind:

1. **First, look for the root.** Think of this as looking for a word inside a larger word. Often a letter or two will be missing.

   EXAMPLES

   un/utter/able   defens/ible

   inter/colleg/iate   re/popular/ize

   post/operat/ive   non/adapt/able

   im/measur/ability   non/commit/tal

2. **If you do not recognize the root, then you will probably not be able to figure out the word.** The next step is to check its meaning in a dictionary.

3. **If you did recognize the root word, look for a prefix.** If there is one, determine how it changes the meaning of the word.

   EXAMPLES

   un/utterable   un- = not

   post/operative   post- = after

4. **Locate the suffix.** Determine how it further adds to or changes the meaning of the root word.

   EXAMPLES

   unutter/able   -able = able to

   postoperat/ive   -ive = state or condition

5. **Next, try out the meaning in the sentence in which the word was used.** Substitute your meaning for the word and see whether the sentence makes sense.

   EXAMPLES

   Some of the victim's thoughts were unutterable at the time of the crime.
   unutterable = not able to be spoken
   My sister was worried about the cost of postoperative care.
   postoperative = state or condition after an operation

EXERCISE 3-19   **Using Word Parts 1**

Directions: Use the steps listed previously to determine the meaning of each boldfaced word. Underline the root in each word and then write a brief definition of the word that fits its use in the sentence.

1. The doctor felt the results of the X-rays were **indisputable.**

_____

2. The **dissimilarity** among the three brothers was surprising.

_____

3. The **extortionist** demanded two payments of $10,000 each.

_____

4. It is **permissible** to camp in most state parks.

_____

5. The student had **retentive** abilities.

_____

6. The **traumatic** event changed the child's attitude toward animals.

_____

7. We were surprised by her **insincerity.**

_____

8. The child's **hypersensitivity** worried his parents.

_____

9. The English instructor told Peter that he had written a **creditable** paper.

_____

10. The rock group's agent hoped to **repopularize** their first hit song.

_____

EXERCISE 3-20   **Using Word Parts 2**

Directions: Read each of the following paragraphs and determine the meaning of each boldfaced word. Write a brief definition for each in the space provided.

    A.   Exercising in hot weather can create stress on the circulatory system due to the high **production** of body heat. In hot weather the **distention** of blood vessels in the skin **diverts** increased quantities of blood to the body surfaces, where heat is released. As the body heats, skin heat evaporates the sweat, cooling the skin and the blood **circulating** near the skin.

—Curtis, Byer, and Shainberg, *Living Well*, p. 360.

1. production _____

2. distention _____

3. diverts _____

4. circulating _____

B.   In addition to being **irreversible**, interpersonal communication is also **unrepeatable.** The reason is simple: Everyone and everything are constantly changing. As a result, you can never **recapture** the exact same situation, frame of mind, or relationship that defined a previous interpersonal act. For example, you can never repeat meeting someone for the first time, comforting a grieving friend, or resolving a specific conflict.

—DeVito, *Building Interpersonal Communication Skills*, p. 22–23.

1. irreversible _____

2. unrepeatable _____

3. recapture _____

C.   People with positive emotional **wellness** can function **independently.** They can think for themselves, make decisions, plan their lives, and follow through with their plans. **Conversely**, people who have difficulty making decisions are often immature and **insecure.** They are afraid to face the consequences of the decisions they make, so they make as few decisions as possible. Growth involves making **mistakes** as well as achieving success. Our mistakes are best viewed as learning experiences. We must take some risks in order to live our lives most fully.

—Curtis, Byer, and Shainberg, *Living Well*, p. 67.

1. wellness _____

2. independently _____

3. conversely _____

4. insecure _____

5. mistakes _____

D.   We could probably greatly reduce the risks associated with nuclear power by simply exercising more care and common sense. There are a **multitude** of published accounts that attest to our carelessness, however. For example, it has been revealed that the Diablo Canyon nuclear power plant in California was built on an earthquake fault line. Of course it was girded for that risk. **Incredibly**, however, the blueprints were somehow **reversed** and the earthquake supports were put in backwards. Furthermore, the mistake was not noticed for four years. At the Comanche Peak Plant in Texas, supports were **constructed** 45 degrees out of line. At the Marble Hill in Indiana, the concrete surrounding the core was found to be full of air bubbles. At the WNP-2 plant in Washington state, the concrete contained air bubbles and pockets of water as well as shields that had been **incorrectly** welded. At the San Onofre plant in California, a 420-ton reactor vessel was installed backwards and the error was not detected for months.

—Wallace, *Biology*, p. 834.

1. multitude _____

2. incredibly _____

3. reversed _____

4. constructed _____

5. incorrectly _____

LEARN IDIOMS

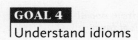

Understand idioms

An **idiom** is a phrase that has a meaning other than the common meaning of the words in the phrase. For example, the phrase *turn over a new leaf* is not about the leaves on a tree. It means to "start fresh" or "begin over again in a new way." You can locate idioms in a dictionary by looking up the key words in the phrase. To find the meaning of the idiom *as the crow flies*, look up the entry for *crow*. Idioms are usually identified by the label "—idiom," followed by the complete phrase and its meaning.

If you need more help figuring out idioms, consult a handbook or dictionary of American idioms, such as *Webster's New World American Idioms Handbook*. It is usually best not to use idioms in your own writing. Many are overused and will not express your ideas in a clear or concise way.

EXERCISE 3-21   Understanding Idioms

Directions: Explain the meaning of each of the following idioms.

1. to keep tabs on _____

   _____

2. to steal someone's thunder _____

   _____

   _____

3. in the dark _____

4. to bite the bullet _____

5. to make no bones about _____

   _____

DEVELOP A SYSTEM FOR LEARNING NEW WORDS

GOAL 5 Develop a system for learning new words

Here are two effective ways to organize and learn specialized or technical vocabulary for each of your courses.

The Vocabulary Card System

One of the most efficient and practical ways to organize the words for study and review is the vocabulary card system. Use a 3-by-5-inch index card for each new term. Record the word on the front and its meaning on the back. If the word is particularly difficult, you might also include a guide to its pronunciation. Underneath the correct spelling of the word, indicate in syllables how the word sounds. For the word *eutrophication* (a term used in chemistry to mean "overnourishment"), you could indicate its pronunciation as "you-tro-fi-kay'-shun." On the back of the card, along with the meaning, you might want to include an example to help you remember the term more easily. A sample vocabulary card, front and back, is shown on the next page.

Sample Vocabulary Card

ostracize (ŏs´ trə sīz)	to banish from social or political favor Ex.: A street gang will ostracize a member who refuses to wear the gang emblem.
Front	**Back**

Use these cards for study, for review, and for testing yourself. Go through your pack of cards once, looking at the front and trying to recall the meaning on the back. Then reverse the procedure; look at the meanings and see whether you can recall the terms. As you go through the pack in this way, sort the cards into two piles: words you know and words you don't know. The next time you review the cards, use only cards in the "don't know" pile for review. This sorting procedure will help you avoid wasting time reviewing words you have already learned. Continue to review the cards until you are satisfied that you have learned each new term. To avoid forgetting a word, review the entire pack of cards periodically.

The Computerized Vocabulary File

Using a word processing program, create a computer file for each of your courses. Daily or weekly, review both textbook chapters and lecture notes and enter specialized and technical terms that you need to learn. Use a two-column or table format, entering the word in one column and its meaning in the other. You might subdivide or code your file by textbook chapter so that you can review easily when exams or quizzes on particular chapters are announced.

Your files can be used in several different ways. If you alphabetize the words, you will have created a glossary that will serve as a handy reference. Keep a print copy handy as you read new chapters and review lecture notes. When studying the words in your file, try scrambling the words to avoid learning them in a fixed order.

Writing in a Visual Age

READING

Research suggests that happiness is one result of living morally and ethically. Dr. Martin Seligman of the University of Pennsylvania pioneered the field of *positive psychology* to discover the causes of happiness. Seligman's research has shown that by identifying your personal strengths and values (Table 1) and applying them every day, you will see an increase in happiness and a decrease in depression. Finding a way to identify and then apply your ethics and values to your daily life really does have an impact on your happiness.

TABLE 1	VIRTUES AND STRENGTHS FOR AUTHENTIC HAPPINESS	
Virtue	**Definition**	**Character Strength**
Wisdom	The acquisition and use of knowledge	Creativity, curiosity, open-mindedness
Courage	The will to accomplish goals in the face of opposition	Authenticity, bravery, persistence, zest
Humanity	Tending to and befriending others	Kindness, love, social intelligence, empathy
Justice	Just behavior or treatment	Fairness, leadership, teamwork
Temperance	Strengths that protect against excess	Forgiveness, modesty, prudence, self-regulation
Transcendence	Forging connections to the larger universe	Gratitude, hope, humor, appreciation of beauty

—Adapted from Solomon, Poatsy, and Martin, *Better Business*, p. 66.

1. In the first column of Table 1, two listed virtues are *temperance* and *transcendence*. Can you use word parts to understand their definitions? Try using Table 3-1 (page 75) and Table 3-3 (page 80).

   _____

   _____

2. Highlight any words in the reading or table that you are not familiar with, and use the techniques you learned in this chapter to discover their meanings.

CRITICAL THINKING AND RESPONSE

3. Write a paragraph answering the following questions: What do you think are the biggest challenges facing society today? Which three of the virtues listed in Table 1 are the most essential to helping people cope with these challenges?

WRITING

4. In a sentence or two, explain how emphasizing your good qualities can help you feel better.

5. Think of a person you respect (friend, relative, or celebrity). Write a paragraph explaining which virtues (listed in Table 1) this person has, and how he or she demonstrates them. By including these examples, you will be providing details that support your topic sentence.

USING VISUALS

6. Suppose you wanted to find three photos to accompany the reading. Choose three virtues from Table 1 and describe the types of photo you might select to illustrate them.

7. Suppose you gave money to the woman in this photo. Which virtue would you be demonstrating? Write a caption to accompany the photo.

WRITING ABOUT A READING

THINKING BEFORE READING

In the following reading, the author examines the history of China's one-child policy, exploring its benefits and drawbacks. Before you read:

1. Preview the reading using the steps listed in Chapter 2, page 35.

2. After you have previewed the reading, connect the reading to your own experience by answering the following questions:

    a. How many siblings (brothers and sisters) do you have?

    b. Do you think the government has the right to tell people how many children they can have?

3. Mark and annotate as you read.

READING
CHINA'S ONE-CHILD POLICY

Jay Withgott and Scott Brennan

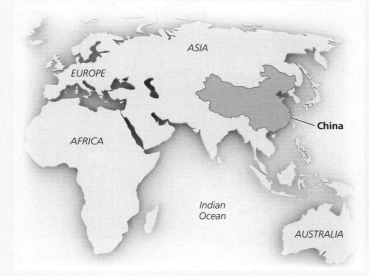

China

"Population growth is analogous to a plague of locusts. What we have on this earth today is a plague of people."

—Ted Turner, media magnate and supporter of the United Nations Population Fund

"As you improve health in a society, population growth goes down. . . . Before I learned about it, I thought it was paradoxical."

—Bill Gates, Chair, Microsoft Corporation

Mao Zedong
longtime leader of the Chinese Communist Party

burgeoning
growing

1   The People's Republic of China is the world's most populous nation, home to one-fifth of the 6.9 billion people living on Earth at the start of 2011.

2   When **Mao Zedong** founded the country's current regime 62 years earlier, roughly 540 million people lived in a mostly rural, war-torn, impoverished nation. Mao believed population growth was desirable, and under his rule China grew and changed. By 1970, improvements in food production, food distribution, and public health allowed China's population to swell to 790 million people. At that time, the average Chinese woman gave birth to 5.8 children in her lifetime.

3   However, the country's **burgeoning** population and its industrial and agricultural development were eroding the nation's soils, depleting its water, leveling its forests, and polluting its air. Chinese leaders realized that the nation might not be able to feed its people if their numbers grew much larger. They saw that continued population growth could exhaust resources and threaten the stability and progress of Chinese society. The government decided to institute a population-control program that prohibited most Chinese couples from having more than one child.

4   The program began with education and outreach efforts encouraging people to marry later and have fewer children (Figure A, p. 90). Along with these efforts, the Chinese government increased the availability of contraceptives and abortion. By 1975, China's annual population growth rate had dropped from 2.8% to 1.8%.

Mother with one son in northern China

Withgott, Jay H.; Brennan, Scott R., *Environment: The Science Behind the Stories,* 4th edition, © 2011. Printed and electronically reproduced by permission of Pearson Education, Inc., Upper Saddle River, New Jersey.

Figure A   *Billboards and murals like this one in the Chinese city of Chengdu promote the national one-child policy. Although the mural shows a baby girl, the policy has resulted in a preference for baby boys, like this one being toted by his grandfather.*

5   To further decrease the birth rate, in 1979 the government took the more drastic step of instituting a system of rewards and punishments to enforce a one-child limit. One-child families received better access to schools, medical care, housing, and government jobs, and mothers with only one child were given longer maternity leaves. In contrast, families with more than one child were subjected to monetary fines, employment discrimination, and social scorn and ridicule. In some cases, the fines exceeded half of a couple's annual income.

6   Population growth rates dropped still further, but public resistance to the policy was simmering. Beginning in 1984, the one-child policy was loosened, strengthened, and then loosened again as government leaders explored ways to maximize population control while minimizing public opposition. Today the one-child program is less strict than in past years and applies mostly to families in urban areas. Many farmers and ethnic minorities in rural areas are **exempted**, because success on the farm often depends on having multiple children.

exempted
released from an obligation

7   In enforcing its policies, China has been conducting one of the largest and most controversial social experiments in history. In purely quantitative terms, the experiment has been a major success: The nation's growth rate is now down to 0.5%, making it easier for the country to deal with its many social, economic, and environmental challenges.

8   However, the one-child policy has also produced unintended consequences. Traditionally, Chinese culture has valued sons because they carry on the family name, assist with farm labor in rural areas, and care for aging parents. Daughters, in contrast, will most likely marry and leave their parents, as the culture dictates. As a result, they cannot provide the same benefits to their parents as will sons. Thus, faced with being limited to just one child, many Chinese couples prefer a son to a daughter. Tragically, this has led to selective abortion, killing of female infants, an unbalanced sex ratio, and a black-market trade in teenaged girls for young men who cannot find wives.

9   Further problems are expected in the near future, including an aging population and a shrinking workforce. Moreover, China's policies have elicited criticism worldwide from people who oppose government intrusion into personal reproductive choices.

10   As other nations become more and more crowded, might their governments also feel forced to turn to drastic policies that restrict individual freedoms?

GETTING READY TO WRITE

Answer each of the following questions using complete sentences.

Reviewing the Reading

1. The reading states that China's annual population growth rate in 1975 was 1.8%. What was it in 1970?

2. In what areas of China today is the one-child policy most enforced?

3. Why are farming families in modern China exempted from the one-child rule?

4. What were the results of Mao Zedong's early policies?

5. What have been some of the negative effects of China's one-child policy?

Examining the Reading Using an Idea Map

Review the reading by completing the missing parts of the idea map shown below.

 Visualize It!

Title **China's One-Child Policy**

Thesis   Due to increasing population figures and the potential for exhausting resources, China instigated a one child policy that has mixed results.

The People's Republic of China: Basic Facts

World's most populous nation, home to one-fifth of the human population

Total population: _____ people

History of One-Child Policy

Mao Zedong originally encouraged population growth: Population grew to _____ in 1970

In early 1970s, Chinese government began to worry about soil, water, _____

Government began a _____ program to prevent people from _____

Components of One-Child Policy

Increased availability of contraceptives and abortion

Rewards: better access to schools, medical care, _____

Punishments: monetary fines, employment discrimination, _____

One-Child Policy Since 1984

Changes in policy: sometimes tighter, sometimes looser

More strict with _____ families

Less strict with _____ families

_____

Population growth rate is now 0.5%

Preference for sons has led to selective abortion, killing of female infants, an unbalanced sex ratio, and black-market trade in teenaged girls

Future problems: aging population and _____

Conclusion   Although the one child policy significantly reduced population numbers, it has led to an imbalance in the ratio of men to women and potential problems as the number of older people grows and the workforce shrinks.

Strengthening Your Vocabulary

Using the word's context, word parts, or a dictionary, write a brief definition of each of the following words or phrases as it is used in the reading.

1. populous (paragraph 1) _____
2. impoverished (paragraph 2) _____
3. depleting (paragraph 3) _____
4. contraceptives (paragraph 4) _____
5. urban (paragraph 6) _____
6. rural (paragraph 6) _____
7. quantitative (paragraph 7) _____
8. sex ratio (paragraph 8) _____
9. black market (paragraph 8) _____

Reacting to Ideas: Discussion and Journal Writing

Get ready to write about the reading by discussing the following:

1. Do the two quotations at the beginning of the reading capture your attention? Why or why not? If not, what could the author have done differently to better interest you in the topic?
2. What words would you use to describe the author's tone in this selection?
3. What does the author mean when he says that China has been conducting "one of the largest and most controversial social experiments in history"?
4. Paragraph 5 outlines some of the rewards and punishments the Chinese government has used to enforce its one-child policy. Suggest some other policies that may be effective in controlling population.

 **Thinking Visually**
5. Why is the billboard shown with the reading not an accurate representation of the results of China's one-child policy?

Thinking Visually
6. Note the world map that accompanies the reading. Which continents are not shown on the map? Does this affect the way you relate to the reading?

 Thinking Visually
7. The photo shows a happy mother with her son. Based on the reading, do you think the mother would be smiling if she were holding a daughter instead? Why or why not?

WRITING ABOUT THE READING

Paragraph Options

1. Summarize the reasons that the Chinese prefer to have sons rather than daughters.
2. The reading begins with two quotations, one from Ted Turner and one from Bill Gates. Choose one of these quotations and write a paragraph explaining it.
3. How would you feel about a government policy that limited you to having only one child? Explain your thinking.

Essay Options

4. Paragraph 9 points out some of the problems that China may experience in the future as a result of its one-child policy, including "an aging population and a shrinking work force." Write an essay in which you explore these two problems.

5. What types of challenges or problems do you think "only children" (that is, children with no brothers or sisters) might face? Write an essay exploring some of these challenges.

6. Write an essay exploring the advantages and disadvantages of the one-child policy for either (a) male children or (b) female children.

CHAPTER REVIEW AND PRACTICE

CHAPTER REVIEW

To review and check your recall of the chapter, select the word or phrase from the box below that best completes each of the following sentences. Keep in mind that three of the words will not be used.

vocabulary log	roots	definition	synonym
etymology	suffixes	thesaurus	prefixes
restrictive	idiom	context	

1. Dictionary meanings that are limited to a special situations are called _____ meanings.

2. _____ is the study of a word's history.

3. A dictionary of synonyms is called a _____.

4. The words, phrases, and sentences around an unknown word are its _____.

5. The beginnings of words that change the meaning of the root word to which they are attached are called _____.

6. The endings of words that change the meaning of the root word to which they are attached are called _____.

7. A(n) _____ is a phrase that has a meaning other than the common meaning of the words in the phrase.

8. A(n) _____ is a method of organizing words you want to learn.

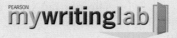 For support in meeting this chapter's objectives, log in to www.mywritinglab.com, go to the Study Plan tab, click on Expanding Your Vocabulary and choose Vocabulary Development from the list of subtopics. Read and view the videos and resources in the Review Materials section, and then complete the Recall, Apply, and Write exercises in the Activities section. You can check your scores and overall progress by using the Gradebook.

WRITERS' WORKSHOPS: Using Words Effectively

The goal of *Pathways* is to help you become a better writer. Learning how to write is an ongoing process. But everyone needs a place to start, and everyone likes to see improvement quickly. The purpose of these Writers' Workshops is to give you some simple, easy-to-remember guidelines that will improve your writing skills immediately.

WRITERS' WORKSHOP

1

YOU'RE A GREAT WRITER? YOUR A GREAT WRITER?

Don't Make These Common Mistakes

The English language can be tricky. Words that sound exactly alike are often spelled different ways and have completely different meanings.

Everyone—including your instructor and potential employers—will be impressed if you avoid the mistakes they see every day. Familiarize yourself with these commonly confused words and phrases, and commit the correct spellings and usage to memory.

affect: A verb meaning "to influence."

The rain *affected* everyone's mood negatively. When will the sun come out and make life worth living again?

effect: A noun meaning "the result."

The medication had many negative *effects* on me. I could live with the sleepiness, but I didn't appreciate all my hair falling out.

a lot: *A lot* is the correct spelling. *Alot* is incorrect.

English teachers correct *a lot* of errors when they grade papers. What a hassle!

all right: *All right* is the correct spelling. *Alright* is incorrect.

As the rock group *The Who* once sang, "The kids are *all right.*"

fewer: Refers to items that can be counted.

The express checkout line is for people buying eight items or *fewer*. Then why do so many people try to get away with nine items or more?

less: Refers to a general amount that cannot be counted.

I consume *less* caffeine now than I used to when I was working full-time.

good: Should be used as an adjective only.

I enjoy a *good* horror movie, but not when I'm alone.

well: Should be used as an adverb. Tip: Many times, *well* is the correct word to use when it appears after the verb.

Thanks to her new hearing aid, she hears *well*. Now I wish she'd get glasses, too.

its: Means "belonging to it."

He absentmindedly scratched the dog behind *its* ears.

it's: A contraction meaning "it is."

It's not unusual for dogs to have fleas in the summer.

Confusing *its* and *it's* is probably the most common mistake in English!

It's great that you stopped the cat from using *its* claws to teach the neighbor's dog a lesson.

loose: An adjective meaning "not tight" or "not securely attached."

In hot weather, *loose* clothing is the way to go.

lose: A verb meaning "misplace" or "not win."

Did you really *lose* your keys again?

their: A possessive form meaning "belonging to them."

The harried store employees kept looking at *their* watches.

there: An adverb indicating place.

She put her computer over *there*, next to the lamp.

they're: Means "they are."

They're here—your Aunt Maud and that awful man she met in Aruba.

to: A preposition indicating direction, or part of an infinitive.

I'm going *to* the mall with Marcie *to* see if I can find something to wear for the office party.

too: Means "also."

Can I come *too*?

two: The number 2.

I'm afraid there's only room for *two* in her car.

whose: The possessive form of *who*.

Whose iPhone is this? I found it in the ladies' room.

who's: Means "who is."

Who's ringing my doorbell?

your: The possessive form of *you*. Used for something belonging to *you*.

I really like *your* shades, but *your* shoes are seriously out of style.

you're: Means "you are."

But *you're* still the best looking guy I know.

An extended list of commonly confused, misunderstood, and misspelled words appears in Part VIII E, pages 608–616.

 TRY IT OUT!

Directions: Underline the word that completes each sentence correctly.

1. (Its / It's) really frustrating when you screen my calls!

2. I would ask you out on a date, but (your / you're) a very boring person.

3. My boss wants me to be more polite. When someone calls, I should ask, "(Whose / Who's) calling, please?" instead of saying, "Who is this and what do you want?"

4. I suspected that the knot in the rope attaching the boat to my car was (loose / lose). That fear was confirmed when my boat went flying into a ditch alongside the highway.

5. Would it be (all right / alright) with you if I bought (a lot / alot) of lottery tickets instead of paying the rent?

WRITERS' WORKSHOP

2

THERE ARE SOME THINGS NOT TO DO . . .

Such as Overusing *There Is* and *There Are*

Sentences beginning with *There is, There are,* or *There were* make use of **expletive construction**. These sentences can be effective when you want to emphasize the subject:

There is a particularly ugly spider spinning an amazingly beautiful web on my window.

There are many good reasons not to eat a carton of ice cream in one sitting.

Often, however, sentences that begin with *There is* or *There are* can be wordy and dull.

Wordy: *There were* errors and unexpected costs that delayed construction of the new football stadium.

Better: Errors and unexpected costs delayed the construction of the new football stadium.

Note: If you must use *There is* or *There are*, be sure to use the correct verb. Use *is* if a singular noun follows. Use *are* if a plural noun follows.

There *is* a woman on the show who lost 150 pounds!

There *are* three benefits of a healthy diet: you live longer, you feel better, and you look great.

→ TRY IT OUT!

Directions: Rewrite each sentence, making it more direct and concise.

1. There were all sorts of delays that caused the airplane to be late, including a rainstorm, thunder, and an antiquated air-traffic control system.

2. There's a great deal of debate over whether or not the average person should take multivitamins.

3. There is a tendency for teenagers to think that everyone is looking at them all the time, something that psychologists call the *spotlight effect*.

4. There are ghosts, poltergeists, wraiths, and phantasms in the dusty old house, but no people.

5. There is no one thing that everyone believes about Twitter accounts: some believe they are fun while others think they are a waste of time.

WRITER'S WORKSHOP

3

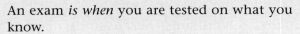

GOOD WRITING IS WHEN . . .

You Don't Use *Is When*

Speech patterns don't always translate well into college writing. Common phrases or sayings that work well in conversation are not necessarily appropriate in essays. Consider the phrases *is when* and *is where*. In a conversation you might hear:

An exam *is when* you are tested on what you know.

A marathon *is where* you run a long distance, ruin your feet, and wonder why you ever thought it was a good idea.

Each sentence provides a definition (which is the function of the verb *is*). In college writing, definitions require nouns on both sides of the verb, which means you must eliminate *is when* and *is where*. Consider the following rewrites.

An examination is a test of what you know. So you'd better read the textbook and attend lectures.

A marathon is a long-distance run that ruins your feet and tests both your endurance and sanity.

Another construction to avoid is *reason is because*. By definition, *reason* equals *because*, so using both together is redundant.

Redundant: *The reason the Yankees lost the game is because* the pitcher doesn't know what he's doing.

Revised: The Yankees lost the game because their pitcher doesn't know how to throw a strike.

→ **TRY IT OUT!**

Directions: Revise the following sentences, eliminating awkward or redundant phrases.

1. A dream that always bothers me is when I dream I am a waiter and everyone in the restaurant is making demands on me at the same time.

2. A "talkback" after a play is where the audience gets to talk to the actors and ask them questions.

3. The reason that I am so irritable is because the baby has kept me awake all night for the last two weeks.

4. A dropped call is when you go into an area with bad cell service, and the phone just loses service.

5. You wonder why I am going to college? The reason is because I want to get a good job, earn a good living, and provide for my family.

WRITERS' WORKSHOP

4

WHAT MAKES A GOOD SENTENCE?

One Possible Answer: Not Using the Verb *Make*

Every sentence has two essential parts—the *subject* and the *verb*. Your sentences will be most effective if they emphasize these two parts. Think of the subject and verb as the key actors in a film. Do you want your actors to be weak and fade into the background, or do you want them to dominate the screen and grab your attention? Do not hide them among phrases that have no significant meaning.

Empty phrases that can almost always be eliminated from your sentences include:

As far as I'm concerned	For all intents and purposes
In my opinion	And stuff
In a manner of speaking	Last but not least

Some particularly weak verbs are *is*, *has*, and *makes*.

Weak: Greenpeace *is* a world leader in environmental awareness.

Revised: Greenpeace leads other environmental groups in making the public aware of ecological issues.

Weak: *Grand Theft Auto has* several different difficulty settings, from easy to impossible.

Revised: *Grand Theft Auto* allows players to choose their level of difficulty, from beginner through expert.

Weak: The climbers *make* slow progress up the steep rock face.

Revised: The climbers progress slowly up the steep rock face.

→ **TRY IT OUT!**

Directions: Rewrite the following sentences, eliminating empty phrases and weak verbs.

1. I was amazed by all the types of food available at the carnival: fried dough, pizza, corn on the cob, Chinese noodles, and stuff.

2. In my opinion, the use of surveillance cameras in public spaces is a threat to the right to privacy.

3. *American Idol* is a trendsetter in terms of the music that young people buy and listen to.

4. All things considered, I'd rather live in the city than in the country.

5. As far as I'm concerned, the chef at Dino's makes the best tacos I've ever eaten.

WRITERS' WORKSHOP

5

AN ESSAY IS NOT A TEXT MESSAGE

Formal Versus Informal Writing

It has been said that the single biggest challenge facing today's college writers is the text message. Text messages have nothing in common with college and professional writing. Why?

1. Text messages are short. College writing requires thought and space to develop your ideas.

2. Text messages are based on abbreviations and shorthand. Serious writing requires you to spell out your words and explain your ideas.

3. Text messages are a form of entertainment. College and professional writing is intended to convey important information and ideas.

4. In a text message, spelling and punctuation don't matter. In college and professional writing, spelling and punctuation matter a great deal.

The way you write a text message should have nothing in common with the way you write a college paper. Text messages are a type of **informal** writing, in which the rules don't matter. In college and the workplace, you are expected to write formally. In **formal** English, the rules do matter. And the better you understand the rules, the better your chances of good grades and a good job offer.

Table 1 outlines some common abbreviations used in text messages. *Never* use these abbreviations in any type of formal writing. Spell out the entire word, and don't forget the capitals and punctuation.

TABLE 1   COMMON TEXT ABBREVIATIONS

Word or Phrase	Abbreviation(s)
as soon as possible	asap
because	cuz
before	b4
by the way	btw
face to face	f2f
great	gr8
I don't know	idk
in my humble/honest opinion	imho
just kidding	jk
laughing out loud	lol
later	l8r
rolling on the floor laughing	rofl
talk to you later	ttyl8r, ttyl, t2yl
tomorrow	2mro
why?	y
you are	u r
your	ur

→ TRY IT OUT!

Directions: Convert the following text messages into formal English sentences.

1. i wuz w1dering how u r doin 2day

    _____

2. can i talk 2 u b4 u leave for the day

    _____

3. my sister cant make it until l8r, what time r u free?

    _____

4. the kidz did gr8 on the test

    _____

5. prof wants 2 know y u wuz late 4 class

    _____

4 Complete Sentences Versus Fragments

Learning Goals

In this chapter, you will learn how to

GOAL 1 Identify sentence fragments

GOAL 2 Recognize and correct fragments caused by missing subjects

GOAL 3 Recognize and correct fragments caused by missing verbs

GOAL 4 Recognize and correct fragments caused by dependent clauses

WWF

Protecting the Future of Nature

Ten million people in sub-Saharan Africa make a living fishing. In the past three decades the number of fish in their waters has declined by 50 percent. Around the world, oceans and the life they support are at risk. WWF is at work in more than 40 countries, developing responsible fishing practices and collaborating with governments and coastal communities on managing their fisheries while safeguarding livelihoods. We can protect marine populations from overfishing and still ensure a catch big enough to feed fishermen, their families and you.

Be Part of Our Work **worldwildlife.org**

WRITE ABOUT IT!

When you read the caption under the picture in the advertisement—"Protecting the Future of Nature"—does it make sense? No doubt your answer is yes. Write a sentence stating the message it communicates about the World Wildlife Federation (WWF). From the caption, the photo, and the accompanying text, you know that the WWF is working toward the development of responsible fishing practices.

Now suppose you saw the caption alone, without the accompanying photograph and text. Would it make sense? Would you understand the message of the advertisement? Probably not. You do not know who is protecting the future of nature. The caption is a sentence fragment. A fragment is an incomplete sentence. It lacks a subject. It does have a verb—*protecting*. How can you make the caption into a complete sentence? You must add a subject.

Here are a few ways to make the caption a complete sentence:

mywritinglab

For more practice with fragments, go to
- Study Plan
- The Writing Process
- Sentence Basics
- Fragments

FRAGMENT	Protecting the future of nature.

subject   verb

COMPLETE SENTENCE   The World Wildlife Federation is protecting the future of nature.

The new version now makes sense even without the photograph. This version has a subject and a verb and expresses a complete thought. In this chapter you will learn to identify fragments and correct them.

NEED TO KNOW
Complete Sentences

Remember that every sentence must have a subject and a verb. The usual word order in **statements** is to put the subject before the verb:

subject   verb

The clowns are coming!

However, occasionally, the verb is put first:

verb   subject   verb   subject

Here come the clowns! There are ten clowns!

The usual **question pattern** has the helping verb before the subject and the main verb after.

helping verb   subject   main verb

Why are ten clowns getting into that little tiny car?

WRITING

WHAT IS A FRAGMENT?

GOAL 1 Identify sentence fragments

A **fragment** is an incomplete sentence that lacks either a subject, a verb, or both. Following are a few more statements taken from magazine ads. Each one is a sentence fragment because each one lacks a subject and a verb and does not express a complete thought. As you read the fragments that follow, notice how difficult they are to understand. Try to guess what product each sentence fragment describes. Correct answers appear at the bottom of p. 105.

FRAGMENT	PRODUCT
1. "Got milk"?	1. _____
2. "Eat Fresh"	2. _____
3. "Mmm mmm Good"	3. _____
4. "Healthy Beautiful Smile for Life"	4. _____

Because advertisers use pictures to complete their messages, they do not have to worry about the confusing nature of sentence fragments. Also, no one requires writers of ads to use complete sentences. Your instructors, however, expect you to write sentences that are complete and correct. You will, therefore, need to know how to spot and correct sentence fragments. To do so, you need to understand three sentence elements:

1. subjects
2. verbs
3. dependent clauses (also called subordinate clauses)

SUBJECTS AND FRAGMENTS

GOAL 2 Recognize and correct fragments caused by missing subjects

The **subject** of a sentence is usually a **noun**. (For a review of nouns, see Part VIII, "Reviewing the Basics," p. 549.)

The <u>Babylonians</u> wrote the first advertisements.

The <u>advertisements</u> were inscribed on bricks.

The <u>kings</u> conducted advertising campaigns for themselves.

NEED TO KNOW

Subjects, Verbs, and Sentence Fragments

- The **subject** of a sentence tells you who or what the sentence is about—who or what does or receives the action of the verb.

- A **verb** expresses action or state of being. Sometimes a verb consists of only one word. (The doorbell *rang*.) Often, however, the main verb has a helping verb. (The guest *had arrived*.)

SUBJECT	VERB
Heat	rises.
Joyce	laughed.
Weeds	grow.
Opportunities	exist.

- A **sentence fragment** is not a complete idea because it lacks either a subject or a verb, or both. It needs to be connected to a nearby sentence, or to be expanded into a new sentence.

The subject of a sentence can also be a **pronoun**, a word that refers to, or substitutes for, a noun. For example, *I, you, he, she, it, they,* and *we* are all familiar pronouns. (For a review of pronouns, see Part VIII, p. 551.)

Early <u>advertisements</u> were straightforward. <u>They</u> carried the names of temples.

The <u>wall</u> was built. <u>It</u> was seen by thousands of people.

The subject of a sentence can also be a group of words:

<u>Inscribing the bricks</u> was a difficult task.

<u>Uncovering the bricks</u> was a surprise.

<u>To build the brick wall</u> was a time-consuming task.

Compound Subjects

Some sentences contain two or more subjects joined together with a coordinating conjunction (*and, but, or, nor, for, so,* or *yet*). The subjects that are linked together form a **compound subject.**

compound subject

<u>Carter's Little Liver Pills</u> and <u>Ivory Soap</u> are examples of early brand-name advertising.

Note that when there are two subjects, there is no comma before the *and.* When there is a series of subjects, however, commas appear after each subject except the last.

compound subject

<u>Calendars</u>, <u>toys</u>, <u>posters</u>, and <u>clocks</u> carried advertisements for early brand-name products.

Distinguishing Subjects from Prepositional Phrases

Do not mistake a noun in a prepositional phrase for the subject of a sentence. The subject of a sentence is *never* in a prepositional phrase. A **prepositional phrase** is a group of words that begins with a preposition (such as *after, in, of*). A prepositional phrase usually ends with a noun or pronoun that tells what or whom is the object of the preposition.

preposition   noun that is object of preposition

<u>on</u> the house

preposition   noun that is object of preposition

<u>from</u> my instructor

Here are a few more prepositional phrases using common prepositions. (For a review of prepositions and more examples, see Part VIII, p. 566.)

<u>across</u> the lawn	<u>until</u> last night
<u>throughout</u> history	<u>to</u> Maria
<u>before</u> the judge	<u>between</u> friends

Tip for Writers

Be sure to use a plural verb with a compound subject even if each of the two nouns or pronouns is singular.

The <u>library</u> and the <u>gym</u> <u>are</u> at the northern end of campus.

Answers to sentence fragments on p. 104: 1. Milk; 2. Subway; 3. Campbell's soup; 4. Crest toothpaste.

Remember, the noun within a prepositional phrase is *never* the subject of a sentence.

PREPOSITIONAL PHRASE   subject

Beneath the chair, the cat dozed.

subject   PREPOSITIONAL PHRASE

The students in the art class painted a mural.

PREPOSITIONAL PHRASE   subject

Inside the house, the temperature was 75 degrees.

It is especially easy to mistake the noun in the prepositional phrase for the subject of the sentence when the prepositional phrase comes between the subject and verb.

subject   PREPOSITIONAL PHRASE

The idea of killing animals disturbs Brian.

EXERCISE 4-1   Identifying Subjects and Prepositional Phrases

Directions: Circle each prepositional phrase. Then underline the subject in each of the following sentences:

EXAMPLE   The superintendent (of our school) was quoted (in the newspaper.)

1. A crowd of teenagers had purchased tickets for the concert.

2. Rows of birds perched on the telephone wires in the cornfields.

3. The strap on my backpack was tattered.

4. Trash from the festival covered the grounds inside the park.

5. Patches of blue sky are visible above the horizon. ■

EXERCISE 4-2   Writing Sentences

Directions: Write a sentence using each of the following words as a subject. Then circle any prepositional phrases in your sentence.

EXAMPLE   sister   My sister has the best sense (of humor.)

1. history _____

2. movie actresses _____

3. dancing _____

4. telephone calls _____

5. studying _____ ■

Fragments Without a Subject

A common sentence-writing error is to write a sentence without a subject. The result is a sentence fragment. Writers often make this mistake when they think the subject of a previous sentence or a noun in a previous sentence applies to the next sentence as well.

COMPLETE SENTENCE   FRAGMENT

Marge lost her keys on Tuesday. And found them on Wednesday.

[The missing subject is *Marge*.]

COMPLETE SENTENCE   FRAGMENT

The instructor canceled class. But did not postpone the quiz.

[The missing subject is *instructor*.]

COMPLETE SENTENCE

Relieved that it had stopped raining, Teresa rushed into the mall.
Then remembered her car window was open.

FRAGMENT

[The missing subject is *Teresa*.]

You can revise a fragment that lacks a subject in two ways:

1. **Add a subject, often a pronoun referring to the subject of the preceding sentence.**

   FRAGMENT   And found them on Wednesday.

   subject

   REVISED   She found them on Wednesday.

   FRAGMENT   Then remembered her car window was open.

   subject

   REVISED   Then she remembered her car window was open.

2. **Connect the fragment to the preceding sentence.**

   FRAGMENT   And found them on Wednesday.

   subject   verb   verb

   REVISED   Marge lost her keys on Tuesday and found them on Wednesday.

   FRAGMENT   But did not postpone the quiz.

   subject   verb   verb

   REVISED   The instructor canceled class but did not postpone the quiz.

Each of these sentences now has a subject and a compound verb (see Part VIII, p. 571).

EXERCISE 4-3   Revising Fragments by Adding Subjects

Directions: Each of the following items consists of a complete sentence followed by a sentence fragment that lacks a subject. Make each fragment into a complete sentence by adding a subject. You may need to take out words, add new ones, capitalize words, or make them lowercase as you revise.

EXAMPLE   Bert threw the basketball. ~~And~~ ^{He} cheered when it went in the hoop.

1. The president waved as he left the building. Then got in the car and drove away.

2. The novel was complex. Was also long and drawn out.

3. The scissors were not very sharp. Were old and rusty, you see.

4. Hundreds of students waited to get into the bookstore. Milled around until the manager unlocked the door.

5. My roommate, whose name is Speed, is an excellent skater. Gets teased sometimes about her name.

6. The computer printed out the list of names. Then beeped loudly.

7. Fans crowded the stadium. And cheered after each touchdown.

8. Many guests arrived early for the wedding. Unfortunately, were not seated until ten o'clock.

9. The delivery man put the large package down. Then rang the doorbell.

10. The big black dog sat obediently. But growled nonetheless. ■

EXERCISE 4-4   Writing About an Advertisement
Writing in Progress

Directions: Write a paragraph describing an advertisement you have seen or heard recently. Explain to whom the advertisement appeals and why. After you have finished revising and proofreading your paragraph, underline the subject of each sentence. Exchange papers with a peer reviewer and see if you agree on the identification of subjects. Discuss any differences of opinion with another peer reviewer or with your instructor. Save your paper. You will need it for another exercise in this chapter. ■

VERBS AND FRAGMENTS

GOAL 3 Recognize and correct fragments caused by missing verbs

A **verb** is a word or word group that indicates what the subject does or what happens to the subject. Most verbs express action or a state of being, for example, *run, invent, build, know, be*. (For a review of verbs, see Part VIII, p. 554.)

Advertising <u>is</u> bland without a slogan.

Slogans <u>promote</u> a specific product.

Sometimes a verb consists of only one word.

The announcer <u>speaks</u>.

Often, however, the main verb is accompanied by one or more **helping (auxiliary) verbs** such as *will, can,* and forms of *be, have,* or *do.* (For a review of helping verbs, see Part VIII, p. 555.)

helping verb   main verb

The announcer <u>will</u> <u>speak</u>.

helping verb   main verb

The announcer <u>will be</u> <u>speaking</u>.

helping verb   main verb

The first trademark <u>was registered</u> in 1870.

helping verb   main verb

<u>Do</u> any companies <u>use</u> animals as trademarks?

helping verb   main verb

The lion <u>has been</u> MGM's trademark for a long time.

Compound Verbs

Some sentences have two or more verbs joined together with a coordinating conjunction (such as *and, or,* or *but*).

subject   compound verb

The "Uncle Sam Wants You" poster <u>stirred</u> patriotism and <u>increased</u> enlistments.

coordinating conjunction

compound verb

The posters <u>appeared</u> on billboards and <u>hung</u> on buildings.

coordinating conjunction

EXERCISE 4-5   Identifying Verbs

Directions: Underline the verb(s), including any helping verb(s), in each of the following sentences:

EXAMPLE

The lectures in psychology <u>have been focusing</u> on instinctive behavior lately.

1. Preschools teach children social and academic skills.

2. Exercise clubs offer instruction and provide companionship.

3. Millions of people have watched soap operas.

4. Essay exams are given in many college classes.

5. The audience will be surprised by the play's ending. ■

Fragments Without Complete Verbs

Fragments often occur when word groups begin with words ending in *-ing* or with phrases beginning with the word *to*. These words and phrases are verb forms and may look like verbs, but they cannot function as verbs in sentences.

-ing *Fragments*

Note the *-ing* word in the fragment below:

FRAGMENT   <u>Walking</u> across campus after lunch.

In this word group, *walking* has no subject. Who is walking? Now let's add a subject and see what happens:

Allison <u>walking</u> across campus after lunch.

The word group still is not a complete sentence; the verb form *walking* cannot be used alone as a sentence verb. You can make the word group a complete sentence by adding a helping verb (for example, *is, was, has been*) or by using a different verb form (*walked* or *walks*).

helping verb added

REVISED   Allison <u>was</u> <u>walking</u> across campus after lunch.

verb form changed to present tense

REVISED   Allison <u>walks</u> across campus after lunch.

Now the word group is a complete sentence.

> **Tip for Writers**
>
> The simple present tense is used for repeated action. "Allison <u>walks</u> across campus after lunch" means she does this regularly. On the other hand, "Allison is walking" (present continuous tense) means right now or at some stated future time (perhaps tomorrow) she is or will be walking.

You can correct fragments beginning with *-ing* words in four ways:

1. **Add a subject and change the verb form to a sentence verb.**

FRAGMENT

FRAGMENT   Morris was patient. Waiting in line at the bank.

subject   verb changed to past tense

REVISED   Morris was patient. He waited in line at the bank.

2. **Add a subject and a form of *be* (such as *am, are, will be, has been, is, was, were*) as a helping verb.**

FRAGMENT

FRAGMENT   Juan was bored. Listening to his sister complain about her boyfriend.

subject   form of *be*   main verb

REVISED   Juan was bored. He was listening to his sister complain about her boyfriend.

3. **Connect the fragment to the sentence that comes before or after it.**

FRAGMENT

FRAGMENT   Mark finished lunch. Picking up his tray. Then he left the cafeteria.

modifies *he*

REVISED   Mark finished lunch. Picking up his tray, he left the cafeteria.

4. **If the *-ing* word is *being*, change its form to another form of *be* (*am, are, is, was, were*).**

FRAGMENT

FRAGMENT   Jayla failed the math quiz. Her mistakes being careless errors.

verb form changed

REVISED   Jayla failed the math quiz. Her mistakes were careless errors.

Fragments with To Phrases

A phrase beginning with *to* cannot be the verb of the sentence. When it stands alone, it is a sentence fragment.

FRAGMENT   To review for the psychology test

This word group lacks a subject and a sentence verb. To make a complete sentence, you need to add a subject and a sentence verb.

subject   verb

REVISED   Deon plans to review for the psychology test.

You can revise fragments that begin with *to* in two ways:

1. **Add a subject and a sentence verb.**

   FRAGMENT   To reach my goal.

                            subject   verb

   REVISED   I hope to reach my goal.

2. **Connect the *to* phrase to a nearby sentence.**

   FRAGMENT   To earn the highest grade. Antonio studied eight hours.

   REVISED   To earn the highest grade, Antonio studied eight hours.

EXERCISE 4-6

Working Together

Correcting Fragments by Adding Verbs

Directions: Each of the following word groups is a fragment. Revise each one to form a complete sentence, and then compare your revisions with those of a classmate.

EXAMPLE

FRAGMENT   Walking along the waterfront.

COMPLETE SENTENCE   Andrea was walking along the waterfront.

1. Photographing the wedding.

   _____

2. To have a family.

   _____

3. Hanging up the suit in the closet.

   _____

4. Deciding what to have for dinner.

   _____

5. To attend the awards ceremony.

   _____

6. Writing the speech.

   _____

7. To sketch a diagram.

   _____

8. To quit her job.

   _____

9. Making the paper less repetitious.

_____

10. Being old and in disrepair.

_____

■

EXERCISE 4-7
Writing in Progress

Revising Your Paragraph

Directions: Go back to the paragraph you wrote in Exercise 4-4 and circle the verb or verbs in each sentence. Exchange papers with a peer reviewer and check each other's work. ■

CLAUSES AND FRAGMENTS

GOAL 4 Recognize and correct fragments caused by dependent clauses

A sentence must not only contain a subject and a verb; *it must also express a complete thought.* That is, a sentence should not leave a question in your mind as to its meaning or leave an idea unfinished. To spot and avoid sentence fragments in your writing, you must be able to recognize the difference between independent and dependent (or subordinate) clauses. A **clause** is a group of related words that contains a subject and its verb. There are two types of clauses, independent and dependent. An **independent clause** expresses a complete thought and can stand alone as a complete sentence. A **dependent (or subordinate) clause** does not express a complete thought. When a dependent clause stands alone, it is a fragment.

Independent Clauses

An **independent clause** has a subject and a verb and can stand alone as a complete and correct sentence. It expresses a complete thought.

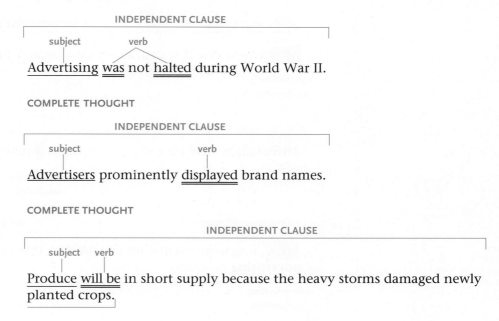

COMPLETE THOUGHT

INDEPENDENT CLAUSE

subject verb

Advertising was not halted during World War II.

COMPLETE THOUGHT

INDEPENDENT CLAUSE

subject verb

Advertisers prominently displayed brand names.

COMPLETE THOUGHT

INDEPENDENT CLAUSE

subject verb

Produce will be in short supply because the heavy storms damaged newly planted crops.

Dependent (or Subordinate) Clauses

A **dependent clause** has a subject and a verb but cannot stand alone as a complete and correct sentence. It does not express a complete thought. A dependent clause makes sense only when it is joined to an independent clause. When a dependent clause stands alone, it is a **dependent clause fragment.** A dependent clause fragment leaves an unanswered question in your mind.

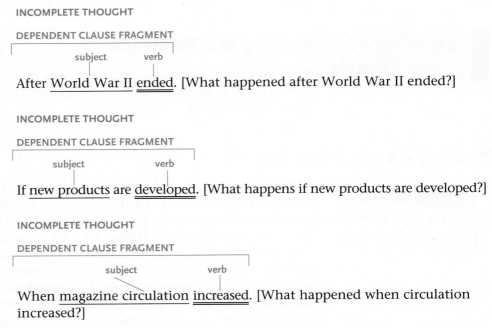

INCOMPLETE THOUGHT

DEPENDENT CLAUSE FRAGMENT

subject   verb

After World War II ended. [What happened after World War II ended?]

INCOMPLETE THOUGHT

DEPENDENT CLAUSE FRAGMENT

subject   verb

If new products are developed. [What happens if new products are developed?]

INCOMPLETE THOUGHT

DEPENDENT CLAUSE FRAGMENT

subject   verb

When magazine circulation increased. [What happened when circulation increased?]

How can you spot dependent clauses? A dependent clause often begins with a word or group of words called a **subordinating conjunction.**

Subordinating conjunctions signal dependent clauses. When you see a clause beginning with one of these words, as shown in the "Need to Know" box on p. 116, make sure the clause is attached to an independent clause. A subordinating conjunction explains the relationship between the dependent clause and the independent clause to which it is joined.

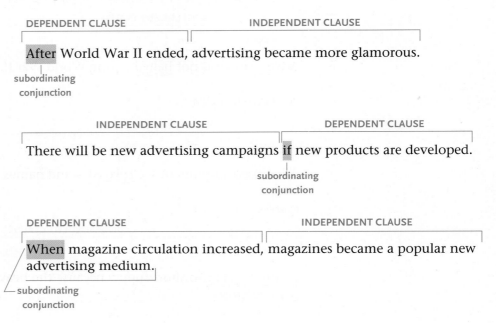

DEPENDENT CLAUSE   INDEPENDENT CLAUSE

After World War II ended, advertising became more glamorous.

subordinating
conjunction

INDEPENDENT CLAUSE   DEPENDENT CLAUSE

There will be new advertising campaigns if new products are developed.

subordinating
conjunction

DEPENDENT CLAUSE   INDEPENDENT CLAUSE

When magazine circulation increased, magazines became a popular new advertising medium.

subordinating
conjunction

EXERCISE 4-8   Identifying Clauses

Directions: Decide whether the following clauses are independent or dependent. Write "I" for independent or "D" for dependent before each clause.

_____   **1.** While Arturo was driving to school.

_____   **2.** *Sesame Street* is a children's educational television program.

_____   **3.** Samantha keeps a diary of her family's holiday celebrations.

_____   **4.** Because Aretha had a craving for chocolate.

_____   **5.** Exercise can help to relieve stress.

_____   **6.** When Peter realized he would be able to meet the deadline.

_____   **7.** A snowstorm crippled the eastern seaboard states on New Year's Eve.

_____   **8.** Unless my uncle decides to visit us during spring break.

_____   **9.** Long-distance telephone rates are less expensive during the evening than during the day.

_____   **10.** As long as Jacqueline is living at home. ■

Correcting Dependent Clause Fragments

You can correct a dependent clause fragment in two ways:

1. **Join the dependent clause to an independent clause to make the dependent clause fragment part of a complete sentence.**

FRAGMENT	Although competition increased.
COMPLETE SENTENCE	Although competition increased, the sales staff was still getting new customers.
FRAGMENT	Because market research expanded.
COMPLETE SENTENCE	The company added new accounts because market research expanded.
FRAGMENT	Although statistics and market research have become part of advertising.
COMPLETE SENTENCE	Although statistics and market research have become part of advertising, consumers' tastes remain somewhat unpredictable.

2. **Take away the subordinating conjunction, and the dependent clause fragment becomes an independent clause that can stand alone as a complete sentence.**

FRAGMENT	Although competition increased.
COMPLETE SENTENCE	Competition increased.

FRAGMENT	Because market research expanded.
COMPLETE SENTENCE	Market research expanded.
FRAGMENT	Although statistics and market research have become part of advertising.
COMPLETE SENTENCE	Statistics and market research have become part of advertising.

Note: When you join a dependent clause to an independent clause, you need to think about punctuation:

1. **If the *dependent* clause comes first, follow it with a comma.** The comma separates the dependent clause from the independent clause and helps you know where the independent clause begins.

   DEPENDENT CLAUSE   INDEPENDENT CLAUSE

   COMMA NEEDED   After World War II ended, humor and sex were used in commercials.

2. **If the *independent* clause comes first, do *not* use a comma between the two clauses.**

   INDEPENDENT CLAUSE

   NO COMMA NEEDED   Humor and sex were used in commercials after World War II ended.

   DEPENDENT CLAUSE

NEED TO KNOW

Subordinating Conjunctions

A clause beginning with a subordinate conjunction is a dependent clause. It cannot stand alone. It must be connected to an independent clause. Here is a list of common subordinating conjunctions:

after	if	though
although	inasmuch as	unless
as	in case	until
as far as	in order that	when
as if	in order to	whenever
as long as	now that	where
as soon as	once	whereas
as though	provided that	wherever
because	rather than	whether
before	since	while
during	so that	
even if	than	
even though	that	

EXERCISE 4-9   **Revising Fragments by Adding Independent Clauses**

Directions: Make each of these dependent clause fragments into a sentence by adding an independent clause before or after the fragment. Add or remove punctuation if necessary.

EXAMPLE   After we got to the beach, we put on sunscreen.

1. Since the surgery was expensive.

    _____

2. As long as my boss allows me.

    _____

3. Because I want to be a journalist.

    _____

4. Until the roof is repaired.

    _____

5. Once I returned the library books.

    _____

6. So that I do not miss class.

    _____

7. Provided that Marietta gets the loan.

    _____

8. Unless you would rather go to the movies.

    _____

9. If the thunderstorm comes during the barbecue.

    _____

10. Although we visited Pittsburgh last summer.

    _____

Dependent Clauses Beginning with Relative Pronouns

Dependent clauses also may begin with **relative pronouns**. (For more information on relative pronouns, see Part VIII, p. 552.)

Relative Pronouns			
RELATIVE PRONOUNS THAT REFER TO PEOPLE		RELATIVE PRONOUNS THAT REFER TO THINGS	
who	whom	that	whichever
whoever	whomever	which	whatever
whose			

The relative pronoun that begins a dependent clause connects the dependent clause to a noun or pronoun in the independent clause. However, the verb in the dependent clause is *never* the main verb of the sentence. The independent clause has its own verb, the main verb of the sentence, and expresses a complete thought.

The following sentence fragments each consist of a noun followed by a dependent clause beginning with a relative pronoun. They are not complete sentences because the noun does not have a verb and the fragment does not express a complete thought.

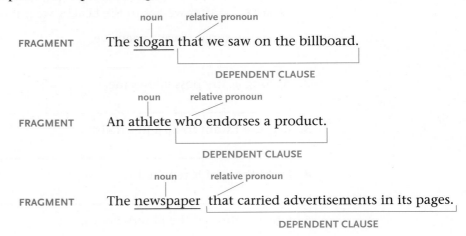

You can correct this type of fragment by adding a verb to make the noun the subject of an independent clause. Often the independent clause will be split, and the dependent clause will appear between its parts.

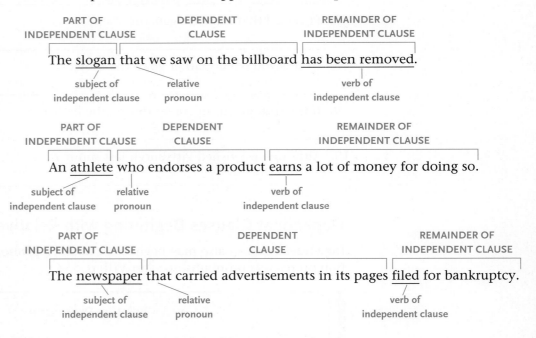

EXERCISE 4-10   Revising Fragments

Directions: Make each of these fragments into a complete sentence. Add words, phrases or clauses, and punctuation as needed.

EXAMPLE   The usher who was available, led us to our seats.

1. The radio that Trevor had purchased last night.

2. The official who had signed the peace treaty.

_____

3. The athlete who won the tennis tournament.

_____

4. Mark, whose nose had been broken in a fight.

_____

5. The advice that his lawyer gave him.

_____

6. The student who needed the scholarship the most.

_____

7. The answering machine that is in the kitchen.

_____

8. Sarah, whom I knew in high school.

_____

9. The problems that the professor assigned.

_____

10. The men who signed the Declaration of Independence.

_____

■

HOW TO SPOT AND REVISE FRAGMENTS: A BRIEF REVIEW

Now that you have learned to identify subjects, verbs, and dependent clauses, you will be able to spot and correct fragments. The "Need to Know" box provides a brief review.

NEED TO KNOW

How to Spot Fragments

Use the following questions to check for fragments:

1. **Does the word group have a subject?** The subject is a noun or pronoun that performs or receives the action of the sentence. To find the subject, ask _who_ or _what_ performs or receives the action of the verb.

2. **Does the word group have a verb?** Be sure that the verb is a complete and correct sentence verb. Watch out for sentences that begin with an _-ing_ word or a _to_ phrase.

3. **Does the word group begin with a subordinating conjunction (_since, after, because, as, while, although,_ and _so forth_) introducing a dependent clause?** Unless the dependent clause is attached to an independent clause, it is a fragment.

4. **Does the word group begin with a relative pronoun (_who, whom, whose, whoever, whomever, that, which, whatever_) introducing a dependent clause?** Unless the dependent clause forms a question, is part of an independent clause, or is attached to an independent clause, it is a fragment.

NEED TO KNOW

How to Revise Fragments

Once you spot a fragment in your writing, correct it in one of the following ways:

1. **Add a subject if one is missing.**

   FRAGMENT   Appeared on television ten times during the game.

   REVISED   The advertisement for Pepsi appeared on television ten times during the game.

2. **Add a verb if one is missing.** Add a helping verb if one is needed, or change the verb form.

   FRAGMENT   An action-packed commercial with rap music.

   REVISED   An action-packed commercial with rap music advertised a new soft drink.

3. **Combine the fragment with an independent clause to make a complete sentence.**

   FRAGMENT   Because advertising is expensive.

   REVISED   Because advertising is expensive, companies are making shorter commercials.

4. **Remove the subordinating conjunction or relative pronoun so the group of words can stand alone as a sentence.**

   FRAGMENT   Since viewers can "zap" out commercials on video-recorders.

   REVISED   Viewers can "zap" out commercials on video-recorders.

EXERCISE 4-11   Revising Fragments

Directions: Make each of the following sentence fragments a complete sentence by combining it with an independent clause, removing the subordinating conjunction or relative pronoun, or adding the missing subject or verb.

EXAMPLE

FRAGMENT   Many environmentalists are concerned about the spotted owl. Which is almost extinct.

COMPLETE SENTENCE   Many environmentalists are concerned about the spotted owl, which is almost extinct.

1. Renting a DVD of the movie *The King's Speech*.

   _____

   _____

2. Spices that had been imported from India.

_____

_____

3. The police officer walked to Jerome's van. To give him a ticket.

_____

_____

4. My English professor, with the cup of tea he brought to each class.

_____

_____

5. After the table was refinished.

_____

_____

6. Roberto memorized his lines. For the performance tomorrow night.

_____

_____

7. A tricycle with big wheels, painted red.

_____

_____

8. On the shelf an antique crock used for storing lard.

_____

_____

9. Because I always wanted to learn to speak Spanish.

_____

_____

10. Looking for the lost keys. I was late for class.

_____

_____

■

 **Analyze It!**

Directions: The following paragraph is correct except that it contains sentence fragments. Underline each fragment. Then revise the paragraph in the space provided by rewriting or combining sentences to eliminate fragments.

Social networks such as Facebook and MySpace appeal to college students for a variety of reasons. Social networks are a way of having conversations. Staying in touch with friends without the inconvenience of getting dressed and meeting them somewhere. Friends can join or drop out of a conversation whenever they want. Social networks also allow college students to meet new people and make new friends. Members can track who is friends with whom. Students may choose to share only portions of their profiles. To protect their privacy. Some students use social networks to form groups. Such as clubs, study groups, or special interest groups. Other students use networks to screen dates. And discover who is interested in dating or who is already taken.

EXERCISE 4-12
Writing in Progress

Revising Sentence Fragments

Directions: Review the paragraph you wrote for Exercise 4-4, checking for sentence fragments. If you find a fragment, revise it. ■

Paragraph Writing Scenarios

Friends and Family

1. Choose a close friend and write a paragraph that explains the characteristics that make him or her a good friend.

2. Write a paragraph that begins with the topic sentence, "There are three main ways to ruin a friendship."

Classes and Campus Life

1. Choose one of your courses and a particular class session for that course. Explain what you learned from that class session. Discuss how you can use what you learned.

2. Which of your classes do you expect to be the most difficult or challenging? Write a paragraph explaining your reasons.

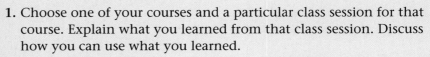

Working Students

1. Write a paragraph on the value of work. Other than a paycheck, what are its benefits?

2. Write a paragraph describing the perfect or ideal job. If you could choose any job you wanted, what would you pick?

Communities and Cultures

1. Everyone belongs to various communities. A community is a group of people who share a common goal or purpose. Clubs, colleges, ethnic groups, and religious groups are all communities. Employees working in the same business form a community, as do members of a sports team or diners in a restaurant. Choose one of your classes and write a paragraph describing why it is a community. That is, explain what you share or have in common with other students.

2. Choose a community (see #1 for a definition of community), other than your classes, that you belong to. Write a paragraph explaining your common goals or purposes.

WRITING ABOUT A READING

THINKING BEFORE READING

In the following reading, the author provides a behind-the-scenes look at prison dog programs. Before you read:

1. Preview the reading, using the steps listed in Chapter 2, p. 35.
2. Connect the reading to your own experience by answering the following questions:
   a. What do you know about dog trainability or canine behavior?
   b. What do you already know about prison inmate training programs?
3. Mark and annotate as you read.

READING

TAILS IN JAIL

A Behind-the-Scenes Look at Prison Dog Programs

Denise Flaim

1   They are the oddest of couples.

2   One is an emblem of violence and lawlessness, of everything that is awry in American society.

3   The other is a greeting-card image of furry innocence, radiating promise and optimism and unsullied loyalty.

4   But together they have forged a bond that has been in the human-canine DNA for millennia, one that transcends steel bars and barbed wire and guard towers, and returns some of society's most isolated and ostracized members to a long-ago place of pride within themselves.

5   Today, there are about a hundred programs around the country that use prisoners to raise and train puppies and dogs for service organizations and rescue groups. Some of the dogs go on to serious jobs, from bomb detection to guiding the blind. Others simply become beloved house pets. But the premise behind using the incarcerated for their caretakers is universal, and starkly simple: Dog training takes time, which is many of these men and women have in abundance.

6   Prison-dog programs are a winning proposition on all sides: For service-dog and adoption groups, they provide full-time foster homes and trainers. Prison officials say the programs increase empathy, lower stress and tension, teach new skills that might one day lead to employment outside the concrete walls, and serve as a powerful motivation to keep a clean disciplinary record. And for the prisoners themselves, the dogs represent something that they had long ago given up any hope of experiencing again: trust.

7   "Dogs show an unconditional love," says Brian Harkness, 41, of Sacramento, Calif., who socialized dogs for Pen Pals of San Quentin during his almost 4-year sentence, which ended only a few months ago. "If you treat them right, they love you, no matter who you are, what you look like," he says. "I can honestly say I never had that before."

8   Sister Pauline Quinn knows firsthand how a bundle of fur can change not only how a person feels inside, but how society values them. Institutionalized 36 times as a youngster, she experienced abuse on the street and at the hands of authority figures that was literally unspeakable—at one point in her life, Quinn, who later became a nun, was so shattered she found herself unable to talk.

9   "I was able to pull myself up after I received a German shepherd named Joni," says Quinn, who had a movie about her life made for cable television, starring Laura Dern in her role. "Through Joni, my self-esteem started to be rebuilt."

10   Quinn calls Joni an "image dog": A big, beautiful, serious shepherd, she commanded respect—something Quinn had had little of in her life–and that transferred to the other end of the leash. "People didn't treat me same way as they did before. It was interesting how a dog can bring back your self-esteem, or empower you if you don't have it within yourself."

11   Recognizing how Joni had transformed her, Quinn decided to do the same for others in the nation's institutions. So in 1981, with the help of a vet-school dean, she started what is believed to be the first prison-dog program in the country, which continues to this day at Washington State Corrections Center for Women in Gig Harbor.

12   "Our own dogs were trained, and we brought them in there so the inmates could have that feeling of success right away," Quinn explains. "The dogs helped the prisoners to become 'other centered'—even if we have pain in our lives, helping others helps our pain."

13   More than a quarter-century after Quinn started her program, today prison-dog programs are flourishing. Here are three, each in a different part of the country, and each training dogs from different backgrounds, for different purposes. But all are rooted in the same belief: That dogs, magical creatures that they are, have the power to bring out the best in us, no matter how far we have strayed.

Inmates at Blackburn Correctional Complex in Lexington, Ky. walk the dogs they have trained (so they will be more adoptable) to the Lexington Humane Society truck after their graduation ceremony on Thursday, March 19, 2009. The inmates are assigned in teams, two per each animal, and are responsible for their dogs 24 hours a day, seven days a week.

Pen Pals of San Quentin

14 San Quentin is no cakewalk: California's only death-row prison was home to the likes of Robert Kennedy's assassin Sirhan Sirhan and mass murderer Charles Manson. But well-behaved inmates in the minimum-security firehouse on the 440-acre island also share their 8-foot-square sleeping quarters with strays from The Marin Humane Society.

15 Larry Carson of the humane society, who coordinates the prison's Pen Pals program, says about 10 to 12 of the firehouse prisoners work with a total of three to four dogs at a time.

16 More than half the dogs are medical fosters, recuperating from everything from heartworm to starvation. Another 20 percent are shy, "shut down" dogs that need more socialization to come out of their shells and be good adoption prospects. And an equivalent amount are adolescent dogs who have never had training or structure.

17 "They really do relate to the dogs," Carson says of the prisoners. "These are homeless dogs, and in some cases dogs that people don't want, and they can relate to that in their own lives."

18 To date, 135 dogs have gone through the San Quentin program. Harkness, the recently released convict, remembers his first dog, Arthur, a Shar-Pei rescued from a Chinese food market where he was likely on the menu.

19 Arthur had a skin condition so severe he had lost all his hair, and he was so gaunt he had lost the breed's characteristic wrinkles. "He was a poor old beat-up dog," Harkness remembers proudly. "But I totally nursed him back to health."

Second Chance Greyhounds

20 Greyhounds who are bred and raised on race tracks have a few things in common with prisoners: Deprived of socialization and life "on the outside," these delicate-looking sighthounds are unfamiliar with everyday objects and occurrences that other dogs simply take for granted.

21 Second Chance Greyhounds is a fledgling rescue group that has partnered with correctional facilities in Georgia and Florida to train former racing greyhounds to transition to life on the couch.

22 Greyhounds from Birmingham Race Course in Alabama spend two months at the minimum-security Gaston Correctional Facility in Florida, whose dormitory set-up is as conducive to a home environment as any prison gets. The prisoners teach basic things that most other dogs know from puppyhood: No, you cannot walk through a sliding glass door. Yes, it's OK to walk across that slippery tile floor. Look, here are steps . . . this is how you climb them. "Sit" means recline back on your haunches; "hurry" means go outside and do your business.

23 Caring for the greyhounds affords the prisoners special privileges, such as taking them outdoors to an enclosed football field to let them exercise. "Watching these greyhounds run is a thrill in itself," says Patti Peterson, who chairs the greyhound group. "They're beautiful runners."

24   The prisoners, many of whom have been incarcerated for fraud or identity theft, write weekly reports on how their dogs have progressed. When dogs finish their stay, they write letters to the new families, who are adopting them sight unseen. And their emotions are displayed in every penstroke.

25   "Please give him lots of love—he needs it. Upon his arrival he had no idea what affection was," reads one neatly scripted letter, written by an inmate named Jenifer on tasteful flower-print stationery. "I hope you have lots of fun, as I have. I will miss him dearly."

Puppies Behind Bars

26   When Gloria Gilbert Stoga founded Puppies Behind Bars 13 years ago, there were all of three prison-dog programs in the country. Today, the program is in place at six correctional facilities in New York, New Jersey and Connecticut, and has graduated almost 600 dogs, many of which have gone on to be service dogs for the disabled, as well as explosives-detection dogs.

27   One concern about any prison-dog program is for the dogs themselves: Are these innocent animals targets for violence and mishandling in a population convicted of serious crimes like murder and rape?

28   Stoga says any potential for abuse is forestalled by a vigorous screening process. "We take into consideration the nature of the crime, length of sentence, disciplinary record and mental health," she says. "And anyone who has directly hurt a child or been convicted of a sex crime is not accepted into the program."

29   Applicants for the program are interviewed using psychologist-written questions, and "puppy raisers," as they are called, are required to sign a contract with Puppies Behind Bars that outlines all of their responsibilities in the program, which include mandatory attendance at weekly puppy class, reading assignments, homework and exams.

30   "This dog is gonna be useful and this dog is gonna love somebody and this dog is just gonna be somebody's everything," says Jasmine, a prisoner at the women's maximum-security Bedford Hills Correctional Facility in Bedford Hills, NY, adding that she thinks her success in training a dog for service or bomb-detection work will translate to employment outside the prison walls. And Stoga confirms that a number of former inmates are working in animal-related fields after their release.

31   In the meantime, the dewy-eyed Golden and Labrador Retriever puppies remind their handlers that that even within their world of lock downs and cinderblock cells, there are ample opportunities for trust, redemption . . . and second chances.

GETTING READY TO WRITE

Answer each of the following questions using complete sentences.

Reviewing the Reading

1. Describe what the dogs in prison programs are trained to do.
2. Who is Sister Pauline Quinn and how did a dog transform her life?
3. Where was the first prison dog training program in the country?
4. Summarize the main points of the three dog training programs described in the article.
5. Describe how prisoners benefit from being involved in dog training programs.

Examining the Reading Using an Idea Map

Review the reading by completing the missing parts of the idea map shown below.

 Visualize It!

Title	**Tails in Jail**
Thesis	Dogs and prisoners both benefit from prison dog training programs.

Prison dog programs are beneficial in several ways.

_____

_____

Prisoners also experience trust and unconditional love from the dogs.

Sister Pauline Quinn experienced how a dog could help transform a life.

Her dog helped her recover from a traumatic early life.

_____

Three different prison programs are described.

Pen Pals of San Quentin:
1. _____
2. _____

Second Chance Greyhounds:
1. _____
2. _____

Puppies Behind Bars:
Almost 600 dogs have graduated from six prisons in the program.

_____

Conclusion	Prison dog programs improve the lives of dogs and prisoners.

Strengthening Your Vocabulary

Using the word's context, word parts, or a dictionary, write a brief definition of each of the following words as it is used in the reading.

1. transcends (paragraph 4) _____

2. ostracized (paragraph 4) _____

3. incarcerated (paragraph 5) _____

4. flourishing (paragraph 13) _____

5. recuperating (paragraph 16) _____

6. fledgling (paragraph 21) _____

7. forestalled (paragraph 28) _____

8. redemption (paragraph 31) _____

Reacting to Ideas: Discussion and Journal Writing

Get ready to write about the reading by discussing the following:

1. How did the author capture your attention in the opening paragraph?

2. The author quotes prison inmates, program coordinators, and a nun in this article. Which of these were most effective in convincing you of the value of prison dog programs?

3. How would you feel about adopting a dog that had been trained by a prisoner?

 **Thinking Visually**

4. What details do you notice about the photograph of the inmates walking with dogs at the Blackburn Correctional Complex? How does this photograph reinforce the author's message?

WRITING ABOUT THE READING

Paragraph Options

1. What questions do you have about the dog training programs that were not answered in this article? Write a paragraph about what else you would like to know about these programs.

2. Write a paragraph discussing pet ownership, including the pros and cons.

3. Do you agree that "dogs . . . have the power to bring out the best in us, no matter how far we have strayed"? Write a paragraph explaining your answer, or substitute a different word for *dogs* and write a paragraph based on that statement.

Essay Options

4. If you support the idea of a prison dog program, compose a letter to the editor of your newspaper, arguing in favor of creating such a program. If you do not see the benefit of a prison dog program, write a letter arguing against it. Be sure to give reasons to support your case.

5. When have you been given a second chance in your life? Write an essay describing your experience.

6. What can you tell about the author's attitude toward dogs and the prison dog programs she describes in the article? Write an essay examining the ways the author reveals her feelings toward the subject, including specific examples from the article. Consider her tone, choice of words, and what she has included as well as what she may have omitted.

CHAPTER REVIEW AND PRACTICE

CHAPTER REVIEW

To review and check your recall of the chapter, match each term in Column A with its meaning in Column B.

COLUMN A

_____ 1. subject

_____ 2. verb

_____ 3. sentence fragment

_____ 4. prepositional phrase

_____ 5. independent clause

_____ 6. compound subject

_____ 7. dependent clause

_____ 8. subordinating conjunctions

_____ 9. clause

_____ 10. relative pronouns

COLUMN B

a. words that express a complete thought and can stand alone as a sentence

b. words such as *who, whom, which, that*

c. words such as *if, as, unless, while*

d. words that have a subject and verb but do not form a complete and correct sentence

e. group of words that contains both a subject and a verb

f. group of words that begins with a preposition

g. incomplete sentence that lacks a subject, a verb, or both

h. word or group of words that indicates what the subject does or what happened to the subject

i. two or more subjects for the same verb

j. part of a sentence that tells you who or what the sentence is about

EDITING PRACTICE

The following paragraph contains numerous fragments. Highlight each fragment and then revise each to eliminate the fragment.

More than 300 million cubic miles. That's how much water covers our planet. However, 97 percent being salty. Which leaves 3 percent fresh water. Three-quarters of that fresh water is in icecaps. And in glaciers. Sixteen thousand gallons. That's how much water the average person drinks in a lifetime. Each family of four, using more than 300 gallons per day. Although the world's demand for water has more than doubled since 1960. There is still a sufficient supply to take care of humanity's needs. However, regular water shortages in certain parts of the world. Because the pattern of rainfall throughout the world is uneven. For instance, 400 inches of rain per year in some parts of India, but no rain for several years in other parts of the world.

PEARSON mywritinglab

For support in meeting this chapter's objectives, log in to www.mywritinglab.com, go to the Study Plan tab, click on Complete Sentences Versus Fragments and choose Fragments from the list of subtopics. Read and view the videos and resources in the Review Materials section, and then complete the Recall, Apply, and Write exercises in the Activities section. You can check your scores and overall progress by using the Gradebook.

5

Run-On Sentences and Comma Splices

Learning Goals

In this chapter, you will learn how to

GOAL 1
Use punctuation correctly within and between sentences

GOAL 2 Recognize and correct run-on sentences

GOAL 3 Recognize and correct comma splices

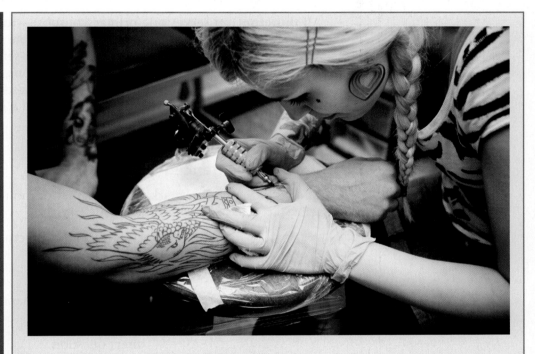

WRITE ABOUT IT!

Study the paragraph below. Why is it difficult to read?

Tattoos are a popular but permanent form of body decoration tattoos similar to body painting used by primitive societies in fact the word *tattoo* comes from the Tahitian word *ta-tu* they are used to communicate things about the wearer to those who view them a tattoo may be used to identify the person wearing the tattoo as part of a group they have recently become popular within a wide range of age groups people getting tattoos are cautioned to be sure to choose a safe, clean tattoo parlor and be sure that sterile procedures are used.

Did you have trouble reading this paragraph? Why? Write a sentence explaining your difficulty.

Most likely you said that the paragraph lacked punctuation. You could not see where one idea ended and another began. It is important to remember this confusion when you are writing. If you run sentences together, you run the risk of confusing your readers. In this chapter you will learn how to avoid this problem. Specifically, you will learn to use punctuation to connect or distinguish separate ideas within a sentence.

WRITING

THE FUNCTION OF PUNCTUATION: HOW TO USE IT CORRECTLY

GOAL 1
Use punctuation correctly within and between sentences

All **punctuation** serves one primary purpose—to separate. Periods, question marks, and exclamation points separate complete sentences from one another. Think of these punctuation marks as *between*-sentence separators. All other punctuation marks—commas, colons, semicolons, hyphens, dashes, quotation marks, and parentheses—separate parts *within* a sentence. To correct and avoid run-on sentences and comma splices, you need a good grasp of both between-sentence and within-sentence punctuation.

Between-Sentence Punctuation

The period, question mark, and exclamation point all mark the end of a sentence. Each has a different function.

BETWEEN-SENTENCE PUNCTUATION

Punctuation	*Function*	*Example*
Period (.)	Marks the end of a statement or command	The lecture is about to begin. Please be seated.
Question mark (?)	Marks the end of a direct question	Are you ready?
Exclamation point (!)	Marks the end of statements of excitement or strong emotion	We are late! I won an award!

Within-Sentence Punctuation

Commas, colons, semicolons, hyphens, dashes, quotation marks, and parentheses all separate parts of a sentence from one another. For a complete review of how and when to use each, refer to Part VIII, "Reviewing the Basics," pp. 588–590.

The **comma** is the most commonly used within-sentence punctuation mark and also the most commonly misused. The comma separates parts of a sentence from one another. In this chapter, we'll be concerned with just one type of separation: the separation of two complete thoughts. *Note:* Some instructors refer to a complete thought as an independent clause. An independent clause has a subject and a verb and can stand alone as a sentence. (For a review of independent clauses, see Chapter 4, p. 113.)

The comma can be used to separate two complete thoughts within a sentence *if and only if* it is used along with one of the coordinating conjunctions (*and, but, for, nor, or, so, yet*). Coordinating conjunctions are words that link and relate equally important parts of a sentence. The comma is not a strong enough separator to be used between complete thoughts without one of the coordinating conjunctions.

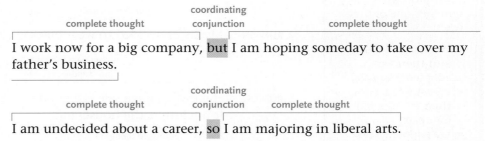

When you do not insert punctuation and a coordinating conjunction between two complete thoughts, you create an error called a **run-on sentence**. (This is sometimes called a **fused sentence** because two sentences are incorrectly fused, or joined together.) When you use *only* a comma to separate two complete thoughts, you make an error called a **comma splice**.

RUN-ON SENTENCES

GOAL 2 Recognize and correct run-on sentences

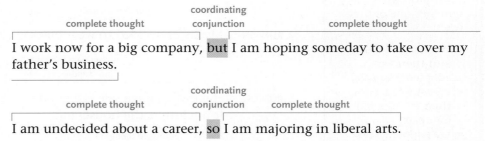

mywritinglab

For more practice with run-ons, go to
■ Study Plan
■ Writing Process
■ Sentence Basics
■ Run-Ons

When you do not separate two complete thoughts (two independent clauses) with the necessary punctuation, the two clauses run together and form a run-on sentence.

How to Recognize Run-On Sentences

1. **Read each sentence aloud.** Listen for a break or change in your voice midway through the sentence. Your voice automatically pauses or slows down at the end of a complete thought. If you hear a break but have no punctuation at that break, you may have a run-on sentence. Try reading the following run-on sentences aloud. Place a slash mark (/) where you hear a pause.

   RUN-ON   The library has a copy machine it is very conveniently located.

   RUN-ON   The Career Planning Center on campus is helpful one of the counselors suggested I take a career-planning course.

   RUN-ON   My major is nursing I do enjoy working with people.

   Did you mark the sentences as follows?

   The library has a copy machine / it is very conveniently located.

   The Career Planning Center on campus is helpful / one of the counselors suggested I take a career-planning course.

   My major is nursing / I do enjoy working with people.

   The pause in each indicates the need for punctuation.

Tip for Writers

Then cannot be used to connect two independent clauses even if it is preceded by a comma. When using *then* as a connector, write the sentence one of these ways:

- We adopted a dog, **and then** we adopted four cats.
- We adopted a dog; **then** we adopted four cats.
- We adopted a dog **and then** four cats.

2. **Look for sentences that contain two complete thoughts (independent clauses) without punctuation to separate them.**

complete thought (independent clause)

RUN-ON   Houseplants are pleasant additions to a home or office they add color and variety.

complete thought (independent clause)

complete thought (independent clause)   complete thought (independent clause)

RUN-ON   My sister decided to wear black   I chose red.

complete thought (independent clause)

RUN-ON   Having a garage sale is a good way to make money it unclutters the house, too.

complete thought (independent clause)

complete thought (independent clause)   complete thought (independent clause)

RUN-ON   We bought a portable phone   then we had to connect the base unit into our phone line.

3. **Look for long sentences.** Not every long sentence is a run-on, but run-ons do tend to occur more frequently in longer sentences than in shorter ones.

RUN-ON   Choosing a mate is one of the most important decisions you will ever make unless you make the right choice, you may be unhappy.

RUN-ON   I plan to work in a day-care center some days taking care of my own kids is enough to make me question my career choice.

EXERCISE 5-1   Identifying Run-On Sentences

Directions: Read each sentence aloud. Place a check mark in the blank before each sentence that is a run-on. Use a slash mark to show where punctuation is needed. Not all of these sentences are run-ons.

_____   1. Parking spaces on campus are limited often I must park far away and walk.

_____   2. Before exercising, you should always stretch and warm up to prevent injury.

_____   3. Theodore's car wouldn't start fortunately Phil was able to use jumper cables to help him get it started.

_____   4. The skydiver jumped from the plane when she had fallen far enough she released her parachute.

_____   5. Radio stations usually have a morning disc jockey whose job is to wake people and cheer them up on their way to work.

NEED TO KNOW

How to Use Coordinating Conjunctions

There are seven coordinating conjunctions. An easy way to remember them is the acronym FANBOYS (for, and, nor, but, or, yet, and so). Choose the one that shows the right relationship between the two complete thoughts in a sentence.

COORDINATING CONJUNCTION	MEANING	EXAMPLE
for	since, because	Sarah is taking math, *for* she is a chemistry major.
and	added to, in addition, along with	Budgeting is important, *and* it is time well spent.
nor	and not, or not, not either	Sam cannot choose a career, *nor* can he decide upon a major.
but	just the opposite, on the other hand	I had planned to visit Chicago, *but* I changed my mind.
or	either	I will major in liberal arts, *or* I will declare myself "undecided."
yet	but, despite, nevertheless	I plan to become a computer programmer, *yet* a change is still possible.
so	as a result, consequently	Yolanda enjoys mathematics, *so* she is considering it as a career.

3. **Use a comma and a coordinating conjunction.** Use a **comma** and a **coordinating conjunction** to separate two complete thoughts placed within one sentence.

   Note: When you separate two complete thoughts by using a coordinating conjunction, you must also use a comma.

   The seven coordinating conjunctions are listed below:

Complete thought	, for	complete thought.
Complete thought	, and	complete thought.
Complete thought	, nor	complete thought.
Complete thought	, but	complete thought.
Complete thought	, or	complete thought.
Complete thought	, yet	complete thought.
Complete thought	, so	complete thought.

   When you use a coordinating conjunction to separate two complete thoughts, be sure to use the right one. Since each coordinating conjunction has a particular meaning, you should choose the one that shows the right relationship between the two thoughts. For example, the conjunction *and* indicates the ideas are equally important and similar. The words *but* and *yet* indicate that one idea is contrary to or in opposition to the other. *For* and *so* emphasize cause-and-effect connections. *Or* and *nor* indicate choice.

The following examples show how to use a comma and a coordinating conjunction to correct a run-on sentence:

RUN-ON   Interests change and develop throughout life you may have a different set of interests 20 years from now.

comma and conjunction so used to show cause-and-effect relationship

CORRECT   Interests change and develop throughout life, so you may have a different set of interests 20 years from now.

RUN-ON   Take courses in a variety of disciplines you may discover new interests.

comma and conjunction for used to show cause-and-effect relationship

CORRECT   Take courses in a variety of disciplines, for you may discover new interests.

RUN-ON   Alexis thought she was not interested in biology by taking a biology course, she discovered it was her favorite subject.

comma and conjunction but used to show contrast

CORRECT   Alexis thought she was not interested in biology, but, by taking a biology course, she discovered it was her favorite subject.

RUN-ON   The weather forecast threatened severe thunderstorms just as the day ended, the sky began to cloud over.

comma and conjunction and used to show addition

CORRECT   The weather forecast threatened severe thunderstorms, and just as the day ended, the sky began to cloud over.

This method of correcting run-ons allows you to indicate to your reader how your two ideas are connected. Use this method for correcting run-on sentences when you want to explain the relationship between the two thoughts.

EXERCISE 5-4
Working Together

Correcting Run-On Sentences Using Commas and Conjunctions

Directions: Working with a classmate, correct each of the following run-on sentences by using a comma and a coordinating conjunction. Think about the relationship between the two thoughts, and then choose the best coordinating conjunction. (These are the coordinating conjunctions you should use: *for, and, nor, but, or, yet, so.*)

EXAMPLE   I thought I had left for class in plenty of time , but I was two minutes late.

1. Jameel got up half an hour late he missed the bus.

2. My creative-writing teacher wrote a book our library did not have a copy.

3. *Ford* is an interesting first name we did not choose it for our son.

4. Smoking cigarettes is not healthy it can cause lung cancer.

5. My paycheck was ready to be picked up I forgot to get it.

6. The window faces north the room gets little sun.

7. I may order Chinese food for dinner I may bake a chicken.

8. Miranda had planned to write her term paper about World War I she switched her topic to the Roaring Twenties.

9. The journalist arrived at the fire she began to take notes.

10. The table is wobbly we keep a matchbook under one leg to stabilize it. ■

4. **Make one thought dependent.** Make one thought dependent by making it a dependent clause. A **dependent clause** depends on an independent clause for its meaning. It cannot stand alone because it does not express a complete thought. In a sentence, a dependent clause must always be linked to an independent clause, which expresses a complete thought. By itself, a dependent clause always leaves a question in your mind; the question is answered by the independent clause to which it is joined.

dependent clause raises a question

Because I missed the bus   [What happened?]

independent clause answers the question

Because I missed the bus, I was late for class.

dependent clause raises a question

When I got my exam back   [What did you do?]

independent clause answers the question

When I got my exam back, I celebrated.

   Did you notice that each dependent clause began with a word that made it dependent? In the above sentences, the words that make the clauses dependent are *Because* and *When*. These words are called subordinating conjunctions. **Subordinating conjunctions** let you know that the sense of the clause that follows them depends on another idea, an idea you will find in the independent clause of the sentence. Some common subordinating conjunctions are *after, although, before, if, since,* and *unless.* (For a more complete list of subordinating conjunctions, see p. 116.)

   You can correct a run-on sentence by changing one of the complete thoughts into a dependent clause and joining the ideas in the two clauses with a subordinating conjunction. This method places more emphasis on the idea expressed in the complete thought (independent clause) and less emphasis on the idea in the dependent clause.

RUN-ON   Aptitudes are built-in strengths they are important in career planning.

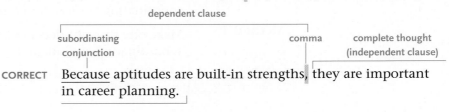

dependent clause

subordinating   comma   complete thought
conjunction   (independent clause)

CORRECT   Because aptitudes are built-in strengths, they are important in career planning.

RUN-ON   Emotional involvement can interfere with job performance be sure to keep work and friends and family separate.

dependent clause

subordinating conjunction

CORRECT   <u>Since</u> emotional involvement can interfere with job performance, be sure to keep work and family and friends separate.

comma   complete thought (independent clause)

Note: A dependent clause can appear before or after an independent clause. If the dependent clause appears first, it must be followed by a comma, as in the examples above. No comma is needed when the complete thought comes first.

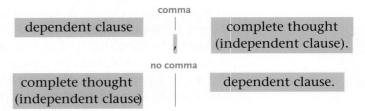

RUN-ON   Personal relationships are enjoyable they should be minimized in the workplace.

dependent clause

subordinating conjunction   comma

CORRECT   <u>Even though</u> personal relationships are enjoyable, they should be minimized in the workplace.

complete thought (independent clause)

complete thought (independent clause)   no comma

CORRECT   Personal relationships should be minimized in the workplace <u>even though</u> they are enjoyable.

subordinating conjunction

dependent clause

NEED TO KNOW

How to Correct Run-On Sentences

You can correct run-on sentences in four ways:

Method 1	Separate the two complete thoughts into two sentences.
Method 2	Separate the two complete thoughts with a semicolon.
Method 3	Join the two complete thoughts with a comma and a coordinating conjunction (*and, but, for, nor, or, so, yet*).
Method 4	Make one thought dependent upon the other by using a subordinating conjunction (see the list on p. 116).

EXERCISE 5-5   **Revising Run-On Sentences Using Subordinating Conjunctions**

Directions: In each of the following run-on sentences, make one thought dependent on the other by using the subordinating conjunction in boldface. Don't forget to use a comma if the dependent clause comes first.

EXAMPLE

until   Until w
                            ∧We called the plumber∧ we were without water.

SUBORDINATING
CONJUNCTION

even though   1. David wants a leather jacket it is very expensive.

so that   2. Margery runs ten miles every day she can try out for the cross-country squad in the spring.

when   3. The television program ended Gail read a book to her son.

because   4. The pool was crowded it was 95 degrees that day.

although   5. Industry is curbing pollution our water supply still is not safe.

because   6. I always obey the speed limit speeding carries a severe penalty in my state.

while   7. The crowd fell silent the trapeze artist attempted a quadruple flip.

since   8. The Cold War with the USSR is over, there are greater opportunities for cultural exchange.

as   9. The storm approached I stocked up on batteries.

whenever   10. The moon is full our dog is restless.   ■

EXERCISE 5-6   **Revising Sentences**

Directions: Write five sentences, each of which has two complete thoughts. Then revise each sentence so that it has one dependent clause and one complete thought (independent clause). Use a comma, if needed, to separate the two clauses. You may want to refer to the list of subordinating conjunctions on p. 116. ■

COMMA SPLICES

GOAL 3 Recognize and correct comma splices

Like run-ons, comma splices are serious sentence errors that can confuse and annoy your readers. Also, like run-ons, they are easy to correct once you know what to look for. In fact, they are corrected in the same way that run-ons are. A comma splice occurs when you use *only* a comma to separate two complete thoughts. A comma alone is not sufficient to divide the two thoughts. A stronger, clearer separation is necessary. You can visualize a comma splice this way:

COMMA SPLICE   Complete thought , complete thought.

COMMA SPLICE   Spatial aptitude is the ability to understand and visualize objects in physical space, it is an important skill for engineers and designers.

COMMA SPLICE   Some people have strong mechanical ability, they often prefer hands-on tasks.

COMMA SPLICE   Verbal reasoning is important to many careers, it is the ability to think through problems.

How to Recognize Comma Splices

To avoid comma splices, you have to make sure that you do not place *only a comma* between two complete thoughts. To test a sentence to see if you have written a comma splice, take the sentence apart at the comma. If the part before the comma is a complete thought and the part after the comma is a complete thought, then you need to check whether the second clause starts with a coordinating conjunction (*for, and, nor, but, or, yet, so*). If you do not have a coordinating conjunction to separate the two complete thoughts, then you have a comma splice.

How to Correct Comma Splices

To correct comma splices, use any one of the four methods you used to correct run-ons:

1. **Separate the thoughts into two complete sentences, deleting the comma.**

   Complete thought.   Complete thought.

2. **Separate the two thoughts with a semicolon, deleting the comma.**

   Complete thought ; complete thought.

3. **Separate the two thoughts by adding a coordinating conjunction after the comma.**

Complete thought	, for	complete thought.
Complete thought	, and	complete thought.
Complete thought	, nor	complete thought.
Complete thought	, but	complete thought.
Complete thought	, or	complete thought.
Complete thought	, yet	complete thought.
Complete thought	, so	complete thought.

4. **Make one thought dependent on the other by using a subordinating conjunction to separate the two thoughts.** (For a complete list of subordinating conjunctions, see p. 116.)

   Subordinating conjunction   dependent clause , independent clause.

   Independent clause   subordinating conjunction   dependent clause.

Paragraph Writing Scenarios

Friends and Family

1. Choose someone close to you. Make a list of how that person looks: his or her eyes, skin, hair, clothing, etc. Now write a paragraph describing that person in detail, using the items from your list. Make sure you write complete sentences and avoid run-on sentences.

2. Write a paragraph that begins with the topic sentence: "If I could change one thing about . . ." Describe what you might change about one of your relatives.

Classes and Campus Life

1. Choose an assignment from one of your courses. Explain what you have been asked to do for that assignment. Discuss three steps you will take in order to complete the assignment.

2. Write a paragraph that explains why you chose to apply to your college. Describe any other colleges that you considered as well.

Working Students

1. Write a paragraph on the kind of work you do. Is it boring or fun; easy or hard? How did you find this job?

2. Write a paragraph describing someone else's job at the same place. Would you rather have that job than the one you currently have? Why or why not?

Communities and Cultures

1. Think about American culture. Write a paragraph describing one thing from another culture that has become part of everyday life in America. It could be a food Americans like, a popular style of dress or music, or words from a language other than English that most Americans would know.

2. Listen to the broadcast of a game, tournament, or other athletic competition. Make a list of dependent clauses the announcer uses in calling the play. Now turn these clauses into complete sentences that describe what is happening in the game.

WRITING ABOUT A READING

THINKING BEFORE READING

In the following reading, the College Board offers some valuable tips on using credit cards and protecting your finances. Before you read:

1. Preview the reading using the steps listed in Chapter 2, page 35.

2. After you have previewed the reading, connect the reading to your own experience by answering the following questions:

   a. Do you currently use a debit card and/or credit card to pay for your purchases?

   b. How much do you generally pay in finance or interest charges per month?

   c. Do you use credit cards to buy things you really cannot afford?

3. Mark and annotate as you read.

READING

CREDIT CARD SMARTS:
TAKE CHARGE OF YOUR CARDS

1   Imagine being 30 years old and still paying off a slice of pizza you bought when you were in college. It may sound crazy, but problems with credit card debt can lead to this scenario. Learning how to use credit cards responsibly now can save you from having to dig yourself out of debt after you graduate. It also helps prevent you from having a bad credit history in the future that will affect other things you want to do. You know that the loans you take out for college need to be paid back once you graduate. If you add a large monthly credit card bill (avoid the temptation to charge your tuition!) to that amount, you may find yourself in a very difficult situation financially.

Credit Cards and College Students

2   Credit cards are an indisputable fact of life and there are many good reasons to have one. They give you protection for your purchases, allow you to shop online, and provide a cushion in case of emergencies. The secret is to use the credit card as a tool to help you when you need it, but not to excess. Discuss with your family what kind of expenses it is reasonable to charge.

3   Credit card abuse has become such a problem that, in February 2010, the federal government recognized the importance of protecting college students from the consequences of misusing credit cards. They enacted legislation changing how credit card companies can do business with students. Although the law provides some protection, it's still up to you to manage credit wisely.

4   The law bans credit card companies from issuing cards to people under the age of 18. If you're under 21 years old, you need an adult cosigner to get a card, unless you can prove that you have the financial means to pay your bill. Other provisions in the law limit some of the fees credit card companies can charge—and, in response, the companies are raising interest rates to avoid losing income. Anyone without an established credit history may face the highest interest rates—and that group typically includes students.

Credit Card Offers on Campus

5   If you don't already have a card, you'll have plenty of opportunities to apply for one once you hit campus. It shouldn't surprise you that the companies are allowed on campus; many colleges earn money by permitting this practice and from creating affinity cards—credit cards that include the name of your college. The law requires that educational institutions and credit card companies let you know about these agreements, but the messages may be subtle. Learn about fees and interest rates to protect yourself.

Carrying a Balance Can Be Very Expensive

6   Credit cards are actually high-interest loans in disguise. Companies may lend you money, but they get it all back and a lot more by charging you fees. Finance charges on the unpaid portion of your bill can be as much as 25 percent each month, and cash-advance fees have even higher interest rates. Annual fees just to carry the card in your wallet range from $20 to $100; there are also late-payment fees, typically $25–$50.

7   Not paying off the entire amount in your account each month can lead to big finance charges. Take the story of Joe: Joe's average unpaid credit card bill during a year is $500, and his finance charge is 20 percent—so he has to pay $100 in interest for the year. He pays a $20 annual fee per year, plus a $25 late fee one month (he was up late studying and forgot to mail in his check). After a year, Joe ends up owing $145 in interest and fees to his credit card company, and he still hasn't paid for any of his actual purchases!

Your Credit Report Matters

8   Your college years are an important time to build the good credit history you need after you graduate. You need to provide a credit report to apply for an apartment or finance a large purchase, such as a car. Employers often review a credit report when they hire and evaluate employees. Problems with credit cards, such as late or missed payments, stay in your credit report for seven years.

Be Credit Smart

9   When you sign up for a credit card, you are responsible for paying the bills. Follow these rules of credit management to lead a financially healthy life:

- Consider using a debit card instead of a credit card. Money is deducted directly from your checking account, so you can't spend more than you actually have.

teaser rate
a low interest rate that increases drastically when the introductory period expires

- Read all application materials carefully—especially the fine print. What happens after the "**teaser rate**" expires? What happens to your interest rate if you're late with a payment or fail to make a payment? What's the interest rate for a cash advance?

- Pay bills promptly to keep finance and other charges to a minimum; pay the balance off if you can.

- Use credit only if you're certain you are able to repay the debt.

- Avoid impulse shopping on your credit card.

- Save your credit card for a money emergency.

Additional Credit Card Advice

10   The Federal Trade Commission provides free information to consumers on dozens of topics related to credit and credit cards.

GETTING READY TO WRITE

Reviewing the Reading

Answer each of the following questions using complete sentences.

1. What is the key difference between a debit card and a credit card?
2. What are three good reasons to own and use a credit card?
3. How are credit card companies responding to new legislation, and how do these changes affect students?
4. Why is it important to have a good credit history?
5. What is an affinity card?

Examining the Reading Using an Idea Map

Review the reading by completing the missing parts of the idea map shown below.

 Visualize It!

Title **Credit Card Smarts: Take Charge of Your Cards**

Thesis   Learning how to use credit cards responsibly now can save you from having to dig yourself out of debt after you graduate.

Credit Cards and College Students

There are three benefits to using credit cards: _____ _____ _____

New laws provide some protection for students, but it's still up to you to manage your credit wisely.

To maintain profits, credit card companies are _____ _____ _____

Credit Card Offers on Campus

Credit card companies work with colleges to offer credit cards to students.

Proceed with caution.

_____

Credit cards are high-interest loans in disguise.

_____ _____

Your Credit Report Matters

You need good credit to make large purchases and sometimes to get a job.

Be Credit Smart

Use a _____ instead of a credit card.

Read application materials carefully.

_____

Use credit only when you can repay the debt.

_____

Save your card for emergencies.

Conclusion   The _____ provides good advice on using credit cards.

Strengthening Your Vocabulary

Using the word's context, word parts, or a dictionary, write a brief definition of each of the following words or phrases as it is used in the reading.

1. indisputable (paragraph 2) _____
2. consequences (paragraph 3) _____
3. means (paragraph 4) _____
4. affinity (paragraph 5) _____

Reacting to Ideas: Discussion and Journal Writing

Get ready to write about the reading by discussing the following.

1. How did the author capture your attention in the opening paragraph?
2. What is the author's purpose in providing the example of Joe's experience with credit-card debt?
3. Write a sentence that summarizes the author's opinion of owning and using credit cards.
4. What words would you use to describe the author's tone? Does this tone add or detract from the reading?
5. How would you describe the author's attitude toward or opinion of credit-card companies?
6. What is the relationship between using a credit card and being able to finance large purchases later in life?

 **Thinking Visually**

7. The photo shows credit cards spilling out of a wallet. Do you think the author of this reading would approve of carrying this many credit cards? What argument might she make in favor of carrying so many credit cards? What argument might she make against carrying multiple credit cards?

WRITING ABOUT THE READING

Paragraph Options

1. Write a paragraph discussing information you would like to have regarding credit cards that was not discussed in the article.
2. Write a paragraph summarizing the pros and cons of carrying and using a credit card.
3. Describe your own experiences with credit cards. Have they been positive, negative, or both? How?
4. Suppose you are offered an affinity card for one of the following organizations: Greenpeace (an Environmental, activist group), PETA (People for the Ethical Treatment of Animals), or the NRA (National Rifle Association). Which would you be most likely to choose, and why? (If none of these groups appeals to you, write about an organization whose affinity card you would be willing to carry.)

Essay Options

5. Do you think your college should allow credit card companies to advertise on campus? Why or why not? What are the benefits and drawbacks to this practice for both you and the college?

6. The reading is about using credit cards to live a financially secure and successful life. Write an essay in which you offer additional advice on how to live within your means and achieve financial security.

7. Add up your expenses for a typical day. How much do you spend on food, snacks, entertainment, gas, and the like? Now write an essay exploring the ways in which you can save half that money by making different choices. (For example, instead of buying a bottle of water, you can bring an empty bottle to campus and fill it from the water fountain.)

CHAPTER REVIEW AND PRACTICE

CHAPTER REVIEW

To review and check your recall of the chapter, select the word or term from the box below that best completes each of the following sentences. Keep in mind that three of the words or terms will not be used.

separate sentences	dependent clause	exclamation point
comma	comma splice	complete thoughts
semicolon	period	dependent
coordinating conjunction	joined	comma splice
	subordinating	

1. A comma is used to separate two _____.

2. A run-on sentence occurs when two complete thoughts are not correctly_____.

3. A(n) _____ occurs when two complete thoughts are separated only by a comma.

4. One way to correct a run-on sentence is to use a _____ to connect the two complete thoughts.

5. Another way to correct a run-on sentence is to create two _____.

6. A third way to correct a run-on sentence is to join the two complete thoughts with a _____ and a coordinating conjunction.

7. A fourth way to correct a run-on sentence is to make one thought _____ on the other by using a subordinating conjunction.

8. A comma splice can be corrected by adding a _____.

9. A _____ cannot stand alone as a sentence.

10. A(n) _____ conjunction is used to join an independent clause and a dependent clause.

EDITING PRACTICE

Revise the following paragraphs, correcting the run-on sentences and comma splices.

1. As in so many other undertakings, the Greeks were ahead of their time in mapmaking their maps showed the world as round rather than flat, the Greeks also developed a system of longitude and latitude for identifying locations. The Romans were excellent administrators and military strategists therefore, it was no surprise that they made reliable road maps and military maps. The most famous mapmaker of ancient times was Claudius Ptolemy of Alexandria, Egypt, he created a comprehensive map of the world.

2. It seems there is a problem on the Internet with certain types of messages that people post. There are people who argue that anyone has the right to say anything on the Internet people do have the right of free speech, but the line should be drawn when it comes to hate messages. It is immoral—and should be illegal—to make remarks that are racist, sexist, and anti-Semitic. After all, these verbal attacks are no longer tolerated in the classroom or in the workplace, why should the Internet be different? The problem with the Internet is that there seem to be no established rules of etiquette among users, maybe there should be some guidelines about what people can and cannot say on the Internet. Why should people be subjected to hate-filled speech in order to preserve the right of free speech?

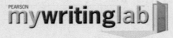

For support in meeting this chapter's objectives, log in to www.mywritinglab.com, go to the Study Plan tab, click on Run-on Sentences and Comma Splices and choose Run-Ons from the list of subtopics. Read and view the videos and resources in the Review Materials section, and then complete the Recall, Apply, and Write exercises in the Activities section. You can check your scores and overall progress by using the Gradebook.

6

Combining and Expanding Your Ideas

Learning Goals

In this chapter, you will learn how to

GOAL 1 Recognize independent and dependent clauses

GOAL 2 Combine ideas of equal importance

GOAL 3 Combine ideas of unequal importance

GOAL 4 Write compound-complex sentences

WRITE ABOUT IT!

Study the six photographs shown above one at a time (cover the others with your hand as you look at them). What is happening in each one? It is probably difficult to tell because there is so little information in each one. Then, look at the six photographs all together. Now it is clear what is happening. Write a sentence that states the main point of the combined photograph.

The six photographs seen separately are difficult to understand because each one contains so little information, and it is unclear if and how each is related to the others. A similar uncertainty can occur in writing when a writer uses too many very short sentences in a paragraph in which the relationship between them is unclear.

In this chapter, you will learn to combine your ideas to make your sentences more effective as well as more interesting. You will also learn how to use sentence arrangement to show the relationships and the logical connections between and among ideas.

WRITING

UNDERSTANDING INDEPENDENT AND DEPENDENT CLAUSES

GOAL 1 Recognize independent and dependent clauses

If you are financially independent, you alone accept full responsibility for your finances. If you are financially dependent, you depend on someone else to pay your living expenses. Clauses, too, are either independent or dependent. (A clause is a group of words that contains a subject and a verb.) Clauses either stand alone and accept responsibility for their own meaning, or they depend on another clause to complete their meaning. Independent clauses can stand alone as sentences. Dependent clauses can never stand alone because they are not complete sentences. The key to combining and expanding your ideas is to recognize this difference between independent and dependent clauses.

The various combinations of independent and dependent clauses shown in the "Need to Know" box on the next page allow you to link your ideas to one another.

COMBINING IDEAS OF EQUAL IMPORTANCE

GOAL 2 Combine ideas of equal importance

For more practice with combining ideas, go to
■ Study Plan
■ The Writing Process
■ Sentence Improvement
■ Combining Sentences

Many times, ideas are of equal importance. For example, in the following sentence, it is just as important to know that the writer never has enough time as it is to know that she always rushes.

I never have enough time, so I always rush from task to task.

Complete thoughts (independent clauses) of equal importance are combined by using a technique called **coordination**. *Co-* means "together." *Coordinate* means "to work together." When you want two complete thoughts to work together equally, you can combine them into a single sentence by using coordination.

Method 1: Use a Comma and a Coordinating Conjunction

The most common way to join ideas is by using a comma and a coordinating conjunction. Use a semicolon only when the two ideas are *very* closely related and the connection between the ideas is clear and obvious. In this section, we will concentrate on using a comma and a coordinating conjunction.

The following two sentences contain equally important ideas:

Samatha works 20 hours per week.

Samatha manages to find time to study.

NEED TO KNOW

Independent and Dependent Clauses

Sentences are made up of various combinations of independent and dependent clauses. Here are the possible combinations:

1. **Simple sentence**   A simple sentence has one independent clause and no dependent clauses.

   independent clause

   Richard hurried to his car.

2. **Compound sentence**   A compound sentence has two or more independent clauses and no dependent clauses.

   independent clause   independent clause

   Richard hurried to his car, but he was already late for work.

3. **Complex sentence**   A complex sentence has one independent clause and one or more dependent clauses.

   independent clause   dependent clause

   Richard hurried to his car because he was late for work.

4. **Compound-complex sentence**   A compound-complex sentence has two or more independent clauses and one or more dependent clauses.

   dependent clause   independent clause

   As Richard hurried to his car, he knew he would be late for work, but he hoped that he would not be docked an hour's pay.

   independent clause   dependent clause

You can combine these ideas into one sentence by using a comma and a coordinating conjunction.

idea 1   comma   conjunction   idea 2

Samatha works 20 hours per week, but she manages to find time to study.

As we saw in the section on correcting run-ons (see Chapter 5, p. 135), a **coordinating conjunction** joins clauses and adds meaning to a sentence. A coordinating conjunction indicates how the ideas are related. Here is a brief review of the meaning of each coordinating conjunction and the relationship it expresses:

COORDINATING CONJUNCTION	MEANING	RELATIONSHIP
and	in addition	The two ideas are added together.
but	in contrast	The two ideas are opposite.
for	because	The idea that follows *for* is the cause of the idea in the other clause.
nor, or	not either, either	The ideas are choices or alternatives.
so	as a result	The second idea is the result of the first.
yet	in contrast	The two ideas are opposite.

Note: Do *not* use the words *also, plus,* and *then* to join complete thoughts. They are *not* coordinating conjunctions.

NEED TO KNOW

How to Join Independent Clauses

There are two basic ways to join two ideas that are equally important:

Method 1.   Join them by using a **comma** and a **coordinating conjunction** (*and, but, for, nor, or, so, yet*).

> Complete thought , coordinating conjunction complete thought.

Method 2.   Join them by using a **semicolon**.

> Complete thought ; complete thought.

Here are a few more examples:

SIMPLE SENTENCES	Time is valuable. I try to use it wisely.
COMBINED SENTENCE	Time is valuable, so I try to use it wisely.
SIMPLE SENTENCES	Many students try to set priorities for work and study. Many students see immediate results.
COMBINED SENTENCE	Many students try to set priorities for work and study, and they see immediate results.
SIMPLE SENTENCES	I tried keeping lists of things to do. My friend showed me a better system.
COMBINED SENTENCE	I tried keeping lists of things to do, but my friend showed me a better system.

Tip for Writers

Sample Sentences Using Coordinating Conjunctions

COORDINATING CONJUNCTION	SAMPLE SENTENCE
and	The sky darkened, <u>and</u> it began to rain.
but	I thought it would rain, <u>but</u> the sun shone instead.
for	Be sure to study both the textbook chapter and your lecture notes, <u>for</u> the instructor may test on both.
nor	You cannot smoke in the lecture hall, <u>nor</u> are you allowed to consume food.
or	In sociology, you can take the written final exam, <u>or</u> you can make an oral presentation instead.
so	I was early for class, <u>so</u> I reread my notes from the previous class.
yet	My brother promised to call, <u>yet</u> I have not heard from him.

EXERCISE 6-1   **Using Coordinating Conjunctions**

Directions: For each of the following sentences, add the coordinating conjunction that best expresses the relationship between the two complete thoughts.

EXAMPLE   I never learned to manage my time, _____*so*_____ I am planning to attend a time-management workshop.

1. I might study math, _____ I might review for my history exam.
2. The average person spends 56 hours a week sleeping, _____ the average person spends seven hours a week eating dinner.
3. Watching television is tempting, _____ I usually shut the set off before I start studying.
4. I do not feel like typing, _____ do I feel like reviewing math.
5. I am never sure of what to work on first, _____ I waste a lot of time deciding.
6. A schedule for studying is easy to follow, _____ it eliminates the need to decide what to study.
7. My cousin has a study routine, _____ she never breaks it.
8. Frank studies his hardest subject first, _____ then he takes a break.
9. I know I should not procrastinate, _____ I sometimes postpone an unpleasant task until the next day.
10. I had planned to study after work, _____ my exam was postponed.

EXERCISE 6-2   **Completing Sentences**

Directions: Complete each of the following sentences by adding a second complete thought. Use the coordinating conjunction shown in bold.

EXAMPLE   I feel torn between studying and spending time with friends, **but** _____*I usually choose to study.*_____

1. My psychology class was canceled, **so** _____
2. I waste time doing unimportant tasks, **and** _____
3. The phone used to be a constant source of interruption, **but** _____

_____

4. I had extra time to study this weekend, **for** _____

_____

5. I had hoped to finish reading my biology chapter, **but** _____
6. Every Saturday I study psychology, **or** _____
7. I had planned to finish work early, **yet** _____
8. I can choose a topic to write about, **or** _____
9. I had hoped to do many errands this weekend, **but** _____

_____

10. I tried to study and watch television at the same time, **but** _____

_____

EXERCISE 6-3   Combining Sentences Using Coordinating Conjunctions

Directions: Combine each of the following pairs of sentences by using a comma and a coordinating conjunction (*and, but, for, nor, or, so, yet*). Change punctuation, capitalization, and words as necessary. Be sure to insert a comma before the coordinating conjunction.

EXAMPLE   **a.** I have a free hour between my first and second classes.
b. I use that free hour to review my biology notes.

I have a free hour between my first and second classes, so I use that

hour to review my biology notes.

1. **a.** Some tasks are more enjoyable than others.
   b. We tend to put off unpleasant tasks.

   _____

   _____

2. **a.** Many people think it is impossible to do two things at once.
   b. Busy students soon learn to combine routine activities.

   _____

   _____

3. **a.** Marita prioritizes her courses.
   b. Marita allots specific blocks of study time for each.

   _____

   _____

4. **a.** Marcus may try to schedule his study sessions so they are several hours apart.
   b. Marcus may adjust the length of his study sessions.

   _____

   _____

5. **a.** Sherry studies late at night.
   b. Sherry does not accomplish as much as she expects to.

   _____

   _____

6. **a.** Marguerite studies without breaks.
   b. Marguerite admits she frequently loses her concentration.

   _____

   _____

7. **a.** Alfonso studies two hours for every hour he spends in class.
   b. Alfonso earns high grades.

   _____

   _____

8. **a.** Deadlines are frustrating.
   b. Deadlines force you to make hasty decisions.

   _____

   _____

9. **a.** Juan thought he was organized.
   b. Juan discovered he was not.

   _____

   _____

10. **a.** Monica sets goals for each course.
    b. Monica usually attains her goals.

    _____

    _____

                                                    ■

Method 2: Use a Semicolon

A semicolon can be used alone or with a transitional word or phrase to join independent clauses. These transitional words and phrases are called **conjunctive adverbs.** Conjunctive adverbs are adverbs that *join*.

Independent clause ; therefore, independent clause.
                   ; however,
                   ; consequently,

I had hoped to earn a good grade; however, I never expected an A.

I lost my wallet; consequently, I had to cancel two credit cards.

As you can see in these examples, a comma follows the conjunctive adverb.

Use this method when the relationship between the two ideas is clear and requires no explanation. Be careful to choose the correct conjunctive adverb. A list of conjunctive adverbs and their meanings follows on the next page.

CONJUNCTIVE ADVERB	MEANING	EXAMPLE
therefore, consequently, thus, hence	cause and effect	I am planning to become a nurse; *consequently*, I'm taking a lot of science courses.
however, nevertheless, nonetheless, conversely	differences or contrast	We had planned to go bowling; *however*, we went to hear music instead.
furthermore, moreover, also	addition; a continuation of the same idea	To save money I am packing my lunch; *also*, I am walking to school instead of taking the bus.
similarly, likewise	similarity	I left class as soon as I finished the exam; *likewise*, other students left.
then, subsequently, next	sequence in time	I walked home; *then* I massaged my aching feet.

Note: If you join two independent clauses with only a comma and fail to use a coordinating conjunction or semicolon, you will produce a comma splice. If you join two independent clauses without using a punctuation mark and a coordinating conjunction, you will produce a run-on sentence.

Tip for Writers

These words mean the same as *and*: *also, besides, furthermore,* and *in addition*. These mean the same as *but*: *however, nevertheless, on the other hand,* and *still*. These mean the same as *so* when it is used to introduce a result: *therefore, consequently,* and *as a result. Otherwise* and *unless* usually mean *if not.*

NEED TO KNOW

How to Use Conjunctive Adverbs

Use a conjunctive adverb to join two equal ideas. Remember to put a semicolon before the conjunctive adverb and a comma after it. Here is a list of common conjunctive adverbs:

also	in addition	otherwise
as a result	instead	similarly
besides	likewise	still
consequently	meanwhile	then
finally	nevertheless	therefore
further	next	thus
furthermore	now	undoubtedly
however	on the other hand	

EXERCISE 6-4   Completing Sentences

Directions: Complete each of the following sentences by adding a coordinating conjunction or a conjunctive adverb and the appropriate punctuation.

EXAMPLE   Teresa vacationed in Denver last year _____*; similarly,*_____ Jan will go to Denver this year.

1. Our professor did not complete the lecture _____ did he give an assignment for the next class.

2. A first-aid kit was in her backpack _____ the hiker was able to treat her cut knee.

3. The opening act performed at the concert _____ the headline band took the stage.

4. I always put a light on when I leave the house _____ I often turn on a radio to deter burglars.

5. Sue politely asked to borrow my car _____ she thanked me when she returned it.

6. My roommate went to the library _____ I had the apartment to myself.

7. Steve and Todd will go to a baseball game _____ they will go to a movie.

8. Cheryl looks like her father _____ her hair is darker and curlier than his.

9. Maureen took a job at a bookstore _____ she was offered a job at a museum.

10. Our neighbors bought a barbecue grill _____ we decided to buy one. ∎

EXERCISE 6-5   Writing Compound Sentences

Directions: Write five compound sentences about how you study for tests or how you spend your weekends. Each sentence should contain two complete thoughts. Join the thoughts by using a comma and a coordinating conjunction. Use a different coordinating conjunction in each sentence. ∎

EXERCISE 6-6   Writing Using Compound Sentences

Directions: Write a paragraph evaluating how well you manage your time. Use at least two compound sentences. ∎

COMBINING IDEAS OF UNEQUAL IMPORTANCE

GOAL 3 Combine ideas of unequal importance

Consider the following two simple sentences:

> Pete studies during peak periods of attention.
>
> Pete accomplishes a great deal.

Reading these sentences, you may suspect that Pete accomplishes a great deal *because* he studies during peak periods of attention. With the sentences separated, however, that cause-and-effect relationship is only a guess. Combining the two sentences makes the relationship between the ideas clear.

> Because Pete studies during peak periods of attention, he accomplishes a great deal.

The combined sentence makes it clear that one event is the cause of another. Let's look at another pair of sentences:

> Yolanda analyzed her time commitments for the week.
>
> Yolanda developed a study plan for the week.

You may suspect that Yolanda developed the study plan *after* analyzing her time commitments. Combining the sentences makes the connection in time clear.

> After Yolanda analyzed her time commitments for the week, she developed a study plan.

In each of these examples, the two complete thoughts were combined so that one idea depended on the other. This process of combining ideas so that one idea is dependent on another is called **subordination**. *Sub-* means "below." Think of subordination as a way of combining an idea of lesser or lower importance with an idea of greater importance.

Ideas of unequal importance can be combined by making the less important idea depend on the more important one. Notice how, in the following sentence, the part before the comma doesn't make sense without the part after the comma.

> While Malcolm was waiting for the bus, he studied psychology.

If you read only the first half of the sentence, you'll find yourself waiting for the idea to be completed, wondering what happened while Malcolm was waiting. The word *while* (a subordinating conjunction) makes the meaning of the first half of the sentence incomplete by itself. Thus, the first half of the sentence is a **dependent clause**. It depends on the rest of the sentence to complete its thought. A dependent clause can never be a complete sentence. It must always be joined to an *independent* clause to make a complete thought. The dependent clause can go at the beginning, in the middle, or at the end of a sentence.

Review the following list for other words that are commonly used to begin dependent clauses. Such words are called **subordinating conjunctions**. Use these words to indicate how a less important idea (a dependent clause) relates to another, more important idea (an independent clause).

SUBORDINATING CONJUNCTION	MEANING	EXAMPLE
before, after, while, during, until, when, once	time	*When* you set time limits, you are working toward a goal.
because, since, so that	cause or effect	*Because* I felt rushed, I made careless errors.
whether, if, unless, even if	condition	*If* I finish studying before nine o'clock, I will read more of my mystery novel.
as, as far as, as soon as, as long as, as if, as though, although, even though, even if, in order to	circumstance	*Even if* I try to concentrate, I still am easily distracted.

Note: Relative pronouns (*who, whom, whose, that, which, whoever, whomever, whichever*) can also be used to show relationships and to join a dependent clause with an independent clause. The topic of relative pronouns is covered in detail in Chapter 8, p. 212.

When you combine a dependent clause with an independent clause, use a comma to separate the clauses if the dependent clause comes *first* in the sentence.

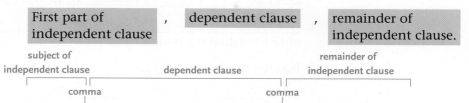

When I follow a study schedule, I accomplish more.

When the dependent clause comes in the *middle* of the sentence, set it off with a *pair* of commas.

| First part of independent clause | , | dependent clause | , | remainder of independent clause. |

Malcolm, while he was waiting for a ride, studied psychology.

If the dependent clause comes at the end of the sentence, do not use a comma to separate it from the rest of the sentence.

| Independent clause | dependent clause. |

I accomplish more when I follow a study schedule.

EXERCISE 6-7   Adding Subordinating Conjunctions

Directions: For each of the following sentences, add a subordinating conjunction that makes the relationship between the two ideas clear. Try to use as many different subordinating conjunctions as possible.

EXAMPLE   _____ When _____ I finish studying, I am mentally exhausted.

1. _____ math requires peak concentration, I always study it first.

2. _____ Andres starts to lose concentration, he takes a short break.

3. Julia never stops in the middle of an assignment _____ she is too tired to finish.

4. _____ she likes to wake up slowly, Shannon sets her alarm for ten minutes before she needs to get up.

5. _____ Maria took a five-minute study break, she felt more energetic.

6. Alan worked on his math homework _____ he did the laundry.

7. _____ Jamille increases his study time, he may not earn the grades he hopes to receive.

8. _____ Marsha completes an assignment, she crosses it off her "To do" list.

9. _____ Robert did not know when he wasted time, he kept a log of his activities for three days.

10. _____ noises and conversation do not interfere with my concentration, I wear a headset with soft music playing. ■

EXERCISE 6-8   Completing Sentences

Directions: Make each of the following sentences complete by adding a complete thought. Be sure the meaning fits the subordinating conjunction used in the sentence.

> EXAMPLE   _____I edited my essay_____ while the ideas were fresh in my mind.

1. _____
   after I finished studying.

2. Because my job is part-time, _____
   _____

3. Once I finish college, _____
   _____

4. _____
   while I was studying.

5. If you schedule blocks of study time, _____
   _____

6. _____
   unless I carry a pocket calendar.

7. Although English is my favorite subject, _____
   _____

8. _____
   as far as I can tell.

9. Even if I finish by eight o'clock, _____
   _____

10. As soon as I decide what to do, _____
    _____

■

EXERCISE 6-9   Combining Sentences

Directions: Combine each of the following pairs of sentences by using a subordinating conjunction and a comma. Change punctuation, capitalization, and words as necessary. You may wish to refer to the list of subordinating conjunctions on p. 116.

> EXAMPLE   **a.** Yi-Min is taking voice lessons.
>   **b.** Yi-Min always sings scales in the shower.
>
>   _Because Ann is taking voice lessons, she always sings scales_
>   _in the shower._

1. **a.** Christine has a six-month-old child.
   b. She must study while the baby sleeps.

   _____

   _____

2. **a.** Taj jots stray thoughts on a notepad to clear them from his mind.
   b. Taj can concentrate through a fire drill.

   _____

   _____

3. **a.** Gary finished a difficult biology assignment.
   b. He rewarded himself by ordering a pizza.

   _____

   _____

4. **a.** It takes Anthony 45 minutes to drive to school.
   b. Anthony records lectures and listens while he drives.

   _____

   _____

5. **a.** Ada felt disorganized.
   b. Ada made a priority list of assignments and due dates.

   _____

   _____

6. **a.** Juanita walked from her history class to her math class.
   b. She observed the brilliant fall foliage.

   _____

   _____

7. **a.** Kevin skipped meals and ate junk food.
   b. Kevin signed up for a cooking class.

   _____

   _____

8. **a.** Lian joined the soccer team.
   b. Lian became the first woman to do so.

   _____

   _____

9. **a.** John ate dinner on Saturday night.
   b. John reviewed his plans for the week with his less-than-fascinated date.

   _____

   _____

10. **a.** Frank waited for his history class to begin.
    b. He wondered if he was in the right room.

    _____

    _____

EXERCISE 6-10
Working Together

Writing Complex Sentences

Directions: Working with a classmate, write ten complex sentences on a subject that interests both of you. Each must contain one dependent clause and one independent clause. Use a comma to separate the clauses when the dependent clause comes first. Use two commas to set off a dependent clause in the middle of the sentence. You do not need a comma when the dependent clause comes last. ■

EXERCISE 6-11

Writing Complex Sentences

Directions: Write a paragraph on one of the following topics. Include at least two complex sentences.

1. Renting videos

2. Catalog shopping

3. Visiting the dentist or doctor

4. Advantages or disadvantages of credit cards

5. A favorite possession or a favorite piece of clothing ■

WRITING COMPOUND-COMPLEX SENTENCES

GOAL 4 Write compound-complex sentences

A compound-complex sentence is made up of two or more independent clauses and one or more dependent clauses. This type of sentence is often used to express complicated relationships. Look at the following examples of compound-complex sentences. Here, a dependent clause is followed by two independent clauses:

dependent clause	independent clause

Even though Marsha needed to be better organized, she avoided weekly study plans, and she ended up wasting valuable time.

independent clause

Here, an independent clause containing a dependent clause is followed by a second independent clause with a dependent clause:

first part of independent clause	dependent clause	remainder of independent clause

The new students who had just arrived wanted a tour of the town; Lamar told them that he had no time.

independent clause   dependent clause

Here, the sentence is made up of a dependent clause, an independent clause containing a dependent clause, and another independent clause:

independent clause

dependent clause	dependent clause

Although Amanda changed her work schedule, she found that she still needed more time to study, and she ended up quitting her job.

independent clause

The key to writing effective and correct compound-complex sentences is to link each clause to the one that follows it in the correct way. The rules you have already learned in this chapter apply. For example, if you have two independent clauses followed by a dependent clause, link the two independent clauses as you would in a compound sentence by using a comma and a coordinating conjunction. Then link the second independent clause to the dependent clause by using a subordinating conjunction.

| independent clause | independent clause | dependent clause |

I got up early, and I left the house before rush hour because I wanted to be on time for my interview.

EXERCISE 6-12   Adding Conjunctions

Directions: Each of the following sentences is made up of at least three clauses. Read each sentence, and then make it correct by adding the necessary subordinating and/or coordinating conjunctions in the blanks.

EXAMPLES   _____Because_____ they both got home from work late, Ted grilled hamburgers _____while_____ Alexa made a salad.

1. _____ Sarah's sociology class required class discussion of the readings, she scheduled time to review sociology before each class meeting _____ she would have the material fresh in her mind.

2. _____ making a "To do" list takes time, Deka found that the list actually saved her time, _____ she accomplished more when she sat down to study.

3. _____ Terry's history lecture was over, he reviewed his notes, _____ when he discovered any gaps, he was usually able to recall the information.

4. Many students have discovered that distributing their studying over several evenings is more effective than studying in one large block of time _____ it gives them several exposures to the material, _____ they feel less pressured.

5. We have tickets for the concert, _____ we may not go _____ Jeff has a bad cold. ■

EXERCISE 6-13   Writing a Compound-Complex Sentence

Directions: Write a compound-complex sentence. Then label its dependent and independent clauses. ■

Analyze It!

Directions: The following paragraph consists of simple sentences and lacks details. Revise the paragraph by expanding or combining sentences. Write your revised paragraph on a separate sheet of paper.

Cell phones cause many problems. Cell phones are a nuisance. They ring all the time. They often ring when I am busy doing something important. They are a distraction. They interrupt me when I am studying. They interrupt me at work. Cell phones are sometimes a safety hazard. I see people talking on their cell phones while doing other things. They are not paying attention. And then there is the social aspect. Cell phones disrupt conversations with friends. My cell phone rings when I am out with friends. I have to ignore them to answer the phone. I try to enjoy dinner in a restaurant. People around me are talking on their cell phones.

Paragraph Writing Scenarios

Friends and Family

1. Choose a casual acquaintance and write a paragraph about what makes you want to know him or her better.

2. Write a paragraph that begins with the topic sentence: "I really hated the way…"

Classes and Campus Life

1. Describe the way you feel before an exam. Explain the difference in how you feel when you are prepared and when you're not.

2. Write a paragraph describing the things you have to carry with you throughout a day on campus.

Working Students

1. Write a paragraph on one thing a working student could do to manage his or her time better. Is there something that you do to stay organized that might work for others?

2. Write a paragraph describing the shoes (or other apparel) you wear to work. Do you choose them for looks or comfort?

Communities and Cultures

1. Choose a culture or country whose people you find particularly interesting or one that you would like to learn more about. Describe what makes this culture or country interesting to you.

2. Describe a family ritual that you know—or guess—came from another country. Who in your family is the one who keeps the ritual going?

WRITING ABOUT A READING

THINKING BEFORE READING

In the following reading, the author describes how music can enhance your workout. As you read, examine how the writer combines ideas into compound and complex sentences. Before you read:

1. Preview the reading, using the steps listed in Chapter 2, p. 35.
2. Connect the reading to your own experience by answering the following questions:

   a. Do you typically listen to music when you are exercising? Why or why not?

   b. What kind of music makes you want to move your body? What kind of music improves your mood?
3. Mark and annotate as you read.

READING

THE PLAYLIST'S THE THING

Choosing the right music can help you crank up the workout

By Carolyn Butler

1   Full disclosure is important; there's quite a lot of Britney Spears on my iPod. Yes, my musical tastes typically run to classic rock and country, but when I head for the gym, suddenly I can't get enough of '80s hits like Wham's "Wake Me Up Before You Go-Go," hip-hop tunes like Kanye West's "Gold Digger," or just about anything by the aforementioned Miss Spears. For some reason, these songs just seem to help me stay on the elliptical machine a little longer, make the time pass faster, and leave me smiling—no matter how tired or achy—post-workout.

2   It turns out that there's some science behind this; new research from the Brunel University School of Sport and Education in England shows that rocking out during cardiovascular exercise can help improve results—from increasing physical endurance and motivation to distracting from negatives like fatigue. The study, published in the February 2009 *Journal of Sport & Exercise Psychology*, found that people who listened to specially selected rock or pop tunes by the likes of Queen, the Red Hot Chili Peppers, and Madonna while on the treadmill—music that was matched to their walking speed—upped their endurance by 15 percent and felt better about the workout than those who chugged along in silence.

3   Researchers also discovered that the right music can help exercisers feel more positive even when they are working out at a level that's close to physical exhaustion, says Brunel's Costas Karageorghis, PhD, an associate professor in sport psychology who has been studying the motivational qualities of music in sports for more than two decades. "The fact that music can still break through even in the midst of much pain and discomfort represents a departure from existing theory," he says.

Choosing the right music can help you crank up the workout.

4   There is another plus. Exercising to a beat may also boost your brainpower. Scientists at Ohio State University recently studied cardiac rehabilitation patients who listened to Vivaldi's "The Four Seasons" while walking on a treadmill for about 30 minutes. The results, published in *Heart & Lung,* showed that all of the participants felt better, both emotionally and mentally, after exercising. But when they listened to the classical composition, they had more than double the **cognitive** gains on a postexercise verbal fluency test than when they worked out in silence.

cognitive
related to mental abilities and processes

5   Of course, music preference is highly personal. So how can you create your own best playlist, one that will keep you moving and motivated for as long as possible? Karageorghis, who created the Brunel Music Rating Inventory, a questionnaire that is used to rate the motivational qualities of music for exercise, offers some tips for picking the right tunes:

percussive
having a strong beat

- MARRY THE MUSIC to your activity and the psychological effect you want to experience. For example, loud, fast, rhythmical, **percussive**, or bass-driven music is great for psyching yourself up before lifting heavy weights.
- CONSIDER THE TEMPO and whether the speed of the music and its rhythm (the pattern of beats over time) are ideal for the speed of the activity you are performing and the heart rate you expect to reach.
- GAUGE YOUR INTENSITY: Generally speaking, you will need faster music if you are training at a higher intensity; a song with 130 to 150 beats per minute (BPM) is ideal for very intense exercise. You can even find software online that organizes your digital music library by BPM.

- FIND YOUR RHYTHM with music that makes you want to move.
- CHECK THE LYRICS for positive affirmations of exercise such as "work your body," "push it," or "run to the beat." Other positive statements such as "moving on up" or "I believe" can help you push yourself.
- LISTEN FOR PLEASURE: Find a pleasing melody and harmony (a combination of notes played at the same time that shapes the emotional "color" of the music) that improves your mood. Generally speaking, major (happy) keys are more appropriate for exercise than minor (sad) keys.
- GET PSYCHED with music that makes you feel excited. Does it evoke a positive state of mind? Are you familiar with the music without finding it tiresome because you've heard it too often?

6   If you're looking for specific song suggestions, check out the box on the next page. And when in doubt, there's always the guiltiest soundtrack pleasure of them all: the theme song from *Rocky*. It never fails to pump me up at a particularly tough treadmill moment. (I mean, remember those stairs?) Others apparently find it inspiring too: Every year for the past three decades, a Brooklyn high school band has played the theme along the New York City Marathon route, encouraging runners to keep on trucking to the finish line. So grab your MP3 player or turn up your stereo and bop your way to an even better, happier workout.

The right music can help exercisers feel more positive even when they are working out at a level that's close to physical exhaustion.

Inspiration for Perspiration

One of the most important elements in choosing music for exercise, says Costas Karageorghis, PhD, is a song's tempo. It should range from about 120 to 140 beats per minute (BPM), a pace like that of most techno and dance music and many rock-and-roll songs. This pace is close to the typical person's heart rate during an everyday, casual workout—say, a long walk or easy jog.

If you're interested in the following playlist for **low-intensity activities like walking** or an easy bike ride. While Karageorghis selected the tracks based on expected heart rate and not on synchronizing your work-rate to the music, some people will be able to achieve both, which is an added bonus.

Track Title	Artist	BPM
The Way I Are	**Timbaland**	115
At the River	**Groove Armada**	116
Umbrella	**Rihanna** *featuring Jay-Z*	116
Don't Stop Movin'	**S Club 7**	117
Lose My Breath	**Destiny's Child**	118
Celebration	**Kool & The Gang**	120
Livin' on a Prayer	**Bon Jovi**	123
I Like to Move It	**Reel 2 Real** *featuring The Mad Stuntman*	123
The Rhythm of the Night	**Corona**	124
Let Me Entertain You	**Robbie Williams**	124

If you're interested in a **more intense aerobic workout like running long distances** or cycling hills, try this playlist from Karageorghis, who helped plan the Sony Ericsson Run to the Beat half-marathon in London in September 2008, which piped scientifically selected live music along the entire 17-mile course for some 12,500 participants.

Track Title	Artist	BPM
Mercy	**Duffy**	127
Don't Stop the Music	**Rihanna**	123
Give It 2 Me	**Madonna**	127
Rise Up	**Yves Larock**	128
Let Me Think About It	**Fedde le Grande** *featuring Ida Corr*	129
Clothes Off!! (*Josh Harris Remix*)	**Gym Class Heroes**	126
Pjanoo	**Eric Prydz**	126
Closer	**Ne-Yo**	125
World, Hold On (Children of the Sky)	**Bob Sinclar**	130
Angel in the Night	**Basshunter**	140

GETTING READY TO WRITE

Reviewing the Reading

Answer each of the following questions using complete sentences.

1. Based on the article, describe at least three positive effects of music on exercise.

2. What type of patients were the subject of the research at Ohio State University? Identify the specific music used in that study.

3. What is the purpose of the Brunel Music Rating Inventory, and who created it?

4. Summarize the seven tips given in the article for choosing the right music for exercise.

5. How does the author define the terms *rhythm* and *harmony*?

6. Which song does the author describe as "the guiltiest soundtrack pleasure of them all"?

7. What range of beats per minute (BPM) is ideal for very intense exercise? Identify which song in the graphic, "Inspiration for Perspiration," has the most BPM and which song has the fewest.

Examining the Reading Using an Idea Map

Review the reading by completing the missing parts of the idea map shown below.

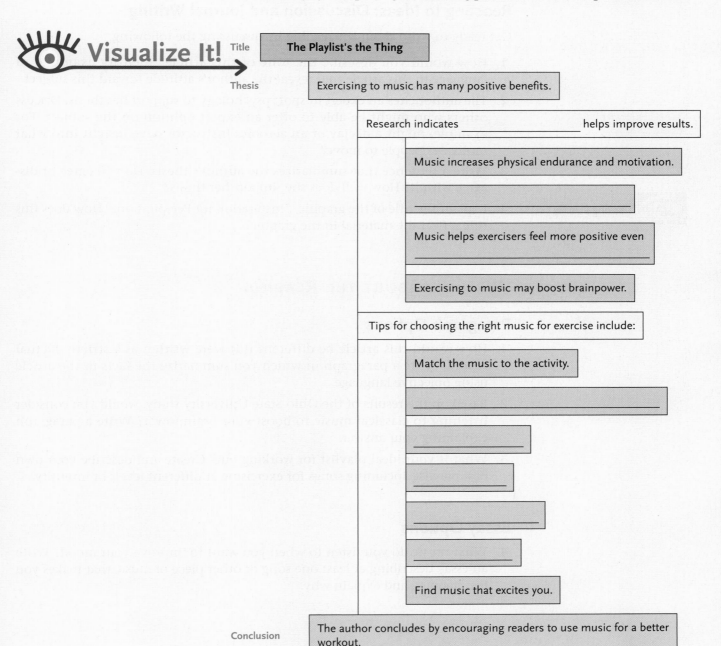

Visualize It!

Title **The Playlist's the Thing**

Thesis Exercising to music has many positive benefits.

Research indicates _____ helps improve results.

Music increases physical endurance and motivation.

_____

Music helps exercisers feel more positive even _____

Exercising to music may boost brainpower.

Tips for choosing the right music for exercise include:

Match the music to the activity.

_____

_____

_____

_____

_____

Find music that excites you.

Conclusion The author concludes by encouraging readers to use music for a better workout.

Strengthening Your Vocabulary

Using the word's context, word parts, or a dictionary, write a brief definition of each of the following words as it is used in the reading.

1. disclosure (paragraph 1) _____
2. fluency (paragraph 4) _____
3. marry (paragraph 5) _____
4. gauge (paragraph 5) _____
5. affirmations (paragraph 5) _____
6. evoke (paragraph 5) _____

Reacting to Ideas: Discussion and Journal Writing

Get ready to write about the reading by discussing the following:

1. How would you describe the tone of this article? Identify examples of language in this article that reveal the author's attitude toward this subject.

2. The author cites an expert in sport psychology to support her thesis. Discuss others who might be able to offer an expert opinion on the subject. For example, might a deejay or an aerobics instructor have insight into what motivates people to move?

3. Write a sentence that summarizes the author's thesis. Do you agree or disagree with it? How well does she support her thesis?

 **Thinking Visually**   4. Explain the title of the graphic, "Inspiration for Perspiration." How does this title reflect the material in the graphic?

WRITING ABOUT THE READING

Paragraph Options

1. How would this article be different if it were written as a strictly factual report? Write a paragraph in which you summarize the facts in the article using objective language.

2. Based on the results of the Ohio State University study, would you consider listening to classical music to boost your brainpower? Write a paragraph explaining your answer.

3. What is your ideal playlist for working out? Create and describe your own best playlist, including songs for exercising at different levels of intensity.

Essay Options

4. What music do you listen to when you want to improve your mood? Write an essay describing at least one song or other piece of music that makes you feel happier, and explain why.

5. This article points to the importance of positive lyrics as affirmations when working out. Write an essay about a song that has meaningful, positive lyrics that help motivate you or improve your mood.

6. Do you seem to work better when you are listening to music, or do you prefer silence? Write an essay exploring the types of tasks or activities that are enhanced by music or sound, and those that are best accomplished in silence.

CHAPTER REVIEW AND PRACTICE

CHAPTER REVIEW

To review and check your recall of the chapter, match each term in Column A with its meaning in Column B.

COLUMN A

_____ 1. independent clause

_____ 2. dependent clause

_____ 3. conjunctive adverb

_____ 4. coordinating conjunction

_____ 5. semicolon

_____ 6. subordinating conjunction

_____ 7. simple sentence

_____ 8. compound sentence

_____ 9. complex sentence

_____ 10. compound-complex sentence

COLUMN B

a. a sentence containing one dependent and one independent clause

b. a word used to begin dependent clauses

c. a group of words containing a subject and verb that can stand alone in a sentence

d. a sentence containing one independent clause

e. a sentence containing two or more independent clauses and one or more dependent clauses

f. a word used with a comma to join two independent clauses

g. a word used with a semicolon to join two equally important ideas

h. a group of words containing a subject and verb that cannot stand alone as a sentence

i. a punctuation mark used to join two independent clauses

j. a sentence containing two or more independent clauses

EDITING PRACTICE

The following student paragraph has had all errors corrected, but it consists mainly of simple sentences and lacks details. Revise it by expanding or combining the sentences.

Many people are homeless. Our country has a problem. Now is the time for the government to take action on the problem of homelessness. The media have focused a great deal of attention on the homeless. This has been happening for the past several years. Many college campuses have been holding "sleepouts." These call attention to the problems of the homeless. Religious groups have been trying to help. They have been opening shelters for them. Still, this is not enough. The problem is only getting worse. The government needs to be pushed to do something about this problem now. Students should write their government officials. Religious groups should put pressure on members of Congress. They should urge them to act upon the problems of the homeless. Concerned citizens should become involved now. This problem is a disgrace to our country.

PEARSON
mywritinglab

For support in meeting this chapter's objectives, log in to www.mywritinglab.com, go to the Study Plan tab, click on Combining and Expanding Your Ideas and choose Combining Sentences from the list of subtopics. Read and view the videos and resources in the Review Materials section, and then complete the Recall, Apply, and Write exercises in the Activities section. You can check your scores and overall progress by using the Gradebook.

Using Adjectives and Adverbs to Describe

Learning Goals

In this chapter, you will learn how to

GOAL 1 Use adjectives to add descriptive details

GOAL 2 Use adverbs to describe actions more vividly

GOAL 3 Use adjectives and adverbs to make comparisons

WRITE ABOUT IT!

Study the photo above and then write a few sentences that describe it in detail.

Some of the words you wrote are probably adjectives—words that describe a noun or pronoun. In this chapter you will learn to use adjectives and adverbs. Adverbs are words that describe verbs or other adverbs. You will see how they are essential to effective communication and how to use them to make your sentences lively and interesting.

WRITING

USING ADJECTIVES TO DESCRIBE

GOAL 1 Use adjectives to add descriptive details

mywritinglab

To practice using adjectives, go to
■ Study Plan
■ Sentence Basics
■ Adjectives

Adjectives describe nouns and pronouns. Notice that the following sample student paragraph uses very few adjectives.

Sample Paragraph

> The congregation had just finished singing a hymn as the minister stepped up to the pulpit. Just as the man asked the congregation to pray, a boy screamed. The grandmother tried to calm the child as she placed a hand over the lips of the child. The child obviously didn't enjoy this because he bit her hand. The minister continued with the prayer and tried to ignore the cries of the boy. Somehow the boy slipped away from the grip of the grandmother and ran down the aisle to the front of the church. The minister walked down from the pulpit and picked up the child. "Lord," he said as he continued the prayer, "help all the children of this world and bless all of the grandmothers, ministers, and members of the congregation who have to put up with them! Amen." With that he ended the service.

This paragraph, which contains no adjectives, gives the bare bones of an interesting story, but how well does it enable you to visualize the people involved? Adjectives give you details about the nouns and pronouns they modify. They can add four kinds of information to your writing:

WHICH?	the <u>young</u> man, the <u>largest</u> stove
WHOSE?	<u>Sam's</u> application, <u>my</u> mug
WHAT KIND?	the <u>job</u> interviewer, the <u>traffic</u> helicopter
HOW MANY?	<u>thirty</u> résumés, <u>no</u> cookies

Thus, we say that adjectives *describe* and *identify* (which? whose?), *qualify* (what kind?), or *limit* (how many?) nouns and pronouns. (For more on adjectives, see Part VIII, "Reviewing the Basics," p. 560.) The following revised version of the above paragraph uses adjectives (underlined) to add interesting and important information.

Revised Paragraph

> The congregation had just finished singing a <u>sacred</u> hymn as the <u>tall</u>, <u>young</u> minister stepped up to the <u>well-lit</u> pulpit. Just as the man asked the <u>reverent</u> congregation to pray, a <u>red-headed</u>, <u>four-year-old</u> boy screamed. His <u>embarrassed</u> grandmother tried to calm the <u>angry</u> child as she placed a <u>firm</u> hand over his <u>quivering</u> lips. The <u>squirming</u> child obviously didn't enjoy this because he bit his <u>grandmother's</u> hand. The <u>calm</u> minister continued with the prayer and tried to ignore the <u>little</u> boy's <u>loud</u>, <u>shrill</u> cries. Somehow, the <u>determined</u>, <u>tearful</u> boy slipped away from his grandmother's <u>firm</u> grip and ran down the <u>long center</u> aisle to the front of the church. The <u>patient</u> minister walked down from the pulpit and picked up the <u>screaming</u> child. "Lord," he said as he continued the prayer, "help all the children of this world and bless all of the <u>loving</u> grandmothers, <u>patient</u> ministers, and <u>long-suffering</u> members of the congregation who have to put up with them! Amen." With that he ended the service.

| EXERCISE 7-1
Working Together | **Writing Adjectives** |

Directions: *The Adjective Contest:* The time limit for this exercise is three minutes. List as many positive adjectives as you can that describe one of your instructors. This is your chance to flatter an instructor! Exchange lists with a partner, verify that each word listed is an adjective, and count the words on the list. The winner is the student who has listed the most positive adjectives.

"The face of the pear-shaped man reminded me of the mashed turnips that Aunt Mildred used to serve alongside the Thanksgiving turkey. As he got out of the strawberry-hued car, his immense fists looked like two slabs of slightly gnawed ham. He waddled over to the counter and snarled at me under his lasagna-laden breath, 'Something, my little bonbon, is fishy in Denmark.' Slowly, I lowered my grilled cheese sandwich . . ."

Using Adjectives Correctly

To use adjectives effectively, you must also use them correctly. Keep the following points in mind:

1. **Adjectives are usually placed in front of the word they describe.**

   the <u>wet</u> raincoat

   the <u>purple</u> dragon

2. **An adjective can follow a <u>linking verb</u>, such as *be, seem,* or *feel.*** A linking verb expresses a state of being.

   Serafina seems <u>sleepy</u>. [*Sleepy* describes Serafina.]

   The room was <u>warm</u>. [*Warm* describes the room.]

3. **Several adjectives can describe the same noun or pronoun.**

   <u>George's</u> <u>three</u> <u>biology</u> assignments

   the <u>worn</u>, <u>ragged</u> <u>denim</u> jacket

4. **When two or more adjectives describe the same noun or pronoun, there are specific rules concerning when to use a comma between the adjectives.**

   • First, *never* place a comma between an adjective and the noun or pronoun it describes.

Tip for Writers

A verb is called a *linking verb* when its subject and the information following the verb both refer to the same person, place, or thing. The word(s) after the linking verb describe or rename the subject.

Joe <u>seems</u> <u>nice</u>. (linking verb + adjective)

Joe <u>is</u> <u>an accountant</u>. (linking verb + noun)

Verbs of sensory perception (taste, smell, etc.) often (but not always) function as linking verbs.

This cake <u>tastes</u> <u>delicious</u>. (linking verb + adjective)

Sam <u>tasted</u> the cake. (In this sentence, <u>tasted</u> is not a linking verb. Sam isn't the cake.)

no comma

a soft-spoken, understanding|counselor

no comma

an interesting, appealing|job

- *Do* place a comma between two adjectives when each describes the same noun (or pronoun) separately.

comma

a soft-spoken, understanding counselor

- *Do not* place a comma between two adjectives when the adjective closest to the noun (or pronoun) describes the noun and the other adjective describes the combination of those two words.

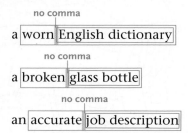

Use the following test to decide whether you need to place a comma between two adjectives: if the word *and* makes sense when placed between the two adjectives, a comma is needed.

MAKES SENSE	a soft-spoken <u>and</u> understanding counselor
USE A COMMA	a soft-spoken, understanding counselor
DOES NOT MAKE SENSE	a new <u>and</u> Mexican restaurant
DO NOT USE A COMMA	a new Mexican restaurant

EXERCISE 7-2   Adding Commas

Directions: If needed, add commas to each of the following phrases.

EXAMPLE   the lazy, sleepy pot-bellied pig

1. an elderly California senator

2. the gentle quiet waves

3. a folded used newspaper

4. the dedicated cancer specialist

5. the sharp cat's claw

6. valuable family photographs

7. a weathered twisted pine tree

8. excited happy children

9. brown leather wallet

10. worthless costume jewelry ■

NEED TO KNOW

Adjectives

- **Adjectives** describe nouns and pronouns.
- An **adjective** is usually placed before the word it describes.
- An **adjective** can follow a linking verb.
- Use **adjectives** to add interest and detail to your sentences.

Using Adjectives to Expand Sentences

Adjectives are powerful words. They can create vivid pictures and impressions in the mind of your reader. Consider the following sentence:

EXAMPLE   The applicant greeted the interviewer.

This sentence has two nouns: *applicant* and *interviewer*. Without adjectives, however, what do we know about them or the situation? With adjectives, the same sentence becomes more informative.

REVISED   The <u>eager</u>, <u>excited</u> applicant greeted the <u>friendly</u>, <u>welcoming</u> <u>job</u> interviewer.

REVISED   The <u>nervous</u>, <u>insecure</u> applicant greeted the <u>cool</u>, <u>polished</u> <u>job</u> interviewer.

Now can you imagine the people and the situation each sentence describes? Let's take another sentence and expand it several ways by using adjectives.

EXAMPLE   The building houses the lab.

REVISED   The <u>ivy-covered</u> <u>brick</u> building houses the <u>well-equipped</u>, <u>up-to-date</u> <u>biology</u> lab.

REVISED   The <u>dilapidated</u>, <u>unpainted</u> building houses the <u>time-worn</u>, <u>outdated</u> <u>biology</u> lab.

As you can see from the examples above, you can drastically alter and expand your meaning by using adjectives. Think of adjectives as words that allow you to choose details that create the impression you want to convey.

EXERCISE 7-3   Expanding and Revising Sentences Using Adjectives

Directions: Expand and revise each of the following sentences in two different ways by adding adjectives. Each of your two revisions should create a different impression. Underline your adjectives.

EXAMPLE   The interviewer asked Julie a question.

REVISED   The <u>skillful</u> interviewer asked Julie an <u>indirect</u> question.

REVISED   The <u>young</u>, <u>inexperienced</u> interviewer asked Julie a <u>personal</u> question.

1. Mr. Lindgren's parrot was able to speak several words.

   a. _____

   b. _____

2. The department store made sales.

   a. _____

   b. _____

3. The Wildlife Rehabilitation Center sponsored an exhibit.

   a. _____

   b. _____

4. A professor published an article on campus reform.

   a. _____

   b. _____

5. The chef prepared a dish.

   a. _____

   b. _____

6. The diner serves food throughout the night.

   a. _____

   b. _____

7. The disc jockey plays music.

   a. _____

   b. _____

8. The book was read by each member of the club.

   a. _____

   b. _____

9. The newspaper lay on the table.

   a. _____

   b. _____

10. The teacher calmed the child by showing her books.

   a. _____

   b. _____

■

■ **EXERCISE 7-4**   **Revising by Adding Adjectives**

Directions: Rewrite the following paragraph by adding adjectives. You can also add new phrases and sentences anywhere in the paragraph—beginning, middle, or end—as long as they have adjectives in them. Underline the adjectives.

> I had been looking forward to my vacation for months. I was going to lie on the beach all day and dance all night. I didn't get off to a good start. On the flight to Miami, I had the middle seat between a big man and a mother with a baby. Then we sat on the ground for two hours because of fog. It was hot and noisy. When we did get off the ground, the flight was very bumpy. Finally we got to Miami. I waited and waited for my suitcase. Needless to say, it didn't arrive. I could just picture all my new clothes sitting in some other city. Actually, though, all I needed for my week in Miami was a raincoat, because it rained every day. I didn't need my party clothes either because the first morning, I slipped getting out of the shower and sprained my ankle. I need a vacation from my vacation. ■

■ **EXERCISE 7-5**   **Writing Using Adjectives**

Directions: Write a paragraph on one of the following topics. After you have written your first draft, revise your paragraph by adding adjectives. Underline your adjectives.

1. A full- or part-time job you held

2. A trip you took

3. A valued possession

4. Searching for _____

5. Interviewing for _____ ■

USING ADVERBS TO DESCRIBE

GOAL 2 Use adverbs to describe actions more vividly

To practice using adverbs, go to
■ Study Plan
■ Sentence Basics
■ Adverbs

Adverbs describe, qualify, or limit verbs, adjectives, or other adverbs. The following paragraph uses no adverbs:

Sample Paragraph

> The old door opened on its rusty hinges. A young woman entered the attic. She searched for the box of costumes. She saw a carton on the shelf across the room. She lifted the box and undid its dusty strings. She opened it. She began laughing. A huge chicken costume was in the box!

Did this paragraph give you enough details to visualize the scene? Imagine you are directing this scene in a movie: How would the rusty door hinges sound? How would the young woman walk when she entered the attic? Where would she look for the costumes? Adverbs give you details about the verbs, adjectives, and other adverbs they modify.

Adverbs can add five kinds of information to your writing:

HOW?	He announced his intentions <u>cautiously</u>.
WHEN?	We will leave <u>tomorrow.</u>
WHERE?	We searched <u>everywhere</u>.
HOW OFTEN?	I exercise <u>daily</u>.
TO WHAT EXTENT?	The caller was <u>very</u> polite.

The following revised version of the above paragraph uses adverbs to add details that let you visualize the scene more fully:

Revised Paragraph

The old door opened <u>creakily</u> on its rusty hinges. A young woman <u>quickly</u> entered the attic. She searched <u>everywhere</u> for the box of costumes. <u>Finally</u>, she saw a carton on the shelf across the room. <u>Gingerly</u>, she lifted the box down and undid its dusty strings. <u>Very carefully</u>, she opened it. She began laughing <u>gleefully</u>. A huge chicken costume was in the box!

From this revision, you can see that adverbs help bring actions alive.

EXERCISE 7-6
Working Together

Writing Adverbs

Directions: *The Adverb Contest:* The time limit for this exercise is ten minutes. Expand the "attic" paragraph above and see how many more adverbs you can add. You can add new phrases and sentences anywhere in the present paragraph—beginning, middle, or end—as long as they have adverbs in them. Underline your adverbs and exchange your expanded story with a partner to verify how many adverbs you have added. The winner is the student who has added the most adverbs. ■

Using Adverbs Correctly

To use adverbs effectively, you must also use them correctly. Keep the following points in mind:

1. **Many adverbs end in -ly.** Some do not, however, such as *often, now, always*, and *not*. To determine whether a word is an adverb, look at how it functions in your sentence.

2. **Adverbs can modify verbs, adjectives, or other adverbs.**

- Here is an adverb describing a verb (a verb expresses action or state of being):

verb

Clara <u>patiently</u> waited for the appointment.

verb

The building crumbled <u>quickly</u>.

verb

The winning team <u>proudly</u> watched the DVD of the playoff game.

- Here is an adverb describing an adjective (an adjective modifies a noun or pronoun):

  adjective

  An extremely long interview is tiring.

  adjective

  The reporters asked briskly efficient questions.

  adjective

  Microscopically small plankton live in the ocean.

- Here is an adverb describing another adverb:

  adverb

  Read a want ad very carefully.

  adverb

  Microscopes allow one to view an object more closely.

  adverb

  The automated door opened quite easily.

3. **Adverbs can be placed almost anywhere in a sentence.** Three common placements are:

AT THE BEGINNING OF THE SENTENCE	Briefly, Mark explained.
IN FRONT OF THE VERB	Mark briefly explained.
AFTER THE VERB	Mark explained briefly.

4. **Adverbs should be followed by a comma only when they begin a sentence.**

   comma

   Slowly, Jim walked into the reception area.

   comma

   Cautiously, he asked to see Mr. Stoneface.

   When adverbs are used elsewhere in a sentence, they are *not* set off by commas.

   no comma   no comma

   Jim walked slowly into the reception area.

   no comma   no comma

   He cautiously asked to see Mr. Stoneface.

Using Adverbs to Expand Sentences

Like adjectives, adverbs are powerful words. Adverbs can create a more complete impression of the action within a sentence. Consider the following sentence and its two revisions:

EXAMPLE	The car runs.
REVISED	The car runs smoothly.
REVISED	The car runs haltingly.

In one revised sentence, the car runs well; in the other revision, the car barely runs at all. Notice how adverbs, like adjectives, let you change the meaning of a sentence.

In the following examples, adverbs provide extra details about the action:

EXAMPLE   The president prepared his State of the Union address.

                         adverb   adverb   adverb
                           | | |
REVISED   The president very carefully and thoroughly prepared his State of the Union address.

EXAMPLE   The swim team accepted the gold medal.

                   adverb   adverb
                     | |
REVISED   Proudly and excitedly, the swim team accepted the gold medal.

Like adjectives, adverbs allow you to choose details that expand your sentences and refine your meaning.

NEED TO KNOW

Adverbs

- **Adverbs** qualify or limit verbs, adjectives, or other adverbs.
- Many adverbs end in *-ly,* but some do not.
- Use a comma after an adverb only when the adverb begins the sentence.
- Use adverbs to qualify and expand your ideas.

EXERCISE 7-7   Expanding and Revising Sentences Using Adverbs

Directions: Expand and revise each of the following sentences in two different ways by adding adverbs. Each revision should create a different impression. Underline your adverbs.

EXAMPLE   The employment agency lists hundreds of management positions.

REVISED   The employment agency usually lists hundreds of management positions.

REVISED   The employment agency seldom lists hundreds of management positions.

1. The gymnast performed his routine.

    a. _____

    b. _____

2. The chemistry experiment was completed.

    a. _____

    b. _____

3. Botanists study newly discovered plant life.

   a. _____

   b. _____

4. The furniture in our office breaks.

   a. _____

   b. _____

5. The businesspeople in my office use cell phones.

   a. _____

   b. _____

6. The professor will post the exam grades.

   a. _____

   b. _____

7. Mirrors should be handled carefully.

   a. _____

   b. _____

8. Many people lived through the Depression.

   a. _____

   b. _____

9. Seat belts have saved thousands of lives.

   a. _____

   b. _____

10. The boat left the dock.

   a. _____

   b. _____
   ■

EXERCISE 7-8   Writing and Revising Using Adverbs

Directions: Write a paragraph on one of the following topics. After you have written your first draft, revise your paragraph by adding adverbs. Underline your adverbs.

1. A long-lasting or vivid memory

2. The lack of privacy in apartments

3. How to make a(n) _____

4. Learning to _____

5. How to avoid _____ ■

EXERCISE 7-9   Revising Using Adjectives and Adverbs

Directions: Rewrite the following paragraph by adding adjectives and adverbs. You can also add phrases and sentences anywhere in the beginning, middle, or end of the paragraph, as long as they have adjectives and adverbs in them. Underline the adjectives and circle the adverbs.

> Every family has someone who's eccentric—someone who's lovable but strange. In my family, that's Aunt Irma. Aunt Irma lives in an apartment filled with souvenirs from her many trips. She has souvenirs of all kinds—big and small—from everywhere in the world. If you want to sit down at Aunt Irma's, you have to move a souvenir, and probably what you're sitting on is a souvenir, too. Aunt Irma also has unusual eating habits. She eats only soup and sandwiches. She always makes her own soups, and they are unusual. The sandwiches are strange, too. You'll never see one on a menu. Aunt Irma is also an exercise nut. She has several sets of weights in different rooms. She runs in place whenever she watches TV. Finally, Aunt Irma has a distinctive way of dressing. I have seen her wear some really strange outfits. But she is lovable and, when all's said and done, what would we do without Aunt Irma stories? ■

USING ADJECTIVES AND ADVERBS TO COMPARE

GOAL 3 Use adjectives and adverbs to make comparisons

Adjectives and adverbs modify, describe, explain, qualify, or restrict the words they modify. **Adjectives** modify nouns and pronouns. **Adverbs** modify verbs, adjectives, and other adverbs; adverbs can also modify phrases, clauses, or whole sentences.

ADJECTIVES   the red car; the quiet one

ADVERBS   quickly finish; only four reasons; very angrily

Comparison Using Adjectives and Adverbs

1. **Positive** adjectives and adverbs modify but do not involve any comparison: *green, bright, lively.*

2. **Comparative** adjectives and adverbs compare two persons, things, actions, or ideas.

   COMPARATIVE ADJECTIVE   Michael is taller than Phoebe.

   COMPARATIVE ADVERB   Antonio reacted more calmly than Robert.

   Here is how to form comparative adjectives and adverbs. (Consult your dictionary if you are unsure of the form of a particular word.)

   • **If the adjective or adverb has one syllable, add** *-er.* **For some two-syllable words, also add** *-er.*

   cold → colder   slow → slower   narrow → narrower

   • **For most words of two or more syllables, place the word** *more* **in front of the word.**

   reasonable → more reasonable   interestingly → more interestingly

- **For two-syllable adjectives ending in -*y*, change the -*y* to -*i* and add -*er*.**

drowsy → drowsier   lazy → lazier

3. **Superlative** adjectives and adverbs compare more than two persons, things, actions, or ideas.

SUPERLATIVE ADJECTIVE   Michael is the <u>tallest</u> member of the team.

SUPERLATIVE ADVERB   Of everyone in the class, she studied the <u>most</u> <u>diligently</u> for the test.

Here is how to form superlative adjectives and adverbs:

- **Add -*est* to one-syllable adjectives and adverbs and to some two-syllable words.**

cold → coldest   slow → slowest   narrow → narrowest

- **For most words of two or more syllables, place the word *most* in front of the word.**

reasonable → most reasonable   interestingly → most interestingly

- **For two-syllable adjectives ending in -*y*, change the -*y* to -*i* and add -*est*.**

drowsy → drowsiest   lazy → laziest

EXERCISE 7-10   Using Adjectives and Adverbs

Directions: Fill in the blank with the comparative form of the adjective or adverb given.

1. seriously   Mary was injured _____ than Tom.
2. lively   I feel a lot _____ than I did yesterday.
3. pretty   This bouquet of flowers is _____ than that one.
4. interesting   My biology teacher is _____ than my history teacher.
5. softly   Speak _____, or you'll wake the baby. ■

EXERCISE 7-11   Using Adjectives and Adverbs

Directions: Fill in the blank with the superlative form of the adjective or adverb given.

1. beautiful   It was the _____ wedding I'd ever seen.
2. slow   I always get in the _____ checkout line at the grocery store.
3. early   This is the _____ Jana has ever arrived.
4. difficult   That is the _____ trick the magician performs.
5. loud   It was by far the _____ band that played last Saturday. ■

Irregular Adjectives and Adverbs

Some adjectives and adverbs form their comparative and superlative forms in irregular ways.

<table>
<tr><td>Positive</td><td>Comparative</td><td>Superlative</td></tr>
<tr><td colspan="3">Adjectives</td></tr>
<tr><td>good</td><td>better</td><td>best</td></tr>
<tr><td>bad</td><td>worse</td><td>worst</td></tr>
<tr><td>little</td><td>littler, less</td><td>littlest, least</td></tr>
<tr><td colspan="3">Adverbs</td></tr>
<tr><td>well</td><td>better</td><td>best</td></tr>
<tr><td>badly</td><td>worse</td><td>worst</td></tr>
<tr><td colspan="3">Adjectives and Adverbs</td></tr>
<tr><td>many</td><td>more</td><td>most</td></tr>
<tr><td>some</td><td>more</td><td>most</td></tr>
<tr><td>much</td><td>more</td><td>most</td></tr>
</table>

Tip for Writers

Littler and *littlest* are used to describe size. *Less* and *least* describe amounts.

Joe is the <u>littlest boy</u> in his class.

I have <u>less money</u> than I had last week.

EXERCISE 7-12   Using Adjectives and Adverbs

Directions: Fill in the blanks with the correct positive, comparative, or superlative form of the adjective or adverb given.

1. good   Bob's barbecue sauce is _____ than Shawna's, but I think Leo's recipe is the _____ of all.

2. little   Please give me just a _____ piece of pie. You can give me even _____ ice cream.

3. well   I don't feel _____ today, but I'm still _____ than I was yesterday.

4. much   I have _____ homework this semester than last semester. Of all my classes, I get the _____ homework in math.

5. bad   It rained _____ on Thursday than on Friday, but it rained the _____ on Saturday. ■

Common Mistakes to Avoid

1. **Do not use adjectives to modify verbs, other adjectives, or adverbs.**

   INCORRECT   Peter and Mary take each other <u>serious</u>.

   CORRECT   Peter and Mary take each other <u>seriously</u>. [Modifies the verb *take*.]

2. **Do not use the adjectives *good* and *bad* when you should use the adverbs *well* and *badly*.**

   INCORRECT   Juan did <u>good</u> on the exam.

   CORRECT   Juan did <u>well</u> on the exam. [Modifies the verb *did*.]

3. **Do not use the adjectives *real* and *sure* when you should use the adverbs *really* and *surely*.**

   INCORRECT   Jan scored <u>real</u> well on the exam.

   CORRECT   Jan scored <u>really</u> well on the exam. [Modifies the verb *well*.]

   INCORRECT   I <u>sure</u> was surprised to win the lottery.

   CORRECT   I <u>surely</u> was surprised to win the lottery. [Modifies the verb *was surprised*.]

4. **Do not use *more* or *most* with the *-er* or *-est* form of an adjective or adverb.** Use one form or the other, according to the rules above.

   INCORRECT   That was the <u>most tastiest</u> dinner I've ever eaten.

   CORRECT   That was the <u>tastiest</u> dinner I've ever eaten.

5. **Avoid double negatives—that is, two negatives in the same clause.**

   INCORRECT   He did <u>not</u> want <u>nothing</u> in the refrigerator.

   CORRECT   He did <u>not</u> want <u>anything</u> in the refrigerator.

6. **When using the comparative and superlative forms of adverbs, do not create an incomplete comparison.**

   INCORRECT   The heater works more <u>efficiently</u>. [More efficiently than what?]

   CORRECT   The heater works <u>more efficiently than it did before we had it repaired</u>.

7. **Do not use the comparative or superlative form for adjectives and adverbs that have no degree.** It is incorrect to write, for example, *more square, most perfect, more equally,* or *most unique*. Do not use a comparative or superlative form for any of the following adjectives and adverbs:

Adjectives				
complete	equal	infinite	pregnant	unique
dead	eternal	invisible	square	universal
empty	favorite	matchless	supreme	vertical
endless	impossible	parallel	unanimous	whole

Adverbs		
endlessly	infinitely	uniquely
equally	invisibly	universally
eternally	perpendicularly	
impossibly	straight	

▌ EXERCISE 7-13   Revising Adjective and Adverb Use

Directions: Revise each of the following sentences so that all adjectives and adverbs are used correctly.

EXAMPLE   I answered the question polite. (ly)

1. Matteo's apartment was more expensive.

2. When I heard the man and woman sing the duet, I decided that the woman sang best.

3. Our local movie reviewer said that the film's theme song sounded badly.

4. The roller coaster was excitinger than the merry-go-round.

5. *The Scarlet Letter* is more good than *War and Peace*.

6. Lia sure gave a rousing speech.

7. Last week's storm seemed badder than a tornado.

8. Some women thought that the Equal Rights Amendment would guarantee that women would be treated more equally.

9. Taking the interstate is the more fast route to the outlet mall.

10. Professor Reed had the better lecture style of all my instructors. ■

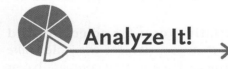 Analyze It!

Directions: Revise the following paragraph by adding adjectives and adverbs. You can also add phrases and sentences anywhere in the beginning, middle, or end of the paragraph, as long as they have adjectives or adverbs in them. Underline the adjectives and circle the adverbs.

When I think back on all my college professors, one stands out as the best. His name was Thomas P. Meyerson, but he was known as Professor M. His lectures were legendary; every student seemed to have at least one story about Professor M's teaching style. I was fortunate to take the last American history class he taught before retiring. At that time, he still had a full head of hair and a moustache with waxed tips. He always wore a suit and tie, with a handkerchief spilling from his pocket. For a lecture on the Revolution, he donned the type of hat worn during that period. For a lecture on Abraham Lincoln, he showed up wearing a stovepipe hat. During a presentation about Civil War battles, he flourished a sword. His lectures were not only entertaining but also educational, as his voice and teaching style brought the past to life, leaving me with images as well as knowledge.

A STUDENT ESSAY
The Student Writer and the Writing Task

The Student Writer

When Gentry Carlson graduated from high school, he joined the Marines. After four years of service, he worked as an automation technician and then decided to attend Itasca College to pursue a career in forestry.

The Writing Task

For his writing class, Carlson was asked to write an essay describing a memorable experience. As you read, note how he uses adjectives and adverbs to make his essay engaging and interesting. In the first two paragraphs the adjectives are underlined and the adverbs are circled.

The Longest Day
Gentry Carlson

Thesis statement	1	My first day in Marine boot camp is a day I'll never forget. From fear of the unknown to the ridiculous antics of the drill instructors, it was an experience I don't believe I want to go through again.
Carlson builds suspense	2	The very first moment while quietly waiting at the San Diego airport was an eerie feeling in itself. All of us Marine Corps recruits were patiently waiting for something to happen, but what? We all waited in fear of the unknown. Then, all of a sudden, I could hear squeaky air brakes. Those air brakes belonged to three large white school buses that had U.S. Marine Corps etched on the side. The time had come; this is what we'd been waiting for.
Series of events begins	3	It was night; we sat quietly as the buses drove us to our new home, where we would live for the next three months. Our fears increased as we rolled into the Marine Corps recruit depot in San Diego. The bus stopped. Again, we all waited for the next thing to happen. All of a sudden, the door flew open; we had entered the life of a Marine Corps recruit.
Suspense builds again		
Series of events continues	4	A dark-complexioned man with razor-sharp creases in his shirt and pants appeared before us. He told us in a commanding tone to quickly, but safely, exit the bus and to find a yellow set of footprints. Upon his command, we all hurriedly exited the bus. After loads of mass confusion, we managed to find our set of yellow footprints. The senior drill instructor proceeded to tell us our agenda for the night.

Next event

Details add interest

5   The agenda he spoke of was not the most appealing. First, we had to sit in a room for about three hours in a time of amnesty, to get rid of anything that's not allowed in boot camp, including cigarettes, candy, lighters, watches, and pictures of our girlfriends. Next, we were given our first military haircut. We lined up in a long line; there were about 120 of us. All of us stood heel to toe with each other, staring at the back of the head of the guy in front of us. Moving, talking, or flinching were all prohibited. I was near the front of the line, so I did not have a long wait. I sat down in the chair; within 60 seconds, I was sheared to the scalp. I had an urge to feel my shaved head, but I did not, due to the fact that a number of the recruits already got chewed out for doing it. Our next stop was supply.

Next event

Details make situation
seem real

6   Once again, we were lined up heel to toe, staring into the back of the head of the guy in front of us as we waited to receive our military issue. Quickly, we shuffled through the line as we yelled out our sizes for everything from our socks up to our cover (Marine Corps jargon for hat). Most of the gear we received was one or two sizes too large. Finally, we got to take a break; we all sat (very quietly) in this large room, trying our best to stay awake. We had no idea what day it was, what time it was; most of us had to be thinking, what the hell am I doing this for? I want to go home!

Next event

7   Finally, the last phase of the day was upon us; it was time to shuffle on to sick bay and get a few shots. Of course, like always, we all formed a long line again, heel to toe, staring at the shaved head in front of us. We went through what seemed to be a gauntlet of shots. One shot in the left arm, one in the right, then two to three more in the left, a couple more in the right, and more and more. Either a needle gun or regular needle was the weapon of choice. Meanwhile, every now and then, someone would pass out; I thought that was hilarious. Finally, to top it all off (or to bottom it all off), we all received one in each cheek of our behinds!

Conclusion

8   After the shots, we headed back to the barracks, each of us praying that we could hit the rack. We were all in such disarray. They shaved us, shot us, and dressed us in white T-shirts, camouflage pants, and tennis shoes, and made us act and look like idiots. This was a long day that I will never forget because it took almost three days to complete.

EXAMINING STUDENT WRITING

1. Underline all the adjectives used in the remainder of the essay.
2. Circle all the adverbs in the remainder of the essay.
3. Try reading the essay by skipping over all the adjectives and adverbs you underlined and circled. How does the essay change?
4. How did Carlson organize his essay?
5. Evaluate the amount of background information Carlson gives at the opening of his essay. Is more needed?
6. Carlson builds suspense throughout the essay. How is this useful?

Paragraph Writing Scenarios

Friends and Family

1. Every family has its own rituals, things they do together over and over again. Write a paragraph on one ritual your family has. It can be the way you practice your religion, share a weekly meal, or celebrate a particular holiday.

2. Write a paragraph that begins with the topic sentence: "My ideal day with my family would be. . . ."

Classes and Campus Life

1. Think of one task you have trouble with in school. Write a paragraph about what makes it difficult.

2. Do you procrastinate or get right to work on your assignments? Write a paragraph that describes the way you approach homework.

Working Students

1. Write a paragraph on what makes good customer service. What personality traits do you have that would make you a good or a poor customer service representative?

2. Write a paragraph describing what you wear to work. Even if it's as simple as a T-shirt and jeans, use plenty of details.

Communities and Cultures

1. Choose a hobby, activity, or interest that introduced you into a new community. What else, if anything, did you have in common with the members of this group?

2. Describe an article of clothing or a fashion trend that came out of a particular culture and is now worn by people of all different cultures.

WRITING ABOUT A READING

THINKING BEFORE READING

In the following reading, the author describes a recent experience on the subway in New York. As you read, notice Doloff's effective use of adjectives and adverbs. Before you read:

1. Preview the reading, using the steps listed in Chapter 2, p. 35.

2. Connect the reading to your own experience by answering the following questions:

   a. Have you ever heard a norteño group or a mariachi band perform? Where did the performance take place and what was your reaction?

   b. When you ride a bus or subway, what (if any) interactions do you typically have with other passengers?

3. Mark and annotate as you read.

READING

NORTEÑO EN MANHATTAN

Steven Doloff

1   At 14th Street on an "N" train heading uptown one recent Friday morning, a three-man norteño band boarded the half-empty subway car I was riding in. Norteño performers are not mariachi (who wear Mexican-style "charro" outfits and use more instruments, like horns), but rather stylistically different "northern" Mexico musicians. And this was an impressive group: short stocky guys in identical black ten gallon hats, fiery red cowboy shirts, black jeans and polished black cowboy boots. Two had acoustic guitars slung over their backs and the third toted a stubby accordion strapped across his stomach.

2   Maybe 30 seconds after they entered the train and without saying a word, they suddenly launched into a driving rendition of "Cielito Lindo" (you know—"ai, ai, aiai"). They were loud, and really good, and did I mention loud? After about two minutes they stopped dead and just stood there silently while one of them changed the position of the **capo** on the neck of his guitar.

3   At the opposite end of the car, sprawled across the "Priority seating for persons with disabilities" bench, a clearly **inebriated** member of the train's captive audience voiced his even clearer indignation at the intrusive performance by provocatively croaking into the palpable quiet after the band stopped, "Wetbacks!"

4   Given the offensive nature of the term, his timing, and the raspiness of his voice, its effect felt almost as thunderous as the previous song. Everyone (maybe 25 people) stared down the car at the drunk and then more indirectly at the performers, who seemed completely oblivious to the **epithet**. But the dissatisfied audience member was not finished. He proceeded to rant incoherently,

capo
a movable device attached to the fingerboard of a guitar to uniformly raise the pitch of all the strings

inebriated
drunk

epithet
a disparaging or abusive word or phrase

half to the other riders and half to the air, about illegal aliens, unemployment, and the current stock market crisis.

5   The accordion player swiveled on his polished heels to look blankly at the drunk. He then hit a single note on his keyboard and the band again slammed into a pounding version of another Mexican standard. At the 28th Street stop, the irate audience member gave up, got up, and lurched off the train.

6   The band finished their second number as the train pulled out of the station. The accordion player then took off his cowboy hat and, with a broad grin, walked down the car holding it out upside down for contributions. Almost everyone started coughing up money—and lots of it. The accordionist just kept smiling and saying "gracias" for each donation, while the other two musicians impassively reslung their guitars over their shoulders. The last person to drop a bill in the hat, who was sitting next to me, mumbled quietly, "Sorry about that guy . . ."

7   At 34th Street, my stop, they got off the car right in front of me, and as they did, they actually spoke, though not very much. My Spanish is minimal, but I made out two sentences. The accordionist said without the slightest inflection of **irony**, "América es un país muy bueno" ("America's a very good country"), to which one of the guitar players responded, "La segunda canción fue muy rápida" ("The second song was too fast").

irony
sarcasm or mockery

8   I know things are going to be economically rough for a while in this country and in this city too. But if the immigrants who pour into the United States every day have this kind of implacable confidence, so can the rest of us, whose parents or grandparents no doubt came here with much the same resolution.

9   I think we'll be okay.

GETTING READY TO WRITE

Reviewing the Reading

Answer each of the following questions using complete sentences.

1. What is a norteño band? Describe how it is different from a mariachi band.
2. What did the norteño band do after it boarded the subway car?
3. What did the drunken passenger call the norteño band? Describe how the band and the other passengers reacted to the outburst.
4. What happened when the norteño band finished playing and asked for contributions?
5. What two comments did the norteño band members make when they got off the train?

Examining the Reading Using an Idea Map

Review the reading by completing the missing parts of the idea map shown below.

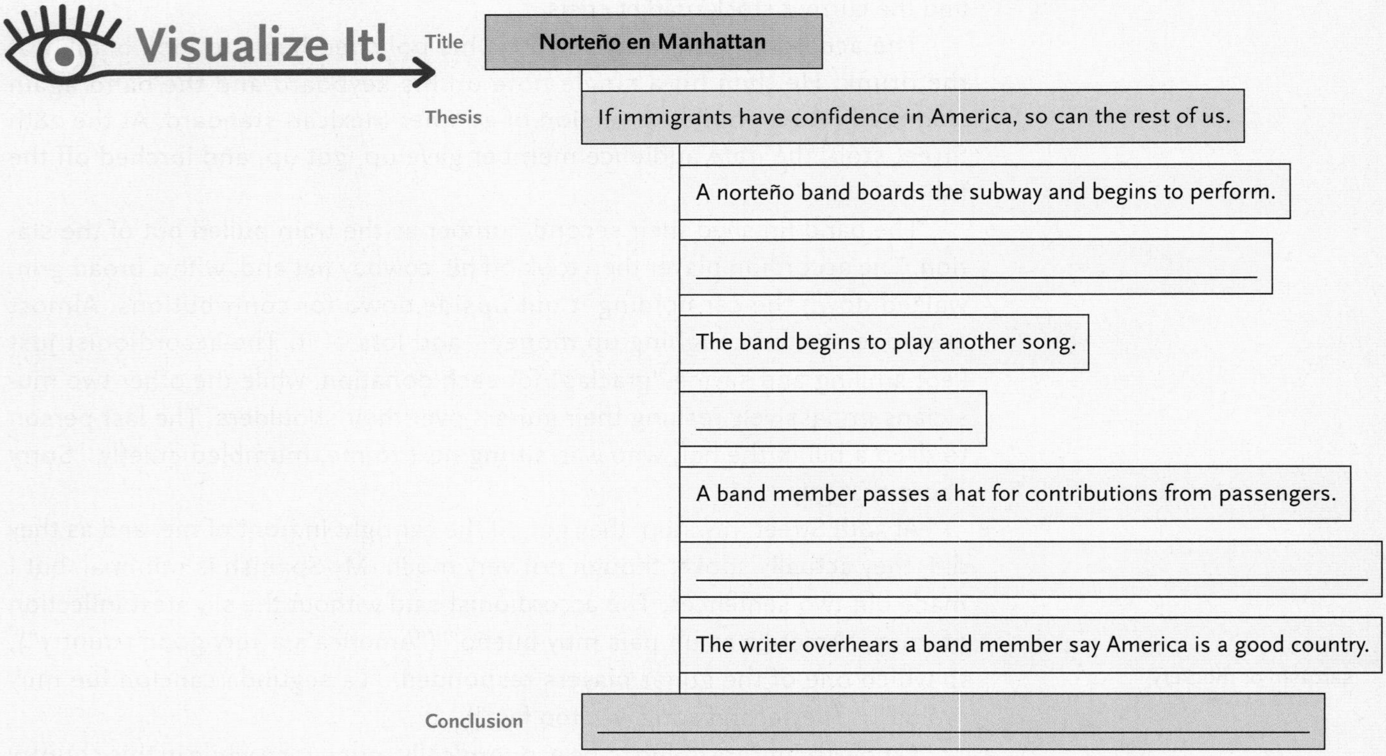

Visualize It!

Title — **Norteño en Manhattan**

Thesis — If immigrants have confidence in America, so can the rest of us.

A norteño band boards the subway and begins to perform.

_____

The band begins to play another song.

_____

A band member passes a hat for contributions from passengers.

_____

The writer overhears a band member say America is a good country.

Conclusion — _____

Strengthening Your Vocabulary

Using the word's context, word parts, or a dictionary, write a brief definition of each of the following words as it is used in the reading.

1. rendition (paragraph 2) _____
2. provocatively (paragraph 3) _____
3. palpable (paragraph 3) _____
4. incoherently (paragraph 4) _____
5. impassively (paragraph 6) _____
6. inflection (paragraph 7) _____
7. implacable (paragraph 8) _____

Reacting to Ideas: Discussion and Journal Writing

Get ready to write about the reading by discussing the following:

1. Consider how the musicians responded to the drunk. Do you think it was the first time they had experienced negative or offensive behavior during a performance? In what ways was the band's response effective?

2. How do you know the other passengers on the subway were more sympathetic to the norteño musicians than to the drunk? Why do you think they were?

3. What was the author's purpose in writing this essay?

4. What effect do you think the setting—a half-empty subway train in Manhattan—has on this story? Discuss how the events might have played out differently in another setting.

5. Consider how the author describes the members of the norteño band. How does that description compare with what he tells the reader about the drunk passenger?

 **Thinking Visually**

6. What aspect of the reading is illustrated by the accompanying photograph? What details do you notice about the photograph that correspond to the reading?

WRITING ABOUT THE READING

Paragraph Options

1. Imagine that you were on the same subway car as the author that day. How would you have reacted to what happened? Write a paragraph describing your response.

2. How would you characterize your interactions with others who behave poorly or inappropriately? Write a paragraph describing how you respond.

3. The drunk's use of the derogatory term *wetbacks* made the other passengers uncomfortable. Think of a time when you heard someone use a disparaging or abusive term and write a paragraph describing your response.

Essay Options

4. What can you tell from this reading about the author's attitudes toward the norteño group and toward the drunk? Write an essay examining the ways in which the author reveals his feelings toward each. Identify specific examples of connotative language that reveal the author's tone, and explain how his tone affects you as the reader.

5. Write an essay describing the same events from the point of view of one of the members of the norteño band.

6. The author uses his experience on the train as a basis for feeling optimistic about the United States. Write an essay explaining whether you agree or disagree with the author's conclusion.

CHAPTER REVIEW AND PRACTICE

CHAPTER REVIEW

To review and check your recall of the chapter, select the word, suffix, or phrase from the box below that best completes each of the following sentences. Keep in mind that eight of the choices will not be used.

in front of	is	is not	*-ly*	end	comparative
adverb	adjective	after	*-ing*	superlative	verbs
begin	lazier	more	lazy	laziest	nouns

1. A(n) _____ is a word that describes a verb, another adjective, or another adverb.

2. A(n) _____ is a word that describes a noun or pronoun.

3. Adjectives usually appear _____ the words they describe.

4. A comma _____ placed between two adjectives that describe the same noun separately.

5. Many adverbs end in _____.

6. Adverbs should be followed by a comma only when they _____ a sentence.

7. _____ adjectives compare two or more things.

8. _____ adjectives compare three or more things.

9. The comparative form of the word *lazy* is _____.

10. The words *good* and *bad* should be used to describe _____.

EDITING PRACTICE

The following student paragraph is correct in every aspect except for the use of adverbs and adjectives. Revise it so that all adverb and adjective problems are corrected.

I am a very impatient person, and my impatience interferes with how easy I can get through a day. For example, when I decide to buy something, such as a new CD, I have to have it right away—that day. I usually drop everything and quick run to the store. Of course, I shortchange myself on studying, and that hurts my grades. My impatience hurts me, too, when I'm waiting for someone, which I hate to do. If my friend Jerome and I agree to meet at noon to work on his car, I get real annoyed if he's even five minutes late. Then I usually end up speaking nasty or sarcastic, saying, "Well, where were *you?*" which I regret later. Perhaps I am the more impatient when I'm behind the steering wheel. If I get behind a slow driver, I get annoyed quick and start honking and beeping my horn. I know this might fluster the other driver, and afterwards I feel guiltily. I've tried talking to myself to calm down. Sometimes it works, so I sure hope I'm overcoming this bad trait.

PEARSON
mywritinglab
For support in meeting this chapter's objectives, log in to www.mywritinglab.com, go to the Study Plan tab, click on Using Adjectives and Adverbs to Describe and choose Adjectives and Adverbs from the list of subtopics. Read and view the videos and resources in the Review Materials section, and then complete the Recall, Apply, and Write exercises in the Activities section. You can check your scores and overall progress by using the Gradebook.

Using Modifiers to Add Detail

Learning Goals

In this chapter, you will learn how to

GOAL 1 Use prepositional phrases to add detail

GOAL 2 Use *-ing* phrases to add detail

GOAL 3 Use relative (*who, which, that*) clauses to add detail

WRITE ABOUT IT!

Compare the two images above. Write a sentence explaining how they differ.

These two images demonstrate what a paragraph looks like without words and phrases that add detail. A paragraph is just a skeleton, as is the first photograph, without words and phrases that explain or change the meaning. In this chapter you will learn to use **modifiers**—words that change or limit the meaning of another word or word group.

WRITING

To further understand the value of modifiers, read this sample paragraph and the revised paragraph that follows it:

Sample Paragraph

Eyes produce tears. Tears wash the eye. Tears clean away dust and germs. People cry sometimes when happy, sad, or in pain. No one knows why. The eye also waters if something touches it or if the person has a cold or other infection. Used tear fluid drains away. It goes to a chamber in the nose. Crying produces a runny nose.

Did this paragraph seem choppy and underdeveloped to you? Now read the revised paragraph below. To add information and improve flow, the writer has used modifiers, such as prepositional phrases, *-ing* phrases, and relative clauses, which are underlined.

Revised Paragraph

Eyes produce tears <u>in the lachrymal glands behind the upper eyelids</u>. <u>Cleaning away dust and germs with every blink</u>, tears wash the eye. <u>For reasons not well understood</u>, people <u>who are happy, sad, or in pain</u> sometimes produce extra tears, <u>which flood down their cheeks</u>. The eye also waters if something touches it or if the person has a cold or other infection. Used tear fluid drains away <u>through two tiny holes in the eyelids near the nose</u>, <u>entering small tubes that are called the tear ducts</u>. These ducts empty into a chamber in the nose. This fact explains why someone <u>who is having a good cry</u> will often get a runny nose as well.

This chapter will help you learn to write more interesting, effective sentences by using three types of modifiers: prepositional phrases, *-ing* phrases, and *who, which,* and *that* relative clauses.

USING PREPOSITIONAL PHRASES TO ADD DETAIL

GOAL 1 Use prepositional phrases to add detail

To practice using modifiers, go to
- Study Plan
- Sentence Basics
- Modifiers

A **preposition** links its object (a noun or pronoun) to the rest of the sentence. Prepositions often show relationships of *time, place, direction,* or *manner.*

TIME	Let's study after class.
PLACE	Meet me behind Hayes Hall.
DIRECTION	Who's that coming toward us?
MANNER	I acted according to my principles.

Prepositions show other relationships as well, usually variations on *time, place, direction,* or *manner.*

DURATION	We walked until dark.
REASON	They were late because of the snow.
RELATION	She looks like her sister.
QUALIFICATION	Everyone attended except Suzanna.
ORIGIN	In the beginning, I thought I couldn't write.
DESTINATION	We're going to the Grand Canyon in May.
LOCATION	The book is in my car.

Become familiar with the following common prepositions. They will help you link your ideas and make your sentences more varied and interesting.

COMMON PREPOSITIONS			
about	beneath	in spite of	round
above	beside	instead of	since
according to	between	into	through
across	beyond	like	throughout
after	by	near	till
against	concerning	next to	to
along	despite	of	toward
along with	down	off	under
among	during	on	underneath
around	except	onto	unlike
as	except for	out	until
aside from	excepting	out of	up
at	for	outside	upon
because of	from	over	with
before	in	past	within
behind	in addition to	regarding	without
below	inside		

A **prepositional phrase** consists of a preposition and the object of the preposition (a noun or pronoun). It may also include words that modify the object.

preposition   object of preposition

Sam sat beside me.

preposition modifier object of preposition

Turn left at the red barn.

You can add a prepositional phrase to a sentence to describe a noun, pronoun, verb, or adjective.

PREPOSITIONAL PHRASE DESCRIBING A . . .

noun

NOUN   The man with the suitcase boarded the train.

pronoun

PRONOUN   Both of the skaters wore red.

verb

VERB   I swam in the ocean.

adjective

ADJECTIVE   I was pleased with my exam grade.

Using Prepositional Phrases to Expand Sentences

Now let's look at how you can use prepositional phrases to add detail to your sentences and expand them:

BASIC SENTENCE	I met an old friend.
ADDITIONAL DETAIL	My old friend was <u>from California</u>. [location]
	We met <u>at a quiet restaurant</u>. [place]
	We met <u>on Saturday night</u>. [time]
EXPANDED SENTENCE	On Saturday night, I met an old friend from California at a quiet restaurant.
BASIC SENTENCE	Molly got a job.
ADDITIONAL DETAIL	Her job is <u>at the bakery</u>. [place]
	The bakery is <u>on Seventh Street</u>. [place]
	She got the job <u>on Monday</u>. [time]
EXPANDED SENTENCE	On Monday, Molly got a job at the bakery on Seventh Street.

Punctuating Prepositional Phrases

To use prepositional phrases effectively, you must also punctuate them correctly. Keep the following points in mind:

1. **A preposition is never separated from its object by a comma.**

   comma

   INCORRECT   <u>According to, the newspaper</u>

   no comma

   CORRECT   <u>According to the newspaper</u>

2. **A prepositional phrase is never a complete sentence.** It lacks both a subject and a verb. Be sure you do not punctuate a prepositional phrase as a sentence. Doing so creates a fragment.

   INCORRECT   We went for a walk. <u>Along the road.</u>

   CORRECT   We went for a walk <u>along the road.</u>

3. **A prepositional phrase that introduces a sentence is set apart from the rest of the sentence by a comma, unless the prepositional phrase is very short (two or three words).**

   comma

   <u>According to my sister and my cousin,</u> the party lasted until midnight.

   no comma

   <u>On Tuesday</u> I missed class.

4. **When a prepositional phrase interrupts a sentence and is not essential to the meaning of the sentence, it is set apart from the sentence with commas.**

   comma   comma

   The president, <u>unlike those before him,</u> intends to establish new policies.

EXERCISE 8-1   Identifying Prepositional Phrases

Directions: Underline each prepositional phrase. Add punctuation if it is needed.

> EXAMPLE   The mayor according to the television news report has approved the proposed school budget.
>
> The mayor, <u>according to the television news report,</u> has approved the proposed school budget.

1. The family walked toward the museum.
2. Throughout the film the man next to me kept sneezing.
3. A tree branch crashed to the ground and slid down the hill.
4. Over the past few years the sculptor has created many works.
5. Barbara bought an iPod instead of a CD player with her bonus check.
6. After dinner Dominic gave me a gift.
7. Over the phone the salesman tried to convince me to buy his product.
8. The dog and the squirrel ran around the tree.
9. We were busy talking and drove past the restaurant.
10. Firemen broke into the building and rescued seven people. ■

EXERCISE 8-2   Expanding Sentences Using Prepositional Phrases

Directions: Expand each of the following basic sentences by using prepositional phrases to add additional detail. Your new sentence should have only one subject and one verb. Add punctuation if it is needed. Underline the prepositional phrases.

> EXAMPLE
>
> BASIC SENTENCE   I ordered a pizza.
>
> ADDITIONAL DETAIL   I ordered it from Mazia's.
>
> I ordered it with mushrooms and anchovies.
>
> I ordered it before noon.
>
> EXPANDED SENTENCE   <u>Before noon</u> I ordered a pizza <u>with mushrooms and anchovies from Mazia's.</u>

1. BASIC SENTENCE   Maria plays the drums.

   ADDITIONAL DETAIL   She plays in a band.

   The band plays at the Rathskeller.

   She plays on weekends.

   EXPANDED SENTENCE   _____

   _____

   _____

2. BASIC SENTENCE   The construction crew is building a skyscraper.

ADDITIONAL DETAIL   They are building it next to a church.

They are building it on Ivy Street.

EXPANDED SENTENCE   _____

_____

_____

3. BASIC SENTENCE   The folders should be organized and filed.

ADDITIONAL DETAIL   They should be organized by subject.

The folders are beside the phone.

They should be filed under "Marketing Ideas."

EXPANDED SENTENCE   _____

_____

_____

4. BASIC SENTENCE   Jason will buy a house.

ADDITIONAL DETAIL   The house is in Williamsville.

He will buy it as an investment.

The house has a two-car garage.

EXPANDED SENTENCE   _____

_____

_____

5. BASIC SENTENCE   The library is a popular place.

ADDITIONAL DETAIL   It is popular for socializing.

The library is in the Humanities Building.

Many students study there during the exam period.

EXPANDED SENTENCE   _____

_____

_____

6. BASIC SENTENCE   The vice president was honored.

ADDITIONAL DETAIL   He was honored for his volunteer work.

He was honored after the staff meeting.

He volunteered throughout his career.

EXPANDED SENTENCE   _____

_____

_____

7. BASIC SENTENCE | Tamara joined a sorority.

ADDITIONAL DETAIL | She joined along with her friend Marion.

This was unlike her sister Shara.

She joined despite her busy schedule.

EXPANDED SENTENCE | _____

_____

_____

8. BASIC SENTENCE | The movie is playing at the theater.

ADDITIONAL DETAIL | The theater is behind the mall.

The movie is about dinosaurs.

It is playing during the afternoon only.

EXPANDED SENTENCE | _____

_____

_____

9. BASIC SENTENCE | Women are waiting to get married.

ADDITIONAL DETAIL | They are waiting until they are older and have careers.

This is happening throughout the country.

This is true according to a recent survey.

EXPANDED SENTENCE | _____

_____

_____

10. BASIC SENTENCE | The museum is famous.

ADDITIONAL DETAIL | The museum is outside the city.

It is famous for its Monet paintings.

It is famous despite its out-of-the-way location.

EXPANDED SENTENCE | _____

_____

_____

■

EXERCISE 8-3   Expanding Sentences Using Prepositional Phrases

Directions: Expand each of the following sentences by adding at least two prepositional phrases anywhere in the sentence. Underline your prepositional phrases.

EXAMPLE

BASIC SENTENCE   Jack rented an apartment.

EXPANDED SENTENCE   Jack rented an apartment <u>with a beautiful view</u> <u>of the waterfront</u>.

1. The bank was recently taken over.

_____

_____

2. The grocery store closed permanently.

_____

_____

3. The publisher uses only recycled paper.

_____

_____

4. The children heard a story.

_____

_____

5. Lightning struck the old oak tree.

_____

_____

6. The tanker spilled oil.

_____

_____

7. Alaskan brown bears catch salmon.

_____

_____

8. The road was being paved.

_____

_____

9. The Bach sonata was played.

_____

_____

10. The show dog won a ribbon.

_____

_____

EXERCISE 8-4
Working Together

Writing a Paragraph Using Prepositional Phrases

Directions: Write a paragraph on one of the following topics. After you have written your first draft, make sure your paragraph includes at least five prepositional phrases. Underline these phrases. Exchange paragraphs with a classmate and evaluate each other's paragraphs. Add additional prepositional phases, if needed.

1. When the unexpected happened
2. Something simple that became difficult
3. A lost and never-found item
4. Signs of laziness
5. A phobia (fear) of _____ ■

USING -*ING* PHRASES TO ADD DETAIL

GOAL 2 Use -*ing* phrases to add detail

Another way to add detail to your writing is to use -*ing* phrases to expand your sentences. An -*ing* phrase begins with the -*ing* verb form (*running, calling*) and functions as an adjective—that is, it modifies a noun or pronoun.

Walking slowly, the couple held hands.

Sitting on the sofa, Sally watched a video.

The phrase *walking slowly* describes the couple. The phrase *sitting on the sofa* describes Sally.

You can also use -*ing* phrases to combine ideas from two sentences into a single sentence.

TWO SENTENCES	Matt grilled a steak.
	He was standing on the patio.
COMBINED	Standing on the patio, Matt grilled a steak.
TWO SENTENCES	The couple discovered an injured pelican.
	The couple searched for sea shells.
COMBINED	Searching for sea shells, the couple discovered an injured pelican.
TWO SENTENCES	The photographer slipped off his step stool.
	He fell two feet.
COMBINED	The photographer slipped off his step stool, falling two feet.

Punctuating -*ing* Phrases

Remember the following rules for punctuating -*ing* phrases:

1. **A comma must follow an -*ing* phrase that appears at the beginning of the sentence.** Its purpose is to separate the -*ing* phrase from the independent thought that follows.

comma

Driving home, I saw a shooting star.

2. **If the -*ing* phrase appears at the end of the sentence, a comma separates the -*ing* phrase from the independent thought that comes before the phrase.**

comma

I explored the flooded basement, wishing I had worn my boots.

3. **When the *-ing* phrase interrupts a sentence and is not essential to the meaning of the sentence, it is set apart from the sentence with commas.**

    ESSENTIAL   The cows munching grass were facing us; the other cows were facing the other way.

    comma   comma

    NOT ESSENTIAL   The cows, munching grass, all stood with their backs to the wind.

EXERCISE 8-5   Combining Sentences

Directions: Combine each pair of sentences into a single sentence that begins with an *-ing* phrase. Underline each *-ing* phrase.

EXAMPLE

TWO SENTENCES   Art wished it would stop raining.

Art was walking home without a raincoat.

COMBINED   <u>Walking home without a raincoat</u>, Art wished it would stop raining.

1. **a.** Kedra did not listen to the lecture.

    b. Kedra was thinking about her essay.

    COMBINED   _____

    _____

2. **a.** Kenyon was driving to the bookstore.

    b. Kenyon was singing to himself.

    COMBINED   _____

    _____

3. **a.** The plumber entered the house.

    b. The plumber carried a toolbox.

    COMBINED   _____

    _____

4. **a.** The baby was crying for her mother.

    b. The baby was standing in her crib.

    COMBINED   _____

    _____

5. **a.** The press secretary held a press conference.

    b. The press secretary was wearing a navy pin-striped suit.

    COMBINED   _____

    _____

EXERCISE 8-6	**Expanding Sentences Using *-ing* Phrases**

Directions: Expand each of the following sentences by adding an *-ing* phrase. You may add your *-ing* phrase at the beginning, in the middle, or at the end of the sentence. Underline each *-ing* phrase.

EXAMPLE	The man stood on a ladder.
EXPANDED SENTENCE	<u>Painting his garage</u>, the man stood on a ladder.

1. The programmer sat at her desk.

   _____

2. The doctor walked through the hospital.

   _____

3. Rafael climbed the tree.

   _____

4. The teenagers walked through the mall.

   _____

5. The instructor returned the exams.

   _____

6. Ellen waited for a bus.

   _____

7. The clerk bagged the groceries.

   _____

8. The movie star accepted the award.

   _____

9. They spent a quiet evening.

   _____

10. The kitten was curled up on the sofa.

   _____

   ■

EXERCISE 8-7	**Writing a Paragraph Using *-ing* Phrases**
Writing in Progress	

Directions: Review the paragraph you wrote for Exercise 8-4. Double-underline any *-ing* phrases. If you have not used any *-ing* phrases, revise your paragraph to include at least one. ■

USING *WHO*, *WHICH*, AND *THAT* RELATIVE CLAUSES TO ADD DETAIL

GOAL 3 Use relative (*who, which, that*) clauses to add detail

A **clause** is a group of words that has a subject and a verb. Clauses that begin with the pronoun *who, which,* or *that* are called **relative** (or **adjective**) **clauses** because they relate one idea to another. The pronoun

   who refers to people.

   which refers to things.

   that refers to people or things.

Relative clauses add variety to your writing, as well as interesting detail. Here are a few examples of relative clauses used to expand sentences by adding detail:

BASIC SENTENCE	My sister is a football fan.
ADDITIONAL DETAIL	She is ten years old.
EXPANDED SENTENCE	My sister, who is ten years old, is a football fan.
BASIC SENTENCE	My favorite movie is *The Fighter*.
ADDITIONAL DETAIL	I saw *The Fighter* ten times.
EXPANDED SENTENCE	My favorite movie is *The Fighter*, which I've seen ten times.
BASIC SENTENCE	I own a large van.
ADDITIONAL DETAIL	The van can haul camping equipment.
EXPANDED SENTENCE	I own a large van that can haul camping equipment.

Placement of Relative Clauses

Who, which, and *that* clauses usually come directly after the words they relate to or modify.

My math instructor, who lives in Baltimore, has a British accent.

Mickey's, which serves 32 varieties of coffee, is part of a national chain.

Punctuating Relative Clauses

Note the following guidelines for punctuating relative clauses:

1. **A relative clause is never a sentence by itself.** Alone, a relative clause is a fragment. It must be combined with a complete sentence.

FRAGMENT	That has two fireplaces.
REVISED	The house that has two fireplaces is for sale.
FRAGMENT	Who lives next door.
REVISED	The woman who lives next door is a plumber.
SENTENCE + FRAGMENT	I needed my notebook. Which I left at home.
REVISED	I needed my notebook, which I left at home.

2. **If the relative clause is essential to the meaning of the sentence, no punctuation is needed.**

   Pens that have refillable cartridges are expensive.

   The sentence above states that not all pens are expensive. Only those pens that have refillable cartridges are expensive. Here the relative clause is essential to the meaning of the sentence, so no commas are needed. Essential relative clauses always use the word *that*.

3. **If the relative clause is *not* essential to the meaning of the sentence, then it should be separated from the remainder of the sentence by commas.** To discover whether the clause is essential, try reading the sentence without the clause. If the basic meaning does not change, the clause is not essential. Nonessential clauses use the word *which* for things and *who* for a person or people.

My car, <u>which is a Nissan</u>, has over 100,000 miles on it.

In this sentence, the additional information that the car is a Nissan does not change the basic meaning of the sentence.

People <u>who talk constantly</u> are annoying.

In this sentence, the clause is essential: only people who talk constantly are annoying.

NEED TO KNOW

Modifiers

- Use *prepositional phrases* to show relationships of time, place, direction, or manner.

- Use *-ing phrases* to describe or modify a noun or pronoun.

- Use *relative clauses* (*who, which,* and *that*) to add detail by showing relationships.

- Be sure to check the punctuation of each of these phrases and clauses.

EXERCISE 8-8   Identifying Relative Clauses

Directions: Underline each relative clause. Add punctuation if it is needed. Circle the word to which each clause relates.

EXAMPLE   My bicycle which I rode all summer needs repair.

REVISED   My (bicycle) which I rode all summer, needs repair.

1. An apartment that has three bedrooms is expensive.

2. The tape that I handed you has a concert recorded on it.

3. Becky who has been there before said the food is terrific.

4. Trees that lose their leaves are called deciduous.

5. Animals that live both on land and in water are called amphibians.

6. The fence which was put up to keep rabbits out of the garden is becoming rusted.

7. My car which I bought at an auction is seven years old.

8. The professor asked a question of Michael who had not done the reading.

9. Bettina reconditions outboard motors which she buys at marinas.

10. Brady who visited France last year speaks six languages fluently. ■

EXERCISE 8-9   Combining Sentences

Directions: Combine each pair of sentences into a single sentence that has a relative clause. Underline the relative clause and circle the word to which each clause relates.

EXAMPLE

TWO SENTENCES   **a.** Sam lives in New Orleans.

b. Sam travels around the country demonstrating computer software.

COMBINED   (Sam) who lives in New Orleans, travels around the country demonstrating computer software.

1. **a.** The trunk was old.

b. The trunk contained antique clothing.

COMBINED _____

_____

2. **a.** The coins were valuable.

b. The coins had sunk on a boat hundreds of years ago.

COMBINED _____

_____

3. **a.** The students attended the Garth Brooks concert.

b. The students enjoy country and western music.

COMBINED _____

_____

4. **a.** Einstein stated the theory of relativity.

b. Einstein was a very humorous man.

COMBINED _____

_____

5. **a.** The truck had a flat tire.

b. The truck was going to the repair shop.

COMBINED _____

_____

6. **a.** The wreath was hung on the door.

b. The wreath was made of dried flowers and leaves.

COMBINED _____

_____

7. **a.** An appointment book was found on the desk.

b. The appointment book was filled with writing.

COMBINED _____

_____

8. **a.** Roberto was hired as an accountant.

   b. Roberto has a degree from this college.

   COMBINED _____

   _____

9. **a.** The pool sold for 300 dollars.

   b. The pool had a tear in its lining.

   COMBINED _____

   _____

10. **a.** Test questions should be approached systematically.

    b. Some test questions are multiple choice.

    COMBINED _____

    _____

   ■

EXERCISE 8-10   Evaluating and Revising Your Writing
Writing in Progress

Directions: Review the paragraph you wrote for Exercise 8-4. Bracket any relative clauses. If you have not included any relative clauses, revise your paragraph to include at least one. ■

EXERCISE 8-11   Expanding Sentences Using Relative Clauses

Directions: Expand each of the following sentences by adding a relative clause. Underline all relative clauses and set off unessential ones with commas.

EXAMPLE	Mr. Schmidt had a heart attack.
EXPANDED SENTENCE	Mr. Schmidt, who had always been healthy, had a heart attack.

1. "The Three Little Pigs" is a popular children's story.

   _____

   _____

2. Our dog is afraid to climb the spiral staircase.

   _____

   _____

3. A paper plate lay in the garbage.

   _____

   _____

4. The stereo was too loud.

   _____

   _____

5. I picked up my screwdriver and tightened the screw.

_____

_____

6. The student called the Records Office.

_____

_____

7. The wineglass shattered.

_____

_____

8. The lottery jackpot is one million dollars.

_____

_____

9. Jackie stepped on the thistle.

_____

_____

10. The train crossed the bridge.

_____

_____

■

EXERCISE 8-12   Expanding Sentences

Directions: Expand the following sentences by adding prepositional phrases, *-ing* phrases, and relative clauses. Underline the phrases and clauses that you add.

EXAMPLE	The sportscaster reported the game.
EXPANDED	The sportscaster, <u>who was wearing a really wild tie</u>, reported the game <u>with great enthusiasm</u>.

1. Randall will graduate.

_____

2. The race began.

_____

3. The Smiths are remodeling.

_____

4. Hillary walked alone.

_____

_____

5. Manuel repairs appliances.

_____

6. The motorcycle was loud.

_____

7. My term paper is due on Tuesday.

_____

_____

8. I opened my umbrella.

_____

9. Austin built a garage.

_____

_____

10. Lucas climbs mountains.

_____

■

EXERCISE 8-13   Writing a Paragraph

Directions: Write a paragraph describing what you think is happening in the photograph below. To make your writing vivid, use adjectives and adverbs, prepositional phrases, *-ing* phrases, and relative clauses.

■

Analyze It!

Directions: Revise the following paragraph by adding modifiers for each blank line.

Going to the dentist terrified me until I discovered an effective strategy for _____. I dreaded dental work so much that I would put off making an appointment _____. At the dentist's office, I would sit nervously in the waiting room, _____. Minutes seemed like hours as I flipped through old magazines, trying to distract myself _____. _____, I would smile weakly at the receptionist, _____. When I finally sat in the dentist's chair, I would literally tremble with fear _____. Recently, a friend suggested that music might calm my fear of the dentist, so I took my MP3 player and headphones _____. In the waiting room, I put on my headphones, _____. Right away I could feel some of the tension leaving my body. In the dentist's chair, I switched to mellow jazz and was amazed that my anxiety remained _____. _____, the dentist even commented on how relaxed I was. When the drilling started, I flinched but soon discovered that the drill was no match for the music _____ .

A STUDENT ESSAY
The Student Writer and the Writing Task

The Student Writer

Kim Hyo-Joo is a student at Our Lady of the Lake University in San Antonio, Texas, and is majoring in psychology.

The Writing Task

Hyo-Joo wrote this essay for a writing class. Her instructor encouraged her to enter her essay in a writing contest sponsored by Longman Publishers, the publisher of this book. Hyo-Joo's essay was selected from among hundreds of essays as a good model essay. As you read, notice Hyo-Joo's use of modifiers—prepositional phrases, adjectives and adverbs, relative clauses, and -*ing* phrases.

English, Friend or Foe?

Kim Hyo-Joo

Thesis statement

Hyo-Joo explains why writing is difficult

I love writing. Frankly, I much prefer writing to talking. I am delighted every time I think up new and striking expressions. However, it is frustrating to me that it is difficult for me to write well in English. I love the delicate shades of meaning that languages have based on their own cultures and traditions, and I do not know many of the delicate meanings of English words. When I try to write something in English, I struggle to find the most appropriate vocabulary, but I am not always convinced that I have made the best choice. On the one hand, this problem makes me feel down, but on the other hand, I think it is unavoidable because I cannot make English my mother tongue. It is also an important reason why I cannot love English. I like to play with words by using and rearranging them, but in English I cannot have this kind of fun.

Topic sentence

Details about learning English

To tell the truth, there is another reason why I hate and fear English. All throughout my school days in Korea, my English scores were low. English was always my weakest point, and most English words were obscure code words to me. I had no interest and felt no necessity to learn English. English was just a subject that I had to memorize. I actually had English phobia. I used to have headaches when I even opened a book related to English. When I was a high school student, I decided that I would never read any more English after graduation. In my university, the Catholic University of Korea, however, some English courses were required and I received bad grades again. My major is psychology, so I had to read many textbooks written in English. I could not avoid English.

Topic sentence

Details about the trip

When I took a trip to Japan, I realized my attitude toward English was wrong. The trip to Japan sparked my interest in foreign cultures and languages. I realized that if I wanted to grow mentally and broaden my experience, it was essential to learn foreign languages, especially English. I came to realize that foreign languages are not just a means for making friends without barriers. As a result, I decided to study English in America. By becoming an exchange student, I started to study English again, but with a new mental attitude and without headaches.

Topic sentence

Details about her
college experience

At the beginning of my first semester in an English-speaking college, Our Lady of the Lake University, I was out of my mind with frustration. It was so difficult to understand what teachers and friends were saying, so sometimes I could not do my assignments or prepare for my tests. I sometimes felt down because of my poor English. I wish I had realized earlier that it was important to learn English. Why didn't it occur to me that if I wanted to experience culture, life, classes, etc., I should make a stronger effort to learn English before I came to the United States?

Topic sentence

Details about people she
has met

Many classes were admirable; my instructors were helpful, and I met many nice and kind people. In Korea I had many large-scale classes. However, here most classes are small-scale, and professors are never authoritative. I can feel their consideration for me. If I were more proficient in English, I could learn more from their teaching. Many people are also very kind. I am often surprised at their intimate conversations with me. Korean people seldom talk to strangers. I am a talkative person, but I am irritated that I can express in English only some of the things I want to say. In addition, I want to enjoy college to the fullest, but the anxiety that my poor English will cause problems makes me waver.

Topic sentence

Details, reasons

Up until now, English was only a school subject to me. I only studied English to earn high scores on exams. Now, I want to be proficient in English in order to expand my world, not just for the high scores on exams. Countries where English is spoken were just foreign countries to me in the old days, but now, if I make English mine, these countries can be included in my world. I will be able to understand people's thoughts and their culture and communicate with them.

Conclusion: Hyo-Joo offers final
positive outlook

I know learning English will not be easy for me, as a matter of course. I believe it will be easier than in the past, because I have a new attitude. I really want to talk confidently to others who live in a foreign country, listen to them, and communicate. Through this, my world will extend and my mental vision will broaden.

EXAMINING STUDENT WRITING

1. Highlight at least two examples each of prepositional phrases and relative clauses.

2. Hyo-Joo uses a wide range of adjectives. Highlight several examples.

3. How did Hyo-Joo organize the essay?

4. What types of supporting information does Hyo-Joo use to promote her thesis?

5. Evaluate the introduction and conclusion. What does each accomplish?

Paragraph Writing Scenarios

Friends and Family

1. Think of something you recently discussed with a friend about which you had very different opinions. Write a paragraph explaining how your viewpoints differed.

2. Write a paragraph about a movie you have seen. Begin with the topic sentence: "My friend (name of friend) has to see (include name of movie)." Describe what you think your friend would like about this film.

Classes and Campus Life

1. Different awards and scholarships are given to students for excellence in various fields of study and activities. Describe something you do very well and what an award for that specialty might be called.

2. Write a paragraph about what you do—or wish you did—to stay in shape. If your campus has a gym, explain what you use it for.

Working Students

1. Write a paragraph on one authority figure at school or work whom you admire. What are the qualities that person has that make him or her a good leader?

2. Make a list of chores you don't ever seem to have the time to do. Which one would you like to get done the most? Why?

Communities and Cultures

1. Describe your family's attitude toward education. How is your own attitude different? How is it the same?

2. Write a paragraph that begins with the phrase "I have always wanted to visit. . . ." Pick a country you've never been to and explain why you'd like to go there.

WRITING ABOUT A READING

THINKING BEFORE READING

The author of the following reading is the mother of basketball legend Shaquille O'Neal. In this excerpt from her autobiography *Walk Like You Have Somewhere to Go*, Lucille O'Neal describes some of the experiences that have shaped her relationship with her famous son. Before you read:

1. Preview the reading, using the steps listed in Chapter 2, p. 35.

2. Connect the reading to your own experience by answering the following questions:

   a. What do you know about your own name and why your parents chose it?

   b. What do you think it would it be like to be the parent of a world-famous person?

3. Mark and annotate as you read.

READING

THE LITTLE WARRIOR

Lucille O'Neal

1   I will always believe that the tough circumstances surrounding his birth are just one of the many reasons Shaquille and I have always had a special bond. Now, that's not to say that I don't share a special bond with all four of my children, because I most certainly do. But as mothers, we often interact differently with each child depending on their needs, personalities, and circumstances. My relationship with my oldest son remains strong to this day, and I know I'm truly blessed to have it.

2   I named him Shaquille, and that's what I call him every time I see him. I've never called him Shaq, and I never will. I don't mind others calling him that, but I named him Shaquille for a reason. More than a few people in my family and a few more outside of it were baffled as to why I decided to give all four of my children Muslim names. I'd grown up in such a strict Christian household that I suppose, in some ways, that was how I chose to rebel against my grandparents' suffocating rules that had irked me all my life—as if being pregnant without the benefit of marriage wasn't enough.

3   Shaquille was born in 1972, an all-at-once thrilling and uncertain time for African Americans everywhere. Black power, black pride, African garb, and Afros were all the

Here, Shaq plays for the Celtics in 2010: his mother's "Little Warrior" has become a basketball superstar.

rage, and I was fascinated by the unity and optimism of the moment. I'd already witnessed the 1967 Newark riots, and along with the rest of the country, I felt deeply the pain of Martin Luther King Jr.'s death in 1968. The world was changing rapidly, and I wanted to be a part of it in any way I could. But what could I do? My family wasn't exactly the activist type, and any civil unrest that led to jail (right or wrong) would result in me staying there. All I knew was that I had to make my mark somehow.

divine intervention
a term referring to God's involvement in human activities

mosque
a Muslim house of worship

4   **Divine intervention** sometimes comes in the most unexpected ways. A few years before I became pregnant with Shaquille, an Islamic **mosque** was built in our neighborhood, no doubt a result of the popularity of the Nation of Islam and Malcolm X. I caught headlines here and there about the Muslim movement, but for the most part, I never fully appreciated what they were doing or what they stood for. In our house, politics were rarely discussed, and when they were, we as children were not included in the conversation. The old adage that children were to be seen and not heard was in full effect in my house, which made the Black Muslim platform seem eons way from my little block in New Jersey.

5   Maybe it was that lack of knowledge that had me so fascinated with the mosque and what it represented in our neighborhood. Its teachings were the polar opposite of all I'd learned as a child, and that was right up my alley. Some days I'd go into the mosque's gift store in the mornings and wander the book aisles for hours, looking for anything that caught my eye. One book that did catch my eye was a collection of Islamic names and their meanings. This was the period when blacks were actually giving their children names that stood for something, and I decided this could be my way of making a statement—giving my firstborn child a name that spoke to the times in which we were living.

6   The name Shaquille stuck in my mind immediately because it meant "little one," and the middle name I gave him, Rashaun, meant "warrior." I liked the idea of my son being a warrior in a world that could be pretty harsh, particularly toward African Americans. Since his father had abandoned his parental responsibilities, my firstborn and I were both going to have to be true warriors together in order to survive.

GETTING READY TO WRITE

Reviewing the Reading

Answer each of the following questions using complete sentences.

1. Why did the author decide to name her son Shaquille? Explain the meaning of his first and middle names.

2. Who raised the author? Describe the household in which she grew up.

3. What were the tough circumstances surrounding Shaquille's birth?

4. How does Shaquille's name reflect the times in which he was born?

Examining the Reading Using an Idea Map

Review the reading by completing the missing parts of the idea map shown below.

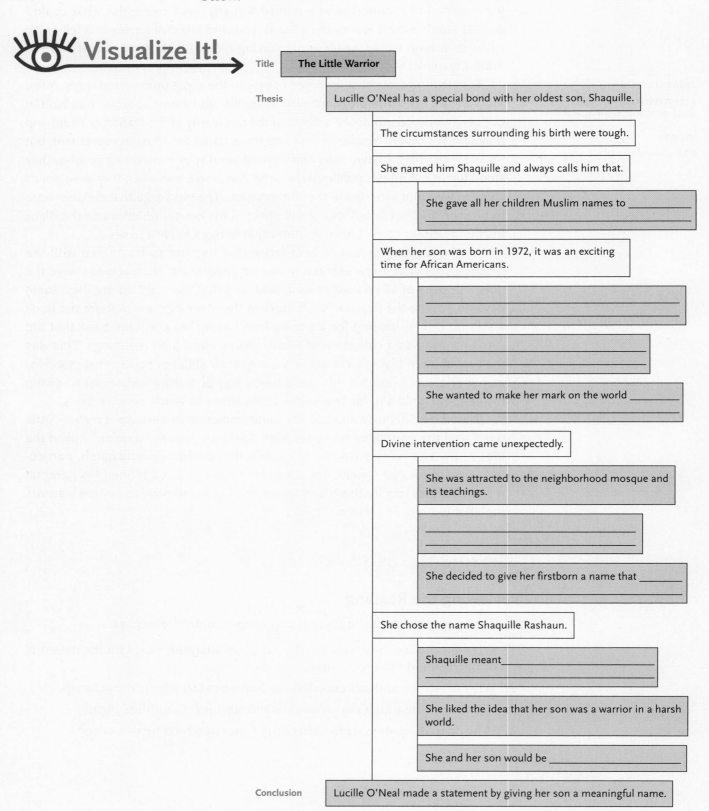

Visualize It!

Title — **The Little Warrior**

Thesis — Lucille O'Neal has a special bond with her oldest son, Shaquille.

The circumstances surrounding his birth were tough.

She named him Shaquille and always calls him that.

She gave all her children Muslim names to _____ _____

When her son was born in 1972, it was an exciting time for African Americans.

_____
_____

_____
_____

She wanted to make her mark on the world _____ _____

Divine intervention came unexpectedly.

She was attracted to the neighborhood mosque and its teachings.

_____
_____

She decided to give her firstborn a name that _____ _____

She chose the name Shaquille Rashaun.

Shaquille meant _____ _____

She liked the idea that her son was a warrior in a harsh world.

She and her son would be _____

Conclusion — Lucille O'Neal made a statement by giving her son a meaningful name.

Strengthening Your Vocabulary

Using the word's context, word parts, or a dictionary, write a brief definition of each of the following words as it is used in the reading.

1. interact (paragraph 1) _____

2. baffled (paragraph 2) _____

3. irked (paragraph 2) _____

4. garb (paragraph 3) _____

5. adage (paragraph 4) _____

Reacting to Ideas: Discussion and Journal Writing

Get ready to write about the reading by discussing the following:

1. How would you describe Lucille's relationship with her son?

2. How did Lucille respond to the strictness of her upbringing?

3. Why did Lucille consider it "divine intervention" when a mosque was built in her neighborhood?

4. Identify some of the descriptive words that were used in this reading. Which words have a strong emotional component or connotative meaning?

 **Thinking Visually**   5. How does the photo of Shaquille playing basketball add to the story?

WRITING ABOUT THE READING

Paragraph Options

1. Have you ever experienced something like divine intervention? Write a paragraph describing what happened.

2. Write a paragraph describing a time when you felt like you had to become a warrior to survive.

Essay Options

3. Write an essay describing the household in which you grew up. How do you think your choices today are influenced by your upbringing?

4. To illustrate her point in paragraph 3, the author mentions people and events that defined the times and signified a changing world. Write an essay describing some of the people and events that define the times you live in today.

CHAPTER REVIEW AND PRACTICE

CHAPTER REVIEW

To review and check your recall of the chapter, match each term in Column A with its meaning in Column B.

COLUMN A	COLUMN B
_____ 1. modifiers	**a.** group of words that contains both a subject and a verb
_____ 2. prepositions	**b.** clause that begins with *who*, *which*, or *that*
_____ 3. prepositional phrase	**c.** group of words containing a preposition and the object of the preposition
_____ 4. *-ing* phrase	**d.** group of words that begins with the *-ing* verb form and modifies a noun or pronoun
_____ 5. clause	**e.** words that show relationships of time, place, direction, or manner
_____ 6. relative clause	**f.** words that change or limit the meaning of other words

EDITING PRACTICE

Revise the following student paragraph by supplying adjectives and adverbs, and by adding prepositional phrases, *-ing* phrases, or relative clauses.

My grandmother lives in an antiques-filled house. She is picky about her furniture. Because of this, nobody puts his or her feet on chairs or sits on beds. When we were little, one of my cousins used to think he could ignore her rules. We would sleep over at Gram's often. Each time, Eric would turn off the lights and swan dive into the bed. This would shove the mattress sideways. It would knock nearly every slat out of place. Of course, Gram noticed and always asked him to stop being so rough on the bed. Anyone else would have changed his or her ways, but Eric thought he was different. My grandmother decided that he needed a lesson. During

the next sleepover, when everyone was in bed, we heard a crash from Eric's room.

We rushed to his room. When we got there, we were surprised to see Eric and the

mattress flat on the floor! Gram had fine-tuned the slats in her bed. She taught Eric

a lesson. He now restricts his diving to beaches and pools.

PEARSON **mywritinglab** For support in meeting this chapter's objectives, log in to www.mywritinglab.com, go to the Study Plan tab, click on Using Modifiers to Add Detail and choose Modifiers and Parts of Speech: Phrases and Clauses from the list of subtopics. Read and view the videos and resources in the Review Materials section, and then complete the Recall, Apply, and Write exercises in the Activities section. You can check your scores and overall progress by using the Gradebook.

WRITERS' WORKSHOPS: Using Language Effectively

WRITERS' WORKSHOP

6

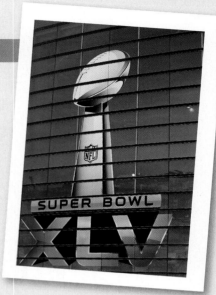

DON'T (-_-) BE (^_^) (TRANSLATION: DON'T WORRY, BE HAPPY)

Convey Your Feelings with Words, Not Emoticons

The smiley ☺ and sad ☹ faces you see all over e-mail and text messages are called **emoticons**, and they play an important role in electronic communication. In face-to-face conversations, you can watch people's faces, and listen to their tone of voice, to understand if they are joking. Without these visual and verbal cues, a joke may be misunderstood. Emoticons developed as a way of indicating tone through images on the computer screen.

Emoticons are never appropriate in college or business writing. Their use implies that the writer is unable to convey his or her feelings through words. Think of it this way: if you need to use an emoticon, you have not expressed your thoughts effectively.

> **Inappropriate/Ineffective:** I'm not feeling so great after flunking that test. ☹
>
> **Appropriate/Effective:** I am feeling depressed after failing that test.
>
> **Inappropriate/Ineffective:** The Cowboys won the Super Bowl!!!!!☺☺☺☺☺
>
> **Appropriate/Effective:** I am overjoyed. The Cowboys won the Super Bowl!

Note also that one piece of punctuation is enough; never use multiple exclamation points or question marks in formal writing.

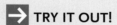 TRY IT OUT!

Directions: Rewrite each sentence in formal English.

1. The Democrats were bummed that they lost control of the Senate. ☹

   _____

   _____

2. Madame Curie must have wondered why she was feeling so sick after she discovered uranium ????

   _____

   _____

3. I am totally looking forward to my vacation!!!!!

   _____

   _____

4. My sister is my favorite sibling, but my brother gives me money when I need it. ☺

_____

_____

5. Howard Stern's autobiography is hilarious. ROFL ☺

_____

_____

WRITERS' WORKSHOP

7

86 THE SLANG, OK?

Write in Standard English

Slang is a set of informal, casual expressions used by a group of people. Many groups have their own slang. Hip-hop artists and their fans sometimes use the term *benjamins* to refer to $100 bills (because Benjamin Franklin's portrait appears on the bill). Skateboarders will say something is *sick* when they think it's cool.

Slang is colorful, expressive, fun, and funny. It shows the living and evolving nature of language, and it often creates feelings of friendship and camaraderie. It is not, however, appropriate for use in any formal writing in college or the workplace, which requires the use of **Standard** English.

Why? Because slang words are not understood by large portions of the population. Consider the title of this workshop. Did you know that "86" means "to get rid of"? Most likely you did not, because the slang term "86" was used by an older generation and is no longer used much. When you write, your goal is to communicate effectively with your readers regardless of their age, gender, or any other category. That's why you need to use Standard English, which everyone understands.

Slang: Jay has a sketchy board, but he can do some sick tricks.

Standard: My friend Jay has a beat up skateboard, but he can do really impressive tricks with it.

Slang: My bro is always *buggin'*. I wish he'd just *marinate*.

Standard: My brother is always nervous about something. I wish he'd just relax.

You know what is slang and what isn't. If you're not sure, you can decide by asking yourself: Would my parents know what this means? Would my teacher? Would I use this word in a job interview?

 TRY IT OUT!

Directions: Rewrite each sentence, converting the slang into Standard English. If you don't understand the slang, check its meaning at **http://www.urbandictionary.com**.

1. I need to get the 411 on that car before I decide to buy it.

_____

_____

2. In Jane Austen's novel *Emma,* Mr. Knightley does a major smackdown on Emma Woodhouse.

_____

_____

3. Of all the people in America with the most dough, Bill Gates is #1.

_____

_____

4. The nutritionist told me to chill on the french fries and eat rabbit food instead.

_____

_____

5. Bud had so much to drink at the party he was yacking all night.

_____

_____

WRITERS' WORKSHOP

8

STOP BEATING A DEAD HORSE

Avoid Trite Expressions and Clichés

Have you ever had a friend who says the same thing over and over again? In writing, a cliché is the equivalent of hearing the same boring words so often that you tune out.

Clichés, sometimes known as *trite expressions,* are words, phrases, and sayings that are used so often that they've become stale. They hurt your writing by making it seem lazy and bland. The following are some clichés you probably have heard or used:

add insult to injury	hit the nail on the head
all work and no play	raining cats and dogs
better late than never	singing the blues
easier said than done	strong as an ox
face the music	work like a dog

Trite expressions like these take the place of original, specific, meaningful descriptions in your writing. When you use a cliché, you have lost a chance to convey a fresh, precise impression. In the following examples, note that the revised version gives much more complete information.

Trite: I worked like a dog to finish my writing assignment.

Revised: I worked until midnight every night last week to finish my writing assignment.

Trite: He smokes like a chimney.

Revised: He smokes two packs of Marlboro Lights a day.

Rewriting clichés is fun. Rethinking them makes you re-visualize them and use words that convey a better mental picture.

→ TRY IT OUT!

Directions: Rewrite the following cliché-ridden sentences to give them fresh meaning. Feel free to add descriptions and further details!

1. The trainer at my gym is fit as a fiddle.

   _____

2. If there's one thing I've learned about clichés, it's that you should avoid them like the plague.

   _____

3. When push comes to shove, Mr. Pearson always has your back.

   _____

4. You need an umbrella; it's raining cats and dogs out there!

   _____

5. Have you ever noticed that people who gossip want you to keep their secrets, but they're always the first to let the cat out of the bag?

   _____

   _____

WRITERS' WORKSHOP

9

STOP REPEATING YOURSELF AND ELIMINATE REDUNDANCY

Say It Once, Effectively

Have you ever known someone who takes way too long to tell a story? The person suffering from **wordiness** uses more words than necessary to get to the point.

Wordiness can be a problem in writing, too. Wordy writers mistakenly believe that more words are better. But the opposite is often true: the clearest writing is short, concise, and sharp.

> **Wordy:** The *rushed and pressured nature of nursing is due to the fact* that hospitals lack adequate staff.

> **Concise:** Nurses are rushed and pressured because hospitals lack adequate staff.

To eliminate wordiness:

1. Look for words that do not add meaning, and eliminate them. You may need to rearrange the words in your sentence, as in the above example.

2. Eliminate empty words and phrases.

Do you need all these words . . .	When you can instead say . . .
spell out in detail	explain
the only difference being that	except
it is clear that	clearly
in the vicinity of	near
on the grounds that	because
for the reason that	because
at this point in time	now

3. Avoid saying the same thing twice in two different ways (redundancy).

square in shape	square [square is a shape]
mental attitude	attitude [the only type of attitude is a mental one]
the year 2009	2009 [2009 is a year]

→ TRY IT OUT!

Directions: Rewrite each sentence, eliminating redundancy and unnecessary words.

1. The "Corn Cob Towers" in Chicago are apartment buildings that are round in shape.

   _____

2. At this stage of the game, Lady Gaga is the most popular singer in the United States.

   _____

3. Stop walking immediately and instantaneously.

   _____

4. I decided to take the introductory psychology course in my first semester of college for the reason that I am giving thought to majoring in the discipline of psychology.

   _____

   _____

5. I am sorry to report that my daughter is sick and is not feeling well.

   _____

WRITERS' WORKSHOP

10

LET EVERYONE INTO YOUR WRITING

Avoiding Sexist Language

The goal of writing is to communicate with as many people as possible: therefore, it is important to use language that includes both women and men. Using gender-specific, or sexist, language can prevent some people from feeling that they are part of the intended audience, or even make them feel excluded. (For more on audience, review Chapter 11, pages 298–299.) Also, by using certain expressions and pronouns, you may unintentionally make unfair statements or offend your readers.

> **Sexist:** A student will get good grades if *he* knows how to take good notes. (This statement fails to recognize that many students are women.)

> **Nonsexist:** A student will get good grades if *he or she* knows how to take good lecture notes. OR *Students* will get good grades if *they* know how to take good lecture notes.

> **Sexist:** The *girl* at the customer service desk was helpful and efficient.
> (The term *girl* implies childishness, immaturity, and perhaps condescension.)

> **Nonsexist:** The *customer service rep* was helpful and efficient. OR
> The *woman* at the customer service desk was helpful and efficient.

> **Sexist:** The *male nurse* gave my grandmother the prescribed medications. (This statement makes an unnecessary distinction between male and female nurses. The nurse's sex doesn't matter.)

> **Nonsexist:** The *nurse* gave my grandmother the prescribed medications.

> Here are a few guidelines to help you to avoid sexist language:

1. When referring to people in general, rewrite your sentence using the phrase *he or she*, *she or he*, or plural nouns.

   > **Sexist:** A writer should proofread *his* paper.

   > **Nonsexist:** A writer should proofread *her or his* paper.
   >   *Writers* should proofread *their* papers.

2. Avoid using the words *man* or *mankind* to refer to people in general. Also avoid occupational terms ending in *-man*.

Sexist	Nonsexist
any man who gives . . .	anyone who gives . . .
policeman	police officer
salesman	salesperson

3. Avoid expressions that make negative or unfair references to men or women.

Sexist	Nonsexist
my old man	my husband
career gal	career-oriented woman

4. Refer to a woman by her own name, not by her husband's name.

   > **Sexist:** Mrs. Samuel Goldstein was named Educator of the Year.

   > **Nonsexist:** Rita Goldstein was named Educator of the Year.

5. When possible, use a term that includes both men and women.

Rather than using . . .	**Use . . .**
actress	actor
stewardess	flight attendant
waitress	server

The key to wring in an inclusive, nonsexist way is to remain focused on your audience. By not excluding people from your writing, you are inviting them into it.

→ **TRY IT OUT!**

Directions: Rewrite each sentence to eliminate sexism or phrases that might exclude certain readers. Convert any slang into Standard English.

1. As your candidate for governor, my goal is to represent the interests of all men in the state.

   _____

   _____

2. The chick at the DMV was way rude.

   _____

3. A doctor should always turn off his cell phone before he sees a patient.

   _____

4. Mrs. Bill Clinton, sometimes known as Hillary, is highly regarded in her role as secretary of state.

   _____

5. The stewardess poured the coffee into my lap before going ballistic and jumping out of the airplane.

   _____

   _____

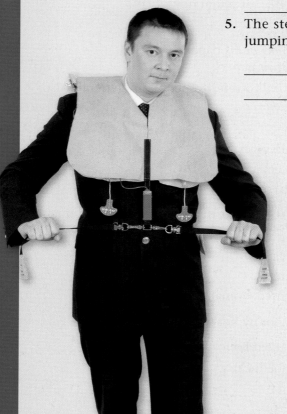

Part III
COMMON
SENTENCE
PROBLEMS
AND HOW TO
AVOID THEM

9 Revising Confusing and Inconsistent Sentences

WRITE ABOUT IT!

The situation shown in the photo does not "seem right." Inconsistencies in your writing can also make it seem "not right" or confusing. Here are a few examples from a book titled *Anguished English* by Richard Lederer that show how errors create confusion and sometimes unintentional humor.

1. We do not tear your clothing with machinery. We do it carefully by hand.

2. Have several very old dresses from grandmother in beautiful condition.

3. Tired of cleaning yourself? Let me do it.

Sometimes sentence errors create unintentional humor, as in Lederer's examples. Most often, though, they distract or confuse your reader. They may also convey the impression that you have not taken time to check and polish your work. In this chapter you will learn to avoid several common types of sentence errors.

WRITING

USING PRONOUNS CLEARLY AND CORRECTLY

GOAL 1
Use pronouns clearly
and correctly

mywritinglab

To practice using pronouns, go to
■ Study Plan
■ Sentence Basics
■ Pronoun Reference and Point of View

A **pronoun** is a word that substitutes for, or refers to, a noun or another pronoun. *I, you, he, she, it, we, they, his, mine, yours, who,* and *whom* are all examples of pronouns. The noun or pronoun to which a pronoun refers is called the pronoun's **antecedent**. To use pronouns correctly, you need to make sure that the antecedent of the pronoun (your pronoun reference) is clear to your reader and that the pronoun and antecedent agree in number (singular or plural) and in gender.

Pronoun Reference

If your pronoun reference is unclear, your sentence may be confusing and difficult to follow. Note the confusing nature of the following sentences:

The aerobics instructor told the student that *she* made a mistake. [Who made the mistake?]

They told Kevin that he was eligible for a Visa card. [Who told Kevin?]

Aaron bought a bowling ball at the garage sale *that* he enjoyed. [Did Aaron enjoy the garage sale or the bowling ball?]

The following suggestions will help you make sure that all your pronoun references are clear:

1. **Make sure there is only one possible *antecedent* for each pronoun.** The antecedent (the word to which the pronoun refers) comes before the pronoun (*ante-* means "before") in the sentence. The reader should not be left wondering what the antecedent of any given pronoun is.

   UNCLEAR   The father told the child that *he* was sunburned.

   REVISED   The father told the child, "I am sunburned."

Tip for Writers

Don't write both a noun and a pronoun for the same subject.

INCORRECT   My teacher she is very tall.

CORRECT   My teacher is very tall. (or) She is very tall.

2. **Avoid using vague pronouns that lack an antecedent.** *They* and *it* are often mistakenly used this way.

   UNCLEAR   *They* told me my loan application needs a cosigner.

   REVISED   The loan officer told me my loan application needs a cosigner.

3. **Eliminate unnecessary pronouns.** If a sentence is clear without a pronoun, delete the pronoun.

   UNCLEAR   The manager, *he* says that the store will close at midnight.

   REVISED   The manager says that the store will close at midnight.

4. **Always place the pronoun as close as possible to its antecedent.**

   UNCLEAR·   Lucia saw a dress at the mall *that* she wanted.

   REVISED   At the mall, Lucia saw a dress that she wanted.

5. **Use the pronoun *you* only if you are directly addressing the reader.**

UNCLEAR   *You* need daily exercise to keep physically fit.

REVISED   Everyone needs daily exercise to keep physically fit.

EXERCISE 9-1   Correcting Pronoun Reference Errors

Directions: Revise each of the following sentences to correct problems in pronoun reference.

EXAMPLE   The glass, ~~it~~ ^was^ filled to the rim.

1. You should try to be honest at all times.

2. When I bought the shirt, I told him that I would pay with my credit card.

3. Jamal told Rob he had received an A in the course.

4. James talked with Bill because he did not know anyone else at the party.

5. The teachers told the school board members, that they needed more preparation time.

6. The board of directors, they decided that the company would have to declare bankruptcy.

7. The gallery owner hung a painting on the wall that was blue.

8. They sent our grades at the end of the semester.

9. The Constitution says you have the right to bear arms.

10. They filled the parking lot on Sunday. ■

EXERCISE 9-2   Revising Sentences

Directions: Revise each of the following sentences to correct problems in pronoun reference. If a sentence contains no errors, write *Correct* beside it.

EXAMPLE   ~~It~~ ^The professor's note^ said that the grades would be posted on Tuesday.

_____   1. On the bulletin board it says there will be a fire drill today.

_____   2. Laverne and Louise they pooled their money to buy a new CD player.

_____   3. They said on the news that the naval base will be shut down.

_____   4. The street that was recently widened is where I used to live.

_____   5. Ivan sat on the couch in the living room that he bought yesterday.

_____   6. "Sarah," the tutor advised, "you should underline in your textbooks for better comprehension."

_____   7. Christina handed Maggie the plate she had bought at the flea market.

_____   8. Bridget found the cake mix in the aisle with the baking supplies that she needed for tonight's dessert.

_____   9. Rick told Larry, he was right.

_____   10. It said in the letter that my payment was late. ■

EXERCISE 9-3
Writing in Progress

Writing a Paragraph

Directions: Write a paragraph on one of the following topics. After you have written your first draft, reread it to be certain your pronoun references are clear. Make corrections if needed.

1. A recent clothing fad
2. Advice columns
3. Horoscopes
4. Remembering names
5. An extreme weather condition (heat wave, storm, blizzard, flood) that you lived through ■

Pronoun-Antecedent Agreement

mywritinglab

To practice pronoun agreement, go to
■ Study Plan
■ Sentence Basics
■ Pronoun-Antecedent Agreement

A pronoun must "agree" with its antecedent—that is, a pronoun must have the same number (singular or plural) as the noun or pronoun it refers to or replaces. Singular nouns and pronouns refer to one person, place, or thing; plural nouns and pronouns refer to more than one.

Always check your sentences for pronoun-antecedent agreement.

                    plural   singular

UNCLEAR   The dogs are in its kennels.

CLEAR   The dogs are in their kennels.

                        plural   singular

UNCLEAR   Marcia and Megan called all her friends about the party.

CLEAR   Marcia and Megan called all their friends about the party.

Use the following guidelines to make sure the pronouns you use agree with their antecedents:

1. **Use singular pronouns with singular nouns.**

   singular noun   singular pronoun

   Teresa sold her bicycle.

2. **Use plural pronouns with plural nouns.**

   plural noun   plural pronoun

   The <u>neighbors</u> always shovel <u>their</u> walks when it snows.

3. **Use a plural pronoun to refer to a compound antecedent joined by *and* unless both parts of the compound refer to the same person, place, or thing.**

   plural antecedent   plural pronoun

   <u>Mark and Keith</u> bought <u>their</u> concert tickets.

   singular antecedent   singular pronoun

   The <u>pitcher and team captain</u> broke <u>her</u> ankle.

4. **When antecedents are joined by *or, nor, either . . . or, neither . . . nor, not . . . but,* or *not only . . . but also,* the pronoun agrees in number with the nearer antecedent.**

   plural noun   plural pronoun

   Either the <u>professor</u> or <u>the students</u> will present <u>their</u> views.

   Note: When one antecedent is singular and the other is plural, avoid awkwardness by placing the plural antecedent second in the sentence.

   AWKWARD   Neither <u>the salespersons nor the manager</u> has received <u>his</u> <u>check</u>.

   REVISED   Neither <u>the manager nor the salespersons</u> have received <u>their</u> checks.

5. **Avoid using *he, him,* or *his* to refer to general, singular words such as *child, person, everyone.*** These words exclude females. Use *he or she, him or her,* or *his or hers,* or rewrite your sentence to use a plural antecedent and a plural pronoun that do not indicate gender.

   INCORRECT   A <u>person</u> should not deceive <u>his</u> friends.

   REVISED   A <u>person</u> should not deceive <u>his or her</u> friends.

   BETTER   <u>People</u> should not deceive <u>their</u> friends.

6. **With collective nouns (words that refer to a group of people, such as *army, class, congregation, audience*), use a singular pronoun to refer to the noun when the group acts as a unit.**

   The <u>audience</u> showed <u>its</u> approval by applauding.

   The <u>team</u> chose <u>its</u> captain.

   Use a plural pronoun to refer to the noun when each member of the group acts individually.

   The <u>family</u> exchanged <u>their</u> gifts.

   The <u>team</u> changed <u>their</u> uniforms.

   To avoid using a plural verb or pronoun after a collective noun, write "the members of the team," which gives you a plural subject (members).

EXERCISE 9-4   Correcting Agreement Errors

Directions: Revise each of the following sentences to correct errors in pronoun-antecedent agreement.

EXAMPLE   Usually when a driver has been caught speeding, ~~they~~ *he or she* readily admit*s* the mistake.

1. Each gas station in town raised their prices in the past week.

2. Neither the waitress nor the hostess received their paycheck from the restaurant.

3. The committee put his or her signatures on the document.

4. An infant recognizes their parents within the first few weeks of life.

5. The Harris family lives by his or her own rules.

6. Lonnie and Jack should put his ideas together and come up with a plan of action.

7. An employee taking an unpaid leave of absence may choose to make their own health-insurance payments.

8. The amount of time a student spends researching a topic depends, in part, on their familiarity with the topic.

9. Alex and Susana lost her way while driving through the suburbs of Philadelphia.

10. Neither the attorney nor the protesters were willing to expose himself to public criticism. ■

Agreement with Indefinite Pronouns

Indefinite pronouns (such as *some, everyone, any, each*) are pronouns without specific antecedents. They refer to people, places, or things in general. When an indefinite pronoun is an antecedent for another pronoun, mistakes in pronoun agreement often result. Use the following guidelines to make your pronouns agree with indefinite pronoun antecedents:

1. **Use singular pronouns to refer to indefinite pronouns that are singular in meaning.**

another	either	nobody	other
anybody	everybody	no one	somebody
anyone	everyone	nothing	someone
anything	everything	one	something
each	neither		

Tip for Writers

Everybody, everyone, and *everything* refer to a group of people or things, but these words are grammatically singular, so use a singular verb with them:

   When there's a snowstorm, <u>everyone gets</u> to class late.

singular antecedent   singular pronoun

<u>Someone</u> left <u>his</u> dress shirt in the locker room.

singular antecedent   singular compound pronoun

<u>Everyone</u> in the office must pick up <u>his or her</u> paycheck.

Note: To avoid the awkwardness of *his or her,* use plural antecedents and pronouns.

plural antecedent   plural pronoun

Office <u>workers</u> must pick up <u>their</u> paychecks.

2. **Use a plural pronoun to refer to indefinite pronouns that are plural in meaning.**

both	few	many	more	several

plural antecedent   plural pronoun

<u>Both</u> of the police officers said that as far as <u>they</u> could tell, no traffic violations had occurred.

3. **The indefinite pronouns *all, any, more, most,* and *some* can be singular or plural, depending on how they are used.** If the indefinite pronoun refers to something that cannot be counted, use a singular pronoun to refer to it. If the indefinite pronoun refers to two or more of something that can be counted, use a plural pronoun to refer to it.

<u>Most</u> of the students feel <u>they</u> can succeed.

<u>Most</u> of the air on airplanes is recycled repeatedly, so <u>it</u> becomes stale.

NEED TO KNOW

Pronouns

- **Pronouns** substitute for, or refer to, nouns or other pronouns.

- The noun or pronoun to which a pronoun refers is called its **antecedent**.

- Make sure that it is always clear to which noun or pronoun a pronoun refers.

- A pronoun must agree with its antecedent in number (singular or plural) and gender. Singular nouns and pronouns refer to one thing; plural nouns and pronouns refer to more than one.

- **Indefinite pronouns** are pronouns without specific antecedents. Follow the rules given in this chapter to make indefinite pronouns agree with their antecedents.

EXERCISE 9-5   Correcting Pronoun-Antecedent Errors

Directions: Revise each of the following sentences to correct errors in pronoun-antecedent agreement.

EXAMPLE   No one could remember their student number.

REVISED   No one could remember his or her student number.

BETTER   The students could not remember their student numbers.

1. Someone left their jacket in the car.

2. Everything Todd said was true, but I did not like the way he said them.

3. In my math class, everyone works at their own pace.

4. When someone exercises, they should drink plenty of liquids.

5. No one should be forced into a curriculum that they do not want.

6. No one will receive their exam grades before Friday.

7. Many of the club members do not pay his or her dues on time.

8. Both of the cooks used her own secret recipes.

9. No one was successful on their first attempt to run the race in less than two hours.

10. Each of the workers brought their own tools. ■

EXERCISE 9-6   Correcting Agreement Errors

Directions: Revise the sentences below that contain agreement errors. If a sentence contains no errors, write *Correct* beside it.

EXAMPLE   Somebody dropped their~~ ~~ring down the drain.
                                    his or her

_____   1. Many of the residents of the neighborhood have had their homes tested for radon.

_____   2. Each college instructor established their own grading policies.

_____   3. The apples fell from its tree.

_____   4. Anyone may enter their painting in the contest.

_____   5. All the engines manufactured at the plant have their vehicle identification numbers stamped on them.

_____   6. No one requested that the clerk gift wrap their package.

_____ 7. Either Professor Judith Marcos or her assistant, Maria, graded the exams, writing their comments in the margins.

_____ 8. James or his parents sails the boat every weekend.

_____ 9. Most classes were not canceled because of the snowstorm; it met as regularly scheduled.

_____ 10. Not only Ricky but also the Carters will take his children to Disneyland this summer. ■

EXERCISE 9-7
Writing in Progress

Revising a Paragraph

Directions: Reread the paragraph you wrote for Exercise 9-3 to be certain that there are no errors in pronoun-antecedent agreement. Revise as needed. ■

AVOIDING SHIFTS IN PERSON, NUMBER, AND VERB TENSE

GOAL 2 Avoid shifts in person, number, and verb tense

The parts of a sentence should be consistent. Shifts in person, number, or verb tense within a sentence make it confusing and difficult to read.

Shifts in Person

Person is the grammatical term used to identify the speaker or writer (**first person**: *I, we*), the person spoken to (**second person**: *you*), and the person or thing spoken about (**third person**: *he, she, it, they,* or any noun, such as *Joan, children*). Be sure to refer to yourself, your audience (or readers), and people you are writing about in a consistent way throughout your sentence or paragraph.

In the following paragraph, note how the writer shifts back and forth when addressing her audience:

> A <u>person</u> should know how to cook. <u>You</u> can save a lot of money if <u>you</u> make your own meals instead of eating out. <u>One</u> can also eat more healthily at home if <u>one</u> cooks according to principles of good nutrition.

Here the writer shifts from sentence to sentence, first using the indefinite phrase *a person*, then the more personal *you*, then the more formal *one*.

In the next paragraph, the writer shifts when referring to himself.

> Arizona has many advantages for year-round living, so <u>I</u> am hoping to move there when <u>I</u> graduate. One reason <u>I</u> want to live in Arizona is that <u>you</u> never need to shovel snow.

In this paragraph, the writer shifts from the direct and personal *I* to the indirect and more general *you*.

To avoid making shifts in references to yourself and others, decide before you begin to write how you will refer to yourself, to your audience, and to those about whom you are writing. Base your decision on whether you want your paragraph to be direct and personal or more formal. In academic writing, most instructors prefer that you avoid using the personal pronoun *I* and try to write in a more formal style.

PERSONAL	I want to live in Florida for a number of reasons.
MORE FORMAL	Living in Florida is attractive for a number of reasons.

PERSONAL	I have difficulty balancing school and a part-time job.
MORE FORMAL	Balancing school and a part-time job is difficult.

Shifts in Number

Number distinguishes between singular and plural. A pronoun must agree in number with its antecedent. Related nouns within a sentence must also agree in number.

SHIFT	All the <u>women</u> wore a <u>dress</u>.
CONSISTENT	All the <u>women</u> wore <u>dresses</u>.

EXERCISE 9-8   Correcting Shift in Person Errors

Directions: Revise each of the following sentences to correct shifts in person or number.

EXAMPLE   I perform better on exams if the professor doesn't hover over ~~you~~. *me*

1. Each student has to plan their schedules for the semester.

2. Eva said she doesn't want to go to the wedding because you would have to bring a gift.

3. In some states, continuing education is required for doctors or lawyers; after you pass the board or bar exam, you are required to take a specified number of credits per year in brush-up courses.

4. Construction workers must wear a hard hats.

5. I swim with a life vest on because you could drown without it.

6. A good friend is always there when you need them most.

7. The first and second relay racers discussed his strategies.

8. I always tell yourself to think before acting.

9. Patients often expect their doctors to have all the answers, but you should realize doctors are not miracle workers.

10. Each giraffe stretched their neck to reach the leaves in the trees. ■

Tip for Writers

When the main clause is in a future tense, the verb in the dependent time clause is put in the present tense even though the entire sentence is about the future.

Shifts in Verb Tense

Use the same verb tense (past, present, future, etc.) throughout a sentence and paragraph unless meaning requires you to make a shift.

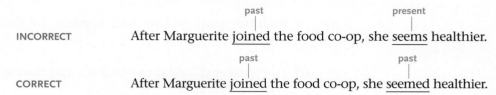

REQUIRED SHIFT   After the moon rises, we will go for a moonlight swim.

Incorrect shifts in verb tense can make a sentence confusing. One of the most common incorrect shifts is between present and past tenses.

INCORRECT   After Marguerite joined the food co-op, she seems healthier.

CORRECT   After Marguerite joined the food co-op, she seemed healthier.

NEED TO KNOW

Shifts in Person, Number, and Verb Tense

- *Person* is a term used to identify the speaker or writer (**first person:** *I, we*), the person spoken to (**second person:** *you*), and the person or thing spoken about (**third person:** *he, she, it, they*, or any noun, such as *desk* or *Robert*).

- Be sure to use a consistent person throughout a piece of writing.

- **Number** distinguishes between singular and plural. A pronoun must agree in number with its antecedent.

- **Verb tense** is the form of a verb that indicates whether the action or state of being that the verb tells about occurs in the past, present, or future. Unless there is a specific reason to switch tenses, be sure to use a consistent tense throughout a piece of writing.

EXERCISE 9-9   Correcting Shifts in Verb Tense

Directions: Revise each of the following sentences to correct shifts in verb tense.

EXAMPLE   I ~~was waiting~~ *waited* for the hailstorm to end, and then I dashed into the restaurant.

1. In the morning, the factory workers punch in, but have not punched out at night.

2. José looked muscular; then he joined a gym and looks even more so.

3. I run two miles, and then I rested.

4. Quinne called me but hangs up on my answering machine.

5. Until I took physics, I will not understand the laws of aerodynamics.

6. While the rain fell, the campers take shelter in their tent.

7. Because the moon will be full, the tide was high.

8. Katie drives me to work, and I worked until 9:30 p.m.

9. Richard went to the mall because he need to buy a suit for his job interview.

10. The speaker stands at the podium and cleared his throat. ■

EXERCISE 9-10   Revising Sentences

Directions: Revise each of the following sentences to correct errors in shift of person, number, or verb tense. If a sentence contains no errors, write *Correct* beside it.

EXAMPLE   Boats along the river were tied to their ~~dock.~~ *docks*

_____ 1. When people receive a gift, you should be gracious and polite.

_____ 2. When we arrived at the inn, the lights are on and a fire is burning in the fireplace.

_____ 3. Before Trey drove to the cabin, he packs a picnic lunch.

_____ 4. The artist paints portraits and weaves baskets.

_____ 5. The lobsterman goes out on his boat each day and will check his lobster traps.

_____ 6. All the cars Honest Bob sells have a new transmissions.

_____ 7. Rosa ran the 100-meter race and throws the discus at the track meet.

_____ 8. Public schools in Florida an have air-conditioning system.

_____ 9. Office workers sat on the benches downtown and are eating their lunches outside.

_____ 10. Before a scuba diver goes underwater, you must check and recheck your breathing equipment. ■

EXERCISE 9-11   Revising a Paragraph
Writing in Progress

Directions: Reread the paragraph you wrote for Exercise 9-3. Check for shifts in person, number, and verb tense. Revise as needed. ■

AVOIDING MISPLACED AND DANGLING MODIFIERS

GOAL 3 Avoid misplaced and dangling modifiers

A **modifier** is a word, phrase, or clause that describes, qualifies, or limits the meaning of another word. Modifiers that are not correctly placed can confuse your reader.

Types of Modifiers

The following list will help you review the main types of modifiers:

1. **Adjectives modify nouns and pronouns.**

   It is an interesting photograph.

   She is very kind.

2. **Adverbs modify verbs, adjectives, or other adverbs.**

   I walked quickly.

   The cake tasted very good.

   The flowers are very beautifully arranged.

3. **Prepositional phrases modify nouns, adjectives, verbs, or adverbs.**

   The woman in the green dress is stunning.

   They walked into the store to buy milk.

4. ***-ing* phrases modify nouns or pronouns.**

   Waiting for the bus, Joe studied his history notes.

5. **Dependent clauses modify nouns, adjectives, verbs, or adverbs.** (A dependent clause has a subject and verb but is incomplete in meaning.)

   After I left campus, I went shopping.

   I left because classes were canceled.

   The kitten that I found in the bushes was frightened.

Misplaced Modifiers

Placement of a modifier in a sentence affects meaning:

   I need only to buy Marcos a gift.

   Only I need to buy Marcos a gift.

   I need to buy only Marcos a gift.

If a modifier is placed so that it does not convey the meaning you intend, it is called a **misplaced modifier.** Misplaced modifiers can make a sentence confusing.

MISPLACED   Anthony found a necklace at the mall <u>that sparkled and glittered</u>. [Which sparkled and glittered—the mall or the necklace?]

MISPLACED   The president announced that the club picnic would be held on August 2 <u>at the beginning of the meeting</u>. [Is the picnic being held at the beginning of the meeting on August 2, or did the president make the announcement at the beginning of the meeting?]

You can avoid a misplaced modifier if you make sure that the modifier immediately precedes or follows the word it modifies.

CORRECT   Anthony found a necklace <u>that sparkled and glittered</u> at the mall.

CORRECT   The club president announced <u>at the beginning of the meeting</u> that the picnic would be held on August 2.

Dangling Modifiers

Dangling modifiers are words or phrases that do not clearly describe or explain any part of the sentence. Dangling modifiers create confusion and sometimes unintentional humor. To avoid dangling modifiers, make sure that each modifying phrase or clause has a clear antecedent.

DANGLING   <u>Uncertain of which street to follow</u>, the <u>map</u> indicated we should turn left. [The opening modifier suggests that the map was uncertain of which street to follow.]

CORRECT   <u>Uncertain of which street to follow</u>, <u>we</u> checked a map, which indicated we should turn left.

DANGLING   My <u>shoes</u> got wet <u>walking across the street</u>. [The modifier suggests that the shoes were walking across the street by themselves.]

CORRECT   My shoes got wet <u>as I crossed the street</u>.

DANGLING   <u>To pass the test</u>, careful review is essential. [Who will pass the test?]

CORRECT   <u>To pass the test</u>, I must review carefully.

There are two common ways to revise dangling modifiers.

1. **Add a word or words that the modifier clearly describes**. Place the new material immediately after the modifier, and rearrange other parts of the sentence as necessary.

   DANGLING   <u>While walking in the garden</u>, <u>gunfire</u> sounded. [The opening modifier implies that the gunfire was walking in the garden.]

   CORRECT   <u>While walking in the garden</u>, <u>Carol</u> heard gunfire.

2. **Change the dangling modifier to a dependent clause**. You may need to change the verb form in the modifier.

   DANGLING   <u>While watching television</u>, the cake burned.

   CORRECT   <u>While Pat was watching television</u>, the cake burned.

NEED TO KNOW

Misplaced and Dangling Modifiers

- A **modifier** is a word, phrase, or clause that describes, qualifies, or limits the meaning of another word.

- A **misplaced modifier** is placed so that it does not convey the intended meaning.

- To avoid misplaced modifiers, be sure that you place the modifier immediately before or after the word it modifies.

- A **dangling modifier** is a word or phrase that does not clearly describe or explain any part of the sentence.

- To revise a dangling modifier you can add a word or words that the modifier clearly describes, or change the dangling modifier to a dependent clause.

EXERCISE 9-12   Correcting Misplaced or Dangling Modifiers

Directions: Revise each of the following sentences to correct misplaced or dangling modifiers.

EXAMPLE   Jerome mailed a bill at the post office that was long overdue.

REVISED   At the post office, Jerome mailed a bill that was long overdue.

1. Running at top speed, dirt was kicked up by the horse.

   _____

   _____

2. Swimming to shore, my arms got tired.

   _____

   _____

3. The helmet on the soldier's head with a red circle represented his nationality.

   _____

   _____

4. In order to answer your phone, the receiver must be lifted.

   _____

   _____

5. Walking up the stairs, the book dropped and tumbled down.

   _____

   _____

6. Twenty-five band members picked their instruments up from chairs that were gleaming and began to play.

_____

_____

7. Laughing, the cat chased the girl.

_____

_____

8. When skating, skate blades must be kept sharp.

_____

_____

9. The ball bounced off the roof that was round and red.

_____

_____

10. Ducking, the snowball hit Andy on the head.

_____

_____

■

EXERCISE 9-13   Correcting Misplaced or Dangling Modifiers

Directions: Revise each of the following sentences to correct misplaced or dangling modifiers.

EXAMPLE   Deciding which flavor of ice cream to order, another customer cut in front of Roger.

REVISED   While Roger was deciding which flavor of ice cream to order, another customer cut in front of him.

1. Tricia saw an animal at the zoo that had black fur and long claws.

_____

_____

2. Before answering the door, the phone rang.

_____

_____

3. I could see large snowflakes falling from the bedroom window.

_____

_____

4. Honking, Felicia walked in front of the car.

_____

_____

5. After leaving the classroom, the door automatically locked.

_____

_____

6. Applauding and cheering, the band returned for an encore.

_____

_____

7. The waiter brought a birthday cake to our table that had 24 candles.

_____

_____

8. Books lined the library shelves about every imaginable subject.

_____

_____

9. While sobbing, the sad movie ended and the lights came on.

_____

_____

10. Turning the page, the book's binding cracked.

_____

_____

■

EXERCISE 9-14
Writing in Progress

Revising a Paragraph

Directions: Reread the paragraph you wrote for Exercise 9-3. Check for dangling or misplaced modifiers. Revise as needed. ■

USING PARALLELISM

GOAL 4
Use parallelism

Study the following pairs of sentences. Which sentence in each pair reads more smoothly?

Pair 1
1. Seth, a long-distance biker, enjoys swimming and drag races cars.
2. Seth enjoys long-distance biking, swimming, and drag racing.

Pair 2
3. The dog was large, had a beautiful coat, and it was friendly.
4. The dog was large, beautiful, and friendly.

mywriting**lab**

To practice parallelism, go to
■ Study Plan
■ Sentence Improvement
■ Parallelism

Do sentences 2 and 4 sound better than 1 and 3? Sentences 2 and 4 have balance. Similar words have similar grammatical form. In sentence 2, *biking, swimming,* and *drag racing* are all nouns ending in *-ing*. In sentence 4, *large, beautiful,* and *friendly* are all adjectives. The method of balancing similar elements within a sentence is called **parallelism.** Parallelism makes your writing smooth and makes your ideas easier to follow.

EXERCISE 9-15   Examining Parallelism

Directions: In each group of words, circle the element that is not parallel.

EXAMPLE   walking, running, (to jog,) dancing

1. intelligent, successful, responsibly, mature

2. happily, quickly, hurriedly, hungry

3. wrote, answering, worked, typed

4. to fly, parachutes, to skydive, to drive

5. were painting, drew, were carving, were coloring

6. sat in the sun, played cards, scuba diving, ate lobster

7. thoughtful, honestly, humorous, quick-tempered

8. rewrote my résumé, arranging interviews, buying a new suit, getting a haircut

9. buy stamps, cash check, dry cleaning, return library books

10. eating sensibly, eight hours of sleep, exercising, drinking a lot of water

What Should Be Parallel?

When you write, be sure to keep each of the following elements parallel:

1. **Nouns in a series**

NOT PARALLEL   The callers on the talk show included a <u>teenager</u>, a <u>man who worked in construction</u>, and a <u>flight attendant</u>.

PARALLEL   The callers on the talk show included a <u>teenager</u>, a <u>construction worker</u>, and a <u>flight attendant</u>.

2. **Adjectives in a series**

| | | adjective | "-ing" phrase |

NOT PARALLEL   The students in the class seemed <u>tired</u> and <u>not paying attention</u>.

PARALLEL   The students in the class seemed <u>tired</u> and <u>inattentive</u>.

(adjective ... adjective)

3. **Verbs in a series** (They should have the same tense.)

simple past   past progressive

NOT PARALLEL   The couple <u>danced</u> and <u>were joking</u>.

simple past   simple past

PARALLEL   The couple <u>danced</u> and <u>joked</u>.

4. **Clauses within sentences**

prepositional phrase

NOT PARALLEL   The students were angry <u>about the parking difficulties</u> and <u>that no one was concerned</u>.

dependent clause

dependent clause

PARALLEL   The students were angry <u>that it was difficult to park</u> and <u>that no one was concerned</u>.

dependent clause

5. **Items being compared or contrasted**

noun   infinitive phrase

NOT PARALLEL   <u>Honesty</u> is better than <u>to be dishonest</u>.

infinitive phrase   infinitive phrase

PARALLEL   It is better <u>to be honest</u> than <u>to be dishonest</u>.

noun   pronoun

NOT PARALLEL   The students wanted <u>parking spaces</u>, not <u>someone to feel sorry for them</u>.

infinitive phrase

noun   noun

PARALLEL   The students wanted <u>parking spaces</u>, not <u>sympathy</u>.

NEED TO KNOW

Parallelism

- **Parallelism** is a method of balancing similar elements within a sentence.
- The following elements of a sentence should be parallel: nouns in a series, adjectives in a series, verbs in a series, clauses within a sentence, and items being compared or contrasted.

EXERCISE 9-16   Correcting Parallelism Errors

Directions: Revise each of the following sentences to correct errors in parallel structure.

EXAMPLE   The instructor ~~was demanding~~ *demanded hard work* and insisted on high standards.

1. Accuracy is more important than being speedy.

2. The teller counted and recounts the money.

3. Newspapers are blowing away and scattered on the sidewalk.

4. Judith was pleased when she graduated and that she received an honors diploma.

5. Thrilled and exhausting, the runners crossed the finish line.

6. Our guest speakers for the semester are a radiologist, a student student medicine, and a hospital administrator.

7. Students shouted and were hollering at the basketball game.

8. We enjoyed seeing the Grand Canyon, riding a mule, and photography.

9. Laughing and relaxed, the co-workers enjoyed lunch at the Mexican restaurant.

10. Professor Higuera is well known for his humor, clear lecturing, and scholarship. ■

EXERCISE 9-17   Correcting Parallelism Errors

Directions: Revise each of the following sentences to achieve parallelism.

EXAMPLE   Rosa has decided to study nursing instead of ~~going into~~ accounting.

1. The priest baptized the baby and congratulates the new parents.

2. We ordered a platter of fried clams, a platter of corn on the cob, and fried shrimp.

3. Lucy entered the dance contest, but the dance was watched by June from the side.

4. Léon purchased the ratchet set at the garage sale and buying the drill bits there, too.

5. The exterminator told Brandon the house needed to be fumigated and spraying to eliminate the termites.

6. The bus swerved and hit the dump truck, which swerves and hit the station wagon, which swerved and hit the bicycle.

7. Channel 2 covered the bank robbery, but a python that had escaped from the zoo was reported by Channel 7.

8. Sal was born when Nixon was president, and Johnson was president when Rob was born.

9. The pediatrician spent the morning with sore throats, answering questions about immunizations, and treating bumps and bruises.

10. Belinda prefers to study in the library, but her brother Marcus studies at home. ■

EXERCISE 9-18
Writing in Progress

Revising a Paragraph

Directions: Reread the paragraph you wrote for Exercise 9-3. Correct any sentences that lack parallelism. ■

EXERCISE 9-19

Revising Sentences

Directions: Now that you have learned about common errors that produce confusing or inconsistent sentences, turn back to the confusing sentences used to introduce the chapter on p. 235. Identify each error, and revise the sentences so they convey the intended meaning. ■

EXERCISE 9-20
Working Together

Revising a Paragraph

Directions: Working with a classmate, revise this student paragraph by correcting all instances of misplaced or dangling modifiers, shifts in verb tense, and faulty parallelism.

Robert Burns said that the dog is "man's best friend." To a large extent, this statement may be more true than you think. What makes dogs so special to humans is their unending loyalty and that they love unconditionally. Dogs have been known to cross the entire United States to return home. Unlike people, dogs never made fun of you or criticize you. They never throw fits, and they seem happy always to see you. This may not necessarily be true of your family, friends, and those who live near you. A dog never lies to you, never betrays your confidences, and never stayed angry with you for more than five minutes. Best of all, he or she never expects more than the basics from you of food and shelter and a simple pat on the head in return for his or her devotion. The world would be a better place if people could only be more like their dogs. ■

Analyze It!

Directions: Revise any sentences in the paragraph that contain errors in pronoun reference, shifts in person, number, or verb tense, or dangling or misplaced modifiers.

In 1994 the Smithsonian Institution received the largest single cash donation in their history; the Mashantucket Pequots presented a 10-million-dollar gift to the Smithsonian to help build the National Museum of the American Indian. That small Connecticut tribe wanted to share the riches from their giant casino and bingo complex. The Pequot tribe owns the Mashantucket Pequot Museum and Research Center, located in Connecticut, in addition to supporting the National Museum of the American Indian; it serves as a major resource on American Native histories and cultures. The Pequots have given donations to many other causes; for example it gave two million dollars to the Special Olympics World Games held in New Haven, Connecticut, in 1995.

Most of the money for the National Museum of the American Indian came from the federal government, but private organizations and individuals also donated his or her share of the construction costs. It says on the museum's website that the facility was designed in consultation with Native peoples. The museum opened their doors on the National Mall in Washington, D.C., in September 2004.

—adapted from the *Cape Cod Times*.

A STUDENT ESSAY
The Student Writer and the Writing Task

The Writer

Kelly Bajier is a student at Avila University in Kansas City, Missouri, where she is majoring in nursing.

The Writing Task

Bajier wrote this essay for a writing class. Her instructor encouraged

her to submit her essay to a writing contest sponsored by Longman Publishers, the publisher of this book. Bajier's essay was selected from among hundreds of essays as a good model essay. As you read, notice Bajier's use of clear and correct sentences throughout.

Rebuilding a Dream

Kelly Bajier

It only took one final strong gust of wind, filled with debris and bullet-like raindrops, to finish the destruction of the home I knew and loved. My perfect beachfront home was a casualty to one of Mother Nature's most monstrous

Background information
about the home

Thesis statement
Topic sentence

Details

Topic sentence

Details

Topic sentence

Details

Conclusion: Bajier reflects
on the rebuilding process.

creations, otherwise known as a hurricane. My father had the house built almost fifteen years ago. I remember him overseeing the construction process as the carpenters and other workers slaved for hours each day. At last the work had been completed. The result was a dream vacation house. The first time I set foot in the brand new entry foyer, I trembled with excitement. I could only imagine the magical moments that would take place over the next years of my life. Some of my most vivid and life-changing memories took place in that house. The first summer ever spent in that house was the most memorable because everywhere I went I had a new adventure waiting for me. I explored the beach for miles. I would run up into the dunes, and my mom would later have to come searching for me to tell me that dinner was ready. After the hurricane destroyed the house, it was up to me and my brother to rebuild it.

After the hurricane, the house was just one big pile of soggy wood. My first task was to clean up the debris, with the help of my brother, David, and plan the rebuilding process. We carried all of the pieces that we could over to a nearby Dumpster. Then we had to break down some of the larger pieces that were still held together by a few screws here and there. Within a couple of months, we had the lot almost completely cleaned up. All that remained of the house was its foundation. David had someone come out to inspect the lot to make sure that it was still buildable. To our delight, it was. First, we had blueprints drawn. Then we ordered wood. The journey had begun and I was on my way to rebuilding the house.

Every day for the next three months, I got up at seven thirty in the morning and picked up where I left off the night before. My hands were burning with exhaustion. Not to mention, I have the world's worst farmer's tan on my shoulders and legs. After five months of hard work, the frame was finally built. Then, I could actually start building the house. I had to get all of the technical work done before I could go any further with the building process. I got the roof done, followed by the siding. Finally, it actually began to look like a house. At the end, I got to decorate it.

The final result was a four-bedroom, two-and-a-half-bath masterpiece. It has all the latest luxuries: a Jacuzzi tub, heated wood floors, and a new alarm system. Every room has its own theme. The kitchen, of course, has the beach theme. The bathrooms all have the same concept of soft and inviting pastels. The master bedroom is my favorite. It has a tribal theme. The blinds are made of bamboo and the bedspread is made of the most intriguing material that is cold and silky to the touch. It has little gold beads imbedded throughout the entire surface. The other three bedrooms are simple. One has a sailboat theme; another has a train theme. The last one has an Indian-like theme, with maroon complemented by gold and various shades of green. This house truly is a dream come true.

A year ago to this day, I stood staring at a pile of trash. After months and months of hard work, I could finally stand back and survey my creation. I stood on the beach facing my new home. The steady waves of wind caressed my face as they made their way past me. The sun's rays beat down on my shoulders and upper back and sent a wave of warmth racing through my entire body. All I could hear was the screeching of seagulls as they glided through the air, surfing in the wind. Clear skies blanketed the ocean for what seemed like forever. All I could think about was how grateful I was for this moment. As a cluster of emotions ran through me, I realized that this was it. My heart and soul belonged in this peaceful place that I called home—my rebuilt home.

EXAMINING STUDENT WRITING

1. Evaluate Bajier's thesis statement and its placement. How could the statement be strengthened?

2. How does Bajier organize her essay?

3. Evaluate the types of details that Bajier includes. Highlight several places where her details help you visualize the situation.

4. Evaluate Bajier's conclusion. Why is it effective?

Paragraph Writing Scenarios

Friends and Family

1. Think of a relative you were close to as a child. Write a paragraph about a time you did something together that made you laugh.

2. Write a paragraph that begins "I thought (choose a person) was my friend, but. . . ."

Classes and Campus Life

1. Think of a place on campus where you usually have to wait in line. Write a paragraph about that place, what you are waiting for, and how you feel about lines.

2. Some instructors allow food and drinks in class; others don't. Write a paragraph expressing your opinion on whether or not you should be allowed to eat in class.

Working Students

1. Write a paragraph about the worst day in your week. What makes this day more difficult than the others?

2. Write a paragraph describing the perfect day off.

Communities and Cultures

1. Think of a country you've never seen but would like to visit. Write a paragraph explaining why you would like to go there. Use your imagination and plenty of details to describe what appeals to you about this country.

2. Transportation varies from place to place. Bus or plane passengers, for example, form a community. Write a paragraph about a kind of transportation you use on a regular basis. What behaviors do you share with other passengers or drivers?

WRITING ABOUT A READING

THINKING BEFORE READING

In the following reading, the author discusses what happens to our discarded electronics. Before you read:

1. Preview the reading, using the steps listed in Chapter 2, p. 35.
2. Connect the reading to your own experience by answering the following questions:
   a. What kinds of things do you typically recycle?
   b. What happens to your old cell phones and other electronic devices when you have finished using them?
3. Mark and annotate as you read.

READING

WASTE WOES

Chris Jozefowicz

1   Matthew Gallagher has skeletons in his attic—and stuffed into a drawer. The 19-year-old from Louisville, Ky., is holding on to the skeletons of electronics past. His family has an old TV and a computer in the attic. Gallagher keeps an obsolete **MP3 player** and a collection of abandoned handheld games in a drawer. While the old electronics languish, Gallagher is dreaming of new gadgets. "Oh, I definitely want to upgrade," he says. He hopes to get a new smart phone and a laptop computer during his first year of college. So why keep the old stuff? "Subconsciously, I guess I think I'll use them again," admits Gallagher. But he rarely does. Instead, they pile up as electronic waste, or e-waste, inside the Gallagher house.

MP3 player
an electronic device that stores, organizes, and plays audio files

2   E-waste is junk with significant electronic components. "Basically, it is anything with a circuit board," says Barbara Kyle, the national coordinator for the Electronics TakeBack Coalition, an organization that fights e-waste. Electronic equipment contains chemicals that can be dangerous if people come in contact with them. Yet tons of electronics are thrown away each day. Some companies even ship e-waste to other countries, where it may be taken apart by people for little money and with a big risk of damage to their health. "The problem is growing exponentially," says Kyle. "Think about all the stuff we have that wasn't even around five years ago."

21st-Century Trash

3   Some consumers, such as the Gallagher family, hoard old equipment, but most electronics end up as part of the waste stream. In 2007, Americans discarded 2.5 million tons of TVs, cell phones, computers, and printers, according to the Environmental Protection Agency (EPA). Worldwide, people throw away 10 to 20 times as much each year. That's enough e-waste to fill a train that stretches around the globe.

4   A fraction of those electronics gets recycled. Greg Spears is vice president of American Industrial Services, an Indiana company involved in recycling e-waste. "We're seeing a lot of TVs because of the switch over to digital TV last year," he says. Recyclers break down electronics and separate the plastic, metal, glass, and other parts to reuse. Spears estimates that 90 percent of appliances, such as TVs or computer monitors, can be recycled, but EPA figures suggest that more than 80 percent of electronics in the United States are not recycled. Some of those electronics end up in landfills close to home. Many more are shipped overseas—sometimes illegally—and left in huge e-waste dumps in Asia, Africa, and Latin America.

Passing the Problem

5   Chemicals can leach into the ground, water, or air if e-waste is not disposed of properly. Professor Valerie Thomas studies recycling at the Georgia Institute of Technology in Atlanta. She says dangerous chemicals are the biggest problem related to e-waste. "E-waste contains chemicals that are toxic," Thomas says. "It can pollute if it goes into a landfill or **incinerator**, and it can pollute if it is recycled because it has to be opened up."

incinerator
a furnace for burning trash

6   So why would other countries take dangerous waste? For money, of course. Spears says junk can often be shipped overseas for less money than it takes to dismantle and sell the parts in the United States. Poor people living in countries such as China or Ghana will then break apart the old electronics and sell the parts for a few dollars a day. Often, children work beside adults in the e-waste scrap yards. In most cases, laws to protect those workers are weak or nonexistent. "The electronics land in places where people earn next to nothing," Kyle says. "The system relies on low-wage workers to basically bash open electronics. People remove the metals and junk the rest. They burn the plastics. It's literally poisoning people."

Will your discarded TV end up in a ditch in Ghana?

7   Those old, thick TVs that are being replaced by flat-screen models can contain more than 5 pounds of lead in each screen. The lead may poison workers who break apart the TVs, and it often pollutes the environment around e-waste dumps. More than 80 percent of kids living in one e-waste recycling town in China had high levels of lead in their blood, according to a recent study. That's a huge health problem because elevated lead levels can damage nerves and kidneys, and slow bone and muscle growth. Lead is

particularly dangerous for kids' brains, which are still developing. Additional studies have shown that people who live and work near e-waste dumps have high levels of other dangerous chemicals in their bodies, raising the risk for cancer and a range of other diseases.

Buyers Beware

8   To prevent e-waste pollution from spreading, people in countries that generate millions of tons of waste—such as the United States—must work to recycle responsibly. Many communities have e-waste recycling collections, but people still need to call the recycler to make sure their e-waste is not shipped overseas. Some large store chains offer free recycling for old electronics and batteries. Even the U.S. Postal Service runs a program that allows people to mail small electronics to a recycler free of charge.

9   Kyle and the Electronics TakeBack Coalition want the federal government to pass laws forbidding the export of e-waste to other nations. "We think manufacturers should take back and recycle our old products when we are done with them, and that the price of the products should include the cost of recycling," Kyle says. "Otherwise, people pay for it [with their health] in China." Consumers can also help solve e-waste problems by buying electronics made with fewer toxic chemicals. Everyone should keep some simple goals in mind to help reduce waste in their electronics, Thomas says. "People should ask themselves, 'Can I upgrade my old one instead of getting a new one? How long will this product last?'"

10   Young people buy and use so many electronic gadgets that they have the power to influence better e-waste practices. One such activist is Jennifer Roberts, who helped fight e-waste at the University of California (UC) in Santa Cruz, where she was recently a student. She helped create Toxic Free UC, a group that succeeded in inspiring the university to commit to buying electronics that are low in toxins and easy to recycle. "Students can make their own campaigns," Roberts says. "There has to be a grassroots campaign of consumers. People have to say, 'I'm not going to support your company if you are putting all these horrible chemicals in your computers and cell phones and not taking care of them at the end of their lives.'"

GETTING READY TO WRITE

Reviewing the Reading

Answer each of the following questions using complete sentences.

1. Define the term *e-waste* and give examples. Why is e-waste dangerous?

2. What happens to most electronic waste? Cite statistics from the article.

3. According to Professor Valerie Thomas, what is the biggest problem related to e-waste? Explain why.

4. Describe some of the specific health effects of exposure to e-waste.

5. List four ways that consumers can help prevent e-waste pollution from spreading and help solve e-waste problems.

Examining the Reading Using an Idea Map

Review the reading by completing the missing parts of the idea map shown below.

Visualize It!

Title **Waste Woes**

Thesis

Discarded electronics often become toxic waste at home and around the world.

E-waste is trash with electronic components.

_____

Americans discarded 2.5 million tons of electronics in 2007.

_____
_____

A fraction of electronics gets recycled.

Most appliances, including TVs and computers, can be recycled.

_____
_____

E-waste can release toxic chemicals into the ground, water, or air.

Other countries accept electronic waste for money.

_____
_____

_____
_____

_____
_____

Consumers can stop e-waste from spreading in several ways.

Work to recycle responsibly.

_____
_____

_____
_____

_____
_____

Conclusion

The author concludes with a call to action for consumers.

Strengthening Your Vocabulary

Using the word's context, word parts, or a dictionary, write a brief definition of each of the following words as it is used in the reading.

1. obsolete (paragraph 1) _____
2. languish (paragraph 1) _____
3. exponentially (paragraph 2) _____
4. hoard (paragraph 3) _____
5. leach (paragraph 5) _____
6. toxic (paragraph 5) _____
7. dismantle (paragraph 6) _____

Reacting to Ideas: Discussion and Journal Writing

Get ready to write about the reading by discussing the following:

1. What was the author's purpose in writing this article?

2. Why do you think some people hoard their old electronics? Why don't more people recycle their old electronics instead of just throwing them away?

3. Analyze the kinds of supporting evidence the author uses in this article. In your opinion, which types of evidence—opinions, facts, statistics, examples— were most persuasive?

 **Thinking Visually**

4. What details do you notice about the photograph of the young boy on page 260? How does this picture add to your understanding of the reading?

WRITING ABOUT THE READING

Paragraph Options

1. Did this article change your opinion about recycling your old electronics? Write a paragraph explaining why or why not.

2. Do you think the federal government should make it illegal to export e-waste to other countries? Write a paragraph explaining your answer.

3. Would you be willing to pay more for an electronic product if the price included the cost of recycling? Write a paragraph explaining why you think this is or is not a good idea.

Essay Options

4. The article describes the power of young people to create campaigns that influence e-waste policies. For what purpose or cause would you be willing to create a grassroots campaign? Write an essay explaining your answer.

5. Write an essay in the form of a letter to the editor of your newspaper, explaining the problem of e-waste and calling for specific actions on the part of consumers.

6. Write an essay examining the ways that you could reduce the amount of e-waste that you generate in your own life.

CHAPTER REVIEW AND PRACTICE

CHAPTER REVIEW

Revising Confusing and Inconsistent Sentences

To review and check your recall of the chapter, select the word or phrase from the box below that best completes each of the sentences that follow. Not all of the words will be used.

adjectives	adverbs	antecedent	dangling	first
indefinite	-ing phrases	misplaced	modifier	number
parallelism	person	plural	precedent	pronoun
second	singular	tense	third	

1. A(n) _____ must always come before the pronoun to which it refers.

2. A pronoun and its antecedent must agree in _____. They must both be either singular or plural.

3. *Any*, *each*, *everyone*, and *some* are examples of _____ pronouns.

4. The grammatical term used to identify the speaker or writer is _____.

5. Verb _____ indicates past, present, or future.

6. A(n) _____ is a word, phrase, or clause that describes, qualifies, or limits the meaning of another word.

7. _____ and -ing phrases modify nouns and pronouns.

8. A(n) _____ modifier is a modifier that has been placed in a sentence where its meaning is unclear.

9. A(n) _____ modifier is a word or phrase that does not clearly describe or explain any part of the sentence it is in.

10. _____ is a method of balancing a series of nouns, verbs, or adjectives in a sentence.

EDITING PRACTICE

Revise the following paragraph so that all words or phrases in a series, independent clauses joined by a coordinating conjunction, and items being compared are parallel. Write your corrections above the lines.

The first practical pair of roller skates was made in Belgium in 1759 and is designed like ice skates. The skates had two wheels instead of being made with four wheels as they are today. The wheels were aligned down the center of the skate, but were containing no ball bearings. The skates had a life of their own. Without ball bearings, they resisted turning, then were turning abruptly, and then refuse to stop. Finally, they jammed to a halt on their own. Until 1884, when ball bearings were introduced, roller-skating was unpopular, difficult, and it was dangerous for people to do. However, when skating technology improved, roller-skates began to compete with ice-skating. Later, an American made roller skates with sets of wheels placed side-by-side rather than by placing them behind one another, and that design lasted until recently. Since 1980, however, many companies have been manufacturing skates based on the older design. In other words, in-line skates are back, and more and more people are discovering Rollerblading joys and that it benefits their health.

PEARSON mywritinglab For support in meeting this chapter's objectives, log in to www.mywritinglab.com, go to the Study Plan tab, click on Revising Confusing and Inconsistent Sentences and choose Pronouns, Pronoun–Antecedent Agreement, Consistent Verb Tense and Active Voice, Misplaced or Dangling Modifiers, and Parallelism from the list of subtopics. Read and view the videos and resources in the Review Materials section, and then complete the Recall, Apply, and Write exercises in the Activities section. You can check your scores and overall progress by using the Gradebook.

10 Using Verbs Correctly

"Then she goes, 'I gotta go,' and I go, 'Okay,' and she goes, 'Later,' and I go, 'Go already!'"

WRITE ABOUT IT!

Have you ever stopped to listen to the way people misuse verbs? Write a sentence evaluating this teenager's use of language.

Did you notice that, in this sentence, the speaker has used *go* instead of more interesting and descriptive verbs like *yelled*, *retorted*, *said*, *replied*, *snorted*, or *exclaimed*? Verbs are words that express action. Using them correctly is essential to good writing and can make the difference between something that is dull or difficult to read and something that is interesting or fun to read. In this chapter you will focus on forming verb tenses with regular and irregular verbs.

WRITING

USING VERB TENSES CORRECTLY

GOAL 1 Use verb
tenses correctly

mywritinglab

To practice using verbs, go to
- Study Plan
- Sentence Improvement
- Consistent Verb Tense and Active Voice

The primary function of verbs is to express action or a condition. However, verbs also indicate time. **Verb tenses** tell us whether an action takes place in the present, past, or future.

The three basic verb tenses are the **simple present**, **simple past**, and **simple future.** There are also nine other verb tenses in English. To review these tenses, see Part VIII, "Reviewing the Basics," p. 557. Using verb tenses consistently (avoiding shifts in tense) is discussed in Chapter 9, on p. 245.

There are two types of verbs: *regular* and *irregular.* The forms of **regular verbs** follow a standard pattern of endings; the forms of **irregular verbs** do not. The English language contains many more regular verbs than irregular verbs.

The Simple Present Tense

The **present tense** indicates action that is occurring at the time of speaking or describes regular, habitual action.

HABITUAL ACTION	Maria works hard.
ACTION AT TIME OF SPEAKING	I see a rabbit on the lawn.

In the **simple present tense**, the verb for first person (*I* or *we*), second person (*you*), or third person plural (*they*) is the same as the infinitive; no ending is added. The verb for third person singular subjects (noun or pronoun) must end in *-s.*

To most third person singular infinitive verbs, just add *-s.* If the verb ends in *-s, -sh, -ch, -x,* or *-z,* add *-es* to make the third person singular form. If the verb ends in a consonant plus *-y,* change the *y* to *i,* and then add *-es* (*I hurry, he hurries*). If the verb ends in a vowel plus *-y,* just add *-s.* (*I stay, he stays*).

Third person singular subjects include the pronouns *he, she,* and *it* and all singular nouns (*a desk, the tall man*). In addition, uncountable nouns (*money, music, homework,* abstractions such as *beauty* and *happiness,* liquids, and so on) are followed by third person singular verbs. (*Water is essential for life.*) Singular collective nouns, such as *family, orchestra, team,* and *class,* also usually take a third person singular verb since they refer to one group.

SIMPLE PRESENT TENSE

Singular		Plural	
Subject	*Verb*	*Subject*	*Verb*
I	like	we	like
you	like	you	like
he, she, it	likes	they	like
Sam	likes	Sam and Brenda	like

In speech we often use nonstandard verb forms, and these are perfectly acceptable in informal conversation. However, these nonstandard forms are *not* used in college writing or in career writing.

In the examples on the next page, note the nonstandard forms of the verb *lift* and the way these forms differ from the correct, standard forms that you should use in your writing.

NONSTANDARD PRESENT	STANDARD PRESENT
Singular	*Singular*
I lifts	I lift
you lifts	you lift
she (he) lift	she (he) lifts
Plural	*Plural*
we lifts	we lift
you lifts	you lift
they lifts	they lift

EXERCISE 10-1   Identifying Verb Forms

Directions: The sentences below are in the simple present tense. First, underline the subject or subjects in each sentence. Then circle the correct verb form.

EXAMPLE   Sal (pick, picks) apples.

1. Planes (take, takes) off from the runway every five minutes.

2. I (enjoy, enjoys) sailing.

3. She (own, owns) a pet bird.

4. We (climb, climbs) the ladder to paint the house.

5. Engines (roar, roars) as the race begins.

6. They always (answer, answers) the phone on the first ring.

7. That elephant (walk, walks) very slowly.

8. You (speak, speaks) Spanish fluently.

9. He (say, says) his name is Luis.

10. Dinosaur movies (scare, scares) me. ■

EXERCISE 10-2   Using the Present Tense

Directions: For each of the following verbs, write a sentence using the simple present tense. Use a noun or *he, she, it,* or *they* as the subject of the sentence.

EXAMPLE   prefer   <u>Art prefers to sit in the front of the bus.</u>

1. call   _____

2. request   _____

3. laugh   _____

4. grow   _____

5. hide   _____

                                                                        ▪

The Simple Past Tense

The **past tense** refers to action that was completed in the past. To form the **simple past tense** of regular verbs, add *-d* or *-ed* to the verb. Note that with the simple past tense, the verb form does not change with person or number.

SIMPLE PAST TENSE			
Singular		**Plural**	
Subject	*Verb*	*Subject*	*Verb*
I	worked	we	worked
you	worked	you	worked
he, she, it	worked	they	worked
Sam	worked	Sam and Brenda	worked

In nonstandard English, the *-d* or *-ed* is often dropped. You may hear "Last night I work all night" instead of "Last night I work*ed* all night." In written English, be sure to include the *-d* or *-ed* ending.

The Simple Future Tense

The **future tense** refers to action that *will* happen in the future. Form the **simple future tense** by adding the helping verb *will* before the verb. Note that the verb form does not change with person or number.

SIMPLE FUTURE TENSE			
Singular		**Plural**	
Subject	*Verb*	*Subject*	*Verb*
I	will work	we	will work
you	will work	you	will work
he, she, it	will work	they	will work
Sam	will work	Sam and Brenda	will work

Tip for Writers

Subject Pronouns

Remember, in English you must include the subject pronoun with the verb. In some languages you do not need to do this because the verb ending indicates the person (first, second, or third) and number (singular or plural) of the sentence's subject.

EXAMPLE   He goes to the store.

Tip for Writers

Occasionally, *shall* (rather than *will*) is used as the first person helping verb in the *simple future* and *future continuous* tenses. It may be used in these situations

TALKING ABOUT A SERIOUS MATTER   Our country shall win this war no matter how long it takes!

MAKING A SUGGESTION OR AN OFFER   Shall we go now? Shall I get you some tea?

NEED TO KNOW
Verb Tense

- **Verb tense** indicates whether an action takes place in the present, past, or future.

- There are three basic verb tenses: **simple present**, **simple past**, and **simple future**.

- The **simple present tense** is used to describe regular, habitual action or can be used for nonaction verbs. It can also indicate action that is occurring at the time of speaking. The ending of a simple present tense verb must agree with the subject of the verb.

- The **simple past tense** refers to action that was completed in the past. For regular verbs, the simple past tense is formed by adding *-d* or *-ed*.

- The **simple future tense** refers to action that will happen in the future. The simple future tense is formed by adding the helping verb *will* before the verb.

EXERCISE 10-3   Using the Simple Past and Simple Future Tenses

Directions: For each of the following verbs, write a sentence using the simple past tense and one using the simple future tense.

EXAMPLE   overcook   The chef overcooked my steak.

I know he will overcook my steak.

1. dance

2. hunt

3. joke

4. watch

5. photograph

EXERCISE 10-4 Writing a Paragraph

Writing in Progress

Directions: Write a paragraph on one of the following topics, using either the simple past tense or the simple future tense.

1. Selecting a movie to rent

2. Cleaning the attic or garage

3. Selecting courses for next semester

4. Buying groceries

5. Caring for a three-year-old child ■

USING IRREGULAR VERBS CORRECTLY

GOAL 2 Use irregular verbs correctly

Errors in verb tense can occur easily with irregular verbs. Irregular verbs do not form the simple past tense according to the pattern we have studied. A regular verb forms the simple past tense by adding *-d* or *-ed*. An irregular verb forms the simple past tense by changing its spelling internally (for example, "I feed" becomes "I fed") or by not changing at all (for example, "I cut" remains "I cut").

Tip for Writers

Helping Verbs

A helping verb is used before the main verb to form certain tenses.

helping verb main verb

Ericka will sit in front of the television for hours.

Common helping verbs include:

have	has	had
be	am	is
do	does	did
are	was	were
being	been	

The following verbs can only be used as helping verbs:

can	could
will	would
shall	should
may	might
must	ought to

EXAMPLE I can leave tomorrow. I may cancel my insurance.

Three Troublesome Irregular Verbs

The verbs *be, do,* and *have* can be especially troublesome. You should master the correct forms of these verbs in both the present tenses and the past tenses since they are used so often.

1. **Irregular Verb: Be**

	PRESENT	PAST
Singular	I am	I was
	you are	you were
	he, she, it is	he, she, it was
Plural	we are	we were
	you are	you were
	they are	they were

• It is nonstandard to use *be* for all present tense forms.

| INCORRECT | I <u>be</u> finished. |
| CORRECT | I <u>am</u> finished. |

| INCORRECT | They <u>be</u> surprised. |
| CORRECT | They <u>are</u> surprised. |

Tip for Writers

The pronoun *you* is always grammatically plural in English. Use plural verbs (*are, have,* or *were*) with *you,* not singular forms such as *is, has,* or *was.* Use a plural verb with *you* even when you are speaking or writing to one person.

- Another error is to use *was* instead of *were* for plural past tenses or with *you.*

| INCORRECT | We <u>was</u> late. |
| CORRECT | We <u>were</u> late. |

| INCORRECT | You <u>was</u> wrong. |
| CORRECT | You <u>were</u> wrong. |

- Note that the verb *to be* never takes an object.

2. Irregular Verb: Do

	PRESENT	PAST
Singular	I do	I did
	you do	you did
	he, she, it <u>does</u>	he, she, it did
Plural	we do	we did
	you do	you did
	they do	they did

Tip for Writers

Does, as a main verb or a helping verb, is used only with third-person singular or uncountable subjects, such as *he, Maria, the book, homework, music,* or *an idea.* Use *do,* not *does,* after *I, you,* or *they.*

- A common error is to use *does* instead of *do* for present plural forms.

| INCORRECT | We <u>does</u> our best. |
| CORRECT | We <u>do</u> our best. |

| INCORRECT | They <u>doesn't</u> know the answer. |
| CORRECT | They <u>don't</u> know the answer. |

- Another error is to use *done* instead of *did* for past plural forms.

| INCORRECT | We <u>done</u> everything. You <u>done</u> finish. |
| CORRECT | We <u>did</u> everything. You <u>did</u> finish. |

3. Irregular Verb: Have

	PRESENT	PAST
Singular	I have	I had
	you have	you had
	he, she, it has	he, she, it had
Plural	we have	we had
	you have	you had
	they have	they had

- A common, nonstandard form uses *has* instead of *have* for the present plural.

| INCORRECT | We <u>has</u> enough. They <u>has</u> a good reason. |
| CORRECT | We <u>have</u> enough. They <u>have</u> a good reason. |

- Another error occurs in the past singular.

    INCORRECT   I <u>has</u> nothing to give you. You <u>has</u> a bad day.

    CORRECT   I <u>had</u> nothing to give you. You <u>had</u> a bad day.

EXERCISE 10-5   Using Standard Verb Forms

Directions: Circle the correct, standard form of the verb in each of the following sentences.

EXAMPLE   Last April Anne (was, were) in Nevada.

1. After I watched the news, I (does, did) my homework.

2. You (be, were) lucky to win the raffle.

3. The electrician (have, has) enough time to complete the job.

4. When I am reading about the Civil War, I (am, be) captivated.

5. All the waitresses I know (have, has) sore feet.

6. We (was, were) at the grocery store yesterday.

7. He (do, does) his studying at the library.

8. We (did, done) the jigsaw puzzle while it rained.

9. Alice Walker (be, is) a favorite author of mine.

10. You (was, were) in the audience when the trophy was awarded. ■

EXERCISE 10-6   Using Irregular Verbs

Directions: Write sentences for each pair of irregular verb shown below. Try to write several sentences that ask questions.

EXAMPLE   am _I am going to the Bulls game tonight._

be _Will you be at home tonight?_

1. do _____

   does _____

2. was _____

   were _____

3. is _____

   be _____

4. do _____

   did _____

5. am _____

   was _____

■

EXERCISE 10-7   Using Irregular Verbs

Directions: Write sentences for each pair of irregular verbs shown below. Use a plural pronoun (*we, you, they*) or a plural noun.

EXAMPLE   be _We will be at my dad's house._

were _They were happy to see us._

1. do _____

   did _____

2. are _____

   be _____

3. have _____

   had _____

4. are _____

   were _____

5. be _____

   were _____

■

EXERCISE 10-8   Correcting Verb Errors
Working Together

Directions: Working with a classmate, read the following student paragraph and correct all verb errors.

Sometimes first impressions of people is very inaccurate and can lead to problems. My brother, Larry, learn this the hard way. When he was 17, Larry and I was driving to the mall. Larry decided to pick up a hitchhiker because he looks safe and trustworthy. After the man got in the car, we notice that he was wearing a knife. A few miles later, the man suddenly tell us to take him to Canada. So my brother said we'd have to stop for gas and explained that he did not have any money. The man get out of the car to pump the gas. When he goes up to the attendant to pay for the gas, we took off. We do not stop until we reach the police station, where we tell the officer in charge what happens. The police caught the man several miles from the gas station. He be serving time in prison for burglary and had escaped over the weekend. Later, Larry said, "I was lucky that my first impression were not my last!" ■

Other Irregular Verbs

Among the other verbs that form the past tense in irregular ways are *become* (*became*), *drive* (*drove*), *hide* (*hid*), *stand* (*stood*), and *wear* (*wore*). For a list of the past-tense forms of other common irregular verbs, see Part VIII, p. 556. If you have a question about the form of a verb, consult this list or your dictionary.

Confusing Pairs of Irregular Verbs

Two particularly confusing pairs of irregular verbs are *lie/lay* and *sit/set*.

Lie/Lay

Lie means to recline. *Lay* means to put something down. The past tense of *lie* is *lay*. The past tense of *lay* is *laid*.

SIMPLE PRESENT	SIMPLE PAST
Command the dog to <u>lie</u> down.	The dog <u>lay</u> down.
<u>Lay</u> the boards over here.	The carpenter <u>laid</u> the boards over there.

Sit/Set

Sit means to be seated. *Set* means to put something down. The past tense of *sit* is *sat*. The past tense of *set* is *set*.

SIMPLE PRESENT	SIMPLE PAST
Please <u>sit</u> over here.	We <u>sat</u> over here.
<u>Set</u> the books on the table.	He <u>set</u> the books on the table.

NEED TO KNOW

Irregular Verbs

- An **irregular verb** does not form the simple past tense with *-d* or *-ed*.

- Three particularly troublesome irregular verbs are *be, do,* and *have*.

- Two confusing pairs of verbs are *lie/lay* and *sit/set*. Each has a distinct meaning.

EXERCISE 10-9   Using Correct Verbs

Directions: Circle the correct verb in each of the following sentences.

EXAMPLE   Eric plans to (lay, (lie)) in bed all day.

1. The chef (sat, set) the mixer on "high" to beat the eggs.

2. I prefer to (lie, lay) on the hammock rather than on a chaise.

3. The students (sit, set) in rows to take the exam.

4. After putting up the wallboard, James (lay, laid) the hammer on the floor.

5. Bags of grain (set, sat) on the truck.

6. I'm going to (lie, lay) down and take a short nap.

7. Because we came late, we (sat, set) in the last row.

8. The kitten (lay, laid) asleep in the laundry basket.

9. Bob (sat, set) the groceries on the counter.

10. Completely exhausted, Shawna (lay, laid) on the sofa. ■

AVOIDING SUBJECT-VERB AGREEMENT ERRORS

GOAL 3 Avoid subject-verb agreement errors

A subject and its verb must agree (be consistent) in person (first, second, third) and in number (singular, plural). (For more on pronoun forms, see p. 551; for more on verb forms in all persons and number, see p. 555.)

The most common problems with subject-verb agreement occur with third-person present tense verbs, which are formed for most verbs by adding -s or -es. (For the present tense and past tense forms of certain irregular verbs, see p. 556.)

Agreement Rules

1. **Use the present tense ending -s or -es if a verb's subject is third-person singular.** For first and second person, no ending is added.

Singular Subject	Verb	Singular Subject	Verb
I	talk	it	talks
you	talk	Sally	talks
he	talks	a boy	talks
she	talks		

2. **For a plural subject (more than one person, place, thing, or idea), use a plural form of the verb.**

Plural Subject	Verb	Plural Subject	Verb
we	talk	Sally and James	talk
you	talk	boys	talk
they	talk		

Common Errors

The following circumstances often lead to errors in subject-verb agreement:

1. **Third-person singular** A common error is to omit the *-s* or *-es* in a third-person singular verb in the present tense. The subjects *he, she,* and *it,* or a noun that could be replaced with *he, she,* or *it,* all take a third-person singular verb.

   INCORRECT   She <u>act</u> like a professional.

   CORRECT   She <u>acts</u> like a professional.

   INCORRECT   <u>Professor Simmons</u> <u>pace</u> while he lectures.

   CORRECT   <u>Professor Simmons</u> <u>paces</u> while he lectures.

2. **Verbs before their subjects** When a verb comes before its subject, as in sentences beginning with *Here* or *There,* it is easy to make an agreement error. *Here* and *there* are never subjects of a sentence and do not determine the correct form of the verb. Look for the subject *after* the verb and, depending on its number, choose a singular or plural verb.

   singular verb   singular subject

   There <u>is</u> a <u>pebble</u> in my shoe.

   plural verb   plural subject

   There <u>are</u> two <u>pebbles</u> in my shoe.

3. **Words between the subject and its verb** Words, phrases, and clauses coming between the subject and its verb do not change the fact that the verb must agree with the subject. To check that the verb is correct, mentally remove everything between the subject and its verb and make sure that the verb agrees in number with its subject.

   singular subject   singular verb

   A <u>list</u> of course offerings <u>is posted</u> on the bulletin board.

   plural subject   plural verb

   <u>Details</u> of the accident <u>were not released</u>.

   Note: Phrases beginning with prepositions such as *along with, together with, as well as,* and *in addition to* are not part of the subject and should not be considered in determining the number of the verb.

   singular subject   singular verb

   The <u>stereo</u>, together with the radios, televisions, and lights, <u>goes</u> dead during electrical storms.

   Note: Using contractions such as *here's* and *there's* leads to mistakes because you cannot "hear" the mistake. "Here's two pens" may not sound incorrect, but "Here is two pens" does.

4. **Compound subjects** Two or more subjects joined by the coordinating conjunction *and* require a plural verb, even if one or both of the subjects are singular.

INCORRECT   Anita and Mark plays cards.

CORRECT   Anita and Mark play cards.

When a compound subject is joined by the conjunctions *or, nor, either . . . or, neither . . . nor, not . . . but,* or *not only . . . but also,* the verb should agree with the subject nearer to it.

Neither the book nor the article was helpful to my research.

Sarah or the boys are coming tomorrow.

NEED TO KNOW

Subject-Verb Agreement

- A **subject** of a sentence must agree (be consistent) with the **verb** in person (first, second, or third) and in number (singular or plural).

- Watch for errors when using the third-person singular, placing verbs before their subjects, using compound subjects, and adding words, phrases, or clauses between the subject and the verb.

EXERCISE 10-10   Choosing Correct Verbs

Directions: Circle the verb that correctly completes each sentence.

EXAMPLE   The newspapers (is, (are)) on the desk.

1. The hubcaps that fell off the car (was, were) expensive to replace.

2. The conductor and orchestra members (ride, rides) a bus to their concerts.

3. A Little League team (practice, practices) across the street each Tuesday.

4. Here (is, are) the computer disk I borrowed.

5. Not only the news reporters but also the weather forecaster (are broadcasting, is broadcasting) live from the circus tonight.

6. Nobody older than 12 (ride, rides) the merry-go-round.

7. The discussion panel (offer, offers) its separate opinions after the debate.

8. Terry's green shorts (hang, hangs) in his gym locker.

9. Several of the cookies (taste, tastes) stale.

10. A mime usually (wear, wears) all-black or all-white clothing. ■

■ EXERCISE 10-11   **Choosing Correct Verbs**

Directions: Circle the verb that correctly completes each sentence.

EXAMPLE   Everybody (like, (likes)) doughnuts for breakfast.

1. Physics (is, are) a required course for an engineering degree.

2. Most of my courses last semester (was, were) in the morning.

3. The orchestra members who (is, are) carrying their instruments will be able to board the plane first.

4. Suzanne (sing, sings) a touching version of "America the Beautiful."

5. Here (is, are) the performers who juggle plates.

6. Kin Lee and his parents (travel, travels) to Ohio tomorrow.

7. A box of old and valuable stamps (is, are) in the safe-deposit box at the bank.

8. The family (sit, sits) together in church each week.

9. Judith and Erin (arrive, arrives) at the train station at eleven o'clock.

10. Directions for the recipe (is, are) on the box. ■

■ EXERCISE 10-12   **Correcting Subject-Verb Agreement Errors**

Directions: Revise any sentences that contain errors in subject-verb agreement.

Los Angeles have some very interesting and unusual buildings. There is the Victorian houses on Carroll Avenue, for example. The gingerbread-style trim and other ornate architectural features makes those houses attractive to tourists and photographers. The Bradbury Building and the Oviatt Building was both part of the nineteenth-century skyline. They was restored as office buildings that now houses twentieth-century businesses. Some of the architecture in Los Angeles seem to disguise a building's function. One of the most startling sights are a building that look like a huge ship. ■

USING ACTIVE INSTEAD OF PASSIVE VOICE

When a verb is in the active voice, the subject performs the action of the verb.

GOAL 4 Use active instead of passive voice in most situations

subject   active-voice verb

ACTIVE VOICE   Mr. Holt opened his briefcase.

When a verb is in the **passive voice**, the subject is the receiver of the action of the verb.

subject   passive-voice verb

PASSIVE VOICE   The <u>briefcase</u> <u>was opened</u>.

This passive-voice sentence does not name the person who opened the briefcase. Passive-voice sentences seem indirect, as if the writer were purposefully avoiding giving information the reader might need or want.

PASSIVE VOICE   The fingerprints <u>had been</u> carefully <u>wiped</u> away.

PASSIVE VOICE   The vase <u>had been broken</u>.

Both active and passive voices are grammatically correct. However, the active voice is usually more effective because it is simpler, more informative, and more direct. Use the active rather than the passive voice unless

1. **you do not know who or what performs the action of the verb.**

   PASSIVE   The broken window <u>had been wiped</u> clean of fingerprints.

2. **you want to emphasize the object of the action rather than who or what performs the action.**

   PASSIVE   The poem "The Chicago Defender Sends a Man to Little Rock" by Gwendolyn Brooks <u>was discussed</u> in class. [Here, exactly who discussed the poem is less important than what poem was discussed.]

As a general rule, try to avoid writing passive-voice sentences. Get in the habit of putting the subject—the person or thing performing the action—at the beginning of each sentence. If you do this, you will usually avoid the passive voice.

NEED TO KNOW

Active and Passive Voices

- When a verb is in the **active voice**, the subject performs the action.

- When a verb is in the **passive voice**, the subject receives the action.

- Because the active voice is straightforward and direct, use it unless you do not know who or what performed the action or want to emphasize the object of the action rather than who or what performed it.

EXERCISE 10-13 Using Active Voice

Directions: Revise each of the following sentences by changing the verb from passive to active voice.

EXAMPLE   The china cups and saucers were painted carefully by Lois and her friends.

REVISED   Lois and her friends carefully painted the china cups and saucers.

1. *Goodnight Moon* was read by the mother to her daughter.

_____

2. The maple tree was trimmed by the telephone company.

_____

3. The vacuum cleaner was repaired by Mr. Fernandez.

_____

4. Many bags of flour were donated by the fraternity.

_____

5. Six quarts of strawberries were made into jam by Alice.

_____

6. Cornrows were braided into Pam's hair by Felicia.

_____

7. Tanya was driven to Weston City by Janice.

_____

8. The transmission was repaired by Mike.

_____

9. Potholes were filled by the city employees.

_____

10. Grapes were pressed into juice by the winemaker.

_____

EXERCISE 10-14   Using Active Voice

Directions: Revise each of the following sentences by changing the verb from passive to active voice.

EXAMPLE   The patient was operated on by an experienced surgeon.

REVISED   An experienced surgeon operated on the patient.

1. The coin collection was inherited by Roderick from his grandfather.

_____

2. A large bunch of roses was cut by my sister.

_____

3. The president's advisers were relied on by the president.

_____

4. Ice cream was served to the children at the birthday party by one of the adults.

_____

5. Tools were packed in a box by Terry.

_____

6. Scuba-diving equipment was handed to the students by the licensed instructor.

_____

7. Alaska was visited by my parents last fall.

_____

8. A large rock bass was caught by James.

_____

9. The newspaper was delivered by a 12-year-old girl on her bike.

_____

10. Trash was collected and disposed of by the picnickers before they left for home.

_____

■

EXERCISE 10-15 Revising a Paragraph
Writing in Progress

Directions: Reread the paragraph you wrote in Exercise 10-4. Check for subject-verb agreement errors and for sentences you wrote in the passive voice. Revise as necessary. ■

 **Analyze It!**

Directions: Revise the following paragraph by correcting all verb usage errors.

The summer I turned ten, I learned the difference between being alone and being lonely. Growing up in a large family, I never had much time to myself, but that summer I visit my aunt for three weeks. She lived in the country, and I was the only kid for miles around. At first, I had felt lonely without my brothers and sisters, but then I discover the boulders in the woods. The jumble of huge rocks was endlessly fascinating. Some days I was an explorer, moving from one rock to another, surveying the countryside from the tallest boulder. Some days, I retired to my secret fort, tucked in a shadowy crevice. I furnished my rocky fort with an old cushion to set on and a cigar box for collecting treasures. On sunny mornings, before the air has lost its early chill, I laid on the flattest boulder, its smooth surface warming my skinny arms and legs. The boulders were my audience when I read aloud the stories I had wrote. I remember many things about my time alone in the woods that summer, but I don't recall ever feeling lonely.

The Writer

Jessica Nantka earned an associate's degree from Erie Community College in Williamsville, New York. She now attends the State University College at Buffalo where she is majoring in elementary education. Her career goal is to become a teacher.

The Writing Task

For her writing class, Nantka was asked to write an essay explaining what she learned from a work experience. As you read, notice that she uses correct and consistent verbs throughout.

Tittle: Identifies the subject of the essay

I Don't Want a Promotion

Jessica Nantka

Background information about her job

Thesis statement

Topic sentence

At every job, there are different levels of seniority. You might think that getting promoted to the highest position is always better. I work at Picasso's Pizzeria and I've been there for almost two years now. I believe a promotion is not always better, and after experiencing and observing different positions at the pizza shop, a promotion doesn't sound good to me.

When I first started, I was promoted quickly. I worked making wings. Within a month I moved up to making subs, and then to being the weekend sub and wing opener. Three months after I started, I became a sub and wing closer and fourteen months into my job, I became a store opener. Now there is talk that I might become the next manager. I have moved from the bottom of the roster to almost the top in a matter of fifteen months. Although it's flattering to be considered for a manager position, I don't think that I want the job.

The positions I've held have shown me that with each promotion comes more responsibility. All new employees start out making wings, and that's all they have to do. Once you're promoted to subs, you not only have to make subs, but you have to be ready to help the wing makers if they need help. The manager will blame you if things go wrong with the wings, so you have to keep an eye on them all the time. There is a lot more to remember on the sub side of the shop and it's a busier job. Promotion to subs comes with a small raise, but a lot more responsibility.

Topic sentence

The manager's job is diverse and has its benefits. It includes cashiering, waiting tables, answering phones, lots and lots of paperwork, and watching over the other employees. Managers get tips for waiting tables, do not have to wear hats, or do any of the dirty jobs. The manager is the one in charge if the owner or general manager is gone, so there is a lot of authority to the job. There's also a nice raise.

Topic sentence

Being manager really is a lot of work, though. The current managers complain about their jobs a lot. Managers are the first to get yelled at if something goes wrong. They even get in trouble if the other workers do something wrong, like making a pizza wrong. Furthermore, if someone forgets to do part of their closing or cleaning list, the managers get in trouble because they are responsible for checking everyone's work. Managers have to put up with rude people on the phone and in the dining room. Managing is really a hard job with a lot of work, especially since managers have to do not only their own work, but have to watch over the work all the other employees do in the entire shop all the time. Sometimes managers even have to step in and do the general manager's work too.

Conclusion:
Nantka explains she prefers to focus her efforts on college.

You can get many raises without getting to the top and that's what I have done. Being in the middle can be a good thing. I like it just where I am. Becoming a manager would mean a lot more responsibility and headaches. I'm glad to have gotten the promotions I've had, but I'm happiest not having all the responsibility in the shop. Some people may think I am not ambitious. That's not true—I am smart, smart enough to spend my time and energy on college where the payoff will be bigger and longer lasting.

EXAMINING STUDENT WRITING

1. Reread Nantka's introduction. Does it draw you into the essay?
2. Reread Nantka's thesis statement. Is it adequately explained and supported throughout the essay?
3. Are Nantka's topic sentences clear? Is each one supported and explained in the remainder of the paragraph?
4. Is more detail or explanation needed? If so, where?

Paragraph Writing Scenarios

Friends and Family

1. Think of a family member who works very hard. Write a paragraph about the kind of dream vacation you would treat this person to if you could.

2. Write a paragraph about a pet owned by someone you know. Use details to describe what makes this animal special, cute, annoying, sweet, or unusual.

Classes and Campus Life

1. Some people are "morning people." Others would describe themselves as "night people." Write a paragraph about your own daily energy levels—when you're the most awake and ready to go and when you're the most sluggish. Include information about what are your ideal times for going to sleep and waking up. Explain how this fits with your college class schedule.

2. Some campuses are sprawling, stately, or spacious places. Others are crammed into cement corners of urban neighborhoods. Write a paragraph that describes the physical place and atmosphere of your school's campus. Use details and plenty of descriptive words to "paint a picture" for your reader.

Working Students

1. Some employers are hesitant about hiring students, while others particularly like having students work for them. Write a paragraph about what you think might make an employer nervous about hiring a student. What would you say about yourself to overcome that employer's fears?

2. A job application asks for references. Choose someone you would use as a reference and write a paragraph describing what you think they would say about you.

Communities and Cultures

1. When we say "culture" we are usually talking about a way of life. Some people identify more closely with the traditional culture of their ancestors, while others follow the trends and fashions of popular culture. Write a paragraph describing which influences you more, the customs, religion, dress, foods, arts, or language of your traditional culture, or the fashions, music, trends, and news from the TV, movies, magazines, or newspapers of popular culture.

2. People migrate from all over the world to the United States in search of the "American dream." To some, this means religious freedom. To others, it means the search for fame and fortune. Write a paragraph describing your idea of the "American dream."

WRITING ABOUT A READING

THINKING BEFORE READING

In the following reading, the author discusses the difficult working conditions faced by workers in the seafood industry in Santa Rosalia, Mexico. Before you read:

1. Preview the reading, using the steps discussed in Chapter 2, p. 35.
2. Connect the reading to your own experience by answering the following questions:
   a. What were working conditions like at your most recent job?
   b. How important is it for you to know the source of the food that you eat?
3. Mark and annotate as you read.

READING
SWEATSHOPS AT SEA

Virginia Sole-Smith

Tecate
a brand of Mexican beer

machete
a large, heavy knife

1   It was a little after eight in the evening, and the sun was just beginning to set over the Gulf of California. Our small motorboat, known here in Santa Rosalia, Mexico, as a *panga*, sped out over the shimmering water. The breezy sea air felt good and clean after the heat of the day, and soon Delmar, the 26-year-old squid fisherman who had agreed to take us out for his night's work, was cracking open cans of Tecate. When we reached Delmar's fishing spot, he cut the engine and flipped on a tiny lightbulb duct-taped to a pole on the middle bench of the *panga*. Floating all around us were dozens of other *pangas*, and as night fell, the dots of light twinkled like a hundred fallen stars. It was beautiful and peaceful. Then we began to fish.

2   Delmar unraveled a glow-in-the-dark plastic tube fitted with sharp metal hooks that was attached to a thousand feet of clear fishing line. He tossed it overboard, wrapping the other end around a piece of scrap wood. When the line went tight after a few minutes, he began to pull, bare hand over bare hand, hauling the line back up through hundreds of feet of water. Seconds later, a 40-pound Humboldt squid splashed up from the depths with an enormous spray of salt water and sticky black ink. From tentacles to tail, it was almost as long as the *panga* was wide.

3   In one fluid movement, Delmar yanked the squid out of the water, slapped it down, grabbed a rusty machete, and chopped off its head. Four hours later, the piles of red squid bodies and heads had grown so large that we had to balance with our feet braced awkwardly against the slick benches. When we had to

Tightening U.S. seafood regulations could improve human rights in Mexico.

move around the boat, we'd slip on spare eyeballs and black slime, and occasionally a spastic tentacle would wrap itself around the odd ankle. To make matters even worse, there were no life vests, radios, or emergency lights on board Delmar's *panga*.

4   It's no wonder that, every season, at least two or three fishermen like Delmar die at sea. The unsafe, grotesque working conditions on the water are just one of the many problems facing the working people of Santa Rosalia, a town of around 10,000 that is located in Baja California Sur. There are no spring break parties here. The dirty waterfront is devoted to three squid factories and the *panga* docks, because fishing the millions of Humboldt squid swimming in 25 square miles of Santa Rosalia's waters is the only game in town.

5   The squid processing plants—Korean-owned Brumar de San Bruno, Korean-owned Hanjin Mexico, and Chinese-owned Pesquera de Longing, SA—buy each day's catch from middlemen who have frozen the price the fishermen receive for their squid at just two pesos per kilo. That means most consider a $50 paycheck for a 10-hour fishing trip to be a good night. And it is, at least when you compare those wages to what the fishermen's wives, mothers, and daughters make working in the plants themselves, which—far from the federal labor offices in Mexico City—operate Wild West style.

6   Rosa Ceseña Ramirez began working in the Hanjin Mexico factory in 1994. She never knew when a shift was going to start or how long it would last. "You can either drink coffee for hours to stay awake, or sleep on the factory floor like an animal," Rosa explains. "Once the squid arrives, we have to work until it's all processed, even if it takes until the next afternoon. Then we go home for a few hours to sleep and see our kids, and have to come right back that evening."

7   The breaking point for Rosa came in November 2002, when Hanjin Mexico allegedly failed to pay its workers a federally mandated annual bonus and shortchanged their weekly paychecks. Rosa gathered signatures and filed a complaint with the Santa Rosalia labor office. Rosa says Hanjin Mexico responded by firing her and more than 90 workers. Eight years later, the former Hanjin Mexico workers are still waiting for the labor office to resolve their dispute, and conditions at all three Santa Rosalia factories have worsened.

8   At the neighboring Pesquera de Longing, workers report that only two toilets are available for more than 80 workers. Conditions at Brumar de San Bruno are no better. Most of the workers are migrant laborers who come from other Mexican states and live at the plant in a long, barracks-style dorm. "There are six of us sleeping in one room and whenever it's time to go back to work, the Koreans just open the door and yell, 'Let's go,'" worker Sonia Sanchez says. "They don't care if you're undressed or sleeping. We're treated like slaves."

9   The owners of the Santa Rosalia factories vehemently deny all of their workers' complaints, which is why Enlace International, a coalition of unions and worker centers in Mexico and the United States, is now approaching year eight of a campaign to create better working conditions for Santa Rosalia's labor force. "There will never be any enforcement of the labor laws in Mexico because this is a country with $212 billion in foreign debts," says Garrett Brown, coordinator of the Maquiladora Health and Safety Support Network. "If Americans want to help these workers, getting our government and banks to forgive Mexico's debt would be a big first step."

10   Another big step would be to tighten U.S. regulation of imported seafood. According to U.S. Department of Agriculture data, imports of processed squid from China totaled more than 1.1 million pounds in 2009 (along with 120 million pounds of unprocessed squid). But figuring out which U.S. retailers to hold accountable for the dire conditions in Santa Rosalia is all but impossible. "Seafood is often shipped from port to port before it reaches the United States, and it can be relabeled upon entry and exit, so we have no way of telling where it originally came from," explains Patrick Woodall of Food and Water Watch, a nonprofit consumer advocacy organization in Washington, D.C. "Companies can catch squid in Mexico, then ship it back to China for processing so they can take advantage of even cheaper labor markets and lower food safety regulations, then send it back to the United States. . . . There's just no way to trace it all."

11   Meanwhile Rosa balances her day job at a local supermarket with raising funds for the local union. She holds meetings for interested workers in the playground of the local school and writes letters to government officials. The process is slow, and more workers suffer every day. But Rosa is not deterred. "We know that one day it will be our daughters working in those factories," she says. "One part of my heart is sad for all the bad things that have happened. But the other part of my heart is happy because I know we are supporting one another."

GETTING READY TO WRITE

Reviewing the Reading

Answer each of the following questions using complete sentences.

1. Explain what a *panga* is and briefly describe the work that occurs on it. What makes this work dangerous?

2. Who owns the squid processing plants described in this essay?

3. Describe conditions at the Hanjin Mexico factory. What caused Rosa Ceseña Ramirez to reach her breaking point and how did her employer respond?

4. What is Enlace International and what is it trying to accomplish?

5. According to the essay, what are two big steps that would help the Mexican workers?

Examining the Reading Using an Idea Map

Review the reading by completing the missing parts of the idea map shown below.

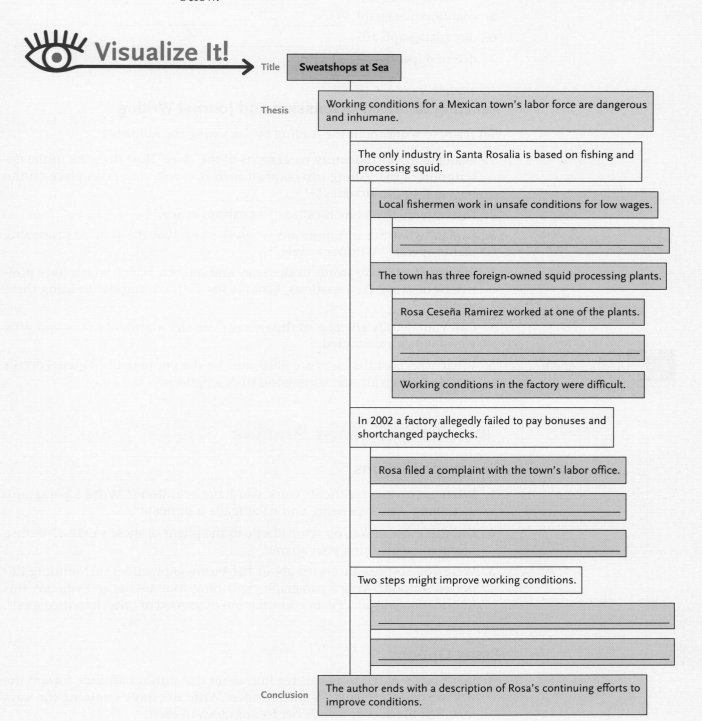

Visualize It!

Title → **Sweatshops at Sea**

Thesis → Working conditions for a Mexican town's labor force are dangerous and inhumane.

The only industry in Santa Rosalia is based on fishing and processing squid.

Local fishermen work in unsafe conditions for low wages.

_____

The town has three foreign-owned squid processing plants.

Rosa Ceseña Ramirez worked at one of the plants.

_____

Working conditions in the factory were difficult.

In 2002 a factory allegedly failed to pay bonuses and shortchanged paychecks.

Rosa filed a complaint with the town's labor office.

_____

_____

Two steps might improve working conditions.

_____

_____

Conclusion → The author ends with a description of Rosa's continuing efforts to improve conditions.

Strengthening Your Vocabulary

Using the word's context, word parts, or a dictionary, write a brief definition of each of the following words as it is used in the reading.

1. grotesque (paragraph 4) _____
2. allegedly (paragraph 7) _____
3. mandated (paragraph 7) _____
4. vehemently (paragraph 9) _____
5. coalition (paragraph 9) _____
6. dire (paragraph 10) _____
7. deterred (paragraph 11) _____

Reacting to Ideas: Discussion and Journal Writing

Get ready to write about the reading by discussing the following:

1. Evaluate the introductory paragraphs of the essay. How does the initial description of the fishing trip contrast with the work that takes place on the boat and in the factories?

2. Discuss why this essay is called "Sweatshops at Sea."

3. Explain what the author means when she says that the seafood processing plants operate "Wild West style."

4. Identify descriptive words in the essay and indicate which words have positive or negative connotations. What is the author's purpose in using these words?

5. Can you identify any bias in this piece? Consider whether facts or opposing viewpoints were omitted.

 **Thinking Visually**　6. What aspects of the essay are illustrated by the photograph? Discuss details in the photograph that correspond to descriptions in the essay.

WRITING ABOUT THE READING

Paragraph Options

1. What is the most difficult work you have ever done? Write a paragraph describing your experience and what made it difficult.

2. Did this essay make you sympathetic to the plight of these workers? Write a paragraph explaining your answer.

3. Were you surprised to learn about the business practices surrounding imported seafood? Write a paragraph explaining your answer and whether this information will affect your consumption of seafood or other imported foods.

Essay Options

4. What can you tell from this reading about the author's attitude toward the workers and the owners of the factories? Write an essay examining the ways in which the author reveals her feelings toward each.

5. Why do you think Rosa Ceseña Ramirez is undeterred after eight years? Write an essay from her point of view explaining her motivations and her commitment to this cause.

6. Consider the two steps that are suggested as ways to improve conditions for the labor force. Do you agree or disagree that these actions should be taken? Can you think of other steps that might be effective? Write an essay explaining your answers.

CHAPTER REVIEW AND PRACTICE

CHAPTER REVIEW

Using Verbs Correctly

To review and check your recall of the chapter, match each term in Column A with its meaning in Column B.

COLUMN A

_____ 1. simple present

_____ 2. simple past

_____ 3. compound subjects

_____ 4. irregular verbs

_____ 5. subject-verb agreement error

_____ 6. active voice

_____ 7. passive voice

_____ 8. wordiness

COLUMN B

a. using more words than necessary to convey a message

b. the verb tense used for action that is happening at the time of the writing

c. when the subject performs the action of the verb

d. verb tense indicating action that has already been completed

e. verbs whose endings do not follow a standard pattern

f. when the subject receives the action of the verb

g. when the subject and verb in a sentence are not consistent in person or number

h. two or more subjects joined by a conjunction and requiring a plural verb

EDITING PRACTICE

The following student paragraph has been revised to correct all errors except for those in subject-verb agreement and shifts in person and number. Complete the revision by correcting all such problems.

Now that the fascination with exercise has been in full swing for a decade, the public are starting to get tired of our nation's overemphasis on fitness. It seems as though every time you turn on the TV or pick up a newspaper or talk with a friend, all we hear about is how we don't exercise enough. The benefits of exercise is clear, but do we really need to have them repeated to us in sermonlike fashion every time we turn around? Each of us are at a point now where we are made to feel almost guilty if we haven't joined a health club or, at the very least, participated in some heavy-duty exercise every day. It may be time you realized that there's better ways to get exercise than these. Americans might be better off just exercising in a more natural way. Taking a walk or playing a sport usually fit in better with our daily routines and isn't so strenuous. It could even be that our obsession with extreme forms of exercise may be less healthy than not exercising at all.

PEARSON
mywritinglab

For support in meeting this chapter's objectives, log in to www.mywritinglab.com, go to the Study Plan tab, click on Using Verbs Correctly and choose Tense, Regular and Irregular Verbs, and Subject-Verb Agreement from the list of subtopics. Read and view the videos and resources in the Review Materials section, and then complete the Recall, Apply, and Write exercises in the Activities section. You can check your scores and overall progress by using the Gradebook.

11 Planning and Organizing

Learning Goals

In this chapter, you will learn how to

GOAL 1
Choose a topic

GOAL 2 Keep your reader in mind as you write

GOAL 3
Generate ideas

GOAL 4
Organize your ideas

WRITE ABOUT IT!

Imagine for a moment that this is your kitchen, and you have only one hour to prepare a meal for someone important. It could be your grandmother, your future in-laws, or someone else you want to impress. Write a sentence describing how you would feel about this task, explaining whether you could pull it together in time and whether it would be as good as you'd like it to be.

You would probably have trouble preparing a meal in an hour because the kitchen is disorganized. Planning and organization are important in writing as well as in meal preparation. First, you have to choose a topic, just as you have to choose a main dish. Next, you have to plan and organize the details you'll write about, just as you have to plan a menu and organize the order in which you prepare each item. Plan properly, and you'll have a delicious meal. Organize well, and you won't be looking for the onions while the garlic burns.

Finally, planning and organizing your paragraph or paper will help to ensure its success, just as planning and organizing the details of your dinner will help to impress your guests. In this chapter you will learn to choose a topic, consider your audience, and generate and organize ideas.

WRITING

CHOOSING A TOPIC

GOAL 1
Choose a topic

mywritinglab

To practice planning and organizing, go to
■ Study Plan
■ The Paragraph
■ Developing and Organizing a Paragraph

Many times, your instructor will assign a topic to write about. Other times, however, instructors will ask you to write a paragraph or essay on a topic of your own choice. The topic you choose often determines how successful your writing will be. The following tips will help you choose a workable topic:

1. **Look for an idea, not just for a topic.** An idea makes a point or states an opinion about a topic. For example, instead of deciding to write about children, start with an idea: "Children often reflect their parents' attitudes." Or, "Children need their own personal space." Or, instead of trying to write about computers, start with the idea that computers are becoming more and more important in everyone's life. Start with an idea!

2. **Look for familiar topics and ideas.** It is easier to think of ideas about topics that you know a lot about. Therefore, examine your own experiences and areas of knowledge.

3. **Look for topics and ideas that interest you.** What subjects or problems grab your attention? What current events or issues spark your interest? You will feel more like writing and will write more successfully if you focus on something interesting and important to you.

4. **Keep an ongoing list of topics.** If a topic doesn't work for one assignment, it may be right for another.

Sources of Ideas

As long as you are aware of, and interacting with, the world around you, you will have ideas to write about. Never think that your ideas are unimportant or worthless. You can develop very simple, ordinary ideas into interesting, effective paragraphs and essays. Here is a list of some good sources of ideas:

SOURCES OF IDEAS	WHAT TO LOOK FOR
daily or weekly activities	likes, dislikes, problems; best, worst, unexpected, exciting events
your physical surroundings	surprising, beautiful, ugly, unusual objects or places
local, national, or world events	memorable, shocking, surprising, interesting, tragic, happy, or amusing occurrences
people (family, friends)	predictable or unpredictable behavior, personalities, actions, histories, insights gained from acquaintances
television or other media	news events, documentaries, trends in programming or advertising, likes, dislikes

"Write about dogs!"

EXERCISE 11-1
Writing in Progress

Choosing a Topic

Directions: Make a list of five to ten topics or ideas that you know about and are interested in.

_____

_____

_____

_____

_____

_____

_____

_____

■

Choosing a Manageable Topic

If your topic is either too broad or too narrow, you will have difficulty writing an effective paragraph or essay about it. If it is too broad, you will have too much to say. If your topic is too narrow, you won't have enough to say. Some warning signals for each situation are as follows:

A TOPIC MAY BE TOO BROAD IF	A TOPIC MAY BE TOO NARROW IF
• you don't know where to start writing.	• you end up repeating ideas.
• you don't know where to stop.	• your paragraph is too short and you have nothing to add.
• you feel as if you are going in circles.	• you find yourself focusing again and again on small details.
• the topic seems overwhelming.	• the topic seems unimportant.

Narrowing a Topic

If your topic is too broad, try to divide it into smaller topics. Just as a large house can be divided into apartments, a large topic can be divided into smaller, more manageable topics.

Suppose you were asked to write a paragraph about a perfect vacation. Let's say you chose New York City as your destination and decided to write a paragraph about your choice. Most likely you would not be able to cover the reasons for your choice in a single paragraph. Because the topic is too broad, you need to divide it into smaller parts. Try to think in terms of ideas, not topics, as shown in the diagram on the next page:

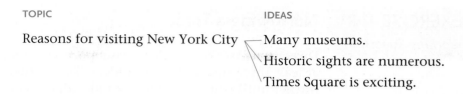

TOPIC   IDEAS

Reasons for visiting New York City —Many museums.

Historic sights are numerous.

Times Square is exciting.

Instead of writing about all of your reasons, you could limit your paragraph to any one of the above reasons.

The diagram below gives you a few other examples of ways to divide large topics into smaller, more manageable ones. Remember to think in terms of *ideas*.

TOPIC   IDEAS

1. parades   Parades are festive, happy occasions.

Parades are often patriotic.

Parades attract crowds.

2. campus newspaper   There are many types of articles.

Advertisements fill the paper.

Announcements are usually important.

3. compliments   There are many types of compliments.

Giving compliments is an art.

Accepting compliments is often awkward.

A **topic** is a thing, a person, or an object. Parades, newspapers, and compliments are things. An **idea** makes a statement about a topic. The statement "Parades are festive, happy occasions" makes a point about parades.

For each topic you consider, think to yourself, "What are the various angles on this subject?" This will help you find *ideas* about the topic. Sometimes more than one narrowing is necessary. Note that the divisions for topics 2 and 3 above can still be considered *topics*, not *ideas*, and that some of them are still too broad to be covered in a single paragraph. For example, in topic 2, "advertisements" (one division of "campus newspaper") is still a topic, not an idea, and is still very broad. The diagram below shows how you can narrow this topic down still further using ideas.

In the diagram above, the first narrowing of the topic "advertisements" yields ideas about the topic (for example, "National advertisers target youthful markets"). Note that each idea is further broken down into examples that support the idea (for instance, "soda ads" and "music ads" are examples of ads that target youthful markets). You'll be working more with supporting your ideas in Chapter 13.

EXERCISE 11-2
Working Together

Narrowing a Topic

Directions: Working with a classmate, divide each of the following topics into at least three smaller topics or ideas. Then, choose one division and narrow it further until you've produced an idea that seems manageable to cover in one paragraph.

1. Child-care problems
2. The importance of holidays
3. The value of friends ■

KEEPING YOUR READER IN MIND

GOAL 2 Keep your reader in mind as you write

Whenever you speak, you are addressing a specific person or group of people. You usually have some knowledge about whom you are addressing. You may know your listeners personally—for example, friends or family. At other times, you may know your listeners in a more distant way. According to your level of familiarity with your listeners and your knowledge about them, you automatically adjust both what you say and how you say it. You speak differently with friends than with your instructors, for example. Suppose the following people made the following comments to you. What would you say to each person? Write your response in the space provided.

PERSON	COMMENT	YOUR RESPONSE
Parent or guardian	"Don't you think you should take a course in psychology?"	_____ _____ _____ _____
Employer	"Have you taken a psychology course yet? If not, you should."	_____ _____ _____ _____
College instructor	"I advise you to register for a psychology course."	_____ _____ _____
Close friend	"Why don't you take a psych class?"	_____ _____ _____ _____

Now analyze your responses. Did you choose different words? Did you express and arrange your ideas differently? Did your tone change? Were some responses casual and others more formal?

Your reaction to each person was different because you took into account who the speaker was as well as what each one said. In writing, your readers are your listeners. They are called your **audience.** As you write, keep your audience in mind. What you write about and how you explain your ideas must match the needs of your audience. Through your language and word choice, as well as through the details you include in your paragraphs, you can communicate effectively with your audience.

Remember, your audience cannot see you when you write. Listeners can understand what you say by seeing your gestures, posture, and facial expressions and hearing your tone of voice and emphasis. When you write, all these nonverbal clues are missing, so you must make up for them. You need to be clear, direct, and specific to be sure you communicate your intended meaning.

EXERCISE 11-3   Considering Your Audience

Directions: Select two people from the list below. For each one, write an explanation of why you decided to attend college.

1. Your best friend

2. Your English instructor

3. Your employer

Do not label which explanation is for which person. In class, exchange papers with a classmate. Ask your classmate to identify the intended audience of each explanation. When you've finished, discuss how the two pieces of writing differ. Then, decide whether each piece of writing is appropriate for its intended audience. ■

GENERATING IDEAS

GOAL 3

Generate ideas

Once you have a topic and an audience in mind, the next step is to generate ideas that you can use to write about that topic. This section describes three techniques for generating ideas.

1. Brainstorming

2. Freewriting

3. Branching

You can use these techniques for both essay and paragraph writing, and they can help you narrow your topic if it is too broad or expand it if it is too narrow. If you are writing an essay, these techniques will help you break your general topic down into paragraphs. In paragraph writing, you can use these techniques for generating details that will fill out your paragraphs and support your main ideas.

Brainstorming

For **brainstorming**, make a list of everything you know about your topic. Include facts, ideas, examples, questions, or feelings. Do not stop to decide if your ideas are good or bad; write down *all* of them. Concentrate on generating *ideas,* not topics. Don't worry about grammar or correctness. Give yourself a time limit. You can brainstorm alone or with another person. After you finish brainstorming, read through your list and mark usable ideas. If you have trouble putting ideas down on paper, consider recording your ideas or discussing ideas with a friend or classmate. The following is a list of ideas a student came up with while brainstorming on the topic of radio talk shows.

Sample Brainstorming

Radio Talk Shows

lots of them

some focus on sports

some deal with issues of the day

some hosts are rude

don't let callers finish talking

some crazy callers, though!

some lack knowledge

some get angry

can learn a lot

get other viewpoints

sometimes hosts get too opinionated

fun to listen to

some topics too controversial

overkill on some issues

The topic of radio talk shows is too broad for a single paragraph. This student's brainstorming produced several paragraph-sized ideas:

characteristics of callers

characteristics of hosts

characteristics of topics covered on radio talk shows

EXERCISE 11-4
Writing in Progress

Brainstorming About a Topic

Directions: Select a topic you listed in Exercise 11-1, or choose one of the following topics. Brainstorm for about five minutes. When you finish, review your work and mark ideas you could use in writing a paragraph.

1. Your dream vacation
2. Physical-education courses
3. Street gangs
4. Photographs
5. Magazines ■

Freewriting

Freewriting is a way to generate ideas on a topic by writing nonstop for a specified period. Here's how it works:

1. **Write whatever comes to your mind, regardless of whether it is about the topic.** If you cannot think of anything to write, rewrite your last interesting phrase or idea until a new idea comes to mind.

2. **Don't worry about complete sentences, grammar, punctuation, or spelling.** Just record ideas as they come to mind. Don't even worry about whether they make sense. If you are writing on a computer, it may be helpful to darken the screen so you aren't distracted by errors and typos.

3. **The most important things are to keep writing and to write fast.**

4. **Give yourself a time limit: three to five minutes is reasonable.**

5. **After you have finished, underline or highlight ideas that might be usable in your paragraph.**

A sample of student freewriting on the topic of visiting the zoo is shown below.

> *Sample Freewriting*
>
> Pat and I went to the zoo Sunday. Great weather. Sunny. Warm. Warm . . . warm . . . warm . . . Oh! I know what I want to say. I didn't have as much fun as I thought I would. I used to love to go to the zoo as a kid. My parents would take us and we'd have a picnic. But I still could get cotton candy at the refreshment stand. It was a really big treat. My dad would carry me on his shoulders and my mother would be pushing my baby brother in the stroller. I loved the giraffes with their long necks and spots. And the tigers. But this time the animals looked so sad. The tiger was in an enclosed area, and he'd worn a path around the edges. He paces constantly. It was awful.

Notice that this sample contains numerous errors, including sentence fragments; this student was focusing on ideas, not correctness. Notice, too, that the student repeats the word *warm,* probably because she was stuck and needed to get her ideas flowing.

This freewriting contains two possible topics:

a childhood memory of the zoo

the quality of life for animals in a zoo

Once you have selected a topic, it may be helpful to freewrite again to generate more ideas.

| EXERCISE 11-5 | **Using Freewriting** |

Directions: Freewrite for five minutes each on two of the following topics. Be sure to write without stopping. When you finish, underline or highlight any ideas that might be usable in writing a paragraph on that topic.

1. Movies
2. Cigarette smoke
3. Common sense
4. Bad motorists
5. Hitchhikers ■

Branching

Branching uses freestyle diagrams to generate ideas. Branching begins with a trunk—that is, with a general topic. Related ideas branch out from the trunk like limbs on a tree. As on a tree, branches also can originate from other branches. To do branching, just follow these simple steps:

1. **Write your general topic in the center of a full sheet of 8.5-by-11-inch paper.** Draw a circle around the topic.

2. **As you think of ideas related to the topic, write them down around the central circle.** Draw a line connecting each idea to the central circle. In the following diagram, a student has used branching to generate ideas on the topic of homeless people.

First Branching Diagram

3. **Now begin to think of ideas that relate to the branches.** Write them down near the appropriate branch. You don't need to work with each branch. Choose only one or two to develop further. You may need to use separate sheets of paper to give yourself room to develop each branch, as in the second branching diagram shown on the next page. Here the student chose to develop further the idea of shelters for the homeless.

4. **Continue to draw branches until you are satisfied you have enough for the assignment at hand.** The student who made the second branching diagram decided to write about one of the experiences she had when she volunteered to serve food in a shelter for the homeless.

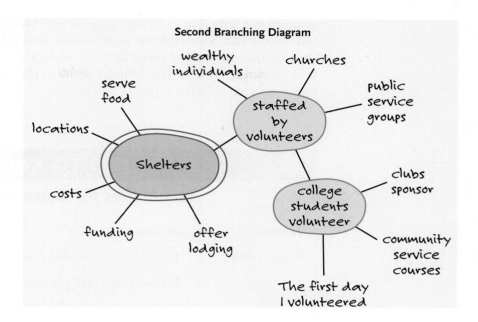

Second Branching Diagram

EXERCISE 11-6   Using Branching

Directions: Use branching to develop two of the following topics:

1. Car-safety devices
2. Noise
3. Borrowing money
4. Sales tax
5. Convenience food stores ■

Choosing a Technique That Works

Now that you have tried these techniques, you may have a sense that one of them works best for you.

However, don't judge the techniques too quickly. Try each of them three or four times. As you continue working with them, another preference may develop. You will also find that for certain topics, one technique may work better than another. For example, suppose you are writing a paragraph about snowmobiling. You may find that freewriting about it does not yield as many fresh ideas as branching. If you're describing a close friend, you may find that branching doesn't work as well as brainstorming or freewriting.

Identifying Usable Ideas

Brainstorming, freewriting, and branching each produce a large assortment of ideas. Your job is to decide which ideas are useful for the writing assignment at hand. Don't feel as if you have to use them all. Sometimes you might select just one idea and develop it further by doing a second freewriting, branching, or brainstorming. For example, suppose you brainstormed on the topic of radio talk shows and selected from your brainstorming list the subtopic of sports talk shows; then you might generate more ideas about sports talk shows by further brainstorming. Your goal is to produce ideas that you can use to develop a paragraph on your selected topic.

NEED TO KNOW

Techniques for Generating Ideas

TECHNIQUE	DESCRIPTION
Brainstorming	1. List all ideas about your topic.
	2. Use words and phrases.
	3. Give yourself a time limit.
Freewriting	1. Write nonstop about your topic.
	2. Write whatever comes to mind.
	3. Give yourself a time limit.
Branching	1. Write your topic in the middle of your page and circle it.
	2. As you think of related ideas, write them down around the center circle. Connect the ideas with lines.
	3. Draw additional branches as needed.

EXERCISE 11-7   Comparing Methods of Generating Ideas

Directions: Select one of the topics listed below. Try brainstorming, freewriting, and branching to generate ideas about it. When you have finished, mark the usable ideas in each method and compare your results. Then answer the questions below.

1. The value of exercise
2. Dressing stylishly
3. Choosing an apartment
4. Managing money
5. Amusement parks

1. Which technique worked best this time? Why?

_____

_____

2. Which technique was least successful this time? Why?

_____

_____

■

ORGANIZING YOUR IDEAS

After you have developed usable ideas to include in your paragraph or essay, the next step is to decide how to organize them. Ideas should flow logically from one to another. There are many ways to group or arrange ideas in both paragraphs and essays so that they are clear and easy to follow. The list below describes three of the most common types of organization:

1. **Least/most arrangement** Arrange your ideas from most to least or least to most, according to some standard. For example, you might arrange ideas from most to least important, likeable, interesting, controversial, serious, or familiar.

2. **Time sequence** Arrange events in the order in which they happened. Whatever happened first is placed first in the paragraph. Whatever occurred last is placed last. A time-sequence organization would be good to use if, for example, you wanted to describe events at a surprise party. This type of organization is also what you would use to describe a process, such as how to change a flat tire.

3. **Spatial arrangement** Arrange descriptions of persons, places, or things according to their positions in space. You could describe your topic from outside to inside, right to left, or top to bottom. For example, you might use a left-to-right organization to describe your psychology classroom, or you might use a front-to-back organization to describe your friend's pickup truck.

These methods of organization are discussed in more detail in Chapter 14.

NEED TO KNOW

Planning and Organizing

Planning and organizing contribute to successful writing. Be sure to

- focus on ideas, not general topics.

- use events, activities, physical surroundings, media, and people around you as sources of ideas.

- make sure your topic is manageable—neither too broad nor too narrow.

- choose a topic that is well suited to your audience.

- use brainstorming, freewriting, and branching to generate ideas.

- organize your ideas using a logical method. Three common methods are least/most arrangement, time sequence, and spatial arrangement.

Analyze It!

Directions: The following is one student's freewriting on the topic of summer camps. Study the freewriting and in the space provided, list possible topics that could be used for a short essay.

The other day my son asked if he could go to summer camp. His friend is going to the YMCA sleep-away camp for two weeks next summer. I didn't know what to say. He's only 8, for crying out loud! I didn't go to camp until I was 10, and man, was I homesick. I cried myself to sleep every night the first week. I guess I'm glad he's curious about it. Adventurous spirit. Unlike me as a kid. Although, come to think of it, camp did build my confidence. And maybe improved my social skills. I loved canoeing and roasting marshmallows around the campfire. Oh, and we played some great pranks! But I got a wicked case of swimmer's ear. I'd be a wreck worrying that my kid might get hurt. He may be ready for sleep-away camp, but I'm not sure I'm ready to let him go. He likes sleeping over at friend's houses. How much does the Y camp cost anyway? I've heard good things about the staff. How DO you decide if your kid's ready? Wonder if there's financial aid available . . .

A STUDENT ESSAY

The Writer

Michael Archer is a student at Greenfield Community College in Greenfield, Massachusetts. He is completing an associate's degree in fine arts. He plans to transfer to art college next year to study sculpture or painting.

The Writing Task

Archer wrote this essay in response to an assignment for his writing class. He was asked to write an essay about a place that was important to him and explain why it was important. As you read, notice how Archer uses detail and descriptive language to develop his ideas.

Listening to the Land

Michael Archer

1   Spirituality is all around us, even in unexpected places. The town I live in has many different religions, from a Cambodian Buddhist monastery up in the hills, to the Quaker meeting house right next door to me. I live on a farm surrounded by woods. I love the land I live on, and I love seeing the woods every morning. I believe this was Native American land. When I was little and I was digging in my yard, I found a stone tool that I think was Native American. Many of the farmers in the area have found many items as well, such as arrowheads.

2   I believe the people who came before us blessed this land, and made it something that is not just beautiful to look at, but a place that has spiritual meaning. It has something you can breathe deep into your soul and hold there. This land has had a great effect on me throughout my life, and even when I was not here, I always carried the memories of it with me.

3   The woods around my home, to me, are as spiritual as a church. You can walk through them and listen to the wind blow through the leaves like a hushed choir, and in the fall the leaves are blown through the air, with a soothing sound like a rain stick. The cool and sometimes dark environment reminds me of being in a church shrouded in shadow, a very relaxing feeling. What is a church if not a place to gather your thoughts and maybe say a prayer? I can follow the trails to a stream and just sit and listen to the sounds of the stream running and the trees creaking in the wind. I can smell the trees, earth, and the stream, which together smell like incense burning. It all creates a spiritual mood, so that it is easy to slip into a meditative state and calm down or think for a while.

4   I sometimes hear drumming from the Sikhs who live just down the road. I can see the Quaker meeting house, and every Sunday morning there are children playing and laughing on the playground, while inside the adults are praying silently. The building is simple but heartwarming to look at, and seeing it from across the field, bordered by trees and tall grass, it seems very welcoming and serene. In each house on my road a different religion could be practiced, or none at all.

5   I think growing up in such a religiously diverse town has had a great effect on my life. It has given me many different viewpoints from which to understand the world I live in. Everywhere I look I see spirituality, which can be found in religious buildings, but also just in the quiet beauty of nature.

EXAMINING STUDENT WRITING

1. How effectively is Michael's thesis statement expressed?
2. How does he group ideas?
3. Evaluate Michael's support for his thesis. Is it relevant, specific, and detailed?
4. How could Michael improve his essay?

Writing in a Visual Age

Caption: _____

_____

_____

READING

In all the controversy and hand-wringing over the lyrics to rap songs, almost nothing has been said about the music. It features a repetitive, heavy bass (often produced electronically) with a hard, high drumbeat (made on a drum machine). Rapid splicing, overdubbing, and heavy engineering produce a glossy, hypnotizing sound. Against this beat-heavy layer, the spoken lyrics stream, sometimes cleverly rhymed, sometimes painfully awkward.

As rap settled into the mainstream, it fell into two categories. The first, "gangsta rap," was angry and often violent, with heavy rhythm and little or no melody. The second, sometimes called "pop rap," spoke of unity more than violence, often featured female singers, and tended to incorporate more traditional melodies, the kind to which you can sing along. Creative blends started to emerge: rap with rock, rap with reggae, and rap with jazz. Rap even became the medium for gospel and Christian music.

—adapted from Yudkin, _Understanding Music_, pp. 302–303.

1. The first sentence refers to the "controversy and hand-wringing" over rap lyrics. Write a sentence or two explaining the controversy.
2. The reading talks about rap music but does not mention hip-hop. Based on your experience, how are rap and hip-hop similar? How are they different?

CRITICAL THINKING AND RESPONSE

3. Why do you think rap and hip-hop music have become so successful? Answer the following questions in a sentence or two: To what emotions does gangsta rap appeal? To what emotions do pop rap songs appeal?

WRITING

4. "Rap music" is a very broad topic. You can see above that the author narrowed his topic by choosing to talk about two types of rap—gangsta and pop. What other facets of rap music might you choose to write about? (Be sure that you have narrowed your topic effectively.)
5. Write a paragraph about your favorite style of music or your favorite performer. Provide at least three reasons why that musical style or performer appeals to you.

USING VISUALS

6. Which type of rap would the photo best illustrate—pop, gangsta, or some other type (note the flowers in the background, the rapper's clothing, and other details)? Write a caption tying the photo to the reading.
7. Suppose you have been given an assignment to write a paragraph or essay based on the photo. Use brainstorming, branching, or freewriting to generate a list of ideas.

Paragraph Writing Scenarios

Friends and Family

1. Choose a friend and write a paragraph about how you met.

2. Think of someone you consider old-fashioned. Write a paragraph about the things this person does or says that are not contemporary or up-to-date.

Classes and Campus Life

1. Imagine that you are filling out a financial aid application. Write a paragraph explaining why you need an extra $1,000 this semester.

2. Write a paragraph about whether you would prefer to live at home with your family, on your own in an apartment or house, or in a dorm.

Working Students

1. You need a day off to prepare for an exam. Write a letter to your boss explaining why this test is so important. Include a suggestion for how you might make up the missed hours.

2. Write a paragraph describing the perfect job.

Communities and Cultures

1. Think of a place you like to go—other than school, work, or home—where you feel like you belong. Write a paragraph about what it is about this place that makes you comfortable.

2. Many Americans originally came from all over the world. Choose a friend or relative, living or deceased, and write a paragraph about where they came from and why they emigrated to this country.

WRITING ABOUT A READING

THINKING BEFORE READING

Christie Scotty's article first appeared in *Newsweek*, a weekly news magazine. The author discusses the ways in which people are treated, based on their professions. Notice how Scotty begins with a thesis and provides evidence to support it.

1. Preview the reading, using the steps discussed in Chapter 2, p. 35.

2. Connect the reading to your own experience by answering the following questions:

   a. How have you been treated by the people you interact with at work?

   b. How do you treat people in the service industry when they are helping you?

3. Mark and annotate as you read.

READING

CAN I GET YOU SOME MANNERS WITH THAT?

So often it was the "professionals" who looked down on me who were lacking in social grace.

Christie Scotty

1 Like most people, I've long understood that I will be judged by my occupation. It's obvious that people care what others do for a living: head into any social setting and introductions of "Hi, my name is . . ." are quickly followed by the ubiquitous "And what do you do?" I long ago realized my profession is a **gauge** that people use to see how smart or talented I am. Recently, however, I was disappointed to see that it also decides how I'm treated as a person.

gauge
a way to evaluate

2 Last year I left a professional position as a small-town reporter and took a job waiting tables while I figured out what I wanted to do next. As someone paid to serve food to people, I had customers say and do things to me I suspect they'd never say or do to their most casual acquaintances. Some people would stare at the menu and mumble drink orders—"Bring me a water, extra lemon, no ice"—while refusing to meet my eyes. Some would interrupt me midsentence to say the air conditioning was too cold or the sun was too bright through the windows. One night a man talking on his cell phone waved me away, then beckoned me back with his finger a minute later, complaining he was ready to order and asking where I'd been.

peon
someone who works in servitude; a slave

3 I had waited tables during summers in college and was treated like a **peon** by plenty of people. But at 19 years old, I sort of believed I deserved inferior treatment from professional adults who didn't blink at handing over $24 for a seven-ounce fillet. Besides, people responded to me differently after I told them I was in college. Customers would joke that one day I'd be sitting at their table, waiting to be served. They could imagine me as their college-age daughter or future co-worker.

4 Once I graduated I took a job at a community newspaper. From my first day, I heard a respectful tone from most everyone who called me, whether they were readers or someone I was hoping to interview. I assumed this was the way the professional world worked—cordially.

5 I soon found out differently. I sat several feet away from an advertising sales representative with a similar name. Our calls would often get mixed up and someone asking for Kristen would be transferred to Christie. The mistake was immediately evident. Perhaps it was because their relationship centered on "gimme," perhaps it was because money was involved, but people used a tone with Kristen that they never used with me.

6 "I called yesterday and you still haven't faxed—"

7 "Hi, this is so-and-so over at the real-estate office. I need—"

8 "I just got into the office and I don't like—"

9 "Hi, Kristen. Why did—"

*AND **MAKE IT SNAPPY**: It seemed that many customers didn't get the difference between server and servant.*

make it snappy
hurry up, do it faster

10   I was just a fledgling reporter, but the governor's press secretary returned my calls far more politely than Kristen's accounts did hers, even though she had worked with many of her clients for years.

11   My job title made people chat me up and express their concerns and complaints with courtesy. I came to expect friendliness from perfect strangers. So it was a shock to return to the restaurant industry. Sure, the majority of customers were pleasant, some even a delight to wait on, but all too often someone shattered that scene.

12   I often saw my co-workers storm into the kitchen in tears or with a mouthful of expletives after a customer had interrupted, degraded or ignored them. In the eight months I worked there, I heard my friends muttering phrases like "You just don't treat people like that!" on an almost daily basis.

13   It's no secret that there's a lot to put up with when waiting tables, and fortunately, much of it can be easily forgotten when you pocket the tips. The service industry, by definition, exists to cater to others' needs. Still, it seemed that many of my customers didn't get the difference between *server* and *servant*.

14   Some days I tried to force good manners. When a customer said hello but continued staring at his menu without glancing up at me, I'd make it a point to say, "Hi, my name is Christie," and then pause and wait for him to make eye contact. I'd stand silent an awkwardly long time waiting for a little respect. It was my way of saying "I am a person, too."

15   I knew I wouldn't wait tables forever, so most days I just shook my head and laughed, pitying the people whose lives were so miserable they treated strangers shabbily in order to feel better about themselves.

modicum
a small amount

16 Three months ago I left the restaurant world and took an office job where some **modicum** of civility exists. I'm now applying to graduate school, which means someday I'll return to a profession where people need to be nice to me in order to get what they want. I think I'll take them to dinner first, and see how they treat someone whose only job is to serve them.

GETTING READY TO WRITE

Reviewing the Reading

Answer each of the following questions using complete sentences.

1. What types of behavior did Scotty encounter from her customers at the restaurant?
2. How does her recent experience as a server compare to her experience as a server during her college days?
3. What types of behavior did the author encounter as a reporter?
4. How was Scotty's experience different from her co-worker, Kristen's?
5. How did Scotty try to force good manners?

Examining the Reading Using an Idea Map

Review the reading by completing the missing parts of the idea map shown on the next page.

Strengthening Your Vocabulary

Using the word's context, word parts, or a dictionary, write a brief definition of each of the following words as it is used in the reading.

1. ubiquitous (paragraph 1) _____
2. inferior (paragraph 3) _____
3. cordially (paragraph 4) _____
4. fledgling (paragraph 10) _____
5. expletives (paragraph 12) _____
6. degraded (paragraph 12) _____

Reacting to Ideas: Discussion and Journal Writing

Get ready to write about the reading by discussing the following:

1. What are some characteristics of jobs in the service industry?
2. Write a journal entry about a time when you were treated poorly by a customer or as a customer.
3. Write a journal entry about one job you would like to have. How would you deal with the people around you?

 **Thinking Visually**

4. What point do the photograph of Christie and its caption make? Why is it a useful addition to the essay?

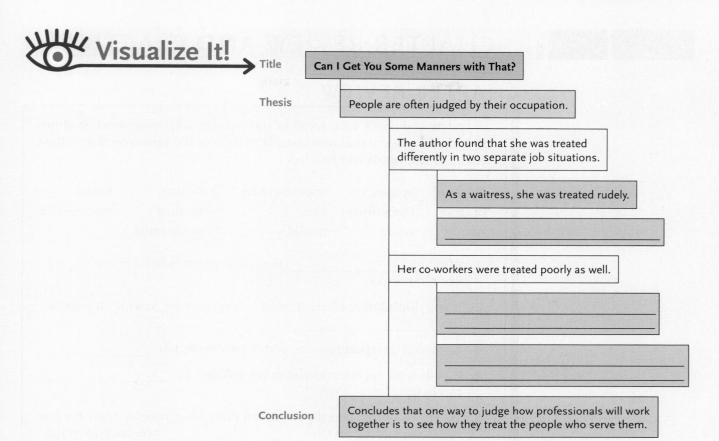

Visualize It!

Title → **Can I Get You Some Manners with That?**

Thesis People are often judged by their occupation.

The author found that she was treated differently in two separate job situations.

As a waitress, she was treated rudely.

Her co-workers were treated poorly as well.

Conclusion Concludes that one way to judge how professionals will work together is to see how they treat the people who serve them.

WRITING ABOUT THE READING

Paragraph Options

1. Write a paragraph about the best or worst restaurant experience you have had.

2. Write a paragraph about a positive experience you had with someone in the service industry.

3. Scotty states that sometimes she tried to "force good manners." Write a paragraph explaining whether you think this is possible. Why or why not?

Essay Options

4. Write an essay about changing manners in our society. Explain whether you feel people are becoming ruder. Support your position with examples.

5. Write an essay defining what good manners are and giving examples. You could also describe situations in which good manners are especially important.

6. Spend some time in a restaurant or café. Observe the ways in which customers and servers interact. Write an essay describing what you saw and how it compares to the experiences of the author, Christie Scotty.

CHAPTER REVIEW AND PRACTICE

CHAPTER REVIEW

To review and check your recall of the chapter, select the word or phrase from the box below that best completes each of the sentences that follow. Not all of the words will be used.

agreeing	audience	brainstorming	branching	broad
diagram	freewriting	idea	least/most	manageable
narrow	reader	spatial	time sequence	

1. A(n) _____ topic is one that is neither too broad nor too narrow.

2. If you don't know where to start or stop writing, your topic may be too _____.

3. If you end up repeating ideas, your topic may be too _____.

4. If your topic seems overwhelming, making a _____ can help.

5. When you write, you should adjust both what you say and how you say it, depending on the _____ you have in mind.

6. _____ consists of making a list of everything you can think of about your topic.

7. Writing nonstop about anything that comes to your mind for a period of time is called _____.

8. Making diagrams with your topic in the center is called _____.

9. Arranging ideas in the order in which they happened is called _____.

10. Arranging descriptions of persons, places, or things according to their position is called _____ arrangement.

EDITING PRACTICE

The following paragraph describing how fog forms is confusing because it is disorganized. Revise it so that it reflects a time-sequence arrangement of the details.

Fog is caused by the natural movement of air from one place to another. When this moist air that was picked up over warm water moves to cool land, or from warmer to cooler water, it cools down. As these warm winds pass over the water, they pick up moisture. When these water molecules condense into a liquid near the ground, fog forms. Warm winds pass over the ocean or another large body of water. As the moist air cools down, the molecules in the water move more slowly and begin to stick together rather than to bounce off each other when they collide.

Drafting and Revising

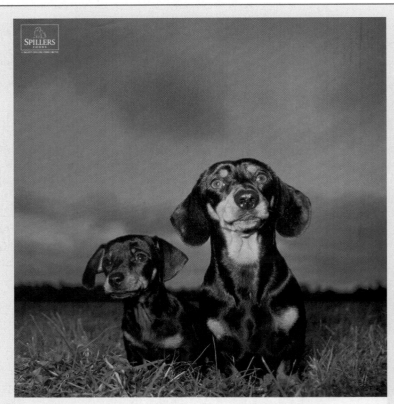

To grow up big and strong like his Dad he should eat Mini Bonio too.

Like Father, like Son, like Mini Bonio a lot. That's because it's been specially made for smaller dogs and puppies. It's also enriched with calcium and minerals for healthy teeth and bones.

And if that's not enough there are four

Spillers takes the biscuit.

other nutritious biscuits in the Spillers range — Mini Chops, Cheese Crunches, Bonio and Shapes.

But even with Mini Bonio he may never grow up to be a Great Dane but he will grow up to be a great Sausage Dog.

WRITE ABOUT IT!

Study the advertisement above. Write a sentence that states what message the advertisement conveys.

Advertisements often begin with a general announcement that catches your interest and suggests what the ad is about. This is called a *headline statement*.

In the ad shown on the preceding page, the headline, "To grow up big and strong like his Dad he should eat Mini Bonio too" catches your attention and suggests the message the ad is trying to convey. The remainder of the ad, called the *body copy,* offers more information about the headline. Ads often end with either a *close* or a *tagline* intended to create a final, lasting impression or to urge action.

Paragraphs follow a similar structure. First, a paragraph must have a sentence that is similar to a headline statement. This sentence identifies the topic of the paragraph, indicates a main point (idea) about the topic, and catches the reader's interest. This sentence is called a **topic sentence**. Writers often place the topic sentence at the beginning of the paragraph. Paragraphs must also have details that support and explain the topic sentence. Finally, like ads, paragraphs need to draw to a close. Usually one or more sentences serve this function. The conclusion of a paragraph makes a strong statement. It leaves the reader with a summary of the paragraph's main point or a point related to what has come before.

In this chapter you will learn how to write topic sentences and develop details to support them. You will also learn how to revise paragraphs to make them more effective.

WRITING

CHOOSING A MANAGEABLE TOPIC

GOAL 1 Choose a manageable topic

The topic you choose for a paragraph must not be too broad or too narrow. It must be the right size to cover in a single paragraph. If you choose a topic that is too broad, you will have too much to say. Your paragraph will wander and seem unfocused. If you choose a topic that is too narrow (too small), you will not have enough to say. Your paragraph will seem skimpy.

Suppose you want to write a paragraph about pollution. You write the following topic sentence:

> Pollution is everywhere.

Clearly, the topic of global pollution is too broad to cover in a single paragraph. Pollution has numerous types, causes, effects, and potential solutions. Would you write about causes? If so, could you write about all possible causes in one paragraph? What about effects? Are you concerned with immediate effects? Long-term effects? You can see that the topic of widespread global pollution is not a manageable one for a single paragraph. You could make this topic more manageable by limiting it to a specific pollutant, an immediate source or effect, and a particular place. Your revised topic sentence might read:

> Fuel emissions from poorly maintained cars greatly increase air pollution in the United States.

This topic may still prove too broad to cover in a single paragraph. You could narrow it further by limiting the topic to a particular city in the United States, or even a particular type of fuel emission.

Shown below are a few more examples of topics that are too broad. Each one has been revised to be more specific.

TOO BROAD	Water conservation
REVISED	Lawn-watering restrictions
TOO BROAD	Effects of water shortages
REVISED	Sinkholes caused by water shortages
TOO BROAD	Crop irrigation
REVISED	A system for allocating water for crop irrigation in the San Joaquin Valley

If your topic is too narrow, you will run out of things to say in your paragraph. You also run the risk of straying from your topic as you search for ideas to include. Suppose you want to write a paragraph about environmental waste. You write the following topic sentence:

Each year Americans discard 2 billion disposable razors.

This sentence is too specific. It could work as a detail, but it is too narrow to be a topic sentence. To turn this statement into a good topic sentence, try to make your topic more general. Your revised topic sentence could be

Each year Americans strain their landfills with convenient but environmentally damaging products.

You then could develop a paragraph such as the following:

Sample Paragraph

    Each year Americans strain their landfills with convenient but environmentally damaging products. For example, Americans discard billions of disposable razors. Disposable diapers are another popular product. Parents use mountains of them on their children instead of washable cloth diapers. Milk, which used to come in reusable glass bottles, is now sold mainly in plastic or cardboard cartons that can only be used once. Other items, such as Styrofoam cups, aluminum cans, disposable cameras, and ballpoint pens, add to the solid-waste problem in this country. Eventually people will need to realize it's not OK to "use it once, then throw it away."

Here are a few other examples of topic sentences that are too narrow. Each one has been revised to be less specific.

TOO NARROW	Americans discard 250 million used tires per year.
REVISED	Several companies are tackling the problem of what to do with used tires.
TOO NARROW	Less than 4 percent of plastics are recycled.
REVISED	Consumers need to take recycling more seriously.
TOO NARROW	Americans in some states are paid five cents per can to recycle aluminum cans.
REVISED	Money motivates many consumers to recycle.

▮ EXERCISE 12-1   Evaluating Sentences

Directions: For each of the following pairs of topic sentences, place a check mark in the blank before the sentence that is more effective (neither too broad nor too narrow):

1. _____ **a.** Power tools can be dangerous.

   _____ **b.** To avoid injury, users of power saws should follow several safety precautions.

2. _____ **a.** A Barbie doll from the 1950s recently sold for $3,000.

   _____ **b.** Barbie dolls from the 1950s are valued by collectors.

3. _____ **a.** Parachuting is a sport.

   _____ **b.** Parachuting is a sport that requires skill and self-confidence.

4. _____ **a.** Learning keyboarding skills requires regular practice.

   _____ **b.** Learning a new skill is difficult.

5. _____ **a.** Children's toys should be fun.

   _____ **b.** A toy should stimulate a child's imagination. ▮

▮ EXERCISE 12-2   Narrowing a Topic
Writing in Progress

Directions: Choose three of the following topics and narrow each one to a topic manageable in a single paragraph. Use branching (p. 302) to help you.

1. Packaging of products
2. The value of parks and "green spaces"
3. Garbage
4. Water pollution or conservation
5. Building environmental awareness
6. Recycling ▮

WRITING TOPIC SENTENCES

GOAL 2 Write an effective topic sentence

An effective **topic sentence** must

1. identify what the paragraph is about (the topic).
2. make a point (an idea) about that topic.

Suppose your topic is acid rain. You could make a number of different points about acid rain. Each of the following is a possible topic sentence:

1. Acid rain has caused conflict between the United States and Canada.
2. Acid rain could be reduced by controlling factory emissions.
3. Acid rain has adversely affected the populations of fish in our lakes.

Each of the sentences identifies acid rain as the topic, but each expresses a different point about acid rain. Each would lead to a different paragraph and be supported by different details.

Think of your topic sentence as a headline; it states what your paragraph will contain. You can also think of a topic sentence as a promise. Your topic sentence promises your reader what you will deliver in the paragraph.

What does each of the following topic sentences promise the reader?

1. There are three basic ways to dispose of sewage sludge.
2. Each year we discard valuable raw materials into landfills.
3. Many people do not understand how easy composting is.

Sentence 1 promises to explain three ways to dispose of sewage sludge. Sentence 2 promises to tell what valuable resources we discard. Sentence 3 promises to explain how easy composting is.

Your topic sentence must be a clear and direct statement of what the paragraph will be about. Use the following suggestions to write effective topic sentences:

1. **Be sure your topic sentence is a complete thought.** If your sentence is a fragment, run-on sentence, or comma splice, your meaning will be unclear or incomplete.

    | FRAGMENT | People who don't throw their litter in the bin. |
    | RUN-ON SENTENCE | The audience was captivated by the speaker no one spoke or moved. |
    | COMMA SPLICE | Many children's games copy adult behavior, playing nurse or doctor is an example. |

    Chapter 4 and Chapter 5 discuss how to spot and correct these errors.

2. **Place your topic sentence first in the paragraph.** You *may* place your topic sentence anywhere in the paragraph, but you will find it easier to develop your paragraph around the topic sentence if you put it first.

3. **Avoid direct announcements or statements of intent.** Avoid sentences that sound like formal announcements, such as the following examples:

    | ANNOUNCEMENT | In this paragraph, I will show that the average American is unaware of the dangers of smog. |
    | REVISED | The average American is unaware of the dangers of smog. |
    | ANNOUNCEMENT | This paragraph will explain why carbon monoxide is a dangerous air pollutant. |
    | REVISED | There are three primary reasons why carbon monoxide is a dangerous air pollutant. |

EXERCISE 12-3 Writing a Topic Sentence

Writing in Progress

Directions: Write a topic sentence for each of the three topics that you selected in Exercise 12-2. ■

DEVELOPING THE PARAGRAPH

| GOAL 3 | Develop a paragraph using supporting details |

Once you've written a preliminary topic sentence, your next step is to include the details that support your sentence. Just as an advertiser provides facts and information that support the headline, so must you provide details that support your topic sentence. Let's look at another advertisement—this time an advertisement for salad dressing.

In the ad shown below, the subject is Newman's Own salad dressing. Now study the body copy. What kinds of information are provided? Notice that only information that supports the subject is included: all the details describe the salad dressing or encourage readers to try a different variety. These are called **relevant details**. *Relevant* means that the details directly relate to or explain the headline. Notice, too, that a reasonable number of facts are included—enough to make the headline believable and convincing. In other words, a **sufficient** number of **details** are provided to make the headline effective. When you select details to support a topic sentence, they must also be *relevant* and *sufficient*. You must provide a sufficient number of details to make your topic sentence understandable and convincing. However, a detail that is interesting and true must be left out if it does not support the topic sentence.

Tip for Writers

Relevant information is about the topic being discussed. The opposite is *irrelevant*. If your teacher marks a sentence *irrelevant*, that means it doesn't belong where you've placed it, so it should be deleted or moved to another paragraph.

Be faithful to your spouse –
Play around with your salad.

Paul Newman

If you're particularly faithful to just one of my delicious all-natural salad dressings, why not loosen up and try something different? Perhaps flavors seasoned with fresh-from-the-garden herbs & spices could persuade you. Just one fling with these tempting alternatives will make you glad you strayed.

NEWMAN'S OWN

Paul Newman and the Newman's Own Foundation donate all profits to charities. Over $200 million has been given to thousands of charities since 1982.

For great recipe ideas, visit
www.newmansown.com
©2006 Newman's Own Inc.

Choosing Relevant Details

Relevant details directly support the topic sentence. The following paragraph contains two details that do not support the topic sentence, which is shaded. Can you spot them?

Sample Paragraph

(1) Corporations are beginning to recognize the importance of recycling. (2) Our landfills are getting too full, and we are running out of room for our garbage. (3) Many companies are selling products with reusable containers. (4) Tide laundry soap and Jergens hand cream, for example, sell refills. (5) It bothers me that some manufacturers charge the same or even more, for refills as for the original containers. (6) I believe all cities and towns should have recycling bins to make it easy for individuals to recycle. (7) By recycling tin, glass, plastic, and paper, companies can save valuable natural resources. (8) Some corporations recycle plastic and paper bags to conserve energy and natural resources. (9) Through these methods, corporations are helping to save our environment.

Sentence 5 is not relevant because what companies charge for reusable containers does not relate to the importance of recycling. Sentence 6 is not relevant because it is about towns and individuals, not corporations.

EXERCISE 12-4

Working Together

Selecting Relevant Details

Directions: Each of the topic sentences listed below is followed by a set of details. Working with a classmate, place check marks in the blanks before those statements that are relevant supporting details.

1. TOPIC SENTENCE   People should take safety precautions when outside temperatures reach 95 degrees or above.

DETAILS

_____ **a.** It is important to drink plenty of fluids.

_____ **b.** If you are exposed to extreme cold or dampness, you should take precautions.

_____ **c.** To prevent heat exhaustion, reduce physical activity.

_____ **d.** Infants and elderly people are particularly at risk for heat exhaustion.

2. TOPIC SENTENCE   Cuba is one of the last nations with a communist government.

DETAILS

_____ **a.** Cuba is an island nation and thus is able to keep out other political philosophies and opponents of communism.

_____ **b.** Cuba earns high revenues from cigar sales despite the U.S. boycott against Cuba.

_____ c. Fidel Castro was not chosen by the Cuban people.

_____ d. The movement to overthrow communism in Cuba is centered in Miami and thus is not very effective within Cuba itself.

3. TOPIC SENTENCE   Freedom of speech, the first amendment to the United States Constitution, does not give everyone the right to say anything at any time.

DETAILS   _____ a. The Constitution also protects freedom of religion.

_____ b. Freedom of speech is a right that citizens of most Western countries take for granted.

_____ c. Freedom of speech is restricted by slander and libel laws, which prohibit speaking or publishing harmful, deliberate lies about people.

_____ d. Citizens may sue if they feel their freedom of speech has been unfairly restricted.

4. TOPIC SENTENCE   Family violence against women is a growing problem that is difficult to control or prevent.

DETAILS   _____ a. Abusive partners will often ignore restraining orders.

_____ b. Violence shown on television may encourage violence at home.

_____ c. New laws make it easier for observers of child abuse to report the violence.

_____ d. Battered women frequently do not tell anyone that they have been battered because they are ashamed.

_____ e. Violence against the elderly is increasing at a dramatic rate. ■

Including Sufficient Details

Including **sufficient details** means including _enough_ details to make your topic sentence believable and convincing. Your details should be as exact and specific as possible. The following paragraph lacks sufficient detail:

Sample Paragraph

Recycling has a lot of positive sides. When you recycle, you receive money if you return used containers. When you recycle, you clean up the earth, and you also save the environment. Less waste and more space are our goals.

Notice that the paragraph is very general. It does not describe any specific benefits of recycling, nor does it explain how recycling saves the environment or creates more space.

A revised version is shown below. Notice the addition of numerous details and the more focused topic sentence.

Revised Paragraph

Recycling offers benefits for consumers and manufacturers, as well as for the environment. Consumers benefit from recycling in several ways. Recycling generates revenue, which should, in the long run, reduce costs of products. Soda bottles and cans returned to the store produce immediate return for cash. Manufacturers benefit, too, since their costs are reduced. Most important, however, are benefits to the environment. Recycling reduces landfills. It also produces cleaner air by reducing manufacturing. Finally, recycling paper saves trees.

If you have difficulty thinking of enough details to include in a paragraph, try brainstorming, freewriting, or branching. Also, try to draft a more focused topic sentence, as the writer did in the paragraph above. You may then find it easier to develop supporting details. If you are still unable to generate additional details, your topic may be too narrow or you may need to do some additional reading or research on your topic. If you use information from printed sources, be sure to give the author credit by using a citation. Indicate the author, title, place of publication, publisher, and year.

NEED TO KNOW

Drafting Paragraphs

To draft effective paragraphs, be sure to

- choose a manageable **topic.** Your topic should be neither too broad nor too narrow.

- write a clear **topic sentence.** Your topic sentence should identify the topic and make a point about that topic.

- develop your paragraph by providing **relevant** and **sufficient details.** Relevant details are those that directly support the topic. Including sufficient details means providing enough details to make your topic sentence believable and convincing.

EXERCISE 12-5   Writing a Paragraph

Writing in Progress

Directions: Write a paragraph developing one of the topic sentences you wrote in Exercise 12-3. Then, check to see if you can improve your topic sentence by making it more focused. Make the necessary changes. Finally, be sure you have included relevant and sufficient details in the rest of your paragraph. ■

Avoiding Plagiarism and Citing Sources

Plagiarism is using another person's words or ideas without giving that person credit. *(Plagiarism* comes from a Latin word meaning "to kidnap.") An author's writing is considered legal property. To take an author's words or ideas and use them as your own is dishonest.

How to Avoid Plagiarism

To avoid plagiarism, keep in mind the following points:

1. **It is not necessary to credit information that is common knowledge—the major facts of history, for example—or information that is available in many reference books.**

2. **You should credit unique ideas, little-known facts, interpretations of facts, and unique wording.**

3. **If you copy in your notes a phrase, sentence, or paragraph from a source, always put quotation marks around it.** Then you'll never make the mistake of presenting it as your own. Following the quotation, indicate the title of the source and the author's name.

4. **When taking notes on someone else's unique ideas, place brackets around your notes to indicate that the information was taken from a source.** In your notes, include information on the source.

How to Credit Sources

When you do use someone else's words or ideas, you must indicate from where and whom you took the information. To credit sources accurately, use the following suggestions.

1. **Be sure to record complete information on each source you use.** On a 3-by-5-inch index card, in a computer file, or on a photocopy of the source materials you have found, write the source's title and author and the page number of the quotation or other information you want to use. If the source is a book, include the publisher and the year and place of publication. If the source is a magazine article, include the volume and issue numbers and the beginning and ending page numbers of the article. For Internet sources, include the author's name, the title, the date of publication, the site's URL, and the date you accessed the site.

2. **In your paper, use the documentation style that your instructor specifies.** Two common documentation methods are the MLA (Modern Language Association) style and the APA (American Psychological Association) style. With both styles, you place a brief reference to the source within your paper, giving the author, the title, and the page number for the material you used. You then give complete information on your sources in a list of references at the end of your paper.

3. **To obtain further information about MLA and APA styles, consult the most recent edition of the *MLA Handbook for Writers of Research Papers* or *the Publication Manual of the American Psychological Association.*** Your library or bookstore will have copies. You can also find summaries of these styles in some writing handbooks or online.

REVISING PARAGRAPHS

GOAL 4 Revise a paragraph by adding, deleting, and changing text

To practice drafting and revising, go to
■ Study Plan
■ The Paragraph
■ Revising the Paragraph

Did you know that it takes an advertising agency months to develop and write a successful ad? Copy writers and editors work through many drafts until they decide on a final version of the ad. Often, too, an agency may test an ad on a sample group of consumers. Then, working from consumer responses, the agency makes further changes in the ad.

To produce an effective paragraph, you will need to revise and test your work. Revision is a process of examining and rethinking your ideas. It involves adding text, deleting text, and changing both *what* you have said and *how* you have said it.

When to Revise

It is usually best, after writing a draft of a paragraph, to wait a day before beginning to revise it. You will have a fresh outlook on your topic and will find that it is easier to see what you need to change.

How to Revise

Sometimes it is difficult to know how to improve your own writing. Simply rereading your own work may not help you discover flaws, weaknesses, or needed changes. This section presents two aids to revision that will help you identify what and how to revise: (1) a **revision map** and (2) a **revision checklist**.

Using Revision Maps

A **revision map** is a visual display of the ideas in your paragraph or essay. It is similar to an idea map (see the facing page). While an idea map shows how ideas in someone else's writing are related, a revision map will show you how ideas in your writing fit together. A revision map will also help you identify ideas that do not fit and those that need further explanation.

To draw a revision map of a paragraph, follow these steps:

1. **Write a shortened topic sentence at the top of your paper, as in the sample revision map on p. 327.** Be sure your topic sentence has both a subject and a verb and expresses an *idea*. Do *not* simply write the topic of your paragraph.

2. **Work through your paragraph sentence by sentence.** On your revision map, underneath the topic sentence, list each detail that directly supports the topic sentence.

3. **If you spot a detail that is an example or a further explanation of a detail already listed, write it underneath the first detail and indent it.**

4. **If you spot a detail that does not seem to support anything you've written, write it to the right of your list, as in the sample revision map.**

The diagram on the next page is a sample revision map.

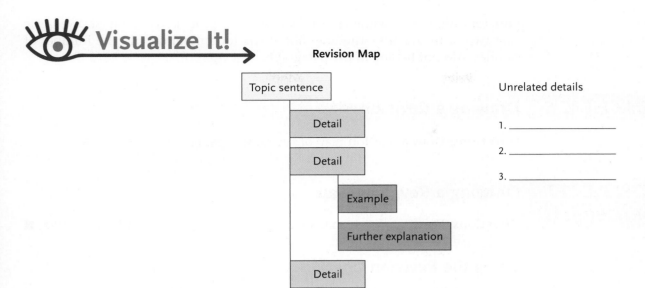

Revision Map

Topic sentence

Detail

Detail

Example

Further explanation

Detail

Unrelated details

1. _____

2. _____

3. _____

The following paragraph is a first draft written by a student named Eric. His revision map follows the paragraph.

Sample First Draft

Pizza is a surprisingly nutritious food. It has cheese, tomato sauce, and crust. Each of these is part of a basic food group. However, nutritionists now talk about the food pyramid instead of food groups. Toppings such as mushrooms and peppers also add to its nutritional value. Pepperoni, sausage, and anchovies provide protein. Pizza is high in calories, though, and everyone is counting calories. But pizza does provide a wide variety of nutrients from vegetables, dairy products, meats, and carbohydrates. And the best part is that it is tasty, as well as nutritious.

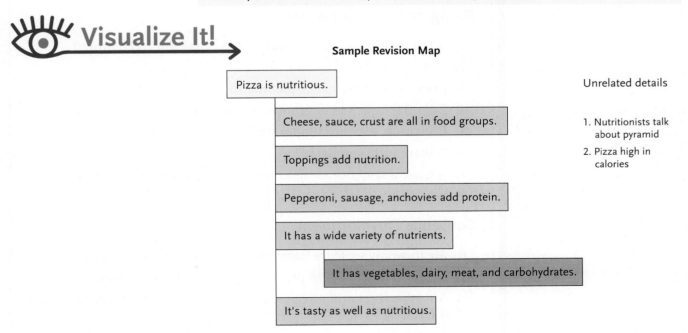

Sample Revision Map

Pizza is nutritious.

Cheese, sauce, crust are all in food groups.

Toppings add nutrition.

Pepperoni, sausage, anchovies add protein.

It has a wide variety of nutrients.

It has vegetables, dairy, meat, and carbohydrates.

It's tasty as well as nutritious.

Unrelated details

1. Nutritionists talk about pyramid

2. Pizza high in calories

Eric's map is a picture of his paragraph. The map reduces his ideas to a brief, skeletonlike form that allows him to concentrate on the ideas themselves. He is not distracted by other revision matters, such as wording, spelling, and punctuation, which come later in the revision process. The map showed Eric that two of his details—the ones about the food pyramid and the number of calories—do not belong in the paragraph.

EXERCISE 12-6 **Drawing a Revision Map**

Directions: Draw a revision map of the sample paragraph on p. 322. ■

EXERCISE 12-7 **Drawing a Revision Map**

Writing in Progress

Directions: Draw a revision map of the paragraph you wrote in Exercise 12-5. ■

Using the Revision Checklist

Focused questions can help you evaluate a piece of writing. The revision checklist is a list of questions in checklist form to help you look closely and critically at your writing and to identify parts that need improvement. It will also help you confirm that you have mastered certain skills. The revision checklist is divided into two parts: paragraph development and sentence development. The sentence development section covers what you learned in Chapter 4 through Chapter 10. As you learn more about writing paragraphs in later chapters, we will add items to the paragraph development section.

Revision Checklist

Paragraph Development

1. Is the topic manageable (neither too broad nor too narrow)?
2. Is the paragraph written with the reader in mind?
3. Does the topic sentence identify the topic?
4. Does the topic sentence make a point about the topic?
5. Does each sentence support the topic sentence?
6. Is there sufficient detail?
7. Is there a sentence at the end that brings the paragraph to a close?

Sentence Development

8. Are there any sentence fragments, run-on sentences, or comma splices?
9. Are ideas combined to produce more effective sentences?
10. Are adjectives and adverbs used to make the sentences vivid and interesting?
11. Are relative clauses and prepositional phrases like *-ing* phrases used to add detail?
12. Are pronouns used correctly and consistently?

Now let's apply the questions from the paragraph development section of the checklist to a sample student paragraph. Read the paragraph and then answer the questions in the revision checklist that follows.

Sample Paragraph

The world is experiencing a steady decline in water quality and availability. About 75 percent of the world's rural population and 20 percent of its urban population have no ready access to uncontaminated water. Many states have a limited water supply, and others waste water. Bans on lawn sprinkling and laws restricting water use would help solve the problem. Building more reservoirs would also help.

Revision Checklist

Paragraph Development

1. Is the topic manageable (neither too broad nor too narrow)?

   _____

2. Is the paragraph written with the reader in mind?

   _____

3. Does the topic sentence identify the topic? (What is the topic?)

   _____

4. Does the topic sentence make a point about the topic? (What is the point?)

   _____

5. Does each sentence support the topic sentence? (List any that do not.)

   _____

6. Is there sufficient detail?

   _____

7. Is there a sentence at the end that brings the paragraph to a close? (What is it?)

   _____

The topic of the paragraph above—water quality and availability throughout the world—is too broad. Water quality and water availability are two separate topics, and both vary greatly throughout the world. To revise this paragraph, the writer first narrowed the topic to one idea. Choosing the topic of increasing water availability in the United States, he wrote the revised paragraph on the following page.

Revised Paragraph

There are several easy-to-take actions that could increase water availability in the United States. First, lawn-sprinkling bans would reduce nonessential use of water in areas in which water is in short supply. Second, laws limiting the total amount of water a household could use would require people to cut down on their water use at home. Increasing the cost of water to households is a third way to restrict its use. Each of these actions could produce an immediate increase in water availability.

NEED TO KNOW

Revising Paragraphs

Revision is a process of examining and rethinking your ideas. It involves adding text, deleting text, and changing both what you say and how you say it. To know what to revise, do the following:

1. Draw a **revision map.** A revision map is similar to an idea map. It shows how your ideas relate to one another.

2. Use a **revision checklist.** The revision checklist offers focused questions that will help you evaluate your writing.

EXERCISE 12-8
Writing in Progress

Using a Revision Checklist

Directions: Apply all the questions in the revision checklist—about both sentences and paragraphs—to the paragraph you wrote in Exercise 12-5. ■

 **Analyze It!**

Directions: In the following paragraph, underline the topic sentence. Then cross out sentences that contain unrelated details that do not support the topic sentence.

If you are a diner who loves to eat a little bit of everything, you should definitely sample the Spanish-based cuisine known as tapas. Tapas originated in Spain as small snacks—olives, almonds, cubes of cheese, slices of ham—eaten while drinking beer or wine in a neighborhood bar during the early evening. According to one legend. Alfonso, the king of Castile, acquired the habit of eating small snacks with wine when he was recovering from an illness, and he later advocated the practice for his subjects. Alfonso was a tyrant and not well-liked. Today, many diners order a selection of tapas for lunch or dinner rather than eating them only as cocktail appetizers. These diners are obviously not concerned with costs or calories Some tapas consist of toasted bread with toppings such as grilled anchovies, smoked ham, or marinated tomatoes. Other tapas are fried and served with sauces: for example, Patatas Brava consists of fried potatoes in a spicy sauce, and Albondigas are meatballs in garlic-to-mato sauce. Spanish cuisine is known for delicious stews and soups as well as tapes If your taste buds are bored, and you want more variety, try some tapas!

WRITING IN PROGRESS: THREE VERSIONS OF "THE EMOTIONAL WALL"

This essay by Tracy Burgio illustrates the process of discovering and narrowing a topic, writing a first draft, and revising. As you read through Burgio's drafts, pay particular attention to the changes she makes.

Topic Selection

Beach

Illuminations

Holiday Inn Grand Island, modeling

Pleasure Island—Planet Hollywood

View from the window

Dinner at Grand Floridian Beach Resort

(Washington, D.C.)

Wash., D.C., changing of the guard

Narrowing a Topic

Washington, D.C.

Capitol

Lincoln Memorial

Visit to White House ———————————————— why it was created

(Vietnam Memorial) ——————————— (my reaction to it)

The Mall ———————————————— response of others

Smithsonian Museum ———————————— construction and location

Georgetown University

First Draft Showing Revisions

The ~~Wall~~ Emotional Wall

Tracy Burgio

This is one of the trips that I went on, that I'll never forget. The place was the Vietnam Memorial in ~~Washington, D.C., about 6:30 P.M. and the sun was going down,~~ so there was a beautiful sunset ~~That means that the sunset was beautiful~~.

I was standing at the beginning of the wall of the Vietnam Memorial. It was the perfect time to be there, because all of a sudden, I felt very emotional being so close to ~~next to~~ the Memorial. The Washington Monument is there, and after that, is ~~its~~ the Capital. Straight in front of the Vietnam Memorial is the Lincoln Memorial.

The way that the sunset was going down, it lit up the whole sky, and the colors were just beautiful from reflecting on the memorials, and the Capitol.

What colors?—add

As I started walking passed the wall, ~~I had a very strange feeling.~~ *certain things started to change* The wall became larger and larger, *and taller than me and seemed as if it were 20-25 feet tall.* I felt very emotional. I couldn't get over how big the wall became. *As I looked at* On the wall, they had all the names of all the men who had died in the Vietnam War.

In what way?

As soon as you start*ed* to look at all the names, you automatically became emotional. *and felt as if I were going to cry. I felt sorry for all the men who died in the Vietnam War.* A lady standing next to me was crying ~~and~~ *as* she put flowers in front of the wall on the ground. I ~~decided~~ *realized* that it was okay to be emotional at that

What did it feel like?

time and at that place. After a little while, I wanted to touch the wall, to see what it was like, ~~and my friend took a picture of me.~~ *and as soon as I did, I had more feelings about it. It felt very smooth, and the names were engraved on the wall.*

Finally I finished walking and the wall became smaller and smaller, as it was in the beginning, which was a little higher above my ankles.

I realized that I'm never going to forget that moment in my life. The scenery was beautiful and the moment was sad, but the view was spectacular. It's something that you~~don't~~ *I won't* want to forget, in fact ~~you will want to~~ *I will* treasure it!

Second Draft Showing Revisions

The Emotional Wall

Tracy Burgio

~~This is one of the trips that I went on that~~ I'll never forget *my trip to* ~~The place was~~ the Vietnam Memorial in Washington, D.C. *It was* about 6:30 P.M. and the sun was going down, so there was a beautiful sunset! It was the perfect time to be ~~their~~ *there* because exactly right behind the memorial *is* the Washington Monument ~~is there,~~ and after that is the Capitol. Straight in front of the Vietnam Memorial is the Lincoln Memorial. The ~~way that the~~ sunset ~~was going down,~~ lit up the whole sky, and the colors were just beautiful, the way they reflected on the memorials and the Capitol. ~~Such as~~ pink, purple, yellow, and green.

As I started walking ~~passed~~ *past* the wall, ~~certain things started to change.~~ The wall became larger and larger, probably 20 to 25 feet taller than ~~me and the width would be about 30 inches.~~ *I am.* All of a sudden, I felt very emotional. I couldn't get over how big the wall became. As I looked on the wall, ~~were~~ *I saw* all the names of all the men *and women* who had died in the Vietnam War. As soon as I started to look at it, I automatically became emotional. *, as* ~~As~~ if I were going to cry, because I felt very sorry for the men and women who died in the war. A lady standing next to me was crying as she put flowers *on the ground* in front of the wall ~~on the ground.~~ I realized that it was okay to be emotional at that time and that place. *¶* After a little while, I wanted to touch the wall, to see what it was like,

and as soon as I did, I had more feelings about it. It felt very smooth and the names
were engraved on the wall. Finally̱ I finished walking ̸and̸ the wall became smaller and
smaller as it was i̶n̶ t̶h̶e̶ b̶e̶g̶i̶n̶n̶i̶n̶g̶ w̶h̶i̶c̶h̶ w̶a̶s̶ a̶ l̶i̶t̶t̶l̶e̶ h̶i̶g̶h̶e̶r̶ a̶b̶o̶v̶e̶ m̶y̶ a̶n̶k̶l̶e̶s̶. *when I first saw it.* *as*

I̶ r̶e̶a̶l̶i̶z̶e̶d̶ t̶h̶a̶t̶ I'm never going to forget that moment in my life. The scenery
was beautiful and the moment was sad, but the view was spectacular. I̶t̶'s̶ s̶o̶m̶e̶-
t̶h̶i̶n̶g̶ t̶h̶a̶t̶ I̶ w̶o̶n̶'t̶ w̶a̶n̶t̶ t̶o̶ f̶o̶r̶g̶e̶t̶,̱ in fact I wilḻ treasure it! *I* *always*

Final Draft

The Emotional Wall

Tracy Burgio

I'll never forget my trip to the Vietnam Memorial in Washington, D.C. It was
about 6:30 P.M., and the sun was going down, so there was a beautiful sunset!
It was the perfect time to be there because exactly right behind the memorial is
the Washington Monument, and after that is the Capitol. Straight in front of the
Vietnam Memorial is the Lincoln Memorial. The sun lit up the whole sky, and the
colors were just beautiful; they reflected on the memorials and the Capitol, pink,
purple, yellow, and green.

As I started walking past the wall, it became larger and larger, probably 20 to
25 feet taller than I am. I couldn't get over how big the wall became. As I looked at
the wall, I saw the names of all the men and women who had died in the Vietnam
War. As soon as I started to look at them, I automatically became emotional, as if
I were going to cry. I felt very sorry for the men and women who died in the war.
A lady standing next to me was crying as she put flowers on the ground in front
of the wall. I realized that it was okay to be emotional at that time and that place.

After a little while, I wanted to touch the wall, to see what it was like, and, as
soon as I did, I had more feelings about it. It felt very smooth, and the names were
engraved on the wall. Finally, as I finished walking, the wall became smaller and
smaller as it was when I first saw it.

I'm never going to forget that moment in my life. The scenery was beautiful, the
view was spectacular, but the moment was sad. In fact, I will always treasure it!

EXAMINING STUDENT WRITING

1. Evaluate the structure and content of the essay.
   a. Does the essay follow a logical plan? Describe its organization.
   b. What is Burgio's thesis?
   c. In what ways does she support her thesis?
   d. Evaluate the effectiveness of the title, introduction, and conclusion.
2. Study the changes Burgio made in her revisions. What kinds of changes did
   she make?
3. What further revisions would you suggest?

A STUDENT ESSAY

The Writer

The following essay was written by Quinne Sember, a student at the State University of New York at Buffalo. She is a pre-med student who devotes time to community internships and volunteering at blood drives.

The Writing Task

Sember submitted this essay as part of a scholarship application. This essay is a good example of the use of concrete details to support a thesis. As you read, highlight particularly informative or interesting details.

Title: suggests purpose of essay

Making a Difference
Quinne Sember

Introduction: begins with a dramatic scene to capture the reader's interest

1   February 12, 2009: a day that lives in infamy in the hearts of Clarence citizens. We all heard the frequent, blaring sirens. The next cold, sunny morning we were shocked as we learned of the tragic deaths of fifty people that had occurred the night before when a plane senselessly crashed in our town. I was overwrought. To think that these people had died in vain upset me to no end. I knew I wanted to do something significant in their memory.

Background information on Sember's involvement in the blood drive

2   The summer following that devastating crash, I was given an opportunity to organize a blood drive for the Upstate New York Transplant Services (UNYTS) through the High School Summer Challenge program. I decided to dedicate it to the memory of the Flight 3407 victims and I held the drive at a small brick church in our town. The experience was humbling: my simple actions held the capacity to save countless lives. I watched as everyday people strolled in to give up a piece of themselves to help another. They would come and sit in the comfortable reclining chair and not bat an eye as a sharp needle was stuck into their vein and the scarlet basis of their life flowed gracefully out of them. All we could offer in return was a cold juice box and a snack, but many refused even this. They knew that their selfless actions would save lives. I was overwhelmed with happiness the entire day. I had found a way to make a difference in the world.

3   This wasn't the first experience I've had with saving lives. I pride myself in my interest in helping people. I hadn't found a way of helping that I was truly passionate about until I became educated about organ, tissue, and blood donation. I believe that these donations are ways that a person can become a bona fide hero. No matter who you are or were during your life, the moment that you make the decision to donate blood or tissue during life, or someone else makes the decision to donate your organs after you die, you become the most

Thesis statement

important person in the world to someone in need. Tens of thousands of lives are saved each year through these donations.

Topic sentence

4   I ran a campaign in my high school to promote organ, tissue, and blood donation through UNYTS for three years. The goal of the campaign was to educate my fellow students about the importance of organ, tissue, and blood donation. This sounds unimportant and bland to most people. But this is not the student council or the Ski Club. This is the business of saving lives.

Topic sentence

5   The goal of the campaign was to spread the word and to educate my peers about donation. Most people look at me with eyes full of wonder when I utter the words "organ donation." Every year a select group of students takes a field trip to the UNYTS administrative facility to learn just what they do. One queasy-looking girl wandered over to me hesitantly while my teacher was explaining the field trip and innocently inquired, "Do I have to donate an organ if I go on the field trip?" Although this struck others as humorous, it was a serious concern to me. If young people do not understand what organ, blood, and tissue donation does and how it can save lives, how can their parents know about the option of donating organs if their child were to be in a car crash and become brain dead? How would they know that they could make a positive situation out of a tragic one? I am motivated to educate the public so that unnecessary deaths can be prevented. If I were to die tomorrow, I would be elated to know that I helped someone else to live by donating my organs and educating other people about what they can do to become a hero.

Conclustion: a striking example brings the essay to a close

6   What really struck a chord with me was a quiet conversation I had with a woman from the church who was there to help us with the blood drive. She was a kind-eyed woman who walked slowly but seemed to have a reserve of energy somewhere within her. She pulled me aside and said in a determined voice, "I just wanted to say thank you for everything you're doing. I received a kidney and a liver two years ago and UNYTS is so important to me because they helped save my life." This moment made me believe in organ donation more than any facts or statistics could have done. The fact that someone gave the gift of life to this woman touched me forever.

EXAMINING STUDENT WRITING

1. Does Sember follow a logical plan of organization? Suggest how the organization could be improved.

2. Do you think further details are needed? If so, suggest which paragraphs need more detail. What types of detail would improve the essay?

3. Do you think the benefits of organ, tissue, and blood donation are adequately explained?

4. Sember's thesis doesn't appear until the third paragraph. Would it be more effective if it were placed elsewhere? Why or why not?

Writing in a Visual Age

READING

Dating has changed, but many aspects of it remain the same. Visit the home of a single man or woman on a typical Saturday night and you will likely witness a familiar routine: the primping and preening in front of the mirror, the nervous glancing at the watch, the hopeful conversations with friends and family members about tonight's date. But apart from the excitement of a night out, what do people get out of dating?

Dating fulfills a number of important functions in people's lives. It is a form of recreation that enables couples to socialize together and have fun. It provides companionship and intimacy. Dating also helps individuals learn social skills, gain self-confidence, and develop one-on-one communication skills. Through their relationships with other people, adolescents in particular develop a sense of their own identity, increasing their feelings of self-worth.

—Kunz, *Think Marriages and Families*, p. 118.

1. Highlight or underline the topic sentence in each paragraph.

2. In the second paragraph, how many details are provided to support the topic sentence? Number each detail.

CRITICAL THINKING AND RESPONSE

3. The reading discusses the benefits of dating. Write a paragraph explaining the drawbacks or challenges of dating. (Be sure to include a topic sentence.)

WRITING

4. Can you think of additional details to add in the second paragraph—that is, additional benefits of dating? Write the details in complete sentences and add them to the paragraph.

5. Write a paragraph describing the difference between "casual dating" and "serious dating." Note that your opinion is called for here. There's no "correct" answer, as different people have different opinions on this matter.

USING VISUALS

6. Examine the photo above. Would you say that the people are on a *good date* or on a *bad date*? Write a sentence or two explaining your choice. (Note that you are examining the *details* of the photo to make your decision.)

7. In this chapter you learned about relevant and irrelevant details. Which details of the photo are *irrelevant* to your decision about whether the couple is having a good time?

Paragraph Writing Scenarios

Friends and Family

1. Write a paragraph describing an ancestor or relative you've never met, but about whom you've heard a lot. Include things others have said about this person that make him or her sound interesting.

2. Every family has its own idea of success. Write a paragraph about something you've done or could do to make your family proud of you.

Classes and Campus Life

1. You have an important assignment due tomorrow, but classes may be canceled because of the weather. Write a paragraph about how you will spend the evening, preparing for classes or hoping for a storm.

2. A book you need from the library has been out for weeks. Write a paragraph explaining how you will solve the problem.

Working Students

1. Imagine you are going to a job interview. Write a paragraph describing specific strengths you have that will enable you to handle both school and work.

2. Describe in a paragraph something you do to pass the time when work is slow.

Communities and Cultures

1. Some people do best as part of a team, and others prefer to do things alone. Write a paragraph describing one thing you'd rather do on your own and another in which you'd rather be part of a group or team.

2. Society has become very casual, with people wearing jeans in most places. Write a paragraph describing one place where you think jeans or other casual clothes are inappropriate.

WRITING ABOUT A READING

THINKING BEFORE READING

The following reading, "Finding a Mate: Not the Same as It Used to Be," is taken from a textbook by James M. Henslin titled *Sociology: A Down-to-Earth Approach to Core Concepts*. As you read this selection, notice how the author uses examples to illustrate his thesis.

1. Preview the reading, using the steps discussed in Chapter 2, p. 35.

2. Connect the reading to your own experience by answering the following questions:

   a. How did your parents meet?

   b. What do you think is the best way to find a mate?

3. Mark and annotate as you read.

READING

FINDING A MATE:
NOT THE SAME AS IT USED TO BE

James M. Henslin

1   THINGS HAVEN'T CHANGED ENTIRELY. Boys and girls still get interested in each other at their neighborhood schools, and men and women still meet at college. Friends still serve as matchmakers and introduce friends, hoping they might click. People still meet at churches and bars, at the mall and at work.

2   But technology is bringing about some fundamental changes.

3   Among traditional people—Jews, Arabs, and in the villages of China and India—for centuries matchmakers have brought couples together. They carefully match a prospective couple by background—or by the position of the stars, whatever their tradition dictates—arranging marriages to please the families of the bride and groom, and, hopefully, the couple, too.

4   In China, this process is being changed by technology. Matchmakers use computerized records—age, sex, personal interests, and, increasingly significant, education and earnings—to identify compatibility and predict lifelong happiness.

5   But parents aren't leaving the process up to technology. They want their input, too. In one park in Beijing, hundreds of mothers and fathers gather twice a week to try to find spouses for their adult children. They bring photos of their children and share them with one another, talking up their kid's virtues while

evaluating the sales pitch they get from the other parents. Some of the parents even sit on the grass, next to handwritten ads they've written about their children.

6   Closer to home, Americans are turning more and more to the Internet. Dating sites advertise that they offer thousands of potential companions, lovers, or spouses. For a low monthly fee, you, too, can meet the person of your dreams.

7   The photos are fascinating in their variety. Some seem to be lovely people, attractive and vivacious, and one wonders why they are posting their photos and personal information online. Do they have some secret flaw that they need to do this? Others seem okay, although perhaps, a bit needy. Then there are the pitiful, and one wonders if they will ever find a mate, or even a **hookup**, for that matter. Some are desperate, begging for someone—anyone—to make contact with them: women who try for sexy poses, exposing too much flesh, suggesting the promise of at least a good time; and men who try their best to look like hulks, their muscular presence promising the same.

8   Many regular, ordinary people post their profiles. And some do find the person of their dreams—or at least adequate matches. With Internet postings losing their stigma, electronic matchmaking is becoming an acceptable way to find a mate.

hookup
a casual relationship

Snapshots

Tall, Dark, and Handsome chats with Buxom Blonde.

9　　Matchmaking sites tout "thousands of eligible prospects." Unfortunately, the prospects are spread over the nation, and few people want to invest in a plane ticket only to find that the "prospect" doesn't even resemble the posted photo. You can do a search for your area, but there are likely to be few candidates from it.

10　　Not to worry. More technology to the rescue.

11　　The ease and comfort of "dating on demand." You sit at home, turn on your TV, and use your remote to search for your partner. Your local cable company has done all the hard work—hosting singles events at bars and malls, where they tape singles talking about themselves and what they are looking for in a mate.

12　　You can view the videos free. And if you get interested in someone, for just a small fee you can contact the individual.

13　　Now all you need to do is to hire a private detective—also available online for another fee—to see if this engaging person is already married, has a dozen kids, has been sued for paternity or child support, or is a child molester or a rapist.

GETTING READY TO WRITE

Answer each of the following questions using complete sentences.

Reviewing the Reading

1. List six criteria that matchmakers in China use to identify compatibility and predict happiness.
2. According to the author, what is the most inconvenient aspect of Internet dating?
3. Explain how "dating on demand" works.
4. How does the author view electronic dating? Is he enthusiastic or skeptical about how technology has changed the process of finding a mate?
5. What is the purpose of the cartoon included with the selection?

Examining the Reading Using an Idea Map

Review the reading by completing the missing parts of the idea map shown on the next page.

 **Visualize It!**

Title → **Finding a Mate: Not the Same as It Used to Be**

Thesis

Technology is changing how people go about _____

_____

Traditional people—Jews, Arabs, those in villages of China and India—have relied for centuries on

_____

In China, technology is changing the matchmaking process.

Computerized records base compatibility on:
- _____
- _____
- _____
- _____
- _____

In America, people are also turning to technology to find a mate.

Internet dating sites offer:
- Wide variety of people
- _____

  _____

  _____
- _____

Dating on demand:
- Cable TV company helps singles make tapes of themselves
- _____
- _____

  _____

  _____

Conclusion

Author concludes with comment about the uncertainty of modern electronic dating.

Strengthening Your Vocabulary

Using the word's context, word parts, or a dictionary, write a brief definition of each of the following words as it is used in the reading.

1. prospective (paragraph 3) _____

2. compatibility (paragraph 4) _____

3. virtues (paragraph 5) _____

4. vivacious (paragraph 7) _____

5. pitiful (paragraph 7) _____

6. stigma (paragraph 8) _____

Reacting to Ideas: Discussion and Journal Writing

Get ready to write about the reading by discussing the following:

1. What do you think of the traditional methods of matchmaking described in this selection? How might technology improve upon these methods?

2. Evaluate the criteria that matchmakers use in China to identify compatibility and predict happiness. What traits would you add to the list? Which ones would you remove?

3. Would you trust the description of a person you met online? Why or why not? If you became interested in a person you met online, would you use a detective service to look into his or her background?

 **Thinking Visually**

4. Why was the cartoon included in the reading? What key point does it emphasize?

WRITING ABOUT THE READING

Paragraph Options

1. Write a paragraph describing how you first met a person who is important in your life.

2. If you are single, have you considered using an electronic dating site? Write a paragraph explaining why or why not.

3. Do you agree that Internet dating sites are losing their stigma? Write a paragraph explaining your answer.

Essay Options

4. Imagine the scene described in paragraph 5, with hundreds of parents trying to make matches for their children in a park in Beijing. If your parents were there, what would they say about you in their "sales pitch" to other parents? Write an essay explaining how you think your parents would describe you. In addition, try writing an ad that your parents might write about you.

5. What can you tell from the reading about the author's attitude toward Internet dating? Write an essay examining the ways the author reveals his feelings toward the subject. Include in your essay specific examples from the

selection that show he is sympathetic, suspicious, disapproving, etc. Also, explain how the selection would be different if it were entirely objective. How does the author's tone add to or detract from the reading?

6. What if you were to make a recording for a dating-on-demand video? Write an essay describing what you would want to include about yourself and the person you are hoping to meet.

Revision Checklist

Paragraph Development

1. Is the topic manageable (neither too broad nor too narrow)?
2. Is the paragraph written with the reader in mind?
3. Does the topic sentence identify the topic?
4. Does the topic sentence make a point about the topic?
5. Does each sentence support the topic sentence?
6. Is there sufficient detail?
7. Is there a sentence at the end that brings the paragraph to a close?

Sentence Development

8. Are there any sentence fragments, run-on sentences, or comma splices?
9. Are ideas combined to produce more effective sentences?
10. Are adjectives and adverbs used to make the sentences vivid and interesting?
11. Are relative clauses and prepositional phrases like -ing phrases used to add detail?
12. Are pronouns used correctly and consistently?

CHAPTER REVIEW AND PRACTICE

CHAPTER REVIEW

To review and check your recall of the chapter, match each term in Column A with its meaning in Column B.

COLUMN A	COLUMN B
——— **1.** topic sentence	**a.** details directly related to or defining the topic
——— **2.** revision map	**b.** process of examining and rethinking written ideas and making changes by rewriting
——— **3.** sufficient	**c.** the subject of a paragraph
——— **4.** revision checklist	**d.** states the main point or idea of a paragraph
——— **5.** relevant details	**e.** enough
——— **6.** topic	**f.** questions to use in evaluating your writing
——— **7.** revision	**g.** a visual display of ideas

EDITING PRACTICE

Paragraph 1

The following student paragraph begins with a topic sentence that is too broad. Revise this topic sentence to make it more specific.

College is different from high school. In high school, there were almost no papers assigned. When we were given writing assignments, we were not expected to type them on a computer. It was acceptable to write papers using pencil and paper. My instructors at college not only expect me to type my papers, but to write papers that provide objective support for an opinion. During my first semester, I spent nearly all of my time at the library trying to figure out how to write an objective paper instead of a paper with just my opinion. It didn't take me long to figure out that the requirements for college papers are very different from those assigned in high school. Furthermore, my high school teachers would take class time to help students review for exams and even small tests. As a result, I did very little studying on my own. In addition, most high school tests were objective tests, and essay questions were found only on final exams. College instructors expect students to prepare themselves for exams, and only rarely are these exams objective ones. It was a real struggle for me to learn how to prepare for college exams and to write good essays, but now that I have two semesters' experience, I think I am on the right track.

Paragraph 2

The following paragraph is a description of a bedroom. It is a weak description because it lacks detail. Revise it by adding details that help the reader to visualize this room.

My favorite room in the house is my bedroom. My room is a shade of blue that contrasts with its white drapes and bedspread. The bed and dressers are made of pine. Plants hang in the windows. The room is always quiet because it is in the back of the house and overlooks the yard.

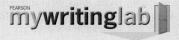

For support in meeting this chapter's objectives, log in to www.mywritinglab.com, go to the Study Plan tab, click on Drafting and Revising and choose The Topic Sentence and Revising the Paragraph from the list of subtopics. Read and view the videos and resources in the Review Materials section, and then complete the Recall, Apply, and Write exercises in the Activities section. You can check your scores and overall progress by using the Gradebook.

Developing, Arranging, and Connecting Details

Learning Goals

In this chapter, you will learn how to

GOAL 1 Develop paragraphs using specific, vivid details

GOAL 2 Arrange details in a logical fashion and use transitions effectively

"It was a dark and stormy night. Rain fell in torrents, soaking through the thin cardboard that passed for a roof in the old mansion. Alone in the attic, Sarah sobbed, imagining her mother dancing while she shivered in the cold."

WRITE ABOUT IT!

The caption below the photograph presents one possible description of what is happening in the house. Write an alternative scenario for what could be happening in the photo. Be as detailed as possible.

What would horror stories or mysteries be without carefully arranged details like those in the caption above and the one you wrote? They would be boring, for one thing. Imagine how quickly you'd lose interest if this story began, "Sarah's mother went out and left her home with a babysitter. But then the babysitter's boyfriend called, so she left, and it was raining and Sarah got scared." Maybe "Sarah" *was* scared, but it's doubtful that you, the reader, feel any tension.

Details—how things happen and when they happen—are what drive a story. The way you arrange details is called **time sequence**. Words and phrases that lead readers from one step in a story to the next are called **transitions**. Your writing will improve as you learn to use details and arrange them well. In this chapter you will learn how to develop details and arrange them using time-sequence, spatial, and least/most arrangements to make your paragraphs clear, lively, and interesting. You will also learn how to use transitions to connect your details.

WRITING

DEVELOPING A PARAGRAPH USING SPECIFIC DETAILS

GOAL 1 Develop paragraphs using specific, vivid details

mywritinglab

To practice using details, go to
■ Study Plan
■ The Paragraph
■ Developing and Organizing a Paragraph

Read the following pairs of statements. For each pair, place a check mark in the blank before the statement that is more vivid and that contains more information.

1. _____ **a.** Professor Valquez gives a lot of homework.

   _____ **b.** Professor Valquez assigns 20 problems during each class and requires us to read two chapters per week.

2. _____ **a.** In Korea, people calculate age differently.

   _____ **b.** In Korea, people are considered to be one year old at birth.

3. _____ **a.** It was really hot Tuesday.

   _____ **b.** On Tuesday the temperature in New Haven reached 97 degrees.

These pairs of sentences illustrate the difference between vague statements and specific statements. Statement a in each pair conveys little information and also lacks interest and appeal. Statement b offers specific, detailed information and, as a result, is more interesting.

As you generate ideas and draft paragraphs, try to include as many specific details as possible. These details (called **supporting details** because they support your topic sentence) make your writing more interesting and your ideas more convincing.

The sample paragraph below lacks detail. Compare it with the revised paragraph that follows it. Notice how the revision has produced a much more lively, informative, and convincing paragraph.

Sample Paragraph

Being a waiter or waitress is a more complicated job than most people think. First of all, you must have a friendly personality. You must be able to maintain a smile no matter what your inner feelings may be. Proper attire and good hygiene are also essential. You have to be good at memorizing what your customers want and make sure each order is made to their specifications. If you are friendly, neat, and attentive to your customers, you will be successful.

Tip for Writers

Concrete is the opposite of *abstract*. Something concrete can be experienced through the senses (by seeing, hearing, tasting, etc.). In contrast, abstractions are ideas, not physical things.

Specific is the opposite of *general*. There are many levels of specificity. For example, *beverage* is more specific than *liquid; coffee* is more specific than *beverage; Joe's black coffee* is even more specific.

Revised Paragraph

Being a waitress is a more complicated job than the average customer thinks. First of all, a friendly, outgoing personality is important. No one wants to be greeted by a waitress who has an angry, indifferent, or "I'm bored with this job" expression on her face. A waitress should try to smile, regardless of the circumstances. When a screaming child hurls a plate of french fries across the table, smile and wipe up the ketchup. Proper attire and good hygiene are important, too. A waitress in a dirty dress and with hair hanging down into the food does not please customers. Finally, attentiveness to customers' orders is important. Be certain that each person gets the correct order and that the food is prepared according to his or her specifications. Pay particular attention when serving salads and steaks, since different dressings and degrees of rareness are easily confused. Following these suggestions will lead to happy customers as well as larger tips.

In this revision, the writer added examples, included more descriptive words, and made all details more <u>concrete</u> and <u>specific</u>.

Here are a few suggestions for how to include more specific details:

1. **Add names, numbers, times, and places.**

   VAGUE — My uncle bought a used car.

   MORE SPECIFIC — Yesterday afternoon my uncle bought a vintage red, two-door 1996 Toyota Tercel at the new "Toy-a-Rama" dealership.

2. **Add more facts and explanation.**

   VAGUE — My fax machine works well.

   MORE SPECIFIC — My fax machine allows me to send letters and documents through a phone line in seconds and at minimal cost.

3. **Use examples.**

   VAGUE — Dogs learn their owners' habits.

   MORE SPECIFIC — As soon as I reach for my wire garden basket, my golden retriever knows this means I'm going outside, and he rushes to the back door.

4. **Draw from your personal experience.**

   VAGUE — People sometimes eat to calm down.

   MORE SPECIFIC — My sister relaxes every evening with a bowl of popcorn.

Depending on your topic, you may need to do research to get more specific details. Dictionaries, encyclopedias, and magazine articles are often good sources. Think of research as interesting detective work and a chance to learn. For example, if you are writing a paragraph about the safety of air bags in cars, you may need to locate some current facts and statistics. Your college library and the Internet will be two good sources; a car dealership and a mechanic may be two others.

EXERCISE 13-1   Revising Sentences

Directions: Revise each of the following statements to make it more specific.

EXAMPLE   Biology is a difficult course.

Biology involves memorizing scientific terms and learning some of life's complex processes.

1. I rode the train.

   _____

   _____

2. Pizza is easy to prepare.

   _____

   _____

3. The Fourth of July is a holiday.

   _____

   _____

4. I bought a lawnmower.

   _____

   _____

5. The van broke down.

   _____

   _____

◼ EXERCISE 13-2   **Writing a Paragraph Using Specific Details**

Directions: Write a paragraph on one of the following topics. Develop a topic sentence that expresses one main point about the topic. Then develop your paragraph using specific details.

1. Your favorite food (or junk food)
2. How pets help people
3. Why shopping is (or is not) fun
4. A sport (or hobby) you would like to take up
5. An annoying habit ◼

METHODS OF ARRANGING DETAILS

GOAL 2 Arrange details in a logical fashion and use transitions effectively

Your paragraph can have many good details in it, but if they are arranged in a jumbled fashion, your writing will lack impact. You must arrange your details logically within each paragraph. Let us look at three common ways of arranging details:

1. Time-sequence arrangement
2. Spatial arrangement
3. Least/most arrangement

Time-Sequence Arrangement

When you are describing an event or series of events, it is often easiest to arrange them in the order in which they happened. This arrangement is called **time sequence**. The following time-sequence map will help you visualize this arrangement of details.

 **Visualize It!**

Time-Sequence Map

Here is how to build a low-fat deli select sandwich.

Start with two slices of whole-grain bread.

Add fat-free smoked chicken breast.

Add low-fat pastrami.

Add one slice of fat-free cheese.

Slather with fat-free mayo.

You can also use time sequence to explain how events happened or to tell a story. For example, you can explain how you ended up living in Cleveland or tell a story about a haunted house. This is called a narrative and is discussed in more detail in Chapter 14, p. 369. In the following sample paragraph, the student has arranged details in time sequence. Read the paragraph and then fill in the blanks in the time-sequence map that follows it.

Sample Time-Sequence Paragraph

   Driving a standard-shift vehicle is easy if you follow these steps. First, push the clutch pedal down. The clutch is the pedal on the left. Then start the car. Next, move the gearshift into first gear. On most cars this is the straight-up position. Next, give the car some gas, and slowly release the clutch pedal until you start moving. Finally, be ready to shift into higher gears—second, third, and so on. A diagram of where to find each gear usually appears on the gearshift knob. With practice, you will learn to start up smoothly and shift without the car making grinding noises or lurching.

 **Visualize It!**

Time-Sequence Map

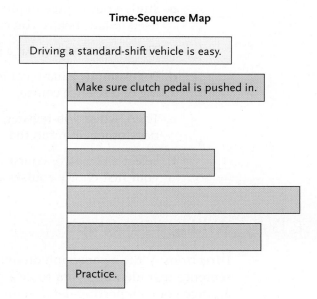

Driving a standard-shift vehicle is easy.

Make sure clutch pedal is pushed in.

Practice.

Time-Sequence Transitions

Look again at the sample paragraph. Notice that transitions are used to lead you from one step to another. Try to pick them out; underline those that you find. Did you underline *first, then, next,* and *finally*? Using transitions like those listed below will help you to link details in a time-sequence paragraph.

NEED TO KNOW

Common Time-Sequence Transitions

first	next	before
second	during	now
third	at the same time	later
in the beginning	following	at last
then	after	finally

EXERCISE 13-3 Arranging Details

Directions: Arrange in time sequence the supporting-detail sentences that follow the topic sentence below. Place a "1" in the blank before the detail that should appear first in the paragraph, a "2" before the detail that should appear second, and so on.

TOPIC SENTENCE   Registration for college classes requires planning and patience.

SUPPORTING-DETAIL SENTENCES

_____ **a.** Find out which of the courses that you need are being offered that particular semester.

_____ **b.** Study your degree requirements and figure out which courses you need to take before you can take others.

_____ **c.** Then start working out a schedule.

_____ **d.** For example, a math course may have to be taken before an accounting or a science course.

_____ **e.** Then, when you register, if one course or section is closed, you will have others in mind that will work with your schedule.

_____ **f.** Select alternative courses that you can take if all sections of one of your first-choice courses are closed. ■

EXERCISE 13-4 Writing a Paragraph

Directions: Write a paragraph on one of the following topics. First, write a topic sentence that identifies your topic and expresses your main point about it. Then arrange your supporting-detail sentences in order. Be sure to use transitions to connect your ideas. When you have finished, draw a time-sequence map of your paragraph (see p. 351 for a model). Use your map to check that you have included sufficient details and that you have presented your details in the correct sequence.

1. Making up for lost time

2. Closing (or beginning) a chapter of your life

3. Getting more (or less) out of an experience than you expected

4. Having an adventure

5. Having an experience that made you feel like saying, "Look who's talking!" ■

Spatial Arrangement

Suppose you are asked to describe a car you have just purchased. You want your reader, who has never seen the car, to visualize it. How would you organize your description? You could describe the car from bottom to top or from top to bottom, or from front to back. This method of presentation is called **spatial arrangement.** For other objects, you might arrange your details from inside to outside, from near to far, or from east to west. Notice how, in the following paragraph, the details are arranged from top to bottom.

Sample Spatial-Arrangement Paragraph

My dream house will have a three-level outdoor deck that will be ideal for relaxing on after a hard day's work. The top level of the deck will be connected by sliding glass doors to the family room. On this level there will be a hot tub, a large picnic table with benches, and a comfortable padded chaise. On the middle level there will be a suntanning area, a hammock, and two built-in planters for a mini-herb garden. The lowest level, which will meet the lawn, will have a built-in stone barbeque pit for big cookouts and a gas grill for everyday use.

Can you visualize the deck?

Spatial-Arrangement Transitions

In spatial-arrangement paragraphs, transitions are particularly important since they often reveal placement or position of objects or parts. Using transitions like those listed in the "Need to Know" box below will help you to link details in a spatial-arrangement paragraph.

NEED TO KNOW

Common Spatial-Arrangement Transitions

above	next to	nearby
below	inside	on the other side
beside	outside	beneath
in front of	behind	the west (or other direction)

EXERCISE 13-5   Using Spatial Arrangement

Directions: Use spatial arrangement to order the supporting-detail sentences that follow the topic sentence below. Write a "1" in the blank before the detail that should appear first in the paragraph, a "2" before the detail that should appear second, and so on.

TOPIC SENTENCE   My beautiful cousin Audry always looks as if she has dressed quickly and given her appearance little thought.

SUPPORTING-DETAIL SENTENCES

_____ **a.** She usually wears an oversized, baggy sweater, either black or blue-black, with the sleeves pushed up.

_____ **b.** Black slip-on sandals complete the look; she wears them in every season.

_____ **c.** On her feet she wears mismatched socks.

_____ **d.** Her short, reddish hair is usually wind-blown, hanging every which way from her face.

_____ **e.** She puts her makeup on unevenly, if at all.

_____ **f.** The sweater covers most of her casual, rumpled skirt. ■

EXERCISE 13-6   Writing a Paragraph Using Spatial Arrangement

Directions: Write a paragraph on one of the following topics. First, write a topic sentence that identifies your topic and expresses your main point about it. Then use spatial arrangement to develop your supporting details.

1. The room you are in now
2. The building where you live
3. A photograph or painting that you like
4. Your dream car
5. Your favorite chair or place ■

Least/Most Arrangement

Another method of arranging details is to present them in order from least to most or most to least, according to some quality or characteristic. For example, you might choose least to most important, serious, frightening, or humorous. In writing a paragraph explaining your reasons for attending college, you might arrange details from most to least important. In writing about an exciting evening, you might arrange your details from most to least exciting.

As you read the following paragraph, note how the writer has arranged details in a logical way.

Sample Least/Most Paragraph

This week has been filled with good news. One night when balancing my checkbook, I discovered a $155 error in my checking account—in my favor, for once! I was even happier when I finally found a buyer for my Chevy Blazer that I had been trying to sell all winter. Then my boss told me he was submitting my name for a 50-cent hourly raise; I certainly didn't expect that. Best of all, I learned that I'd been accepted into the Radiology curriculum for next fall.

In this paragraph, the details are arranged from least to most important.

Least/Most Transitions

In least/most paragraphs, transitions help your reader to follow your train of thought. Using transitions like those listed in the "Need to Know" box below will help you link details in a least/most paragraph.

NEED TO KNOW

Common Least/Most Transitions

most important	particularly important	moreover
above all	even more	in addition
especially	best of all	not only . . . but also

EXERCISE 13-7   Writing a Paragraph Using Least/Most Arrangement

Directions: Write a paragraph on one of the following topics. First, write a topic sentence that identifies your topic and expresses your main point about it. Then use a least/most arrangement to order your details. When you have finished, draw a map of your paragraph. Use your map to check that you have included sufficient details and that you have arranged your details in least/most order.

1. Your reasons for choosing the college you are attending
2. Changes in your life since you began college
3. Three commercials you saw on television recently
4. Why you like a certain book or movie
5. Good (or bad) things that have happened to you recently ■

EXERCISE 13-8   Writing Topic Sentences
Working Together

Directions: Working with a classmate, write a topic sentence for each of the following topics. Then indicate what method (time sequence, spatial, or least/most) you would use to arrange supporting details.

TOPIC	relationship with a friend
TOPIC SENTENCE	Whenever George and I get together,
	he always takes over the conversation.
METHOD OF ARRANGEMENT	time sequence

1. TOPIC   animals that have humanlike behaviors

   TOPIC SENTENCE _____

   _____

   METHOD OF ARRANGEMENT _____

2. TOPIC   a difficulty that I faced

   TOPIC SENTENCE _____

   _____

   METHOD OF ARRANGEMENT _____

3. TOPIC   feeling under pressure

   TOPIC SENTENCE _____

   _____

   METHOD OF ARRANGEMENT _____

4. TOPIC   a favorite dinner menu

   TOPIC SENTENCE   _____

                               _____

   METHOD OF   _____
   ARRANGEMENT

5. TOPIC   an exciting sporting event

   TOPIC SENTENCE   _____

                               _____

   METHOD OF   _____
   ARRANGEMENT   ■

EXERCISE 13-9   Identifying Methods of Arrangement
Working Together

Directions: Find several magazine or newspaper ads. Working in a group, identify the method of arrangement of the advertising copy. ■

NEED TO KNOW

Developing, Arranging, and Connecting Details

Be sure to use interesting and lively **details** to support your topic sentence.

- Choose details that are specific and concrete.

- Within your paragraphs, arrange details in a **logical order.** Three techniques for arranging details are
    - **time-sequence arrangement;** information is presented in the order in which it happened.
    - **spatial arrangement;** descriptive details are arranged according to their position in space.
    - **least/most arrangement;** ideas are arranged from least to most or most to least according to some quality or characteristic.

- Use **transitions** to help your reader move easily from one key detail to the next.

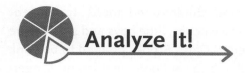

Analyze It!

Directions: The following paragraph lacks concrete details to make it interesting and informative. Revise the paragraph by adding details to help readers visualize the writer's shopping experience.

If I go grocery shopping before supper, without taking a list of items that I really need, the results can be disastrous. Because I'm hungry, everything looks good, and I tend to overload my cart. The problem starts in the produce department. Perhaps I need bananas and broccoli. After placing these items in my cart, I find myself adding a lot of other fruits and vegetables. Then I go to the fish department, where I get two kinds of fish instead of one. I proceed to the cereal aisle and put three boxes in my cart. On the way to get yogurt, I end up buying ice cream. "This has got to stop!" I say to myself, but myself does not listen.

A STUDENT ESSAY

The Writer

The following essay was written by Maya Prestwich, a student at Northwestern University, in Evanston, Illinois.

The Writing Task

Prestwich submitted an essay to her college newspaper, the *Daily Northwestern*, where it was published. This essay is a good example of the use of concrete details to support a thesis. As you read, highlight particularly informative or interesting details.

Halloween: Fun Without Cultural Guilt

Maya Prestwich

Title: suggests main point of the essay

Introduction: tells story of three children—essay opens with details

1   "What are you gonna be?" That's the question circulating around school yards this week. I overheard a group of children talking about Halloween costumes as I walked by the school three blocks from my house.

2   The lone girl of the group was going as a ballerina, and the boys were fighting it out over who could be Batman. All feelings about feminism and gender stereotypes aside, the whole scene made me smile. I'd forgotten how much children love Halloween and how much I love it, too. Years of being immersed in campus life had left me feeling as if Halloween really was just another day, but moving off-campus has allowed me to rediscover it.

Thesis statement

3   What is it about Halloween that seems to put everyone in a happier, more adventurous mood? There's that feeling in the air (beneath the chill), a festive feeling, a primitive feeling, a pagan feeling. October 31 is really the only time when we allow ourselves to freely embrace that aspect of our humanity.

Topic sentence

4   It's also a very rare chance for everyone, children and adults, to reinvent themselves a little. School teachers get to be witches, little boys and girls can be superheroes. Country farm girls who listen to Garth Brooks pretend to be punk rock fans, and for one night, I can pretend to be a confident, indifferent, dangerous black cat. It seems sort of ridiculous on the surface, but it's important to me to have this day when coloring outside the lines is acceptable. I believe it is crucial that we help our children learn that doing things they wouldn't normally do can be fun and exhilarating and liberating.

Intersting details

Topic sentence

5   For grown-ups, and us almost-grown-ups, it's important to remember on Halloween that you can change what you are "going to be" if you know you made the wrong decision. Being a cat or a ghost or a globe or a Power Ranger is a decision I would agonize over for a full month, but it was still just a decision. A different costume could easily be thrown together or an old one dragged out of the closet, and I could take the evening in a different direction.

Topic sentence

6   Similarly, all of those big adult things that we agonize over, what career to choose, which job to go for, whom to marry, are still just decisions. Reinventing yourself, changing your life is not quite as simple as changing your costume, but it's not quite as difficult as we make it out to be, either.

Topic sentence

7   There's another pretty spiffy thing about Halloween, and that's the way that it unifies us, Catholic, Jewish, or unaffiliated, rich or middle class, city or country, believers in one god, believers in many gods, believers in no gods. We can share this one holiday without having to go through sensitivity training. Every kid gets dressed up and hopes for a good haul, everyone who can leaves the porch light on and answers the doorbell bearing Tootsie Rolls, and every mom decides that a crime wave is going to hit their small town and participates in the ritual "inspecting of the candy."

Good use of detail

Conclusion: refers back to the title

8   Halloween is freer of culture clash than even Independence or Columbus days. Face it, it is a really awesome holiday, a day for fun and spontaneity without any of the ramifications of cultural guilt and that is cause for celebration, or at least the consumption of candy.

EXAMINING STUDENT WRITING

1. Does Prestwich follow a logical plan of organization? Suggest how the organization could be improved.

2. Do you think further details are needed? If so, suggest which paragraphs need more detail.

3. Prestwich's thesis is in the form of a question. Is this format effective or would a statement be more effective? Give reasons for your answer.

4. Do you think the notion of cultural guilt is adequately explained?

Writing in a Visual Age

READING

The old saying "It's a small world, after all" is the essence of what business people call globalization. The term *globalization* refers to the movement toward a more interconnected world. It is one of the most profound factors affecting people today. Without a doubt, whatever happens in the United States (the world's largest economy) has a significant impact on people around the world. The reverse is also true. What happens in other countries often has a ripple effect on U.S. consumers, businesses, and workers.

Consider an example: The booming economies of India and China are a major reason for the growing global demand for energy. Increased energy demand leads to rising oil and gas prices, which have created higher prices for other things, such as groceries. (It costs more to ship supplies to stores, and these businesses must then pass on the increased costs to their customers.) As a result, people have less money to spend on entertainment, such as eating out. Local restaurants and other businesses feel the pinch. Their sales fall, and they lay off workers.

—adapted from Solomon, Boatsy, and Martin, *Better Business*, p. 96.

1. Which method of arranging details (time sequence, spatial, or least/most) do the authors use in the second paragraph?

CRITICAL THINKING AND RESPONSE

2. The reading offers examples from economics and business, but globalization affects many other areas of society, too. Where do you see the influences of other countries in the United States? Write a sentence or two offering an example.

WRITING

3. Complete the following map for the second paragraph of the reading.

Consequences of growing global demand for energy

_____

_____

People have less money to spend on entertainment

_____

Local businesses lay off workers

4. The reading talks about the influence of international factors on U.S. jobs. Write a paragraph explaining your dream career or dream job, the one you're going to college to prepare for. Write a paragraph using the most/least arrangement, spelling out the reasons for your choice from most important to least important.

USING VISUALS

5. This photo shows how a very successful U.S. business, McDonald's, operates in other countries, illustrating how U.S. businesses affect people in other countries. Look closely at the photo details and try to determine which country this McDonald's is located in. Write a sentence explaining how you came to this conclusion.

6. Your town or city probably has a number of ethnic restaurants. Which restaurant or cuisine is your favorite and why? When considering the details to include in your paragraph, use the techniques you learned in this chapter: use examples, add facts and explanations, and draw from your personal experience.

Paragraph Writing Scenarios

Friends and Family

1. Think of a good friend with whom you once had a major argument. Write a paragraph explaining what that argument was about and how you got over it.

2. Write a paragraph describing a relative other than your parents who you were close to as a child.

Classes and Campus Life

1. Think about the teachers you have this year. Write a paragraph comparing two of them. What are the main differences in their styles of teaching?

2. If there is a campus store, write a paragraph about the things you regularly would buy there or would not buy there. If there is not a store on your campus, write a paragraph explaining why you think your school should add one.

Working Students

1. Write an imaginary letter to your boss explaining what you would do to improve your workplace.

2. Write a paragraph explaining why you deserve a raise.

Communities and Cultures

1. People often form ideas about a culture without knowing anyone from that culture. Describe one incorrect idea, misconception, or stereotype that people have about a culture.

2. People live in a variety of communities. Choosing from urban, suburban, rural, or small-town neighborhoods, write a paragraph describing the one you'd most like to live in and why.

WRITING ABOUT A READING

THINKING BEFORE READING

The following reading, "A Brother's Murder," explains how a man feels about the circumstances surrounding the death of his street-smart younger brother. As you read this selection, notice that Brent Staples uses specific details to make his essay vivid and real. Also notice that he arranges his details logically, mainly using the time-sequence pattern.

1. Preview the reading, using the steps discussed in Chapter 2, p. 35.

2. Connect the reading to your own experience by answering the following questions:

   a. If you grew up in a neighborhood filled with crime, run-down buildings, and hopelessness, would you remain part of the community or move away from it?

   b. What could you say or do to help a relative or friend headed for trouble?

3. Mark and annotate as you read.

READING

A BROTHER'S MURDER

Brent Staples

1   It has been more than two years since my telephone rang with the news that my younger brother Blake—just 22 years old—had been murdered. The young man who killed him was only 24. Wearing a ski mask, he emerged from a car, fired six times at close range with a massive .44 Magnum, then fled. The two had once been inseparable friends. A senseless rivalry—beginning, I think, with an argument over a girlfriend—escalated from posturing, to threats, to violence, to murder. The way the two were living, death could have come to either of them from anywhere. In fact, the assailant had already survived multiple gunshot wounds from an incident much like the one in which my brother lost his life.

2   I left the East Coast after college, spent the mid- and late-1970s in Chicago as a graduate student, taught for a time, then became a journalist. Within 10 years of leaving my hometown, I was overeducated and "upwardly mobile," ensconced on a quiet, tree-lined street where voices raised in anger were scarcely ever heard. The telephone, like some grim umbilical, kept me connected to the old world with news of deaths, imprisonings, and misfortune. I felt emotionally beaten up. Perhaps to protect myself, I added a psychological dimension to the physical distance I had already achieved. I rarely visited my hometown. I shut it out.

3   As I fled the past, so Blake embraced it. On Christmas of 1983, I traveled from Chicago to a black section of Roanoke, Virginia, where he then lived. The desolate public housing projects, the hopeless, idle young men crashing

posturing
putting on an attitude, posing

umbilical
connecting cord, similar to the cord that joins a baby to the placenta in the womb

against one another—these reminded me of the embittered town we'd grown up in. It was a place where once I would have been comfortable, or at least sure of myself. Now, hearing of my brother's forays into crime, his scrapes with police and street thugs, I was scared, unsteady on foreign terrain.

4   I saw that Blake's romance with the street life and the hustler image had flowered dangerously. One evening that late December, standing in some Roanoke dive among drug dealers and grim, hair-trigger losers, I told him I feared for his life. He had affected the image of the tough he wanted to be. But behind the dark glasses and the swagger, I glimpsed the baby-faced toddler I'd once watched over. I nearly wept. I wanted desperately for him to live. The young think themselves immortal, and a dangerous light shone in his eyes as he spoke laughingly, of making fools of the policemen who had raided his apartment looking for drugs. He cried out as I took his right hand. A line of stitches lay between the thumb and index finger. Kickback from a shotgun, he explained, nothing serious. Gunplay had become part of his life.

5   I lacked the language simply to say: Thousands have lived this for you and died. I fought the urge to lift him bodily and shake him. This place and the way you are living smells of death to me, I said. Take some time away, I said. Let's go downtown tomorrow and buy a plane ticket anywhere, take a bus trip, anything to get away and cool things off. He took my alarm casually. We arranged to meet the following night—an appointment he would not keep. We embraced as though through glass. I drove away.

6   As I stood in my apartment in Chicago holding the receiver that evening in February 1984, I felt as though part of my soul had been cut away. I questioned myself then, and I still do. Did I not reach back soon or earnestly enough for him? For weeks I awoke crying from a recurrent dream in which I chased him, urgently trying to get him to read a document I had, as though reading it would protect him from what had happened in waking life. His eyes shining like black diamonds, he smiled and danced just beyond my grasp. When I reached for him, I caught only the space where he had been.

—from *Bearing Witness.*

swagger
boastful show of fearlessness

Immortal
unable to die

recurrent
returning, repeating

GETTING READY TO WRITE

Answer each of the following questions using complete sentences.

Reviewing the Reading

1. How and why did Blake, Staples's younger brother, die?
2. Why was Staples so worried about Blake?
3. Describe Staples's attempts to help Blake when he visited him in 1983 in Roanoke, Virginia.
4. What effects did Blake's death have on Staples?

Examining the Reading Using an Idea Map

Review the reading by completing the missing parts of the idea map shown below.

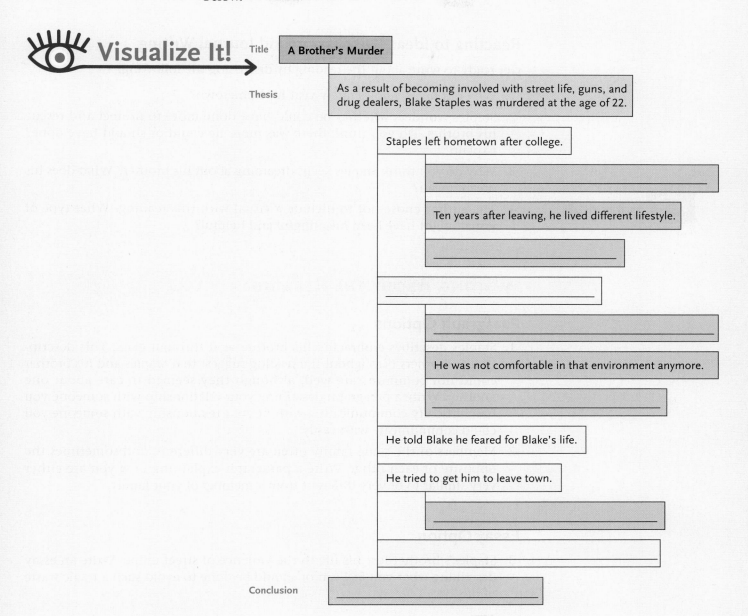

Strengthening Your Vocabulary

Using the word's context, word parts, or a dictionary, write a brief definition of each of the following words as it is used in the reading.

1. rivalry (paragraph 1) _____

2. escalated (paragraph 1) _____

3. ensconced (paragraph 2) _____

4. desolate (paragraph 3) _____

5. forays (paragraph 3) _____

6. terrain (paragraph 3) _____

Reacting to Ideas: Discussion and Journal Writing

Get ready to write about the reading by discussing the following:

1. Why did Brent Staples rarely visit his hometown?

2. Staples wonders whether he could have done more to protect and rescue his brother. Do you think there was more he could or should have done? Explain.

3. Why do you think Staples keeps dreaming about his brother? What does his dream mean?

 **Thinking Visually**

4. The author chose not to include a visual with this reading. What type of visual might have been meaningful and helpful?

WRITING ABOUT THE READING

Paragraph Options

1. Staples describes embracing his brother as if through glass. This description and others throughout the reading suggest that Staples and his brother could not communicate well, although they seemed to care about one another. Write a paragraph describing your relationship with someone you had difficulty communicating with or your relationship with someone you could communicate with easily.

2. Members of the same family often are very different, and sometimes the opposite of each other. Write a paragraph explaining how you are either very similar to or very different from a member of your family.

Essay Option

3. Staples's brother lost his life to the violence of street crime. Write an essay describing what you feel can or should be done to avoid such a tragic waste of life.

Revision Checklist

Paragraph Development

1. Is the topic manageable (neither too broad nor too narrow)?
2. Is the paragraph written with the reader in mind?
3. Does the topic sentence identify the topic?
4. Does the topic sentence make a point about the topic?
5. Does each sentence support the topic sentence?
6. Is there sufficient detail?
7. Is there a sentence at the end that brings the paragraph to a close?

Sentence Development

8. Are there any sentence fragments, run-on sentences, or comma splices?
9. Are ideas combined to produce more effective sentences?
10. Are adjectives and adverbs used to make the sentences vivid and interesting?
11. Are relative clauses and prepositional phrases like *-ing* phrases used to add detail?
12. Are pronouns used correctly and consistently?

CHAPTER REVIEW AND PRACTICE

CHAPTER REVIEW

To review and check your recall of the chapter, select the word or phrase from the box below that best fits in each of the following sentences. Keep in mind that each word or phrase may be used more than once.

least/most	spatial	time-sequence

1. "The following steps should be taken before you turn on your new computer. First, make sure it is plugged in. Next, turn on all peripherals." This is an example of a _____ paragraph.

2. *To the east, beside, on the other side*, and *beneath* are all examples of _____ arrangement transitions.

3. "Talk about a disaster! It was bad enough that the dress I wanted to wear had a stain. The bus came late, and I spilled coffee on my application. To make things even worse, I sneezed on the interviewer!" The writer chose to tell this story using a _____ arrangement.

(continued)

4. The following is an example of a _____ map:
   How to Bake a Cake

   a. butter pan

   b. preheat oven

   c. assemble, measure, and combine ingredients

   d. pour batter into pan and place pan in oven

   e. bake

5. "The model is wearing a lovely ensemble that begins with a chic scarf knotted at the neck. Below it, the notched collar of the jacket adds a tailored look. This look is further enhanced by the trim belt at the waist." The announcer described the outfit using a _____ arrangement.

6. In a _____ arrangement, ideas are organized according to a particular quality, such as importance.

7. *During, later, first,* and *at last* are all examples of _____ transitions.

8. To supply descriptive details according to their physical relationship to each other is to use _____ arrangement.

9. *Best of all, moreover, especially,* and *in addition* are all examples of _____ transitions.

10. The _____ arrangement is used to present information in the order in which it occurred.

EDITING PRACTICE

The following paragraph lacks transitions to connect its details. Revise it by adding transitional words or phrases where useful.

Registering a used car with the Department of Motor Vehicles requires several steps. You should be sure you have proper proof of ownership. You must have the previous owner's signature on the "transfer of ownership" stub of his or her registration or on an ownership certificate to show that you purchased the car. You also need a receipt for the amount you paid for the car. You must provide proof that the vehicle is insured. You need to obtain forms from your insurance company showing you have the required amount of insurance. You must have the car inspected if the old inspection sticker has expired. Take the previous owner's registration form or ownership certificate, insurance forms, and proof of inspection to the Department of Motor Vehicles office. Here, you will fill out a new registration form and pay sales tax and a registration fee. Then you will be issued a temporary registration. Within two weeks, you will receive your official vehicle registration in the mail.

PEARSON
mywritinglab

For support in meeting this chapter's objectives, log in to www.mywritinglab.com, go to the Study Plan tab, click on Developing, Arranging, and Connecting Details and choose Developing and Organizing a Paragraph and Summary Writing from the list of subtopics. Read and view the videos and resources in the Review Materials section, and then complete the Recall, Apply, and Write exercises in the Activities section. You can check your scores and overall progress by using the Gradebook.

14

Using Methods of Organization

Learning Goals

In this chapter, you will learn how to

GOAL 1 Write using narration

GOAL 2 Write using description

GOAL 3 Write using example

GOAL 4 Write using definition

GOAL 5 Write using comparison and contrast

GOAL 6 Write using classification

GOAL 7 Write using process

GOAL 8 Write using cause and effect

GOAL 9 Write using argument

WRITE ABOUT IT!

Study the photograph above and then write a paragraph about it.

You could have developed your paragraph in a number of ways. For example, perhaps you told a story about the special occasion for which the cake was served. If so, you used a method of development called **narration** (discussed in Section A of this chapter). If your paragraph described the delicious taste, texture, or flavors of the cake, you used a method of development called **description** (Section B of this chapter). There are other possible ways to write a paragraph about the cake, using different methods of development. In this chapter you will learn the different methods for developing and organizing a paragraph.

WRITING

METHODS OF ORGANIZATION

Separate sections of this chapter are devoted to each of the following methods of development:

Section A: Narration	Tells a story that involves cake
Section B: Description	Describes the taste, texture, or flavor of cake
Section C: Example	Gives examples of celebrations in which cake is often served.
Section D: Definition	Defines what cake is to someone unfamiliar with it
Section E: Comparison and Contrast	Compares different flavors of cake
Section F: Classification	Explains the different types of cake (chocolate, layer, pound cakes, etc.)
Section G: Process	Explains how cake is made or explains how to make a cake
Section H: Cause and Effect	Explains why people enjoy cake
Section I: Argument	Makes the case that cake should be on every restaurant menu

Each of these methods of development produces an entirely different paragraph. The method you use depends on what you want to say and how you want to say it. For example, if you wanted your readers to visualize or imagine something, you might use description. If you wanted your readers to understand how something works, you would use process. If you wanted to convince your readers of something, you would use argument. The method you choose, then, should suit your purpose for writing. The nine methods of development described in this chapter offer you a wide range of choices for developing and organizing your writing. By learning to use each of them, you will develop a variety of new approaches to paragraph writing.

A: NARRATION

GOAL 1 Write using narration

What Is Narration?

The technique of making a point by telling a story is called **narration**. Narration is *not* simply listing a series of events—"this happened, then that happened." Narration shapes and interprets events to make a point. Notice the difference between the two paragraphs below.

mywritinglab

To practice using narration, go to
■ Study Plan
■ The Paragraph
■ Paragraph Development: Narration

Paragraph 1: Series of Events

Last Sunday we visited the National Zoo in Washington, D.C. As we entered, we decided to see the panda bear, the elephants, and the giraffes. All were outside enjoying the springlike weather. Then we visited the bat cave. I was amazed at how closely bats pack together in a small space. Finally, we went into the monkey house. There we spent time watching the giant apes watch us.

Paragraph 2: Narrative

Last Sunday's visit to the National Zoo in Washington, D.C., was a lesson to me about animals in captivity. First, we visited the panda, the elephants, and the giraffes. All seemed slow moving and locked into a dull routine—pacing around their yards. Then we watched the seals. Their trainer had them perform stunts for their food; they would never do these stunts in the wild. Finally, we stopped at the monkey house, where sad, old apes stared at us and watched kids point at them. The animals did not seem happy or content with their lives.

The first paragraph retells events in the order in which they happened, but with no shaping of the story. The second paragraph, a narrative, also presents events in the order in which they happened, but uses these events to make a point: animals kept in captivity are unhappy. Thus, all details and events work together to support that point. You can visualize a narrative paragraph as follows. Study the model and the map for paragraph 2.

 Visualize It!

Model Idea Map for Narration

```
Topic sentence
     │
     ├── Event 1
     │
     ├── Event 2
     │
     └── Event 3
```

Note: The number of events will vary.

Idea Map of Paragraph 2

```
The visit to the zoo was a lesson to me.
     │
     ├── Pandas, elephants, and giraffes followed a dull routine.
     │
     ├── Seals performed stunts.
     │
     └── Kids pointed at sad, old apes.
```

How to Develop a Narrative Paragraph

Developing a narrative paragraph involves writing a topic sentence and presenting sufficient details to support it.

Write a Clear Topic Sentence

Your topic sentence should accomplish two things:

1. **It should identify your topic.**
2. **It should reveal your attitude toward your topic.**

For example, suppose you are writing about visiting a zoo. Your topic sentence could take your narrative in a variety of directions, each of which would reveal a very different attitude toward the experience.

- During my recent visit to the zoo, I was saddened by the animals' behavior in captivity.
- A recent visit to the zoo gave my children a lesson in geography.
- My recent visit to the zoo taught me more about human nature than about animals.

Directions: The following paragraph uses the narrative method of development. Study its annotations to discover how the writer supports the topic sentence and organizes her ideas.

Author establishes the importance of the narrative

Topic sentence

> I can't eat. I can't sleep. And I certainly can't study. I stare at a single paragraph for a quarter of an hour but can't absorb it. How can I, when behind the words, on the white background of the paper, I'm watching an endless loop of my parents' deaths? Watching as their cream-colored

Description of events

> Buick flies through the guardrail and over the side of the bridge to avoid old Mr. McPherson's red truck? Old Mr. McPherson, who confessed as he was led from the scene that he wasn't entirely sure what side of the road he should have been on and thinks that maybe he hit the gas instead of the brake? Old Mr. McPherson, who showed up at church

Final comment reveals McPherson's mental state

> one legendary Easter without trousers?

—Gruen, *Water for Elephants*, p. 21.

EXERCISE A-1
Writing in Progress

Writing Topic Sentences

Directions: Complete three of the following topic sentences by adding information that describes an experience you have had related to the topic.

EXAMPLE   My first job <u>was an experience I would rather forget.</u>

1. Holidays _____
2. A frightening event _____
3. My first day on campus _____
4. Cell phones _____
5. My advisor/instructor _____

Include Sufficient Details

A narrative paragraph should include enough detail to support your topic sentence and allow your reader to understand fully the experience you are writing about. Be sure you have answered most of the following questions:

- *What* events occurred?
- *Where* did they happen?
- *When* did they happen?
- *Who* was involved?
- *Why* did they happen?
- *How* did they happen?

EXERCISE A-2   Brainstorming Details
Writing in Progress

Directions: Using one of the topic sentences you wrote in Exercise A-1, brainstorm a list of relevant and sufficient details to support it. ■

How to Organize a Narrative Paragraph

The events in a narrative are usually arranged in the order in which they happened. This method of organization is called **time-sequence arrangement** (see Chapter 13, p. 350, for a discussion of this method). Transitions are especially important in narrative paragraphs because they identify and separate events from one another. Useful transitions are shown below.

Narration: Useful Transitions			
first	then	in the beginning	next
second	later	after	during
third	at last	following	after that
finally			while

EXERCISE A-3   Using Time-Sequence Order
Writing in Progress

Directions: Using the topic sentence you wrote in Exercise A-1, and the relevant and sufficient details you generated in Exercise A-2, present your details in time-sequence order, using transitions as needed. ■

Analyze It!

Directions: The paragraph on the left is a professional example of a narrative paragraph. Read the paragraph and then complete the idea map below.

Foxy came over early in the evening of July 3 to help Dayton load Babe into the back of the pickup for her ride to the rodeo. Fencing had been fixed to the sides of the bed, which was pulled against the open gate of the corral. A runway made of thick boards covered with a piece of shag carpet was rigged to the tailgate. I watched from the open window while Dayton spread the flat bottom of the truck with fresh hay, then waited while Foxy rustled and spooked Babe. It took awhile. She raced by the ramp, flicking her tail and shaking her head, kicking dust into Foxy's new rodeo clothes. Her hooves struck the ground hard as hammers, and she shook the bit, flapping the rope out of Foxy's reach. Finally, as if she knew what she was doing, she charged into the truck so fast that Dayton backed against the cab and waved his arms to ward her off, but the next minute, she had lowered her head to chew some hay, her heaving sides the only sign she was excited.

—Dorris, *A Yellow Raft in Blue Water*, pp. 276–277.

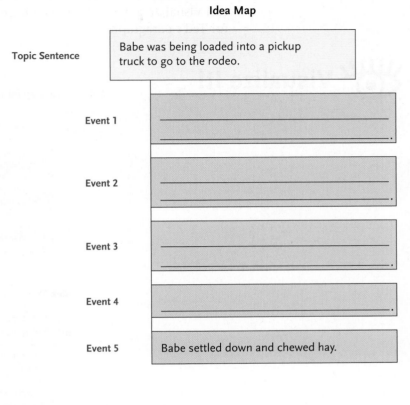

Idea Map

Topic Sentence — Babe was being loaded into a pickup truck to go to the rodeo.

Event 1 — _____

Event 2 — _____

Event 3 — _____

Event 4 — _____

Event 5 — Babe settled down and chewed hay.

B: DESCRIPTION

GOAL 2 Write using description

mywritinglab

To practice using description, go to
- Study Plan
- The Paragraph
- Paragraph Development: Describing

What Is Description?

Descriptive writing uses words and phrases that appeal to the senses—taste, touch, smell, sight, hearing. Descriptive writing helps your reader imagine an object, person, place, or experience. The details you use should also leave your reader with an overall impression of what you are describing. Here is a sample descriptive paragraph written by a student, Ted Sawchuck. Notice how he makes you feel as if you are in the kitchen with him as he prepares chili.

My favorite chili recipe requires a trip to the grocery store and a day to hang around the kitchen stirring, but it is well worth the expense and time. Canned, shiny red kidney beans and fat, great white northern beans simmer in the big pot, while ground beef and kielbasa sizzle and spit in a cast-iron skillet. Raw white onions bring tears to one's eyes, and they are quickly chopped. Plump yellow and orange peppers are chopped to add fiber and flavor, while six cloves of garlic, smashed, make simmering all day a necessity. When it cooks, this chili makes the whole house smell mouthwateringly good. When eaten, chunks of kielbasa stand out in a spicy, garlicky sauce with small nuggets of ground beef.

Notice that this paragraph describes tastes, smells, sounds, and colors. You even learn how it feels to chop an onion. Notice, too, that all of the details directly support an overall impression that is expressed in the first sentence. You can visualize a descriptive paragraph as follows. Study the model and the map for Ted's paragraph.

Model Idea Map for Description

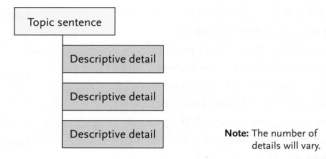

Note: The number of details will vary.

Idea Map of Sawchuck's Paragraph on Chili

How to Develop a Descriptive Paragraph

A descriptive paragraph has three key features, an overall impression, sensory details, and descriptive language.

1. **Create an overall impression.** The **overall impression** is the *one* central idea you want to present to your reader. It is the single, main point that all of your details prove or support. For example, if you are writing a paragraph about your math instructor's sense of humor, then all of your details should be about amusing things he or she has said or done. Your overall impression should be expressed in your topic sentence, usually at the beginning of the

paragraph. Notice that each of the following topic sentences expresses a different overall impression of Niagara Falls:

a. Niagara Falls is stunningly beautiful and majestic.

b. The beauty of Niagara Falls is hidden by its tourist-oriented, commercial surroundings.

c. Niagara Falls would be beautiful to visit if I could be there alone, without the crowds of tourists.

Your overall impression is often your first reaction to a topic. Suppose you are writing about your college snack bar. Think of a word or two that sums up how you feel about it. Is it noisy? Smelly? Relaxing? Messy? You could develop any one of these descriptive words into a paragraph. For example, your topic sentence might be:

The snack bar is a noisy place that I try to avoid.

The details that follow would then describe the noise—the clatter of plates, loud conversations, chairs scraping the floor, and music blaring.

Examine It!

Directions: The following paragraph, about the eruption of Mount St. Helens, a volcano in Washington state, uses the descriptive method of development. Notice how each of the highlighted words and phrases helps you visualize the eruption.

The slumping north face of the mountain produced the greatest landslide witnessed in recorded history; about 2.75 km³ (0.67 mi³) of rock, ice, and trapped air, all fluidized with steam, surged at speeds approaching 250 kmph (155 mph). Landslide materials traveled for 21 km (13 mi) into the valley, blanketing the forest, covering a lake, filling the rivers below. The eruption continued with intensity for 9 hours, first clearing out old rock from the throat of the volcano and then blasting new material.

—Christopherson, *Geosystems*, p. 368.

EXERCISE B-1

Writing in Progress

Brainstorming, Reacting, and Writing Topic Sentences

Directions: Brainstorm a list of words that sum up your reaction to each of the following topics. Then develop each list of words into a topic sentence that expresses an overall impression and could lead to a descriptive paragraph.

TOPIC	A parent or guardian
REACTION	Dad: loving, accepting, smart, helpful, calm, generous
TOPIC SENTENCE	My whole life, my father has been generous and helpful in the way he let me be myself.

1. TOPIC   A library, gym, or other public place that you have used

   REACTION   _____

   TOPIC SENTENCE _____

   _____

   _____

2. TOPIC   A part-time job, past or present

   REACTION   _____

   TOPIC SENTENCE _____

                  _____

                  _____

3. TOPIC   A small shop or a shopkeeper familiar to you

   REACTION   _____

   TOPIC SENTENCE _____

                  _____

                  _____

4. TOPIC   A music video, movie, or song

   REACTION   _____

   TOPIC SENTENCE _____

                  _____

                  _____

5. TOPIC   A person in the news

   REACTION   _____

   TOPIC SENTENCE _____

                  _____

                  _____

                  _____

2. **Include sensory details. Sensory details** appeal to your senses—your sense of touch, taste, sight, sound, and smell. Try to imagine your topic—the person, place, thing, or experience. Depending on what your topic is, write down what it makes you see, hear, smell, taste, or feel.

EXERCISE B-2   Brainstorming Details
Writing in Progress

Directions: Using one of the topic sentences you wrote in Exercise B-1, brainstorm details that support the overall impression it conveys.

3. **Use descriptive language. Descriptive language** uses words that help your readers imagine your topic and make it exciting and vivid to them. Consider the following sentences. The first is dull and lifeless; the second describes what the writer sees and feels.

   NONDESCRIPTIVE   The beach was crowded with people.

   DESCRIPTIVE   The beach was overrun with teenage bodies wearing neon Lycra suits and slicked with sweet-smelling oil. ■

Making your details more descriptive is not difficult. Use the guidelines below.

NEED TO KNOW

Using Descriptive Details

1. **Use verbs that help your reader picture the action.**

   NONDESCRIPTIVE   The boy walked down the beach.

   DESCRIPTIVE   The boy ambled down the beach.

2. **Use exact names.** Include the names of people, places, brands, animals, flowers, stores, streets, products—whatever will make your description more precise.

   NONDESCRIPTIVE   Kevin parked his car near the deserted beach.

   DESCRIPTIVE   Kevin parked his maroon Saturn convertible at Burke's Garage next to the deserted beach.

3. **Use adjectives to describe.** Adjectives are words that describe nouns. Place them before or after nouns to add detail.

   NONDESCRIPTIVE   The beach was deserted.

   DESCRIPTIVE   The remote, rocky, windswept beach was deserted.

4. **Use words that appeal to the senses.** Use words that convey touch, taste, smell, sound, and sight.

   NONDESCRIPTIVE   I saw big waves roll on the beach.

   DESCRIPTIVE   Immense black waves rammed the shore, releasing with each crash the salty, fishy smell of the deep ocean.

How to Organize a Descriptive Paragraph

Among the common methods of ordering details in descriptive writing are

- **Spatial arrangement.** You organize details according to their physical location. (See Chapter 13, p. 352, for a discussion of this method.) For example, you could describe a favorite newsstand by arranging your details from right to left or from front to back.

- **Least/most arrangement.** You organize details in increasing or decreasing order, according to some quality or characteristic, such as importance. (See Chapter 13, p. 354, for a discussion of this method.) Suppose your overall impression of a person is that she is disorganized. You might start with some minor traits (she can never find a pen) and move to more serious and important characteristics of disorganization (she misses classes and forgets appointments).

Whatever method you choose to arrange your details, you will want to use good transitional words and phrases between details.

Description: Useful Transitions

SPATIAL	LEAST/MOST
above, below, inside, outside, beside	first, second, primarily, secondarily
next to, facing, nearby, to the right, to the left, in front of, across	most important, also important

---

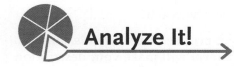

Analyze It!

Directions: The paragraph on the left is a professional example of a descriptive paragraph. For each part of the house listed below, list several descriptive words that help you visualize its appearance.

The earth by the front door was worn flat, smoothed by the dumping and drying of dishwater. Shingles were blown off the roof in an irregular pattern that reminded me of notes on a music sheet, and tan cardboard replaced glass in a pane of the attic window. The house and the land had been through so many seasons, shared so much rain and sun, so much expanding and shrinking with heat and cold, that the seams between them were all but gone. Now the walls rose from the ground like the sides of a short, square hill, dug out by the wind and exposed.

—Dorris, *A Yellow Raft in Blue Water*, p. 251.

Roof: _____

_____

Attic window: _____

_____

Walls: _____

_____

EXERCISE B-3
Writing in Progress

Writing a Descriptive Paragraph

Directions: Using the details you developed in Exercise B-2, write a paragraph. Assume that your reader is unfamiliar with what you are describing. Use descriptive language and organize your paragraph using a spatial or least/most arrangement, and use transitions as needed. ■

C: EXAMPLE

GOAL 3 Write using example

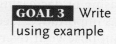

To practice using illustration, go to
■ Study Plan
■ The Paragraph
■ Paragraph Development: Illustrating

What Is an Example?

An **example** is a specific instance or situation that explains a general idea or statement. Apples and grapes are examples of fruit. Martin Luther King Day and Thanksgiving Day are examples of national holidays. Here are a few sample general statements along with specific examples that illustrate them:

GENERAL STATEMENT	EXAMPLES
1. I had an exciting day.	**a.** My sister had her first baby.
	b. I got a bonus check at work.
	c. I reached my goal of 20 laps in the pool.
2. Joe has annoying habits.	**a.** He interrupts me when I am talking.
	b. He is often late and makes no apologies.
	c. He talks with his mouth full.

Here is a sample paragraph written by Annie Lockhart that uses examples to explain the general idea of superstitious beliefs:

> Superstition affects many people on a daily basis. For example, some people think it is very unlucky if a black cat crosses their path, so they go to great lengths to avoid one. Also, according to another superstitious belief, walking under a ladder brings bad luck. Putting shoes on a bed is thought to be a sign that a death will occur in the family. People tend either to take superstitions very seriously or to reject them out of hand as fanciful imagination; regardless, they play an important part in our culture.

Notice that the paragraph gives three examples of superstitions. You can visualize an example paragraph as follows. Study the model and the map for the paragraph on superstitions.

 Visualize It!

Model Idea Map for Example

Topic sentence

Example

Example

Example

Note: The number of examples will vary.

Idea Map for Lockhart's Paragraph on Superstition

Superstition affects many people on a daily basis.

Black cats are unlucky.

Walking under ladders brings bad luck.

Shoes on a bed mean death.

How to Develop an Example Paragraph

Developing an example paragraph involves writing a topic sentence and selecting appropriate examples to support it.

Write a Topic Sentence

Your topic sentence should accomplish two things:

1. **It should identify your topic.**
2. **It should make a general statement that the examples support.**

   Here are a few examples of topic sentences. Can you predict the types of examples each paragraph would contain?

   - Consumers often purchase brand names they have seen advertised in the media.
   - Advertisers use attention-getting devices to make a lasting impression in the minds of their consumers.
   - Some teenagers are obsessed with instant messaging, using it to the extreme and forsaking other forms of communication.

Choose Appropriate Examples

Make sure the examples you choose directly support your topic sentence. Use the following guidelines in choosing examples:

1. **Choose clear examples.** Do not choose an example that is complicated or has too many parts; your readers may not be able to see the connection to your topic sentence clearly.

2. **Use a sufficient number of examples to make your point understandable.** The number you need depends on the complexity of the topic and your readers' familiarity with it. One example is sufficient only if it is well developed. The more difficult and unfamiliar the topic, the more examples you will need. For instance, if you are writing about how purchasing books at the college bookstore can be viewed as an exercise in patience, two examples may be sufficient. However, if you are writing about religious intolerance, you probably will need more than two examples.

3. **Include examples that your readers are familiar with and understand.** If you choose an example that is out of the realm of your readers' experience, the example will not help them understand your main point.

4. **Vary your examples.** If you are giving several examples, choose a wide range from different times, places, people, etc.

5. **Choose typical examples.** Avoid outrageous or exaggerated examples that do not accurately represent the situation you are discussing.

6. **Each example should be as specific and vivid as possible, accurately describing an incident or situation.** Include as much detail as is necessary for your readers to understand how the situation illustrates your topic sentence.

7. **Make sure the connection between your example and your main point is clear to your readers.** If the connection is not obvious, include an explanation. For instance, if it is not clear that poor time management is an example of poor study habits, explain how the two relate.

Examine It!

Directions: The following paragraph is a good model of an example paragraph. Study its annotations to discover how the writers use examples to develop their paragraph.

Alternative Energy Sources

Topic sentence

Example 1 (new technology)

Example 2 (wind power)

Example 3 (applications)

New technologies are helping to make alternative sources of energy cost effective. In Pennsylvania and Connecticut, *for example,* the waste from landfills is loaded into furnaces and burned to generate electricity for thousands of homes. Natural sources of energy, *such as* the sun and the wind, are also becoming more attractive. The electricity produced by 300 wind turbines in northern California, *for instance,* has resulted in a savings of approximately 60,000 barrels of oil per year. Solar energy also has many applications, from pocket calculators to public telephones to entire homes, and is even used in spacecraft, where conventional power is unavailable.

—adapted from Bergman and Renwick, *Introduction to Geography,* p. 343, and Carnes and Garraty, *The American Nation,* p. 916.

EXERCISE C-1
Writing in Progress

Brainstorming Examples

Directions: Select one of the topics listed below, narrow it, and write a topic sentence for it. Then brainstorm a list of examples that support it.

1. The behavior of professional athletes
2. The value of travel or a vacation
3. People's eating habits
4. Television commercials
5. Restaurant dining ■

How to Organize an Example Paragraph

Be sure to arrange your examples logically. You might arrange them from most to least important or least to most important. (See Chapter 13, p. 354 and section B of this chapter, p. 377.) You might also arrange them chronologically, in order of time, if the examples are events in the past. For example, if you are reporting on how early educational experiences influenced you, you might begin with the earliest situation and progress to the most recent.

Regardless of the order you use, be sure to connect your examples with transitional words and phrases like those shown below.

Example: Useful Transitions		
for example	for instance	to illustrate
one example	another example	such as
also		

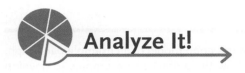

Analyze It!

Directions: The following paragraph is a good model of an example paragraph. Read the paragraph and highlight each example. Then, underline the sentences that the examples support.

Controlling Information and Using Technology

To maintain their positions of power, elites try to control information. Fear is a favorite tactic of dictators. To muffle criticism, they imprison, torture, and kill reporters who dare to criticize their regime. Under Saddam Hussein, the penalty for telling a joke about Hussein was having your tongue cut out. Lacking such power, the ruling elites of democracies rely on more covert means. The new technology is another tool for the elite. Telephones can be turned into microphones even when they are off the hook. Machines can read the entire contents of a computer in a second, without leaving evidence that they have done so. Security cameras—"Tiny Brothers"—have sprouted almost everywhere. Face-recognition systems can scan a crowd of thousands, instantly matching the scans with digitized files of individuals. With these devices, the elite can monitor citizens' activities without anyone knowing that they are being observed. Dictatorships have few checks on how they employ such technology, but in democracies, checks and balances, such as requiring court orders for search and seizure, at least partially curb their abuse. The threat of bypassing such restraints on power are always present, as with the Homeland Security laws.

—Henslin, *Sociology*, p. 249.

EXERCISE C-2
Writing in Progress

Writing an Example Paragraph

Directions: Using the topic sentence and examples you generated in Exercise C-1, write an example paragraph. Present your details in a logical order, using transitions as needed. ■

D: DEFINITION

GOAL 4 Write using definition

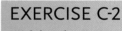

To practice using definition, go to
■ Study Plan
■ The Paragraph
■ Paragraph Development: Definition

What Is Definition?

A **definition** is an explanation of what something is. It has three essential parts:

1. The term being defined
2. The group, or category, to which the term belongs
3. Its distinguishing characteristics

Suppose you had to define the term *cheetah*. If you said it was a cat, then you would be stating the group to which it belongs. **Group** means the general category of which something is a part. If you said a cheetah lives in Africa and southwest Asia, has black-spotted fur, is long-legged, and is the fastest animal on land, you would be giving some of its distinguishing characteristics. **Distinguishing characteristics** are those details that allow you to tell an item apart from others in its same group. The details about the cheetah's fur, long legs, and speed enable a reader to distinguish it from other large cats in Africa and southwest Asia. Here are a few more examples:

TERM	GROUP	DISTINGUISHING CHARACTERISTICS
opal	gemstone	greenish blue colors
comedian	entertainer	makes people laugh
fear	emotion	occurs when a person feels threatened or in danger

Here is a sample definition paragraph written by a student, Ted Sawchuck.

> Sushi is a Japanese food consisting of small cakes of cooked rice wrapped in seaweed. While it is commonly thought of as raw fish on rice, it is actually any preparation of vinegared rice. Sushi can also take the form of conical hand rolls and the more popular sushi roll. The roll is topped or stuffed with slices of raw or cooked fish, egg, or vegetables. Slices of raw fish served by themselves are commonly mistaken for sushi but are properly referred to as *sashimi*.

In the paragraph above, the term being defined is *sushi*. Its group is Japanese food, and its distinguishing characteristics are detailed. You can visualize a definition paragraph as follows. Study the model and the map for the paragraph on sushi shown below.

 **Visualize It!**

Model Idea Map for Definition

> Topic sentence (term and general class)
>> Distinguishing characteristic
>>
>> Distinguishing characteristic
>>
>> Distinguishing characteristic

Note: The number of characteristics will vary.

Idea Map of Sawchuck's Paragraph on Sushi

> Sushi is a Japanese food consisting of rice wrapped in seaweed.
>> Uses vinegared rice
>>
>> Conical or sushi-roll shape
>>
>> Topped or stuffed with raw or cooked fish, eggs, or vegetable
>>
>> Sushi is not just slices of raw fish served alone.

Examine It!

Directions: The following paragraph is a good model of a definition paragraph. Study the annotations to discover how the writer defines the term *nervous system*

The Nervous System

Topic sentence	
First distinguishing feature	The nervous system, the master controlling and communicating system of the body, has three overlapping functions. (1) It uses millions of sensory receptors to monitor changes occurring both inside and outside the body. These changes are called stimuli and the gathered
Second distinguishing feature	information is called *sensory input*. (2) It processes and interprets the sensory input and decides what should be done at each moment—a
Third distinguishing feature	process called *integration*. (3) It causes a response by activating our muscles or glands; the response is called *motor output*. An example will
Example	illustrate how these functions work together. When you are driving and see a red light ahead (sensory input), your nervous system integrates this information (red light means "stop"), and your foot goes for the brake (motor output).

—Marieb, *Anatomy and Physiology*, p. 387.

EXERCISE D-1   Classifying Terms

Directions: For each term listed below, give the group it belongs to and at least two of its distinguishing characteristics.

TERM	GROUP	DISTINGUISHING CHARACTERSTICS
1. baseball	_____	_____
2. a role model	_____	_____
3. blogging	_____	_____
4. terrorism	_____	_____
5. facial expressions	_____	_____

How to Develop a Definition Paragraph

Developing a definition paragraph involves writing a topic sentence and adding explanatory details.

Write a Topic Sentence

The topic sentence of a definition paragraph should accomplish two things:

1. **It should identify the term you are explaining.**
2. **It should place the term in a general group. It may also provide one or more distinguishing characteristics.**

In the topic sentence below, the term being defined is *psychiatry*, the general group is "a branch of medicine," and its distinguishing feature is that it "deals with mental and emotional disorders."

Psychiatry is a branch of medicine that deals with mental and emotional disorders.

EXERCISE D-2
Writing in Progress

Writing a Topic Sentence

Directions: Write a topic sentence that includes a group and a distinguishing characteristic for each of the following items.

1. shirt _____
2. horror _____
3. hip-hop _____
4. age discrimination _____
5. ballroom dancing _____

■

Add Explanatory Details

Your topic sentence will usually *not* be sufficient to give your reader a complete understanding of the term you are defining. You will need to explain it further in one or more of the following ways:

1. **Give examples.** Examples can make a definition more vivid and interesting to your reader. (To learn more about using examples, see section C of this chapter, p. 378.)
2. **Break the term into subcategories.** Breaking your subject down into subcategories helps to organize your definition. For example, you might explain the term *discrimination* by listing some of its types: racial, gender, and age.
3. **Explain what the term is not.** To bring the meaning of a term into focus for your reader, it is sometimes helpful to give counterexamples, or to discuss in what ways the term means something different from what one might expect. Notice that Sawchuck does this in the paragraph on sushi.
4. **Trace the term's meaning over time.** If the term has changed or expanded in meaning over time, it may be useful to trace this development as a way of explaining the term's current meaning.
5. **Compare an unfamiliar term to one that is familiar to your readers.** If you are writing about rugby, you might compare it to football, a more familiar sport. Be sure to make the connection clear to your readers by pointing out characteristics that the two sports share.

How to Organize a Definition Paragraph

You should logically arrange the distinguishing characteristics of a term. You might arrange them from most to least familiar or from more to less obvious, for example. Be sure to use strong transitional words and phrases to help your readers follow your presentation of ideas, guiding them from one distinguishing characteristic to another. Useful transitional words and phrases are shown below.

Definition: Useful Transitions			
can be defined as	means	is	
one	a second	another	also

Analyze It!

Directions: The paragraph on the left is a good model of a paragraph that uses definition as a method of development. Complete the outline below using information given in the paragraph.

What Is a Tale?

The name *tale* is sometimes applied to any story, whether short or long, true or fictitious. But defined in a more limited sense, a **tale** is a story, usually short, that sets forth strange and wonderful events in more or less bare summary, without detailed character-drawing. *Tale* implies a story in which the goal is to reveal something marvelous rather than to reveal the character of someone. In the English folk tale "Jack and the Beanstalk," for instance, we take away a more vivid impression of the miraculous beanstalk and the giant who dwells at its top than of Jack's mind or personality.

—adapted from Kennedy and Gioia, *Literature*, p. 7.

I.   Tale

A.   Often defined as _____
     _____.

B.   In a more limited sense, it has specific characteristics.

1.   It is usually _____.

2.   It describes events _____ form.

3.   Its goal is to _____, rather than to reveal someone's character.

a.   Example: _____:
     the _____ is memorable, but Jack's personality is not.

EXERCISE D-3   Writing a Definition Paragraph

Writing in Progress

Directions: Select one of the topic sentences you wrote for Exercise D-2. Write a paragraph defining that topic, using transitions as needed. ■

E: COMPARISON AND CONTRAST

GOAL 5 Write using comparison and contrast

What Are Comparison and Contrast?

Comparison and contrast are two ways of organizing information about two or more subjects. **Comparison** focuses on similarities; **contrast** focuses on differences. When writing paragraphs, it is often best to focus either on similarities or on differences, instead of trying to cover both in a short piece of writing.

To practice using comparison and contrast, go to

- Study Plan
- The Paragraph
- Paragraph Development: Comparing and Contrasting

Essay-length pieces can focus on both similarities and differences, but it is often easier to concentrate on one or the other. Here is a sample contrast paragraph written by Ted Sawchuck:

> Every time I go out for Mexican food, I have to choose between tacos de carne asada and tacos al pastor—they are tasty, but different. The tacos de carne asada are three small tortillas stuffed with chopped steak, served with a dish each of cilantro, onion, tomato, and fiery salsa. The tacos al pastor are similar, but chorizo is added to the chopped steak. While the tacos al pastor are a little greasier, they also have more spice and heat. Tacos de carne asada are drier with less flavor, but there's more room to add the vegetables, and that often makes for more dynamic flavor possibilities.

In this paragraph, Sawchuck discusses the differences between two types of tacos. He examines their ingredients, their spiciness, and their overall flavor. You can visualize a comparison or contrast paragraph as follows. Study the models and the map for Sawchuck's paragraph.

Model Idea Map for Comparison

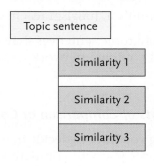

Note: The number of similarities will vary.

Model Idea Map for Contrast

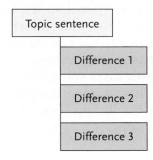

Note: The number of differences will vary.

Idea Map for Sawchuck's Paragraph on Tacos

Tacos de carne asada and tacos al pastor taste different.

Contents: de carne asada have steak; al pastor have steak and chorizo

Texture: al pastor are greasier

Heat: al pastor have more heat

Vegetables: de carne asada have more room for vegetables

How to Develop a Comparison or Contrast Paragraph

Developing a comparison or contrast paragraph involves writing a topic sentence and developing points of comparison or contrast.

Write a Topic Sentence

Your topic sentence should do two things:

1. **It should identify the two subjects that you will compare or contrast.**
2. **It should state whether you will focus on similarities, differences, or both.**

Here are a few sample topic sentences that meet the requirements above:

- Judaism is one of the smallest of the world's religions; Hinduism is one of the largest.
- Neither Judaism nor Hinduism limits worship to a single location, although both hold services in temples.
- Unlike Hinduism, Judaism teaches belief in only one God.

Be sure to avoid topic sentences that announce what you plan to do. Here's an example: "I'll compare network news and local news and show why I prefer local news."

Develop Points of Comparison or Contrast

The first thing you have to decide in writing a comparison or contrast paragraph is on what bases you will compare your two subjects. These bases are called **points of comparison** or **contrast.** Suppose you are comparing two different jobs that you have held. Points of comparison could be your salary, work schedule, required tasks, responsibilities, relationships with other employees, relationship with your boss, and so forth. The points of comparison you choose should depend on what you want your paragraph to show—your purpose for writing. If your purpose is to show what you learned from the jobs, then you might compare the tasks you completed and your responsibilities. If you want to make a case that working conditions in entry level jobs are poor, then you might use responsibilities, work schedule, and relationship with your boss as points of comparison.

Examine It!

Directions: The following paragraph is a good model of a comparison and contrast paragraph. Study the annotations to discover how the writer explains the differences between two types of tumors.

Malignant and Benign Tumors

Topic Sentence

Difference #1

Not all tumors are **malignant** (cancerous); in fact, more are **benign** (noncancerous). Benign and malignant tumors differ in several key ways. Benign tumors are generally composed of ordinary-looking cells enclosed in a fibrous shell or capsule that prevents their spreading to other body areas. Malignant tumors, in contrast, are

Difference #2

> usually not enclosed in a protective capsule and can therefore spread to other organs. Unlike benign tumors, which merely expand to take over a given space, malignant cells invade surrounding tissue, emitting clawlike protrusions that disrupt chemical processes within healthy cells.

—adapted from Donatelle, *Health*, p. 324.

EXERCISE E-1
Writing in Progress

Brainstorming and Writing Topic Sentences

Directions: For two of the topics below, brainstorm lists of similarities or differences. Review your lists and choose points of comparison. Then write topic sentences for them.

1. Two special places
2. Two favorite pastimes
3. Two styles of dress
4. Two cars
5. Two public figures
6. Two sports
7. Two college classes
8. Two relatives ■

How to Organize a Comparison or Contrast Paragraph

Once you have identified similarities or differences and drafted a topic sentence, you are ready to organize your paragraph. There are two ways you can organize a comparison or contrast paragraph:

- subject by subject
- point by point

Subject-by-Subject Organization

In the **subject-by-subject method**, you write first about one of your subjects, covering it completely, and then about the other, covering it completely. Ideally, you cover the same points of comparison or contrast for both and in the same order. With subject-by-subject organization, you begin by discussing your first job—its salary, working conditions, and responsibilities. Then you discuss your second job—its salary, working conditions, and responsibilities. You can visualize the arrangement with the idea map shown on p. 390.

To develop each subject, focus on the same kinds of details and discuss the same points of comparison in the same order. Organize your points within each topic, using a most-to-least or least-to-most arrangement.

 **Visualize It!**

Model Idea Map for Subject-by-Subject Organization

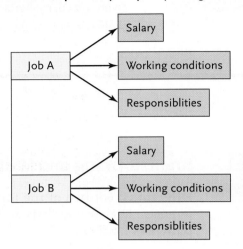

 **Analyze It!**

Directions: The paragraph on the left is a good model of a paragraph that uses comparison and contrast as a method of development. Complete the map below using information given in the paragraph.

Types of Leaders

Groups have two types of leaders. The first is easy to recognize. This person, called an **instrumental leader** (or *task-oriented leader*), tries to keep the group moving toward its goals. These leaders try to keep group members from getting sidetracked, reminding them of what they are trying to accomplish. The **expressive leader** (or *socioemotional leader*), in contrast, usually is not recognized as a leader, but he or she certainly is one. This person is likely to crack jokes, to offer sympathy, or to do other things that help to lift the group's morale. Both type of leadership are essential: the one to keep the group on track, the other to increase harmony and minimize conflicts.

—Henslin, *Sociology,* p. 169.

Types of Leaders

Instrumental leader or task-oriented leader

_____

_____

_____

Reminds them of their goals

_____

_____

Not recognized as a leader, but is one

_____

EXERCISE E-2

Writing in Progress

Writing a Paragraph

Directions: Using the subject-by-subject method of organization, write a comparison or contrast paragraph on one of the topics you worked with in Exercise E-1. ■

Point-by-Point Organization

In the **point-by-point method of organization**, you discuss both of your subjects together for each point of comparison or contrast. For the paragraph on jobs, you would write about the salary for Job A and Job B, and then you would write about working conditions for Job A and Job B, and so on.

You can visualize the organization this way:

Visualize It!

Model Idea Map for Point-by-Point Organization

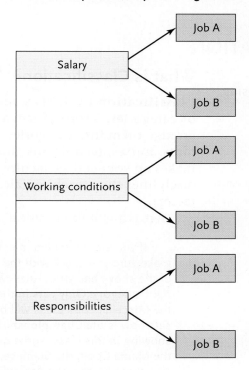

When using this organization, maintain consistency by discussing the same subject first for each point. (For example, always discuss Job A first and Job B second.)

If your paragraph focuses only on similarities or only on differences, arrange your points in a least-to-most or most-to-least pattern.

Transitions are particularly important in comparison and contrast writing. Because you are discussing two subjects and covering similar points for each, your readers can easily become confused. Useful transitions are shown below.

Comparison and Contrast Useful Transitions

To show similarities	likewise, similarly, in the same way, too, also
To show differences	however, on the contrary, unlike, on the other hand, but, although

---

EXERCISE E-3
Writing in Progress

Using Transitions

Directions: Review the paragraph you wrote for Exercise E-2. Add transitions, as needed. ■

F: CLASSIFICATION

GOAL 6 Write using classification

mywritinglab

To practice using classification, go to
■ Study Plan
■ The Paragraph
■ Paragraph Development: Division/Classification

What Is Classification?

Classification explains a subject by identifying and describing its types or categories. For instance, a good way to discuss medical personnel is to arrange them into categories: doctors, nurse practitioners, physician's assistants, nurses, technicians, and nurse's aides. If you wanted to explain who makes up your college faculty, you could classify the faculty members by the disciplines they teach (or, alternatively, by age, level of skill, or some other factor).

Here is a sample classification paragraph written by Elsie Hunter:

> If you are interested in entering your pedigreed pet in the upcoming cat show, make sure you check with the Cat Fanciers' Association first. The CFA, sponsor of the show, has strict rules regarding eligibility. You must enter your cat in the right category. Only cats in the Championship Class, the Provisional Class, or the Miscellaneous Class will be allowed to participate. The first category in every cat show is the Championship Class. There are 37 pedigreed breeds eligible for showing in this class, some of which may sound familiar, such as the Abyssinian, the Maine Coon, the Siamese, and the Russian Blue. The Provisional Class allows only three breeds: the American Bobtail, a breed that looks like a wildcat but acts like a pussycat; the LaPerm, a curly-haired cutie that's descended from early American barn cats; and the semi-longhaired Siberian, a breed that was first imported from Russia in 1990. The Miscellaneous Class allows only one breed—the big Ragamuffin with its silky, rabbitlike coat. So, before you rush out and pay the entry fee, make sure you have something fancy enough for the Cat Fanciers' Association.

This paragraph explains the eligibility for a cat show by describing the three categories of cats allowed to enter the show.

You can visualize the process of classification as follows. Study the model and the map for Hunter's paragraph below.

Model Idea Map for Classification

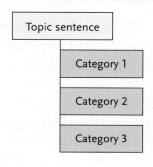

Topic sentence

Category 1

Category 2

Category 3

Note: The number of categories will vary.

Idea Map for Hunter's Paragraph on Cats

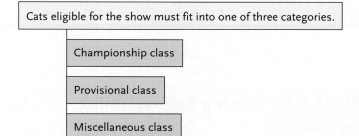

Cats eligible for the show must fit into one of three categories.

Championship class

Provisional class

Miscellaneous class

How to Develop a Classification Paragraph

Developing a classification paragraph involves deciding on a basis of classification for the subject you are discussing, writing a topic sentence, and explaining each subgroup.

Decide on What Basis to Classify Information

To write a paper using classification, you must first decide on a basis for breaking your subject into subgroups. Suppose you are given an assignment to write about some aspect of campus life. You decide to classify the campus services into groups. You could classify them by benefit, location, or type of facility, depending on what you wanted the focus of your writing to be.

The best way to plan your classification paragraph is to find a good general topic and then brainstorm different ways to break it into subgroups or categories.

Examine It!

Directions: The following paragraph is a good model of a classification paragraph. Study the annotations to discover how the writers classify strategies used by companies.

Company Strategies

Topic sentence

Category 1

Category 2

Category 3

Three types of strategy are usually considered by a company. The purpose of **corporate strategy** is to determine the firm's overall attitude toward growth and the way it will manage its businesses or product lines. A company may decide to *grow* by increasing its activities or investment or to *retrench* by reducing them. **Business (or competitive) strategy**, which takes place at the level of the business unit or product line, focuses on improving the company's competitive position. At the level of **functional strategy**, managers in specific areas decide how best to achieve corporate goals by being as productive as possible.

—adapted from Ebert and Griffin, *Business Essentials*, p. 117.

EXERCISE F-1
Working Together

Using Brainstorming

Directions: For each of the following topics, brainstorm to discover different ways you might classify them. Compare your work with that of a classmate and select the two or three most effective classifications.

1. TOPIC Crimes

   WAYS TO CLASSIFY _____

   _____

   _____

2. TOPIC Movies

   WAYS TO CLASSIFY _____

   _____

   _____

3. TOPIC Web sites

   WAYS TO CLASSIFY _____

   _____

   _____

Most topics can be classified in a number of different ways. Stores can be classified by types of merchandise, prices, size, or customer service provided, for example. Use the following tips for choosing an appropriate basis of classification:

- **Consider your audience.** Choose a basis of classification that will interest them. Classifying stores by size may not be as interesting as classifying them by merchandise, for example.

- **Choose a basis that is uncomplicated.** If you choose a basis that is complicated or lengthy, your topic may be difficult to write about. Categorizing stores by prices may be unwieldy, since there are thousands of products sold at various prices.

- **Choose a basis with which you are familiar.** While it is possible to classify stores by the types of customer service they provide, you may have to do some research or learn more about available services in order to write about them.

EXERCISE F-2
Writing in Progress

Using Brainstorming

Directions: Choose one of the following topics. Brainstorm a list of possible ways to classify the topic.

1. Professional athletes or their fans

2. Bad drivers

3. Diets

4. Cell phone users

5. Friends ■

Write a Topic Sentence

Once you have chosen a way to classify a topic and have identified the subgroups you will use, you are ready to write a topic sentence. Your topic sentence should accomplish two things:

1. **It should identify your topic.**
2. **It should indicate how you will classify items within your topic.**

The topic sentence may also mention the number of subgroups you will use. Here are a few examples:

- Three relatively new types of family structures are single-parent families, blended families, and families without children.

- Since working as a waiter, I've discovered that there are three main types of customer complaints.

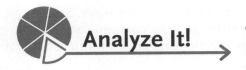 **Analyze It!**

Directions: The paragraph on the left is a good model of a paragraph that uses classification as a method of development. Complete the chart on the right using information given in the paragraph.

Types of Burns

Burns are classified according to their severity (depth) as first-, second-, or third-degree burns. In **first-degree burns,** only the epidermis is damaged. The area becomes red and swollen. Except for temporary discomfort, first-degree burns are not usually serious and generally heal in two to three days without any special attention. **Second-degree burns** involve injury to the epidermis and the upper region of the dermis. The skin is red and painful, and *blisters* appear. Because sufficient numbers of epithelial cells are still present, regrowth (regeneration) of the epithelium can occur. Ordinarily, no permanent scars result if care is taken to prevent infection. **Third-degree burns** destroy the entire thickness of the skin. The burned area appears blanched (gray-white) or blackened, and because the nerve endings in the area are destroyed, the burned area is not painful. In third-degree burns, regeneration is not possible, and skin grafting must be done to cover the underlying exposed tissues.

—Marieb, *Essentials of Human Anatomy and Physiology,* p.124.

Characteristic	First-Degree Burns	Second-Degree Burns	Third-Degree Burns
Appearance	_____ _____	_____	_____
Degree of Skin Damage	_____ _____	_____	_____
Healing Properties	_____ _____	_____	_____

EXERCISE F-3
Writing in Progress

Writing a Topic Sentence

Directions: For one of the topics in Exercise F-2, write a topic sentence that identifies the topic and explains your method of classification. ■

Explain Each Subgroup

The details in your paragraph should explain and provide further information about each subgroup. Depending on your topic and/or your audience, it may be necessary to define each subgroup. If possible, provide an equal amount of detail for each subgroup. If you define or offer an example for one subgroup, you should do the same for each of the others.

How to Organize a Classification Paragraph

The order in which you present your categories depends on your topic. Possible ways to organize the categories include from familiar to unfamiliar, from oldest to newest, or from simpler to more complex. Be sure to use transitions to signal your readers that you are moving from one category to another. Useful transitions are shown below.

Classification: Useful Transitions		
first	second	third
one	another	also
in addition	then	last

EXERCISE F-4
Writing in Progress

Writing a Classification Paragraph

Directions: For the topic sentence you wrote in Exercise F-3, write a classification paragraph. Be sure to identify and explain each group. Use transitions, as needed. ■

G: PROCESS

GOAL 7 Write using process

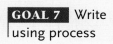

To practice using process, go to
■ Study Plan
■ The Paragraph
■ Paragraph Development: Process

What Is Process?

A process is a series of steps or actions that one follows in a particular order to accomplish something. When you assemble a toy, bake a cake, rebuild an engine, or put up a tent, you do things in a specific order. A **process paragraph** explains the steps to follow in completing a process. The steps are given in the order in which they are done. Here is a sample process paragraph. In it, the student writer, Ted Sawchuck, explains how copyediting is done at his college's student newspaper.

> The Fourth Estate's copyediting process is not very complicated. First, articles are submitted in electronic format and are read by Merren, the copy editor. Next, she makes changes and ensures all the articles are in their proper place. Then, section editors have a day to read the stories for their sections and make changes. Finally, all articles, photographs, cartoons, and anything else to be included in the upcoming issue is read and fact-checked by the editor-in-chief.

In this paragraph the writer identifies four steps. Notice that they are presented in the order in which they happen. You can visualize a process paragraph as follows. Study the model and the map on the following page for the paragraph above.

There are two types of process paragraphs—a "how-to" paragraph and a "how-it-works" paragraph:

- **A "how-to" paragraph explains how something is done.** For example, it may explain how to change a flat tire, aid a choking victim, or locate a reference source in the library.

- A "how-it-works" paragraph explains how something operates or happens. For example, it may explain the operation of a pump, how the human body regulates temperature, or how children acquire speech.

 Visualize It!

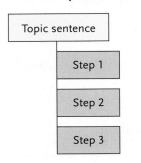

Model Idea Map for Process

Topic sentence

Step 1

Step 2

Step 3

Note: The number of steps will vary.

Idea Map of Sawchuck's Essay on Copyediting

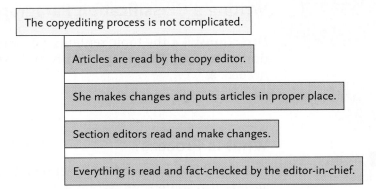

The copyediting process is not complicated.

Articles are read by the copy editor.

She makes changes and puts articles in proper place.

Section editors read and make changes.

Everything is read and fact-checked by the editor-in-chief.

How to Develop a Process Paragraph

Developing a process paragraph involves writing a topic sentence and explaining each step clearly and thoroughly.

Write a Topic Sentence

For a process paragraph, your topic sentence should accomplish two things:

1. **It should identify the process or procedure.**
2. **It should explain to your reader why familiarity with it is useful, interesting, or important (*why* he or she should learn about the process).** Your topic sentence should state a goal, offer a reason, or indicate what can be accomplished by using the process.

Here are a few examples of topic sentences that contain both of these important elements:

- Reading maps, a vital skill if you are taking vacations by car, is a simple process, except for the final refolding.
- Because reading is an essential skill, all parents should know how to interest their children in recreational reading.
- To locate information on the Internet, you must know how to use a search engine.

Examine It!

Directions: The following paragraph is a good model of a process paragraph. Study the annotations to discover how the writer describes the process of digestion.

Heading announces topic
Step 1: stretching of wall

Step 2: gastric juices

Step 3: pummelling and compression

Comparison to something familiar helps reader understand three steps

The Digestive Process

The digestive process involves three basic steps. As food enters and fills the stomach, its wall begins to stretch. At the same time the gastric juices are being secreted. Then the three muscle layers of the stomach wall become active. They compress and pummel the food, breaking it apart physically, all the while continuously mixing the food with the enzyme-containing gastric juice so that the semifluid chyme is formed. The process looks something like the preparation of a cake mix, in which the floury mixture is repeatedly folded on itself and mixed with the liquid until it reaches uniform texture.

—Marieb, *Essentials of Human Anatomy and Physiology*, p. 487.

EXERCISE G-1
Writing in Progress

Writing a Topic Sentence

Directions: Write a topic sentence for one of the topics listed below. Then write a paragraph using the techniques listed below.

1. How to have an exciting vacation
2. How to cure an illness
3. How to shop on the Internet
4. How to build or repair _____
5. How _____ works ■

Explain the Steps

Use the following tips when explaining each step in a process:

1. **Include only essential, necessary steps.** Avoid comments, opinions, and unnecessary information because they may confuse your reader.
2. **Assume that your reader is unfamiliar with your topic** (unless you know otherwise). Be sure to define unfamiliar terms and describe clearly any technical or specialized tools, procedures, or objects.
3. **Use a consistent point of view.** Use either the first person ("I") or the second person ("you") throughout. Don't switch between them.
4. **List needed equipment.** For how-to paragraphs, tell your readers what they will need to complete the process. For a how-to paragraph on making chili, list the ingredients, for example.
5. **Identify pitfalls and problems.** Alert your readers about potential problems and places where confusion or error may occur. For instance, warn your chili-making readers to add chili peppers gradually and to taste the chili frequently along the way.

How to Organize a Process Paragraph

Process paragraphs should be organized sequentially according to the order in which the steps are done or occur. It is usually a good idea to place your topic sentence first. Placing it in this position provides your reader with a purpose for reading. Be sure to use transitional words and phrases to signal your readers that you are moving from one step to another. Useful transitions are listed below.

Process: Useful Transitions		
first	then	next
second	later	after
third	while	following
after	finally	afterward
before		

Analyze It!

Directions: The paragraph on the left is a good model of a paragraph that uses process as a method of development. On the right, list the steps in the method of loci process using information given in the paragraph.

The Method of Loci

The *method of loci* is a memory device that can be used when you want to remember a list of items such as a grocery list or when you give a speech or a class report and need to make your points in order without using notes. The word *loci* (pronounced "LOH-sye") is the plural form of *locus,* which means "location" or "place." Here's how to use the method of loci. Select any familiar place—your home, for example—and simply associate the items to be remembered with locations there. Progress in an orderly fashion. For example, visualize the first item or idea you want to remember in its place on the driveway, the second in the garage, the third at the front door, and so on, until you have associated each item you want to remember with a specific location. You may find it helpful to conjure up oversized images of the items that you place at each location. When you want to recall the items, take an imaginary walk starting at the first place—the first item will pop into your mind. When you think of the second place, the second item will come to mind, and so on.

—Wood et al., *Mastering the World of Psychology,* p. 181.

List the steps involved in the method of loci memory device.

Step 1: _____

_____

Step 2: _____

Step 3: _____

_____

Step 4: _____

_____

EXERCISE G-2
Writing in Progress

Adding Transitions

Directions: Revise the draft you wrote for Exercise G-1. Check transitional words and phrases and add more, if necessary, to make your ideas clearer. ■

H: CAUSE AND EFFECT

GOAL 8 Write using cause and effect

To practice using cause and effect, go to
■ Study Plan
■ The Paragraph
■ Paragraph Development: Cause & Effect

What Are Cause and Effect?

Causes are explanations of why things happen. **Effects** are explanations of what happens as a result of an action or event. Each day we face situations that require cause-and-effect analysis. Some are daily events; others mark important life decisions. Why won't my car start? Why didn't I get my student loan check? What will happen if I skip class today? How will my family react if I decide to get married? Here is a sample cause-and-effect paragraph. The student writer, Ted Sawchuck, discusses what can go wrong when preparing guacamole.

> Adding too many ingredients to guacamole will ruin the delicate flavor created by the interplay between fatty avocado, spicy peppers, and sweet tomatoes. Adding yogurt, for example, dilutes the dip to an almost souplike consistency and ruins the flavor. Dumping in salsa overpowers the delicate avocado so that you don't know what you are eating. Another common error, adding too much salt, masks the luxurious flavor of the avocado found in the best guacamole.

In this paragraph the student writer identifies three causes and three effects. You can visualize a cause-and-effect paragraph as follows. Study the model and the map for Sawchuck's paragraph.

Visualize It!

Model Idea Map for Cause and Effect

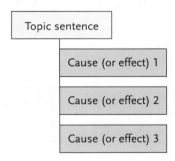

Topic sentence

Cause (or effect) 1

Cause (or effect) 2

Cause (or effect) 3

Note: The number of causes or effects will vary.

Idea Map of Sawchuck's Paragraph on Guacamole

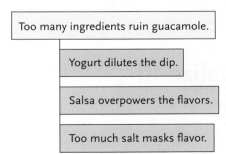

Too many ingredients ruin guacamole.

Yogurt dilutes the dip.

Salsa overpowers the flavors.

Too much salt masks flavor.

How to Develop a Cause-and-Effect Paragraph

Developing a cause and effect paragraph involves distinguishing between causes and effects, writing a topic sentence, and providing relevant and sufficient details.

Distinguish Between Cause and Effect

How can you distinguish between causes and effects? To determine causes, ask:

"Why did this happen?"

To identify effects, ask:

"What happened because of this?"

Let's consider an everyday situation: you lost your set of keys, so you are locked out of your apartment. This is a simple case in which one cause produces one effect. You can diagram this situation as follows:

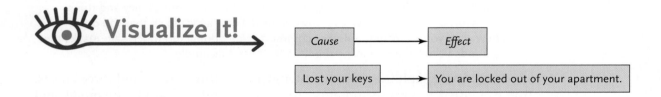

Most situations, however, are much more complicated than the one shown above. Sometimes cause and effect work like a chain reaction: one cause triggers an effect, which in turn becomes the cause of another effect. In a chain reaction, each event in a series influences the next, as shown in the following example:

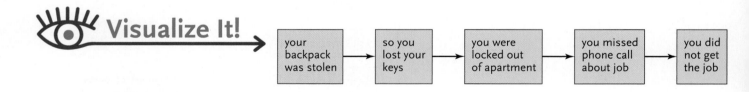

At other times, many causes may contribute to a single effect, as shown in the following diagram.

For example, there may be several reasons why you decided to become a veterinarian:

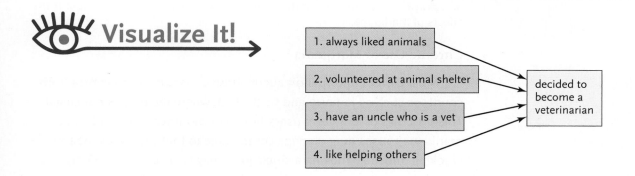

At other times, a single cause can have multiple effects, as shown below:

Suppose, for example, you decide to take a second part-time job:

When analyzing a cause-and-effect situation that you plan to write about, ask yourself the following questions:

1. What are the causes? What are the effects? (To help answer these questions, draw a diagram of the situation.)
2. Which should be emphasized—cause or effect?
3. Are there single or multiple causes? Single or multiple effects?
4. Is a chain reaction involved?

Examine It! →

Directions: The following paragraph is a good model of a cause-and-effect paragraph. Study the annotations to discover how the writers explain the effects of marijuana.

Chronic Use of Marijuana

Most current information about chronic marijuana use comes from countries such as Jamaica and Costa Rica, where the drug is not illegal.

Effect #1 — These studies of long-term users (for 10 or more years) indicate that marijuana causes lung damage comparable to that caused by tobacco

Effect #2 — smoking. Indeed, smoking a single joint may be as bad for the lungs as smoking three tobacco cigarettes. Other risks associated with marijuana include suppression of the immune system, blood pressure changes,

and impaired memory function. Recent studies suggest that pregnant women who smoke marijuana are at a higher risk for stillbirth or miscar-

Effect #3 — riage and for delivering low–birth weight babies and babies with abnormalities of the nervous system. Babies born to marijuana smokers are five times more likely to have features similar to those exhibited by children with fetal alcohol syndrome.

—Donatelle, *Access to Health*, p. 436.

EXERCISE H-1   Identifying Causes and Effects

Writing in Progress

Directions: Identify possible causes and effects for three of the following situations:

1. Spending too much time surfing the Internet
2. Academic cheating or dishonesty
3. An important decision you made
4. The popularity of cell phones
5. Earning good grades ■

Write a Topic Sentence

To write effective topic sentences for cause-and-effect paragraphs, do the following:

1. **Clarify the cause-and-effect relationship.** Before you write, carefully identify the causes and the effects. If you are uncertain, divide a sheet of paper into two columns. Label one column "Causes" and the other "Effects." Brainstorm about your topic, placing your ideas in the appropriate column.

2. **Decide whether to emphasize causes or effects.** In a single paragraph, it is best to focus on either causes or effects—not both. For example, suppose you are writing about students who work two part-time jobs. You need to

decide whether to discuss why they work two jobs (causes) or what happens to students who work two jobs (effects). Your topic sentence should indicate whether you are going to emphasize causes or effects. (In essays, you may consider both causes and effects.)

3. **Determine whether the events are related or independent.** Analyze the causes or effects to discover if they occurred as part of a chain reaction or are not related to one another. Your topic sentence should suggest the type of relationship you are writing about. If you are writing about a chain of events, your topic sentence should reflect this—for example, "A series of events led up to my brother's decision to join the military." If the causes or effects are independent, then your sentence should indicate that—for example, "Young men and women join the military for a number of different reasons."

 **Analyze It!**

Directions: The paragraph on the left is a good model of a paragraph that uses cause and effect as a method of development. Read it and then complete the outline on the right using information given in the paragraph.

Risk Factors for Ulcers

Although ulcers are commonly associated with stress, they can be brought on by other risk factors. Chronic use of aspirin and other nonsteroidal anti-inflammatory drugs increases the risk of ulcer because these agents suppress the secretion of both mucus and bicarbonate, which normally protect the lining of the GI tract from the effects of acid and pepsin. The risk of ulcer is also increased by chronic alcohol use or the leakage of bile from the duodenum into the stomach, both of which can disrupt the mucus barrier. Surprisingly, ulcers are usually not associated with abnormally high rates of stomach-acid secretion; more often than not, acid secretion is normal or even below normal in most people with ulcers.

—adapted from Germann and Stanfield, *Principles of Human Physiology*, p. 622.

A. List four causes of ulcers.

1. _____

_____

2. _____

_____

3. _____

_____

4. _____

_____

EXERCISE H-2   **Writing a Topic Sentence**

Writing in Progress

Directions: For one of the topics you chose in Exercise H-1, decide whether you will focus on causes or effects. Then write a topic sentence for a paragraph that will explain either causes *or* effects. ■

Provide Relevant and Sufficient Details

Each cause or effect you describe must be relevant to the situation introduced in your topic sentence. Each cause or reason requires explanation, particularly if it is *not* obvious. Jot down a list of the causes or reasons you plan to include.

This process may help you think of additional ones and will give you a chance to consider how to explain or support each cause or reason. You might decide to eliminate one or to combine several.

How to Organize a Cause-and-Effect Paragraph

There are several ways to arrange the details in a cause-and-effect paragraph. The method you choose depends on your purpose in writing, as well as on your topic. Suppose you are writing a paragraph about the effects of a hurricane on a coastal town. Several different arrangements of details are possible:

1. **Chronological** A chronological organization arranges your details in the order in which situations or events happened. For example, the order in which damage occurs during the course of a hurricane would become the order in which you present your details about the event. This arrangement is similar to the arrangement you learned in section A of this chapter, "Narration," p. 372. A chronological arrangement works for situations and events that occurred in a specific order.

2. **Order of importance** In an order-of-importance organization, the details are arranged from least to most important or from most to least important. In describing the effects of a hurricane, you could discuss the most severe damage first and then describe lesser damage. Alternatively, you could build up to the most important damage for dramatic effect.

3. **Spatial** Spatial arrangement of details uses physical or geographical position as a means of organization. In recounting the hurricane damage, you could start by describing damage to the beach and then work toward the center of town.

4. **Categorical** This method of arrangement divides the topic into parts or categories. Using this arrangement to describe hurricane damage, you could recount what the storm did to businesses, roads, city services, and homes.

Because cause-and-effect relationships can be complicated, be sure to use transitional words and phrases to signal your reader which are causes and which are effects. Useful transitions are shown below.

Cause and Effect: Useful Transitions	
FOR CAUSES	FOR EFFECTS
because, due to, one cause is . . . , another is . . . , since, for, first, second	consequently, as a result, thus, resulted in, one result is . . . , another is . . . , therefore

EXERCISE H-3
Writing in Progress

Writing a Cause-and-Effect Paragraph

Directions: Write a paragraph developing the topic sentence you wrote for Exercise H-2. Be sure to include relevant and sufficient details. Organize your paragraph according to one of the methods described above. ■

I: ARGUMENT

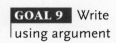

GOAL 9 Write using argument

To practice using argument, go to
- Study Plan
- The Paragraph
- Paragraph Development: Argument

What Is Argument?

An **argument** is a line of reasoning intended to persuade the reader or listener to agree with a particular viewpoint or to take a particular action. An argument presents reasons and evidence for accepting a belief or position or for taking a specific action. For example, you might argue that testing cosmetic products on animals is wrong, or that a traffic signal should be installed at the end of your street. An argument has three essential parts:

- **An issue** This is the problem or controversy that the argument addresses. It is also the topic of an argument paragraph. Gun control legislation is an example of an issue.

- **A position** A position is the particular point of view a writer has on an issue. There are always at least two points of view on an issue—pro and con. For example, you may be for or against gun control. You may favor or oppose lowering the legal drinking age.

- **Support** Support consists of the details that demonstrate your position is correct and should be accepted. There are three types of support: reasons, evidence, and emotional appeals.

Here is a sample argument paragraph:

> I strongly urge residents to vote "NO" on a referendum to withdraw funding for the proposed renovation of the Potwine town soccer fields. The town's other available fields are at capacity, and the number of children trying out for soccer is still growing. There are now more than 2,000 children between the ages of 6 and 13 playing on recreational and travel soccer teams. Meanwhile, the number of fields the college is willing to let us use has been reduced from 19 to 2. We are now having to rent fields in neighboring towns to accommodate all of the teams playing on Saturday afternoons! Opponents of the renovation always cite money as an obstacle. In fact, the money to fix the fields has been sitting in a Community Preservation Act fund for more than 15 years. Let the upcoming election be the final one, and make it one for the children—our own and the generations to come. Vote NO.

In this paragraph, the issue is the renovation of soccer fields. The writer's claim is that the renovation is necessary. The paragraph then offers reasons for the renovation.

Study the model and the map for this paragraph on the following page.

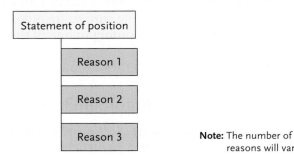

Model Idea Map for Argument

Statement of position

Reason 1

Reason 2

Reason 3

Note: The number of reasons will vary.

Idea Map of Paragraph on Soccer Fields

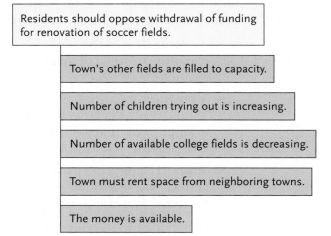

Residents should oppose withdrawal of funding for renovation of soccer fields.

Town's other fields are filled to capacity.

Number of children trying out is increasing.

Number of available college fields is decreasing.

Town must rent space from neighboring towns.

The money is available.

How to Develop an Argument Paragraph

Developing an argument paragraph involves writing a topic sentence, supporting your position with reasons and evidence, and addressing opposing viewpoints.

Write a Topic Sentence

Your topic sentence should do the following:

1. **Identify the issue.**
2. **State your position on the issue.**

The following topic sentence makes it clear that the writer will argue against the use of animals for medical research:

> The testing of cosmetics on animals should be outlawed because it is cruel, unnecessary, and disrespectful of animals' place in the chain of life.

Notice that this thesis identifies the issue and makes it clear that the writer opposes animal testing. It also suggests the three major reasons she will present: (1) it is cruel, (2) it is unnecessary, and (3) it is disrespectful. You do not always have to include the major points of your argument in your topic sentence statement, but including them does help the reader know what to expect. This topic sentence also makes clear what action the author thinks is appropriate: using animals in medical research should be outlawed.

Here are a few more topic sentences. Notice that they use the verbs *must,* *would,* and *should.*

- if owe expect industries to be environmentally responsible, then we should provide tax breaks to help cover their costs.
- It would be a mistake to assume sexual discrimination has been eliminated or even reduced significantly over the decade.
- The number of women on our college's Board of Trustees must be increased.

Examine It!

Directions: The following paragraph is a good model of an argument paragraph. Study the annotations to discover how the writer argues that animals should be used in medical research.

Heading announces the issue

Animals Should Be Used in Medical Research

Topic sentence: States a position

Laboratory animal research is fundamental to medical progress. Vaccines for devastating human diseases like polio and smallpox and equally serious animal diseases like rabies, feline leukemia, and distemper were all developed through the use of research animals.

Reason 1

Reason 2

The discovery, development, and refinement of drugs that could arrest, control, or eliminate such human diseases as AIDS, cancer, and heart disease all require the use of laboratory animals whose physiological mechanisms are similar to humans. I have only noted above a few of the many examples where animals have been used in human and veterinary medical research. It's also important to note that studies in behavior, ecology, physiology, and genetics all require the use of animals, in some capacity, to produce valid and meaningful knowledge about life on this planet.

Reason 3

—Tuff, "Animals and Research" from *NEA Higher Education Advocate.*

EXERCISE I-1

Writing in Progress

Writing a Topic Sentence

Directions: For three of the following issues, take a position and write a topic sentence.

1. Professional athletes' salaries

2. Drug testing in the workplace

3. Using cell phones while driving

4. Mandatory counseling for drug addicts

5. Buying American-made products

6. Adopting shelter animals

7. A topic of your choice ■

Support Your Position

There are two primary types of support that you can use to explain why your position should be accepted:

- **Reasons** Reasons are general statements that back up a position. Here are a few reasons to support an argument in favor of parental Internet controls:

  The Internet contains sites that are not appropriate for children.

  The Internet is a place where sexual predators can find victims.

  No one else polices the Internet, so parents must do so.

- **Evidence** The most common types of evidence are facts and statistics, quotations from authorities, examples, and personal experience.

Use a Variety of Evidence

Facts and Statistics

When including facts and statistics, be sure to do the following:

1. **Obtain statistics from reliable online or print sources.** These include databases, almanacs, encyclopedias, articles in reputable journals and magazines, or other trustworthy reference materials from your library.
2. **Use up-to-date information, preferably from the past year or two.** Outdated statistics may be incorrect or misleading.
3. **Make sure you define terms and units of measurement.** For example, if you say that 60 percent of adults regularly play the lottery, you should define what "regularly" means.

Quotations from Authorities

You can also support your position by using expert or authoritative statements of opinion or conclusions. Experts or authorities are those who have studied a subject extensively, conducted research on it, or written widely about it. For example, if you are writing an essay calling for stricter preschool-monitoring requirements to prevent child abuse, the opinion of a psychiatrist who works extensively with abused children would provide convincing support.

Examples

Examples are specific situations that illustrate a point. Refer to section C of this chapter for a review of how to use them as supporting details. In a persuasive essay, your examples must represent your position and should illustrate as many aspects of your position as possible. Suppose your position is that a particular television show should be cancelled because it contains excessive use of inappropriate language. The evidence you choose to support this position should be specific examples of the language used.

Personal Experience

If you are knowledgeable about a subject, your personal experiences can be convincing evidence. For example, if you were writing an essay supporting the position that being a child in a single-parent household encourages a teenager or young adult to mature earlier, you could discuss your own experiences with assuming new responsibilities.

Analyze It!

Directions: The paragraph on the left is a good model of a paragraph that uses argument as a method of development. Complete the map on the right using information given in the paragraph.

Animals Should Not Be Used in Medical Research

I cannot accept the argument that research on animals is necessary to discover "cures" for humans. Many diseases and medications react very differently in animals than they do in humans. Aspirin, for example, is toxic to cats, and there are few diseases directly transmittable from cats to humans. I particularly abhor the "research" conducted for cosmetic purposes. The Draise test—where substances are introduced into the eyes of rabbits and then examined to see if ulcers, lesions or other observable reactions take place—is archaic and inefficient. Other alternatives exist that are more accurate and do not cause unnecessary suffering to our fellow creatures. Household products are also tested needlessly on animals using the LD-50 test. Animals, in many cases puppies, are force-fed these toxic chemicals to determine the dosage at which exactly 50 percent of them die. These tests are not necessary and do not give very useful information.

—adapted from Molina, "Animals and Research"
from *NEA Higher Education Advocate.*

Statement of position: _____

_____

Reason 1: _____

_____

Reason 2: _____

_____

Reason 3: _____

_____

EXERCISE 1-2

Writing in Progress

Generating Reasons and Evidence

Directions: Generate reasons and evidence to support one of the topic sentences you wrote for Exercise I-1. ■

Address Opposing Viewpoints

An opposing viewpoint is the position that is the opposite of the one you take. It is effective to recognize opposing viewpoints because it builds your credibility and shows that you are open-minded. For example, suppose you are arguing that children should wear uniforms to school. You could also recognize or acknowledge that opponents believe uniforms stifle creativity and individuality. You may also decide to refute, or argue against, opposing viewpoints. *Refute* means "to present evidence that a statement is wrong." You could refute the notion that uniforms stifle individuality by stating that children will find more useful and important ways of expressing their individuality if uniforms are required. Think of refutation as a process of finding weaknesses in your opponent's argument.

How to Organize an Argument Paragraph

There are two common ways to organize an argument paragraph.

1. **Place the topic sentence first and then give the supporting evidence and reasons.**

2. **Give your evidence and reasons first and conclude with the topic sentence.**

Because argumentation is complex, be sure to use transitional words and phrases to guide your reader from one reason or piece of evidence to another. Useful transitions are shown below.

Argument: Useful Transitions		
one reason	furthermore	therefore
a second reason	another reason	because

EXERCISE 1-3   Writing an Argument Paragraph

Directions: Using the reasons and evidence you generated in Exercise I-2, write an argument paragraph. Be sure to recognize and/or refute opposing viewpoints. ■

A STUDENT ESSAY

The Writer

James Sturm is a graduate of Kalamazoo College with a degree in international and area studies. Currently he is in Taiwan teaching high school English as part of a fellowship from Princeton in Asia. He plans to continue working abroad and is considering starting a career with the Foreign Service.

The Writing Task

Sturm wrote this essay while in college for a writing class. His assignment was to identify an event that made a major change in his life and explain why it made it a difference and how he coped with the transition.

Title: identifies the subject of the essay

Handling Transition

James Lawrence Sturm III

Introduction: Sturm engages the reader by describing an event

1   I stepped off the train and I could already feel my feet going numb from the cold. I had arrived in the dead of winter in Harbin, China, a city far removed

from anything remotely Western. That transition helped me learn I can live a normal, full life completely immersed in a foreign language and culture.

Background information on Harbin and explanation of why it is a challenging environment

2   The city of Harbin, which lies twelve hours north of Beijing by train, is known for its Soviet influence and freezing cold weather. Dubbed the "Paris of the East" by travelers passing through, much of the architecture retains markings of the Soviet era. The geographic location of Harbin places it near the southern border of Russia, hence the cold. For these reasons, Harbin is a place few Westerners choose to make their home away from home.

Topic sentence

Reasons for his choice

3   This isolation from the West is why I chose to go there. After studying Chinese for two and a half years, culminating in a six-month study abroad in Beijing, I chose to leave my friends behind and spend my second semester abroad in Harbin because I knew the best way to improve my Chinese and connect with the local culture was to place myself beyond the reach of Western comfort.

Topic sentence

Reasons why the transition was difficult

4   It was a difficult transition for many reasons. The day I arrived in February, the temperature was negative 15 degrees Celsius. The absence of Westerners in Harbin meant it was difficult to find Western-style leisure activities. And finally, all twenty of us in the program took a Chinese language pledge: for the entire semester we would speak only Chinese unless talking to family on the phone (which was done out of earshot of classmates to preserve the pure language environment). It was the most intense and challenging immersion experience of my life.

Topic sentence

5   This challenge paid off because it taught me to thrive in a foreign culture. I chose to be involved in campus life by joining a Chinese traditional dance class. As the only foreigner in the class, I attracted enough attention to make some friends; before long, I found myself noticing familiar faces when I strolled through campus. I also frequented various local coffee shops. In that way, I formed casual friendships with many a Chinese barista, making me feel at home. But the most significant relationship I cultivated was with my Chinese roommate, Obama. He chose his English name after our president, which led to many conversations about the American culture and system of thought. In return, I learned the reason behind his nightly foot-washing ritual, among other aspects of Chinese culture.

How Sturm handled the transition

Conclusion: reflection on the event and the transition

6   Looking back, I wouldn't change anything I did. I would only ask for more time to spend in Harbin because when it comes to immersion, time spent is proportional to personal growth and adaptation.

EXAMINING STUDENT WRITING

1. Does Sturm provide an adequate number of relevant details? What types of details could be added?

2. Evaluate Sturm's introduction. What other ways could he have introduced his topic while building interest?

3. Examine Sturm's thesis statement. How accurately does it suggest the topics Sturm covers?

4. Choose a paragraph from the essay and evaluate it with the paragraph development questions on page 420.

Writing in a Visual Age

READING

Perhaps the shrewdest philanthropists in the contemporary film industry are Angelina Jolie and Brad Pitt. Their Jolie-Pitt Foundation has contributed millions of dollars to such causes as rebuilding New Orleans after it was devastated by Hurricane Katrina. They have provided grants to such humanitarian groups as Doctors Without Borders. They have visited refugee camps in war-torn areas in Africa, Afghanistan, and Iraq. Knowing that the press will hound them anyway, they have sold the rights to exclusive photos of their newborn children to magazines like *People* for a reported $14 million—which was then channeled into the Jolie-Pitt Foundation. When the photos appeared in *People*, sales of the magazine went up 45 percent.

—adapted from Giannetti, *Understanding Movies*, p. 260.

Angelina Jolie speaks to Chechen refugees at the Bella refugee camp in Ingushetia, a region bordering Chechnya.

1. Underline the topic sentence in the paragraph.
2. Which method of organization does this reading use?

CRITICAL THINKING AND RESPONSE

3. What do you think of Angelina Jolie and Brad Pitt's decision to sell photos of their newborn children to a magazine? Do you think children's privacy should be protected, or do you think that Jolie and Pitt made the right decision? Write a paragraph explaining your position, and be sure to include a clear topic sentence.

WRITING

4. Suppose you were given a million dollars to donate to a charity. Write a paragraph explaining which charity or type of charity you would choose and why.
5. The reading offers examples of the way Hollywood celebrities can have a positive influence. Write a paragraph suggesting some other ways that film stars can have a positive impact on the world.

USING VISUALS

6. Using the photo to guide you, write a descriptive paragraph about either Angelina Jolie or Brad Pitt.
7. Write a paragraph in which you compare and contrast Brad Pitt and Angelina Jolie. The photo may help you get started.

Paragraph Writing Scenarios

Friends and Family

1. Write a paragraph defining friendship.

2. Choose a parent or close family member whom you admire. Write a paragraph giving examples that demonstrate this person's admirable characteristics.

Classes and Campus Life

1. Write a paragraph classifying the types of problems that may lead to dropping out of college.

2. Write a paragraph explaining how you studied for a particular exam.

Working Students

1. Write a paragraph describing an employer or supervisor for whom you have worked. Be sure to create an overall impression about this person.

2. Write a paragraph comparing or contrasting two co-workers.

Communities and Cultures

1. Write a paragraph about a tradition that you value. Write a narrative paragraph that details the events related to the tradition.

2. Choose a community to which you belong. Write a paragraph about an activity that you share with other members. Be sure to explain why you chose to participate.

WRITING ABOUT A READING

THINKING BEFORE READING

In this selection from *Newsweek* magazine, Leticia Salais writes about how she changed her mind and decided to embrace her native language in "Saying 'Adios' to Spanglish." As you read, pay attention to the organization of the essay and to the reasons Salais gives for her decision.

1. Preview the reading, using the steps discussed in Chapter 2, p. 35.

2. Connect the reading to your own experience by answering the following questions:

   a. Has your ethnic background or cultural heritage played an important role in your own life?

   b. When you were younger, did you want to change anything about the circumstances in which you grew up?

3. Mark and annotate as you read.

READING
SAYING 'ADIOS' TO SPANGLISH

Leticia Salais

Growing up, I wanted nothing to do with my heritage.
My kids made me see how wrong that was.

adios
Spanish for good-bye

Spanglish
an informal language that
combines Spanish and English

1   *Niños, vengan a comer.* My 18-month-old son pops out from behind the couch and runs to his high chair. My 7-year-old has no idea what I just said. He yells out from the same hiding spot: "What did you say?" My older son does not suffer from hearing loss. He is simply not bilingual like his brother, and did not understand that I was telling him to come eat.

2   Growing up in the poorest neighborhoods of El Paso, Texas, I did everything I could to escape the poverty and the color of my skin. I ran around with kids from the west side of town who came from more affluent families and usually didn't speak a word of Spanish. I spoke Spanish well enough, but I pretended not to understand it and would not speak a word of it. In school, I refused to speak Spanish even with my Hispanic friends. I wanted nothing to do with it. While they joined Chicano clubs, all I wanted to do was be in the English literacy club. Even at home, the only person to whom I spoke Spanish was my mom, and that's only because she wouldn't have understood me otherwise.

Anglo
a white American of
non-Hispanic descent

3   After I got married and moved to Tucson, Ariz., I thought I was in heaven. Though I was actually in the minority, I felt right at home with my **Anglo** neighbors. When I got pregnant with my first son, I decided that English would be his first language and, if I could help it, his only language. I never spoke a word of Spanish around him, and when his grandparents asked why he did not understand what they were saying, I made excuses. He understands but he's very shy. He understands the language but he refuses to speak it. In reality, I didn't want him to speak it at all.

telenovelas
Spanish soap operas on
television

4   In a land of opportunity, I soon realized I had made a big mistake. I was denying my son one of the greatest gifts I had to offer: the ability to be bilingual. I saw the need for interpreters on a daily basis in the health field where I worked. Even trips to the grocery store often turned into an opportunity to help someone who could not understand English or vice versa.

5   In the nursing home where I worked, I met a wonderful group of Spanish-speaking individuals, whom I bonded with right away. I longed to speak like they did, enunciating the words correctly as they rolled off their tongues. It sounded like music to me. I started watching Spanish **telenovelas** and listening to Spanish morning shows on the radio just to improve my

vocabulary. I heard words that had never been uttered around me growing up in a border town where people spoke a mixture of Spanish and English. A co-worker from Peru had the most eloquent way of speaking in a language that I recognized as Spanish yet could not fully comprehend. Did I also cheat myself of being bilingual?

6   Today I can take any English word and, like magic, easily find its Spanish equivalent. I now live a life that is fully bilingual. I hunger for foreign movies from Spain and the interior of Mexico just to challenge myself by trying to guess what all the words mean. I even surprise my mom when she doesn't understand what I'm saying. I know she is proud that I no longer speak Spanglish, and I am no longer embarrassed to speak Spanish in public. I see it as a secret language my husband and I share when we don't want those around us to understand what we are saying. I quickly offer the use of my gift when I see someone struggling to speak English or to understand Spanish, and I quietly say a prayer of thanks that I am not in his or her shoes. I feel empowered and blessed that I can understand a conversation in another language and quickly translate it in my head.

7   My second son has benefited from my bilingual tongue. I speak only Spanish to him while my husband speaks only English; I am proud to say that his first language was Spanish. My 7-year-old, on the other hand, still has a way to go. I'm embarrassed that I foolishly kept my beautiful native language from him. I hope I have not done irreversible damage. A couple of years ago, I began speaking to him only in Spanish, but I had not yet heard him utter a complete sentence back.

8   Then, as if my prayers were answered, from behind the couch, I heard a tiny voice exclaim, *Ven, mira esto*. It was my older son instructing his little brother to come look at what he was doing. Maybe I won't be his first bilingual teacher, but it looks like he's already learning from another expert—his bilingual brother. Maybe it's not too late after all.

GETTING READY TO WRITE

Reviewing the Reading

Answer each of the following questions using complete sentences.

1. Where did the author grow up?

_____

2. List three examples of how the author tried to escape her heritage while she was growing up.

_____

_____

_____

3. How did the author feel about her first son learning Spanish?

_____

4. How did the author improve her Spanish?

_____

5. How did the author and her husband teach their second son to be bilingual?

_____

Examining the Reading Using An Idea Map

Review the reading by completing the missing parts of the idea map shown below.

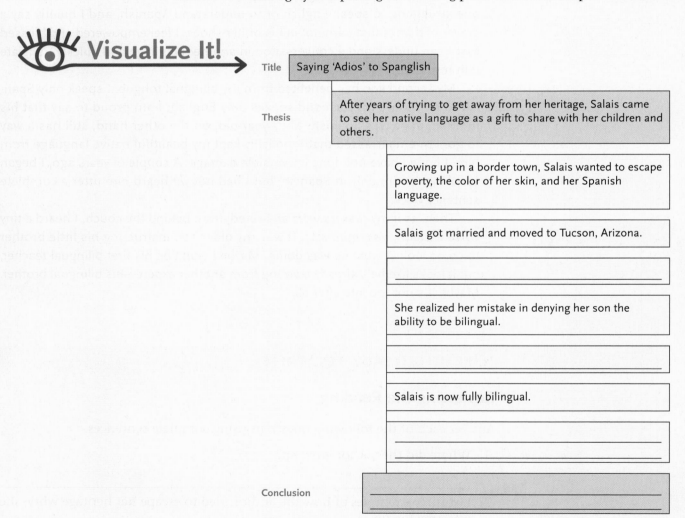

Visualize It!

Title   Saying 'Adios' to Spanglish

Thesis   After years of trying to get away from her heritage, Salais came to see her native language as a gift to share with her children and others.

Growing up in a border town, Salais wanted to escape poverty, the color of her skin, and her Spanish language.

Salais got married and moved to Tucson, Arizona.

_____

She realized her mistake in denying her son the ability to be bilingual.

_____

Salais is now fully bilingual.

_____
_____

Conclusion   _____
_____

Strengthening Your Vocabulary

Using the word's context, word parts, or a dictionary, write a brief definition of each of the following words as it is used in the reading.

1. bilingual (paragraph 1) _____

2. affluent (paragraph 2) _____

3. bonded (paragraph 5) _____

4. enunciating (paragraph 5) _____

5. eloquent (paragraph 5) _____

6. empowered (paragraph 6) _____

7. irreversible (paragraph 7) _____

Reacting to Ideas: Discussion and Journal Writing

Get ready to write about the reading by discussing the following questions:

1. What is the author's purpose for writing this article?

2. Why did the author think she was "in heaven" when she moved to Arizona?

3. Why did the author feel like she had to make excuses about her son not speaking Spanish? Why was the author's mother proud when her daughter no longer spoke Spanglish?

4. How did the author come to view her bilingual ability as a gift? In what ways does she share her gift outside of her family?

 **Thinking Visually**   5. What does the photograph add to the reading? What other photographs might have been more interesting or informative?

WRITING ABOUT THE READING

Paragraph Options

1. Write a paragraph describing your own ethnic background or cultural heritage.

2. The author described her efforts to escape the circumstances in which she grew up. Were there any aspects of your childhood that you wanted to escape or change? Write a paragraph explaining your answer.

3. Having children caused the author to have a change of heart about speaking Spanish. Think of a time when you had a significant change of heart, and write a paragraph about your experience.

Essay Options

4. The author views her ability to speak two languages as a gift she can give to her children. Write an essay describing a "gift" you would like to pass on to your children. It may be the ability to speak another language, a tradition from your own childhood, or a personal quality such as your sense of humor or love of sports. Be sure to explain why you would choose this particular gift, for example, how would it benefit your child?

5. The author describes several advantages to being bilingual. Write an essay identifying the ones in the article as well as any other benefits you can think of. If you are able to speak more than one language, include examples from your own experience. For example, have you ever been able to assist someone else because of your ability to speak another language?

6. What cultural or ethnic background did each of your parents come from? How did those influences emerge in the family in which you grew up? Write an essay about how your parents' separate experiences in their own families affected the family they formed together.

Revision Checklist

Paragraph Development

1. Is the topic manageable (neither too broad nor too narrow)?
2. Is the paragraph written with the reader in mind?
3. Does the topic sentence identify the topic?
4. Does the topic sentence make a point about the topic?
5. Does each sentence support the topic sentence?
6. Is there sufficient detail?
7. Is there a sentence at the end that brings the paragraph to a close?

Sentence Development

8. Are there any sentence fragments, run-on sentences, or comma splices?
9. Are ideas combined to produce more effective sentences?
10. Are adjectives and adverbs used to make the sentences vivid and interesting?
11. Are relative clauses and prepositional phrases like *-ing* phrases used to add detail?
12. Are pronouns used correctly and consistently?

CHAPTER REVIEW AND PRACTICE

CHAPTER REVIEW

To review and check your recall of the chapter, match each term in Column A with its meaning in Column B.

COLUMN A	COLUMN B
_____ 1. classification	**a.** focuses on similarities and differences
_____ 2. definition	**b.** describes the order in which things are done or how they work
_____ 3. process	**c.** takes a position on an issue
_____ 4. narration	**d.** presents, supports an impression with sensory details
_____ 5. description	**e.** makes a point by telling a story
_____ 6. example	**f.** explains by giving situations that illustrate the topic sentence
_____ 7. cause and effect	**g.** explains why things happen or explains what happens as a result of an action
_____ 8. argument	**h.** explains a term by giving its class and distinguishing characteristics
_____ 9. comparison and contrast	**i.** explains by dividing something into groups or categories

EDITING PRACTICE

The following informative paragraph comparing two types of skis is not organized logically. Revise this paragraph so that its main idea is developed logically.

> Cross-country skis and downhill skis are different in many aspects. Cross-country skis are intended for gliding over fairly level terrain. Unlike cross-country skis, downhill skis have steel edges and their bindings keep the entire boot clamped

(continued)

to the ski. Downhill skis are broader and heavier, and they have a flatter bottom. Cross-country skis are lightweight and very narrow, and their bottoms are curved so the skis do not lie flat on the snow. Downhill skis are meant for skiing down steep slopes using frequent turns. The bindings on cross-country skis do not keep the heel clamped down, since the long, running strides used in cross-country skiing depend on free movement of the heel.

PEARSON
mywritinglab

For support in meeting this chapter's objectives, log in to www.mywritinglab.com, go to the Study Plan tab, click on Using Methods of Organization and choose Paragraph Development-Narrating, Describing, Illustrating, Definition, Comparison and Contrast, Classification, Process, Cause and Effect, and Argument from the list of subtopics. Read and view the videos and resources in the Review Materials section, and then complete the Recall, Apply, and Write exercises in the Activities section. You can check your scores and overall progress by using the Gradebook.

Part V
COMMON
PARAGRAPH
PROBLEMS
AND HOW TO
AVOID THEM

15 Revising Underdeveloped Paragraphs

Learning Goals

In this chapter, you will learn how to

GOAL 1 Revise ineffective topic sentences

GOAL 2 Revise underdeveloped paragraphs

WRITE ABOUT IT!

Write a sentence describing the garden in the upper left photograph. No doubt you had trouble doing so. Now write a sentence describing the garden in the second photograph. How do your descriptions differ?

Many ineffective paragraphs are like the first photograph above. They do not provide enough information and leave the reader frustrated and confused. In this chapter you will learn how to revise paragraphs so they provide your readers with plenty of information.

WRITING

REVISING INEFFECTIVE TOPIC SENTENCES

GOAL 1 Revise ineffective topic sentences

mywriting**lab**

To practice paragraph revision, go to
■ Study Plan
■ The Paragraph
■ Revising the Paragraph

Your topic sentence is the most important sentence in the paragraph. It promises what the remainder of the paragraph will deliver. A weak topic sentence usually produces a weak paragraph. Your topic sentence will be weak if it (1) lacks a viewpoint or attitude, (2) is too broad, or (3) is too narrow.

Topic Sentences that Lack a Point of View

A topic sentence should identify your topic *and* express an attitude or viewpoint. It must make a point about the topic.

If your topic is the old roller coaster at Starland Park, it is not enough to make a general statement of fact in your topic sentence.

LACKS POINT OF VIEW   There is an old roller coaster at Starland Park.

Your reader would rightly ask in this case, "So what?" A topic sentence needs to tell the reader what is important or interesting about your topic. It should state the point you are going to make in the rest of the paragraph. For every topic, you can find many points to make in a topic sentence. For example:

EXPRESSES POINT OF VIEW   The old roller coaster at Starland Park is unsafe and should be torn down.

The old roller coaster at Starland Park no longer seems as frightening as it did when I was young.

Three types of people go on the old roller coaster at Starland Park: the brave, the scared, and the stupid.

If you write a topic sentence that does not express a viewpoint, you will find you have very little or nothing to write about in the remainder of the paragraph. Look at these topic sentences:

LACKS POINT OF VIEW   Pete works at the YMCA.

EXPRESSES POINT OF VIEW   Pete got over his shyness by working at the YMCA.

If you used the first topic sentence, "Pete works at the YMCA," what else could you include in your paragraph? If you instead used the second topic sentence, you would have something to write about. You could describe Pete before and after he began working at the YMCA, discuss positive aspects of the job, or give examples of friends Pete has made through his work.

Notice how the following topic sentences have been revised to express a point of view.

LACKS POINT OF VIEW   Mark plays soccer.

REVISED   Mark's true personality comes out when he plays soccer. [Details can explain Mark's personality as revealed by his soccer game.]

LACKS POINT OF VIEW	Professor Cooke teaches accounting.
REVISED	Professor Cooke makes accounting practical. [Details can describe how Professor Cooke makes accounting skills relevant to everyday life.]

LACKS POINT OF VIEW	I read newspapers.
REVISED	I recommend reading newspapers from back to front. [Details can give reasons why this method is best.]

The following suggestions will help you revise your topic sentence if you discover that it lacks a point of view:

1. **Use brainstorming, freewriting, or branching.** Try to generate more ideas about your topic. Study your results to discover a way to approach your topic.

2. **Ask yourself questions about your topic sentence.** Specifically, ask "Why?" "How?" "So what?" or "Why is this important?" Answering your own questions will give you ideas for revising your topic sentence.

EXERCISE 15-1
Working Together

Revising Topic Sentences

Directions: The following topic sentences lack a point of view. Working with a classmate, revise each one to express an interesting view on the topic.

SENTENCE	I took a biology exam today.
REVISED	The biology exam that I took today contained a number of surprises.

1. I am taking a math course this semester.

    REVISED _____

    _____

2. I purchased a video camera last week.

    REVISED _____

    _____

3. Soft rock was playing in the dentist's office.

    REVISED _____

    _____

4. Sam has three televisions and four radios in his household.

    REVISED _____

    _____

5. There is one tree on the street where I live.

    REVISED _____

    _____

6. Many people wear headphones on their way to work.

   REVISED _____

   _____

7. Our sociology professor will give us three exams.

   REVISED _____

   _____

8. The first hurricane of the season is predicted to strike land tomorrow.

   REVISED _____

   _____

9. My four-year-old son has learned the alphabet.

   REVISED _____

   _____

10. Juanita enrolled her son in a day-care center.

    REVISED _____

    _____

■

Topic Sentences that Are Too Broad

Some topic sentences express a point of view, but they are too broad in scope.

TOO BROAD   The death penalty is a crime against humanity.

This statement cannot be supported in a single paragraph. Lengthy essays, even entire books, have been written to argue this opinion.

A broad topic sentence promises more than you can reasonably deliver in a single paragraph. It leads to writing that is vague and rambling. With a broad topic sentence, you will end up with too many facts and ideas to cover or too many generalities (general statements) that do not sufficiently explain your topic sentence. In the following example, note the broad topic sentence and its effects on paragraph development.

Sample Paragraph

All kinds of violent crimes in the world today seem to be getting worse. Sometimes I wonder how people could possibly bring themselves to do such horrible things. One problem may be the violent acts shown on television programs. Some people think crime has a lot to do with horror movies and television programs. We have no heroes to identify with other than criminals. News reporting of crimes is too "real"; it shows too much. Kids watch these programs without their parents and don't know what to make of them. Parents should spend time with their children and supervise their play.

The topic sentence above promises more than a good paragraph can reasonably deliver: to discuss all violent crimes in the world today and their worsening nature. If you reread the paragraph, you will see that in the supporting sentences the author wanders from topic to topic. She first mentions violence on television, then moves to lack of heroes. Next she discusses news reporting that is too graphic, then switches to children watching programs alone. Finally, she ends with parental supervision of children. Each point about possible causes of violence or ways to prevent it seems underdeveloped.

An effective topic sentence needs to be more focused. For example, the topic sentence for a paragraph about crime might focus on one type of crime in one city and one reason for its increase.

FOCUSED   Home burglaries are increasing in Owensville because of increased drug usage.

Another effective topic sentence for a paragraph on crime could focus on one possible cause of rising violence in the workplace.

FOCUSED   The mass layoffs in the past few years have led to more criminal acts by desperate, unemployed workers.

The topic sentence of the following paragraph is also too broad.

Sample Paragraph

People often forget the spirit and value of life and concentrate on worldly goods. These people buy things for show—nice cars, nice clothes, nice houses. These people are scraping their pennies together just to live well. They do not realize that things not from the store are just as nice. Their health, their families, and the people they care about are far more important than money. You can be rich and poor at the same time.

Because the topic was too broad, the writer continued to use general statements throughout the paragraph and to repeat the same or similar ideas. A more effective approach might be to select one worldly good and show how it affects one person.

FOCUSED   My sister is so concerned with dressing stylishly that she ignores everyone around her.

Now the writer can explain how an emphasis on clothing detracts from her sister's relationship with others.

Another effective topic sentence might focus the paragraph on not taking good health for granted:

FOCUSED   I used to think I could buy my way to happiness, but that was before I lost my good health.

The following suggestions will help you revise your topic sentence if you discover that it is too broad:

1. **Narrow your topic.** A topic that is too broad often produces a topic sentence that is too broad. Narrow your topic by subdividing it into smaller topics. Continue subdividing until you produce a topic that is manageable in a single paragraph.

2. **Rewrite your topic sentence to focus on one aspect or part of your topic.** Ask yourself, "What is the part of this topic that really interests me or that I care most about? What do I know most about the topic and have the most to say about?" Then focus on *that* aspect of the topic.

3. **Apply your topic sentence to a specific time and place.** Ask yourself, "How does this broad topic that I'd like to write about relate to some particular

time and place that I know about? How can I make the general topic come alive by using a well-defined example?"

4. **Consider using one of your supporting sentences as a topic sentence.** Reread your paragraph; look for a detail that could be developed or expanded.

EXERCISE 15-2
Writing in Progress

Revising Topic Sentences

Directions: Turn each of the following broad topic sentences into a well-focused topic sentence that could lead to an effective paragraph. Remember that your topic sentence must also include a point of view. Then compare your answers with your classmates' answers to see the variety of effective topic sentences that can come from a broad one.

TOO BROAD	Hunting is a worthwhile and beneficial sport.
REVISED	Hunting deer in overpopulated areas is beneficial to the herd.

1. I would like to become more creative.

REVISED _____

_____

2. Brazil is a beautiful country.

REVISED _____

_____

3. Pollution is a big problem.

REVISED _____

_____

4. The space program is amazing.

REVISED _____

_____

5. It is very important to learn Japanese.

REVISED _____

_____

6. We must protect the environment.

REVISED _____

_____

7. Lani is a good mother.

REVISED _____

_____

8. The book was interesting.

REVISED _____

_____

9. Lots of magazines are published.

REVISED _____

_____

10. Honesty is important.

REVISED _____

_____

■

Topic Sentences that Are Too Narrow

If your topic sentence is too narrow, you will realize it right away because you won't have enough to write about to complete your paragraph. Topic sentences that are too narrow also frequently lack a point of view.

TOO NARROW	My birdfeeder attracts yellow songbirds.
REVISED	Watching the different birds at our feeder is a pleasant diversion enjoyed by our entire family, including our cat.
TOO NARROW	My math instructor looks at his watch frequently.
REVISED	My math instructor has a number of nervous habits that detract from his lecture presentations.

The following suggestions will help you revise your topic sentence when it is too narrow:

1. **Broaden your topic to include a wider group or range of items or ideas.** For example, do not write about one nervous habit; write about several. Look for patterns and trends that could form the basis of a new, broader topic sentence.

2. **Broaden your topic so that it takes in both causes and effects or makes comparisons or contrasts.** For example, do not write only about how fast an instructor lectures. Also write about the effect of his lecture speed on students trying to take notes, or contrast that instructor with others who have different lecture styles.

3. **Brainstorm and research; try to develop a more general point from your narrower one.** Ask yourself, "What does this narrow point mean? What are its larger implications?" Suppose you've written the following topic sentence:

I wanted to buy a CD this week, but it was not in my budget.

You could expand this idea to discuss the importance or value of making and following a weekly budget.

NEED TO KNOW

Topic Sentences

Ineffective paragraphs may frustrate, confuse, or bore your reader.

A weak topic sentence may

- lack a point of view or attitude toward the topic.
- be too broad.
- be too narrow.

To revise a topic sentence that lacks a point of view

- use brainstorming, freewriting, or branching.
- ask yourself questions about your topic sentence to focus on a particular viewpoint.

To narrow a topic sentence that is too broad, consider

- narrowing your topic.
- rewriting your topic sentence to focus on one aspect of your topic.
- applying your topic sentence to a specific time and place.
- using one of your supporting sentences as a topic sentence.

To broaden a topic sentence that is too narrow, consider

- broadening your topic to make it more inclusive.
- broadening your topic to consider causes and effects or to make comparisons or contrasts.
- brainstorming and researching to develop a more general point.

EXERCISE 15-3   Broadening Topic Sentences

Directions: Turn each of the following narrow topic sentences into a broader, well-focused topic sentence that could lead to an effective paragraph. Remember that your topic sentence must also include a point of view. Then compare your answers with your classmates' answers to see the variety of effective topic sentences that can come from a narrow one.

TOO NARROW   Football players wear protective helmets.

REVISED   Football players wear several types of protective equipment to guard against injuries.

1. I planted a tomato plant in my garden.

REVISED   _____

_____

2. The cafeteria served hot dogs and beans for lunch.

REVISED _____

_____

3. Orlando sings in a low key.

REVISED _____

4. Suzanne bought a stapler for her desk.

REVISED _____

_____

5. Koala bears are really marsupials, not bears.

REVISED _____

_____

6. On our vacation, we stopped at a small town called Boothbay Harbor.

REVISED _____

_____

7. Homemade bread contains no preservatives.

REVISED _____

8. At Halloween, the girl dressed as a witch.

REVISED _____

_____

9. The comedian told a joke about dental floss.

REVISED _____

_____

10. We had a family portrait taken for Christmas.

REVISED _____

_____

■

REVISING PARAGRAPHS TO ADD SUPPORTING DETAILS

GOAL 2 Revise underdeveloped paragraphs

The details in a paragraph should give your reader sufficient information to make your topic sentence believable. Paragraphs that lack necessary detail are called **underdeveloped paragraphs.** Underdeveloped paragraphs lack supporting sentences to prove or explain the point made in the topic sentence. As you read the following student paragraph, keep the topic sentence in mind and consider whether the rest of the sentences support it.

Sample Student Paragraph

I am a very impatient person, and my impatience interferes with how easily I can get through a day. If I ask for something, I want it immediately. If I'm going somewhere and I'm ready and somebody else isn't, I get very upset. I hate driving behind someone who drives slowly when I cannot pass. I think that annoys me the most, and it never happens unless I am in a hurry. If I were less impatient, I would probably feel more relaxed and less pressured.

This paragraph begins with a topic sentence that is focused (it is neither too broad nor too narrow) and that includes a point of view. It promises to explain how the writer's impatience makes it difficult for him to get through a day. However, the rest of the paragraph does not fulfill this promise. Instead, the writer gives two very general examples of his impatience: (1) wanting something and (2) waiting for someone. The third example, driving behind a slow driver, is a little more specific, but it is not developed well. The last sentence suggests, but does not explain, that the writer's impatience makes him feel tense and pressured.

Taking into account the need for more supporting detail, the author revised his paragraph as follows:

Revised Paragraph

I am a very impatient person, and my impatience interferes with how easily I can get through a day. For example, when I decide to buy something, such as a new CD, I *have* to have it right away—that day. I usually drop everything and run to the store. Of course, I shortchange myself on studying, and that hurts my grades. My impatience hurts me, too, when I'm waiting for someone, which I hate to do. If my friend Alex and I agree to meet at noon to work on his car, I get annoyed if he's even five minutes late. Then I usually end up saying something nasty or sarcastic like "Well, where *were* you?" which I regret later. Perhaps I am most impatient when I'm behind the steering wheel. If I get behind a slow driver, I get annoyed and start honking and beeping my horn. I know this might fluster the other driver, and afterwards I feel guilty. I've tried talking to myself to calm down; sometimes it works, so I hope I'm overcoming this bad trait.

Did you notice that the writer became much more specific in the revised version? He gave an example of something he wanted—a CD—and he described his actions and their consequences. The example of waiting for someone was provided by the incident involving his friend Alex. Finally, the writer explained the driving example in more detail and stated its consequences. With the extra details and supporting examples, the paragraph is more interesting and effective.

The following suggestions will help you revise an underdeveloped paragraph:

1. **Analyze your paragraph sentence by sentence.** If a sentence does not add new, specific information to your paragraph, delete it or add to it so that it becomes relevant.

2. **Think of specific situations, facts, or examples that illustrate or support your topic.** Often you can make a general sentence more specific.

3. **Brainstorm, freewrite, or branch.** To come up with additional details or examples to use in your paragraph, try some prewriting techniques. If necessary, start fresh with a new approach and new set of ideas.

4. **Reexamine your topic sentence.** If you are having trouble generating details, your topic sentence may be the problem. Consider changing the approach.

EXAMPLE   Rainy days make me feel depressed.

REVISED   Rainy days, although depressing, give me a chance to catch up on household chores.

5. **Consider changing your topic.** If a paragraph remains troublesome, look for a new topic and start over.

EXERCISE 15-4   Revising a Paragraph

Directions: The following paragraph is poorly developed. What suggestions would you make to the writer to improve the paragraph? Write them in the space provided. Be specific. Which sentences are weak? How could each be improved?

> I am attending college to improve myself. By attending college, I am getting an education to improve the skills that I'll need for a good career in broadcasting. Then, after a successful career, I'll be able to get the things that I need to be happy in my life. People will also respect me more.

_____

_____

_____

_____

_____

EXERCISE 15-5   Evaluating a Paragraph

Directions: Evaluate the following paragraph by answering the questions that follow it.

> One of the best ways to keep people happy and occupied is to entertain them. Every day people are being entertained, whether it is by a friend for a split second or by a Broadway play for several hours. Entertainment is probably one of the nation's biggest businesses. Entertainment has come a long way from the past; it has gone from plays in the park to films in eight-screen movie theaters.

1. Evaluate the topic sentence. What is wrong with it? How could it be revised?

_____

_____

2. Write a more effective topic sentence on the topic of entertainment.

_____

_____

3. Evaluate the supporting details. What is wrong with them?

_____

_____

What should the writer do to develop her paragraph?

_____

_____

4. Use the topic sentence you wrote in question 2 above to develop a paragraph about entertainment.

_____

_____

_____

_____

_____

_____

_____

■

EXERCISE 15-6

Writing in Progress

Writing a Paragraph

Directions: Develop one of the topic sentences you wrote in Exercise 15-2 into a paragraph that uses good supporting details. Then draw an idea map of your paragraph, and revise your paragraph as needed. ■

NEED TO KNOW

Adding Supporting Details

To revise an underdeveloped paragraph,

- analyze your paragraph sentence by sentence.

- think of specific situations, facts, or examples that illustrate or support your main point.

- use brainstorming, freewriting, or branching.

- reexamine your topic sentence.

- consider changing your topic.

 **Analyze It!**

Directions: The topic sentence on the left is ineffective because it is too broad. On the right, rewrite the topic sentence to be more specific. Then rewrite the paragraph so that it contains concrete details that support the topic sentence.

There are a wide variety of books available for leisure reading. Many people find that thrillers—novels that have an exciting plot—make great "escape" literature. Thrillers are usually easy to read. Thrillers sometimes overlap with mysteries, another popular genre. Then there are science fiction and romances, too. When choosing a book for leisure reading, a person should consider the difficulty level of the book. Some people find it relaxing to read nineteenth-century novels, but other readers are frustrated by the unfamiliar language and slow action. It is not always easy to find the perfect book, but the library offers helpful resources for the determined leisure reader.

Topic Sentence: _____

_____

_____

_____

_____

_____

_____

_____

_____

A STUDENT ESSAY

The Writer

Fidel Sanchez was a student at Richard J. Daley College in Chicago, Illinois when he wrote this essay.

The Writing Task

Sanchez wrote this essay for a writing class. His instructor encouraged him

to enter his essay in a writing contest sponsored by Longman Publishers, the publisher of this book. Sanchez's essay was selected from among hundreds of essays as a good model essay. As you read, notice that each of Sanchez's paragraphs is well developed.

The Worst and Best Jobs of My Life

Fidel Sanchez

1 Depending on what job you choose, that choice can greatly influence your life either positively or negatively. Jobs have the power to give you a feeling of hope, meaning, accomplishment, and fulfillment or to leave you feeling broken, devastated, depressed, with a sense of hopelessness that never seems to go away. I have had two jobs in my life that have greatly affected me; one job made me feel important and useful, while the other job made me feel the exactly the opposite.

2 The first job I had was as a teacher's clerical assistant in high school. The credit hours were essential if I were to graduate so I took the job. I would help my teacher, Ms. Witherspoon, with the hordes of student papers that came her way. She would decorate them with soul-crushing F's or award-winning A's, along with little tidbits on how to do better next time. I would then leisurely type in all the information about each student's poor or near perfect academic performance into the computer. Correcting the piles of homework assignments and multiple-choice tests was time-consuming because she had so many students, but this task became easier once I had all the answers in my head. That line of work made me feel important, and, furthermore, I knew what I was doing, and I felt I was making a difference.

3 Now, my second job was the exact opposite of the first. I wanted to go to college, and my parents wanted to help me by paying my tuition. However my parents, due to medical reasons, could not work, so it became my responsibility to support them and to earn money for college. I started to search for job openings around my neighborhood. Finally, I found employment at a company called Sun Optics; there I would make a fair amount of money.

4 The company made glasses for people with visual problems. I thought the job would be exhilarating since I was trying something new in my life. I would receive clear, see-through bags of frames along with an ophthalmologist's description of what the customer wanted for his or her glasses. Then I would put them on a specified colored tray with a round circular piece of plastic that soon would become lenses. My first day on the job was atrocious. Nearly cutting my finger as I tried to dull the sharp edges of freshly cut lenses did not impress my boss. Learning how to heat plastic frames with burning hot sand in order to put in the lens was challenging, too. Sometimes the job required a little something extra like drilling a hole in the lens. My employers were supposed to teach me how to do these extra things, but they never did. When I talked to them about it, all they did was bellow at me and make hostile remarks.

5 I was more of a liability than an asset as I continued to work for Sun Optics. Dread came over me as I would get up every morning to go to work. This anxiety left me the day my parents told me they could start working again, so I was able to quit this job and start college. The thought that I might have to

face unpleasant jobs later in life made me realize that I had better start making good, sensible, and well-thought-out choices about what I want to do with my life and what career I want. We're all employees of an enterprise called life, so it's up to me to choose a career that will make this enterprise enjoyable and rewarding.

EXAMINING STUDENT WRITING

1. What is Sanchez's purpose for writing the essay?
2. How is the essay organized?
3. Highlight the transitions that move the reader from one topic to another.
4. What additional details could Sanchez have provided?

Writing in a Visual Age

READING

The growing influence of street gangs has had a harmful impact on our country, even though the media do not highlight gang violence as often today as they did some years ago. Drug abuse, gang shootings, beatings, thefts, carjackings, and the possibility of being caught in the crossfire have caused entire neighborhoods to live in fear. Once thought to occur only in urban areas, gang violence now appears in rural and suburban communities, particularly in southeastern, southwestern, and western states.

Experts believe that young people join gangs for a number of reasons. Although the reasons are complex, gangs seem to meet many of their needs. Gangs provide a sense of belonging to a family that gives them self-worth, companionship, security, and excitement. In other cases, gangs provide economic security through criminal activity such as drug sales. Once young people become involved in the gang subculture it is hard for them to leave. Threats of violence or fear of not making it on their own dissuade even those who are most seriously trying to get out.

—adapted from Donatelle, *Health*, p. 106.

1. In what parts of the United States are you least likely to find gangs in rural and suburban towns?

2. The reading provides a balanced view of gangs. Write a topic sentence with a strong point of view that expresses your feelings about gangs.

CRITICAL THINKING AND RESPONSE

3. Write a comparison or contrast paragraph answering one of these questions: How is a gang like a family? How is a gang different from a family?

WRITING

4. The reading classifies gangs as a "subculture," or a smaller group with a specific identity within a larger group. Other subcultures in the United States include skateboarders and punk rockers. Write a paragraph about a subculture you have observed, encountered, or taken part in. Include a topic sentence with a strong point of view.

5. While the first paragraph of the reading provides good basic information, it might be improved with additional details. What types of additional details might the author include to make the paragraph more interesting or informative?

USING VISUALS

Caption: _____

6. Two of the most violent and deadly gangs in the United States are the Crips and the Bloods. Gang members often mark their "turf" with graffiti. Examine this photo. Which gang do you think spray-painted the graffiti? Write a caption to accompany the photo, tying it into the reading.

7. Suppose you are looking for a photo to accompany the reading. You want the photo to illustrate the ways in which a gang can function as a "family" for its members. What type of photo would you look for? Search the Internet to see if you can find such a photo, and bring it to class. Write a caption to accompany the photo.

Paragraph Writing Scenarios

Friends and Family

1. Write a paragraph about someone in the past who encouraged you to do your best and how they would feel about you now.

2. Write a paragraph that begins "My friends would say my best feature is . . ."

Classes and Campus Life

1. Which would you like to do more, get a job or go on to get another degree?

2. Students have different learning styles. Some learn best from lectures, others by reading, and still others by doing hands-on experiments. Write a paragraph explaining how you learn best.

Working Students

1. Imagine a friend was stealing from your workplace. Would you tell your boss about it, even if it meant losing that friend? Why or why not?

2. Write a paragraph about how your current job does or does not have anything in common with the career you'd like to pursue in the future.

Communities and Cultures

1. Which would best describe the role you play in your community: peacemaker, troublemaker, or the one who stays out of the way?

2. Choose a holiday that is important in your culture and describe how it is typically celebrated.

WRITING ABOUT A READING

THINKING BEFORE READING

This essay, which originally appeared in *The Chronicle of Higher Education*, was written by a 2009 graduate of Stanford University. Read the selection to find out what he believes is most important for college students to focus on when choosing a major. As you read, identify the author's topic, his thesis, and the types of details he includes to support his point.

1. Preview the reading, using the steps discussed in Chapter 2, p. 35.

2. Connect the reading to your own experience by answering the following questions:

   a. Have you chosen a major?

   b. Do you feel it is important for college students to choose a major during their first year or before beginning college?

3. Mark and annotate as you read.

READING

STOP ASKING ME MY MAJOR

Scott Keyes

Scott Keyes, a recent college graduate, advises against gearing one's study concentration to fickle job prospects. Instead, he says, follow your intellectual passion.

1   One of my best friends from high school, Andrew, changed majors during his first semester at college. He and I had been fascinated by politics for years, sharing every news story we could find and participating in the Internet activism that was exploding into a new political force. Even though he was still passionate about politics, that was no longer enough. "I have to get practical," he messaged me one day, "think about getting a job after graduation. I mean, it's like my mom keeps asking me: What can you do with a degree in political science anyway?"

2   I heard the same question from my friend Jesse when students across campus were agonizing about which major was right for them. He wasn't quite sure what he wanted to study, but every time a field sparked his interest, his father would pepper him with questions about what jobs were available for people in that discipline. Before long, Jesse's dad had convinced him that the only way he could get a job and be successful after college was to major in pre-med.

3   My friends' experiences were not atypical.

4   Choosing a major is one of the most difficult things students face in college. There are two main factors that most students consider when making

this decision. First is their desire to study what interests them. Second is the fear that a particular major will render them penniless after graduation and result in that dreaded postcollege possibility: moving back in with their parents.

5   All too often, the concern about a major's practical prospects are pushed upon students by well-intentioned parents. If our goal is to cultivate students who are happy and successful, both in college as well as in the job market, I have this piece of advice for parents: Stop asking, "What can you do with a degree in (fill in the blank)?" You're doing your children no favors by asking them to focus on the job prospects of different academic disciplines, rather than studying what interests them.

6   It is my experience, both through picking a major myself and witnessing many others endure the process, that there are three reasons why parents (and everyone else) should be encouraging students to focus on what they enjoy studying most, rather than questioning what jobs are supposedly available for different academic concentrations.

7   The first is psychological. For his first two years of college, Jesse followed his dad's wishes and remained a pre-med student. The only problem was that he hated it. With no passion for the subject, his grades slipped, hindering his chances of getting into medical school. As a result his employability, the supposed reason he was studying medicine in the first place, suffered.

8   The second reason to stop asking students what they can do with a major is that it perpetuates the false notion that certain majors don't prepare students for the workplace. The belief that technical majors such as computer science are more likely to lead to a job than a major such as sociology or English is certainly understandable. It's also questionable. "The problem," as my friend Jose explained to me, "is that even as a computer-science major, what I learned in the classroom was outdated by the time I hit the job market." He thought instead that the main benefit of his education, rather than learning specific skills, was gaining a better way of thinking about the challenges he faced. "What's more," he told me, "no amount of education could match the specific on-the-job training I've received working different positions."

9   Finally, it is counterproductive to demand that students justify their choice of study with potential job prospects because that ignores the lesson we were all taught in kindergarten (and shouldn't ignore the closer we get to employment): You can grow up to be whatever you want to be. The jobs people work at often fall within the realm of their studies, but they don't have to. One need look no further than some of the most prominent figures in our society to see illustrations. The TV chef Julia Child studied English in college. Author Michael Lewis, whose best sellers focus on sports and the financial industry, majored in art history. Matt Groening, creator of *The Simpsons*, got his degree in philosophy, as did the former Hewlett Packard chief executive Carly Fiorina. Jeff Immelt, chief executive of General Electric, focused on mathematics. Indeed, with the Department of Labor estimating that on average people switch careers (not just jobs) two or three times in their lives, relying on a college major as career preparation is misguided.

10   I'm not saying any applicant can get any job. Job seekers still need market-able skills if they hope to be hired. However, in a rapidly changing economy, which majors lead to what jobs is not so clear cut. Many employers look for applicants from a diverse background—including my friend who has a degree in biochemistry but was just hired at an investment consulting firm.

11   That doesn't mean that majors no longer matter. It is still an important decision, and students are right to seek outside counsel when figuring out what they want to study. But questioning how a particular major will affect their employability is not necessarily the best approach. Although parents' intentions may be pure—after all, who doesn't want to see their children succeed after graduation?—that question can hold tremendous power over impressionable freshmen. Far too many of my classmates let it steer them away from what they enjoyed studying to a major they believed would help them get a job after graduation.

12   One of those friends was Andrew. He opted against pursuing a degree in political science, choosing instead to study finance because "that's where the jobs are." Following graduation, Andrew landed at a consulting firm. I recently learned with little surprise that he hates his job and has no passion for the work.

13   Jesse, on the other hand, realized that if he stayed on the pre-med track, he would burn out before ever getting his degree. During his junior year he changed tracks and began to study engineering. Not only did Jesse's grades improve markedly, but his enthusiasm for the subject recently earned him a lucrative job offer and admission to a top engineering master's program.

14   Andrew and Jesse both got jobs. But who do you think feels more successful?

GETTING READY TO WRITE

Reviewing the Reading

Answer each of the following questions using complete sentences.

1. What are the two main factors students consider when choosing a major, according to the author? _____
_____

2. According to the author, why should people stop asking students about the job prospects of different majors? _____

_____

3. What kindergarten lesson does the author believe should not be ignored?

_____

4. What point do the examples Julia Child, Matt Groening, and Carly Fiorina help prove?

_____

5. What does the author believe his two friends, Jesse and Andrew, demonstrate?

_____

Examining the Reading Using an Idea Map

Examine the reading by completing the missing parts of the following idea map.

Visualize It!

Title	Stop Asking Me My Major
Thesis	College students should choose a major based on what interests them.

Many students feel pressure from parents to select a major that will make them employable.

_____
_____

Concerns about a major are pushed on a student by parents.

_____
_____

_____
_____

Students should not ignore the lesson that you can grow up to be whatever you want.

The jobs people hold often do not fall within the realm of their studies, but they don't have to as evidenced by many famous success stories.

Many employers look for applicants with a diverse background.

Concludes with the comparison: _____

Conclusion _____
_____

Strengthening Your Vocabulary

Using the word's context, word parts, or a dictionary, write a brief definition of each of the following words as it is used in the reading.

1. atypical (paragraph 3) _____
2. render (paragraph 4) _____
3. perpetuates (paragraph 8) _____
4. misguided (paragraph 9) _____
5. lucrative (paragraph 13) _____

Reacting to Ideas: Discussion and Journal Writing

Get ready to write about the reading by discussing the following:

1. How does the author try to influence your opinions in this selection? Is he successful?

2. What arguments could you make against the author's assertion that people should study only what interests them?

3. How did you decide what your major will be? What factors influenced your decision? What did your parents have to say?

4. The author points to his friend Jesse as support for his argument, but why might he not be a good example?

 **Thinking Visually**   5. Explain the purpose of the photograph included with the selection. Is the photograph effective?

WRITING ABOUT THE READING

Paragraph Options

1. Reread Jose's statements in paragraph 8. Write a paragraph presenting your response to Jose's point of view.

2. Replace the underlined words in the following quote from paragraph 5 so the statement reflects your own philosophy: "If our goal is to cultivate students who are happy and successful, both in college as well as in the job market, I have this piece of advice for parents: Stop asking 'What can you do with a degree in (fill in the blank)?'" Write a paragraph explaining your revised statement.

3. Write a paragraph describing your ideal job. How will the classes you take now prepare you for this job?

Essay Options

4. Write an essay explaining how you would give advice to a younger friend or relative about choosing a major. Rely on your personal experience and that of people you know.

5. According to the author, parents' opinions heavily influence students' choices in college. How have your parents influenced your choices in college and in life? Write an essay exploring this.

Revision Checklist

Paragraph Development

1. Is the topic manageable (neither too broad nor too narrow)?
2. Is the paragraph written with the reader in mind?
3. Does the topic sentence identify the topic?
4. Does the topic sentence make a point about the topic?
5. Does each sentence support the topic sentence?
6. Is there sufficient detail?
7. Is there a sentence at the end that brings the paragraph to a close?

Sentence Development

8. Are there any sentence fragments, run-on sentences, or comma splices?
9. Are ideas combined to produce more effective sentences?
10. Are adjectives and adverbs used to make the sentences vivid and interesting?
11. Are relative clauses and prepositional phrases like *-ing* phrases used to add detail?
12. Are pronouns used correctly and consistently?

CHAPTER REVIEW AND PRACTICE

CHAPTER REVIEW

To review and check your recall of the chapter, select the word or phrase from the box below that best completes each of the following sentences. Not all of the words and phrases will be used.

too narrow	too broad	time sequence	point of view	place
questions	answers	causes and effects	sentence	paragraph

1. A topic sentence should express a _____.

2. A topic sentence that covers too much information is _____.

3. To revise a topic sentence that lacks a point of view, ask yourself _____ about the topic.

4. A topic sentence is _____ if you discover you do not have enough to write about.

(continued)

5. One way to revise a topic sentence that is too narrow is to consider _____ or comparisons and contrasts.

6. One way to revise a topic sentence that is too broad is to limit your topic to a specific time or _____.

7. One way to revise an underdeveloped paragraph is to analyze each _____ to determine what it contributes to the paragraph.

EDITING PRACTICE

This paragraph is skimpy and underdeveloped. Revise it by adding details.

In our family, Thanksgiving Day is one of the most important holidays of the year. Last year our large extended family, including children as well as adults, gathered at a relative's farmhouse in New Hampshire. People started arriving the day before Thanksgiving. It was a cold day. Everyone helped complete a multitude of chores. The next morning, preparations for the big dinner began in earnest. First we stuffed the turkey. While the turkey was roasting in the oven, we prepared a number of side dishes and dessert. When Thanksgiving dinner was finally served, the food itself seemed less important than the simple fact of being together. For that, we gave thanks.

PEARSON
mywritinglab   For support in meeting this chapter's objectives, log in to www.mywritinglab.com, go to the Study Plan tab, click on Revising Underdeveloped Paragraphs and choose Topic Sentence and Revising the Paragraph from the list of subtopics. Read and view the videos and resources in the Review Materials section, and then complete the Recall, Apply, and Write exercises in the Activities section. You can check your scores and overall progress by using the Gradebook.

16 Using an Idea Map to Spot Revision Problems

Learning Goals

In this chapter, you will learn how to

GOAL 1 Identify when you have strayed off topic

GOAL 2 Identify and eliminate irrelevant details

GOAL 3 Revise to ensure that details are logically arranged and developed

GOAL 4 Revise to ensure your paragraph is balanced

GOAL 5 Identify and eliminate unnecessary repetition

WRITE ABOUT IT!

How many shots do you suppose it takes to get the perfect photograph? Write a list of the factors a photographer might consider in choosing the right photograph.

Photographers take many shots to get just the right one. As a writer, you need to take many "shots" at a paragraph or essay to get it right. That is, you need to write several drafts before the paragraph or essay says what you want it to say.

Some students find revision a troublesome step because it is difficult for them to see what is wrong with their own work. After working hard on a first draft, it is tempting to say to yourself that you've done a great job and to think, "This is fine." Other times, you may think you have explained and supported an idea clearly when actually you have not. In other words, you may be blind to your own paper's weaknesses. Almost all writing, however, needs and benefits from revision. An idea map can help you spot weaknesses and discover what you may not have done as well as you thought.

An idea map will show how each of your ideas fits with and relates to all of the other ideas in a paragraph or essay. When you draw an idea map, you reduce your ideas to a skeleton form that allows you to see and analyze them more easily.

In this chapter you will learn how to use an idea map to (1) discover problems in a paragraph and (2) guide your revision. This chapter will discuss five questions to ask that will help you identify weaknesses in your writing, and it will suggest ways to revise your paragraphs to correct each weakness.

1. **Does the paragraph stray from the topic?**
2. **Does every detail belong?**
3. **Are the details arranged and developed logically?**
4. **Is the paragraph balanced?**
5. **Is the paragraph repetitious?**

WRITING

DOES THE PARAGRAPH STRAY FROM THE TOPIC?

GOAL 1 Identify when you have strayed off topic

mywritinglab

To practice essay revision, go to
■ Study Plan
■ The Essay
■ Revising the Essay

When you are writing a first draft of a paragraph, it is easy to drift away from the topic. As you write, one idea triggers another, and that idea another, and eventually you end up with ideas that have little or nothing to do with your original topic, as in the following first-draft student paragraph.

Sample Student Paragraph

One Example of Toxic Waste

The disposal of toxic waste has caused serious health hazards. Love Canal is one of the many toxic dump sites that have caused serious health problems. This dump site in particular was used by a large number of nearby industries. The canal was named after a man named Love. Love Canal, in my opinion, was an eye-opener on the subject of toxic dump sites. It took about ten years to clean the dump site up to a livable condition. Many people living near Love Canal developed cancers. There were many miscarriages and birth defects. This dump site might have caused irreversible damage to our environment, so I am glad it has been cleaned up.

The following idea map shows the topic sentence of the paragraph and, underneath it, the supporting details that directly relate to the topic sentence. All the unrelated details are in a list to the right of the map. Note that the concluding sentence is also included in the map, since it is an important part of the paragraph.

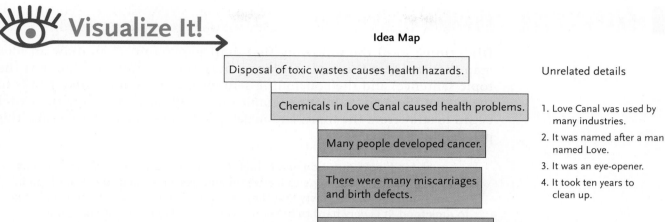

Visualize It!

Idea Map

Disposal of toxic wastes causes health hazards.

Chemicals in Love Canal caused health problems.

Many people developed cancer.

There were many miscarriages and birth defects.

I am glad it has been cleaned up.

Unrelated details

1. Love Canal was used by many industries.
2. It was named after a man named Love.
3. It was an eye-opener.
4. It took ten years to clean up.

In this paragraph the author began by supporting her topic sentence with the example of Love Canal. However, she began to drift when she explained how Love Canal was named. To revise this paragraph, the author could include more detailed information about Love Canal health hazards or examples of other disposal sites and their health hazards.

You can use an idea map to spot where you begin to drift away from your topic. To do this, take the last idea in the map and compare it with your topic sentence.

Last idea ←——→ Topic sentence

Does the last idea directly support your topic sentence? If not, you may have drifted from your topic. Check the second-to-last detail, going through the same comparison process. Working backward, you'll see where you started to drift. This is the point at which to begin revising.

What to Do If You Stray Off Topic

Use the following suggestions to revise your paragraph if it strays from your topic:

1. **Locate the last sentence that does relate to your topic, and begin your revision there.** What could you say next that *would* relate to the topic?

2. **Consider expanding your existing ideas.** If, after two or three details, you have strayed from your topic, consider expanding the details you have, rather than searching for additional details.

3. **Reread your brainstorming, freewriting, or branching to find more details.** Look for additional ideas that support your topic. Do more brainstorming, if necessary.

4. **Consider changing your topic.** Drifting from your topic is not always a loss. Sometimes by drifting you discover a more interesting topic than your original one. If you decide to change topics, revise your entire paragraph. Begin by rewriting your topic sentence.

■ **EXERCISE 16-1**   **Drawing an Idea Map**

Directions: Read the following first-draft paragraph. Then draw an idea map that includes the topic sentence, only those details that support the topic sentence, and the concluding sentence. List the unrelated details to the side of the map, as in the example on p. 449. Identify where the writer began to stray from the topic, and make specific suggestions for revising this paragraph.

> Junk food lacks nutrition and is high in calories. Junk food can be anything from candy and potato chips to ice cream and desserts. All of these are high in calories. But they are so tasty that they are addictive. Once a person is addicted to junk food, it is very hard to break the addiction. To break the habit, one must give up any form of sugar. And I have not gone back to my old lifestyle in over two weeks. So it is possible to break an addiction, but I still have the craving. ■

■ **EXERCISE 16-2**   **Writing a Paragraph**

Writing in Progress

Directions: Write a paragraph on one of the following topics. Then draw an idea map of it. Use the same procedure you used in Exercise 16-1. If you have strayed from your topic, revise your paragraph using the suggestions given above.

1. A memorable sight, sound, or meal

2. City language or country language

3. Trends in TV ads

4. A crowd you have watched or been a part of

5. The way that a certain friendship developed ■

DOES EVERY DETAIL BELONG?

GOAL 2 Identify and eliminate irrelevant details

Every detail in a paragraph must directly support the topic sentence or one of the other details. Unrelated information should not be included, a mistake one student made in the following first-draft paragraph.

Sample Student Paragraph

> In a world where stress is an everyday occurrence, many people relieve stress through entertainment. There are many ways to entertain ourselves and relieve stress. Many people watch movies to take their minds off day-to-day problems. However, going to the movies costs a lot of money. Due to the cost, some people rent movies at video stores. Playing sports is another stress reliever. Exercise always helps to give people a positive attitude and keeps them in shape. Racquetball really keeps you in shape because it is such a fast game. A third form of entertainment is going out with friends. With friends, people can talk about their problems and feel better about them. But some friends always talk and never listen, and such conversation creates stress instead of relieving it. So if you are under stress, be sure to reserve some time for entertainment.

The following idea map shows that this writer included four unrelated details:

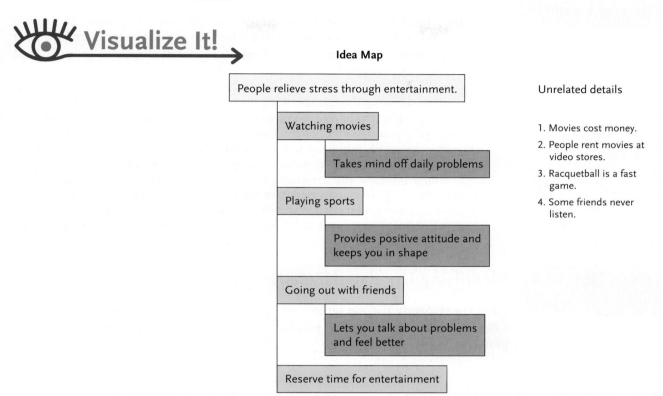

Visualize It!

Idea Map

People relieve stress through entertainment.

Watching movies

Takes mind off daily problems

Playing sports

Provides positive attitude and keeps you in shape

Going out with friends

Lets you talk about problems and feel better

Reserve time for entertainment

Unrelated details

1. Movies cost money.
2. People rent movies at video stores.
3. Racquetball is a fast game.
4. Some friends never listen.

To spot unrelated details, draw an idea map. To decide whether a detail is unrelated, ask, "Does this detail directly explain the topic sentence or one of the other details?" If you are not sure, ask, "What happens if I take this out?" If meaning is lost or if confusion occurs, the detail is important. Include it in your map. If you can make your point just as well without the detail, mark it "unrelated."

In the sample student paragraph on p. 450, the high cost of movies and the low-cost alternative of renting videos do not directly explain how or why movies are entertaining. The racquetball detail does not explain how exercise relieves stress. The detail about friends not listening does not explain how talking to friends is helpful in reducing stress.

Making Sure Every Detail Belongs

The following suggestions will help you use supporting details more effectively:

1. **Add explanations to make the connections between your ideas clearer.** Often a detail may not seem to relate to the topic because you have not explained *how* it relates. For example, health-care insurance may seem to have little to do with the prevention of breast cancer deaths until you explain that mammograms, which are paid for by some health-care plans, can prevent deaths.

2. **Add transitions.** Transitions make it clearer to your reader how one detail relates to another.

3. **Add new details.** If you've deleted several nonessential details, your paragraph may be too sketchy. Return to the prewriting step to generate more details you can include.

EXERCISE 16-3   Identifying Unrelated Details
Working Together

Directions: Read the following paragraph and draw an idea map of it. Underline any unrelated details and list them to the side of your map. Compare your results with those of a classmate and then decide what steps the writer should take to revise this paragraph.

> Your credit rating is a valuable thing that you should protect and watch over. A credit rating is a record of your loans, credit card charges, and repayment history. If you pay a bill late or miss a payment, that information becomes part of your credit rating. It is, therefore, important to pay bills promptly. Some people just don't keep track of dates; some don't even know what date it is today. Errors can occur in your credit rating. Someone else's mistakes can be put on your record, for example. Why these credit-rating companies can't take more time and become more accurate is beyond my understanding. It is worthwhile to get a copy of your credit report and check it for errors. Time spent caring for your credit rating will be time well spent. ■

EXERCISE 16-4   Identifying Unrelated Details
Writing in Progress

Directions: Study the paragraph and the idea map you drew for Exercise 16-2. Check for unrelated details. If you find any, revise your paragraph using the suggestions given above. ■

ARE THE DETAILS ARRANGED AND DEVELOPED LOGICALLY?

GOAL 3 Revise to ensure that details are logically arranged and developed

Details in a paragraph should follow some logical order. As you write a first draft, you are often more concerned with expressing your ideas than with presenting them in the correct order. As you revise, however, you should make sure you have followed a logical arrangement. Chapter 13 discusses various methods of arranging and developing details. The following "Need to Know" box reviews these arrangements:

NEED TO KNOW

Methods of Arranging and Developing Details

Method	Description
1. Time sequence	Arranges details in the order in which they happen.
2. Spatial	Arranges details according to their physical location.
3. Least/most	Arranges details from least to most or from most to least, according to some quality or characteristic.

Chapter 14 discusses several methods of organizing and presenting material. The "Need to Know" box on the next page reviews these arrangements.

NEED TO KNOW

Methods of Organizing and Presenting Material

Method	Description
1. Narration	Arranges events in the order in which they occurred.
2. Description	Arranges descriptive details spatially or uses the least/most arrangement.
3. Example	Explains by giving situations that illustrate a general idea or statement.
4. Definition	Explains by giving a subject's category or distinguishing characteristics.
5. Comparison and contrast	Explains an idea by comparing or contrasting it with another, usually more familiar, idea.
6. Classification	Explains by identifying types or categories.
7. Process	Arranges steps in the order in which they are to be completed.
8. Cause and effect	Explains why something happened or what happened as a result of a particular action.
9. Argument	Takes a position on an issue.

Your ideas need a logical arrangement to make them easy to follow. Poor organization creates misunderstanding and confusion. After drafting the following paragraph, a student drew an idea map that showed her organization was haphazard.

Sample Student Paragraph

When I was pregnant with my son, I wondered if life would ever be normal again. There were the nights I couldn't sleep because of all the kicking and the baby moving up to my lungs so I couldn't breathe. That was when I really had it! Each month I got bigger and bigger, and after a while I was so big I couldn't bend over or see my feet. Then there was the morning sickness. I don't know why they call it that because you're sick all the time for the first two months. Then there were all those doctor visits during which she told me, "Not for another week or two." Of course, when I realized my clothes didn't fit, I broke down and cried. But all of a sudden everything started up, and I was at the hospital delivering the baby two weeks early, and it's like it happened so fast and it was all over, and I had the most beautiful baby in my arms and I knew it was worth all that pain and suffering.

An idea map lets you see quickly when a paragraph has no organization or when an idea is out of order. This student's map, on the next page, showed that her paragraph did not present the events of her pregnancy in the most logical

 **Visualize It!**

Idea Map

When I was pregnant, I wondered if life would ever be normal.

Couldn't sleep—baby kicking, breathing difficult

Got bigger and bigger

Morning sickness

Doctor: "Not for another week"

Clothes didn't fit

Birth

arrangement: time sequence. She therefore reorganized the events in the order in which they happened and revised her paragraph as follows:

Revised Paragraph

When I was pregnant with my son, I wondered if life would ever be normal again. First there was the morning sickness. I don't know why they call it that because I was sick all the time for the first two months. Of course, when I realized my clothes didn't fit, I broke down and cried. Each month I got bigger and bigger, and finally I was so big I couldn't bend over or see my feet. Then there were the nights I couldn't sleep because of all the kicking and the baby moving up to my lungs so I couldn't breathe. That was when I really had it. Finally, there were all those doctor visits during which she told me, "Not for another week or two." But all of a sudden everything started to happen, and I was at the hospital delivering the baby two weeks early. Everything happened so fast. It was all over, and I had the most beautiful baby in my arms. Then I knew it was worth all that pain and suffering.

Arranging and Developing Details Logically

The following suggestions will help you revise your paragraph if it lacks organization:

1. **Review the methods of arranging and developing details and of organizing and presenting material** (see the "Need to Know" boxes on pp. 452–453). Will one of those arrangements work? If so, number the ideas in your idea map according to the arrangement you choose. Then begin revising your paragraph.

   If you find one or more details out of logical order in your paragraph, do the following:

   • **Number the details in your idea map to indicate the correct order, and revise your paragraph accordingly.**
   • **Reread your revised paragraph and draw another idea map.**
   • **Look to see if you've omitted necessary details.** After you have placed your details in a logical order, you are more likely to recognize gaps.

2. **Look at your topic sentence again.** If you are working with a revised arrangement of supporting details, you may need to revise your topic sentence to reflect that arrangement.

3. **Check whether additional details are needed.** Suppose, for example, you are writing about an exciting experience, and you decide to use the time-sequence arrangement. Once you make that decision, you may need to add details to enable your reader to understand exactly how the experience happened.

4. **Add transitions.** Transitions help make your organization obvious and easy to follow.

EXERCISE 16-5   Evaluating Arrangement of Ideas

Directions: Read the following student paragraph, and draw an idea map of it. Evaluate the arrangement of ideas. What revisions would you suggest?

> The minimum wage is not an easily resolved problem; it has both advantages and disadvantages. Its primary advantage is that it does guarantee workers a minimum wage. It prevents the economic abuse of workers. Employers cannot take advantage of workers by paying them less than the minimum. Its primary disadvantage is that the minimum wage is not sufficient for older workers with families to support. For younger workers, such as teenagers, however, this minimum is fine. It provides them with spending money and some economic freedom from their parents. Another disadvantage is that as long as people, such as a teenagers, are willing to work for the minimum, employers don't need to pay a higher wage. Thus, the minimum wage prevents experienced workers from getting more money. But the minimum wage does help our economy by requiring a certain level of income per worker. ■

EXERCISE 16-6   Evaluating Arrangement of Ideas

Writing in Progress

Directions: Review the paragraph and idea map you produced for Exercise 16-2. Evaluate the logical arrangement of your points and details, and revise if needed. ■

IS THE PARAGRAPH BALANCED?

GOAL 4 Revise to ensure your paragraph is balanced

An effective paragraph achieves a balance among its points. That is, each idea receives an appropriate amount of supporting detail and emphasis. The following student paragraph lacks balance, as its idea map on the following page shows.

Sample Student Paragraph

Waiting

Waiting is very annoying, exhausting, and time-consuming. Waiting to buy books at the college store is an example of a very long and tiresome task. I need to buy books, and so does everyone else. This causes the lines to be very long. Most of the time I find myself leaning against the wall daydreaming. Sometimes I will even leave the line and hope to come back when the store isn't extremely busy. But that never works because everyone else seems to get the same idea. So I finally realize that I just have to wait. Another experience is waiting for a ride home from school or work. My ride always seems to be the last car to pull up in the parking lot. When I am waiting for my ride, I often wonder what it would be like to own a car or if I will ever make it home. Waiting in line at a fast-food restaurant is also annoying because, if it is fast, I shouldn't have to wait. Waiting for an elevator is also no fun. Waiting just seems to be a part of life, so I might as well accept it.

456 Chapter 16 ■ Using an Idea Map to Spot Revision Problems

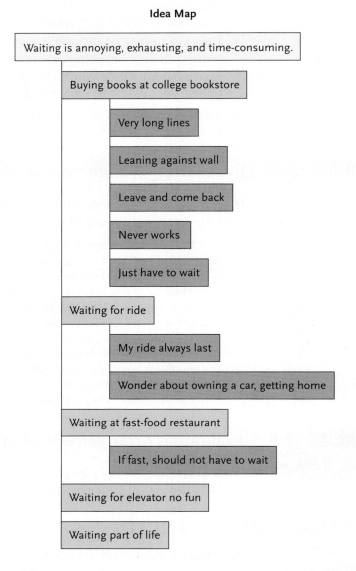

Idea Map

As the idea map above shows, a major portion of the paragraph is devoted to waiting in line to buy books. The second example, waiting for a ride, is not as thoroughly explained. The third example, waiting at a fast-food restaurant, is treated in even less detail, and the fourth, waiting for an elevator, has the least detail. To revise, the writer should expand the treatment of waiting for rides, fast food, and elevators, and perhaps decrease the treatment of the bookstore experience. An alternative solution would be for the writer to expand the bookstore experience and eliminate the other examples. In this case, a new topic sentence would be needed.

Making Sure Your Paragraph Is Balanced

The following suggestions will help you revise your paragraph for balance:

1. **Not every point or example must have the *same* amount of explanation.** For example, more complicated ideas require more explanation than simpler, more obvious ones. When you are using a least/most arrangement, the more important details may need more coverage than the less important ones.

2. **If two ideas are equally important and equally complicated, they should receive similar treatment.** For instance, if you include an example or statistic in support of one idea, you should do so for the other.

EXERCISE 16-7   Evaluating Balance of Details

Directions: Read the following paragraph, and draw an idea map of it. Evaluate the balance of details and indicate where more details are needed.

> I am considering buying a puppy. There are four breeds I am looking at: golden retrievers, beagles, Newfoundlands, and cocker spaniels. Cocker spaniels are cute, but golden retrievers are cute *and* intelligent. Golden retrievers are very gentle with children, and I have two sons. They are also very loyal. But they have a lot of fur, and they shed, unlike beagles, which have short fur. Newfoundlands are very large, and they have dark-colored fur that would show up on my rug. Newfoundlands also drool a lot. My apartment is small, so a Newfoundland is probably just too big, furry, and clumsy. ■

EXERCISE 16-8   Evaluating Balance of Details
Writing in Progress

Directions: Review your paragraph and idea map for Exercise 16-2. Evaluate the balance of details, and revise if necessary. ■

IS THE PARAGRAPH REPETITIOUS?

GOAL 5 Identify and eliminate unnecessary repetition

In a first draft, you may express the same idea more than once, each time in a slightly different way. As you are writing a first draft, repetitive statements may help you stay on track. They keep you writing and help generate new ideas. However, it is important to eliminate repetition at the revision stage. Repetitive statements add nothing to your paragraph. They detract from its clarity. An idea map will bring repetition to your attention quickly because it makes it easy to spot two or more very similar items.

As you read the following first-draft student paragraph, see if you can spot the repetitive statements. Then notice how the idea map on the next page clearly identifies the repetition.

Sample Student Paragraph

> Chemical waste dumping is an environmental concern that must be dealt with, not ignored. The big companies care nothing about the environment. They would just as soon dump waste in our backyards as not. This has finally become a big issue and is being dealt with by forcing the companies to clean up their own messes. It is incredible that large companies have the nerve to dump just about anywhere. The penalty should be steep. When the companies are caught, they should be forced to clean up their messes.

The idea map shows that points 1, 2, and 4 say nearly the same thing—that big companies don't care about the environment and dump waste nearly anywhere. Because there is so much repetition, the paragraph lacks development. To revise, the writer first needs to eliminate the repetitious statements. Then she needs to generate more ideas that support her topic sentence and explain why or how chemical waste dumping must be dealt with.

Visualize It!

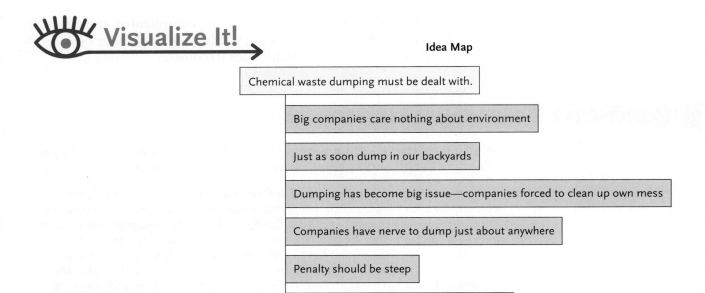

Idea Map

Chemical waste dumping must be dealt with.

Big companies care nothing about environment

Just as soon dump in our backyards

Dumping has become big issue—companies forced to clean up own mess

Companies have nerve to dump just about anywhere

Penalty should be steep

When caught, clean up should be required

How to Avoid Repetition

The following suggestions will help you revise a paragraph with repetitive ideas:

1. **Try to combine ideas.** Select the best elements and wording of each idea and use them to produce a revised sentence. Add more detail if needed.

2. **Review places where you make deletions.** When you delete a repetitious statement, check to see whether the sentence before and the sentence after the deletion connect. Often a transition will be needed to help the paragraph flow easily.

3. **Decide whether additional details are needed.** Often we write repetitious statements when we don't know what else to say. Thus, repetition often signals lack of development. Refer to Chapter 15 for specific suggestions on revising underdeveloped paragraphs.

4. **Watch for statements that are only slightly more general or specific than one another.** For example, although the first sentence below is general and the second is more specific, they repeat the same idea.

   Ringing telephones can be distracting. The telephone that rang constantly throughout the evening distracted me.

   To make the second sentence a specific example of the idea in the first sentence, rather than just a repetition of it, the writer would need to add specific details about how the telephone ringing throughout the evening was a distraction.

EXERCISE 16-9   Identifying and Revising Repetitive Statements

Directions: Read the following paragraph and delete all repetitive statements. Make suggestions for revision.

Children misbehaving is an annoying problem in our society. I used to work as a waiter at Denny's, and I have seen many incidences in which parents allow their children to misbehave. I have seen many situations that you would just not believe. Once I served a table at which the parents allowed their four-year-old to make his toy spider crawl up and down my pants as I tried to serve the food. The parents just laughed. Children have grown up being rewarded for their actions, regardless of whether they are good or bad. Whether the child does something the parents approve of or whether it is something they disapprove of, they react in similar ways. This is why a lot of toddlers and children continue to misbehave. Being rewarded will cause the child to act in the same way to get the same reward. ■

NEED TO KNOW

Using Idea Maps

An idea map is a visual display of the ideas in your paragraph. It allows you to see how ideas relate to one another and to identify weaknesses in your writing. You can use idea maps to answer the following five questions that will help you revise your paragraphs:

- Does the paragraph stray from the topic?

- Does every detail belong?

- Are the details arranged and developed logically?

- Is the paragraph balanced?

- Is the paragraph repetitious?

EXERCISE 16-10   Identifying and Revising Repetitive Statements

Writing in Progress

Directions: Review your paragraph and idea map for Exercise 16-2. Identify and revise any repetitive statements. ■

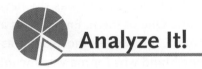 Analyze It!

Directions: The following paragraph strays from its topic and includes details that do not belong. Revise the paragraph by deleting all sentences that do not directly support the thesis.

Do you have trouble getting out of the house on time in the morning? If you are not a naturally well-organized person, you may need to overcompensate by being super organized in the morning. A detailed checklist can help you accomplish the seemingly impossible goal of leaving home exactly when you are supposed to. It is especially difficult to leave on time if you are tired or feeling lazy. When making such a checklist, most people find it helpful to backtrack to the previous evening. Do you have clean clothes for the next day, or do you need to do a load of laundry? Are your materials for school or work neatly assembled, or is there a landslide of papers covering your desk? Do you need to pack a lunch? You get the picture. In your checklist, include tasks to complete the night before as well as a precise sequence of morning tasks with realistic estimates of the time required for each task. If you have children, help them make checklists to keep track of homework assignments. Child development experts stress the importance of predictable structure in children's lives. If you live with a friend or spouse, make sure to divide all chores in an equitable way. Often one person tends to be neater than the other, so you may need to make compromises, but having an explicit agreement about household responsibilities can help prevent resentment and conflict at home.

A STUDENT ESSAY

The Student Writer

Zoë Cole is a student athlete majoring in elementary education.

The Writing Task

Zoë Cole was taking a writing class and was asked to write an essay about a childhood experience. She chose to write about her experiences playing soccer. Cole's first draft is shown below, along with the idea map she drew to help her revise. Study the first draft, her idea map, and the section titled "Evaluating the Idea Map" before you read her final draft.

Sports and Life

Zoë Cole

First Draft

1   I started playing soccer when I was four. Most of the girls in my preschool were playing, and two of their dads were the coaches, Danny and Chuck. The first time I played soccer I didn't know anything about it, except that it looked like it was fun. I didn't know about winning and losing, except in Candyland, the first board game I ever played. I just had a good time chasing the ball and trying to kick it. So I was surprised when some of the other girls on my team started talking about "Oh, we lost. It's not fair."

2   When I was seven we moved. I got on a town team, and some of the girls were good. They had been playing together for three years and I was the new kid. Some of them already thought they were stars. One of them, Emma, was a bully. She thought she was better than the rest of us. But Annie, whose dad was one of the coaches, was really nice. I didn't understand why Emma was mean, especially since she wasn't as good as Annie.

3   In fact, this early experience playing soccer was my first lesson in how different people can be. I realized that not all of my friends were nice all the time. I also realized that someone could be nice one-on-one but not so nice on a team. Like Emma, who was fun to play with at home but who just got meaner and more bossy during games. That wasn't true of Annie: she was nice all the time. If I had to give an example of a bad sport, it would be Emma. Unlike Annie, she never stopped telling us what to do and pointing out our mistakes. And if we lost, she threw a fit. It made the other kids not like her, which only made her worse. I haven't stayed in touch with Emma, but I've met people like her and I usually avoid them. I don't like being criticized or blamed when things go wrong, especially by someone who has room for improvement herself!

4   Despite some of the unpleasant players, I did enjoy the game. I enjoyed the competition, but I also just liked being outside with other kids. It was also a break in the routine of my very traditional household. Dinner at 6, bath at 8, bed at 8:30. My parents were always there to watch me play, which made me feel important. My older brother, who was also a soccer player, thought I wasn't very good, but I didn't care.

5   Annie is still my friend. Eighteen years have gone by since we met at recreation league, and she's still the same easygoing person. She was never bossy or critical like Emma, and she played really well, too. Some of the other girls were nice and would compliment you after a good play, like saying "good try" if you missed, but Annie never said much. She just grinned. She looked cute when she did it, because she had one tooth missing in the front. She grinned at you when you kicked in a goal and she grinned at you when you missed the ball completely. She never got upset and would do her silly victory dance even when we lost. She was first on line to slap hands with the other team. And she's still like that. Whether things are going really well or bad, I can always count on that Annie grin. You could say Annie is a trustworthy player, but she's more than that because she's like that when there's not a game. She's just Annie and she's everyone's friend and if she doesn't like you, she keeps it to herself.

6   There were other girls on the team who were sort of in between Annie and Emma. A couple of them were like, really insecure and neurotic and thought that everything they did mattered, good or bad. They wouldn't pass when someone was clear, but would try and take the ball alone down to the goal and then get upset when the other team took it away. They thought it was more about *them* and not the team. Some of them didn't go on playing and by high school a few had quit completely. One who didn't quit should have, because she was always scared of getting hurt. She would only go after the ball if other people on the team were there first.

7   Me, I still love soccer, but I am a different type of player than all of those whom I have described. I may not be as good as Annie, but I always play hard and try my best. I never walk away from the field feeling like I should have done something I didn't do. And I care about my teammates and the opposing players, too. I guess that's what life is all about; trying your best. If you do, you'll never let yourself down.

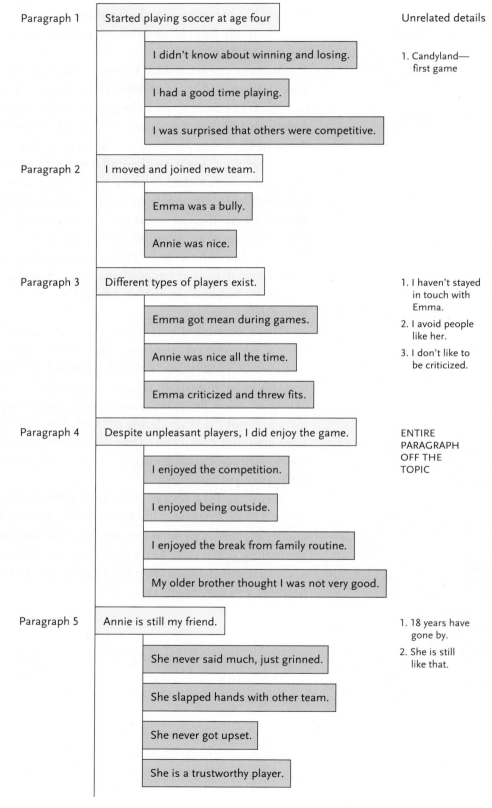

Idea Map

Paragraph 1 — Started playing soccer at age four

    I didn't know about winning and losing.

    I had a good time playing.

    I was surprised that others were competitive.

Paragraph 2 — I moved and joined new team.

    Emma was a bully.

    Annie was nice.

Paragraph 3 — Different types of players exist.

    Emma got mean during games.

    Annie was nice all the time.

    Emma criticized and threw fits.

Paragraph 4 — Despite unpleasant players, I did enjoy the game.

    I enjoyed the competition.

    I enjoyed being outside.

    I enjoyed the break from family routine.

    My older brother thought I was not very good.

Paragraph 5 — Annie is still my friend.

    She never said much, just grinned.

    She slapped hands with other team.

    She never got upset.

    She is a trustworthy player.

Unrelated details

1. Candyland— first game

1. I haven't stayed in touch with Emma.
2. I avoid people like her.
3. I don't like to be criticized.

ENTIRE PARAGRAPH OFF THE TOPIC

1. 18 years have gone by.
2. She is still like that.

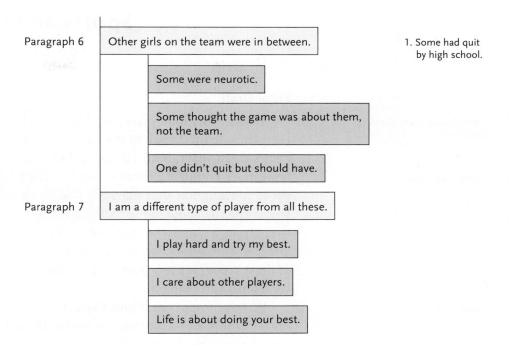

EVALUATING THE IDEA MAP

Cole studied her idea map and realized the following:

1. She jumped from player to player, instead of concentrating on one at a time.

2. She also felt the essay was a story about individual people but did not make any points about them.

3. For the topic of paragraph 3, she had written, "Different types of players exist." She decided to make this statement her thesis. She decided to use specific players as examples of types of players instead of writing about the players as topics themselves. She created names for her categories.

4. She decided to include herself as an example of a Team Player.

5. She realized she needed to include an example of the insecure player in paragraph 6.

6. She eliminated paragraph 4, since it was not about types of players.

7. In all of the paragraphs, she eliminated the unrelated details that she identified.

Sports and Life
Zoë Cole

Final Draft

Introduction: background
information

Thesis statement

1   When I was four years old, I began playing soccer on my neighborhood recreation team. I took to the sport right away and continued to play for the next sixteen years, both on school teams and with independent and increasingly more competitive travel leagues. From these years of experience, I have come to recognize that there are four basic types of athletes, each with a different attitude about being part of a team. To make it simple, I've given each of these types a name: the Insecure Player, the Poor Sport, the Trustworthy Player, and the Team Player. No matter what the game, I believe you'll find one of each of these types on every team, field, court, or blacktop. I'll use my own girls' soccer team as an example.

Topic sentence

Example: Kayla

2   I'd have to put my friend Kayla in the first category, which is the Insecure Player group. Kayla worried so much about her ability that she had trouble connecting with the rest of the team. She rarely stayed in position, but would charge at the ball no matter where it went. Some people accused her of being a "hot dog," but I knew how insecure she felt. Because she was afraid of letting the team down, she overcompensated, trying to make plays that weren't hers to make in order to prove her worth on the team. When the play failed, or we lost a game, Kayla would slink off, ashamed and too embarrassed to face the rest of the team. No matter how many times the coach would tell her she wasn't solely responsible for whatever went wrong, she couldn't let up. In trying too hard, she upset the balance of the team and continued to feel awful. I put her in the category of Insecure Player because she never could step back and see herself as only one part of the team.

Topic sentence
Example: Emma

3   Another type of player is the Poor Sport. Emma was a good example of a Poor Sport. She was a good player—one of the best we had, in fact—but, nonetheless, she had a negative effect on the team. She was quick to yell at other players during games when they made a mistake or neglected to do something *she* thought they should have done. No matter how many times the coach told Emma to stop, she didn't, becoming in effect the team bully. She took this bad attitude a step further, letting everyone know who she deemed worthy of being her friend and ostracizing those whose abilities she considered inferior. If we lost a game, she was the first to point out whose responsibility it was, reciting a list of bad plays and who made them. Never mind that we were only ten years old; Emma was already the ultimate Poor Sport.

Topic sentence
Example: Annie

4   Then there is the Trustworthy Player—the one you can always count on. Annie was a completely neutral player who never let her emotions show. She showed up on time, said little, and played hard. She was consistent, strong, and unafraid. When Annie played defense, no one worried; we knew she wouldn't let the ball get by. When we won, she smiled. When we lost, she shrugged. There was no celebration and no mourning by Annie. She was like an efficient machine, always on, never distracted. This attitude carried over into her everyday

life, and we have remained friends. She is still as steady as she was at ten, and I appreciate her reliable, calm presence.

Topic sentence

Example: the writer herself

5   And finally there is the Team Player. This type of player puts the team first and herself second. I am a good example of a Team Player. I stopped playing soccer in college but never lost my love of the game. I also never forgot I was part of a team. Sure, I liked to win, but I knew that we were only human. Exhaustion, illness, and injury all contributed to how we played. And there were simply teams who were better. Maybe they had better coaching, maybe they practiced more, maybe they were older; there were just times when we were beaten, fair and square. But I never felt down or angry. I loved the game so much that I was able to admire a competitor who showed heart and skill on the field—even as she was contributing to our defeat!

Conclusion: comments on the value of sports

6   I've tried to carry this understanding of sportsmanship with me throughout my adult life. Playing on a team helped me understand people better—especially myself. I find that my early exposure to teamwork has made me a good collaborator and therefore more valuable at work. Sure, I hate to lose. But I think losing has a lot to do with attitude. As long as you always play your best or work your hardest, you never really lose.

EXAMINING STUDENT WRITING

1. What was the most important revision that Cole made?

2. Evaluate the title. Could she have chosen a more descriptive title?

3. Do you think it was effective for Cole to use herself as a example of one of the categories?

4. What other revisions do you feel are needed?

Writing in a Visual Age

READING

Large collections of animals, which were originally called menageries, have existed since the times of the ancient Chinese, Egyptians, and Aztecs. Modern zoos, sometimes called zoological parks, now come in many sizes and can be found throughout the world. The Philadelphia Zoo was the first (1859) location in the United States dedicated to the large-scale collection and display of animals. Although this facility is still popular, it has been eclipsed by more spectacular zoos such as the Bronx Zoo and the San Diego Zoo. Historically, most zoos were established as not-for-profit organizations, but that form of operation is changing. All of these zoos are large, creating a great deal of public interest as well as generating significant international tourism traffic. This interest is based on unusual exhibits, collections of animal species, and efforts to re-create the natural settings found in the wild.

—Cook, Yale, and Marqua, *Tourism*, p. 211.

1. The reading is a collection of facts about zoos, but it does not appear to have a topic sentence. Write a topic sentence and indicate where you would insert it.

   _____

   _____

   _____

2. Which sentence in the reading could be eliminated because it provides an unnecessary detail?

CRITICAL THINKING AND RESPONSE

3. The reading offers an overview of zoos, but it does not address any of the controversies surrounding zoos. Write a sentence or two in which you explain some of the criticisms that can be directed against zoos. (*Hint:* Think about animal rights.)

WRITING

4. You win a free trip and must choose among three types of tourist attractions: a zoo, an aquarium, and an art museum. Which trip would you choose and why? Write a paragraph examining your choice, providing details that support your topic sentence.

USING VISUALS

5. Write a descriptive paragraph about the photo. Make sure your description is balanced and not repetitious.

6. Write two captions for the photo. The first caption should be supportive of zoos and their mission. The second caption should be critical of zoos.

Caption: _____

_____

Paragraph Writing Scenarios

Friends and Family

1. Write a paragraph that begins "The most important thing I learned from my mother is . . ."

2. Write about an event that stands out in the history of your family.

Classes and Campus Life

1. Which of the "Three R's" (Reading, Writing, and Arithmetic) is the most difficult for you? What are you doing to make it easier?

2. Do you think race should be considered in awarding financial aid? Why or why not?

Working Students

1. Write a paragraph that begins "When I go to bed at night, I worry about . . ."

2. Write an imaginary job description that fits you perfectly.

Communities and Cultures

1. What is a typical weekend activity you enjoy doing with a group?

2. Write a paragraph about what you would miss most about your present community if you had to move away.

WRITING ABOUT A READING

THINKING BEFORE READING

The following reading, "You Can't Be Thin Enough: Body Images and the Mass Media," is from the book *Sociology: A Down-to-Earth Approach to Core Concepts*, by James M. Henslin. As you read, notice the variety of evidence that the author includes to support his thesis.

1. Preview the reading, using the steps discussed in Chapter 2, p. 35.

2. Connect the reading to your own experience by answering the following questions:

   a. How would you describe the ideal body type?

   b. Are most people content or dissatisfied with their body type? Why?

3. Mark and annotate as you read.

READING

YOU CAN'T BE THIN ENOUGH: BODY IMAGES AND THE MASS MEDIA

James M. Henslin

1   When you stand before a mirror, do you like what you see? To make your body more attractive, do you watch your weight or work out? You have ideas about what you should look like. Where did you get them?

2   TV and magazine ads keep pounding home the message that our bodies aren't good enough, that we've got to improve them. The way to improve them, of course, is to buy the advertised products: hair extensions for women, hairpieces for men, hair transplants, padded bras, diet programs, anti-aging products, and exercise equipment. Muscular hulks show off machines that magically produce "six-pack abs" and incredible biceps—in just a few minutes a day. Female movie stars effortlessly go through their own tough workouts without even breaking into a sweat. Women and men get the feeling that attractive members of the opposite sex will flock to them if they purchase that wonder-working workout machine.

3   Although we try to shrug off such messages, knowing that they are designed to sell products, the messages still get our attention. They penetrate our thinking and feelings, helping to shape ideal images of how we "ought" to look. Those models so attractively clothed and coiffed as they walk down the runway, could they be any thinner? For women, the message is clear: You can't be thin enough. The men's message is also clear: You can't be muscular enough.

All of us contrast the reality we see when we look in the mirror with our culture's ideal body types. The thinness craze encourages some people to extremes, as with Paris Hilton. It also makes it difficult for larger people to have positive self-images. Overcoming this difficulty, Queen Latifah is in the forefront of promoting an alternative image.

4   Woman or man, your body isn't good enough. It sags where it should be firm. It bulges where it should be smooth. It sticks out where it shouldn't, and it doesn't stick out enough where it should.

5   And—no matter what your weight is—it's too much. You've got to be thinner. Exercise takes time, and getting in shape is painful. Once you do get in shape, if you slack off it seems to take only a few days for your body to sag into its previous slothful, drab appearance. You can't let up, you can't exercise enough, and you can't diet enough.

6   But who can continue at such a torrid pace, striving for what are unrealistic cultural ideals? A few people, of course, but not many. So **liposuction** is appealing. Just lie there, put up with a little discomfort, and the doctor will vacuum the fat right out of your body. Surgeons can transform flat breasts into super breasts overnight. They can lower receding hairlines and smooth furrowed brows. They remove lumps with their magical tummy tucks, and can take off a decade with their rejuvenating skin peels, face lifts, and **Botox** injections.

7   With impossibly shaped models at *Victoria's Secret* and skinny models showing off the latest fashions in *Vogue* and *Seventeen*, half of U.S. adolescent girls feel fat and count calories. Some teens even call the plastic surgeon. Anxious lest their child violate peer ideals and trail behind in her race for popularity, parents foot the bill. Some parents pay $25,000 just to give their daughters a flatter tummy.

8   With peer pressure to alter the body already intense, surgeons keep stoking the fire. A sample ad: "No Ifs, Ands or Butts. You Can Change Your Bottom

liposuction

a surgical procedure in which fat is removed from under the skin by means of suction

Botox

a cosmetic form of botulinum toxin that temporarily paralyzes the muscles that cause wrinkles, making the skin appear smoother

Line in Hours!" Some surgeons even offer gift certificates—so you can give your loved ones liposuction or Botox injections along with their greeting card.

9   The thinness craze has moved to the East. Glossy magazines in Japan and China are filled with skinny models and crammed with ads touting diet pills and diet teas. In China, where famine used to abound, a little extra padding was valued as a sign of good health. Today, the obsession is thinness. Not-so-subtle ads scream that fat is bad. Some teas come with a package of diet pills. Weight-loss machines, with electrodes attached to acupuncture pressure points, not only reduce fat but also build breasts—or so the advertisers claim.

10   Not limited by our rules, advertisers in Japan and China push a soap that supposedly "sucks up fat through the skin's pores." What a dream product! After all, even though our TV models smile as they go through their paces, those exercise machines do look like a lot of hard work.

11   Then there is the other bottom line: Attractiveness does pay off. U.S. economists studied physical attractiveness and earnings. The result? "Good-looking" men and women earn the most, "average-looking" men and women earn more than "plain" people, and the "ugly" earn the least. In Europe, too, the more attractive workers earn more. Then there is that potent cash advantage that "attractive" women have: They attract and marry higher-earning men.

12   More popularity *and* more money? Maybe you can't be thin enough after all. Maybe those exercise machines are a good investment. If only we could catch up with the Japanese and develop a soap that would suck the fat right out of our pores. You can practically hear the jingle now.

jingle
a catchy song used in advertising

GETTING READY TO WRITE

Reviewing the Reading

Answer each of the following questions using complete sentences.

1. According to the reading, what message is sent by TV and magazine ads?

   _____

2. How is the men's message different from the women's message?

   _____

3. What statistic is cited for how many adolescent girls in the United States feel fat and count calories? _____

4. In addition to the United States, what other countries are described as having an obsession with thinness? _____

5. List two financial advantages associated with physical attractiveness.

   _____

   _____

Examining the Reading Using an Idea Map

Review the reading by completing the missing parts of the idea map shown below.

 **Visualize It!** →

Title — You Can't Be Thin Enough: Body Images and the Mass Media

Thesis — TV and magazine ads send the message that our bodies aren't good enough and we've got to improve them.

_____
_____
_____

The messages penetrate our thinking and feelings, shaping ideal images of how we "ought" to look.

Women should be thinner; men should be more muscular.

_____
_____

Unrealistic cultural ideals make liposuction, cosmetic surgery, and other procedures appealing.

_____

Attractiveness pays off financially.

_____
_____

_____
_____

Conclusion — Concluding reference to the title and to the Japanese fat-sucking soap.

Strengthening Your Vocabulary

Using the word's context, word parts, or a dictionary, write a brief definition of each of the following words as it is used in the reading.

1. penetrate (paragraph 3) _____

2. coiffed (paragraph 3) _____

3. slothful (paragraph 5) _____

4. torrid (paragraph 6) _____

5. receding (paragraph 6) _____

6. furrowed (paragraph 6) _____

7. rejuvenating (paragraph 6) _____

8. violate (paragraph 7) _____

9. potent (paragraph 11) _____

Reacting to Ideas: Discussion and Journal Writing

Get ready to write about the reading by discussing the following questions:

1. Discuss Western culture's ideal body types. How do these "ideal" bodies affect your own body image?

 **Thinking Visually**

2. What is the purpose of the photograph included with the selection?

3. Would you consider cosmetic surgery or any of the other procedures described in the article? Why or why not?

4. Discuss the last paragraph of the reading. What do you think the author is revealing about his attitude toward the subject?

WRITING ABOUT THE READING

Paragraph Options

1. Write a paragraph answering the first question posed in paragraph 1: "When you stand before a mirror, do you like what you see?"

2. Who or what shapes or influences your ideas about what you should look like? Write a paragraph explaining your answer.

3. What is your opinion of teenagers having cosmetic surgery as described in the reading? Write a paragraph explaining your answer.

Essay Options

4. Look through a popular magazine and study the ads it contains. Identify several that send the message that "our bodies aren't good enough," and choose two to write about in an essay. Describe the product being marketed and the ideal body type featured in the ad. Be sure to evaluate the effectiveness of each ad.

5. Choose a TV program to analyze. What body images are portrayed on the show? How realistic are these images? Is there evidence of cultural stereotypes on the show? Pay particular attention to the commercials that air during the show. What products are being advertised? What body images are featured in the commercials? Write an essay describing your observations.

Revision Checklist

Paragraph Development

1. Is the topic manageable (neither too broad nor too narrow)?
2. Is the paragraph written with the reader in mind?
3. Does the topic sentence identify the topic?
4. Does the topic sentence make a point about the topic?
5. Does each sentence support the topic sentence?
6. Is there sufficient detail?
7. Is there a sentence at the end that brings the paragraph to a close?

Sentence Development

8. Are there any sentence fragments, run-on sentences, or comma splices?
9. Are ideas combined to produce more effective sentences?
10. Are adjectives and adverbs used to make the sentences vivid and interesting?
11. Are relative clauses and prepositional phrases like *-ing* phrases used to add detail?
12. Are pronouns used correctly and consistently?

CHAPTER REVIEW AND PRACTICE

CHAPTER REVIEW

To review and check your recall of the chapter, select the word or phrase from the box below that best completes each of the following sentences. Not all of the words and phrases will be used.

logically	unrelated	forward	idea map	repetitive
strayed	backward	sequentially	balanced	

1. A(n) _____ can help you spot weaknesses in your writing.

2. When your paragraph has little or nothing to do with your original topic, you have _____ from the topic.

3. When drawing an idea map, list _____ details to the right of the map.

4. To identify where you drifted from your topic, read your paragraph _____, and compare each idea with your topic sentence.

5. You should arrange details in a paragraph _____.

6. A paragraph is _____ if each idea receives an appropriate amount of detail and emphasis.

7. A paragraph that states information more than once is _____.

EDITING PRACTICE

Paragraph 1

The following first draft of a student's paragraph has a number of problems in paragraph development and organization. Draw an idea map for this paragraph, and then revise the paragraph using the map.

Sudents attend my college for financial, social, and academic reasons. The college I attend is a community college, and most of the students still live at home. Attending a community college gives them the opportunity to experiment for a couple of years before they decide about careers. Also, it is a state school, so the cost of tuition is more reasonable than it might be in a private college. The college is located in a beautiful setting in the countryside on the site of a former landscape nursery. Since the students commute to school and the student body is small, it is easy to get to know a lot of people. The commute takes most students less than 30 minutes. Most of the students come from a few local high schools, so there is not a long period of social adjustment. My college has an excellent reputation because of our sports teams that are usually in contention for a state title. Many of the students who attend my college are either committed to a particular vocational program, or they have not yet made up their minds about a career.

Paragraph 2

The following paragraph is underdeveloped. Draw an idea map and revise the paragraph by expanding on and adding details in order to support its main point.

The average American worker is worse off today than at any time in the past decade. There are fewer good jobs now. Living expenses and taxes have increased. Workers' salaries have declined. More families need both spouses to work. Clearly, we are worse off today.

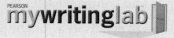

For support in meeting this chapter's objectives, log in to www.mywritinglab.com, go to the Study Plan tab, click on Using an Idea Map to Spot Revision Problems and choose Revising the Paragraph and Editing the Paragraph from the list of subtopics. Read and view the videos and resources in the Review Materials section, and then complete the Recall, Apply, and Write exercises in the Activities section. You can check your scores and overall progress by using the Gradebook.

17 Essay Basics and Development

Learning Goals

In this chapter, you will learn how to

GOAL 1 Structure an effective essay

GOAL 2 Select a topic and plan an essay

GOAL 3 Write an effective thesis statement

GOAL 4 Locate specific, relevant evidence to support your thesis

GOAL 5 Use transitions to clearly relate ideas

GOAL 6 Write effective titles, introductions, and conclusions

GOAL 7 Analyze essay questions and plan answers

WRITE ABOUT IT!

The photograph above shows a building under construction. Write a sentence explaining how constructing a building is similar to the task of writing.

Your sentence probably included the idea that writing is a work in progress; it is a series of steps. In this chapter you will learn how to write essays. You will learn how to structure an essay, write an effective thesis statement, support your thesis with evidence, and write effective introductions, conclusions, and titles.

WRITING

AN OVERVIEW OF THE ESSAY

If you can write a paragraph, you can write an essay. The structure is similar, and they have similar parts. A paragraph expresses one main idea, called the **topic**, and is made up of several sentences that support that idea. The main idea is expressed in a sentence called the **topic sentence**. An essay also expresses one key idea called the **thesis**. This is expressed in a sentence called the **thesis statement**. The chart below shows how the parts of the paragraph are very much like the parts of an essay.

Tip for Writers

The prefix *trans-* means "across" or "from one place to another." A transitional sentence carries the reader from the idea before it to the idea that follows it, making the connection between them easier to understand.

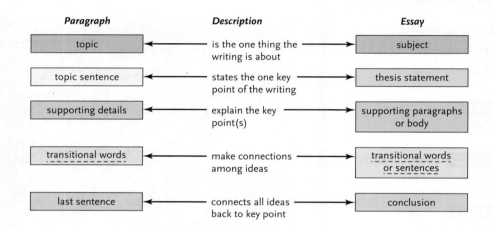

Paragraph	Description	Essay
topic	is the one thing the writing is about	subject
topic sentence	states the one key point of the writing	thesis statement
supporting details	explain the key point(s)	supporting paragraphs or body
transitional words	make connections among ideas	transitional words or sentences
last sentence	connects all ideas back to key point	conclusion

THE STRUCTURE OF AN ESSAY

GOAL 1 Structure an effective essay

To practice essay organization, go to
- Study Plan
- The Essay
- Essay Organization

Think of the organization of an essay as modeling the organization of a paragraph, with one idea being explained by supporting details. Because an essay is usually at least three paragraphs long, and often more, it needs an opening paragraph, called the **introduction**, that focuses the reader and provides necessary background information before the thesis is presented. The paragraphs that support the thesis are called the **body** of the essay. Due to length and complexity, an essay also needs a final paragraph, called the **conclusion**, to draw the ideas discussed together and bring it to an end. You can visualize the organization of an essay as shown on the following page.

PLANNING YOUR ESSAY

GOAL 2 Select a topic and plan an essay

An essay requires more time spent in planning and organization than does a single paragraph, although the process is the same. It involves selecting an appropriate topic and generating ideas. The topic for an essay should be broader than for a single paragraph. For more information on broadening or narrowing topics, see Chapter 18, pp. 501–503. To generate ideas for an essay, use the techniques you learned in Chapter 11 for generating ideas for paragraphs.

 Visualize It!

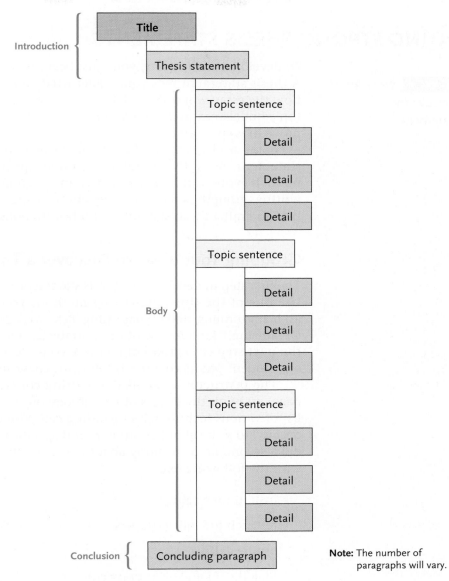

Idea Map Showing
Essay Structure

Introduction { Title — Thesis statement

Topic sentence — Detail, Detail, Detail

Body { Topic sentence — Detail, Detail, Detail

Topic sentence — Detail, Detail, Detail

Conclusion { Concluding paragraph

Note: The number of paragraphs will vary.

EXERCISE 17-1
Working Together

Narrowing a Topic and Generating Ideas

Directions: Choose one of the following topics, narrow it down, and generate ideas for a two-page essay. Exchange your work with a classmate and evaluate each others' work.

1. Organic or health foods

2. Natural disasters

3. Predictable or unpredictable behaviors

4. Teenage fads or fashions

5. Controlling stress

6. Valued possessions

7. An unfortunate accident or circumstance

8. A technological advance ■

WRITING STRONG THESIS STATEMENTS

GOAL 3 Write an effective thesis statement

To develop a sound essay, you must begin with a well-focused thesis statement. A **thesis statement** tells your reader what your essay is about and gives clues to how the essay will unfold. The thesis statement should not only identify your topic but also express the main point about your topic that you will explain or prove in your essay.

Some students think they should be able to just sit down and write a thesis statement. But a thesis statement rarely springs fully formed into a writer's mind: it evolves and, in fact, may change significantly during the process of pre-writing, grouping ideas, drafting, and revising. The next section will show you how to draft a thesis statement and how to polish it into a focused statement.

Grouping Your Ideas to Discover a Thesis Statement

The first step in developing a thesis statement is to generate ideas to write about. Use one of the three prewriting methods you have studied: (1) freewriting, (2) brainstorming, and (3) branching. Refer to p. 299 of Chapter 11, "Planning and Organizing," for a review of these strategies. Once you have ideas to work with, the next step is to group or connect your ideas to form a thesis. Let's see how one student produced a thesis following these steps.

The instructor in Tsoukalas' writing course assigned a short (one-to-two-page) essay on the effects of technology on modern life. After brainstorming a list of various technologies including cell phones, iPods, and video games, she decided to write about computers and specifically about the Internet. She then did a second brainstorming about uses and effects of the Internet. She came up with the following list:

instant messaging

research for college papers

online dating

Match.com and eHarmony.com

Mapquest to find directions

chat rooms

meet new friends

college Web site

e-mail—socializing with friends

Facebook

Google to find the answer to anything

online profiles

accuracy of online profiles

Tsoukalas's next step in writing her essay was to select usable ideas and try to group or organize them logically. In the brainstorming list on the previous page, Tsoukalas saw three main groups of ideas: communicating, socializing, and online dating. She sorted her list into categories:

> **Communicating:** instant messaging, chat rooms, completing assignments
>
> **Socializing:** Facebook, online profiles, friending new people
>
> **Online Dating:** Match.com, eHarmony.com

Once Tsoukalas had grouped her ideas into these categories, she could write a thesis statement:

> The Internet has become an excellent means of communicating, socializing, and meeting potential dates.

This thesis statement identifies her topic—the Internet—and suggests three ways in which it has affected her life. You can see how this thesis statement grew out of her idea groupings. Furthermore, this thesis statement gives her readers clues as to how she will organize the essay. A reader knows from this preview which uses she will discuss and in what order.

How to Group Ideas

How do you know which ideas to group? Look for connections and relationships among ideas that you generate during prewriting. Here are some suggestions:

1. **Look for categories.** Try to discover how you can classify and subdivide your ideas. Think of categories as titles or slots in which you can place ideas. Look for a general term that is broad enough to cover several of your ideas. For example, Tsoukalas broke down the many uses of the Internet into communicating, socializing, and online dating. Suppose you were writing a paper on favoritism. You could break down the topic by a category, such as place.

   SAMPLE THESIS STATEMENT   Whether it's practiced in the workplace, in a classroom, or on Capitol Hill, favoritism is unfair.

2. **Try organizing your ideas chronologically.** Group your ideas according to the clock or calendar.

   SAMPLE THESIS STATEMENT   From the ancient Mayans to King Henry VIII's court to present-day Congress, personal relationships have always played a role in professional achievement.

3. **Look for similarities and differences.** When working with two or more topics, see if you can approach them by looking at how similar or different they are.

   SAMPLE THESIS STATEMENT   The two great pioneers of psychotherapy, Freud and Jung, agreed on the concept of the libido but completely disagreed on other issues.

4. **Separate your ideas into causes and effects or problems and solutions.** You can often analyze events and issues in this way.

SAMPLE THESIS STATEMENT   The phrase "it takes a village to raise a child" means that birth parents alone do not determine what an individual will grow up to be.

5. **Divide your ideas into advantages and disadvantages, or pros and cons.** When you are evaluating a proposal, product, or service, this approach may work.

SAMPLE THESIS STATEMENT   Deciding on a major before starting college can either help a student stay focused and on track or keep him or her from discovering new interests.

6. **Consider several different ways to approach your topic or organize and develop your ideas.** As you consider what your thesis statement is going to be, push yourself to see your topic from a number of different angles or from a fresh perspective.

For example, Tsoukalas could have examined her brainstorming list and decided to focus only on the Internet as an information source, looking more deeply into search engines and informational Web sites. In other words, within every topic lie many possible thesis statements.

Guidelines for Writing Thesis Statements

A thesis statement should explain what your essay is about, and it should also give your readers clues to its organization. Think of your thesis statement as a promise; it promises your reader what your paper will deliver. Here are some guidelines to follow for writing an effective thesis statement:

1. **It should state the main point of your essay.** It should not focus on details; it should give an overview of your approach to your topic.

TOO DETAILED   Because babies don't know anything about the world around them, parents should allow them to touch toys and other objects.

REVISED   Because babies don't know anything about the world around them when they are born, they need to spend lots of time touching, holding, and exploring the everyday things we take for granted.

2. **It should assert an idea about your topic.** Your thesis should express a viewpoint or state an approach to the topic.

LACKS AN ASSERTION   Advertisers promote beer during football games.

REVISED   One of the reasons you see so many beer ads during ball games is that men buy more beer than women.

3. **It should be as specific and detailed as possible.** For this reason, it is important to review and rework your thesis *after* you have written and revised drafts.

TOO GENERAL   You need to take a lot of clothes with you when you go camping.

REVISED   Because the weather can change so quickly in the Adirondacks, it is important to pack clothing that will protect you from both sun and rain.

4. **It may suggest the organization of your essay.** Mentioning key points that will be discussed in the essay is one way to do this. The order in which you mention them should be the same as the order in which you discuss them in your essay.

DOES NOT SUGGEST ORGANIZATION   Learning to read is important for your whole life.

REVISED   Literacy is a necessary tool for academic, professional, and personal success.

5. **It should not be a direct announcement.** Do not begin with phrases such as "In this paper I will . . ." or "My assignment was to discuss . . ."

DIRECT ANNOUNCEMENT   What I am going to write about is how working out can make you better at your job.

REVISED   Exercise can dramatically improve the performance of everyone, from front office to assembly-line workers.

6. **It should offer a fresh, interesting, and original perspective on the topic.** A thesis statement can follow the guidelines discussed above, but, if it seems dull or predictable, it needs more work.

PREDICTABLE   Complex carbohydrates are good for you.

REVISED   Diets that call for cutting out carbohydrates completely are overlooking the tremendous health benefits of whole grains.

EXERCISE 17-2   Writing a Thesis Statement

Writing in Progress

Directions: Using the topic you chose and the ideas you generated about it in Exercise 17-1, develop a thesis statement. ■

SUPPORTING YOUR THESIS WITH SUBSTANTIAL EVIDENCE

GOAL 4 Locate specific, relevant evidence to support your thesis

Every essay you write should offer substantial evidence in support of your thesis statement. This evidence makes up the body of your essay. **Evidence** can consist of personal experience, anecdotes (stories that illustrate a point), examples, reasons, descriptions, facts, statistics, and quotations (taken from sources).

Many students have trouble locating concrete, specific evidence to support their theses. Though prewriting yields plenty of good ideas and helps you focus your thesis, prewriting ideas may not always provide sufficient evidence. Often you need to brainstorm again for additional ideas. At other times, you may need to consult one or more sources to obtain further information on your topic.

The table on the next page lists ways to support a thesis statement and gives an example of how Tsoukalas could use each one in her essay on different ways to use the Internet.

TABLE 17-1   WAYS TO ADD EVIDENCE

Topic: The Internet's Impact

Support Your Thesis by	Example
Telling a story (narration)	Relate a story about a couple who met using an online dating service.
Adding descriptive detail (description)	Give details about one person's Facebook profile.
Giving an example	Give an example of types of personal likes and dislikes that are included in one person's online profile.
Giving a definition	Explain the meaning of the term "friendship status."
Making comparisons	Compare two online dating sites.
Making distinctions (contrast)	Compare instant messaging with face-to-face conversations.
Discussing types or kinds (classification)	Discuss the types of information that can be found on the Internet.
Explaining how something works (process)	Explain how to register on Facebook.
Giving reasons (causes)	Explain what factors contribute to the popularity of chat rooms.
Analyzing effects	Explain why online profiles can be misleading.

The table offers a variety of ways Tsoukalas could add evidence to her essay, but she would not need to use all of them. Instead, she should choose the one that is the most appropriate for her audience and purpose. Tsoukalas could also use different types of evidence in combination. For example, she could *describe* a particular online dating site and *tell a story* that illustrates its use.

Use the following guidelines in selecting evidence to support your thesis:

1. **Be sure your evidence is relevant.** That is, it must directly support or explain your thesis.

2. **Make your evidence as specific as possible.** Help your readers see the point you are making by offering detailed, concrete information. For example, if you are explaining the dangers of driving while intoxicated, include details that make that danger seem immediate: victims' names and injuries, types of vehicle damage, statistics on the loss of life, and so on.

3. **Be sure your information is accurate.** It may be necessary to check facts, verify stories you have heard, and ask questions of individuals who may have provided information.

4. **Locate sources that provide evidence.** Because you may not know enough about your topic and lack personal experience, you may be unable to provide strong evidence. When this happens, locate several sources on your topic.

5. Be sure to document any information that you borrow from other sources. See Chapter 12, p. 325, "Avoiding Plagiarism and Citing Sources" for more information.

EXERCISE 17-3   Writing a First Draft
Writing in Progress

Directions: Write a first draft of an essay for the thesis statement you wrote in Exercise 17-2. Support your thesis statement with at least three types of evidence. ■

 Analyze It!

Directions: On the left is the brainstorming one student did on the topic of space exploration. Study the brainstorming and use the key on the right to identify and group the ideas into three sets of related ideas that could be used in an essay. Choose one of the topics, create a topic sentence, and list the ideas you would use in the order in which you would use them.

Space Exploration

what if Columbus and other explorers hadn't taken the risk to explore new worlds?
space travel inspires younger generation
space travel a luxury when poverty, famine, and war on Earth
recent Gallup poll shows 71% of Americans support the space program
why not just use robots—why risk human lives?
achievements of Hubble telescope, International Space Station, humans on moon
national trauma from shuttle disasters
space shuttle Challenger and Columbia deaths
basic scientific research often leads to unexpected practical applications
exploring space could involve discoveries that solve energy crisis and other problems
natural resources on other planets
NASA-developed technologies (led to laptop computers, solar power cells)
no matter how advanced the technology, human error will always cause problems
satellite enabled telephone and TV communications, global navigation, weather forecast
adverse health effects of weightlessness (bone loss, muscle damage, loss of red blood cells)
is it worth it to go to the moon?
travel to other planets takes too long
astronauts vulnerable to cosmic radiation

| V = value of space program |
| R = risks of space program |
| D = disadvantages of space program |
| |
| |
| |
| |
| |
| |
| |
| |
| |
| |
| |
| |
| |
| |

A STUDENT ESSAY

The Writer

Markella Tsoukalas is a student at Fairleigh Dickinson University in Teaneck, New Jersey. She is a junior and is majoring in business management with a concentration in human resources.

The Writing Task

Now let's take a look at how Tsoukalas developed her essay on the impact of the Internet. As you read her draft, notice in particular the types of evidence she uses and how her thesis statement promises what her essay delivers.

Title

Expanding My World Through the Internet

Markella Tsoukalas

1   The Internet has revolutionized America's way of communicating and of meeting new and interesting people. When the Internet was first introduced to American society, only the rich and famous had access to it because only they could afford computers; now, the majority of U.S. households have computer and Internet access. The Internet has become an excellent means of communicating, socializing, and meeting one's soul mate.

Thesis statement

Topic sentence

Personal experience or evidence

2   When I first started using the Internet, I was obsessed with the instant messaging and chat rooms. They were new ways of communicating with my friends without worrying about increasing the phone bill. My parents thought it was the best thing ever invented because I wasn't going out as much with my friends, which meant that I wasn't spending as much money. There was no need for them to be worrying constantly about where I was and if I was okay. For about a year, I was glued to the computer because I was fascinated with all the different techniques and programs that were available. Now I socialize on the Internet at a more moderate level and use it for school-related assignments and finding needed information, as well.

Topic sentence

Explanation of how Facebook works

3   Facebook is one of the most widely used social networking sites. Each user creates a profile detailing his or her likes and dislikes, and posts a picture, if desired. If the user sees someone attractive on Facebook, a simple request is sent requesting friendship status. Facebook allows people to socialize with people they know and with people they have just met. Facebook offers a safe way of meeting people without face-to-face encounters. However, Facebook also has its disadvantages. Users do not know if a posted profile is truthful and accurate, and keeping up with friends on Facebook can be quite time-consuming.

4   Topic sentence

There is a soul mate for every person in the world, but it is harder for some than others to find that special person. Match.com and eHarmony.com were created for those "hard to find" soul mates. When a user creates a profile that includes a list of the user's interests, the user is matched with someone who is perceived to have similar interests. A major advantage of both of the sites is that they allow the matched couple to get to know one another before meeting in person, if they choose. The couple can decide if there is sufficient mutual connection for a face-to-face meeting. There have been many relationships made through Match.com and eHarmony.com; some have led to marriage. They are great sites to try out if you are having troubles in the love department.

Details about online dating sites

Conclusion: Tsoukalas recaps three main points and comments on how each has affected her

5   I am fortunate that the Internet has found its way into my life. It's one of the most convenient sources for communication and information sharing. Socializing on the Internet has put me in touch with people from all different countries. As for finding a soul mate, I'll leave you guessing on that one. Overall, as the Internet continues to expand throughout the world, our experiences will also expand.

EXAMINING STUDENT WRITING

1. How effectively is Tsoukalas thesis statement expressed?

2. Evaluate Tsoukalas's support for her thesis. Is it relevant, specific, and detailed? What other types of evidence might she have used to strengthen her essay?

3. Evaluate the essay's title. Is it interesting and engaging? Suggest other titles that might be effective.

4. Were the three categories that Tsoukalas used to devise her thesis statement well chosen and effectively carried through in the essay?

5. Overall, how could Tsoukalas improve her essay?

MAKING CONNECTIONS AMONG YOUR IDEAS CLEAR

GOAL 5
Use transitions to clearly relate ideas

To produce a well-written essay, be sure to make it clear how your ideas relate to one another. There are several ways to do this:

1. **Use transitional words and phrases.** The transitional words and phrases that you learned in Chapter 14 for connecting ideas are helpful for making your essay flow smoothly and communicate clearly. Table 17-2 on the next page lists useful transitions for each method of organization. Notice the use of these transitional words and phrases in Tsoukalas's essay: *when, now,* and *however.*

2. **Write a transitional sentence.** This sentence is usually the first sentence in the paragraph. It might come before the topic sentence or it might *be* the topic sentence. Its purpose is to link the paragraph in which it appears with the paragraph before it. Sometimes it comes at the end of the paragraph and links the paragraph to the following one.

TABLE 17-2   USEFUL TRANSITIONAL WORDS AND PHRASES

Method of Development	Transitional Words and Phrases
Least/Most or Most/Least	most important, above all, especially, particularly important, less important
Spatial	above, below, behind, beside, next to, inside, outside, to the west (north, etc.), beneath, near, nearby, next to
Time Sequence	first, next, now, before, during, after, eventually, finally, at last, later, meanwhile, soon, then, suddenly, currently, after, afterward, after a while, as soon as, until
Narration/Process	first, second, then, later, in the beginning, when, after, following, next, during, again, after that, at last, finally
Description	see Spatial and Least/Most or Most/Least above
Example	for example, for instance, to illustrate, in one case
Definition	means, can be defined as, refers to, is
Classification	one, another, second, third
Comparison	likewise, similarly, in the same way, too, also
Contrast	however, on the contrary, unlike, on the other hand, although, even though, but, in contrast, yet
Cause and Effect	because, consequently, since, as a result, for this reason, therefore, thus

3. **Repeat key words.** Repeating key words from either the thesis statement or the preceding paragraph helps your reader see connections among ideas. In Tsoukalas's essay, notice the repetition of key words and phrases such as *Internet* and *Facebook*.

EXERCISE 17-4   Analyzing Your Draft

Writing in Progress

Directions: Review the draft you wrote for Exercise 17-3. Analyze how effectively you have connected your ideas. Add key words or transitional words, phrases, or sentences, as needed. ■

WRITING THE INTRODUCTION, CONCLUSION, AND TITLE

GOAL 6 Write effective titles, introductions, and conclusions

The introduction, conclusion, and title each serve a specific function. Each one strengthens your essay and helps your reader better understand your ideas.

Writing the Introduction

An introductory paragraph has three main purposes.

1. **It presents your thesis statement.**

2. **It interests your reader in your topic.**

3. **It provides any necessary background information.**

Although your introductory paragraph appears first in your essay, it does *not* need to be written first. In fact, it is sometimes best to write it last, after you have developed your ideas, written your thesis statement, and drafted your essay.

We have already discussed writing thesis statements earlier in the chapter (see p. 478). Here are some suggestions on how to interest your reader in your topic:

TABLE 17-3 WAYS TO INTEREST YOUR READER	
Technique	**Example**
Ask a provocative or controversial question	How would you feel if the job you had counted on suddenly fell through?
State a startling fact or statistic	Last year, the United States government spent a whopping billion dollars a day on interest on the national debt.
Begin with a story or an anecdote	The day Liam Blake left his parka on the bus was the first day of what would become the worst snowstorm the city had ever seen.
Use a quotation	Robert Frost wrote "Two roads diverged in a wood, and I—/I took the one less traveled by,/And that has made all the difference."
State a little-known fact, a myth, or a misconception	What was Harry S. Truman's middle name? Stephen? Samuel? Simpson? Actually, it's just plain "S." There was a family dispute over whether to name him for his paternal or maternal grandfather, an argument that was settled by simply using the common initial "S."

A straightforward, dramatic thesis statement can also capture your reader's interest, as in the following example:

The first day I walked into Mr. Albierto's advanced calculus class, I knew I had made a huge mistake.

An introduction should also provide the reader with any necessary background information. Consider what information your reader needs to understand your essay. You may, for example, need to define the term *genetic engineering* for a paper on that topic. At other times, you might need to provide a brief history or give an overview of a controversial issue.

Now reread the introduction to Tsoukalas's essay on p. 484. How does she introduce her topic?

EXERCISE 17-5   Revising Your Introduction
Writing in Progress

Directions: Revise the introduction to the essay you wrote for Exercise 17-3. ■

Writing the Conclusion

The final paragraph of your essay has two functions: It should reemphasize your thesis statement and draw the essay to a close. It should not be a direct announcement, such as "This essay has been about . . ." or "In this paper I hoped to show that . . ."

It's usually best to revise your essay at least once *before* working on the conclusion. During your first or second revision, you often make numerous changes in both content and organization, which may, in turn, affect your conclusion.

Here are a few effective ways to write a conclusion. Choose one that will work for your essay.

1. **Look ahead.** Project into the future and consider outcomes or effects.

2. **Return to your thesis.** If your essay is written to prove a point or convince your reader of the need for action, it may be effective to end with a sentence that recalls your main point or calls for action. If you choose this way to conclude, be sure not to merely repeat your first paragraph. Be sure to reflect on the thoughts you developed in the body of your essay.

3. **Summarize key points.** Especially for longer essays, briefly review your key supporting ideas. Notice how Tsoukalas's concluding paragraph touches upon each of her three main points: communication, socializing, and dating online.

If you have trouble writing your conclusion, it's probably a tip-off that you need to work further on your thesis or organization.

EXERCISE 17-6
Writing in Progress

Revising Your Conclusion

Directions: Write or revise a conclusion for the essay you wrote for Exercise 17-3. ■

Selecting a Title

Although the title appears first in your essay, it is often the last thing you should write. The title should identify the topic in an interesting way, and it may also suggest the focus. To select a title, reread your final draft, paying particular attention to your thesis statement and your overall method of development. Here are a few examples of effective titles:

"Which Way Is Up?" (for an essay on mountain climbing)

"A Hare Raising Tale" (for an essay on taking care of rabbits)

"Topping Your Bottom Line" (for an essay on how to increase profitability)

To write accurate and interesting titles, try the following tips:

1. **Write a question that your essay answers.** For example: "What Are the Signs That It's Safe to Approach a Strange Dog?"

2. **Use key words that appear in your thesis statement.** If your thesis statement is "Diets rich in lean beef can help teenagers maintain higher levels of useable iron," your title could be "Lean Beef Is Good for Teens."

3. **Use brainstorming techniques to generate options.** Don't necessarily go with the first title that pops into your mind. If in doubt, try out some options on friends to see which is most effective.

| **EXERCISE 17-7** | **Choosing a Title** |
| *Writing in Progress* | **Directions:** Come up with a good title for the essay you wrote for Exercise 17-3. ■ |

WRITING ESSAY-EXAM ANSWERS

GOAL 7 Analyze essay questions and plan answers

You can master the art of writing good essay-exam answers. The following suggestions and strategies will help:

1. **Read the directions carefully.** They may, for example, tell you to answer only two out of four questions.

2. **Plan your time.** For example, if you have to answer two essay questions in a 50-minute class session, give yourself 20 to 25 minutes for each one.

3. **Answer the easiest question first.** Doing so may take you less time than you budgeted, and consequently, you can spend additional time on harder questions.

4. **Analyze each question.** Look for words that tell you what to write about and how to organize your answer. If an exam question says, "Trace the history of advertising in the United States," the word *trace* tells you to organize your essay using a time-sequence arrangement. The question also identifies and focuses the topic—the history of advertising.

5. **Plan your answer.** On the back of the exam or on a separate sheet of paper that you will not turn in, jot down ideas you will include in your essay. Arrange your ideas to follow the method of development suggested in the question.

6. **Write your thesis statement.** A thesis statement is like a topic sentence. It announces what your essay will be about. Thesis statements in essay-exam answers should be simple and straightforward. Start by rewording the question.

SAMPLE ESSAY QUESTION	SAMPLE THESIS STATEMENT
Describe the psychological factors that may affect a person's decision to change jobs.	There are five psychological factors that may affect a person's decision to change jobs.
Define and give an example of age discrimination.	Age discrimination takes place whenever people are mistreated or unfairly judged simply because of how old they are.

7. **Present adequate supporting details.** Write a separate paragraph for each major supporting detail. Begin each paragraph with a topic sentence that introduces each new point. Each paragraph should provide relevant and sufficient support for the topic sentence.

8. **Proofread your answer.** Be sure to leave enough time to proofread your answer. Check for errors in spelling, punctuation, and grammar.

9. **If you run out of time . . .** If you run out of time before you have finished answering the last question, don't panic. Take the last minute or two to make a list or outline of the other points you planned to cover. Some instructors will give you partial credit for this outline.

Writing in a Visual Age

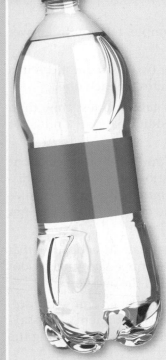

READING

Bottled water has become increasingly popular during the past 20 years. It is estimated that Americans drink almost 8 billion gallons of bottled water each year. Many people prefer the taste of bottled water to tap water. They also feel that bottled water is safer than tap water. But is it true that bottled water is safer than tap water?

The Environmental Protection Agency (EPA) sets and monitors the standards for city water systems. The EPA does not monitor water from private wells, but it publishes recommendations for well owners to help them maintain a safe water supply. In contrast, the Food and Drug Administration (FDA) regulates bottled water. It does not require that bottled water meet higher quality standards than public water. Bottled water is often treated and filtered differently than tap water, which changes its taste and appearance. But bottled water often comes from the same sources as city water.

Although bottled water may taste better than tap water, there is no evidence that it is safer to drink. Look closely at the label of your favorite bottled water. If the label states, "From a public water source," it has come directly from the tap! Some bottled waters may have more minerals than tap water, but there are no other additional nutritional benefits of drinking bottled water.

—Thompson and Manore, *Nutrition for Life*, p. 240.

1. Many essays have a thesis statement, but this reading has a "thesis question"—that is, it asks a question that the essay promises to answer. Underline the thesis question.

2. What do you think the benefits of using a "thesis question" might be for the reader? For the writer?

CRITICAL THINKING AND RESPONSE

3. The reading talks about the purity and taste of bottled water, but it does not mention one of the common criticisms of bottled water. Write a sentence in which you explain this criticism. (*Hint*: Think about the amount of garbage generated by all those bottles.)

WRITING

4. Write an effective, interesting title for the reading.

5. This reading contains an introduction and body paragraphs. Write a concluding paragraph that expresses your opinion about the topic.

USING VISUALS

6. Write a caption to accompany the illustration. Be sure it reflects the content of the essay, as well as your conclusion.

7. What other photos might have been useful to explain and illustrate this essay?

Essay Writing Scenarios

Friends and Family

1. Describe a family item you would save in the event of a natural disaster. Whose was it, and why is it special to you?

2. Write an essay that begins "The best vacation my family ever took together was . . ."

Classes and Campus Life

1. Mark Twain wrote, "The person who *does* not read good books has no advantage over the person who *can't* read them." Write a short essay explaining what you think he meant.

2. Where do you do your best work, in class discussions or alone on a computer? Why?

Working Students

1. Explain which you'd prefer, a job in which you deal with people or with things.

2. Describe something you do in your daily life that you would never do at work.

Communities and Cultures

1. Community leaders can be elected officials or ordinary citizens. Write an essay about one person who makes (or has made) a difference in your community.

2. Describe one thing you did as a teenager to fit in with a particular group.

WRITING ABOUT A READING

THINKING BEFORE READING

This selection first appeared in a December 2009 issue of *Forbes* magazine. Read the article to find out how and why one man is working to transform the field of artificial limbs. As you read, notice how the author structures the essay by developing a thesis statement and using supporting evidence and detail. Also notice the effective title, introduction, and conclusion.

1. Preview the reading, using the steps listed on p. 35.

2. Connect the reading to your own experience by answering the following questions:

   a. What recent medical advances are you aware of that are changing people's lives?

     b. Do you think injuries veterans of recent wars in the Middle East have suffered will put pressure on the U.S. government to increase funding and research in the field of prosthetics?

3. Mark and annotate as you read.

READING

A STEP BEYOND HUMAN

Andy Greenberg

1   On his way to a lunch meeting a few years ago Hugh Herr was running late. So he parked his Honda Accord in a handicapped parking spot, sprang out of the car and jogged down the sidewalk. Within seconds a policeman called out, asking to see his disability permit. When Herr pointed it out on his dashboard, the cop eyed him suspiciously. "What's your affliction?" he asked dryly.

2   Herr, a slim and unassuming 6-footer with dark, neatly parted hair, took a step toward the officer and responded in an even tone: "I have no [expletive] legs."

3   Blurring the boundaries of disability is a trick that Herr, director of the **biomechatronics** group at MIT's Media Lab, has spent the last 27 years perfecting. At age 17 both of Herr's legs were amputated 6 inches below the knee after a rock climbing trip ended in severe frostbite. Today he's one of the world's preeminent prosthetics experts. His goal: to build artificial limbs that are superior to natural ones. His favorite test subject: himself. "I like to say that there are no disabled people," says Herr, 45. "Only disabled technology."

4   Herr swaps his feet out to suit his needs. He generally walks on flat carbon-fiber springs inside his shoes but sometimes replaces them with longer carbon bows for jogging. When he goes rock climbing—often scaling cliffs of expert-level difficulty—he switches to one of multiple pairs of climbing legs he's built himself, including small, rubber feet on aluminum poles that stretch his height beyond 7 feet, spiked aluminum claws that replace **crampons** for ice climbing or tapered polyethylene hatchets that wedge into crevices. "The fact that I'm missing lower limbs is an opportunity," he says. "Between my residual limb and the ground, I can create anything I want. The only limits are physical laws and my imagination."

5   Over the last several years that imagination has been working overtime. Late next year iWalk, a company Herr founded in 2006, plans to release the PowerFoot One, the world's most advanced robotic ankle and foot. Most prosthetic feet are fixed at a clumsy 90 degrees. The PowerFoot, equipped with three internal microprocessors and 12 sensors that measure force, **inertia** and position, automatically adjusts its angle, stiffness and damping 500 times a second.

biomechatronics

an applied science combining biology, mechanics, and electronics

crampons

spikes attached to shoes for ice climbing.

inertia

the tendency of a body to stay at rest unless acted upon by an outside force.

Employing the same sort of sensory feedback loops that the human nervous system uses, plus a library of known patterns, the PowerFoot adjusts for slopes, dips its toe naturally when walking down stairs, even hangs casually when the user crosses his or her legs.

6   The PowerFoot is the only foot and ankle in the world that doesn't depend on its wearer's energy. With a system of passive springs and a half-pound rechargeable lithium iron phosphate battery, the foot—made of aluminum, titanium, plastic and carbon fiber—provides the same 20-joule push off the ground that human muscles and tendons do. It automatically adjusts the power to the walker's speed, but users can also dial that power up or down with a Bluetooth-enabled phone. (And soon, Herr says, with an iPhone application.) One test subject told Herr that his nonamputated leg often tires before his prosthetic-enhanced one. "This is the first time that the prosthesis is driving the human, instead of the other way around," says Herr.

7   Herr frequently wears a pair of his new creations. The next to try the PowerFoot will be the Department of Defense, which is looking for prostheses for the nearly 1,000 soldiers who have lost limbs in Iraq and Afghanistan. The Veterans Administration and the Army are among the investors who funded his MIT research. Veterans, he argues, also make the perfect early adopters, given their athletic, active lifestyles. "These are remarkable people," says Herr. "If the PowerFoot can work for them, it can work for anyone." iWalk hopes to put the PowerFoot on the general market in 2010, priced in the low five figures. The startup has raised $10.2 million from investors, including General Catalyst Partners and WFD Ventures.

8   Herr's motives extend beyond profit. In 1982 he and a friend climbed Mount Washington in New Hampshire, a place infamous for its unpredictable and nasty weather. They were caught in a snowstorm, losing their way in a near-complete whiteout and subzero temperatures. After three and a half days of crawling along a frozen river, Herr's lower legs were practically destroyed by cold. A member of the rescue team sent after them, 28-year-old Albert Dow, was killed in an avalanche. "I feel a responsibility to use my intellect and resources to do as much as I can to help people. That's Albert Dow's legacy for me," says Herr.

Cyborg evangelist: Herr wears a pair of his disability-defying PowerFoot devices.

9   Within three months of his amputations Herr was rock climbing with simple prosthetics. Within six months he was in a machine shop, building new feet, using the skills he'd learned at a vocational high school in Lancaster, Pa., where he grew up.

10   While he had previously focused on merely working a trade, Herr became a nearly obsessive student, earning a master's in mechanical engineering at MIT and a Ph.D. in biophysics at Harvard. Once, when his hands suffered from repetitive stress disorder while he was writing his doctoral thesis, he attached a pencil to a pair of sunglass frames and typed with his head. "He's driven to the point of exhaustion, physical degradation," says Rodger Kram, a professor of integrative physiology at the University of Colorado at Boulder, who worked with Herr at Harvard. "Every step he takes, he's forced to think about making prosthetics better."

11   Herr wants to transform how people define disability. Last year he sat on a panel of scientists that confirmed that Oscar Pistorius, a South African sprinter with no legs below the knee, should be allowed to compete in the Olympics. Herr helped discredit arguments that Pistorius got a metabolic advantage from his carbon-fiber legs. (Pistorius missed qualifying by a fraction of a second.)

12   Herr has tasted athletic discrimination, too. Because he uses special climbing prosthetics, many dispute his claim to be the second in the world to free-climb a famously challenging pitch near Index Mountain, Wash. "When amputees participate in sports, they call it courageous," he says. "Once you become competitive, they call it cheating." Herr even believes that in the coming decades **Paralympic** athletes will regularly outperform Olympic athletes. We may need special disability laws for humans who decline to have their bodies mechanically enhanced, he says.

Paralympic
related to an international competition for athletes with disabilities

13   "Disabled people today are the test pilots for technology that will someday be pervasive," Herr explains. "Eliminating disability and blurring man and machine will be one of the great stories of this century."

GETTING READY TO WRITE

Reviewing the Reading

Answer each of the following questions, using complete sentences.

1. Why were Herr's legs amputated?
2. How has Herr turned his disability into an advantage?
3. How does the Department of Defense plan to use Herr's invention?
4. How does Albert Dow motivate Herr?
5. How are prosthetics changing athletics?
6. What does Herr predict will be the future of prosthetics?

Examining the Reading Using an Idea Map

Review the reading by completing the missing parts of the idea map.

Title — **A Step Beyond Human**

Thesis — Hugh Herr had his legs amputated due to frostbite, and now spearheads research and development of artificial limbs.

_____

_____

He plans to release the Power Foot One, the most advanced robotic foot and ankle.

_____

_____

Herr is energetic and driven.

Herr was back climbing six months after his amputation.

Herr got several degrees to be able to do this type of work.

_____

Herr wants to transform how people define disability.

_____

_____

Conclusion — The technology used by disabled people today will someday be used by all people to expand their abilities.

Strengthening Your Vocabulary

Using the word's context, word parts, or a dictionary, write a brief definition of each of the following words or phrases as it is used in the reading.

1. affliction (paragraph 1) _____

2. preeminent (paragraph 3) _____

3. residual (paragraph 4) _____

4. vocational (paragraph 9) _____

5. degradation (paragraph 10) _____

6. pitch (paragraph 12) _____

7. pervasive (paragraph 13) _____

Reacting to Ideas: Discussion and Journal Writing

Get ready to write about the reading by discussing the following:

1. Write a paragraph about a time you turned a disadvantage into an advantage. How did you do so?

2. Explain how the title of the article relates to the subject. Can you think of another title that would also work for this article?

 **Thinking Visually**

3. What does the photograph on page 493 reveal about about Herr? What type of person do you think he is based on the photograph?

WRITING ABOUT THE READING

Paragraph Options

1. Write a paragraph about how you think most people tend to think about those who have prosthetic limbs. What is a common reaction?

2. Write a paragraph discussing whether a person should take on any responsibility when someone dies trying to help him or her.

3. Herr engaged in risky behavior and suffered the consequences. Write a paragraph explaining either the benefits or drawbacks of a risky situation in which you or someone you know was involved.

Essay Options

4. There have been advances in robotics that allow humans to exceed their biological limitations. Write an essay discussing the advantages and disadvantages of these technologies.

5. Herr is motivated to do his work because of what happened in his life. Write an essay explaining what in your life has motivated you to pursue an education in your field of study.

6. There are many movies, games, and books that fantasize about what could happen if human/robot combinations got out of control. Write an essay expressing and explaining your point of view about whether these combinations might be useful or dangerous, or both, and whether they should be controlled, and if so, how.

Revision Checklist

Paragraph Development

1. Is the topic manageable (neither too broad nor too narrow)?
2. Is the paragraph written with the reader in mind?
3. Does the topic sentence identify the topic?
4. Does the topic sentence make a point about the topic?
5. Does each sentence support the topic sentence?
6. Is there sufficient detail?
7. Is there a sentence at the end that brings the paragraph to a close?

Sentence Development

8. Are there any sentence fragments, run-on sentences, or comma splices?
9. Are ideas combined to produce more effective sentences?
10. Are adjectives and adverbs used to make the sentences vivid and interesting?
11. Are relative clauses and prepositional phrases like *-ing* phrases used to add detail?
12. Are pronouns used correctly and consistently?

Essay Development

13. Does the essay accomplish its purpose?
14. Is the essay appropriate for the audience?
15. Is the thesis statement clearly expressed?
16. Does each paragraph support the thesis?
17. Is the essay logically organized?
18. Are transitions used to connect your ideas?
19. Are the introduction, conclusion, and title effective?

CHAPTER REVIEW AND PRACTICE

CHAPTER REVIEW

To review and check your recall of the chapter, select the word or phrase from the box below that best fits in each of the following sentences. Keep in mind that not all words or phrases will be used.

direct announcements	paragraph	relevant	reemphasize
essay	group	interest	
topic	identify	main point	
delete	generate ideas	redirect	

1. One function of a thesis statement is to identify the _____.

2. You should _____ about your topic before writing your thesis statement.

3. An essay is similar to a _____ in structure.

4. One way to discover a thesis statement is to _____ your ideas generated by brainstorming or freewriting.

5. In writing thesis statements, you should avoid _____.

6. A thesis statement expresses the _____ of your essay.

7. Evidence that supports the thesis should be _____ and specific.

8. One function of an introduction is to _____ your reader.

9. The conclusion should _____ your thesis.

10. The title of an essay should _____ the topic of the essay.

 ## EDITING PRACTICE

The following paragraph lacks transitions to connect its details. Revise it by adding transitional words or phrases where useful.

Anyone who has been to a professional hockey game has a right to be disgusted. It is especially true if you have attended one in the past five years. Players are permitted to bash each other on the ice. They are allowed to get away with it. Sometimes players are encouraged to do this. Often they are encouraged by their coaches or other players. People are starting to object to paying good money to attend a game. This is especially true when most of what you get to see is a street fight. Hockey is a contact sport. It is understandable that arguments will break out among players. This causes tempers to flare. It is unfair to subject fans to a dramatic show of violence. Most of the fans have paid good money to watch the game, not the fights. The National Hockey League should fine and suspend players. They should do this each time they get into a fight. If they did this, soon the players would be playing hockey with appropriate sportsmanlike conduct instead of fighting.

PEARSON
mywritinglab

For support in meeting this chapter's objectives, log in to www.mywritinglab.com, go to the Study Plan tab, click on Essay Basics and Development and choose Recognizing the Essay, Thesis Statement, and Essay Introductions, Conclusions, and Titles from the list of subtopics. Read and view the videos and resources in the Review Materials section, and then complete the Recall, Apply, and Write exercises in the Activities section. You can check your scores and overall progress by using the Gradebook.

18

Avoiding Common Problems in Essays

WRITE ABOUT IT!

The skating rink sign shown above humorously demonstrates writing that is unclear and ineffective. Revise the sign to express what you think the writer probably meant. In your own writing, be sure to watch for errors and search for ways to make your sentences and paragraphs more effective. Once you know what to look for, it is also easy to spot errors and areas that need improvement in your essays. Even the best writers run into problems; it is not uncommon for writers to make several starts and numerous revisions before they are satisfied with what they have written. Sometimes they even scrap what they have written and start afresh. In this chapter you will learn how to identify and fix five key problems you may encounter in writing essays. Specifically, you will learn to identify and fix topics that are too broad or too narrow, ineffective thesis statements, underdeveloped essays, and disorganized essays. You will also learn to use revision maps to evaluate your essays.

WRITING

PROBLEM #1: THE TOPIC IS TOO BROAD

GOAL 1 Choose a topic that is not too broad

mywritinglab

To practice essay revision, go to
■ Study Plan
■ The Essay
■ Revising the Essay

One common mistake in writing an essay is choosing a topic that is too broad. No matter how hard you work, if you begin with a topic that is too broad, you will not be able to produce a successful essay. If your topic is too broad, there will be too much information to include, and you will not be able to cover all the important points with the right amount of detail.

Suppose you are taking a sociology class and have been asked to write a two-page paper on your impression of campus life so far. If you just wrote down the title "Campus Life" and started writing, you would find that you had too much to say and probably would not know where to start. Should you write about your classes, meeting new friends, adjusting to differences between high school and college, or managing living arrangements? Here are a few more examples of topics that are too broad:

- Pollution (Choose one type and focus on causes or effects.)
- Vacations (Choose one trip and focus on one aspect of the trip, such as meeting new people.)
- Movies (Choose one movie and concentrate on one feature, such as character development, plot, or humor.)

How to Identify the Problem

Here are the symptoms of a topic that is too broad:

1. **You have too much to say.** If it seems as if you could go on and on about the topic, it is probably too broad.

2. **You feel overwhelmed.** If you feel the topic is too difficult or the task of writing about it is unmanageable, you may have too much to write about. Another possibility is that you have chosen a topic about which you do not know enough.

3. **You are not making progress.** If you feel stuck, your topic may be too broad. It also may be too narrow (see Problem #2 above).

4. **You are writing general statements and not explaining them.** Having too much to cover forces you to make broad, sweeping statements that you cannot explain in sufficient depth.

How to Narrow a Broad Topic

One way to narrow a topic that is too broad is to divide it into subtopics using the topic-narrowing techniques shown in Chapter 11, p. 296. Then choose one subtopic and use it to develop new ideas for your essay.

Another way to limit a broad topic is to answer questions that will limit it. Here are six questions that are useful in limiting your topic to a particular place, time, kind, or type:

1. Who?
2. What?
3. When?
4. Where?
5. Why?
6. How?

Suppose your topic is job hunting. You realize it is too broad and apply the questions below.

	Topic: Job Hunting
QUESTIONS	EXAMPLES
Who?	Who can help me with job hunting? (This question limits the topic to people and agencies that offer assistance.)
What?	What type of job am I seeking? (This question limits the topic to a specific occupation.)
When?	When is the best time to job hunt? (This question limits the topic to a particular time frame, such as right after graduation.)
Where?	Where is the best place to find job listings? (This question limits the topic to one source of job listings, such as the Internet.)
Why?	Why is it important to network with friends and family? (This question limits the topic to one way to search for jobs.)
How?	How should I prepare my résumé? (This question limits the topic to one aspect of job hunting.)

EXERCISE 18-1
Working Together

Narrowing a Topic

Directions: Working with a classmate, narrow three of the following topics to one aspect that is manageable in a two-page essay.

1. Athletics
2. Public education
3. The military
4. The change of seasons
5. Television programming
6. Crime
7. Principles to live by
8. Children's toys ■

PROBLEM #2: THE TOPIC IS TOO NARROW

GOAL 2 Choose a topic that is not too narrow

Another common mistake is to choose a topic that is too narrow. If you decide to write about the effects of the failure of Canada geese to migrate from western New York during the winter, you will probably run out of ideas, unless you are prepared to do extensive library or Internet research. Instead, broaden your topic to the migration patterns of Canada geese. Here are a few more examples of topics that are too narrow:

- The history of corn mazes in the Ohio River valley
- Shopping on eBay for designer handbags
- The attitude of a nasty receptionist at the veterinarian's office

How to Identify the Problem

Here are the symptoms of a topic that is too narrow:

1. **After a paragraph or two, you have nothing left to say.** If you run out of ideas and keep repeating yourself, your topic is probably too narrow.

2. **Your topic does not seem important.** If your topic seems insignificant, it probably is. One reason it may be insignificant is that it focuses on facts rather than ideas.

3. **You are making little or no progress.** A lack of progress may signal a lack of information.

4. **Your essay is too factual.** If you find you are focusing on small details, your topic may be too narrow.

How to Broaden a Narrow Topic

To broaden a topic that is too narrow, try to extend it to cover more situations or circumstances. If your topic is the price advantage of shopping for your chemistry textbook on the Internet, broaden it to include various other benefits of Internet shopping for textbooks. Discuss price, but also consider convenience and free shipping. Do not limit yourself to one type of textbook. Specifically, to broaden a topic that is too narrow:

1. **Think of other situations, events, or circumstances that illustrate the same idea.**

2. **Think of a larger concept that includes your topic.**

EXERCISE 18-2   Broadening a Topic

Directions: Broaden three of the following topics to ones that are manageable in a two-page essay.

1. A groom who wore sneakers to his formal wedding
2. Materials needed for _____ (a craft or hobby)
3. Your parents' attitude toward crime
4. Your local high school's dress code that prohibits short skirts
5. An annoying advertisement
6. A friend's pet peeve
7. A child's first word
8. Missing a deadline for a college psychology paper ■

PROBLEM #3: THE THESIS STATEMENT NEEDS REVISION

GOAL 3 Revise your thesis statement so it clearly states your purpose

The best time to evaluate and, if necessary, revise your thesis statement is after you have written a first draft. At that time you can see if your essay delivers what your thesis promises. If it does not, it needs revision, or you need to refocus your essay.

How to Identify the Problem

Here are the characteristics of a weak thesis statement:

1. **The essay does not explain and support the thesis.**
2. **The thesis statement does not cover all the topics included in the essay.**
3. **The thesis statement is vague or unclear.**
4. **The thesis statement makes a direct announcement.**

How to Revise Your Thesis Statement

When evaluating your thesis statement, ask the following questions:

1. **Does my essay develop and explain my thesis statement?** As you write an essay, its focus and direction may change. Revise your thesis statement to reflect any changes. If you discover that you drifted away from your original thesis and you want to maintain it, work on revising so that your paper delivers what your thesis statement promises.

2. **Is my thesis statement broad enough to cover all the points I made in the essay?** As you develop your first draft, you may find that one idea leads naturally to another. Both must be covered by the thesis statement. For example, suppose your thesis statement is "Because of the number of patients our clinic sees in a day, the need for nurse practitioners has increased dramatically." If, in your essay, you discuss lab technicians and interns as well as nurses, then you need to broaden your thesis statement.

3. **Does my thesis statement use vague or unclear words that do not clearly focus the topic?** For example, in the thesis statement "Physical therapy can help bursitis," the word *help* is vague and does not suggest how your essay will approach the topic. Instead, if your paper discusses the effectiveness of physical therapy, this approach should be reflected in your thesis: "When it comes to chronic bursitis, deep tissue massage by a trained physical therapist can be very effective."

EXERCISE 18-3   Evaluating and Revising Thesis Statements

Directions: Identify what is wrong with each of the following thesis statements and revise each one to make it more effective.

1. Most people like to dance.
2. Call the doctor when you're sick.
3. Everyone should read the newspaper.
4. It's important to keep your receipts.
5. Driving in snow is dangerous. ■

EXERCISE 18-4

Writing in Progress

Writing a Thesis Statement

Directions: Choose one of the topics you worked with in Exercise 18-1 or 18-2. Generate ideas about the topic and write a tentative thesis statement. ■

PROBLEM #4: THE ESSAY IS UNDERDEVELOPED

GOAL 4 Add evidence to under-developed essays

An underdeveloped essay is one that lacks sufficient information and evidence to support the thesis.

How to Identify the Problem

Here are the characteristics of an underdeveloped essay:

Tip for Writers

Ramble means "talk or write a lot without staying on one point or making your main idea clear." *Unfocused* suggests the same problem.

1. The essay seems to ramble or is <u>unfocused.</u>
2. The essay repeats information or says the same thing in slightly different ways.
3. The essay makes general statements but does not support them.
4. The essay lacks facts, examples, comparisons, or reasons.

How to Revise an Underdeveloped Essay

Use the following suggestions to revise an underdeveloped essay:

1. **Delete sentences that are repetitious and add nothing to the essay.** If you find you have little or nothing left, do additional brainstorming, freewriting, or branching to discover new ideas. If this technique does not work, consider changing your topic to one about which you have more to say.
2. **Make sure your topic is not too broad or too narrow.** If it is, use the suggestions for topic revision given earlier in the chapter on p. 501 and p. 503.
3. **Go through your essay sentence by sentence and highlight any ideas that you could further develop and explain.** Develop these ideas into separate paragraphs.
4. **Make sure each topic sentence is clear and specific.** Then add details to each paragraph that make it sharp and convincing.

EXERCISE 18-5

Writing in Progress

Writing an Essay

Directions: Using the thesis statement you wrote in Exercise 18-4, write an essay. Then evaluate and revise it, if necessary, using the suggestions given above. ■

PROBLEM #5: THE ESSAY IS DISORGANIZED

GOAL 5 Restructure disorganized essays and add transitions

A disorganized essay is one that does not follow a logical method of development. A disorganized essay makes it difficult for your readers to follow your train of thought. If readers must struggle to follow your ideas, they may stop reading or lose their concentration. In fact, as they struggle to follow your thinking, they may miss important information or misinterpret what you are saying.

How to Identify the Problem

Use the following questions to help you evaluate the organization of your essay:

1. Does every paragraph in the essay support or explain your thesis statement?
2. Do you avoid straying from your topic?
3. Does each detail in each paragraph explain the topic sentence?
4. Do you make it clear how one idea relates to another by using transitions?

How to Revise Disorganized Essays

To improve the organization of your essay, use one of the methods of organization discussed in Chapter 14. Here is a brief review:

METHOD OF ORGANIZATION	PURPOSE
Narration	Presents events in the order in which they happened
Description	Gives descriptive, sensory details
Example	Explains a situation or idea by giving circumstances that illustrate it
Definition	Explains the meaning of a term by giving its class and distinguishing characteristics
Comparison and Contrast	Focuses on similarities and differences
Classification	Explains by organizing a topic into groups or categories
Process	Describes the order in which things are done
Cause and Effect	Explains why things happen or what happens as a result of something else
Argument	Gives reasons to support a claim

Once you have chosen and used a method of development, be sure to use appropriate transitions to connect your ideas.

Another way to spot and correct organizational problems is to draw an idea or revision map as discussed on the next page. Using a map will help you visualize the progression of your ideas graphically and see which ideas fit and which do not.

EXERCISE 18-6	**Evaluating Organization**
Writing in Progress	**Directions:** Evaluate the organization of the essay you wrote in Exercise 18-5. Revise it using the suggestions given above. ■

USING MAPS TO GUIDE YOUR REVISION

GOAL 6 Use idea maps as revision tools

In Chapter 16, "Using an Idea Map to Spot Revision Problems," you learned to draw revision maps to evaluate paragraphs. The same strategy works well for essays, too. A revision map will help you evaluate the overall flow of your ideas as well as the effectiveness of individual paragraphs.

To draw an essay revision map, begin by listing your title at the top of the page. Write your thesis statement underneath it, and then list the topic of each paragraph. Next, work through each paragraph, recording your ideas in abbreviated form. Then write the key words of your conclusion. If you find details that do not support the topic sentence, record those details to the right of the map. Use the model on p. 508 as a guide.

When you've completed your revision map, conduct the following tests:

1. **Read your thesis statement along with your first topic sentence.** Does the topic sentence clearly support your thesis? If not, revise it to make the relationship clearer. Repeat this step for each topic sentence.

2. **Read your topic sentences, one after the other, without reading the corresponding details.** Is there a logical connection between them? Have you arranged them in the most effective way? If not, revise to make the connection clearer or to improve your organization.

3. **Examine each individual paragraph.** Are there enough relevant, specific details to support the topic sentence?

4. **Read your introduction and then look at your topic sentences.** Does the essay deliver what the introduction promises?

5. **Read your thesis statement and then your conclusion.** Are they compatible and consistent? Does the conclusion agree with and support the thesis statement?

EXERCISE 18-7	**Drawing a Revision Map**
Writing In Progress	**Directions:** Draw a revision map of the essay you wrote and revised in Exercises 18-5 and 18-6. Make further revisions as needed. ■

 **Visualize It!**

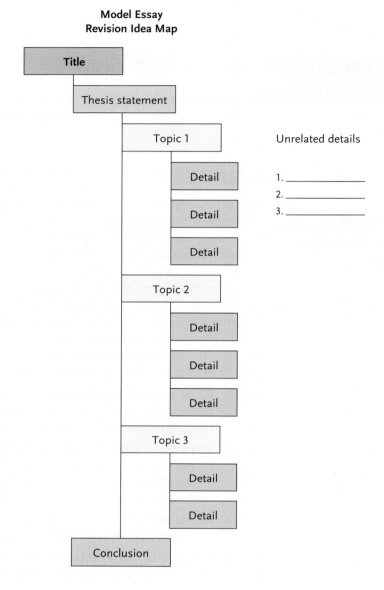

Model Essay
Revision Idea Map

SEEKING FURTHER HELP

GOAL 7 Seek help from classmates, your instructors, and a writing lab

If the suggestions offered in this chapter do not help you solve a problem with a particular essay, be sure to use the following resources:

- **Your classmates.** Ask a classmate to read your essay and make comments and suggestions.
- **Your instructor.** Visit your instructor during office hours. Take a draft of your paper with you and have specific questions in mind.
- **The writing lab.** Many campuses have a writing lab where students can get help with papers. Take your draft with you and ask for feedback and revision ideas.

Analyze It!

Directions: A student wrote the following outline for an essay on American beauty pageants. Study the outline and identify what is wrong with it. Cross out details that do not support the thesis statement or do not belong where they are placed in the outline. You may add new details, if needed.

Essay Title: "Women's Beauty Pageants in the United States"

I. **Introduction**
   A. History of U.S. beauty pageants
      1. Miss America Pageant
      2. International Beauty Pageants
      3. Miss USA Pageant

   B. **Thesis statement: Woman's beauty pageants are unfair to women and unhealthy for their participants.**

II. **Body of Essay**
   A. Drawbacks outweigh benefits
      1. Such entertainment is harmful to women
      2. Not best way to support charities and worthy causes

   B. Content rules
      1. Swimsuit and evening gown competition
      2. Age limitations
      3. Talent contests
      4. Men not similarly judged on their looks

   C. Pageants create biased, unfair standards of beauty
      1. Western standards of beauty are used
      2. Racial and ethnic groups not widely represented
      3. Talent and congeniality carry little weight in judging

   D. Contest sponsors
      1. Commercial advertisers
      2. Other types of promoters

   E. Pageants are degrading for women
      1. Create "cattle show" mentality
      2. Undermine the goals and progress of women's rights

   F. Pageants promote physically unhealthy practices
      1. Pressure to become thin creates health problems
         a. Anorexia
         b. Other eating disorders
         c. Liposuction
      2. Little emphasis on women's intelligence, talent, character, skills

III. **Conclusion**
   A. Surprising that beauty pageants are still so popular worldwide
   B. Women should not support these pageants

A STUDENT ESSAY

The Writer

Aurora Gilbert attends Columbia University, where she plans to major in Sociology. She hopes to attend graduate school for public health and go on to work for global health in Latin America.

The Writing Task

Gilbert wrote this essay as part of her application process to Columbia University. She was careful to write a coherent, correct essay that also demonstrated that she is a serious, intellectually capable student with diverse interests and goals.

Title suggests thesis

From Ignorant Bliss to Painful Awareness
Aurora Gilbert

Introduction: Gilbert describes an engaging scene to interest her readers

1   Warmth and sunlight washed over me as I cracked open my eyes, still trapped in the serenity between sleep and consciousness. I smelled the smoky warmth of the cooking fire and I heard what sounded like a million voices chattering in Spanish on the other side of my bedroom wall. A gaggle of young children came bouncing into my room and swarmed my bed, jumping up and down, yelling "¡Aurora, Aurora!" I pretended to still be asleep, yet the enthusiasm in their voices overwhelmed my emotions and forced a smile to my face, and I could no longer lie in bed. Pushing through my mosquito net, I yelled "¡Buenos días!" to anyone who could hear me, and I was ready to take on the day that awaited.

Topic sentence

Background information on living in DR

2   For one month, I followed this same routine as I stayed with a family in the small village of Gualete in the Dominican Republic (DR). I held daily English classes for the locals and attempted to immerse myself in a culture completely different from my own. Though I had been doing service work at food banks and shelters around Seattle for years, I was new to the experience of immersion. For the first time, I lived the lives of the people I served. The concept of complete isolation from my world in the United States was terrifying at first, but I soon found myself infatuated with the DR.

Topic sentence

3   The love, the music, and the dancing of this culture overtook and enveloped me, but not for long. They swept me into a place where suffering is obscured from view, and I forgot that the world around me was anything but a perfect dream. Then one day, I saw the boy across the street come home late, carrying a familiar-looking wooden box. I realized that he was one of the shoeshine boys who begged me for money in the larger towns and who are often forced into prostitution. I learned that some of the local children had just been abandoned by their mother for four days, left alone in their house, starving and dirty. I noticed that food was running short because my family barely had enough money for three meals a day.

Thesis statement   4   What once was ignorant bliss became painful awareness. I was furious that these Dominicans must live in such undeserved despair, and frustrated with myself for not realizing earlier the dark truth behind the veil of carefree customs. Every act of generosity shown to me by these people made me feel sick with guilt. I felt discouraged and lost in the face of such a severe situation, yet a glint of hope revealed itself in my clouded perspective. Although the people of Gualete are the most impoverished people I've ever met, they are also the most compassionate and grateful, which inspired me like nothing ever had before.

Conclusion: Gilbert reflects on her experience and its meaning   5   As I stood outside of my house on the last day of my trip with my sisters in my arms and tears streaming down my cheeks, I promised myself that I would never forget these people. The feeling that pervaded my senses was no longer one of blind happiness or anger, but one of understanding and determination. Now home in Seattle, when I help the Latinos at the food bank or work with Spanish-speaking kids at the local elementary school, I am momentarily transported back to that land of love and life, poverty and despair; the flame of passion in my heart flares even higher as I am reminded that my work is completely worth it, but only just beginning.

EXAMINING STUDENT WRITING

1. How did Gilbert organize her essay?
2. The thesis statement appears relatively late in the essay. Evaluate this placement.
3. Highlight several transitional words and phrases that Gilbert uses to connect her ideas.
4. Highlight three places where Gilbert uses descriptive details effectively.
5. Examine Gilbert's last sentence. Is this an effective conclusion?

Writing in a Visual Age

READING

Do unto others as you would have them do unto you. This golden rule is something that is often heard but also often forgotten when we deal with other people. Respect in the workplace encompasses many things, but first and foremost it must result in a comfortable workplace environment. A comfortable work environment is one in which team members feel they are evaluated and judged by their performance and not their race, gender, or personal beliefs. It is a work environment that develops all team members to their fullest potential. Team members in a golden rule environment will not do things because they fear the consequences. Rather, team members will do things because they want success for everyone, including themselves and the business. One admirable goal is to drive fear out of the workplace, so that everyone may work effectively. Chris Allen, a spokesman for the successful Chipotle restaurant chain, stated in an interview that "A funny thing happens when you treat people like responsible, capable, and highly performing individuals: That's exactly how they operate."

—adapted from Chesser and Cullen, *The World of Culinary Supervision, Training, and Management*, p. 76.

1. According to the authors, what is the "golden rule" of creating a comfortable workplace environment?

2. The reading includes one example of sexist language. Underline it.

CRITICAL THINKING AND RESPONSE

3. The authors say that fear must be driven out of the workplace. What do they mean by "fear"? Can you think of any instances where fear would actually be a good thing in the workplace?

WRITING

4. The authors have condensed an entire essay into one paragraph! Using what you have learned in this chapter, rewrite the essay, adding an introduction, body paragraphs, and a conclusion. Feel free to use examples from your own experience.

5. Write an essay in which you describe your favorite job or your least favorite job. Include all the elements of a good essay: a title, a thesis statement, support for your topic sentences, and a conclusion.

USING VISUALS

6. Look at the photo and write a note to the man on the left telling him what he is doing wrong.

7. Write a caption for the photo, linking the photo to the reading or to your revision of the reading.

Caption: _____

_____

_____

8. Sometimes writers will include two photos—one showing the right way to do something and one showing the wrong way. What type of photo would you choose to show your readers the proper way to develop respect in the workplace?

Essay Writing Scenarios

Friends and Family

1. Compare the jobs your grandparents held with those your parents hold. How has the level and type of job changed over time? What does this change suggest about family growth and change?

2. Write an essay about where you preferred to play as a child; at a park or playground, in a backyard, on a street, at a friend's house, etc.

Classes and Campus Life

1. What kind of person is attracted to your major? Describe the qualities someone should have if he or she is interested in this field.

2. Write an essay about something you did really well in high school.

Working Students

1. Many students work and attend college at the same time. What skills does it take to balance school and work?

2. Write an essay about what you will look for in your next job. How will it be different from the job you have currently?

Communities and Cultures

1. Traditionally, men and women have had very different roles in different cultures. Write an essay about one thing that only women used to do in your culture that men now also do, or vice versa.

2. People do many things to show off their status in a community. Describe one thing that people buy, drive, or wear to show that they are important.

WRITING ABOUT A READING

THINKING BEFORE READING

Humorist Brian Doyle write this piece, "Irreconcilable Dissonance: The Threat of Divorce as the Glue of Marriage," about marriage and divorce. As you read, pay attention to the author's use of humor.

1. Preview the reading, using the steps discussed in Chapter 2, p. 35.

2. Connect the reading to your own experience by answering the following questions:

   a. Are you or anyone you know divorced? What were the reasons for the divorce?

   b. What do you think makes a marriage last?

3. Mark and annotate as you read.

READING

IRRECONCILABLE DISSONANCE: THE THREAT OF DIVORCE AS THE GLUE OF MARRIAGE

Brian Doyle

irreconcilable
incompatible, not capable of getting along

dissonance
clashing of things that are very different

pregnant
full of, filled

chaotic
confused, disoriented

1   I have been married once to the woman to whom I am still married, so far, and one thing I have noticed about being married is that it makes you a lot more attentive to divorce, which used to seem like something that happened to other people, but doesn't anymore, because of course every marriage is **pregnant** with divorce, and also now I know a lot of people who are divorced, or are about to be, or are somewhere in between those poles, for which shadowy status there should be words like mivorced or darried or sleeperated or schleperated, but there aren't, so far.

2   People seem to get divorced for all sorts of reasons, and I find myself taking notes, probably defensively, but also out of sheer amazement at the **chaotic** wilderness of human nature. For example, I read recently about one man who got divorced so he could watch all sixty episodes of *The Wire* in chronological order. Another man got divorced after thirty years so he could, he said, fart in peace. Another man got divorced in part because he told his wife he had an affair, but he didn't have an affair, he just couldn't think of any other good excuse to get divorced, and he didn't want to have an affair, or be with anyone else other than his wife, because he liked his wife, and rather enjoyed her company as a rule, he said, but he just didn't want to be married to her every day anymore, he preferred to be married to her every second or third day, but she did not find that a workable arrangement, and so they parted company, confused.

3   Another man I read about didn't want to get divorced, he said, but when his wife kept insisting that they get divorced because she had fallen in love with another guy, he, the husband, finally agreed to get divorced, and soon after he found himself dating the other guy's first wife; as the first guy said, who could invent such a story?

4   I read about a woman who divorced her husband because he picked his nose. I read about a woman who got divorced because her husband never remembered to pay their property taxes and finally, she said, it was just too much. Is it so very much to ask, she asked, that the person who shares responsibility for your life remembers to pay your joint taxes? Does this have to be a crisis every year? She seemed sort of embarrassed to say what she said, but she said it.

5   It seems to me that the reasons people divorce are hardly ever for the dramatic reasons that we assume are the reasons people get divorced, like snorting cocaine for breakfast or discovering that the minister named Bernard who you married ten years ago is actually

...honestly I just feel like we don't communicate like we used to!

a former convict named Ezzard with a wife in Wisconsin, according to the young detective who sat down in your office at the accounting firm one morning and sounded embarrassed about some things he had come to tell you that you should know.

6   I read about a couple who got divorced because of "irresolute differences," a phrase that addled me for weeks. Another couple filed for divorce on the grounds of irreconcilable dissonance, which seemed like one of those few times in life when the exact right words are applied to the exact right reason for those words. I read about another woman who divorced her husband because one time they were walking down the street, the husband on the curb side in accordance with the ancient courteous male custom of being on that side so as to receive the splatter of mud or worse from the street and keep such splatter from the pristine acreage of his beloved, and as they approached a fire hydrant he lifted his leg, puppylike, as a joke, and she marched right to their lawyer's office and instituted divorce proceedings. That particular woman refused to speak to reporters about the reasons for divorce, but you wonder what the iceberg was under that surface, you know?

7   The first divorce I saw up close, like the first car crash you see up close, is imprinted on the inside of my eyelids, and I still think about it, not because it happened, but because years after it happened it seems so fated to have happened. How could it be that two people who really liked each other, and who took a brave crazy leap on not just living together, which lots of mammals do, but swearing fealty and respect in front of a huge crowd, and filing taxes as a joint entity, and spawning a child, and cosigning mortgages and car loans, how could they end up signing settlement papers on the dining room table and then wandering out into the muddy garden to cry? How could that be?

8   The saddest word I've heard wrapped around divorce like a tattered blanket is tired, as in "We were both just tired," because being tired seems so utterly normal to me, so much the rug always bunching in that one spot no matter what you do, the slightly worn dish rack, the belt with extra holes punched with an ice pick that you borrowed from your cousin for exactly this purpose, the flashlight in the pantry that has never had batteries and never will, that the thought of tired being both your daily bread and also grounds for divorce gives me the willies. The shagginess of things, the way they never quite work out as planned and break down every other Tuesday, necessitating wine and foul language and duct tape and the wrong-size screw quietly hammered into place with the bottom of the garden gnome, seems to me the very essence of marriage; so if what makes a marriage work (the constant shifting of expectations and eternal parade of small surprises) is also what causes marriages to dissolve, where is it safe to stand?

9   Nowhere, of course. Every marriage is pregnant with divorce, every day, every hour, every minute. The second you finish reading this essay, your spouse could close the refrigerator, after miraculously finding a way to wedge the juice carton behind the milk jug, and call it quits, and the odd truth of the matter is that because she might end your marriage in a moment, and you might end hers, you're still married. The instant there is no chance of death is the moment of death.

GETTING READY TO WRITE

Reviewing the Reading

Answer each of the following questions using complete sentences.

1. Why does Doyle begin his essay by explaining his marital status in the way that he does?

2. What does Doyle think about the reasons he has heard about for divorces?

3. What is Doyle's response to the idea that people divorce because they are tired?

Examining the Reading Using an Idea Map

Review the reading by filling in the missing parts of the idea map below.

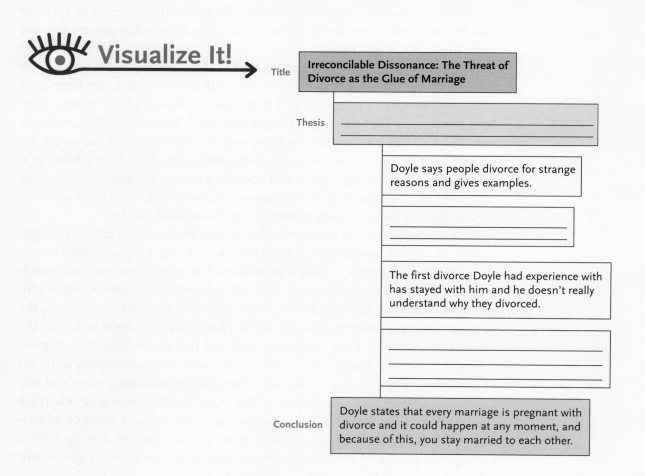

Visualize It!

Title — **Irreconcilable Dissonance: The Threat of Divorce as the Glue of Marriage**

Thesis — _____

Doyle says people divorce for strange reasons and gives examples.

_____

The first divorce Doyle had experience with has stayed with him and he doesn't really understand why they divorced.

_____

Conclusion — Doyle states that every marriage is pregnant with divorce and it could happen at any moment, and because of this, you stay married to each other.

Strengthening Your Vocabulary

Using the word's context, word parts, or a dictionary, write a brief definition of each of the following words as it is used in the reading.

1. irresolute (paragraph 6) _____

2. pristine (paragraph 6) _____

3. fealty (paragraph 7) _____

4. spawning (paragraph 7) _____

5. willies (paragraph 8) _____

Reacting to Ideas: Discussion and Journal Writing

Get ready to write about the reading by discussing the following:

1. Consider what we expect divorce to be. Must it always be chaotic and angry?

2. Discuss Doyle's writing. Do you think he's funny? Do you think divorce is a topic appropriate for humor?

3. Write about the reasons that caused you to suddenly not like a friend or family member at one point. Were those reasons enough to end your relationship with each other?

 **Thinking Visually**   4. Discuss how the cartoon relates and adds to the article.

WRITING ABOUT THE READING

Paragraph Options

1. Write a paragraph describing a divorce you know about. What were the reasons? Do you think they were justified? How do they compare to the reasons Doyle offers?

2. Doyle compares marriage and divorce with life and death. How are they alike? How does the prospect of divorce or death make marriage or life better? Write a paragraph discussing this.

Essay Options

3. Do you believe that any marriage could just suddenly end without warning? Do you think people who are married think about divorce often as Doyle suggests? Write an essay discussing this.

4. Why do you think the divorce rate is so high? Write an essay discussing the reasons.

Revision Checklist

Paragraph Development

1. Is the topic manageable (neither too broad nor too narrow)?
2. Is the paragraph written with the reader in mind?
3. Does the topic sentence identify the topic?
4. Does the topic sentence make a point about the topic?
5. Does each sentence support the topic sentence?
6. Is there sufficient detail?
7. Is there a sentence at the end that brings the paragraph to a close?

Sentence Development

8. Are there any sentence fragments, run-on sentences, or comma splices?
9. Are ideas combined to produce more effective sentences?
10. Are adjectives and adverbs used to make the sentence vivid and interesting?
11. Are relatives claused and prepositional phrases lice -*ing* phrases used to add detail?
12. Are pronouns used correctly and consistently?

Essay Development

13. Does the essay accomplish its purpose?
14. Is the essay appropriate for the audience?
15. Is the thesis statement clearly expressed?
16. Does each paragraph support the thesis?
17. Is the essay logically organized?
18. Are there transitions to connect the ideas?
19. Are the introduction, conclusion, and title effective?

CHAPTER REVIEW AND PRACTICE

CHAPTER REVIEW

To review and check your recall of the chapter, match each item in Column A with its meaning in Column B.

COLUMN A

_____ 1. underdeveloped essay

_____ 2. broad topic

_____ 3. narrow topic-

_____ 4. disorganized essay

_____ 5. revision map

_____ 6. ineffective thesis statement

_____ 7. vague thesis statement

_____ 8. an essay that repeats the same information over and over

_____ 9. asking the questions Who?, What?, When?, Where?, Why?, and How?

_____ 10. thinking of other situations or events that illustrate your topic

COLUMN B

a. an essay that does not follow a logical train of thought

b. an essay in which the topic is too narrow

c. method for broadening a topic

d. an essay that does not support and explain its thesis

e. one that does not cover all the points made in the essay

f. a topic that covers too much

g. ways to narrow a topic that is too broad

h. a topic that is too specific or detailed

i. a diagram that helps you evaluate and improve your essay

j. one that does not suggest how the essay will approach the topic

EDITING PRACTICE

Paragraph 1

The narrative paragraph on the next page is weak because it lacks focus and only retells events. Revise it by fleshing out the details and focusing them so they make a point.

Last summer my family took a trip to the Canadian Rockies. We flew to Chicago and then to Calgary. Then we took a train into the mountains. We stopped at Banff first. The next part of the trip was long and very scenic. We crossed a number of rivers, rode along riverbanks, and went through tunnels. At the end of the first day, we stayed in Kamloops, British Columbia. The next day, we traveled down the mountains to Vancouver and arrived there in the afternoon. We were tired, but we had fun.

Paragraph 2

The following paragraph contains a weak topic sentence. Revise this sentence to make it stronger.

It is good to study history. First, studying history gives you a new way of looking at your own life. When you learn about the past, you begin to see that your lifetime is only part of a larger picture. Second, history can help you understand problems better. You begin to see why the world is as it is and what events caused it to be this way. Finally, history allows you to think of yourself in a different way. In looking at everything that has happened before us, we as individuals seem small and unimportant.

PEARSON
mywritinglab

For support in meeting this chapter's objectives, log in to www.mywritinglab.com, go to the Study Plan tab, click on Avoiding Common Problems in Essays and choose Essay Organization, Revising the Essay, and Editing the Essay from the list of subtopics. Read and view the videos and resources in the Review Materials section, and then complete the Recall, Apply, and Write exercises in the Activities section. You can check your scores and overall progress by using the Gradebook.

PART VII

Readings: Read and Respond

WRITING ABOUT A READING

Thinking Before Reading

The author of this article has written several books on the link between diet and health. In the following reading, he examines a new partnership between a famous fried chicken restaurant chain and a breast cancer advocacy group. Before you read:

1. Preview the reading, using the steps discussed in Chapter 2, p. 35.

2. Connect the reading to your own experience by answering the following questions:

    a. How often do you eat fast food? Are you concerned about the effects of fast food on your health?

    b. What do you already know about Susan G. Komen for the Cure?

3. Mark and annotate as you read.

READING

GREED, CANCER, AND PINK KFC BUCKETS

John Robbins

grassroots
involving ordinary people at a local or community level

1   We live in a world of profound contradictions. Some things are just unbelievably strange. At times I feel like I've found a way to adapt to the weirdness of the world, and then along comes something that just boggles my mind. The largest **grassroots** breast cancer advocacy group in the world, a group called "Susan G. Komen for the Cure," has now partnered with the fast food chain KFC in a national "Buckets for the Cure" campaign. The program began last month and runs through the end of May.

2   KFC is taking every chance it can manufacture to trumpet the fact that it will donate 50 cents to Komen for every pink bucket of chicken sold. For its part, Komen is announcing on its website that "KFC and Susan G. Komen for the Cure are teaming up . . . to . . . spread educational messaging via a major national campaign which will reach thousands of communities served by nearly 5,000 KFC restaurants."

3   Educational messaging, indeed. How often do you think this "messaging" provides information about the critical importance a healthy diet plays in maintaining a healthy weight and preventing cancer? How often do you think it refers in any way to the many studies that, according to the National Cancer Institute's website, "have shown that an increased risk of developing colorectal, pancreatic, and breast cancer is associated with high intakes of well-done, fried or barbecued meats?" If you guessed zero, you're right.

4   Meanwhile, the American Institute for Cancer Research reports that 60 to 70 percent of all cancers can be prevented with lifestyle changes. Their number one dietary recommendation is to: "Choose predominantly plant-based diets rich in a variety of vegetables and fruits, legumes and minimally processed

egregious
outrageously bad

pinkwashing
using support for breast cancer research to sell products, especially products that can be linked with cancer

starchy staple foods." Does that sound like pink buckets of fried chicken?

5 Pardon me for being cynical, but I have to ask, if Komen is going to partner with KFC, why not take it a step further and partner with a cigarette company? They could sell pink packages of cigarettes, donating a few cents from each pack while claiming "each pack you smoke brings us closer to the day cancer is vanquished forever."

6 Whose brilliant idea was it that buying fried chicken by the bucket is an effective way to fight breast cancer? One breast cancer advocacy group, Breast Cancer Action, thinks the Komen/ KFC campaign is so **egregious** that they call it "**pinkwashing**," another sad example of commercialism draped in pink ribbons. "Make no mistake," they say, "every pink bucket purchase will do more to benefit KFC's bottom line than it will to cure breast cancer."

7 One thing is hard to dispute. In partnering with KFC, Susan G. Komen for the Cure has shown itself to be numbingly oblivious to the role of diet in cancer prevention. Of course it's not hard to understand KFC's motives. They want to look good. But recent publicity the company has been getting hasn't been helping. For one thing, the company keeps taking hits for the unhealthiness of its food. Just last month, when KFC came out with its new Double Down sandwiches, the products were derided by just about every public health organization for their staggering levels of salt, calories and artery-clogging fat.

8 Then there's the squeamish matter of the treatment of the birds who end up in KFC's buckets, pink or otherwise. People for the Ethical Treatment of Animals (PETA) has an entire website devoted to what they call Kentucky Fried Cruelty, but you don't have to be an animal activist to be horrified by how the company treats chickens, if you lift the veil of the company's PR and see what actually takes place.

9 When PETA sent investigators with hidden cameras into a KFC "Supplier of the Year" slaughterhouse in Moorefield, West Virginia, what they found was enough to make KFC choke on its own pink publicity stunts. Workers were caught on video stomping on chickens, kicking them and violently slamming them against floors and walls. Workers were also filmed ripping the animals' beaks off, twisting their heads off, spitting tobacco into their eyes and mouths, spray-painting their faces, and squeezing their bodies so hard that the birds expelled feces—all while the chickens were still alive.

10 KFC, naturally, did everything they could to keep the footage from being aired, but their efforts failed. In fact, the video from the investigation ended up being broadcast by TV stations around the world, as well as on all three national evening news shows, *Good Morning America*, and every one of the major cable news networks. Plus, more than a million people subsequently watched the footage on PETA's website.

11 It wasn't just animal activists who condemned the fast food chain for the level of animal cruelty displayed at KFC's "Supplier of the Year" slaughterhouse. Dr. Temple Grandin, perhaps the meat industry's leading

ethology

the branch of zoology that studies the behavior of animals in their natural habitats

farmed-animal welfare expert, said, "The behavior of the plant employees was atrocious." Dr. Ian Duncan, a University of Guelph professor of applied **ethology** and an original member of KFC's own animal-welfare advisory council, wrote, "This tape depicts scenes of the worst cruelty I have ever witnessed against chickens . . . and it is extremely hard to accept that this is occurring in the United States of America."

12   KFC claims, on its website, that its animal-welfare advisory council "has been a key factor in formulating our animal welfare program." But Dr. Duncan, along with five other former members of this advisory council, say otherwise. They all resigned in disgust over the company's refusal to take animal welfare seriously. Adele Douglass, one of those who resigned, said in an SEC filing reported on by the *Chicago Tribune* that KFC "never had any meetings. They never asked any advice, and then they touted to the press that they had this animal-welfare advisory committee. I felt like I was being used."

13   You can see why KFC would be eager to jump on any chance to improve its public image, and why the company would want to capitalize on any opportunity to associate itself in the public mind with the fight against breast cancer. What's far more mystifying is why an organization with as much public trust as Susan G. Komen for the Cure would jeopardize public confidence in its authenticity. As someone once said, it takes a lifetime to build a reputation, but only 15 minutes to lose it.

GETTING READY TO WRITE

Reviewing the Reading

Answer each of the following questions using complete sentences.

1. Describe the "Buckets for the Cure" campaign.

2. According to the American Institute for Cancer Research, what percentage of all cancers can be prevented with lifestyle changes?

3. What is the number one dietary recommendation of the American Institute for Cancer Research?

4. What is "pinkwashing" and what does it have to do with the Komen/KFC campaign?

5. Give a brief summary of what PETA investigators found at the KFC "Supplier of the Year" slaughterhouse in West Virginia. How did KFC's animal-welfare advisory council react?

Examining the Reading Using an Idea Map

Draw an idea map of the reading, using the guidelines on p. 47.

Strengthening Your Vocabulary

Using the word's context, word parts, or a dictionary, write a brief definition of each of the following words as it is used in the reading.

1. profound (paragraph 1) _____

2. contradictions (paragraph 1) _____

3. advocacy (paragraph 1) _____

4. predominantly (paragraph 4) _____

5. cynical (paragraph 5) _____

6. vanquished (paragraph 5) _____

7. derided (paragraph 7) _____

8. atrocious (paragraph 11) _____

9. jeopardize (paragraph 13) _____

10. authenticity (paragraph 13) _____

Reacting to Ideas: Discussion and Journal Writing

Get ready to write about the reading by discussing the following:

1. Discuss why Komen chose to partner with KFC. Do you think the "Buckets for the Cure" campaign will be considered successful?

2. Did the description of animal abuse at KFC's supplier affect your opinion of fast food in general and KFC in particular? Why or why not?

3. Write a sentence that summarizes the author's opinion regarding the partnership between Komen and KFC. Do you agree or disagree with his opinion?

4. The author included both facts and opinions to support his thesis in this essay. Find examples of both and evaluate their effectiveness. Can you find any examples of bias in this piece?

 **Thinking Visually**   5. How does the photo accompanying this essay add to or detract from the material? Do you think a more graphic picture would be more effective?

WRITING ABOUT THE READING

Paragraph Options

1. How would this essay be different if it were written as a strictly factual report? Write a paragraph in which you summarize the facts of the essay in objective language.

2. Write a paragraph explaining whether you agree or disagree that Susan G. Komen for the Cure has "jeopardize[d] public confidence in its authenticity" by partnering with KFC.

3. The author points to the importance of a healthy diet in preventing cancer. Do you think most people (including yourself) make that connection? Write a paragraph explaining your answer.

Essay Options

4. Is it appropriate for advocacy organizations such as Komen to promote their causes using commercial means? Write an essay explaining why or why not. Try to think of other advocacy groups that have formed such partnerships, on either a national or a local level.

5. What responsibility do restaurants and other commercial enterprises have toward consumer health? Write an essay exploring this question. In your

own experience, what effect does "educational messaging" from advertising campaigns have on your lifestyle choices?

6. Imagine that you are a member of an animal-welfare advisory council for a large company. What guidelines would you promote for the company to follow regarding animal welfare? Write an essay describing your ideas for animal welfare in a commercial setting.

WRITING ABOUT A READING

Thinking Before Reading

This reading selection from a textbook titled *Society in Focus* describes the increasing use of surveillance monitoring systems in public places. Read the selection to discover the benefits and risks of high-tech surveillance.

1. Preview the reading, using the steps discussed in Chapter 2, page 35.

2. Connect the reading to your own experience by answering the following questions:

    a. Have you noticed surveillance cameras monitoring you anywhere? How did it make you feel?

    b. Consider a world in which everything everyone does is caught on tape. How do you feel about that?

3. Mark and annotate as you read.

READING

A SURVEILLANCE SOCIETY

William E. Thompson and Joseph V. Hickey

1   The cameras are familiar to most people, perhaps even comforting to some. They are perched high atop almost every lamppost, rooftop, and street light. Elsewhere, they are undetectable, except to the authorities. Video cameras are never turned off. They pan up and down, left and right, surveying traffic, pedestrians, and everything else in public view, day and night.

Growing Trends

2   You might be thinking that this scene offers a glimpse of the future. Perhaps it is a dark, futuristic vision, much like George Orwell's nightmare of **Big Brother** monitoring and controlling people's lives down to the smallest details. But by now you are aware that *things are not necessarily what they seem.*

Big Brother
a fictional character from George Orwell's futuristic novel *Nineteen Eighty-Four* who is the dictator of a totalitarian state

dystopian
nightmarish worst case
scenario

3   This is not some grim, **dystopian** vision of the future, but a growing trend almost everywhere in the world—including most shopping malls and stores, almost all government and corporate offices, and many other social arenas. In the name of public security, the British have been most active of all nations in installing surveillance monitoring systems. In the beginning, they were tried in a handful of "trouble spots." Now more than 4.2 million cameras have been installed throughout Britain, and the average Londoner can expect his or her picture to be taken hundreds of times each day. Alarmed at the amount of surveillance and the astonishing amount of personal data that is hoarded by the state and by commercial organizations, Ross Clark asks whom should we fear most: the government agencies that are spying on us or the criminals who seem to prosper in the swirling fog of excessive data collection?

4   Since the 9/11 terrorist attacks, the United States has been trying to catch up. Times Square in New York and the nation's capital have seen a proliferation of surveillance cameras installed in public places. Experiments in face-recognition technology have been expanded, and "photo radar" that uses cameras and computers to photograph license plates, identify traffic violators, and issue citations is catching on as well. And in all cases, the technology has also grown more sophisticated. The USA PATRIOT Act, passed after 9/11 and renewed in 2006, expanded the government's authority to "spy" on private citizens.

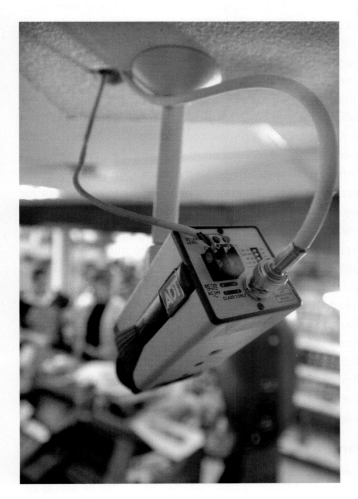

5   In the private sector, cameras and computers are abundant and socially accepted. Today, there are millions of tiny private security cameras at hotels, malls, parking lots—everywhere businesses and shoppers can be found. The new digital surveillance systems are more sophisticated than those from just a few years ago. Today's technology not only can scan businesses and malls, but also analyze what it is watching and recording and, if something is unusual, alert security. Likewise, digital security systems can now record, store, and index images, making it possible for security personnel to "instantly retrieve images of every person who passed through a door on any given day."

Surveillance Technologies

6   High-tech surveillance devices are becoming more common across the urban landscape. Although many people may be wary of these devices, few are aware that they are but a small part of surveillance technologies that now routinely monitor all of our personal histories, daily routines, and tastes. And 9/11 and global terrorist threats have increased public willingness for added security and new surveillance technologies.

7   Police and military surveillance is impressive—with video scanners, electronic ankle monitors,

night-vision goggles, and pilotless airborne spy vehicles, to name just a few. But high-tech surveillance has expanded well beyond the police and military to thousands of corporations, government agencies, and even individuals who routinely monitor the workplace, marketplace, and almost all other social arenas. As one sociologist noted, "Being able to hide and remain anonymous has become more difficult . . . we are moving toward a glass village in which everyone is available for view online."

Information Sharing

8   Today, corporations and government agencies routinely share databases. In "computer matching," organizations swap back and forth personal information on different kinds of populations and combine them to suit their own needs. The Pentagon's "Total Information Awareness Program" is one of the most ambitious plans to combine computer databases. The Pentagon maintains that it relies mainly on information from government, law enforcement, and intelligence databases to "forestall terrorism," but its use of other kinds of data—like personal financial and health records—remains unresolved. Critics argue that because such a system could (and some say already has) tap into e-mail, culling records, and credit card and banking transactions as well as travel documents, it poses a direct threat to civil liberties.

9   Similar arguments were made after the Passage of the USA PATRIOT Act in 2001, which gave the government the right to "search suspected terrorists' library records—and add them to government databases—without the patron ever knowing." By early 2002, one study found that over 85 libraries had already been asked for information on patrons in connection with the 9/11 investigation.

10   Post-9/11 surveillance surfaced as a controversial political issue in 2006 when it was discovered that after the 9/11 attacks the government gave approval to the highly secretive National Security Agency (NSA) to solicit phone records of private citizens from the nation's largest phone companies. Only weeks later it was revealed that the government also had begun monitoring the banking habits of private citizens in an effort to thwart terrorist activities. Open debates developed over how much personal privacy Americans were willing to relinquish for the promise of safety from terrorism. Nevertheless, the act was renewed in 2006.

11   The government is not the only one in the spying business. Some of the most sophisticated surveillance devices are available to the public and can be ordered from retail catalogues. For example, night-vision goggles can be had for the price of a good video camera. High-tech scanners are available that can trace ink patterns and read the content of letters "without ever breaking the seal" (Brin, 1996: 308). Brin believes that there is a good possibility that as cameras get smaller and more mobile we should expect "mosquito-scale drones" that fly in and out of office and home windows, making privacy difficult or impossible. Of course, cell phones and other mobile devices with digital cameras have proliferated, as have pinhole cameras, microvideo systems, and wireless video that potentially could make everyone part of the security apparatus.

The Impact of Surveillance

12   Journalists have largely focused their attention on how surveillance relates to political citizenship and "privacy" issues, but much more is involved. According to sociologist David Lyon, new surveillance systems have expanded

to the point at which they have become a major social institution that affects all social relationships, as well as people's very identities, personal space, freedom, and dignity. Increasingly, data images—computer-integrated profiles of each individual's finances, health, consumer preferences, ethnicity, neighborhood, education, criminal record, and other "significant" characteristics—are the "looking-glass" that provide social judgments about "who we are" and our life changes. Using the old South Africa as his guide, Lyon asks, will the new "non-persons," segregated by surveillance systems, be bankrupt individuals or perhaps nonconsumers?

13   Many people see the benefits of new surveillance as far outweighing the risks and argue that only criminals and terrorists should be concerned about the intensification of surveillance. They assert, "Why should I worry about privacy? I have nothing to hide." Lyon himself makes the point that dark visions about corporate and government Big Brothers may be counterproductive in that they may produce nothing more than paranoia, fatalism, and inaction. New surveillance, in fact, both constrains and enables. Although it is unequally distributed, with large organizations controlling most information technologies, these same technologies have given ordinary people access to many new channels of participation and protest, not only nationally but globally. Today's increases in identity theft, spying, selling of personal information, and other technological invasions of privacy prompted one sociologist to conclude that "public access to private information has taken on even more ominous tones."

fatalism
the belief that events are determined by fate and cannot be changed by human actions

GETTING READY TO WRITE

Reviewing the Reading

Answer each of the following questions using complete sentences.

1. What kinds of information do corporations and governments share?
2. What does the Pentagon's Total Information Awareness Program plan to do?
3. What impact did 9/11 have on libraries?
4. What kinds of monitoring did the government institute after 9/11?
5. What types of surveillance devices are available to the public?

Examining the Reading Using an Idea Map

Draw an idea map of the reading, using the guidelines on p. 47.

Strengthening Your Vocabulary

Using the word's context, word parts, or a dictionary, write a brief definition of each of the following words as it is used in the reading.

1. wary (paragraph 6) _____
2. culling (paragraph 8) _____
3. thwart (paragraph 10) _____
4. apparatus (paragraph 11) _____
5. paranoia (paragraph 13) _____

Reacting to Ideas: Discussion and Journal Writing

Get ready to write about the reading by discussing the following questions:

1. How might information from surveillance cameras be misused? How can this be prevented?
2. How do we balance the government's need to gather information with our need for privacy?
3. What other threats to privacy occur in today's society?

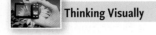 **Thinking Visually**   4. What point in the reading does the photo reinforce?

WRITING ABOUT THE READING

Paragraph Options

1. Write a paragraph explaining your views on whether or not private citizens should have access to surveillance equipment for their own personal use.
2. Do you agree that corporations and government agencies should be permitted to share surveillance information with each other? Write a paragraph exploring this.

Essay Options

3. Write an essay explaining how you feel about the government being able to access information about you from health, financial, and even library records. Do you believe this is a violation of your privacy?
4. Do you agree with those who say only criminals and terrorists should be worried about government surveillance? Write an essay expressing your views.

WRITING ABOUT A READING

Thinking Before Reading

The following reading is from a sociology textbook. In this selection, the author discusses the implications of genetic testing.

1. Preview the reading, using the steps discussed in Chapter 2, page 35.
2. Connect the reading to your own experience by answering the following questions:
   a. Does anyone in your family have an illness or condition that may be genetic? If so, does this make you concerned about how it could affect you or other people in your family?
   b. What do you know about the advances in genetic testing? What kinds of testing are possible that you know of?
3. Mark and annotate as you read.

READING

THE GENETIC CRYSTAL BALL: DO WE REALLY WANT TO LOOK?

John J. Macionis

FELISHA: Before I get married, I want my partner to have a genetic screening. It's like buying a house or a car—you should check it out before you sign on the line.

EVA: Do you expect to get a warranty, too?

1   The liquid in the laboratory test tube seems ordinary enough, like a syrupy form of water. But this liquid is one of the greatest medical break-throughs of all time; it may even hold the key to life itself. The liquid is deoxyribonucleic acid, or DNA, the spiraling molecule found in cells of the human body that contains the blueprint for making each one of us human as well as different from every other person.

2   The human body is composed of some 100 million cells, most of which contain a nucleus of twenty-three pairs of chromosomes (one of each pair comes from each parent). Each chromosome is packed with DNA, in segments called genes. Genes guide the production of protein, the building block of the human body.

3   If genetics sounds complicated (and it is), the social implications of genetic knowledge are even more complex. Scientists discovered the structure of the DNA molecule in 1952, and in recent years they have made great gains in "mapping" the human **genome**. Charting the genetic landscape may lead to understanding how each bit of DNA shapes our being.

genome
the full DNA sequence of an organism

4   But do we really want to turn the key unlock the secrets of life itself? And what do we do with this knowledge once we have it? Research has already iden-tified genetic abnormalities that cause sickle-cell anemia, muscular dystrophy, **Huntington's disease**, cystic fibrosis, some forms of cancer, and other crip-pling and deadly afflictions. Genetic screening—gazing into a person's genetic "crystal ball"—could let people know their medical destiny and allow doctors to manipulate segments of DNA to prevent diseases before they appear.

Huntington's disease
a hereditary nervous system disease involving brain deterioration

5   But many people urge caution in such research, warning that genetic in-formation can easily be abused. At its worst, genetic mapping opens the door to Nazi-like efforts to breed a "super-race." In 1994, the People's Republic of China began to use genetic information to regulate marriage and childbirth with the purpose of avoiding "new births of inferior quality."

6   It seems inevitable that some parents will want to use genetic testing to evaluate the health (or even the eye color) of their future children. What if they want to abort a fetus be-cause it falls short of their standards? Should parents be allowed to use genetic manipula-tion to create "designer children"?

Scientists are learning more and more about the genetic factors that prompt the eventual development of serious diseases. If offered the opportunity, would you want to undergo a genetic screening that would predict the long-term future of your own health?

7   Then there is the issue of "genetic privacy." Can a prospective spouse request a genetic evaluation of her fiancé before agreeing to marry? Can a life insurance company demand genetic testing before issuing a policy? Can an employer screen job applicants to weed out those whose future illnesses might drain the company's health care funds? Clearly, what is scientifically possible is not always morally desirable. Society is already struggling with questions about the proper use of our expanding knowledge of human genetics. Such ethical dilemmas will multiply as genetic research moves forward in the years to come.

What Do You Think?

1. Traditional wedding vows join couples "in sickness and in health." Do you think individuals have a right to know the future health of their potential partner before tying the knot? Why or why not?

2. Do you think parents should be able to genetically "design" their children? Why or why not?

3. Is it right that private companies doing genetic research are able to patent their discoveries so that they can profit from the results, or should this information be made available to everyone? Explain your answer.

Sources: D. Thompson (1999) and Golden & Lemonick (2000)

GETTING READY TO WRITE

Reviewing the Reading

Answer each of the following questions using complete sentences.

1. How could science use genetic screening to benefit people?
2. Why did the author mention China's use of genetic information?
3. What does the term "designer children" mean?

Examining the Reading Using an Idea Map

Draw an idea map of the reading, using the guidelines on p. 47.

Strengthening Your Vocabulary

Using the word's context, word parts, or a dictionary, write a brief definition of each of the following words as it is used in the reading.

1. spiraling (paragraph 1) _____
2. abnormalities (paragraph 4) _____
3. manipulate (paragraph 4) _____
4. inevitable (paragraph 6) _____
5. prospective (paragraph 7) _____
6. dilemmas (paragraph 7) _____

Reacting to Ideas: Discussion and Journal Writing

Get ready to write about the reading by discussing the following questions:

1. What other technologies have risks and benefits that must be carefully weighed?

2. If routine genetic testing becomes standard, how do you think that information should be controlled? What kinds of new laws will be needed?

3. How would knowing you are going to have a genetic disease change the way you live your life?

 **Thinking Visually**

4. What function does the caption accompanying the photograph serve?

WRITING ABOUT THE READING

Paragraph Options

1. How would you respond if a partner wanted you to have a genetic screening before marriage? Write a paragraph describing your reaction.

2. Write a paragraph answering this question from the photo caption: "If offered the opportunity, would you want to undergo a genetic screening that would predict the long-term future of your own health?"

Essay Options

3. Reread the questions in the box at the end of the selection. Choose one and write an essay explaining your answer.

4. Write an essay exploring as many ways as you can think of that genetic screening could be used with regard to unborn children.

WRITING ABOUT A READING

Thinking Before Reading

The following reading is taken from a web site called WebMD Health News. Notice how the author uses research to illustrate her points.

1. Preview the reading, using the steps discussed in Chapter 2, p. 35.

2. Connect the reading to your own experience by answering the following questions:

   a. What do you know about cyberbullying?

   b. What effects of cyberbullying have you seen?

3. Mark and annotate as you read.

READING

EMOTIONAL TROUBLES FOR 'CYBERBULLIES' AND VICTIMS

Denise Mann

1   New research sheds important light on the prevalence, extent, and consequences of "cyberbullying" as well as some of the emotional and physical characteristics of cyberbullies and their victims. Both the cyberbullies and those who they bully online are more likely to report a host of physical and mental problems, according to a new study in the July issue of the *Archives of General Psychiatry*.

2   A relatively new phenomenon, cyberbullying is defined as "an aggressive intentional act carried out by a group or individual using electronic forms of contact repeatedly and over time against a victim who cannot easily defend him or herself," according to the study. The increase in cyberbullying **dovetails** with the explosion in the use of computers, cell phones, and other electronic devices by children. Unlike traditional bullying, which largely relies on physical threats, rumors, and exclusion, cyberbullies can reach larger audiences via social media and other technology, making it difficult for the intended victim to escape their bullies. Cyberbullies can also do so relatively anonymously.

dovetails
fits together closely

3   The new study included information on 2,215 Finnish teens aged 13 to 16. Overall, 4.8% of the teens said that they were victimized by cyberbullies, 7.4% admitted to being cyberbullies, and 5.4% said they were both cyberbullies and had been cyberbullied. Most of the cyberbullying was done via computer instant messages and discussion groups, the study showed. Cyberbullies often harassed peers of the same age. Sixteen percent of girls surveyed said they were bullied by boys, whereas just 5% of boys said they were cyberbullied by girls.

Emotional and Physical Issues

4   Victims of cyberbullying reported emotional, concentration, and behavioral issues, as well as trouble getting along with their peers. These teens were also more likely to report frequent headaches, recurrent stomach pain, and difficulty sleeping; one in four said they felt unsafe at school. What's more, those teens who were victimized by cyberbullies were less likely to be living with both biological parents, the researchers report.

5   Cyberbullies also reported emotional difficulties, concentration and behavior issues and difficulty getting along with others. They were also more likely to be hyperactive, have conduct problems, abuse alcohol, and smoke cigarettes. In addition, cyberbullies also reported frequent headaches and feeling unsafe at school. Those teens who were both cyberbullies and victims reported all of these physical and mental health issues, the study found.

6   "Policy makers, educators, parents, and adolescents themselves should be aware of the potentially harmful effects of cyberbullying," conclude the researchers, who were led by Andre Sourander, MD, PhD, a child psychiatrist at Turku University in Finland. "Future research is needed on whether anti-bullying policies, materials, interventions and mobile telephone and Internet user guidelines are effective for reducing cyberbullying."

Staying Safe Online

7   Parry Aftab's life mission is to keep children and teens safe online. An Internet privacy and security lawyer in Fort Lee, N.J., Aftab is the executive director of wiredsafety.org, an online safety and educational site which is the parent group for a charity called stopcyberbullying.org. "Cyberbullying is when a minor uses technology as a weapon to hurt another," she says. It can take many forms such as stealing another kid's password or his or her points in an online game or digitally adding a peer's face to a photo of a naked body and then posting it online (where it can quickly go viral), she says. "There are millions of different ways to [cyberbully]; it is limited only by the bandwidth and creativity of kids."

8   Cyberbullying changes the typical playground or schoolyard social structure. "It brings a whole different group of kids into the problem," she says. "Real-life victims can become online bullies because it is rarely a matter of size," she explains. "It gets the girls and geeks involved and they are normally the ones being bullied." There is no escape from cyberbullies, she says. If a child was bullied at school, home was often a safe haven. But "teens are always connected, and technology follows you everywhere you are, 24-7," she says. "Cyberbullying can have devastating consequences and parents need to understand that most kids have been cyberbullied at least once."

9   The question becomes what to do about it. Aftab's advice to teens who are victims of cyberbullies? "Stop, block, and tell," she says. "Do not reply. Block the message and then tell a trusted adult," she says. Other tips include using non-obvious passwords and changing them after breakups to discourage hackers, she suggests. Parents of children who are bullied online need to take a deep breath before they overreact and make things worse, she says. "If there is a teacher or guidance counselor with whom you have a good relationship, call that person first so your child won't be blamed as a tattletale," she advises. But "if there is a threat, you have to call the police."

10   Aftab's group is planning to release a free stop cyberbullying toolkit for schools in August. Child psychoanalyst Leon Hoffman, MD, the executive

director of the Bernard L. Pacella Parent Child Center in New York City, agrees with Aftab. "This [research] paper stresses the importance of a no-tolerance policy that the adults have to enforce vigorously." "This paper verifies that cyberbullying is a significant problem," Aftab tells WebMD. "More importantly, it promotes the idea that school and mental health personnel need to be aware of its existence."

perpetrator
one who commits a wrong action

11   More research is needed to get a better handle on some of the physical and mental characteristics of cyberbullies and their victims, he says. "Whether cyberbullying [victim or **perpetrator** or both] is the cause of a variety of problems or whether kids with a variety of psychosocial and medical problems are prone to bullying, victimization or both is a question that has to be studied."

GETTING READY TO WRITE

Reviewing the Reading

Answer each of the following questions using complete sentences.

1. How is cyberbullying different from traditional bullying?
2. What effects do victims of cyberbullying commonly report?
3. How does cyberbullying change the typical school structure?
4. What should adults do about cyberbullying, according to this article?

Examining the Reading Using an Idea Map

Draw an idea map of the reading, using the guidelines on p. 47.

Strengthening Your Vocabulary

Using the word's context, word parts, or a dictionary, write a brief definition of each of the following words as it is used in the reading.

1. prevalence (paragraph 1) _____
2. phenomenon (paragraph 2) _____
3. harassed (paragraph 3) _____
4. hyperactive (paragraph 5) _____

Reacting to Ideas: Discussion and Journal Writing

Get ready to write about the reading by discussing the following questions:

1. Why do you think people who cyberbully experience negative emotional and physical consequences?
2. Why do you think people cyberbully others? How is it different from regular bullying?

3. What do you think further research will show—that cyberbullying is caused by problems kids already have or that cyberbullying creates those problems?

Thinking Visually

4. Why is the photograph a useful addition to the reading?

WRITING ABOUT THE READING

Paragraph Options

1. Write a paragraph describing cyberbullying you or someone you know experienced.

2. What should a school no-tolerance cyberbullying policy include in your opinion? Describe it in a paragraph.

3. How can parents prevent cyberbullying? Offer some suggestions in a paragraph.

Essay Options

4. How else has modern technology changed the way teens deal with each other? Write an essay explaining how technology has changed teen behavior.

5. Before there was cyberbullying, there was bullying. Why do you think kids and teens do this kind of thing to each other? What purpose does it serve? Write an essay explaining your thoughts.

WRITING ABOUT A READING

Thinking Before Reading

The following reading, "The Struggle to Be an All-American Girl," uses adjectives and adverbs effectively to bring vividness and realism to the events of the author's childhood story.

1. Preview the reading, using the steps discussed in Chapter 2, page 35.

2. Connect the reading to your own experience by answering the following questions:

   a. Think about your family heritage or ethnic background. What is your attitude toward it?

   b. Consider your childhood education. Do you have mostly positive or mostly negative memories?

3. Mark and annotate as you read.

READING

THE STRUGGLE TO BE AN ALL-AMERICAN GIRL

Elizabeth Wong

1   It's still there, the Chinese school on Yale Street where my brother and I used to go. Despite the new coat of paint and the high wire fence, the school I knew ten years ago remains remarkably, stoically the same.

2   Every day at 5 P.M., instead of playing with our fourth- and fifth-grade friends or sneaking out to the empty lot to hunt ghosts and animal bones, my brother and I had to go to Chinese school. No amount of kicking, screaming, or pleading could dissuade my mother, who was solidly determined to have us learn the language of our heritage.

3   Forcibly, she walked us the seven long, hilly blocks from our home to school, depositing our defiant tearful faces before the stern principal. My only memory of him is that he swayed on his heels like a palm tree, and he always clasped his impatient twitching hands behind his back. I recognized him as a repressed maniacal child killer, and knew that if we ever saw his hands we'd be in big trouble.

4   We all sat in little chairs in an empty auditorium. The room smelled like Chinese medicine, an imported faraway mustiness, like ancient mothballs or dirty closets. I hated that smell. I favored crisp new scents, like the soft French perfume that my American teacher wore in public school.

5   There was a stage far to the right, flanked by an American flag and the flag of the Nationalist Republic of China, which was also red, white and blue but not as pretty.

6   Although the emphasis at the school was mainly language—speaking, reading, writing—the lessons always began with an exercise in politeness. With the entrance of the teacher, the best student would tap a bell and everyone would get up, kowtow, and chant, "Sing san ho," the phonetic for "How are you, teacher?"

7   Being 10 years old, I had better things to learn than ideographs copied painstakingly in lines that ran right to left from the tip of a *moc but,* a real ink pen that had to be held in an awkward way if blotches were to be avoided. After all, I could do the multiplication tables, name the satellites of Mars, and write reports on *Little Women* and *Black Beauty*. Nancy Drew, my favorite book heroine, never spoke Chinese.

8   The language was a source of embarrassment. More times than not, I had tried to disassociate myself from the nagging loud voice that followed me wherever I wandered in the nearby American supermarket outside Chinatown. The voice belonged to my grandmother, a fragile woman in her seventies who could outshout the best of the street vendors. Her humor was raunchy; her Chinese rhythmless, patternless. It was quick; it was loud; it was unbeautiful. It was not like the quiet, lilting romance of French or the gentle refinement of the American South. Chinese sounded pedestrian. It sounded public.

9   In Chinatown, the comings and going of hundreds of Chinese on their daily tasks sounded chaotic and frenzied. I did not want to be thought of as mad, as talking gibberish. When I spoke English, people nodded at me, smiled sweetly,

kowtow
kneel, touching forehead to ground

ideographs
symbols representing ideas or objects

said encouraging words. Even the people in my culture would cluck and say that I'd do well in life. "My, doesn't she move her lips fast," they would say, meaning that I'd be able to keep up with the world outside Chinatown.

10   My brother was even more fanatical than I about speaking English. He was especially hard on my mother, criticizing her, often cruelly, for her pidgin speech—smatterings of Chinese scattered like chop suey in her conversation. "It's not 'What it is,' Mom," he'd say in exasperation. "It's 'What *is* it, what *is* it!'" Sometimes Mom might leave out an occasional "the" or "a," or perhaps a verb of being. He would stop her in mid-sentence: "Say it again, Mom. Say it right." When he tripped over his own tongue, he'd blame it on her: "See, Mom, it's all your fault. You set a bad example."

11   What infuriated my mother most was when my brother cornered her on her consonants, especially "r." My father had played a cruel joke on Mom by assigning her an American name that her tongue wouldn't allow her to say. No matter how hard she tried, "Ruth" always ended up "Luth" or "Roof."

12   After two years of writing with a *moc but* and reciting words with multiples of meanings, I finally was granted a cultural divorce. I was permitted to stop Chinese school.

13   I thought of myself as multicultural. I preferred tacos to egg rolls; I enjoyed **Cinco de Mayo** more than Chinese New Year.

14   At last, I was one of you; I wasn't one of them.

15   Sadly, I still am.

Cinco de Mayo
Mexican holiday celebrating the defeat of Napoleon III in the Battle of Puebla

GETTING READY TO WRITE

Reviewing the Reading

Answer each of the following questions using complete sentences.

1. At the end of the essay, Wong says, "At last, I was one of you; I wasn't one of them." To whom do the *you* and the *them* refer?

2. Summarize Wong's attitude toward her Chinese heritage.

3. Why do you think Wong's mother insisted she attend Chinese school?

Examining the Reading Using an Idea Map

Draw an idea map of the reading, using the guidelines on p. 47.

Strengthening Your Vocabulary

Using the word's context, word parts, or a dictionary, write a brief definition of each of the following words as it is used in the reading.

1. stoically (paragraph 1) _____

_____

2. dissuade (paragraph 2) _____

_____

3. repressed (paragraph 3) _____

_____

4. maniacal (paragraph 3) _____

_____

5. disassociate (paragraph 8) _____

_____

6. chaotic (paragraph 9) _____

_____

7. frenzied (paragraph 9) _____

_____

Reacting to Ideas: Discussion and Journal Writing

Get ready to write about the reading by discussing the following questions:

1. Why do you think Wong's brother criticized his mother's inability to speak English?
2. Why does Wong say she prefers tacos to egg rolls?
3. Explain the meaning of the title of the essay.
4. What photograph might be used to illustrate this article?

 **Thinking Visually**

WRITING ABOUT THE READING

Paragraph Options

1. Wong was embarrassed by her Chinese heritage. Write a paragraph describing a situation in which you were proud of or embarrassed by your heritage or by the cultural behavior of a member of your family.

2. Write a paragraph in which you describe a family tradition. Use plenty of adjectives and adverbs in your description.

Essay Options

3. Wong states that Nancy Drew, the main character in an American mystery novel series, was her heroine. Write an essay describing a person, real or fictional, whom you admire. Be sure to describe the specific characteristics that make this person your hero or heroine.

4. Clearly, Wong and her brother viewed their heritage from a different perspective than that of their parents and grandparents. Write an essay in which you evaluate generational differences within your own family. Choose one topic or issue and consider how different your family's generations view the matter.

WRITING ABOUT A READING

Thinking Before Reading

The following reading, "Are Latinos Different?" was written by Sandra Márquez, a Los Angeles–based journalist. In this article, which appeared on HispanicMagazine.com, Márquez addresses the health differences between Hispanics and non-Hispanic whites in the United States, as well as the implications for medical research.

1. Preview the reading, using the steps discussed in Chapter 2, page 35.
2. Connect the reading to your own experience by answering the following questions:
   a. What is racial or ethnic profiling?
   b. Do health issues vary among different ethnic groups?
3. Mark and annotate as you read.

READING

ARE LATINOS DIFFERENT?

Sandra Márquez

taboo
forbidden

1   Profiling, the practice of compiling data for the purpose of making generalizations about a particular race or ethnic group, is considered **taboo**, or at least politically incorrect, when it comes to criminal behavior or traffic stops. In terms of science, most anyone who received a U.S. public school education was taught that, despite different skin colors, all human bodies were created equally. There was no genetic difference among races.

2   So why the growing trend toward "medical profiling"? Why the need to do medical research that specifically looks at health patterns of Hispanics? The answer is simple, according to Dr. David Hayes-Bautista, director of the Center for the Study of Latino Health and Culture at the University of California Los Angeles. The more than 38 million Latinos living in the United States represent an "**epidemiological paradox**." Despite popular conceptions, Latinos live longer and have a lower incidence of heart attacks, the leading forms of cancer and strokes than the general public.

epidemiological
referring to the branch of medicine that studies the causes, distribution, and control of diseases in populations

3   The difference isn't a genetic one, according to the doctor. His research on the topic has convinced him that the generally good health of Hispanics is rooted in **cultura**. And by studying Latino health patterns, he believes that the general public will benefit.

paradox
a statement that seems contradictory but is true

cultura
culture

4   "Although Latino populations may generally be described as low-income and low-education with little access to care, Latino health outcomes are generally far better than those of non-Hispanic whites," Hayes-Bautista writes in *Latinos: Remaking America*, published in 2002 by Harvard University and the University of California Press. "This paradox has been observed in so many

Latino populations in so many regions over so many years that its existence cries out to be explained," states Hayes-Bautista.

5   The flip side of his research also merits further inquiry. Hispanics have a high incidence of diabetes—64 percent higher than white Americans—AIDS and cirrhosis of the liver, the latter of which is higher among Hispanics than any other group. Recent studies looking specifically at Hispanic health patterns have been conducted by the American Cancer Society, the American Heart Association and the National Alliance of State and Territorial AIDS Directors.

6   The Cancer Society study found that Hispanics are less likely than white Americans to develop and die from lung, breast, prostate and colon cancer—while being more prone to the less common cancer of the cervix, liver and gall bladder. The Heart Association study found that Type 2 diabetes has reached epidemic proportions among Hispanics. And the AIDS study found that Hispanics, who comprise 13 percent of the U.S. population, account for 20 percent of those living with AIDS.

7   But the issue of medical profiling is not without controversy. The debate is reflected in a California ballot measure to be decided Oct. 7. Proposition 54, dubbed the Racial Privacy Act, would bar state officials from gathering data on race and ethnicity. The initiative's website (www.racialprivacy.org) claims the measure is a step toward creating a "colorblind society." "As the most ethnically diverse state in the Union, California has the most to gain by compelling its government to treat all citizens equally and without regard to race. The latest U.S. Census divides Americans into a whopping 126 different ethnic/racial categories. How many categories should Californians put up with?" it asks.

8   Although Proposition 54's backers say the new law would include an exemption for medical research, prominent groups, such as Kaiser Permanente and the California Health Association, appear unconvinced and have opposed the measure.

9   Oscar Cisneros, a policy analyst for the Latino Issues Forum, a public policy and advocacy institute in San Francisco, said the medical research exemption would only apply to clinical settings. If approved, he said the measure would

make it harder for public health officials who rely on government data to tailor messages to specific risk groups. It would also have implications for tracking a public health threat such as SARS, which originated in China, Cisneros says. "It's not like they force people to reveal their race," Cisneros says of government demographic data. "It's all voluntary information that allows them to get a better picture of what is really going on."

10   Lorenzo Abundiz, 50, a retired Santa Ana, California, firefighter who was told he had just weeks to live after being diagnosed with a rare form of sarcoma cancer five years ago, said he would like to see medical research focus

on one thing—finding a cure for all cancers. "Cancer has no preference. It will get everyone: black, white, Mexican. It will nail you. I want to see where everybody bonds together, like cancer survivors like me, and says, 'Let's find a cure,'" says Abundiz, who in July underwent a CAT scan indicating he was in full remission.

11   Abundiz received a state firefighter medal of valor for rescuing two fellow firefighters from a tire shop fire by single-handedly lifting a 500-pound wall without wearing protective breathing gear. He has also been lauded for rescuing pets from burning homes and in June 2001, he married his sweetheart, Peggy, in New York's Times Square in front of millions of viewers on ABC's *Good Morning America*. He believes toxic exposure on the job made him susceptible to cancer. Nonetheless, it does run in his family. His father died of prostate cancer. He credits the love of his wife, a vegetarian diet, and learning to live more with nature by "letting butterflies land on my fingers and seeing God in nature" for his survival.

12   Dr. Hayes-Bautista says a "Latino norm" is apparent in all of his medical research. He believes "something that Latinos do each day" explains Hispanic health patterns and further study could lead to a reduction of heart disease, cancer and strokes in the population at large. "At the larger level, it has to be culture, which would include what people eat. It probably has to include family or social networks, and it [even] might have something to do with spirituality, the mind-body connection," he says.

GETTING READY TO WRITE

Reviewing the Reading

Answer each of the following questions using complete sentences.

1. Define the term *profiling*.
2. Briefly compare Latinos with non-Hispanic whites on the following health issues discussed in the article. (The first one is done for you.)
     a. length of life: _____
     b. heart attacks: _____
     c. diabetes: _____
     d. AIDS: _____
     e. cirrhosis of the liver: _____
     f. lung, breast, prostate, and colon cancer: _____
     _____
3. What does Dr. Hayes-Bautista believe is at the root of Hispanics' generally good health?
4. What is the purpose of California's Proposition 54?
5. Why was Lorenzo Abundiz awarded a medal of valor?
6. What does Lorenzo Abundiz believe made him susceptible to cancer?

Examining the Reading Using an Idea Map

Draw an idea map of the reading, using the guidelines on p. 47.

Strengthening Your Vocabulary

Using the word's context, word parts, or a dictionary, write a brief definition of each of the following words as it is used in the reading.

1. epidemic (paragraph 6) _____

2. controversy (paragraph 7) _____

3. exemption (paragraph 8) _____

4. remission (paragraph 10) _____

    _____

5. valor (paragraph 11) _____

6. lauded (paragraph 11) _____

7. susceptible (paragraph 11) _____

Reacting to Ideas: Discussion and Journal Writing

Get ready to write about the reading by discussing the following questions:

1. What is controversial about medical profiling?

2. Why does the good health of Hispanics present a paradox?

3. Explain what is meant by the phrase "a colorblind society" (paragraph 7).

4. Evaluate the quality of the supporting evidence in this article. What sources does the author draw upon for information? How credible are they?

 **Thinking Visually**   5. How does the photo support the thesis of the article?

WRITING ABOUT THE READING

Paragraph Options

1. Why do you think the author wrote about Lorenzo Abundiz in this article? Write a paragraph explaining who he is and why his story is significant.

2. Have you ever felt that you were stereotyped—or even profiled—based on some aspect of your identity (for example, age, ethnicity, or gender)? Write a paragraph describing your experience.

3. Do you think Proposition 54 should have been passed (it wasn't)? Write a paragraph explaining why or why not.

Essay Options

4. In the context of Dr. Hayes-Bautista's research, *culture* includes what people eat, their family or social networks, and spirituality. Write an essay describing these aspects of your culture and how they could affect your own health. Feel free to include other aspects of your culture that may be relevant to your health.

5. In addition to medical profiling, many other medical issues provoke debate and/or controversy. Choose an issue, such as stem-cell research or medicinal marijuana, and write an essay taking a stand on one side of the issue. Be sure to include evidence to support your argument and to persuade your readers to accept your point of view.

6. According to the article, supporters of Proposition 54 object to the U.S. census's "whopping 126 different ethnic/racial categories" for Americans. How do you feel about being asked to place yourself in a particular category? Write an essay describing your response to requests for personal information about yourself, whether in a national census or on a college application or some other type of form. Are you ever concerned about how the information will be used?

PART VIII

Reviewing the Basics

GUIDE TO REVIEWING THE BASICS

OVERVIEW

Most of us know how to communicate in our own language. When we talk or write, we put our thoughts into words and, by and large, we make ourselves understood. But many of us do not know the specific terms and rules of grammar. Grammar is a system that describes how language is put together. Grammar must be learned, almost as if it were a foreign language.

Why is it important to study grammar, to understand grammatical terms like *verb, participle,* and *gerund* and concepts like *agreement* and *subordination?* There are several good reasons. Knowing grammar will allow you to

- **recognize an error in your writing and correct it.** Your papers will read more smoothly and communicate more effectively when they are error free.

- **understand the comments of your teachers and peers.** People who read and critique your writing may point out a "fragment" or a "dangling modifier." You will be able to revise and correct the problems.

- **write with more impact.** Grammatically correct sentences are signs of clear thinking. Your readers will get your message without distraction or confusion.

As you will see in this section, "Reviewing the Basics," the different areas of grammatical study are highly interconnected. The sections on parts of speech, sentences, punctuation, mechanics, and spelling fit together into a logical whole. To recognize and correct a run-on sentence, for example, you need to know both sentence structure *and* punctuation. To avoid errors in capitalization, you need to know parts of speech *and* mechanics. If grammar is to do you any good, your knowledge of it must be thorough. As you review the following "basics," be alert to the interconnections that make language study so interesting.

Grammatical terms and rules demand your serious attention. Mastering them will pay handsome dividends: error-free papers, clear thinking, and effective writing.

Understanding the Parts of Speech

The eight parts of speech are **nouns, pronouns, verbs, adjectives, adverbs, conjunctions, prepositions,** and **interjections.** Each word in a sentence functions as one of these parts of speech. Being able to identify the parts of speech in sentences allows you to analyze and improve your writing and to understand grammatical principles discussed later in this section.

It is important to keep in mind that *how* a word functions in a sentence determines *what* part of speech it is. Thus, the same word can be a noun, a verb, or an adjective, depending on how it is used.

NOUN
He needed some blue wallpaper.

VERB
He will wallpaper the hall.

ADJECTIVE
He went to a wallpaper store.

A.1 NOUNS

A **noun** names a person, place, thing, or idea.

People	*woman, winner, Maria Alvarez*
Places	*mall, hill, Indiana*
Things	*lamp, ship, air*
Ideas	*goodness, perfection, harmony*

The form of many nouns changes to express **number** (**singular** for one, **plural** for more than one): *one bird, two birds; one child, five children.* Most nouns can also be made **possessive** to show ownership by the addition of *-'s: city's, Norma's.*

Sometimes a noun is used to modify another noun:

NOUN MODIFYING DIPLOMA
Her goal had always been to earn a college diploma.

Nouns are classified as **proper**, **common**, **collective**, **concrete**, **abstract**, **count**, and **noncount**.

1. **Proper nouns** name specific people, places, or things and are always capitalized: *Martin Luther King Jr.; East Lansing; Ford Taurus*. Days of the week and months are considered proper nouns and are capitalized.

   > PROPER NOUN   PROPER NOUN   PROPER NOUN
   > In September Allen will attend Loyola University.

2. **Common nouns** name one or more of a general class or type of person, place, thing, or idea and are not capitalized: *president, city, car, wisdom*.

   > COMMON NOUN COMMON NOUN   COMMON NOUN   COMMON NOUN
   > Next fall the students will enter college to receive an education.

3. **Collective nouns** name a whole group or collection of people, places, or things: *committee, team, jury*. They are usually singular in form.

   > COLLECTIVE NOUN   COLLECTIVE NOUN
   > The flock of mallards is flying over the herd of bison.

4. **Concrete nouns** name tangible things that can be tasted, seen, touched, smelled, or heard: *sandwich, radio, pen*.

   > CONCRETE NOUN   CONCRETE NOUN
   > The frozen pizza was stuck in the freezer.

5. **Abstract nouns** name ideas, qualities, beliefs, and conditions: *honesty, goodness, poverty*. Use a singular verb with an abstract noun.

   > ABSTRACT NOUNS ABSTRACT NOUN
   > Their marriage was based on love, honor, and trust.

   > ABSTRACT NOUN
   > Poverty is a major problem in the United States.
   > SINGULAR VERB

6. **Count nouns** name items that can be counted. Count nouns can be made plural, usually by adding *-s* or *-es: one river, three rivers; one box, ten boxes*. Some count nouns form their plural in an irregular way: *man, men; goose, geese*.

   > COUNT NOUN   COUNT NOUN   COUNT NOUN
   > The salespeople put the invoices in their files.

7. **Noncount nouns** name ideas or qualities that cannot be counted. Noncount nouns almost always have no plural form: *air, knowledge, unhappiness*.

   > NONCOUNT NOUN   NONCOUNT NOUN
   > As the rain pounded on the windows, she tried to find the courage to walk home from work.

A.2 PRONOUNS

A **pronoun** is a word that substitutes for or refers to a noun or another pronoun. The noun or pronoun to which a pronoun refers is called the pronoun's **antecedent**. A pronoun must agree with its antecedent in person, number, and gender (these terms are discussed later in this section).

> After the campers discovered the cave, they mapped it for the next group, which was arriving next week. [The pronoun *they* refers to its antecedent, *campers;* the pronoun *it* refers to its antecedent, *cave;* the pronoun *which* refers to its antecedent, *group.*]

The eight kinds of pronouns are **personal, demonstrative, reflexive, intensive, interrogative, relative, indefinite,** and **reciprocal.**

1. **Personal pronouns** take the place of nouns or pronouns that name people or things. A personal pronoun changes form to indicate **person, gender, number,** and **case.**

   Person is the grammatical term used to distinguish the speaker (**first person:** *I, we*); the person spoken to (**second person:** *you*); and the person or thing spoken about (**third person:** *he, she, it, they*). **Gender** is the term used to classify pronouns as **masculine** (*he, him*); **feminine** (*she, her*); or **neuter** (*it*). **Number** classifies pronouns as **singular** (one) or **plural** (more than one). Some personal pronouns also function as adjectives modifying nouns (*our house*).

PERSON	SINGULAR	PLURAL
First person	I, me, my, mine	we, us, our, ours
Second person	you, your, yours	you, your, yours
Third person		
Masculine	he, him, his	
Feminine	she, her, hers	they, them, their, theirs
Neuter	it, its	

I called my manager about my new clients. She wanted to know as soon as they placed their first orders. "Your new clients are important to us," she said.

[1ST PERSON SINGULAR · 1ST PERSON SINGULAR (PRONOUN/ADJECTIVE) · 1ST PERSON SINGULAR (PRONOUN/ADJECTIVE) · 3RD PERSON SINGULAR · 3RD PERSON PLURAL · 3RD PERSON PLURAL (PRONOUN/ADJECTIVE) · 2ND PERSON SINGULAR (PRONOUN/ADJECTIVE) · 1ST PERSON PLURAL · 3RD PERSON SINGULAR]

A pronoun's **case** is determined by its function as a subject (**subjective** or **nominative case**) or an object (**objective case**) in a sentence. A pronoun that shows ownership is in the **possessive case.**

2. **Demonstrative pronouns** refer to particular people or things. The demonstrative pronouns are *this* and *that* (singular) and *these* and *those* (plural). (*This, that, these,* and *those* can also be demonstrative adjectives when they modify a noun.)

> This is more thorough than that.

> The red shuttle buses stop here. These go to the airport every hour.

3. **Reflexive pronouns** indicate that the subject performs actions to, for, or upon itself. Reflexive pronouns end in *-self* or *-selves*.

> We excused ourselves from the table and left.

PERSON	SINGULAR	PLURAL
First person	myself	ourselves
Second person	yourself	yourselves
Third person	himself	
	herself	themselves
	itself	

4. **An intensive pronoun** emphasizes the word that comes before it in a sentence. Like reflexive pronouns, intensive pronouns end in *-self* or *-selves*.

> The filmmaker herself could not explain the ending.

> They themselves repaired the copy machine.

Note: A reflexive or intensive pronoun should not be used as a subject of a sentence. An antecedent for the reflexive pronoun must appear in the same sentence.

> INCORRECT   Myself create colorful sculpture.

> CORRECT   I myself create colorful sculpture.

5. **Interrogative pronouns** are used to introduce questions: *who, whom, whoever, whomever, what, which, whose.* The correct use of *who* and *whom* depends on the role the interrogative pronoun plays in a sentence or clause. When the pronoun functions as the subject of the sentence or clause, use *who.* When the pronoun functions as an object in the sentence or clause, use *whom.*

> What happened?

> Which is your street?

> Who wrote *Ragtime?* [*Who* is the subject of the sentence.]

> Whom should I notify? [*Whom* is the object of the verb *notify: I should notify whom?*]

6. **Relative pronouns** relate groups of words to nouns or other pronouns and often introduce adjective clauses or noun clauses (see p. 586). The relative pronouns are *who, whom, whoever, whomever,* and *whose* (referring to people) and *that, what, whatever,* and *which* (referring to things).

In 1836 Charles Dickens met John Forster, <u>who</u> became his friend and biographer.

We read some articles <u>that</u> were written by former astronauts.

7. **Indefinite pronouns** are pronouns without specific antecedents. They refer to people, places, or things in general.

<u>Someone</u> has been rearranging my papers.

<u>Many</u> knew the woman, but <u>few</u> could say they knew her well.

Here are some frequently used indefinite pronouns:

SINGULAR		PLURAL
another	nobody	all
anybody	none	both
anyone	no one	few
anything	nothing	many
each	one	more
either	other	most
everybody	somebody	others
everyone	someone	several
everything	something	some
neither		

8. **The reciprocal pronouns** *each other* and *one another* indicate a mutual relationship between two or more parts of a plural antecedent.

Dión and Sharon congratulated <u>each other</u> on their high grades.

EXERCISE 1   Identifying Nouns and Pronouns

Directions: In each of the following sentences (a) circle each noun and (b) underline each pronoun.

EXAMPLE   When <u>we</u> finished the (project), <u>our</u> (manager) celebrated by ordering (pizza) for <u>everyone</u> in the (office).

1. I know the course will be challenging, but I will do whatever it takes to succeed.

2. The blue whale can weigh up to 150 tons; its heart alone weighs as much as a car.

3. Victor and his co-workers collaborated on the report, but he wrote the final version himself.

4. Whoever calls to identify the song playing on the radio will win a free ticket to a concert.

5. My son and daughter both love sports: his favorite sport is basketball, and hers is baseball.

6. Anybody who owns a car can save a small fortune on repairs by taking a basic course in automotive mechanics.

7. Whose leftover food is making the refrigerator smell bad?

8. Kayla is president of a club that promotes environmental awareness and encourages students to use their bikes instead of cars.

9. During the horror movie my friend and I kept screaming and grabbing each other.

10. This is a busy time of year, but that is no excuse for skipping your workout.

■

A.3 VERBS

Verbs express action or state of being. A grammatically complete sentence has at least one verb in it.

There are three kinds of verbs: **action verbs**, **linking verbs**, and **helping verbs** (also known as **auxiliary verbs**).

1. **Action verbs** express physical and mental activities.

Mr. Ramirez <u>dashed</u> for the bus.

The incinerator <u>burns</u> garbage at high temperatures.

I <u>think</u> that seat is taken.

The programmer <u>worked</u> until 3:00 A.M.

Action verbs are either **transitive** or **intransitive**. The action of a **transitive verb** is directed toward someone or something, called the **direct object** of the verb. Direct objects receive the action of the verb. Transitive verbs require direct objects to complete the meaning of the sentence.

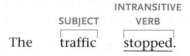

	TRANSITIVE	DIRECT
SUBJECT	VERB	OBJECT
Amalia	made	clocks.

An **intransitive verb** does not need a direct object to complete the meaning of the sentence.

		INTRANSITIVE
	SUBJECT	VERB
The	traffic	stopped.

Some verbs can be both transitive and intransitive, depending on their meaning and use in a sentence.

INTRANSITIVE   The traffic <u>stopped</u>. [no direct object]

DIRECT OBJECT

TRANSITIVE   The driver <u>stopped</u> the <u>bus</u> at the corner.

2. A **linking verb** expresses a state of being or a condition. A linking verb connects a noun or pronoun to words that describe the noun or pronoun.

Common linking verbs are forms of the verb *be* (*is, are, was, were, being, been*), *become, feel, grow, look, remain, seem, smell, sound, stay,* and *taste*.

Their child <u>grew</u> tall.

The office <u>looks</u> messy.

Mr. Davenport <u>is</u> our accountant.

3. **A helping (auxiliary) verb** helps another verb, called the **main verb**, to convey when the action occurred (through verb tense) and to form questions. One or more helping verbs and the main verb together form a **verb phrase**. Some helping verbs, called **modals**, are always helping verbs:

can, could	shall, should
may, might	will, would
must, ought to	

The other helping verbs can sometimes function as main verbs as well:

am, are, be, been, being, did, do, does

had, has, have

is, was, were

The verb *be* is a very irregular verb, with eight forms instead of the usual five: *am, is, are, be, being, been, was, were.*

HELPING   MAIN
VERB   VERB

The store <u>will</u> <u>close</u> early on holidays.

HELPING   MAIN
VERB   VERB

<u>Will</u> the store <u>close</u> early on New Year's Eve?

Forms of the Verb

All verbs except *be* have five forms: the **base form** (or dictionary form), the **past tense**, the **past participle**, the **present participle**, and the **-s form**. The first three forms are called the verb's **principal parts**. The **infinitive** consists of *to* plus a base form: *to go, to study, to talk.* For **regular verbs**, the past tense and past participle are formed by adding *-d* or *-ed* to the base form. **Irregular verbs** follow no set pattern to form their past tense and past participle.

TENSE	REGULAR	IRREGULAR
Base form	work	eat
Past tense	worked	ate
Past participle	worked	eaten
Present participle	working	eating
-s form	works	eats

Verbs change form to agree with their subjects in person and number (see p. 276); to express the time of their action (**tense**); to express whether the action is a fact, command, or wish (**mood**); and to indicate whether the subject is the doer or the receiver of the action (**voice**).

A. Parts of Speech

Principal Parts of Irregular Verbs

Consult the following list and your dictionary for the principal parts of irregular verbs.

BASE FORM	PAST TENSE	PAST PARTICIPLE
be	was, were	been
become	became	become
begin	began	begun
bite	bit	bitten
blow	blew	blown
burst	burst	burst
catch	caught	caught
choose	chose	chosen
come	came	come
dive	dived, dove	dived
do	did	done
draw	drew	drawn
drive	drove	driven
eat	ate	eaten
fall	fell	fallen
find	found	found
fling	flung	flung
fly	flew	flown
get	got	gotten
give	gave	given
go	went	gone
grow	grew	grown
have	had	had
know	knew	known
lay	laid	laid
lead	led	led
leave	left	left
lie	lay	lain
lose	lost	lost
ride	rode	ridden
ring	rang	rung
rise	rose	risen
say	said	said
set	set	set
sit	sat	sat
speak	spoke	spoken
swear	swore	sworn
swim	swam	swum
tear	tore	torn
tell	told	told
throw	threw	thrown
wear	wore	worn
write	wrote	written

Tense

The **tenses** of a verb express time. They convey whether an action, process, or event takes place in the present, past, or future.

The three **simple tenses** are **present**, **past**, and **future**. The **simple present** tense is the base form of the verb (and the -s form of third-person singular subjects; see p. 267); the **simple past** tense is the past-tense form; and the **simple future** tense consists of the helping verb *will* plus the base form.

The **perfect tenses**, which indicate completed action, are **present perfect**, **past perfect**, and **future perfect**. They are formed by adding the helping verbs *have* (or *has*), *had*, or *will have* to the past participle.

In addition to the simple and perfect tenses, there are six progressive tenses. The **simple progressive tenses** are the **present progressive**, the **past progressive**, and the **future progressive**. The progressive tenses are used for continuing actions or actions in progress. These progressive tenses are formed by adding the present, past, and future forms of the verb *be* to the present participle. The **perfect progressive tenses** are the **present perfect progressive**, the **past perfect progressive**, and the **future perfect progressive**. They are formed by adding the present perfect, past perfect, and future perfect forms of the verb *be* to the present participle.

The following chart shows all the tenses for a regular verb and an irregular verb in the first person. (For more on tenses, see p. 267.)

TENSE	REGULAR	IRREGULAR
Simple present	I talk	I go
Simple past	I talked	I went
Simple future	I will talk	I will go
Present perfect	I have talked	I have gone
Past perfect	I had talked	I had gone
Future perfect	I will have talked	I will have gone
Present progressive	I am talking	I am going
Past progressive	I was talking	I was going
Future progressive	I will be talking	I will be going
Present perfect progressive	I have been talking	I have been going
Past perfect progressive	I had been talking	I had been going
Future perfect progressive	I will have been talking	I will have been going

Mood

The mood of a verb indicates the writer's attitude toward the action. There are three moods in English: **indicative, imperative,** and **subjunctive.**

The **indicative mood** is used for ordinary statements of fact or questions.

The light <u>flashed</u> on and off all night.

<u>Did</u> you <u>check</u> the batteries?

The **imperative mood** is used for commands, suggestions, or directions. The subject of a verb in the imperative mood is *you,* though it is not always included.

<u>Stop</u> shouting!

<u>Come</u> to New York for a visit.

<u>Turn</u> right at the next corner.

The **subjunctive mood** is used for wishes, requirements, recommendations, and statements contrary to fact. For statements contrary to fact or for wishes, the past tense of the verb is used. For the verb *be,* only the past-tense form *were* is used.

If I <u>had</u> a million dollars, I'd take a trip around the world.

If my supervisor <u>were</u> promoted, I would be eligible for her job.

To express suggestions, recommendations, or requirements, the base form is often used.

I recommend that the houses <u>be</u> sold after the landscaping is done.

The registrar required that Maureen <u>pay</u> her bill before attending class.

Voice

Transitive verbs (those that take objects) may be in either the active voice or the passive voice (see p. 279). In an **active-voice** sentence, the subject performs the action described by the verb; that is, the subject is the actor. In a **passive-voice** sentence, the subject is the receiver of the action. The passive voice of a verb is formed by using an appropriate form of the helping verb *be* and the past participle of the main verb.

SUBJECT IS   ACTIVE
ACTOR   VOICE

Dr. Hillel <u>delivered</u> the report on global warming.

SUBJECT IS RECEIVER   PASSIVE VOICE

The report on global warming <u>was delivered</u> by Dr. Hillel.

EXERCISE 2   **Changing Verb Tense**

Directions: Revise the following sentences, changing each verb from the present tense to the tense indicated.

EXAMPLE   I <u>check</u> the inventory of office supplies.

PAST TENSE   I checked the inventory of office supplies. _____

1. They <u>explain</u> the problem to the computer technician.

   SIMPLE FUTURE _____

2. Kwan <u>reads</u> fairy tales to his daughter.

   PRESENT PROGRESSIVE _____

3. I <u>sell</u> the most product replacement plans.

   PAST PERFECT _____

4. The carefree days of summer <u>come</u> to an end.

   FUTURE PROGRESSIVE _____

5. Scientists <u>detect</u> evidence of liquid water on one of Saturn's moons.

   PRESENT PERFECT _____

   _____

6. Robert <u>laughs</u> at his cat's attempt to catch a fly.

   PAST PROGRESSIVE _____

7. I <u>complete</u> my degree requirements in May.

   FUTURE PERFECT _____

8. Darren <u>prepares</u> his final presentation for the course.

   PAST PERFECT PROGRESSIVE _____

   _____

9. The campus singing groups <u>rehearse</u> for two months.

   FUTURE PERFECT PROGRESSIVE _____

   _____

10. Emily and Teresa <u>play</u> soccer on the weekends.

    PRESENT PERFECT PROGRESSIVE _____

    _____

A.4 ADJECTIVES

Adjectives modify nouns and pronouns. That is, they describe, identify, qualify, or limit the meaning of nouns and pronouns. An adjective answers the question *Which one?, What kind?,* or *How many?* about the word it modifies.

WHICH ONE?	The <u>twisted</u>, <u>torn</u> umbrella was of no use to its owner.
WHAT KIND?	The <u>spotted</u> owl has caused <u>heated</u> arguments in the Northwest.
HOW MANY?	<u>Many</u> customers waited for <u>four</u> days for Internet service to be restored.

In form, adjectives can be **positive** (implying no comparison), **comparative** (comparing two items), or **superlative** (comparing three or more items). (See p. 188 for more on the forms of adjectives.)

POSITIVE

The computer is <u>fast</u>.

COMPARATIVE

Your computer is <u>faster</u> than mine.

SUPERLATIVE

This is the <u>fastest</u> computer I have ever used.

There are two general categories of adjectives. **Descriptive adjectives** name a quality of the person, place, thing, or idea they describe: *<u>mysterious</u> man, <u>green</u> pond, <u>healthy</u> complexion.* **Limiting adjectives** narrow the scope of the person, place, or thing they describe: *<u>my</u> computer, <u>this</u> tool, <u>second</u> try.*

Descriptive Adjectives

A **regular** (or **attributive**) adjective appears next to (usually before) the word it modifies. Several adjectives can modify the same word.

The <u>enthusiastic</u> <u>new</u> hairstylist gave <u>short</u>, <u>lopsided</u> haircuts.

The <u>wealthy</u> dealer bought an <u>immense</u> <u>blue</u> vase.

Sometimes nouns function as adjectives modifying other nouns: *<u>tree</u> house, <u>hamburger</u> bun.*

A **predicate adjective** follows a linking verb and modifies or describes the subject of the sentence or clause (see p. 574; see p. 583 on clauses).

PREDICATE ADJECTIVE

The meeting was <u>long</u>. [modifies the subject, *meeting*]

Limiting Adjectives

1. The **definite article**, *the,* and the **indefinite articles,** *a* and *an,* are classified as adjectives. *A* and *an* are used when it is not important to specify a particular noun or when the object named is not known to the reader (*A radish adds color to a salad*). *The* is used when it is important to specify one or more of a particular noun or when the object named is known to the reader or has already been mentioned (*The radishes from the garden are on the table*).

   A squirrel visited the feeder that I just built. The squirrel tried to eat some bird food.

2. When the possessive pronouns *my, your, his, her, its, our,* and *their* are used as modifiers before nouns, they are considered **possessive adjectives.**

   Your friend borrowed my laptop for his trip.

3. When the demonstrative pronouns *this, that, these,* and *those* are used as modifiers before nouns, they are called **demonstrative adjectives.** *This* and *these* modify nouns close to the writer; *that* and *those* modify nouns more distant from the writer.

   Buy these wireless headsets, not those wired ones.

   This freshman course is a prerequisite for those advanced courses.

4. **Cardinal adjectives** are words used in counting: *one, two, twenty,* and so on.

   I read four biographies of Jack Kerouac and seven articles about his work.

5. **Ordinal adjectives** note position in a series.

   The first biography was too sketchy, whereas the second one was too detailed.

6. **Indefinite adjectives** provide nonspecific, general information about the quantities and amounts of the nouns they modify. Some common indefinite adjectives are *another, any, enough, few, less, little, many, more, much, several,* and *some.*

   Several people asked me if I had enough blankets or if I wanted the thermostat turned up a few degrees.

7. The **interrogative adjectives** *what, which,* and *whose* modify nouns and pronouns used in questions.

   Which radio station do you like? Whose music do you prefer?

8. The words *which* and *what,* along with *whichever* and *whatever,* are **relative adjectives** when they modify nouns and introduce subordinate clauses.

   She couldn't decide which job she wanted to take.

9. **Proper adjectives** are adjectives derived from proper nouns: *Spain* (noun), *Spanish* (adjective); *Freud* (noun), *Freudian* (adjective). Most proper adjectives are capitalized.

   Shakespeare lived in Elizabethan England.

   The speaker used many French expressions.

EXERCISE 3   Revising by Adding Adjectives

Directions: Revise each of the following sentences by adding at least three adjectives.

EXAMPLE	My jacket provided little protection from the wind.
REVISED	My flimsy jacket provided little protection from the bitter, gusting wind.

1. The aroma of freshly baked bread greeted us as we entered the farmhouse.

_____

_____

2. Amalie's goal is to establish a preschool program that will meet the needs of children.

_____

_____

3. The barking of my neighbor's dog kept me awake for most of the night.

_____

_____

4. In the lab, students must follow rules about the use of equipment and materials.

_____

_____

5. I could hear my friend's laugh rising above the voices of other people at the reception.

_____

_____

6. A customer service representative must have communication skills and a patient personality.

_____

_____

7. My daughter constructs buildings out of blocks to house her collection of toy animals.

_____

_____

8. The painting that Akiko exhibited at the student art show was a success.

   _____

   _____

9. The lights of the aurora borealis created a display in the night sky.

   _____

   _____

10. As a volunteer at the local animal shelter, Susan solicits donations and helps find owners for the pets.

    _____

    _____

    ■

A.5 ADVERBS

Adverbs modify verbs, adjectives, other adverbs, or entire sentences or clauses (see p. 583 on clauses). Like adjectives, adverbs describe, qualify, or limit the meaning of the words they modify.

An adverb answers the question *How?, When?, Where?, How often?,* or *To what extent?* about the word it modifies.

HOW?	Cheryl moved <u>awkwardly</u> because of her stiff neck.
WHEN?	I arrived <u>yesterday</u>.
WHERE?	They searched <u>everywhere</u>.
HOW OFTEN?	He telephoned <u>repeatedly</u>.
TO WHAT EXTENT?	Simon was <u>rather</u> slow to answer his e-mail.

Many adverbs end in *-ly* (*lazily, happily*), but some adverbs do not (*fast, here, much, well, rather, everywhere, never, so*), and some words that end in *-ly* are not adverbs (*lively, friendly, lonely*). Like all other parts of speech, an adverb may best be identified by examining its function within a sentence.

I <u>quickly</u> skimmed the book. [modifies the verb *skimmed*]

<u>Very</u> angry customers crowded the service desk. [modifies the adjective *angry*]

He was injured <u>quite</u> seriously. [modifies the adverb *seriously*]

<u>Apparently</u>, the job was bungled. [modifies the whole sentence]

Like adjectives, adverbs have three forms: **positive** (does not suggest any comparison), **comparative** (compares two actions or conditions), and **superlative** (compares three or more actions or conditions; see also p. 188).

POSITIVE   POSITIVE

Noah rose early and crept downstairs quietly.

COMPARATIVE   COMPARATIVE

Levi rose earlier than Noah and crept downstairs more quietly.

SUPERLATIVE

Bill rose the earliest of anyone in the house and crept downstairs
most quietly.

SUPERLATIVE

Some adverbs, called **conjunctive adverbs** (or **adverbial conjunctions**)—
such as *however, therefore,* and *besides*—connect the ideas of one sentence or
clause to those of a previous sentence or clause. They can appear anywhere in
a sentence. (See p. 159 for how to punctuate sentences containing conjunctive
adverbs.)

CONJUNCTIVE ADVERB

James did not want to go to the library on Saturday; however, he knew
the books were overdue.

The sporting-goods store was crowded because of the sale. Leila,
therefore, was asked to work extra hours.

CONJUNCTIVE ADVERB

Some common conjunctive adverbs are listed below, including several
phrases that function as conjunctive adverbs.

accordingly	for example	meanwhile	otherwise
also	further	moreover	similarly
anyway	furthermore	namely	still
as a result	hence	nevertheless	then
at the same time	however	next	thereafter
besides	incidentally	nonetheless	therefore
certainly	indeed	now	thus
consequently	instead	on the contrary	undoubtedly
finally	likewise	on the other hand	

EXERCISE 4   Using Adverbs

Directions: Write a sentence using each of the following comparative or
superlative adverbs.

EXAMPLE   earlier: *The library is open until 5:00 on weekdays, but it*

closes earlier on weekends.

1. fastest: _____

_____

2. less carefully: _____

_____

3. most cheaply: _____

_____

4. higher: _____

_____

5. best: _____

_____

6. more generously: _____

_____

7. hardest: _____

_____

8. closer: _____

_____

9. least efficiently: _____

_____

10. better: _____

_____

■

A.6 CONJUNCTIONS

Conjunctions connect words, phrases, and clauses. There are three kinds of conjunctions: **coordinating, correlative,** and **subordinating. Coordinating** and **correlative conjunctions** connect words, phrases, or clauses of equal grammatical rank. (A **phrase** is a group of related words lacking a subject, a predicate, or both. A **clause** is a group of words containing a subject and a predicate; see pp. 571 and 572.)

1. The **coordinating conjunctions** are *and, but, nor, or, for, so,* and *yet*. These words must connect words or word groups of the same kind. Therefore, two nouns may be connected by *and,* but a noun and a clause cannot be. *For* and *so* can connect only independent clauses.

COORDINATING

NOUN   CONJUNCTION   NOUN

We studied the novels of Toni Morrison and Alice Walker.

A. Parts of Speech

COORDINATING
CONJUNCTION

VERB | VERB

The copilot successfully flew and landed the disabled plane.

COORDINATING   INDEPENDENT
INDEPENDENT CLAUSE   CONJUNCTION   CLAUSE

The carpentry course sounded interesting, so Meg enrolled.

COORDINATING   SUBORDINATE
INDEPENDENT CLAUSE   CONJUNCTION   CLAUSE

We hoped that the mail would come soon and that it would contain our bonus check.

2. **Correlative conjunctions** are pairs of words that link and relate grammatically equivalent parts of a sentence. Some common correlative conjunctions are *either/or, neither/nor, both/and, not/but, not only/but also,* and *whether/or.* Correlative conjunctions are always used in pairs.

CORRELATIVE CONJUNCTIONS

Either the electricity was off, or the bulb had burned out.

3. **Subordinating conjunctions** connect dependent, or subordinate, clauses to independent clauses (see p. 113). Some common subordinating conjunctions are *although, because, if, since, until, when, where,* and *while.*

SUBORDINATING CONJUNCTION

Although the movie got bad reviews, it drew big crowds.

SUBORDINATING CONJUNCTION

She received a lot of mail because she was a reliable correspondent.

A.7 PREPOSITIONS

A **preposition** links and relates its **object** (a noun or a pronoun) to the rest of the sentence. Prepositions often show relationships of time, place, direction, and manner.

PREPOSITION   OBJECT OF PREPOSITION

I walked around the block.

PREPOSITION   OBJECT OF PREPOSITION

She called during our meeting.

COMMON PREPOSITIONS				
along	besides	from	past	up
among	between	in	since	upon
around	beyond	near	through	with
at	by	off	till	within
before	despite	on	to	without
behind	down	onto	toward	
below	during	out	under	
beneath	except	outside	underneath	
beside	for	over	until	

Some prepositions consist of more than one word; they are called **phrasal prepositions** or **compound prepositions**.

PHRASAL PREPOSITION   OBJECT OF PREPOSITION

According to our records, you have enough credits to graduate.

PHRASAL PREPOSITION   OBJECT OF PREPOSITION

We decided to make the trip in spite of the snowstorm.

COMMON PHRASAL PREPOSITIONS		
according to	in addition to	on account of
aside from	in front of	out of
as of	in place of	prior to
as well as	in regard to	with regard to
because of	in spite of	with respect to
by means of	instead of	

The object of the preposition often has modifiers.

                                        OBJ. OF   OBJ. OF

          PREP.   MODIFIER PREP. PREP. MODIFIER PREP.

Not a sound came from the child's room except a gentle snoring.

Sometimes a preposition has more than one object (a **compound object**).

COMPOUND OBJECT OF PREPOSITION

PREPOSITION

The laundromat was between campus and home.

Usually the preposition comes before its object. In interrogative sentences, however, the preposition sometimes follows its object.

OBJECT OF PREPOSITION   PREPOSITION

What did your supervisor ask you about?

The preposition, object or objects of the preposition, and the object's modifiers all form a **prepositional phrase**.

PREPOSITIONAL PHRASE

The scientist conducted her experiment throughout the afternoon and early evening.

There may be many prepositional phrases in a sentence.

PREPOSITIONAL PHRASE   PREPOSITIONAL PHRASE

The water from the open hydrant flowed into the street.

The noisy kennel was underneath the beauty salon, despite the complaints of customers.

Alongside the weedy railroad tracks, an old hotel with faded grandeur stood near the abandoned brick station on the edge of town.

Prepositional phrases frequently function as adjectives or adverbs. If a prepositional phrase modifies a noun or pronoun, it functions as an adjective. If it modifies a verb, adjective, or adverb, it functions as an adverb.

The auditorium inside the conference center has a special sound system. [adjective modifying the noun *auditorium*]

The doctor looked cheerfully at the patient and handed the lab results across the desk. [adverbs modifying the verbs *looked* and *handed*]

EXERCISE 5   Using Prepositional Phrases

Directions: Expand each of the following sentences by adding a prepositional phrase in the blank.

EXAMPLE   Hummingbirds sip nectar *from flowers* .

1. The meteorologist predicts that the heat wave will continue
   _____.

2. _____, Kate sat in the front row and took careful notes.

3. I cautiously stepped _____ to keep my new shoes dry.

4. The batter hit the ball so hard that it flew _____.

5. If you misplace your house key, use the extra key located
   _____.

6. The orchestra conductor walked _____ and raised his baton.

7. My daughter always hides _____ when we play hide and seek.

8. When Sofia walks _____, she often picks up seashells.

9. Our manager said the report must be completed _____.

10. When Jamal opened the door, the cat ran _____ and escaped outside.

A.8 INTERJECTIONS

Interjections are words that express emotion or surprise. They are followed by an exclamation point, comma, or period, depending on whether they stand alone or serve as part or all of a sentence. Interjections are used in speech more than in writing.

<u>Wow</u>! What an announcement!

<u>So</u>, was that lost letter ever found?

<u>Well</u>, I'd better be going.

PEARSON
mywritinglab ┤ For support in mastering these topics, log in to
www.mywritinglab.com, go to the Study Plan tab,
click on Understanding the Parts of Speech and
choose Nouns, Pronouns, Verbs, Adjectives, Adverbs, and Prepositions from the
list of subtopics. Read and view the videos and resources in the Review Materials
section, and then complete the Recall, Apply, and Write exercises in the Activities
section. You can check your scores and overall progress by using the Gradebook.

Understanding the Parts of Sentences

A **sentence** is a group of words that expresses a complete thought about something or someone. A sentence must contain a **subject** and a **predicate**.

Subject	*Predicate*
Telephones	ring.
Cecilia	laughed.
Time	will tell.

Depending on their purpose and punctuation, sentences are **declarative, interrogative, exclamatory,** or **imperative.**

A **declarative sentence** makes a statement. It ends with a period.

SUBJECT PREDICATE

The snow fell steadily.

An **interrogative sentence** asks a question. It ends with a question mark (?).

SUBJECT PREDICATE

Who called?

An **exclamatory sentence** conveys strong emotion. It ends with an exclamation point (!).

SUBJECT PREDICATE

Your photograph is in the company newsletter!

An **imperative sentence** gives an order or makes a request. It ends with either a period or an exclamation point, depending on how mild or strong the command or request is. In an imperative sentence, the subject is *you,* but this often is not included.

PREDICATE

Get me a fire extinguisher now! [The subject *you* is understood: (*You*) get me a fire extinguisher now!]

B.1 SUBJECTS

Tip for Writers

A *sentence* is a group of words containing both a subject and a predicate. The subject is the part of the sentence that tells you whom or what the sentence is about.

The predicate is the part of the sentence that contains the main verb. It is also the part of the sentence that tells you what the subject is doing or that describes the subject.

The **subject** of a <u>sentence</u> is whom or what the sentence is about. It is who or what performs or receives the action expressed in the predicate. The subject is often a **noun**, a word that names a person, place, thing, or idea.

<u>Julia</u> worked on her math homework.

The rose <u>bushes</u> must be watered.

<u>Honesty</u> is the best policy.

The subject of a sentence can also be a **pronoun**, a word that refers to or substitutes for a noun.

<u>She</u> revised the memo three times.

<u>I</u> will attend the sales meeting.

Although the ink spilled, <u>it</u> did not get on my shirt.

The subject of a sentence can also be a group of words used as a noun.

<u>Reading e-mail from friends</u> is my idea of a good time.

Simple Versus Complete Subjects

The **simple subject** is the noun or pronoun that names what the sentence is about. It does not include any **modifiers**—that is, words that describe, identify, qualify, or limit the meaning of the noun or pronoun.

SIMPLE SUBJECT

The bright red concert <u>poster</u> caught everyone's eye.

SIMPLE SUBJECT

Online <u>banking</u> has revolutionized the banking industry.

When the subject of a sentence is a proper noun (the name of a particular person, place, or thing), the entire name is considered the simple subject.

SIMPLE SUBJECT

<u>Martin Luther King Jr.,</u> was a famous leader.

The simple subject of an imperative sentence is *you*.

SIMPLE SUBJECT

[<u>You</u>] Remember to bring the sales brochures.

The **complete subject** is the simple subject plus its modifiers.

COMPLETE SUBJECT

SIMPLE SUBJECT

<u>The sleek, black limousine</u> waited outside the church.

COMPLETE SUBJECT

Fondly remembered as a gifted songwriter, fiddle player, and storyteller, Quintin Lotus Dickey lived in a cabin in Paoli, Indiana.

SIMPLE SUBJECT

Compound Subjects

Some sentences contain two or more subjects joined with a coordinating conjunction (*and, but, nor, or, for, so, yet*). Those subjects together form a **compound subject.**

COMPOUND SUBJECT

Maria and I completed the marathon.

COMPOUND SUBJECT

The computer, the printer, and the DVD player were unusable during the blackout.

B.2 PREDICATES

The **predicate** indicates what the subject does, what happened to the subject, or what is being said about the subject. The predicate must include a **verb**, a word or group of words that expresses an action or a state of being (for example, *run, invent, build, know, will decide, become*).

Joy swam sixty laps.

The thunderstorm replenished the reservoir.

Sometimes the verb consists of only one word, as in the previous examples. Often, however, the main verb is accompanied by a **helping verb** (see p. 555).

HELPING   MAIN
VERB   VERB

By the end of the week, I will have worked 25 hours.

HELPING MAIN
VERB   VERB

The training session had begun.

HELPING MAIN
VERB   VERB

The professor did return the journal assignments.

Simple Versus Complete Predicates

The **simple predicate** is the main verb plus its helping verbs (together known as the **verb phrase**). The simple predicate does not include any modifiers.

SIMPLE PREDICATE

The proctor hastily <u>collected</u> the blue books.

SIMPLE PREDICATE

The moderator <u>had introduced</u> the next speaker.

The **complete predicate** consists of the simple predicate, its modifiers, and any complements (words that complete the meaning of the verb; see p. 574). In general, the complete predicate includes everything in the sentence except the complete subject.

COMPLETE PREDICATE
SIMPLE PREDICATE

The music <u>sounds</u> better from the back of the room.

COMPLETE PREDICATE
SIMPLE PREDICATE

Hannah <u>decided</u> to change the name of her company to something less controversial and confusing.

Compound Predicates

Some sentences have two or more predicates joined by a coordinating conjunction (*and, but, nor*). These predicates together form a **compound predicate**.

COMPOUND PREDICATE

Marcia <u>unlocked</u> her bicycle and <u>rode</u> away.

COMPOUND PREDICATE

The supermarket owner <u>will survey</u> his customers and <u>order</u> the specialized foods they desire.

EXERCISE 6   Identifying Sentence Parts

Directions: Underline the simple or compound subject and circle the simple or compound predicate in each of the following sentences.

EXAMPLE   Elizabeth Cady Stanton (championed) women's rights.

1. The coffee in the staff lounge tastes even worse than vending-machine coffee!
2. Of all the pediatricians in the clinic, Dr. Alvarez has the gentlest beside manner.
3. Students in the nursing program and staff of the local hospital are organizing a community health fair.

4. In their reviews of the new Italian restaurant, food critics praised the linguini with clam sauce and raved about the lobster ravioli.

5. By the end of next year, I will have repaid most of my student loans.

6. For many film stars of the 1940s, singing and dancing were essential job skills.

7. Kenji and his friend jog for thirty minutes most mornings and lift weights at least twice a week.

8. Last spring my sister took a criminal justice course and audited a sociology course.

9. Many well-known actors and other media celebrities made appearances at the political fund-raiser.

10. The art of modern sculptor Claes Oldenburg includes giant replicas of small, mundane objects such as a button or a lipstick. ■

B.3 COMPLEMENTS

A **complement** is a word or group of words used to complete the meaning of a subject or object. There are four kinds of complements: **subject complements**, which follow linking verbs; **direct objects** and **indirect objects**, which follow transitive verbs (verbs that take an object); and **object complements**, which follow direct objects.

Linking Verbs and Subject Complements

A linking verb (such as *be, become, seem, feel, taste*) links the subject to a **subject complement**, a noun or adjective that renames or describes the subject. (See p. 554 for more about linking verbs.) Nouns that function as complements are called **predicate nominatives** or **predicate nouns**. Adjectives that function as complements are called **predicate adjectives**.

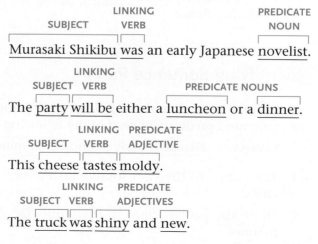

SUBJECT | LINKING VERB | PREDICATE NOUN
Murasaki Shikibu was an early Japanese novelist.

SUBJECT | LINKING VERB | PREDICATE NOUNS
The party will be either a luncheon or a dinner.

SUBJECT | LINKING VERB | PREDICATE ADJECTIVE
This cheese tastes moldy.

SUBJECT | LINKING VERB | PREDICATE ADJECTIVES
The truck was shiny and new.

Direct Objects

A **direct object** is a noun or pronoun that receives the action of a transitive verb (see p. 554). A direct object answers the question *What?* or *Whom?*

TRANSITIVE VERB   DIRECT OBJECT

The pharmacist helped us. [The pharmacist helped *whom*?]

TRANSITIVE VERB   DIRECT OBJECTS

Jillian borrowed a bicycle and a visor. [Jillian borrowed *what*?]

Indirect Objects

An **indirect object** is a noun or pronoun that receives the action of the verb indirectly. Indirect objects name the person or thing *to whom* or *for whom* something is done.

TRANSITIVE   INDIRECT   DIRECT
VERB   OBJECT   OBJECT

The computer technician gave me the bill. [He gave the bill *to whom*?]

TRANSITIVE VERB   INDIRECT OBJECTS   DIRECT OBJECTS

Eric bought his wife and son some sandwiches and milk. [He bought food *for whom*?]

Object Complements

An **object complement** is a noun or adjective that modifies (describes) or renames the direct object. Object complements appear with verbs like *name, find, think, elect, appoint, choose,* and *consider.*

DIRECT OBJECT   NOUN AS OBJECT COMPLEMENT

We appointed Joshua our representative. [*Representative* renames the direct object, *Joshua*.]

DIRECT OBJECT   ADJECTIVE AS OBJECT COMPLEMENT

The judge found the defendant innocent of the charges. [*Innocent* modifies the direct object, *defendant*.]

B.4 BASIC SENTENCE PATTERNS

There are five basic sentence patterns in English. They are built with combinations of subjects, predicates, and complements. The order of these elements within a sentence may change, or a sentence may become long and complicated when modifiers, phrases, or clauses are added. Nonetheless, one of five basic patterns stands at the heart of every sentence.

PATTERN 1

Subject	+	*Predicate*
I		shivered.
Brittany		swam.

PATTERN 2

Subject	+	*Predicate*	+	*Direct Object*
Anthony		ordered		a new desk.
We		wanted		freedom.

PATTERN 3

Subject	+	*Predicate*	+	*Subject Complement*
The woman		was		a welder.
Our course		is		interesting.

PATTERN 4

Subject	+	*Predicate*	+	*Indirect Object*	+	*Direct Object*
My friend		loaned		me		a laptop.
The company		sent		employees		a questionnaire.

PATTERN 5

Subject	+	*Predicate*	+	*Direct Object*	+	*Object Complement*
I		consider		her singing		exceptional.
Lampwick		called		Jiminy Cricket		a beetle.

EXERCISE 7   Using Complements

Directions: Complete each sentence with a word or words that will function as the type of complement indicated.

> EXAMPLE   The students elected Liang <u>president of the Student Senate</u>.
> object complement

1. These gardenias smell so _____ that they are making me sneeze.
predicate adjective

2. Matt checked the _____ of the previous meeting to verify that the
direct object
committee had reached agreement on the issue.

3. When my kids were young, I always sang _____ lullabies at bedtime.
indirect object

4. Some fans were not impressed by the band's latest releases, but I found the
new songs _____ and _____.
object complements

5. My grandparents have been _____ for 50 years, and they are still
in love.
predicate adjective

6. Caitlin e-mailed her _____ a map showing the location of her new
   indirect object

apartment.

7. As I spend more time with my co-worker, we are becoming closer
   _____.
   predicate noun

8. When Damian walked across the stage to receive his diploma, he seemed
   very _____ and _____.
   predicate adjectives

9. Latoya and her business partner are planning to open a new _____.
   direct object

10. The professor warned students that keeping up with the assigned reading in
    this course could be a _____. ■
    predicate noun

B.5 EXPANDING THE SENTENCE WITH ADJECTIVES AND ADVERBS

A sentence may consist of just a subject and a verb.

   Lei studied.

   Rumors circulated.

Most sentences, however, contain additional information about the subject and the verb. Information is commonly added in three ways:

- **by using adjectives and adverbs**
- **by using phrases** (groups of words that lack either a subject or a predicate or both)
- **by using clauses** (groups of words that contain both a subject and a predicate)

Using Adjectives and Adverbs to Expand Your Sentences

Adjectives are words used to modify or describe nouns and pronouns (see p. 560). Adjectives answer questions about nouns and pronouns such as *Which one?, What kind?, How many?* Using adjectives is one way to add detail and information to sentences.

WITHOUT ADJECTIVES   Dogs barked at cats.

WITH ADJECTIVES   Our three large, brown dogs barked at the two terrified spotted cats.

Note: Sometimes nouns and participles are used as adjectives (see p. 579 on participles).

NOUN USED AS ADJECTIVE

People are rediscovering the milk bottle.

PRESENT PARTICIPLE   PAST PARTICIPLE
USED AS ADJECTIVE   USED AS ADJECTIVE

Mrs. Simon had a swimming pool with a broken drain.

Adverbs add information to sentences by modifying or describing verbs, adjectives, or other adverbs (see p. 563). An adverb usually answers the question *How?, When?, Where?, How often?,* or *To what extent?*

WITHOUT ADVERBS   I will clean.

The audience applauded.

WITH ADVERBS   I will clean very thoroughly tomorrow.

The audience applauded loudly and enthusiastically.

B.6 EXPANDING THE SENTENCE WITH PHRASES

A **phrase** is a group of related words that lacks a subject, a predicate, or both. A phrase cannot stand alone as a sentence. Phrases can appear at the beginning, middle, or end of a sentence.

WITHOUT PHRASES   I noticed the stain.

Sal researched the topic.

Manuela arose.

WITH PHRASES   Upon entering the room, I noticed the stain on the expensive carpet.

At the local aquarium, Sal researched the topic of shark attacks.

An amateur astronomer, Manuela arose in the middle of the night to observe the lunar eclipse but, after waiting ten minutes in the cold, gave up.

There are eight kinds of phrases: **noun; verb; prepositional;** three kinds of **verbal phrases (participial, gerund,** and **infinitive); appositive;** and **absolute.**

Noun and Verb Phrases

A noun plus its modifiers is a **noun phrase** (*red shoes, the quiet house*). A main verb plus its helping verb is a **verb phrase** (*had been exploring, is sleeping;* see p. 555 on helping verbs.)

Prepositional Phrases

A **prepositional phrase** consists of a preposition (for example, *in, above, with, at, behind*), an object of the preposition (a noun or pronoun), and any modifiers of the object. (See p. 567 for a list of common prepositions.) A prepositional phrase functions like an adjective (modifying a noun or pronoun) or an adverb (modifying a verb, adjective, or adverb). You can use prepositional phrases to tell more about people, places, objects, or actions. A prepositional phrase usually adds information about time, place, direction, manner, or degree.

As Adjectives

The woman <u>with the briefcase</u> is giving a presentation <u>on meditation techniques</u>.

Both <u>of the telephones</u> <u>behind the partition</u> were ringing.

As Adverbs

The fire drill occurred <u>in the morning</u>.

I was curious <u>about the new human resources director</u>.

The conference speaker came <u>from Australia</u>.

<u>With horror</u>, the crowd watched the rhinoceros's tether stretch <u>to the breaking point</u>.

A prepositional phrase can function as part of the complete subject or as part of the complete predicate but should not be confused with the simple subject or simple predicate.

COMPLETE SUBJECT   COMPLETE PREDICATE

SIMPLE   PREPOSITIONAL PHRASE   SIMPLE
SUBJECT   PHRASE   PREDICATE

The red leather-bound volumes <u>on the dusty shelf</u> were filled with obscure facts.

PREPOSITIONAL PHRASE

COMPLETE PREDICATE

SIMPLE PREDICATE   PREPOSITIONAL PHRASE

Pat ducked quickly <u>behind the potted fern</u>.

Verbal Phrases

A **verbal** is a verb form that cannot function as the main verb of a sentence. The three kinds of verbals are **participles, gerunds,** and **infinitives.** A **verbal phrase** consists of a verbal and its modifiers.

Participles and Participial Phrases

All verbs have two participles: present and past. The **present participle** is formed by adding -*ing* to the base form (*walking, riding, being*). The **past participle** of regular verbs is formed by adding -*d* or -*ed* to the base form (*walked, baked*). The past participle of irregular verbs has no set pattern (*ridden, been*). (See p. 556 for a list of common irregular verbs and their past participles.) Both the present participle and the past participle can function as adjectives modifying nouns and pronouns.

PAST PARTICIPLE
AS ADJECTIVE

PRESENT PARTICIPLE
AS ADJECTIVE

Irritated, Natalia circled the confusing traffic rotary once again.

A **participial phrase** consists of a participle and any of its modifiers.

PARTICIPIAL PHRASE

PARTICIPLE

We listened for Isabella climbing the rickety stairs.

PARTICIPIAL PHRASE

PARTICIPLE

Disillusioned with the whole system, Kay sat down to think.

PARTICIPIAL PHRASE

PARTICIPLE

The singer, having caught a bad cold, canceled his performance.

Gerunds and Gerund Phrases

A **gerund** is the present participle (the *-ing* form) of the verb used as a noun.

Shoveling is good exercise.

Rex enjoyed gardening.

A **gerund phrase** consists of a gerund and its modifiers. A gerund phrase, like a gerund, is used as a noun and can therefore function in a sentence as a subject, a direct or indirect object, an object of a preposition, a subject complement, or an appositive.

GERUND PHRASE

Photocopying the report took longer than Alice anticipated. [subject]

GERUND PHRASE

The director considered making another monster movie. [direct object]

GERUND PHRASE

She gave running three miles daily credit for her health. [indirect object]

GERUND PHRASE

Before learning Greek, Omar spoke only English. [object of the preposition]

GERUND PHRASE

Her business is designing collapsible furniture. [subject complement]

GERUND PHRASE

Gabriel's trick, memorizing license plates, has come in handy. [appositive]

Infinitives and Infinitive Phrases

The **infinitive** is the base form of the verb as it appears in the dictionary preceded by the word *to*. An **infinitive phrase** consists of the infinitive and any modifiers. An infinitive phrase can function as a noun, an adjective, or an adverb. When it is used as a noun, an infinitive phrase can be a subject, object, complement, or appositive.

INFINITIVE PHRASE
To love one's enemies is a noble goal. [noun used as subject]

INFINITIVE PHRASE
The season to sell bulbs is the fall. [adjective modifying *season*]

INFINITIVE PHRASE
The chess club met to practice for the state championship. [adverb modifying *met*]

Sometimes the *to* in an infinitive phrase is not used.

Tyler helped us learn the new accounting procedure. [The *to* before *learn* is understood.]

Note: Do not confuse infinitive phrases with prepositional phrases beginning with the preposition *to*. In an infinitive phrase, *to* is followed by a verb; in a prepositional phrase, *to* is followed by a noun or pronoun, or an adjective and a noun.

Appositive Phrases

An **appositive** is a noun that explains, restates, or adds new information about another noun. An **appositive phrase** consists of an appositive and its modifiers. (See p. 592 for punctuation of appositive phrases.)

APPOSITIVE
Claude Monet completed the painting *Water Lilies* around 1903. [adds information about the noun *painting*]

APPOSITIVE PHRASE
APPOSITIVE
Francis, my neighbor with a large workshop, lent me a wrench. [adds information about the noun *Francis*]

Absolute Phrases

An **absolute phrase** consists of a noun or pronoun and any modifiers followed by a participle or a participial phrase. An absolute phrase modifies an entire sentence, not any particular word within the sentence. It can appear anywhere in a sentence and is set off from the rest of the sentence with a comma or commas. There may be more than one absolute phrase in a sentence.

ABSOLUTE PHRASE

The winter being over, the geese returned.

ABSOLUTE PHRASE

Senator Arden began his speech, his voice rising to be heard over the loud applause.

ABSOLUTE PHRASE

A vacancy having occurred, the hotel manager called the first name on the reservations waiting list.

EXERCISE 8   Expanding Sentences

Directions: Expand each of the following sentences by adding adjectives, adverbs, and/or phrases (prepositional, verbal, appositive, or absolute).

EXAMPLE   Mike and Chen studied.

EXPANDED   *The day before the exam, Mike and Chen studied together for three hours without a single break.*

1. I hung a poster. _____

_____

2. The squirrel snatched a seed. _____

_____

3. Thomas invited Monica. _____

_____

4. Midori demonstrated. _____

_____

5. I am working. _____

_____

6. Tyrell included graphs. _____

_____

7. Canoeing was an experience. _____

_____

8. The leader scheduled a meeting. _____

_____

9. Angelina helped her grandfather. _____

_____

10. I walked. _____

_____

■

B.7 EXPANDING THE SENTENCE WITH CLAUSES

A **clause** is a group of words that contains a subject and a predicate. A clause is either **independent** (also called **main**) or **dependent** (also called **subordinate**).

An **independent clause** can stand alone as a grammatically complete sentence.

INDEPENDENT CLAUSE   INDEPENDENT CLAUSE

SUBJECT PREDICATE   SUBJECT PREDICATE

The alarm sounded, and I awoke.

INDEPENDENT CLAUSE   INDEPENDENT CLAUSE

SUBJECT PREDICATE   SUBJECT   PREDICATE

The scientist worried. The experiment might fail.

INDEPENDENT CLAUSE   INDEPENDENT CLAUSE

SUBJECT PREDICATE   SUBJECT   PREDICATE

He bandaged his ankle. It had been sprained.

A **dependent clause** has a subject and a predicate, but it cannot stand alone as a grammatically complete sentence because it does not express a complete thought. Most dependent clauses begin with either a **subordinating conjunction** or a **relative pronoun**. These words connect the dependent clause to an independent clause.

SUBORDINATING

CONJUNCTION SUBJECT PREDICATE

because the alarm sounded

SUBORDINATING

CONJUNCTION SUBJECT   PREDICATE

that the experiment might fail

RELATIVE PRONOUN

(SUBJECT)   PREDICATE

which had been sprained

These clauses do not express complete thoughts and therefore cannot stand alone as sentences. When joined to independent clauses, however, dependent clauses function as adjectives, adverbs, and nouns and are known as **adjective** (or **relative**) **clauses, adverb clauses,** and **noun clauses.** Noun clauses can function as subjects, objects, or complements.

Common Subordinating Conjunctions		
after	inasmuch as	that
although	in case that	though
as	in order that	unless
as far as	insofar as	until
as if	in that	when
as soon as	now that	whenever
as though	once	where
because	provided that	wherever
before	rather than	whether
even if	since	while
even though	so that	why
how	supposing that	
if	than	
Relative Pronouns		
that	which	
what	who (whose, whom)	
whatever	whoever (whomever)	

Adjective Clause

DEPENDENT CLAUSE

He bandaged his ankle, which had been sprained. [modifies *ankle*]

Adverb Clause

DEPENDENT CLAUSE

Because the alarm sounded, I awoke. [modifies *awoke*]

Noun Clause

DEPENDENT CLAUSE

The scientist worried that the experiment might fail. [direct object of *worried*]

Sometimes the relative pronoun or subordinating conjunction is implied or understood rather than stated. Also, a dependent clause may contain an implied predicate. When a dependent clause is missing an element that can clearly be supplied from the context of the sentence, it is called an **elliptical clause.**

ELLIPTICAL CLAUSE

Reality TV is more entertaining than dramas [are]. [*Are* is the understood predicate in the elliptical dependent clause.]

ELLIPTICAL CLAUSE

Canadian history is among the subjects [that] the book discusses. [*That* is the understood relative pronoun in the elliptical dependent clause.]

Relative pronouns are generally the subject or object in their clauses. *Who* and *whoever* change to *whom* and *whomever* when they function as objects.

B.8 BASIC SENTENCE CLASSIFICATIONS

Depending on its structure, a sentence can be classified as one of four basic types: **simple**, **compound**, **complex**, or **compound-complex**.

Simple Sentences

A **simple sentence** has one independent (main) clause and no dependent (subordinate) clauses (see p. 113). A simple sentence contains at least one subject and one predicate. It may have a compound subject, a compound predicate, and various phrases, but it has only one clause.

SUBJECT PREDICATE

Sap rises.

SUBJECT   COMPOUND PREDICATE

In the spring the sap rises in the maple trees and is boiled to make a thick, delicious syrup.

Compound Sentences

A **compound sentence** has at least two independent clauses and no dependent clauses (see p. 154). The two independent clauses are usually joined with a comma and a coordinating conjunction (*and, but, nor, or, for, so, yet*). Sometimes the two clauses are joined with a semicolon and no coordinating conjunction or with a semicolon and a conjunctive adverb like *nonetheless* or *still* followed by a comma. (See p. 564 on conjunctive adverbs and p. 159 on punctuation.)

INDEPENDENT CLAUSE

Reading a novel by Henry James is not like reading a thriller, but with patience the rewards are greater.

INDEPENDENT CLAUSE

INDEPENDENT CLAUSE   INDEPENDENT CLAUSE

I set out to explore the North River near home; I ended up at Charlie's Clam Bar.

Complex Sentences

A **complex sentence** has one independent clause and one or more dependent clauses (see p. 156). The clauses are joined by subordinating conjunctions or relative pronouns (see p. 119).

INDEPENDENT CLAUSE   DEPENDENT CLAUSE

We tried to find topics to talk about while we waited for the bus.

INDEPENDENT CLAUSE   DEPENDENT CLAUSE

The receptionist greeted me warmly as I entered the office
because I hadn't seen her in a long time.

DEPENDENT CLAUSE

Compound-Complex Sentences

A **compound-complex sentence** contains two or more independent clauses
and one or more dependent clauses (see p. 154).

DEPENDENT CLAUSE   INDEPENDENT CLAUSE

If students work part-time, they must plan their studies carefully,
and they must limit their social lives.

INDEPENDENT CLAUSE

INDEPENDENT CLAUSE   INDEPENDENT CLAUSE   INDEPENDENT CLAUSE

It was mid-March, and the pond had begun to melt; I walked toward
it expectantly as I wondered if I could go skating one last time.

DEPENDENT CLAUSE   DEPENDENT CLAUSE

EXERCISE 9   Combining Sentences

Directions: Combine each of the following pairs of sentences into a single sentence by forming independent and/or dependent clauses. You may need to add,
change, or delete words.

EXAMPLE   **a.** The flip-flops were not selling well.

b. The store marked down the price of the flip-flops.

COMBINED   The flip-flops were not selling well, so the store marked down
the price.

1.   **a.** Alicia is good at making minor plumbing repairs.

b. Alicia does not attempt to fix electrical problems.

_____

_____

2.   **a.** My brother, an excellent gourmet cook, tried a new dessert recipe.

b. The new dessert recipe was a total disaster.

_____

_____

3.   **a.** Yuan previewed the course syllabus online.

b. Yuan decided to take a different course instead.

_____

_____

4. **a.** First the clay tiles must be thoroughly dried in the sun.

   b. Then the clay tiles are fired in the kiln.

   _____

5. **a.** Only a few people signed up for the summer course.

   b. The summer course has been canceled.

   _____

6. **a.** Ezra, the host of the potluck barbecue, will grill hamburgers and veggie dogs.

   b. Each guest will bring soda or a side dish.

   _____

   _____

7. **a.** Rachel is enrolled in the local community college.

   b. Rachel is studying to become an emergency medical technician.

   _____

   _____

8. **a.** Keisha will babysit her sister's kids on Saturday.

   b. Keisha will take the kids to the park.

   _____

9. **a.** The Meals On Wheels program is looking for volunteers to deliver meals.

   b. The volunteers must use their own cars to deliver the meals.

   _____

   _____

10. **a.** Some students study best late at night.

    b. Other students do their best studying in the morning.

    _____

    _____

    ■

Using Punctuation Correctly

C.1 END PUNCTUATION

When to Use Periods

Use a period in the following situations:

1. **To end a sentence unless it is a question or an exclamation.**

   We washed the car even though we knew a thunderstorm was imminent.

Note: Use a period to end a sentence that states an indirect question or indirectly quotes someone's words or thoughts.

INCORRECT	Courtney wondered if she would be on time?
CORRECT	Courtney wondered if she would be on time.

2. **To punctuate many abbreviations.**

   M.D.   B.A.   P.M.   B.C.   Mr.   Ms.

Do not use periods in acronyms, such as *NATO* and *AIDS,* or in abbreviations for most organizations, such as *NBC* and *NAACP.*

Note: If a sentence ends with an abbreviation, the sentence has only one period, not two.

   The train was due to arrive at 7:00 P.M.

When to Use Question Marks

Use question marks after direct questions.

   How long can a coral snake grow?

If a quotation ends in a question mark, place the question mark within the closing quotation marks.

   She asked the barista, "Do you have white mocha?"

If a quotation is included in a sentence that asks a question, the question mark goes after the closing quotation mark.

   Did you say Amber said, "I will not come"?

Tip for Writers

Punctuation

Practice recognizing punctuation marks, and make sure you know what they mean and how to use them. Using punctuation incorrectly can sometimes change the meaning of your sentences. Here are two examples:

1. When your friends help, you stop working.

   When your friends help you, stop working.

2. Did she finally marry Roger?

   Did she finally marry, Roger?

Note: Use a period, not a question mark, after an indirect question.

> She asked the barista if they had white mocha.

When to Use Exclamation Points

Use an exclamation point at the end of a sentence that expresses particular emphasis, excitement, or urgency. Use exclamation points sparingly, however, especially in academic writing.

> What a beautiful day it is!   Dial 911 right now!

C.2 COMMAS

The comma is used to separate parts of a sentence from one another. If you omit a comma when it is needed, you risk making a clear and direct sentence confusing.

When to Use Commas

Use a comma in the following situations:

1. **Before a coordinating conjunction that joins two independent clauses** (see p. 133).

   Terry had planned to leave work early, but he was delayed.

2. **To separate a dependent (subordinate) clause from an independent clause when the dependent clause comes first in the sentence** (see p. 163).

   After I left the library, I went to the computer lab.

3. **To separate introductory words and phrases from the rest of the sentence.**

   Unfortunately, I forgot my umbrella.

   To pass the baton, I will need to locate my teammate.

   Exuberant over their victory, the football-team members carried the quarterback on their shoulders.

4. **To separate a nonrestrictive phrase or clause from the rest of a sentence.** A **nonrestrictive** phrase or clause is added to a sentence but does not change the sentence's basic meaning.

   To determine whether an element is nonrestrictive, read the sentence without the element. If the meaning of the sentence does not essentially change, then the commas are *necessary*.

   My sister, who is a mail carrier, is afraid of dogs. [The essential meaning of this sentence does not change if we read the sentence without the subordinate clause: *My sister is afraid of dogs.* Therefore, commas are needed.]

Mail carriers who have been bitten by dogs are afraid of them. [If we read this sentence without the subordinate clause, its meaning changes considerably: *Mail carriers are afraid of (dogs).* It seems to say that *all* mail carriers are afraid of dogs. In this case, adding commas is incorrect.]

5. **To separate three or more items in a series.**

   Note: A comma is *not* used *after* the last item in the series.

   I plan to take math, psychology, and writing next semester.

6. **To separate coordinate adjectives: two or more adjectives that are not joined by a coordinating conjunction and that equally modify the same noun or pronoun.**

   The thirsty, hungry children returned from a day at the beach.

   To determine if a comma is needed between two adjectives, use the following test. Insert the word *and* between the two adjectives. Also try reversing the order of the two adjectives. If the phrase makes sense in either case, a comma is needed. If the phrase does not make sense, do not use a comma.

   The tired, angry child fell asleep. [*The tired and angry child* makes sense; so does *The angry, tired child.* Consequently, the comma is needed.]

   Sarah is an excellent psychology student. [*Sarah is an excellent and psychology student* does not make sense, nor does *Sarah is a psychology, excellent student.* A comma is therefore not needed.]

7. **To separate parenthetical expressions from the clauses they modify.** Parenthetical expressions are added pieces of information that are not essential to the meaning of the sentence.

   Most students, I imagine, can get jobs on campus.

8. **To separate a transition from the clause it modifies.**

   In addition, I will revise the bylaws.

9. **To separate a quotation from the words that introduce or explain it.**
   Note: The comma goes *inside* the closing quotation marks.

   "Shopping," Jade explained, "is a form of relaxation for me."

   Jade explained, "Shopping is a form of relaxation for me."

10. **To separate dates, place names, and long numbers.**

    October 10, 1994, is my birthday.

    Dayton, Ohio, was the first stop on the tour.

    Participants numbered 1,777,716.

11. **To separate phrases expressing contrast**

    Sam's good nature, not his wealth, explains his popularity.

■ EXERCISE 10   Adding Commas

Directions: Revise each of the following sentences by adding commas where needed.

EXAMPLE   If you feel like seeing a movie tonight, give me a call.

1. According to the American Red Cross Hurricane Katrina and Hurricane Rita destroyed more than 350,000 homes.

2. Many fans who attended the rock concert thought the band sounded great but some were disappointed that the concert was so short.

3. "If you're feeling brave" said Lin "we could ski down the black-diamond trail."

4. Diego met with his academic advisor who is the chair of the computer science department to discuss career options.

5. When I switched to a vegan diet I quit eating meat fish eggs and milk.

6. During Ben's performance review the manager commended him for his positive respectful interactions with patrons.

7. Tonight as you may recall is your night to do the dishes.

8. Volunteering for Habitat for Humanity has been a pleasure not a burden.

9. I don't have time to go swimming right now; besides it looks like it's going to rain.

10. Shauna is planning to visit her friend in Washington D.C. when the cherry trees bloom.

■

C.3 UNNECESSARY COMMAS

It is as important to know where *not* to place commas as it is to know where to place them. The following rules explain where it is incorrect to place them:

1. **Do not place a comma between a subject and its verb, between a verb and its complement, or between an adjective and the word it modifies.**

   ADJECTIVE   SUBJECT

   INCORRECT   The stunning, imaginative, and intriguing, painting, became the hit of the show.

   VERB

   CORRECT   The stunning, imaginative, and intriguing painting became the hit of the show.

2. **Do not place a comma between two verbs, subjects, or complements used as compounds.**

   COMPOUND VERB

   INCORRECT   Kaitlin called, and asked me to come by her office.

   CORRECT   Kaitlin called and asked me to come by her office.

3. **Do not place a comma before a coordinating conjunction joining two dependent clauses.**

DEPENDENT CLAUSE

INCORRECT   The city planner examined blueprints that the park designer had submitted, and that the budget officer had approved.

DEPENDENT CLAUSE

CORRECT   The city planner examined blueprints that the park designer had submitted and that the budget officer had approved.

4. **Do not place commas around restrictive clauses, phrases, or appositives.** Restrictive clauses, phrases, and appositives are modifiers that are essential to the meaning of the sentence.

INCORRECT   The girl, who grew up down the block, became my lifelong friend.

CORRECT   The girl who grew up down the block became my lifelong friend.

5. **Do not place a comma before the word *than* in a comparison or after the words *like* and *such* as in an introduction to a list.**

INCORRECT   Some snails, such as, the Oahu tree snail, have more colorful shells, than other snails.

CORRECT   Some snails, such as the Oahu tree snail, have more colorful shells than other snails.

6. **Do not place a comma next to a period, a question mark, an exclamation point, a dash, or an opening parenthesis.**

INCORRECT   "When will you come back ?," Dillon's son asked him.

CORRECT   "When will you come back ?" Dillon's son asked him.

INCORRECT   The bachelor button, (also known as the cornflower) grows well in ordinary garden soil.

CORRECT   The bachelor button (also known as the cornflower) grows well in ordinary garden soil.

7. **Do not place a comma between cumulative adjectives.** Cumulative adjectives, unlike coordinate adjectives (see p. 590), cannot be joined by *and* or rearranged.

INCORRECT   The light, yellow, rose blossom was a pleasant birthday surprise. [*The light and yellow and rose blossom* does not make sense, so the commas are incorrect.]

CORRECT   The light yellow rose blossom was a pleasant birthday surprise.

C.4 COLONS AND SEMICOLONS

When to Use a Colon

A colon follows an independent clause and usually signals that the clause is to be explained or elaborated on. Use a colon in the following situations:

1. **To introduce items in a series after an independent clause.** The series can consist of words, phrases, or clauses.

   I am wearing three popular colors: gray, black, and white.

2. **To signal a list or a statement introduced by an independent clause ending with *the following* or *as follows*.**

   The directions are as follows: take Main Street to Oak Avenue and then turn left.

3. **To introduce a quotation that follows an introductory independent clause.**

   My brother made his point quite clear: "Never borrow my car without asking me first!"

4. **To introduce an explanation.**

   Mathematics is enjoyable: it requires a high degree of accuracy and peak concentration.

5. **To separate titles and subtitles of books.**

   Biology: A Study of Life

Note: A colon must always follow an independent clause. It should not be used in the middle of a clause.

   INCORRECT   My favorite colors are: red, pink, and green.

   CORRECT   My favorite colors are red, pink, and green.

When to Use a Semicolon

Use a semicolon in the following situations:

1. **To separate two closely related independent clauses not connected by a coordinating conjunction** (see p. 135).

   Sam had a 99 average in math; he earned an A in the course.

2. **To separate two independent clauses joined by a conjunctive adverb** (see p. 159).

   Margaret earned an A on her term paper; consequently, she was exempt from the final exam.

3. **To separate independent clauses joined with a coordinating conjunction if the clauses are very long or if they contain numerous commas.**

   By late afternoon, having tried on every pair of black checked pants in the mall, Maribel was tired and cranky; but she still had not found what she needed to complete her outfit for the play.

4. **To separate items in a series if the items are lengthy or contain commas.**

   The soap opera characters include Marianne Loundsberry, the heroine; Maya and Sarah, her children; Barry, her ex-husband; and Louise, her best friend.

5. **To correct a comma splice or run-on sentence** (see pp. 135, 142).

EXERCISE 11   Adding Colons and Semicolons

Directions: Correct each of the following sentences by placing colons and semicolons where necessary. Delete any incorrect punctuation.

EXAMPLE   Even when I'm busy, I try to make time for my three favorite hobbies: reading, gardening, and biking.

1. When Kyoko plans a hike, she makes sure her backpack contains the following items; water, power bars, sunscreen, bug repellent, a windbreaker, and a cell phone.
2. Mark Twain said it best, "The difference between the almost right word and the right word . . . 'tis the difference between the lightning-bug and the lightning."
3. Consider this amazing fact, the superheated air, that surrounds a bolt of lightning, is about four times hotter than the surface of the sun.
4. I couldn't have made it through college without coffee; in fact, if I were writing a memoir about that period, the title would probably be "College, The Coffee Years."
5. The classic movie, *Casablanca*, had a stellar cast; Humphrey Bogart, who played the role of Rick, Ingrid Bergman, who played Ilsa, and Claude Rains, who played Louis.
6. It is certainly reassuring when a pediatrician tells you not to worry about your sick child, however, you also need to trust your own instincts and advocate for your child.
7. Any decent job should provide: a fair salary, reasonable working hours, and a safe work environment, these elements are nonnegotiable.
8. When I was a child, my grandfather gave me clear instructions for picking strawberries, pick the berries that are bright red, but leave the light, red berries.

9. The last thing Jasper needed was responsibility for another pet, never-theless, the large, dark, pleading, eyes of the abandoned puppy, proved irresistible.

10. For my son's birthday, his two cousins, and several children from the neigh-borhood joined us for a picnic in the park, everyone had a great time.

C.5 DASHES, PARENTHESES, HYPHENS, APOSTROPHES, QUOTATION MARKS

Dashes (—)

The dash is used to (1) separate nonessential elements from the main part of the sentence, (2) create a stronger separation, or interruption, than commas or parentheses, and (3) emphasize an idea, create a dramatic effect, or indicate a sudden change in thought.

My sister—the friendliest person I know—will visit me this weekend.

My brother's most striking quality is his ability to make money—or so I thought until I heard of his bankruptcy.

Do not leave spaces between the dash and the words it separates.

Parentheses ( )

Parentheses are used in pairs to separate extra or nonessential information that often amplifies, clarifies, or acts as an aside to the main point. Unlike dashes, parentheses de-emphasize information.

Some large breeds of dogs (golden retrievers and Newfoundlands) are susceptible to hip deformities.

The prize was dinner for two (maximum value, $50.00) at a restaurant of one's choice.

Hyphens (-)

Hyphens have the following primary uses:

1. **To split a word when dividing it between two lines of writing or typing** (see p. 602).

2. **To join two or more words that function as a unit, either as a noun or as a noun modifier.**

mother-in-law   single-parent families
twenty-year-old   school-age children
state-of-the-art sound system

Apostrophes (')

Use apostrophes in the following situations:

1. **To show ownership or possession.** When the person, place, or thing doing the possessing is a singular noun, add -'s to the end of it, regardless of what its final letter is.

   The man's DVD player   John Keats's poetry
   Aretha's best friend

   • With plural nouns that end in -s, add only an apostrophe to the end of the word.

   the twins' bedroom   postal workers' hours
   teachers' salaries

   With plural nouns that do not end in -s, add -'s.

   children's books   men's slacks

   • Do not use an apostrophe with the possessive adjective *its*.

   INCORRECT   It's frame is damaged.
   CORRECT   Its frame is damaged.

2. **To indicate omission of one or more letters in a word or number.** Contractions are used in informal writing but usually not in formal academic writing.

   it's [it is]   hasn't [has not]
   doesn't [does not]   '57 Ford [1957 Ford]
   you're [you are]   class of '12 [class of 2012]

Quotation Marks (" ")

Quotation marks separate a direct quotation from the sentence that contains it. Here are some rules to follow in using quotation marks.

1. **Quotation marks are always used in pairs.**

   Note: A comma or period goes at the end of the quotation, inside the quotation marks.

   Shana declared, "I never expected D'Andre to give me a watch for Christmas."

   "I never expected D'Andre to give me a watch for Christmas," Shana declared.

2. **Use single quotation marks for a quotation within a quotation.**

   My literature professor said, "Byron's line 'She walks in beauty like the night' is one of his most sensual."

   Note: When quoting long prose passages of more than four typed lines, do not use quotation marks. Instead, set off the quotation from the rest of the text by indenting each line one inch from the left margin. This format is called a **block quotation.**

The opening lines of the Declaration of Independence establish the purpose of the document:

> When in the Course of human events it becomes necessary for one people to dissolve the political bonds which have connected them with another, and to assume among the powers of the earth, the separate and equal station to which the Laws of Nature and of Nature's God entitle them, a decent respect to the opinions of mankind requires that they should declare the causes which impel them to the separation.

3. **Use quotation marks to indicate titles of songs, short stories, poems, reports, articles, and essays.** Books, movies, plays, operas, paintings, statues, and the names of television series are italicized.

"Rappaccini's Daughter" (short story)

American Idol (television series)

"The Road Not Taken" (poem)

Huckleberry Finn (book)

4. **Colons, semicolons, exclamation points, and question marks, when not part of the quoted material, go outside of the quotation marks.**

What did George mean when he said, "People in glass houses shouldn't throw stones"?

EXERCISE 12   Adding Punctuation

Directions: To the following sentences, add dashes, apostrophes, parentheses, hyphens, and quotation marks where necessary.

EXAMPLE   All faculty members' e-mail addresses are listed in the college directory.

1. Whenever my friend has a personal problem, he just buys another self help book.
2. What famous play includes the line, I have always relied on the kindness of strangers?
3. If a movie is rated PG parental guidance suggested, I preview it myself to make sure that its appropriate for my eight year old son.
4. When asked to identify the greatest rock song of all time, the music critic replied, That's easy the song Stairway to Heaven by the band Led Zeppelin.
5. Answering customers questions about computer products is Aarons responsibility.
6. One of Maya Angelous most beloved poems is I Know Why the Caged Bird Sings; equally inspirational is her poem I Rise.
7. Be careful if you see the horses ears flattened against its head, as this may mean that the horse is about to kick.

8. If you can wait a minute, said Serena, Id be happy to check that price for you."

9. Alfred Hitchcocks film *Psycho* possibly the greatest horror movie of all time has terrified generations of viewers since its release in 1960.

10. The professor assigned two more Hemingway stories, in addition to My Old Man : Hills Like White Elephants and A Clean Well-Lighted Place.

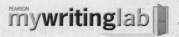 For support in mastering these topics, log in to www.mywritinglab.com, go to the Study Plan tab, click on Using Punctuation Correctly and choose Final Punctuation, Commas, Semicolons, Colons, Dashes and Parentheses, Apostrophes, and Quotation Marks from the list of subtopics. Read and view the videos and resources in the Review Materials section, and then complete the Recall, Apply, and Write exercises in the Activities section. You can check your scores and overall progress by using the Gradebook.

Managing Mechanics and Spelling

D.1 CAPITALIZATION

In general, capital letters are used to mark the beginning of a sentence, to mark the beginning of a quotation, and to identify proper nouns. Here are some guidelines on capitalization:

What to Capitalize	*Example*
1. First word in every sentence	Prewriting is useful.
2. First word in a direct quotation	Sarah commented, "That exam was difficult!"
3. Names of people and animals, including the pronoun *I*	Aladdin Michelle Obama Spot
4. Names of specific places, cities, states, nations, geographic areas, or regions	New Orleans the Southwest Lake Erie
5. Government and public offices, departments, buildings	Williamsville Library House of Representatives
6. Names of social, political, business, sporting, cultural organizations	Boy Scouts Buffalo Bills
7. Names of months, days of the week, holidays	August Tuesday Halloween
8. In titles of works: the first word following a colon, the first and last words, and all other words except articles, prepositions, and conjunctions	*Biology: A Study of Life* "Once More to the Lake"
9. Races, nationalities, languages	African-American, Italian, English
10. Religions, religious figures, sacred books	Hindu, Hinduism, God, Allah, the Bible
11. Names of products	Tide, Buick

599

12. Personal titles when they come right before a name	Professor Rodriguez Senator Hatch
13. Major historic events	World War I
14. Specific course titles	History 201 Introduction to Psychology

<hr>

EXERCISE 13   **Capitalizing Words**

Directions: Capitalize words as necessary in the following sentences.

EXAMPLE   Henry Thoreau said, "to regret deeply is to live afresh."

1. Artist Georgia O'Keeffe lived for many years in new mexico, painting images that captured the stark beauty of the american southwest.

2. I haven't completed my paper for professor Stern yet, so I will have to finish writing it over the thanksgiving break.

3. On april 9, 1865, the american civil war drew to a close when confederate general Robert E. Lee surrendered at appomattox court house.

4. The springfield city library now offers free access to wireless internet service.

5. The first five books of the old testament of the bible form the sacred jewish text of the pentateuch.

6. Science is not my strongest subject, so I took the course physics for poets to fulfill my science requirement.

7. Baseball legend Jackie Robinson, who played for the brooklyn dodgers, told the story of his life in the book *I never had it made: an autobiography of Jackie Robinson.*

8. The great salt lake, located in northern utah, is much saltier than the pacific ocean; the salty water makes swimmers unusually buoyant, so they float very easily.

9. The novel *all quiet on the western front* tells the story of a young soldier's experience during world war I.

10. My daughter refuses to eat anything but kellogg's frosted flakes for breakfast; while she eats, she studies the picture of tony the tiger on the cereal box. ■

<hr>

D.2 ABBREVIATIONS

An abbreviation is a shortened form of a word or phrase that is used to represent the whole word or phrase. The following is a list of common acceptable abbreviations:

What to Abbreviate	*Example*
1. Some titles before or after people's names	Mr. Ling Samuel Rosen, M.D. *but* Professor Ashe
2. Names of familiar organizations, corporations, countries	CIA, IBM, VISTA, USA

3. Time references preceded or followed by a number

7:00 A.M.
3:00 P.M.
A.D. 1973

4. Latin terms when used in footnotes, references, or parentheses

i.e. [*id est*, "that is"]
et al. [*et alii*, "and others"]

Here is a list of things that are usually *not* abbreviated in a paragraph or essay:

	Example	
What Not to Abbreviate	*Incorrect*	*Correct*
1. Units of measurement	thirty in.	thirty inches
2. Geographic or other place names when used in sentences	N.Y. Elm St.	New York Elm Street
3. Parts of written works when used in sentences	Ch. 3	Chapter 3
4. Names of days, months, holidays	Tues.	Tuesday
5. Names of subject areas	psych.	psychology

EXERCISE 14   Revising Abbreviations

Directions: Correct the inappropriate use of abbreviations in the following sentences. If a sentence contains no errors, write "C" beside it.

EXAMPLE   The tiny lizard is only about four ~~em~~ long.

centimeters

_____ 1. Homer Hickam, a boy known for building homemade rockets during the 1950s, became a NASA engineer as an adult.

_____ 2. A great sprinter, Susan is expected to win the fifty-yd. dash.

_____ 3. Spicy foods—e.g., hot peppers—sometimes disagree with me.

_____ 4. My English lit. class meets Tues. and Th. at 2:00.

_____ 5. Some convicted criminals have been freed from prison after DNA testing proved they were innocent.

_____ 6. The co. I work for is located on Walnut St. in Phila.

_____ **7.** I stayed up until 3:00 A.M to finish reading the final chap. of this exciting novel.

_____

_____ **8.** The *Aeneid,* Virgil's epic poem about the founding of Rome, was written about 30 B.C.E.

_____

_____ **9.** During Aug., the heat in TX can be brutal.

_____

_____ **10.** Prof. Jenkins has a very engaging lecture style.

_____

■

D.3 HYPHENATION AND WORD DIVISION

On occasion you may want to divide and hyphenate a word on one line and continue it on the next. Here are some guidelines for dividing words.

1. **Divide words only when necessary.** Frequent word divisions make a paper difficult to read.

2. **Divide words between syllables.** Consult a dictionary if you are unsure how to break a word into syllables.

    di-vi-sion   pro-tect

3. **Do not divide one-syllable words.**

4. **Do not divide a word so that a single letter is left at the end of a line.**

    INCORRECT   a-typical

    CORRECT   atyp-ical

5. **Do not divide a word so that fewer than three letters begin the new line.**

    INCORRECT   visu-al

    CORRECT   vi-sual

    INCORRECT   caus-al [This word cannot be divided at all.]

6. **Divide compound words only between the words.**

    some-thing   any-one

7. **Divide words that are already hyphenated only at the hyphen.**

    ex-policeman

EXERCISE 15   Dividing Words

Directions: Insert a diagonal (/) mark where each word should be divided. Write "N" in the margin if the word should not be divided.

EXAMPLE   fic/tion

———————— 1. crashing   ———————— 6. elite

———————— 2. splurge   ———————— 7. unsteady

———————— 3. cross-reference ———————— 8. sandpaper

———————— 4. amorphous   ———————— 9. x-ray

———————— 5. glory   ———————— 10. property ■

D.4 NUMBERS

Numbers can be written as numerals (600) or words (six hundred). Here are some guidelines for when to use numerals and when to use words:

When to Use Numerals	*Example*
1. Numbers that are spelled with more than two words	375 students
2. Days and years	August 10, 1993
3. Decimals, percentages, fractions	56.7 59 percent 1¾ cups
4. Exact times	9:27 A.M.
5. Pages, chapters, volumes; acts and lines from plays	chapter 12 volume 4
6. Addresses	122 Peach Street
7. Exact amounts of money	$5.60
8. Scores and statistics	23–6 5 of every 12

When to Use Words	*Example*
1. Numbers that begin sentences	Two hundred ten students attended the lecture.
2. Numbers of one or two words	sixty students, two hundred women

■ EXERCISE 16   **Revising Misused Numbers**

Directions: Correct the misuse of numbers in the following sentences. If a sentence contains no errors, write "C" next to it.

EXAMPLE   I planned to read fifty pages last night, but I only made it to page ~~forty-two~~. 42

_____ 1. When we rehearse Act 6 of the play, I keep messing up line sixteen.

_____ 2. Beat one and three-quarters cups of sugar into the softened butter.

_____ 3. In 2011 a Gallup survey showed that roughly 7 out of 10 Americans own a dog or a cat.

_____ 4. Lola ran the race in fourteen point three seconds.

_____ 5. 46 percent of Americans have used the Internet, e-mail, or text messaging to participate in the political process.

_____ 6. The world's population is expected to reach almost nine billion by the year 2042.

_____ 7. According to the syllabus, we need to read chapters seven and eight by next week.

_____ 8. Jian's daughter proudly reported that she had saved two dollars and twenty-seven cents in her piggy bank.

_____ 9. On weekdays, I always set my alarm for 7:10 A.M., but I generally hit the snooze bar and sleep for another 15 or 20 minutes.

_____ 10. When I was ten years old, my goal was to read every volume of the encyclopedia, but I only finished part of volume 1.

D.5 SUGGESTIONS FOR IMPROVING SPELLING

Correct spelling is important in a well-written paragraph or essay. The following suggestions will help you submit papers without misspellings:

1. **Do not worry about spelling as you write your first draft.** Checking a word in a dictionary at this point will interrupt your flow of ideas. If you do not know how a word is spelled, spell it the way it sounds. Circle or underline the word so you remember to check it later.

2. **Keep a list of words you commonly misspell.** This list can be part of your error log.

3. **Every time you catch an error or find a misspelled word on a paper returned by your instructor, add it to your list.**

4. **Study your list.** Ask a friend to quiz you on the words. Eliminate words from the list after you have passed several quizzes on them.

5. **Develop a spelling awareness.** You'll find that your spelling will improve just by your being aware that spelling is important. When you encounter a new word, notice how it is spelled and practice writing it.

6. **Pronounce words you are having difficulty spelling.** Pronounce each syllable distinctly.

7. **Review basic spelling rules.** Your college library or learning lab may have manuals, workbooks, or computer programs that cover basic rules and provide guided practice.

8. **Be sure to have a dictionary readily available when you write.**

9. **Read your final draft through once, checking only for spelling errors.** Look at each word carefully, and check the spelling of those words of which you are uncertain.

D.6 SIX USEFUL SPELLING RULES

The following six rules focus on common spelling trouble spots:

1. **Is it *ei* or *ie*?**

   Rule: Use *i* before *e*, except after *c* or when the syllable is pronounced *ay* as in the word *weigh.*

   EXAMPLE   *i* before *e:* bel<u>ie</u>ve, n<u>ie</u>ce

   except after *c:* rec<u>ei</u>ve, conc<u>ei</u>ve

   or when pronounced *ay:* n<u>ei</u>ghbor, sl<u>ei</u>gh

Exceptions:	either	neither	foreign	forfeit
	height	leisure	seize	weird

2. **When adding an ending, do you keep or drop the final *e*?**

   Rules: **a.** Keep the final *e* when adding an ending that begins with a consonant. (Vowels are *a, e, i, o, u,* and sometimes *y;* all other letters are consonants.)

   hope → hop<u>ef</u>ul   aware → awar<u>en</u>ess

   live → liv<u>el</u>y   force → forc<u>ef</u>ul

   b. Drop the final *e* when adding an ending that begins with a vowel.

   hope → hop<u>in</u>g   file → fil<u>in</u>g

   note → not<u>ab</u>le   write → writ<u>in</u>g

Exceptions:	argument	truly	changeable
	awful	manageable	courageous
	judgment	noticeable	outrageous
	acknowledgment		

3. **When adding an ending, do you keep the final _y_, change it to _i_, or drop it?**

   Rules: **a.** Keep the _y_ if the letter before the _y_ is a vowel.

   de<u>lay</u> → de<u>lay</u>ing   b<u>uy</u> → b<u>uy</u>ing   pr<u>ey</u> → pr<u>ey</u>ed

   b. Change the _y_ to _i_ if the letter before the _y_ is a consonant, but keep the _y_ for the _-ing_ ending.

   de<u>fy</u> → de<u>fi</u>ance   mar<u>ry</u> → mar<u>ri</u>ed
         → de<u>fy</u>ing   → mar<u>ry</u>ing

4. **When adding an ending to a one-syllable word, when do you double the final letter if it is a consonant?**

   Rules: **a.** In one-syllable words, double the final consonant when a single vowel comes before it.

   dr<u>op</u> → dr<u>opp</u>ed   sh<u>op</u> → sh<u>opp</u>ed   p<u>it</u> → p<u>itt</u>ed

   b. In one-syllable words, _don't_ double the final consonant when two vowels or a consonant comes before it.

   rep<u>air</u> → rep<u>air</u>able   so<u>und</u> → so<u>und</u>ed
   r<u>eal</u> → r<u>eal</u>ize

5. **When adding an ending to a word with more than one syllable, when do you double the final letter if it is a consonant?**

   Rules: **a.** In multisyllable words, double the final consonant when a single vowel comes before it _and_ the stress falls on the last syllable. (Vowels are _a, e, i, o, u,_ and sometimes _y._ All other letters are consonants.)

   be<u>gin</u>´ → be<u>ginn</u>ing   tran<u>smit</u>´ → tran<u>smitt</u>ed
   re<u>pel</u>´ → re<u>pell</u>ing

   b. In multisyllable words, do _not_ double the final consonant when (a) a vowel comes before it _and_ (b) the stress is not on the last syllable once the new ending is added.

   refer → reference

   admit → admitance

6. **To form a plural, do you add _-s_ or _-es_?**

   Rules: **a.** For most nouns, add _-s._

   cat → cat<u>s</u>   house → house<u>s</u>

   b. Add _-es_ to words that end in _-o_ if the _-o_ is preceded by a consonant.

   her<u>o</u> → her<u>oes</u>   potat<u>o</u> → potat<u>oes</u>

   Exceptions: _zoos, radios, ratios,_ and other words ending with two vowels.

   c. Add _-es_ to words ending in _-ch, -sh, -ss, -x,_ or _-z._

   chur<u>ch</u> → chur<u>ches</u>   fo<u>x</u> → fo<u>xes</u>   di<u>sh</u> → di<u>shes</u>

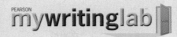 For support in mastering these topics, log in to www.mywritinglab.com, go to the Study Plan tab, click on Managing Mechanics and Spelling and choose Capitalization, Abbreviations and Numbers, and Spelling from the list of subtopics. Read and view the videos and resources in the Review Materials section, and then complete the Recall, Apply, and Write exercises in the Activities section. You can check your scores and overall progress by using the Gradebook.

Commonly Misused Words and Phrases

This list is intended as a guide to words and phrases that often are confusing. If the word or phrase you seek is not here, check in a good dictionary.

a, an   Use *an* before words that begin with a vowel sound (the vowels are *a, e, i, o,* and *u*) or a silent *h: an airplane, an honor.* Use *a* before words that begin with a consonant sound: *a book, a house.*

a while, awhile   *A while* is a phrase containing an article and a noun; *awhile* is an adverb meaning "for some time." *A while* can be used following a preposition, such as *for: Wait here for a while. Awhile* is used to modify a verb: *We need to rest awhile.*

accept, except   *Accept* is a verb that means "receive"; *She accepted the gift gratefully. Except* is usually a preposition meaning "other than," "but," or "excluding": *Everyone has left except me.*

advice, advise   *Advice* is a noun: *He gave me his best advice about health insurance. Advise* is a verb: *I can only advise you about it.*

affect, effect   *Affect* is almost always a verb meaning "influence": *Smoking affects one's health. Effect* can be either a verb or a noun. In its usual use, as a noun, it means "result": *The drug has several side effects.* When *effect* is used as a verb, it means "cause" or "bring about": *The committee was able to effect a change in the law.*

all ready, already   *All ready* means "completely prepared." *Already* means "by this time" or "previously."

all right, alright   Although the form *alright* is often used, most authorities regard it as a misspelling of *all right.*

all together, altogether   *All together* means "as a group" or "in unison": *The workers presented their grievance all together to the supervisor. Altogether* is an adverb that means "completely" or "entirely": *His answer was not altogether acceptable.*

allusion, illusion   An *allusion* is an indirect reference or a hint: *Her allusions about his weight embarrassed him.* An *illusion* is a false idea or appearance: *Cosmetic surgery is intended to create the illusion of youth.*

almost, most   See *most, almost.*

alot, lots, lots of   *Alot* should be written only as two words: *a lot.* It is an informal substitute for *many* or *much,* as are *lots* and *lots of.* You should avoid all three in formal writing.

among, between   See *between, among*.

amount of, number of   Use *amount of* to refer to quantities that cannot be counted: *A large <u>amount of</u> milk had been left in the refrigerator.* Use *number of* with quantities that can be counted: *A large <u>number of</u> eggs had been left in the carton.*

and/or   Avoid using *and/or* unless your writing is of a technical, business, or legal nature. Remember that in these types of writing *and/or* indicates *three* options: one *or* the other *or* both.

anybody, any body; anyone, any one   *Anybody* and *anyone* are indefinite pronouns that mean "any person at all": *Does <u>anybody (anyone)</u> have change for a dollar? Any body* consists of a noun modified by the adjective *any: Is <u>any body</u> of government responsible for this injustice? Any one,* the pronoun *one* modified by *any,* refers to a certain person or thing in a group: *You may choose <u>any one</u> of the desserts with your entree.*

anyone, any body   See *anybody, any body; anyone, any one*.

anyplace, anywhere   *Anyplace* is informal for *anywhere* and should be avoided in formal writing.

anyways, anywheres, nowheres; anyway, anywhere, nowhere   Use *anyway, anywhere,* and *nowhere* rather than the forms ending in *-s.*

as   Using *as* instead of *because, since,* or *while* can lead to confusion: *The ball game was canceled <u>as</u> it started raining.* Here, *as* could mean either "because" or "when." Avoid using *as* rather than *whether* or *who:*

> whether
> We are not sure ~~as~~ we can be there.

> who
> She is the person ~~as~~ interrupted my lunch hour.

as, as if, as though, like   See *like, as, as if, as though*.

bad, badly   *Bad* is an adjective; *badly* is an adverb. *Badly* should be used to modify verbs: *They sang quite <u>badly</u>. Bad* can be used to modify nouns or pronouns: *The <u>bad</u> behavior irritated the child's hostess.* In addition, *bad* should be used after linking verbs, such as *am, is, become, feel,* or *seem: She felt <u>bad</u> last night.*

being as, being that   Use *because* or *since* rather than these expressions. Besides being informal, they can make sentences awkward.

between, among   Use *between* when referring to two things or people: *My wife and I divide the household chores <u>between</u> us.* Use *among* for three or more things or people: *The vote was evenly divided <u>among</u> the four candidates.*

bring, take   Use *bring* to describe the movement of an object toward you: *<u>Bring</u> me the newspaper, please.* Use *take* when the movement is away from you: *Will you <u>take</u> these letters to the mailbox?*

can, may   In formal writing you should make a distinction between *can* and *may. Can* refers to the ability to do something: *He <u>can</u> run a mile in less than five minutes. May* indicates permission: *You <u>may</u> choose whichever DVD you want.*

censor, censure   *Censor* as a verb means "edit or ban from the public for moral or political reasons": *The school board voted not to <u>censor</u> the high school reading lists but to recommend novels with literary merit.* The verb *censure* means "criticize or condemn publicly": *The member of Congress was <u>censured</u> because of questionable fund-raising practices.*

complement, compliment   *Complement* is a verb meaning "complete, add to, or go with": *They make a good couple; their personalities* complement *each other.* *Compliment* as a verb means "praise or flatter": *I must* compliment *you on your quick wit.* As a noun it means "flattering remark": *You should not regard his* compliments *as sincere.*

conscience, conscious   *Conscience* is a noun meaning "sense of moral right or wrong": *His* conscience *required him to return the lost wallet. Conscious* is an adjective meaning "alert, aware, awake": *Were you* conscious *of the change in temperature?*

continual, continuous   *Continual* means "happening regularly": Continual *calls by telemarketers are a nuisance. Continuous* means "happening for a long period of time without interruption": *The car alarm made a* continuous, *high-pitched noise.*

could have, could of   See *of, have.*

data   *Data,* the plural form of the Latin noun *datum,* means "facts or information." *Data* is often accepted as either a plural or a singular noun: *These data* are *conclusive. This data* is *conclusive.* Though technically correct, the singular form *datum* is rarely used.

different from, different than   *Different from* is the preferred expression: *Today is* different from *yesterday.* However, when *different from* leads to an awkward construction, *different than* is becoming acceptable: *Today Cheryl is* different than *she was last month* (avoids *from what she was last month*).

disinterested, uninterested   *Disinterested* means "objective or impartial": *The dispute was mediated by a* disinterested *party. Uninterested* means "not interested": *She was so* uninterested *in the football game that she nearly fell asleep.*

doesn't, don't   *Don't* is the contraction for *do not,* not for *does not: We* don't *want it.*

$\qquad$ *doesn't*
She ~~don't~~ have any.

due to   The phrase *due to* should be used only when it functions as a predicate adjective after a linking verb (usually a form of *be*): *His ill health was* due to *his poor diet.* It should not be used as a preposition meaning "because of" or "on account of":

$\qquad$ *because of*
The ball game was canceled ~~due to~~ bad weather.

effect, affect   See *affect, effect.*

elicit, illicit   *Elicit* is a verb meaning "draw out" or "bring to light": *The police were unable to* elicit *any information from the accomplice. Illicit* is an adjective meaning "illegal": *The suspect had* illicit *drugs on his person.*

emigrate, immigrate   See *immigrate, emigrate.*

etc.   This is the abbreviation for the Latin *et cetera,* meaning "and so on." Ending a list with *etc.* is acceptable in informal writing and in some technical writing and business reporting. However, in formal writing it is preferable to end a list with an example or with *and so on.*

everyday, every day   *Everyday* is an adjective that means "ordinary" or "usual": *They decided to use their* everyday *dishes for the party. Every day,* an adjective and a noun, means "occurring on a daily basis": Every day, *he walks the dog in the morning.*

explicit, implicit   *Explicit* is an adjective that means "clearly stated": *I left explicit instructions for the worker. Implicit* means "indirectly stated or implied": *The fact that he didn't object indicated his implicit approval of the arrangement.*

farther, further   When referring to distance, use *farther: He lives farther from work than she does.* When you mean "additional," use *further: Upon further consideration, I accept the position.*

fewer, less   *Fewer* refers to items that can be counted: *There are fewer people here today than yesterday. Less* refers to a general amount that cannot be counted: *We have less orange juice than I thought.*

firstly, secondly, thirdly   Use *first, second, third* instead to avoid sounding pretentious and needing to add *-ly* to remaining numbers in a list.

further, farther   See *farther, further.*

get   *Get* is a verb used in many slang and colloquial expressions. Avoid the following uses:

> That really ~~got to~~ me.   [*annoyed (moved)*]

> We've ~~got to~~ go now.   [*must*]

> I ~~got back at~~ her.   [*took revenge on*]

> Don't ~~get~~ sick.   [*become*]

> ~~Get moving on~~ that.   [*Start doing*]

> We ~~got to~~ the party late.   [*arrived at*]

> We ~~got done~~ early.   [*finished*]

good, well   *Good* is an adjective: *I enjoy a good workout.* It should not be used as an adverb. *Well* should be used instead:

> We ate ~~good~~ on our vacation.   [*well*]

Well can also be an adjective when used with verbs expressing feeling or state of being: *She feels well today.*

got to   See *get.*

hanged, hung   *Hanged* is the past tense and past participle form of the verb *hang,* meaning "execute": *He was hanged as a traitor. Hung* is the past tense and past participle form of the verb *hang* in all its other meanings: *We hung the picture above the fireplace.*

have, of   See *of, have.*

have got to   See *get.*

he/she, his/her; he or she, his or her   At one time, it was permissible to use *he* to mean *he or she.* Now, this is seldom appropriate. Use *he or she* and *his or her,* rather than *he/she, his/her,* when referring to a person whose gender is unknown: *Everyone must learn to walk before he or she runs.* If using these or other "double" pronouns becomes awkward, revise your sentence by using the plural pronoun or by refocusing the sentence.

> When you meet ~~each guest~~, ask ~~him to her~~ to show ~~his or her~~   [*guests* / *them* / *their*]
> ID ~~card.~~   [*cards*]

> When you meet each guest, ask to see an ID card.

hisself   *Hisself* is nonstandard. Use *himself.*

hung, hanged   See *hanged, hung.*

if, whether   Use *if* when expressing a condition: *If I leave early, I can beat the rush hour traffic.* Use <u>whether</u> when expressing an alternative: *I don't know whether to stay or to leave.*

illicit, elicit   See *elicit, illicit.*

illusion, allusion   See *allusion, illusion.*

immigrate, emigrate   *Immigrate (to)* means "come to a country": *They recently <u>immigrated</u> to the United States. Emigrate (from)* means "leave a country": *They <u>emigrated</u> from Mexico for economic reasons.*

implicit, explicit   See *explicit, implicit.*

imply, infer   Speakers or writers *imply.* They suggest or hint at something: *He <u>implied</u> that he was unhappy with my work.* Listeners or readers *infer* by drawing conclusions from what they have read, heard, or seen: *I <u>inferred</u> that I need to become more conscientious.*

in, into, in to   Use *in* to indicate position or location: *Your book is <u>in</u> the drawer.* Use *into* to show movement: *They were led <u>into</u> a winding corridor.* Sometimes *in* and *to* are used close together as separate words: *They gave <u>in to</u> our requests.*

in regard to, in regards to   *In regards to* confuses two other phrases—*in regard to* and *as regards.* Use either of the last two or use *regarding: <u>In regard to</u> (as regards; regarding) your last phone call, I will arrive in time for the 2:30 meeting.*

infer, imply   See *imply, infer.*

irregardless, regardless   *Irregardless* is nonstandard. Use *regardless* instead.

is when, is where   *When* and *where* are often used incorrectly in sentences that define. Using just *is* or rewording your sentence can correct this faulty construction:

> A touchdown ~~is when~~ you cross your opponent's goal line with
> *is scored when* ⋀
>
> the ball in your possession.

> A touchdown ~~is when you cross~~ your opponent's goal line with
> *is crossing* ⋀
>
> the ball in your possession.

> Art history ~~is where you study~~ the world's great art treasures.
> *is the study of* ⋀

its, it's   *Its* is the possessive case form of the pronoun *it;* no apostrophes are used to show possession with personal pronouns (*his, hers, its, theirs*). *The poodle scratched <u>its</u> ear. It's* is the contraction for *it is: <u>It's</u> time for a change.*

kind, sort, type   These words are singular and should be used with singular modifiers and verbs: *<u>This kind</u> of book <u>is</u> expensive.* They should be used in their plural forms with plural modifiers and verbs: *<u>These types</u> of pens <u>work</u> best.* Using *a* following *type of, kind of,* or *sort of* is incorrect:

> What type of a dog is that?

Also, omitting *of* is nonstandard:

I can't guess what type~of~car that is.

kind of, sort of   Avoid using *kind of* or *sort of* in formal speech or writing to mean "somewhat" or "rather":

The movie was ~kind of~ scary.
rather

The traffic was ~sort of~ slow this morning.
somewhat

lay, lie   *Lay* is a transitive verb meaning "put or place." Its principal parts are *lay, laid, laid*: *Lay your bag here. She laid her bag here. She has laid her bag here every day. Lie* is an intransitive verb meaning "recline or be situated." Its principal parts are *lie, lay, lain*: *Lie down for a while. He lay down for a while. He has lain down every few hours.*

leave, let   *Leave* is a verb that means "depart," "exit," or "let be": *We will leave the room, so that you can be left alone. Let* means "permit or allow": *They would not let me go.*

less, fewer   See *fewer, less.*

like, as, as if, as though   *Like* is a preposition and should be used only with a noun or a noun phrase: *You look like your mother.* Do not use *like* as a conjunction to introduce subordinate clauses. Use *as, as if,* or *as though.*

Do ~like~ I tell you.
as

She looks ~like~ she is ready to fall asleep.
as if (as though)

loose, lose   *Loose* is an adjective meaning "not tight" or "not attached securely": *A loose brick fell into the fireplace. Lose* is a verb that means "misplace" or "not win": *Don't lose your way in the woods. They will lose the game unless they score soon.*

lots, lots of   See *alot, lots, lots of.*

may, can   See *can, may.*

may be, maybe   *May be* is a verb phrase: *The train may be late this morning. Maybe* is an adverb meaning "perhaps" or "possibly": *Maybe we can have lunch together tomorrow.*

may have, may of   See *of, have.*

media, medium   *Media* is the plural form of *medium: Of all the broadcast media, television is the medium that reaches most households.*

might have, might of   See *of, have.*

most, almost   *Most* should not be used in place of *almost.* When you mean "nearly," use *almost;* when you mean "the greatest number or quantity" use *most: She gets most of her exercise by walking to work almost every day.*

nowhere, nowheres   See *anyways, anywheres, nowheres.*

number of, amount of   See *amount of, number of.*

of, have   *Of* is spelled the way the contraction *'ve*, for *have*, sounds. Always write *could have, may have, might have, should have,* and *would have.*

off, off of   Use *off* or *from* instead of *off of:*

The poodle jumped off ~~of~~ the bed as I entered the room.

OK, O.K., okay   All three of these spellings are acceptable in informal writing, but they should be avoided in formal writing or speech.

percent (per cent), percentage   *Percent* should be used with a specific number: *Less than 40* <u>percent</u> *of the class passed the exam. Percentage* is used when no number is referred to: *A large* <u>percentage</u> *of adults cannot program a VCR.*

plus   *Plus* is used as a preposition meaning "in addition to." *His skill* <u>plus</u> *his compassion made him a fine surgeon.* It should not be used as a conjunction in place of *and.*

He is very skillful, ~~plus~~ ^and^ he is compassionate.

principal, principle   The noun *principal* can mean "sum of money (excluding interest)" or "important person in an organization": *At any time, you can pay the* <u>principal</u> *on this loan. The high school* <u>principal</u> *distributed the awards.* As an adjective, *principal* means "most important": *His* <u>principal</u> *concern was their safety. Principle* is a noun meaning "rule or standard": *The* <u>principles</u> *stated in the Constitution guide our democracy.*

raise, rise   *Raise* is a transitive verb meaning "lift." Its principal parts are *raise, raised,* and *raised:* <u>Raise</u> *the flag at sunrise. He* <u>raised</u> *the flag at sunrise. They* <u>have raised</u> *the flag at sunrise for years. Rise* is an intransitive verb meaning "go higher" or "get to one's feet." Its principal parts are *rise, rose,* and *risen: I* <u>rise</u> *early on weekends. The sun gradually* <u>rose</u> *in the sky. The bread dough* <u>has</u> *already* <u>risen.</u>

real, really   *Real* is an adjective meaning "genuine" or "actual": *He found a* <u>real</u> *gold coin. Really* is an adverb meaning "very or extremely": *He is* <u>really</u> *proud of his discovery.*

reason is because, reason is that   Use *that* rather than *because* in formal speech and writing:

The reason I am late is ~~because~~ ^that^ my car broke down.

regardless, irregardless   See *irregardless, regardless.*

set, sit   *Set* is a transitive verb meaning "put or place." Its principal parts are *set, set, set: Please* <u>set</u> *the pitcher on the table. I* <u>set</u> *it on the counter, instead. I will* <u>set</u> *it on the table later. Sit* is an intransitive verb meaning "be seated." Its principal parts are *sit, sat,* and *sat: I* <u>sit</u> *in the front row. He* <u>sat</u> *behind me. They* <u>have sat</u> *for too long.*

shall, will   *Shall* was once preferred for use with *I* or *we* and for expressing determination. Today, *will* and *shall* are practically interchangeable for these instances, so *will* is acceptable for expressing future time with *be*, in all uses. *Shall* is now used primarily in polite questions: <u>Shall</u> *we dance?*

should have, should of   See *of, have.*

sometime, some time, sometimes   *Sometime* is an adverb meaning "at an unspecified point in the future": *We'll see that movie* <u>sometime</u>. *Some time* is an adjective (*some*) and a noun (*time*), and as a phrase it means "a period of time": *We'll find some time for that later.* *Sometimes* is an adverb meaning "now and then": *Sometimes recreation must be viewed as important.*

sort   See *kind, sort, type.*

sort of   See *kind of, sort of.*

stationary, stationery   *Stationary* is an adjective meaning "not moving": *Attach the birdhouse to a stationary object, such as a tree.* *Stationery* is a noun meaning "writing paper": *She sent a note on her personal stationery.*

suppose to, use to, supposed to, used to   *Suppose to* and *use to* are nonstandard and unacceptable substitutes for *supposed to* and *used to.*

sure, surely   *Sure* is an adjective: *She was sure she was correct.* *Surely* is an adverb: *She is surely correct.*

sure and, try and, sure to, try to   *Sure to* and *try to* are the correct forms.

take, bring   See *bring, take.*

than, then   *Than* is a conjunction that is used to make a comparison: *That is larger than I thought.* *Then* is an adverb used to indicate time: *Let's finish this first and then have dinner.*

that, which, who   Frequently, there is confusion about these relative pronouns. *That* refers to persons, animals, and things; *which* refers to animals and things; and *who* (and *whom*) refer to persons. To keep the distinctions clear, follow these guidelines.

1. Use *who* (*whom*) when referring to persons: *He is the one who won the contest.*

2. Use *which* for animals and things when it introduces nonrestrictive clauses: *My iPod, which I bought at Wal-Mart, works perfectly.*

3. Use *that* for animals and things when introducing restrictive relative clauses: *Everything that I did was misunderstood.*

their, there, they're   *Their* is a possessive pronoun: *They gave their tickets to the usher.* *There* is an adverb indicating place: *Put the chair over there, please.* *They're* is the contraction of *they are: They're going to be disappointed.*

theirself, theirselves, themself, themselves   *Theirself, theirselves,* and *themself* are nonstandard substitutes for *themselves: They built the boat by themselves.*

these kind(s), these sort(s), these type(s)   See *kind, sort, type.*

to, too, two   *To* is either a preposition indicating direction or part of an infinitive: *I'm going to the store to buy groceries.* *Too* is an adverb meaning "also" or "more than enough": *She is too thin to be healthy. Can I come too?* *Two* is a number: *I'll be home in two hours.*

toward, towards   These words are interchangeable, but *toward* is preferred in American English. Use consistently whichever form you choose.

try and, try to   See *sure and, try and, sure to, try to.*

type   See *kind, sort, type.*

use to, used to   See *suppose to, use to, supposed to, used to.*

wait for, wait on   *Wait for* means "await" or "pause in expectation": *Wait for me at the bus stop.* *Wait on* means "serve" or "act as a waiter": *The restaurant owner waited on us.*

way, ways   *Ways* is a colloquial substitute for *way*. In formal writing and speech, use *way:*

We have a long ~~ways~~^(way) to go.

well, good   See *good, well.*

whether, if   See *if, whether.*

which, who, that   See *that, which, who.*

who's, whose   *Who's* is the contraction of *who is:* <u>Who's</u> *knocking on the door?* *Whose* is the possessive form of *who:* <u>Whose</u> *car is that? Naomi is the one* <u>whose</u> *mother is the famous writer.*

will, shall   See *shall, will.*

would have, would of   See *of, have.*

your, you're   *Your* is a possessive pronoun: <u>Your</u> *apology is accepted. You're* is the contraction of *you are:* <u>You're</u> *welcome to join us for dinner.*

PEARSON
mywritinglab   For support in mastering these topics, log in to www.mywritinglab.com, go to the Study Plan tab, click on Commonly Confused Words and choose Easily Confused Words from the list of subtopics. Read and view the videos and resources in the Review Materials section, and then complete the Recall, Apply, and Write exercises in the Activities section. You can check your scores and overall progress by using the Gradebook.

Credits

Photo Credits

Thinking Visually Icon: kak2s/Shutterstock; **Paragraph Writing Scenarios Box, top to bottom:** Blend Images/Alamy; Jason Molyneaux/Masterfile; Masterfile; mangostock/Shutterstock; **p. 1, left to right:** Corbis/SuperStock; Exactostock/SuperStock; Blend Images/Alamy; **p. 6:** Danita Delimont/Alamy; **p. 9:** Mehmet Dilsiz/Shutterstock; **p. 10:** andresr/Shutterstock; **p. 17:** Benjamin Rondel/age fotostock; **p. 31, left to right:** Mauritius/SuperStock; Just ASC/Shutterstock; guaitiero boffi/Shutterstock; alphaspirit/Shutterstock; Diego Cervo/Shutterstock; **p. 34, left to right:** Blend Images/SuperStock; Corbis/SuperStock; **p. 51:** AP Images/Aiden Pellett; **p. 54:** Marcelo Rudini/Alamy; **p. 87:** andresr/Shutterstock; **p. 88:** BananaStock/Thinkstock; **p. 89:** eprom_is/iStockphoto; **p. 90:** Louise Gubb/The Image Works; **p. 96:** woodsy/Shutterstock; **p. 97:** John Pagliuca/Shutterstock; **p. 98, left to right:** Darren Hubley/Shutterstock; mpanch/Shutterstock; **p. 99:** Frances Roberts/Alamy; **p. 100:** Mehmet Dilsiz/Shutterstock; **p. 101:** djgis/Shutterstock; **p. 102:** Courtesy World Wildlife Fund; **p. 125:** I61/Zuma Press/Newscom; **p. 131:** Balono/iStockphoto; **p. 147:** Michael Willis/Alamy; **p. 153:** Danita Delimont/Alamy; **p. 170:** Priscilla Gragg/Autora Open/Alamy; **p. 171:** I Love Images/age fotostock; **p. 177:** Ninette Maumus/Alamy; **p. 179:** © The New Yorker Collection 1983 Jack Ziegler from cartoonbank.com. All Rights Reserved.; **p. 197:** SUNNYphotography.com/Alamy; **p. 202:** Paulcowan/Dreamstime; **p. 218:** AP Images/Rafiq Maqbool; **p. 222:** Zou Zheng/Xinhua News Agency/Newscom; **p. 228:** Ken Durden/Shutterstock; **p. 229:** Angelo Gilardelli/Shutterstock; **p. 230:** GoodMoodPhoto/Shutterstock; **p. 231:** iofoto/Shutterstock; **p. 233:** iofoto/Shutterstock; **p. 234:** Shmeliova Natalia/Shutterstock; **p. 235:** Tony Lilley/Alamy; **p. 260:** Peter Essick/Aurora Photos/Corbis; **p. 266:** Image Source/age fotostock; **p. 287:** WaterFrame/Alamy; **p. 293:** Michael Blann/Getty Images; **p. 295:** © The New Yorker Collection 1976 George Booth from cartoonbank.com. All Rights Reserved.; **p. 308:** AP Images/NBC/NBCU Photobank; **p. 311:** Robbie McClaran; **p. 316:** The Advertising Archives; **p. 321:** Courtesy Newman's Own and Gotham Advertising; **p. 336:** Flirt/SuperStock; **p. 339:** Jason Love/Cartoon Stock; **p. 346:** Topham/The Image Works; **p. 359:** NASA; **p. 360:** Asia Photopress/Alamy; **p. 368:** Dave King/DK Images; **p. 414, top to bottom:** AP Images/Tanya Makeyeva/UNHCR Pool; DFree/Shutterstock; **p. 416:** age fotostock/SuperStock; **p. 423, left and right:** Andrea Jones/Garden Exposures Photo Library; **p. 438:** Andrejs Pidjass/Shutterstock; **p. 439:** Ryan McGinnis/Alamy; **p. 442:** Blend Images/Alamy; **p. 447:** Niall McDarmid/Alamy; **p. 466:** vblinov/Shutterstock; **p. 467:** Adrian Sherratt/Alamy; **p. 469:** Ouzounova/Splash News/Newscom; **p. 475:** Exactostock/SuperStock; **p. 490, top to bottom:** Kayros Studio "Be Happy!"/Shutterstock; Elena Elisseeva/Shutterstock; **p. 493:** Len Rubinstein; **p. 500:** Alex Hinds/Alamy; **p. 512, top to bottom:** SOMOS/SuperStock; Juice Images/Alamy; **p. 514:** Chris "ROY" Taylor/Cartoon Stock; **p. 523:** PBurch/Tulane University; **p. 527:** Adrian Sherratt/Alamy; **p. 531:** Deco Images II/Alamy; **p. 534:** Rawdon Wyatt/Alamy; **p. 542:** Blend Images/Alamy.

Text Credits

Chapter 1

p. 23: Adapted from Henslin, *Sociology*, pp. 380–381.

p. 31: Gini Stepens Frings, *Fashion: From Concept to Consumer*, Ninth Edition, Pearson Prentice Hall, p. 6.

Chapter 2

p. 36: Saul Kassin, *Psychology*, Fourth Edition, pp. 244–245. © 2004. Adapted by permission of the author.

p. 44: James M. Henslin, *Sociology: A Down-to-Earth Approach*, Tenth Edition, © 2010. Printed and electronically reproduced by permission of Pearson Education, Inc., Upper Saddle River, New Jersey.

p. 45: Byer and Shainberg, *Living Well: Health in Your Hands*, © 1995, pp. 78–79.

p. 46: Cook, Yale, and Marqua, *Tourism: The Business of Travel*, Fourth Edition, © 2010, Upper Saddle River, NJ: Prentice Hall, p. 214.

p. 47: Byer and Shainberg, *Living Well: Health in Your Hands*, © 1995, p. 311.

p. 50: James M. Henslin, *Sociology: A Down-to-Earth Approach*, Tenth Edition, © 2010. Printed and electronically reproduced by permission of Pearson Education, Inc., Upper Saddle River, New Jersey.

p. 51: Rebecca J. Donatelle, *Health: The Basics*, Green Edition, p. 255.

p. 54: Wright and Boorse, *Environmental Science: Toward a Sustainable Future*, Eleventh Edition, © 2011 Pearson Education, p. 604.

p. 55: David Ropeik, "What Really Scares Us," *Parade Magazine*, March 30, 2003. Reprinted by permission of the author.

Chapter 3

p. 61: Gerald Audesirk, Teresa Audesirk, and Bruce E. Byers, *Biology: Life on Earth*, Eighth Edition, © 2008, p. 381. Reprinted by permission of Pearson Education, Inc., Upper Saddle River, NJ.

p. 62: Copyright © 2010 by Houghton Mifflin Harcourt Publishing Company. Reproduced by permission from *The American Heritage Dictionary of the English Language*, Fourth Edition.

p. 64: Copyright © 2010 by Houghton Mifflin Harcourt Publishing Company. Reproduced by permission from *The American Heritage Dictionary of the English Language*, Fourth Edition.

p. 67: Copyright © 2004 by Houghton Mifflin Harcourt Publishing Company. Reproduced by permission from *The American Heritage College Thesaurus*.

p. 68: Barbara Miller, *Anthropology,* Second Edition, © 2008 Pearson Education, Upper Saddle River, NJ, p. 484.

p. 72: Adapted from H. L. Capron, *Computers: Tools for an Information Age*, Fifth Edition, 1998.

p. 83: Byer and Shainberg, *Living Well: Health in Your Hands*, © 1995, p. 360.

p. 84: DeVito, *Messages: Building Interpersonal Communication Skills*, Third Edition, © 1996 HarperCollins Publishers, pp. 22–23.

p. 84: Byer and Shainberg, *Living Well: Health in Your Hands*, © 1995, p. 67.

p. 84: Wallace, *Biology: The World of Life*, Sixth Edition, p. 834.

p. 87: Adapted from Solomon, Poatsy, and Martin, *Better Business*, © 2010, Pearson Prentice Hall, p. 66.

p. 89: Jay H. Withgott and Scott R. Brennan, *Environment: The Science Behind the Stories*, Fourth Edition, © 2011. Printed and electronically reproduced by permission of Pearson Education, Inc., Upper Saddle River, New Jersey.

Chapter 4

p. 123: Denise Flam, "Tails in Jail," © 2011 Denise Flam. Reprinted with permission of the author.

Chapter 5

p. 146: "Credit Card Smarts: Take Charge of Your Cards." Source: http://www.collegeboard.com/student/plan/college-success/9139.html. Copyright © 2011 The College Board. www.collegeboard.com. Reproduced with permission.

Chapter 6

p. 169: Copyright 2009 American Diabetes Association. From *Diabetes Forecast Magazine*, 2009, pp. 31–33. Reprinted with permission from The American Diabetes Association.

Chapter 7

p. 193: Gentry Carlson, "The Longest Day." Reprinted by permission of the author.

p. 196: Steven Doloff, "Norteno en Manhatten," *The Epoch Times*, January 9, 2009. Steven Doloff is a professor of English at Pratt Institute and his essays have appeared in *The New York Times, The Washington Post, The Boston Globe, The Philadelphia Inquirer, The Chicago Sun-Times,* and *The Los Angeles Times.* Reprinted with permission of the author.

Chapter 8

p. 219: Kim Hyo-Joo, "English, Friend or Foe?" Reprinted by permission of the author.

p. 222: Lucille O'Neil, "The Little Warrior." Reprinted by permission. From *Walk Like You Have Somewhere to Go* by Lucille O'Neal and Allison Samuels, © 2010, Thomas Nelson Inc., Nashville, Tennessee. All rights reserved.

Chapter 9

p. 256: Adapted from the *Cape Cod Times*, October 25, 1994.

p. 256: Kelly Bajier, "Rebuilding a Dream." Reprinted by permission of the author.

p. 259: Chris Jozefowicz, "Waste Woes," *Current Health*, January 2, 2010. Special permission granted by *Weekly Reader*, published and copyrighted by Weekly Reader Corporation. All rights reserved.

Chapter 10

p. 283: Jessica Nantka, "I Don't Want a Promotion." Reprinted by permission of the author.

p. 286: Virginia Sole-Smith, "Sweatshops at Sea," *UTNE Reader*, September–October 2010. Research support for this article provided by The Nation Institute's Investigative Fund. Reprinted by permission of the author.

Chapter 11

p. 307: Michael Archer, "Listening to the Land." Reprinted by permission of the author.

p. 308: Jeremy Yudkin, *Understanding Music*, Prentice Hall, © 2010, pp. 202–203.

p. 310: Christie Scotty, "Can I Get You Some Manners with That?" from *Newsweek*, October 18, 2004. © 2004 The Newsweek/Daily Beast Company LLC. All rights reserved. Used by permission and protected by the Copyright Laws of the United States. The printing, copying, redistribution, or retransmission of the Material without express written permission is prohibited. www.newsweek.com

Chapter 12

p. 331: Tracy Burgio, "The Emotional Wall." Reprinted by permission of the author.

p. 334: Quinne Sember, "Making a Difference." Reprinted by permission of the author.

p. 336: Jenifer Kunz, *Think Marriages and Families*, Boston: Pearson, © 2011, p. 118.

p. 338: Henslin, James M., *Sociology: A Down-to-Earth Approach, Core Concepts*, Third Edition, © 2009, p. 303. Reprinted by permission of Pearson Education, Inc., Upper Saddle River, NJ.

Chapter 13

p. 357: Maya Prestwich, "Halloween Fun Without Cultural Guilt," *The Daily Northwestern*, October 30, 1997. Reprinted with permission.

p. 359: Kendall Martin, Mary Anne Poatsy, and Michael R. Soloman, *Better Business*, First Edition, Prentice Hall, © 2010. Reprinted with permission of Pearson Education, Inc.

p. 361: Brent Staples, "A Brother's Murder," *The New York Times Magazine*, March 30, 1986. Reprinted with permission. © 1986 *The New York Times*. All rights reserved. Used by permission and protected by the Copyright Laws of the United States. The printing, copying, redistribution, or retransmission of the Material without express written permission is prohibited.

Chapter 14

p. 371: Sara Gruen, *Water for Elephants,* Chapel Hill, NC: Algonquin Books of Chapel Hill, 2006, p. 21.

p. 373: Michael Dorris, *A Yellow Raft in Blue* Water, New York: Henry Holt and Company, 1987, pp. 276–277.

p. 375: Robert W. Chrisopherson, *Geosystems: An Introduction to Physical Geography*, Fourth Edition, Upper Saddle River, NJ: Prentice Hall, 2000, p. 368.

p. 378: Michael Dorris, *A Yellow Raft in Blue* Water, New York: Henry Holt and Company, 1987, p. 251.

p. 381: Bergman and Renwick, *Introduction to Geography*, Second Edition, Upper Saddle River, NJ: Prentice Hall, p. 356. Carnes and Garraty, *The American Nation*, Tenth Edition, New York: Longman, 2000, p. 916.

p. 382: James M. Henslin, *Sociology: A Down-to-Earth Approach*, Ninth Edition, Boston: Pearson/Allyn and Bacon, 2008, p. 249.

p. 384: Elaine Marieb, *Human Anatomy and Physiology*, Fifth Edition, San Francisco: Benjamin Cummings, 2001, p. 387.

p. 386: X.J. Kennedy and Dana Gioia, *Literature: An Introduction to Fiction, Poetry, and Drama*, Third Compact Edition, New York: Longman, 2003, p. 7.

p. 388: Rebecca J. Donatelle, *Health: The Basics*, Fifth Edition, San Francisco: Benjamin Cummings, 2003, p. 324.

p. 390: James M. Henslin, *Sociology: A Down-to-Earth Approach*, Ninth Edition, Boston: Pearson/Allyn and Bacon, 2008, p. 169.

p. 394: Ronald J. Ebert and Ricky W. Griffin, *Business Essentials*, Fourth Edition, Upper Saddle River, NJ: Prentice Hall, 2003, p. 117.

p. 396: Elaine Marieb, *Essentials of Human Anatomy and Physiology*, Ninth Edition, San Francisco: Pearson/Benjamin Cummings, 2009, p. 124.

p. 399: Elaine Marieb, *Essentials of Human Anatomy and Physiology*, Ninth Edition, San Francisco: Pearson/Benjamin Cummings, 2009, p. 487.

p. 400: Wood, Wood, and Boyd, *Mastering the World of Psychology*, Third Edition, Boston: Pearson/Allyn and Bacon, 2008, p. 181.

p. 401: Paragraph by Ted Sawchuck. Reprinted by permission of the author.

p. 404: Rebecca J. Donatelle, *Health: The Basics*, Eighth Edition, San Francisco: Pearson/Benjamin Cummings, 2009, p. 205.

p. 405: William J. Germann and Cindy Stanfield, *Principles of Physiology*, First Edition, San Francisco: Benjamin Cummings, 2002, p. 622.

p. 409: Donald W. Tuff, "Animals and Research," *NEA Higher Education Advocate*, Vol. X, No. 5, March 1994.

p. 411: Angela Molina, "Animals and Research," *NEA Higher Education Advocate*, Vol. X, No. 5, March 1994.

p. 412: James Lawrence Sturm III, "Handling Transition." Reprinted with permission of the author.

p. 414: Louis Giannetti, *Understanding Movies*, Twelfth Edition, Boston: Allyn and Bacon, © 2011, p. 260.

p. 416: Leticia Salais, "Saying 'Adios' to Spanglish," from *Newsweek*, December 8, 2007, My Turn. © 2007 The Newsweek/Daily Beast Company LLC. All rights reserved. Used by permission and protected by the Copyright Laws of the United States. The printing, copying, redistribution, or retransmission of the Material without express written permission is prohibited. www.newsweek.com

Chapter 15

p. 436: Fidel Sanchez, "The Worst and Best Jobs of My Life." Reprinted by permission of the author.

p. 438: Rebecca Donatelle, *Health: The Basics*, Green Edition, Boston: Benjamin Cummings, © 2011, p. 106.

p. 440: Scott Keyes, "Stop Asking Me My Major," *The Chronicle of Higher Education*, January 10, 2010. Reprinted by permission of the author.

Chapter 16

p. 460: Zoë Cole, "Sports and Life." Reprinted by permission of the author.

p. 466: Cook, Yale, and Marqua, *Tourism: The Business of Travel*, Fourth Edition, Upper Saddle River, NJ: Prentice Hall, © 2010, p. 211.

p. 468: James M. Henslin, *Sociology: A Down-to-Earth Approach, Core Concepts*, Third Edition, © 2009, p. 303. Reprinted by permission of Pearson Education, Inc., Upper Saddle River, NJ.

Chapter 17

p. 484: Markella Tsoukalas, "Expanding My World Through the Internet." Reprinted by permission of the author.

p. 490: Thompson and Manore, *Nutrition for Life*, Second Edition, San Francisco: Benjamin Cummings, © 2010, p. 240.

p. 492: Andy Greenberg, "A Step Beyond Human" from *Forbes*, December 14, 2009, Vol. 184, Issue 11. Reprinted by permission of Forbes Media LLC © 2011.

Chapter 18

p. 510: Aurora Gilbert, "From Ignorant Bliss to Painful Awareness." Reprinted with permission of the author.

Index